Microsoft® Office Excel® 2007

ILLUSTRATED

COMPLETE

J/K

FINAL

1) pg 227
   229
pg 231
readover
add pic to
chart

(J) enthanol chart

pg 121 payment 4 car

pg 64 unit c conditional formatting

sorting

table (G)

(skip I)

no trendlines

Microsoft® Office Excel® 2007

ILLUSTRATED

COMPLETE

Elizabeth Eisner Reding/Lynn Wermers

COURSE TECHNOLOGY
CENGAGE Learning

Australia • Brazil • Japan • Korea • Mexico • Singapore • Spain • United Kingdom • United States

COURSE TECHNOLOGY
CENGAGE Learning™

Microsoft® Office Excel® 2007—Illustrated Complete
Elizabeth Eisner Reding/Lynn Wermers

Senior Acquisitions Editor: Marjorie Hunt

Senior Product Manager: Christina Kling Garrett

Associate Product Manager: Rebecca Padrick

Editorial Assistant: Michelle Camisa

Senior Marketing Manager: Joy Stark

Contributing Author: Harry Phillips

Marketing Coordinator: Jennifer Hankin

Developmental Editors: Barbara Clemens, MT Cozzola

Production Editor: Daphne Barbas

Copy Editor: Gary Michael Spahl

QA Manuscript Reviewers: Nicole Ashton, John Frietas, Jeff Schwartz, Susan Whalen

Cover Designers: Elizabeth Paquin, Kathleen Fivel

Cover Artist: Mark Hunt

Composition: GEX Publishing Services

For product information and technology assistance, contact us at
Cengage Learning Customer & Sales Support, 1-800-354-9706

For permission to use material from this text or product, submit all requests online at **cengage.com/permissions**
Further permissions questions can be emailed to
permissionrequest@cengage.com

ISBN-13: 978-1-4239-0522-6

ISBN-10: 1-4239-0522-9

Course Technology
25 Thomson Place
Boston, Massachusetts 02210
USA

Cengage Learning is a leading provider of customized learning solutions with office locations around the globe, including Singapore, the United Kingdom, Australia, Mexico, Brazil, and Japan. Locate your local office at:
international.cengage.com/region

Cengage Learning products are represented in Canada by Nelson Education, Ltd.

For your lifelong learning solutions, visit **course.cengage.com**

Purchase any of our products at your local college store or at our preferred online store **www.ichapters.com**

Trademarks:
Some of the product names and company names used in this book have been used for identification purposes only and may be trademarks or registered trademarks of their respective manufacturers and sellers.

Microsoft and the Office logo are either registered trademarks or trademarks of Microsoft Corporation in the United States and/or other countries. Course Technology is an independent entity from Microsoft Corporation, and not affiliated with Microsoft in any manner. Microsoft product screen shot(s) reprinted with permission from Microsoft Corporation.

Printed in the United States of America
5 6 7 8 9 11 10 09

About This Book

Welcome to *Microsoft Office Excel—Illustrated Complete!* Since the first edition of this book was published in 1994, millions of students have used various Illustrated texts to master software skills and learn computer concepts. We are proud to bring you this new Illustrated book on the most exciting version of Microsoft Office ever to release.

As you probably have heard by now, Microsoft completely redesigned this latest version of Office from the ground up. No more menus! No more toolbars! The software changes Microsoft made were based on years of research during which they studied users' needs and work habits. The result is a phenomenal and powerful new version of the software that will make you and your students more productive and help you get better results faster.

Before we started working on this new edition, we also conducted our own research. We reached out to nearly 100 instructors like you who have used previous editions of this book and our Microsoft Office texts. Some of you responded to one of our surveys, others of you generously spent time with us on the phone, telling us your thoughts. Seven of you agreed to serve on our Advisory Board and guided our decisions.

As a result of all the feedback you gave us, we have preserved the features that you love, and made improvements that you suggested and requested. And of course we have covered all the key features of the new software. (For more details on what's new in this edition, please read the Preface.) We are confident that this book and all its available resources will help your students master Microsoft Office Excel 2007.

Advisory Board

We thank our Advisory Board who enthusiastically gave us their opinions and guided our every decision on content and design from beginning to end. They are as follows:

Kristen Callahan, Mercer County Community College

Paulette Comet, Assistant Professor, Community College of Baltimore County

Barbara Comfort, J. Sargeant Reynolds Community College

Margaret Cooksey, Tallahassee Community College

Rachelle Hall, Glendale Community College

Hazel Kates, Miami Dade College

Charles Lupico, Thomas Nelson Community College

Author Acknowledgments

Elizabeth Eisner Reding Creating a book of this magnitude is a team effort. I would like to thank my husband, Michael, as well as Christina Kling Garrett, the project manager, and my development editor, MT Cozzola, for her suggestions and corrections. I would also like to thank the production and editorial staff for all their hard work that made this project a reality.

Lynn Wermers I would like to thank Barbara Clemens for her insightful contributions, great humor, and patience. I would also like to thank Christina Kling Garrett for her encouragement and support in guiding and managing this project.

Preface

Welcome to *Microsoft Office Excel 2007—Illustrated Complete*. If this is your first experience with the Illustrated series, you'll see that this book has a unique design: each skill is presented on two facing pages, with steps on the left and screens on the right. The layout makes it easy to digest a skill without having to read a lot of text and flip pages to see an illustration.

This book is an ideal learning tool for a wide range of learners—the rookies will find the clean design easy to follow and focused with only essential information presented, and the hotshots will appreciate being able to move quickly through the lessons to find the information they need without reading a lot of text. The design also makes this a great reference after the course is over! See the illustration on the right to learn more about the pedagogical and design elements of a typical lesson.

What's New in This Edition

We've made many changes and enhancements to this edition to make it the best ever. Here are some highlights of what's new:

- **New Getting Started with Microsoft Office 2007 Unit**—This unit begins the book and gets students up to speed on features of Office 2007 that are common to all the applications, such as the Ribbon, the Office button, and the Quick Access toolbar.

- **Real Life Independent Challenge**—The new Real Life Independent Challenge exercises offer students the opportunity to create projects that are meaningful to their lives, such as a budget for buying a house.

- **New Case Study**—A new case study featuring Quest Specialty Travel provides a practical and fun scenario that students can relate to as they learn skills. This fictional company offers a wide variety of tours around the world.

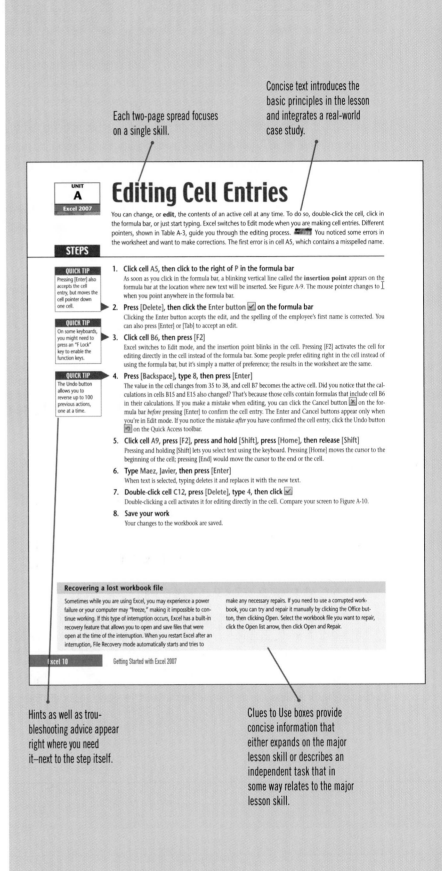

Each two-page spread focuses on a single skill.

Concise text introduces the basic principles in the lesson and integrates a real-world case study.

Hints as well as troubleshooting advice appear right where you need it—next to the step itself.

Clues to Use boxes provide concise information that either expands on the major lesson skill or describes an independent task that in some way relates to the major lesson skill.

- **Content Improvements**—All of the content in the book has been updated to cover Office 2007 and also to address instructor feedback. See the instructor resource CD for details on specific content changes for Excel.

Assignments

The lessons use Quest Specialty Travel, a fictional adventure travel company, as the case study. The assignments on the light purple pages at the end of each unit increase in difficulty. Data files and case studies provide a variety of interesting and relevant business applications. Assignments include:

- **Concepts Reviews** consist of multiple choice, matching, and screen identification questions.
- **Skills Reviews** provide additional hands-on, step-by-step reinforcement.
- **Independent Challenges** are case projects requiring critical thinking and application of the unit skills. The Independent Challenges increase in difficulty, with the first one in each unit being the easiest. Independent Challenges 2 and 3 become increasingly open-ended, requiring more independent problem solving.
- **Real Life Independent Challenges** are practical exercises in which students create documents to help them with their every day lives.
- **Advanced Challenge Exercises** set within the Independent Challenges provide optional steps for more advanced students.
- **Visual Workshops** are practical, self-graded capstone projects that require independent problem solving.

Every lesson features large, full-color representations of what the screen should look like as students complete the numbered steps.

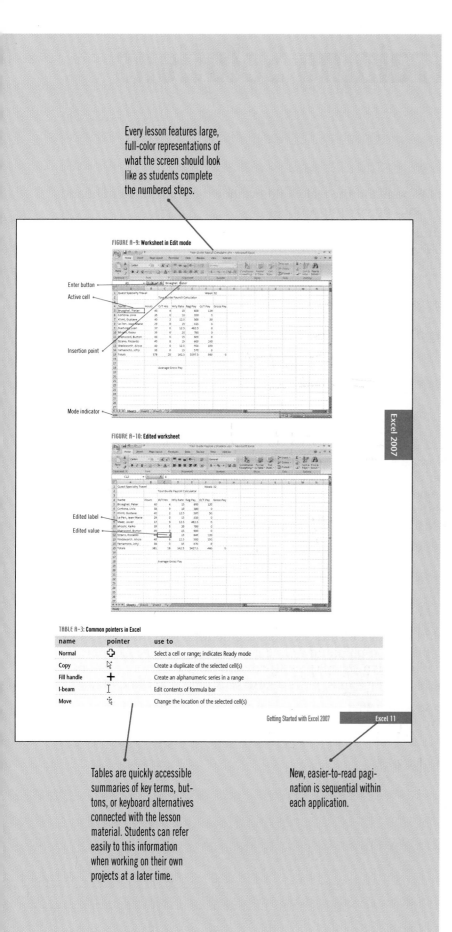

FIGURE A-9: Worksheet in Edit mode

FIGURE A-10: Edited worksheet

TABLE A-3: Common pointers in Excel

name	pointer	use to
Normal	⊕	Select a cell or range; indicates Ready mode
Copy	⟍	Create a duplicate of the selected cell(s)
Fill handle	✛	Create an alphanumeric series in a range
I-beam	I	Edit contents of formula bar
Move	⟰	Change the location of the selected cell(s)

Getting Started with Excel 2007

Excel 11

Tables are quickly accessible summaries of key terms, buttons, or keyboard alternatives connected with the lesson material. Students can refer easily to this information when working on their own projects at a later time.

New, easier-to-read pagination is sequential within each application.

Assessment & Training Solutions

SAM 2007 helps bridge the gap between the classroom and the real world by allowing students to train and test on important computer skills in an active, hands-on environment.

SAM 2007's easy-to-use system includes powerful interactive exams, training or projects on critical applications such as Word, Excel, Access, PowerPoint, Outlook, Windows, the Internet, and much more. SAM simulates the application environment, allowing students to demonstrate their knowledge and think through the skills by performing real-world tasks.

Designed to be used with the Illustrated series, SAM 2007 includes built-in page references so students can print helpful study guides that match the Illustrated textbooks used in class. Powerful administrative options allow instructors to schedule exams and assignments, secure tests, and run reports with almost limitless flexibility.

Student Edition Labs

Our Web-based interactive labs help students master hundreds of computer concepts, including input and output devices, file management and desktop applications, computer ethics, virus protection, and much more. Featuring up-to-the-minute content, eye-popping graphics, and rich animation, the highly interactive Student Edition Labs offer students an alternative way to learn through dynamic observation, step-by-step practice, and challenging review questions. Also available on CD at an additional cost.

Online Content   Blackboard

Blackboard is the leading distance learning solution provider and class-management platform today. Course Technology has partnered with Blackboard to bring you premium online content. Instructors: Content for use with *Microsoft Office Excel 2007–Illustrated Complete* is available in a Blackboard Course Cartridge and may include topic reviews, case projects, review questions, test banks, practice tests, custom syllabi, and more.

Course Technology also has solutions for several other learning management systems. Please visit *www.course.com* today to see what's available for this title.

Instructor Resources

The Instructor Resources CD is Course Technology's way of putting the resources and information needed to teach and learn effectively into your hands. With an integrated array of teaching and learning tools that offers you and your students a broad range of technology-based instructional options, we believe this CD represents the highest quality and most cutting edge resources available to instructors today. Many of these resources are available at *www.course.com*. The resources available with this book are:

- **Instructor's Manual**—Available as an electronic file, the Instructor's Manual includes detailed lecture topics with teaching tips for each unit.

- **Sample Syllabus**—Prepare and customize your course easily using this sample course outline.

- **PowerPoint Presentations**—Each unit has a corresponding PowerPoint presentation that you can use in lecture, distribute to your students, or customize to suit your course.

- **Figure Files**—The figures in the text are provided on the Instructor Resources CD to help you illustrate key topics or concepts. You can create traditional overhead transparencies by printing the figure files. Or you can create electronic slide shows by using the figures in a presentation program such as PowerPoint.

- **Solutions to Exercises**—Solutions to Exercises contain every file students are asked to create or modify in the lessons and end-of-unit material. Also provided in this section, there is a document outlining the solutions for the end-of-unit Concepts Review, Skills Review, and Independent Challenges. An Annotated Solution File and Grading Rubric accompany each file and can be used together for quick and easy grading.

- **Data Files for Students**—To complete most of the units in this book, your students will need Data Files. You can post the Data Files on a file server for students to copy. The Data Files are available on the Instructor Resources CD, the Review Pack, and can also be downloaded from *www.course.com*. In this edition, we have included a lesson on downloading the Data Files for this book, see page xxiv.

Instruct students to use the Data Files List included on the Review Pack and the Instructor Resources CD. This list gives instructions on copying and organizing files.

- **ExamView**—ExamView is a powerful testing software package that allows you to create and administer printed, computer (LAN-based), and Internet exams. ExamView includes hundreds of questions that correspond to the topics covered in this text, enabling students to generate detailed study guides that include page references for further review. The computer-based and Internet testing components allow students to take exams at their computers, and also saves you time by grading each exam automatically.

CourseCasts—Learning on the Go. Always available...always relevant.

Want to keep up with the latest technology trends relevant to you? Visit our site to find a library of podcasts, CourseCasts, featuring a "CourseCast of the Week," and download them to your mp3 player at *http://coursecasts.course.com*.

Our fast-paced world is driven by technology. You know because you're an active participant—always on the go, always keeping up with technological trends, and always learning new ways to embrace technology to power your life.

Ken Baldauf, a faculty member of the Florida State University Computer Science Department, is responsible for teaching technology classes to thousands of FSU students each year. He knows what you know; he knows what you want to learn. He's also an expert in the latest technology and will sort through and aggregate the most pertinent news and information so you can spend your time enjoying technology, rather than trying to figure it out.

Visit us at *http://coursecasts.course.com* to learn on the go!

Brief Contents

Contents

EXCEL 2007

Unit I: Automating Worksheet Tasks   **201**

EXCEL 2007

Unit J: Enhancing Charts   **225**

| EXCEL 2007 | **Unit M: Exchanging Data with Other Programs** | **297** |

| EXCEL 2007 | **Unit N: Sharing Excel Files and Incorporating Web Information** | **321** |

Read This Before You Begin

Frequently Asked Questions

What are Data Files?

A Data File is a partially completed Excel workbook, or another type of file that you use to complete the steps in the units and exercises to create the final document that you submit to your instructor. Each unit opener page lists the Data Files that you need for that unit.

Where are the Data Files?

Your instructor will provide the Data Files to you or direct you to a location on a network drive from which you can download them. Alternatively, you can follow the instructions on the next page to download the Data Files from this book's Web page.

What software was used to write and test this book?

This book was written and tested using a typical installation of Microsoft Office 2007 installed on a computer with a typical installation of Microsoft Windows Vista. The browser used for any steps that require a browser is Internet Explorer 7.

If you are using this book on Windows XP, please see the next page "Important notes for Windows XP users." If you are using this book on Windows Vista, please see the Appendix at the end of this book.

Do I need to be connected to the Internet to complete the steps and exercises in this book?

Some of the exercises in this book assume that your computer is connected to the Internet. If you are not connected to the Internet, see your instructor for information on how to complete the exercises.

What do I do if my screen is different from the figures shown in this book?

This book was written and tested on computers with monitors set at a resolution of 1024 × 768. If your screen shows more or less information than the figures in the book, your monitor is probably set at a higher or lower resolution. If you don't see something on your screen, you might have to scroll down or up to see the object identified in the figures.

The Ribbon—the blue area at the top of the screen—in Microsoft Office 2007 adapts to different resolutions. If your monitor is set at a lower resolution than 1024 × 768, you might not see all of the buttons shown in the figures. The groups of buttons will always appear, but the entire group might be condensed into a single button that you need to click to access the buttons described in the instructions. For example, the figures and steps in this book assume that the Editing group on the Home tab in Word looks like the following:

1024 × 768 Editing Group

Editing Group on the
Home Tab of the
Ribbon at 1024 × 768

If your resolution is set to 800 × 600, the Ribbon in Word will look like the following figure, and you will need to click the Editing button to access the buttons that are visible in the Editing group.

800 × 600 Editing Group

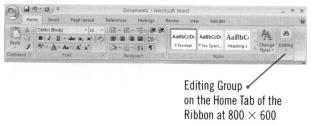

Editing Group
on the Home Tab of the
Ribbon at 800 × 600

800 × 600 Editing Group clicked

Editing Group on the Home Tab of the Ribbon at
800 × 600 is selected to show available buttons

Important Notes for Windows XP Users

The screenshots in this book show Microsoft Office 2007 running on Windows Vista. However, if you are using Microsoft Windows XP, you can still use this book because Office 2007 runs virtually the same on both platforms. There are a few differences that you will encounter if you are using Windows XP. Read this section to understand the differences.

Dialog boxes

If you are a Windows XP user, dialog boxes shown in this book will look slightly different than what you see on your screen. Dialog boxes for Windows XP have a blue title bar, instead of a gray title bar. However, beyond this superficial difference in appearance, the options in the dialog boxes across platforms are the same. For instance, the screen shots below show the Font dialog box running on Windows XP and the Font dialog box running on Windows Vista.

FIGURE 1: Dialog box in Windows XP

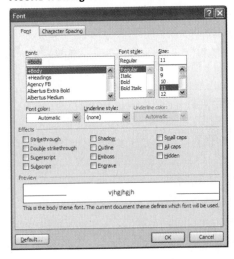

FIGURE 2: Dialog box in Windows Vista

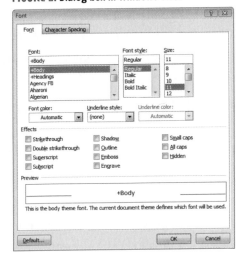

Alternate Steps for Windows XP Users

Nearly all of the steps in this book work exactly the same for Windows XP users. However, there are a few tasks that will require you to complete slightly different steps. This section provides alternate steps for a few specific skills.

Starting a program

1. Click the **Start button** on the taskbar
2. Point to **All Programs**, point to **Microsoft Office**, then click the application you want to use

FIGURE 3: Starting a program

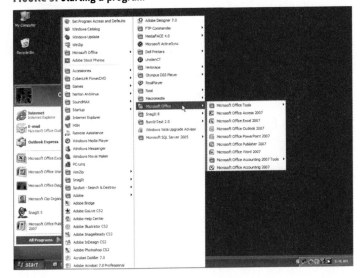

Saving a file for the first time

1. Click the **Office button**, then click **Save As**
2. Type a name for your file in the File Name text box
3. Click the **Save in list arrow**, then navigate to the drive and folder where you store your Data Files
4. Click **Save**

FIGURE 4: Save As dialog box

Opening a file

1. Click the **Office button**, then click **Open**
2. Click the **Look in list arrow**, then navigate to the drive and folder where you store your Data Files
3. Click the file you want to open
4. Click **Open**

FIGURE 5: Open dialog box

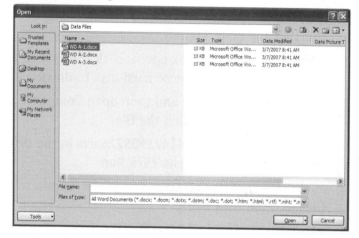

Downloading Data Files for This Book

In order to complete many of the lesson steps and exercises in this book, you are asked to open and save Data Files. A **Data File** is a partially completed Word document, Excel workbook, Access database, PowerPoint presentation, or another type of file that you use as a starting point to complete the steps in the units and exercises. The benefit of using a Data File is that it saves you the time and effort needed to create a file; you can simply open a Data File, save it with a new name (so the original file remains intact), then make changes to it to complete lesson steps or an exercise. Your instructor will provide the Data Files to you or direct you to a location on a network drive from which you can download them. Alternatively, you can follow the steps below to download the Data Files from this book's Web page.

1. **Start Internet Explorer, type www.cengage.com/coursetechnology/ in the address bar, then press [Enter]**

2. **Click in the Enter ISBN Search text box, type 9781423905226, then click Search**

3. **When the page opens for this textbook, click the About this Product link for the Student, point to Student Downloads to expand the menu, and then click the Data Files for Students link**

4. **If the File Download – Security Warning dialog box opens, click Save. (If no dialog box appears, skip this step and go to Step 6)**

5. **If the Save As dialog box opens, click the Save in list arrow at the top of the dialog box, select a folder on your USB drive or hard disk to download the file to, then click Save**

6. **Close Internet Explorer and then open Computer and display the contents of the drive and folder to which you downloaded the file**

7. **Double-click the file 9781423905226.exe in the drive or folder, then, if the Open File – Security Warning dialog box opens, click Run**

8. **In the WinZip Self-Extractor window, navigate to the drive and folder where you want to unzip the files to, then click Unzip**

9. **When the WinZip Self-Extractor displays a dialog box listing the number of files that have unzipped success-fully, click OK, click Close in the WinZip Self-Extractor dialog box, then close Computer**

    The Data Files are now unzipped in the folder you specified in Step 8 and ready for you to open and use.

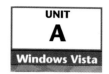

Getting Started with Windows Vista

Microsoft Windows Vista, or **Windows**, is an **operating system**—software that manages the complete operation of your computer. When you start a computer, Windows sets it up for use and then displays the **desktop**—a graphical user interface (GUI) that you use to interact with Windows and the other software on your computer. The Windows desktop displays **icons**, or small images, that represent items such as the Recycle Bin and Computer. When you open a program or document, Windows displays the program or document in a rectangular-shaped work area known as a **window**. Windows helps you organize **files** (collections of stored electronic data, such as text, pictures, video, music, and programs) in **folders** (containers for files) so that you can easily find them later. Windows also keeps all the computer hardware and software working together properly.  As a new Oceania tour guide for Quest Specialty Travel (QST), you need to develop basic Windows skills to keep track of all the tour files on your company laptop computer.

OBJECTIVES

Start Windows Vista

Use a pointing device

Start a program

Move and resize windows

Use menus, toolbars, and
keyboard shortcuts

Use dialog boxes

Use scroll bars

Use Windows Help and Support

End a Windows Vista session

Starting Windows Vista

When you start your computer, Windows steps through a process called **booting** to get the computer up and running. During this time, you might need to select your user account and enter your password. This information identifies you to Windows as an authorized user of the computer and helps keep your computer secure. After booting is complete, Windows displays the Windows desktop. The desktop, shown in Figure A-1, provides a way for you to interact with Windows Vista and to access its tools. The desktop appears with preset, or **default**, settings; however, you can change these settings to suit your needs. The image that fills the desktop background is called **wallpaper**. The desktop contains an icon for the Recycle Bin, which stores deleted files and folders. The desktop also displays **gadgets** (mini-programs for performing everyday tasks, such as a Clock) on the **Sidebar**. The **taskbar**, the horizontal bar at the bottom of the screen, displays information about open programs, folders, and files. You click the **Start button** on the left side of the taskbar to start programs, find and open files, access Windows Help and Support, and more. The **Quick Launch toolbar**, located on the taskbar, includes buttons for showing the desktop when it is not currently visible, switching between windows (the work areas for open programs), and starting the Internet Explorer Web browser. Table A-1 identifies the default icons and elements found on a desktop. Your supervisor, Nancy McDonald, Oceania's tour developer, asks you to become familiar with Windows Vista and its features before your upcoming tour.

STEPS

1. **If your computer and monitor are turned off, press the Power button on the front of the system unit, then press the Power button on the monitor**

   After your computer starts, you see either a **Welcome screen** with icons for each user account on the computer or the Windows desktop. If you see the Welcome screen, continue with Step 2. If you see the Windows desktop, compare it to the one shown in Figure A-1, then continue with Step 4.

2. **If necessary, click the icon for your user account**

   If you use a password with your user account, Windows prompts you for the password. If not, continue with Step 4.

3. **If prompted for a password, type your password in the Password box, then click the Next button**

   After Windows verifies your password, you see the Windows desktop. See Figure A-1. Your Windows desktop may look slightly different.

   TROUBLE

   If you don't know your password, ask your instructor or technical support person. If you don't use a password, leave the Password box empty and click the Next button

4. **If the Welcome Center opens, click the Close button [X] in the upper-right corner of the Welcome Center window**

TABLE A-1: Common desktop components

desktop element	icon	allows you to
Recycle Bin		Store folders and files you delete from your hard drive(s) and restore them
Windows Sidebar (or Sidebar)		View the current time on a clock, view a slide show, and more
Taskbar		Switch between open programs, folders, and files; and resize windows
Notification area		Check the time, adjust the volume of your speakers, connect to the Internet, check problems identified by Windows Vista, and more
Quick Launch toolbar		Show the desktop, switch between windows, and open the Internet Explorer Web browser
Start button		Start programs, search for files, open documents, view pictures, listen to music, play games, get help, and more

FIGURE A-1: Windows Vista desktop

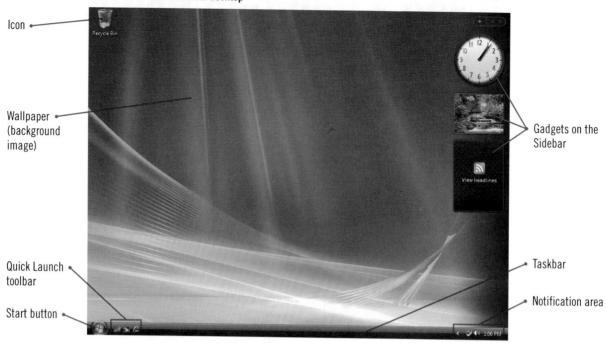

Icon

Wallpaper (background image)

Quick Launch toolbar

Start button

Gadgets on the Sidebar

Taskbar

Notification area

Using Windows Vista with Aero

Some editions of Windows Vista support **Windows Aero**, a new graphical user-interface feature that enhances the transparency (referred to as **translucency**) of the Start menu, taskbar, windows, and dialog boxes, as shown in Figure A-2. These transparency features also enable you to locate content by seeing through one window to the next window. **Windows Flip** allows you to display a set of thumbnails or miniature images of all open windows. **Windows Flip 3D** allows you to

display stacked windows at a three-dimensional angle to see even more of the content of all open windows. Likewise, **live taskbar thumbnails** display the content within open, but not visible, windows, including live content such as video. These features provide three different ways to quickly view, locate, and select windows with the content you need. To view these effects, your version of Windows Vista and your computer's hardware must support the use of Windows Aero.

FIGURE A-2: Windows Aero features

Translucent Start menu

Translucent window frame and borders

Live thumbnail

Live taskbar thumbnail for a minimized window

Using a Pointing Device

The most common way to interact with your computer and the software you are using is with a **pointing device**, such as a mouse, trackball, touch pad, or pointing stick, as shown in Figure A-3. If touch input is available on your computer, you can also use an onscreen **touch pointer** to perform pointing operations with a finger. As you move your pointing device, a small arrow or other symbol on the screen, called a **pointer**, moves in the same direction. Table A-2 illustrates common pointer shapes and their functions. You press the left and right buttons on the pointing device to select and move objects (such as icons and desktop windows); open programs, windows, folders, and files; and select options for performing specific tasks, such as saving your work. Table A-3 lists the five basic ways in which you can use a pointing device. Pointing devices can work with your computer through a cable or through a wireless connection that transmits data using radio waves. ▰▰▰▰ You'll practice using your pointing device so you can work more efficiently.

STEPS

QUICK TIP

Left-handed users can change the Button configuration setting in the Mouse Properties dialog box to switch the primary and secondary (left and right) mouse buttons.

1. **Locate the pointer on the desktop, then move your pointing device**

   The pointer moves across the Windows desktop in the same direction as you move your pointing device.

2. **Move the pointer so the tip is directly over the Recycle Bin icon** 🗑

   Positioning the pointer over an item is called **pointing**. The Recycle Bin icon is highlighted and a **ToolTip**, or label, identifies its purpose.

3. **With the pointer over** 🗑, **press and release the left button on your pointing device**

   Pressing and releasing the left button, called **clicking** or **single-clicking**, selects an icon on the desktop or in a window and selects options and objects within a program. In this case, the Recycle Bin icon is selected.

TROUBLE

If the Recycle Bin window opens, you may have pressed the left button twice. Click the Close button in the title bar to close the window.

4. **With** 🗑 **still selected, press and hold down the left button on your pointing device, move your pointing device to another location on the desktop, then release the left button**

   A copy of the Recycle Bin icon moves with the pointer. When you release the left button on your pointing device, the Recycle Bin is placed on the desktop in a different location. You use this technique, called **dragging**, to move icons and windows.

5. **Drag** 🗑 **back to its original desktop location**

6. **Position the pointer over** 🗑, **then press and release the right button on your pointing device**

   This action, called **right-clicking**, opens a shortcut menu, as shown in Figure A-4. A **shortcut menu** lists common commands for an object. A **command** is an instruction to perform a task, such as renaming an object. If a command is dimmed, such as "Empty Recycle Bin," it is not currently available for you to use.

QUICK TIP

When a step says "click," use the left button on your pointing device. When it says "right-click," use the right button.

7. **Click the desktop background**

   The shortcut menu closes and Windows selects the desktop background.

8. **Point to** 🗑, **then quickly press the left button on your pointing device twice and release it**

   Quickly clicking the left button twice is called **double-clicking**, which opens a window or a program. In this case, the Recycle Bin window opens to display any folders and files deleted from the hard disk.

QUICK TIP

Be sure to hold your pointing device still as you double-click.

9. **Click the Close button** ❎ **in the upper-right corner of the Recycle Bin window**

   The Recycle Bin window closes. Every window has a Close button; clicking it is the fastest way to close a window.

FIGURE A-3: Common pointing devices

Mouse

Trackball

Touch pointer

Touchpad

Pointing stick

FIGURE A-4: Shortcut menu

Selected object

Dimmed command is unavailable

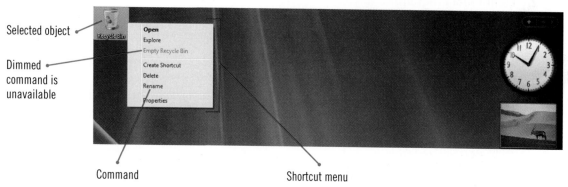

Command

Shortcut menu

TABLE A-2: Common pointer shapes

shape	name	description
⟋	Normal Select	Points to an object and chooses a command
◯	Busy	Indicates that Windows or another program is busy and you must wait before continuing
⟋◯	Working in Background	Indicates that Windows or another program is busy and the computer's response time is slower, but you can still perform other operations
I	Text Select (also called I-Beam)	Identifies where you can type, select, insert, or edit text
☞	Link Select	Identifies a link you can click to jump to another location, such as a Help topic or a Web site

TABLE A-3: Basic pointing device techniques

technique	what to do
Pointing	Move the pointing device to position the tip of the pointer over an object, option, or item
Clicking	Quickly press and release the left button
Double-clicking	Quickly press and release the left button twice
Dragging	Point to an object, press and hold the left button, move the object to a new location, then release the left button
Right-clicking	Point to an object, then quickly press and release the right button

Starting a Program

From the Start menu, you can open programs or software products on your computer. In addition to other software that you purchase and install on the computer, Windows Vista includes a variety of programs, such as Windows Calendar, Windows Mail, Windows Movie Maker, and Windows Photo Gallery. Windows also comes with **accessories**, which are simple programs to perform specific tasks, such as the Windows Calculator accessory for performing quick calculations. Table A-4 describes the organization of the Start menu. 🔲🔳 Because you need to develop QST tour proposals and brochures with photographs of exotic Pacific islands, you want to try the Windows Photo Gallery.

STEPS

QUICK TIP
You can also press the Windows logo key to open or close the Start menu.

1. **Click the Start button 🟦 on the taskbar**

   The Start menu opens, as shown in Figure A-5. From the left pane, you can start programs installed on your computer. From the right pane, you can open specific folders, open Windows tools, change Windows settings, get Help and Support, and shut down Windows. Some of the options on your Start menu will differ.

2. **Point to All Programs**

   The All Programs menu opens in the left pane, with an alphabetical listing of the programs installed on your computer followed by groups of related programs, such as Accessories. See Figure A-6. Your list of programs will differ.

TROUBLE
If you see an Info Pane on the right side of the window, close it by clicking the Hide Info Pane button.

3. **Click Windows Photo Gallery on the All Programs menu**

   The Windows Photo Gallery window opens, displaying thumbnails of images in the Sample Pictures folder on your computer. See Figure A-7. A **thumbnail** is a smaller image of the actual contents of a file that contains a picture. Windows also displays a Windows Photo Gallery button on the taskbar for the now open Windows Photo Gallery.

4. **Leave the Photo Gallery window open for the next lesson**

TABLE A-4: Start menu components

component	description
Pinned Items List	Contains the two programs commonly used for a Web browser and e-mail: Internet Explorer and a version of Microsoft Outlook; you can change these two programs and you can add other programs to this list
Recently-opened Programs List	Lists programs you have recently opened so you can quickly return to them.
All Programs	Displays a list of programs installed on your computer
Search Box	Quickly locates programs, folders, and files, and shows the search results in the left pane of the Start menu
User Folders	Provides quick access to your Documents, Pictures, Music, and Games folders, plus the folder for your user account (your username at the top of the right pane)
Windows Tools	Search quickly locates programs, folders, and files Recent Items displays the names of up to 15 files you recently opened Computer opens a Windows Explorer window and shows the drives and other hardware on your computer Network provides access to computers and other hardware on your network Connect To shows your Internet and network connections
Settings & Help	Control Panel provides tools for viewing and changing Windows settings and installing hardware and software Default Programs lets you specify the programs and program settings you prefer to use Help and Support opens the Windows Help and Support Center to provide you with assistance and Help information
Power & Lock Buttons	Power button puts your computer to sleep (your computer appears off and uses very little power) Lock button locks your computer (a security measure for when you are not using the computer), and displays shut-down options

FIGURE A-5: **Start menu**

Pinned items list

Recently-
opened
programs

Power, Lock,
and Lock menu
buttons

User account
icon

Your important
folders

Windows tools,
settings, and Help

FIGURE A-6: **All Programs menu**

Installed
programs
(your list
will differ)

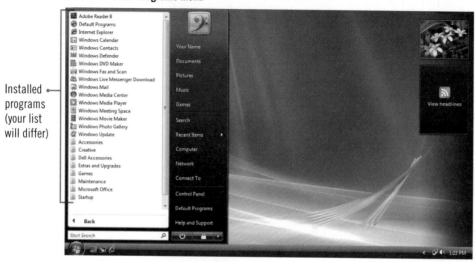

FIGURE A-7: **Windows Photo Gallery window**

Thumbnail of
an image

Taskbar button
for Windows
Photo Gallery
window

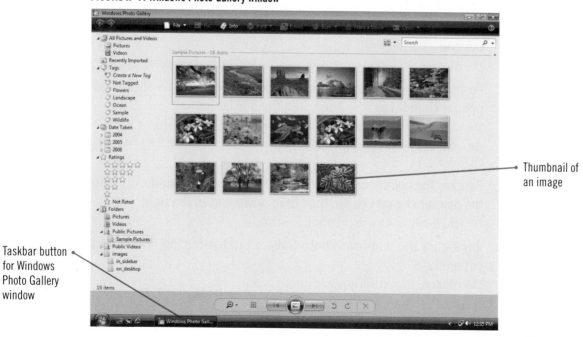

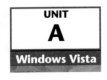
Moving and Resizing Windows

Each program you start opens in its own window. As you work, you will invariably need to move and resize windows so that you can see more of one window or view two or more windows at the same time. To resize a window, you use the **resizing buttons**—Maximize 🔲, Restore Down 🗗, and Minimize 🔲 —in the upper-right corner of the window. To adjust a window's height or width (or both), you drag a window border or window corner. To move a window, you drag its **title bar**—the area across the top of the window that displays the window name or program name. If you open more than one program at once, you are **multitasking**—performing several tasks at the same time—and each program appears in a different window. The **active window** is the window you are currently using. An **inactive window** is another open window that you are not currently using. 📇 As you examine photos for a new tour brochure, you need to move and resize the Windows Photo Gallery window.

STEPS

QUICK TIP

You can also maximize or restore down a window by double-clicking its title bar.

1. **If the Windows Photo Gallery window does not fill the desktop, click the Maximize button 🔲 in the upper-right corner of the Windows Photo Gallery window**

   The Windows Photo Gallery window is maximized. A **maximized window** fills your desktop and you cannot see its borders. After you maximize a window, the Maximize button changes to a Restore Down button.

2. **Click the Restore Down button 🗗 in the upper-right corner of the Windows Photo Gallery window**

   The Windows Photo Gallery window returns to its previous size and position on the desktop. The window borders are visible, and the Restore Down button changes to a Maximize button.

3. **Click the Minimize button 🔲 in the upper-right corner of the Windows Photo Gallery window**

   The Windows Photo Gallery window is still open, just not visible. See Figure A-8. A **minimized window** shrinks to a button on the taskbar. You can use this feature to hide a window that you are not currently using, but may use later.

4. **Click the Windows Photo Gallery taskbar button**

   The Windows Photo Gallery window returns to its original size and position on the desktop.

5. **Drag the title bar on the Windows Photo Gallery window to the upper-left corner of the desktop**

   The Windows Photo Gallery window is repositioned on the desktop.

6. **Position the pointer on the right border of the Windows Photo Gallery window until the pointer changes to ⟺, then drag the border left**

   The width of the Windows Photo Gallery window narrows. See Figure A-9. To widen the window, you drag the right window border to the right. To decrease or increase a window's height, you drag the bottom border up or down.

7. **Position the pointer on the lower-right corner of the Windows Photo Gallery window until the pointer changes to ⬊, then drag down and to the right**

   Both the height and width of the window change.

8. **Right-click the Windows Photo Gallery taskbar button, then click Close on the shortcut menu**

   The Windows Photo Gallery window closes.

FIGURE A-8: Minimized window

Windows Photo Gallery
is open, but not visible

FIGURE A-9: Restored down window being resized

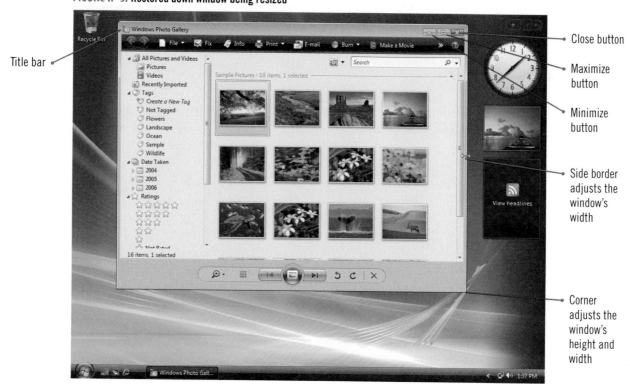

Title bar

Close button

Maximize button

Minimize button

Side border adjusts the window's width

Corner adjusts the window's height and width

Using Menus, Toolbars, and Keyboard Shortcuts

A **menu** displays a list of commands you use to accomplish a task. Menus organize commands into groups of related tasks. In some program windows, you open menus from a **menu bar** located below the window's title bar. At other times, you open menus from a **toolbar**, a set of buttons you can click to open menus or select common commands that may also be available from a menu bar. Some menu commands and toolbar buttons have a **keyboard shortcut**, which is a key or a combination of keys that you press to perform a command. 🖼️ As you prepare for your first tour, Nancy recommends that you examine the Slide Show gadget and the Windows Photo Gallery.

STEPS

1. **Point to the Slide Show gadget on the Sidebar, resting the pointer on the displayed image**

   The Slide Show toolbar appears at the bottom of the slide show image, and the Slide Show gadget toolbar appears to the right of the Slide Show gadget. See Figure A-10. The left border of the Sidebar is now visible.

2. **Click the View button 🔲 on the Slide Show toolbar**

   The Windows Photo Gallery window opens and displays an enlarged view of the image displayed in the Slide Show gadget. The title bar identifies the filename of the image and the name of the open program. A toolbar appears below the title bar, with options for working with the image.

3. **Click the File button 🔲 File ▾ on the toolbar**

   The File menu lists commands related to working with the files. See Figure A-11. A keyboard shortcut appears to the right of some commands.

4. **Click Exit**

   The Windows Photo Gallery window closes.

5. **Point to the Slide Show gadget on the Sidebar, then click 🔲 on the Slide Show toolbar**

   The Photo Gallery Viewer window opens again.

6. **Click the Play Slide Show button 🔲 on the Slide Show toolbar at the bottom of the window**

   Windows Photo Gallery displays a full-screen slide show of each image in your Sample Pictures folder, one at a time.

7. **Press [Esc]**

   The slide show stops and you return to the Windows Photo Gallery window.

8. **Press and hold [Alt], press and release [F4], then release [Alt]**

   The Windows Photo Gallery window closes. The keyboard shortcut [Alt][F4] closes any active window.

FIGURE A-10: Windows Sidebar

Add Gadget button

Slide Show gadget

View button

FIGURE A-11: File menu

File button

Commands on File menu

Play Slide Show button

Toolbar

Keyboard shortcut

Dimmed command is unavilable

Exit command

Using keyboard shortcuts

Keyboard shortcuts allow you to work more quickly and efficiently because you can keep your hands on the keyboard rather than moving between the keyboard and your pointing device. Many programs use the same keyboard shortcuts for common operations, such as [Ctrl][O] for opening a file and [Ctrl][S] for saving a file. Taking the time to learn the keyboard shortcuts for the actions you perform frequently will improve your productivity. Keyboard shortcuts are shown on menus with a plus sign separating the keys you need to press at the same time, such as Ctrl+S for saving a file. Remember, you do not press the plus sign when you use a keyboard shortcut

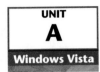

Using Dialog Boxes

When you select a command from a menu or toolbar, the program may perform the operation immediately. Or, it may open a **dialog box**, a type of window in which you specify how you want to complete the operation. Although dialog boxes are similar to a window, they do not contain Maximize, Minimize, and Restore Down buttons, and you usually cannot resize a dialog box. Figure A-12 shows a Print dialog box with two **tabs**—General and Options—that separate groups of settings into related categories. Dialog boxes provide different ways to select options. Table A-5 lists common types of options found in dialog boxes. ░░░░░ You want to review the Sidebar default settings to determine whether they meet your needs while you work.

STEPS

1. **Right-click the background of the Sidebar under the last gadget, then click Properties**
    The Windows Sidebar Properties dialog box opens, as shown in Figure A-13. **Properties** are characteristics or settings of a component of the graphical user interface. The first setting in the dialog box is a check box for starting the Sidebar whenever Windows starts. A **check box** turns an option on (checked) or off (unchecked). You click the check box to change the option's status. As you can see from the check mark in the Start Sidebar when Windows starts check box, it is already turned on.

2. **Click the Sidebar is always on top of other windows check box**
    A check mark is added to the check box, which sets the Sidebar to remain visible when you open a window.

3. **In the Arrangement section, click the Left option button**
    You click one **option button** to select from several options. In this case, you clicked the option button to display the Sidebar on the left side of the desktop. You can select only one option button for a setting. The "Display Sidebar on monitor" button is a **drop-down list button** that you click to open a list that shows one or more options to choose. The **link** at the bottom of the Maintenance section opens a Help topic about how to customize the Sidebar. At the bottom of the dialog box are **command buttons**, which you click to complete or cancel any changes you make in the dialog box. Clicking OK closes the dialog box and applies the settings you selected. Clicking Apply applies the settings you selected, but keeps the dialog box open for additional changes. Clicking Cancel leaves the settings unchanged and closes the dialog box.

QUICK TIP
In a dialog box, pressing [Enter] is the same as clicking OK; pressing [Esc] is the same as clicking Cancel.

4. **Click Cancel**
    The dialog box closes without changing any of the settings for the Sidebar.

FIGURE A-12: Print dialog box

Tab

List box

Option buttons

Text box

Close button

Check box

Buttons that open another dialog box

Spin box

Command buttons

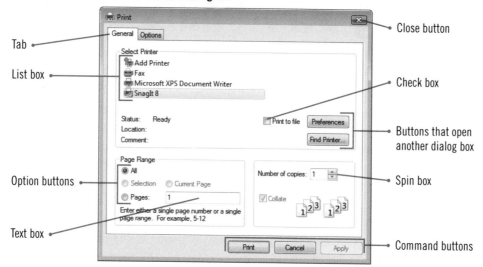

FIGURE A-13: Windows Sidebar Properties dialog box

Tab

Check boxes

Option buttons

Link to Help information

Drop-down list box

Command buttons

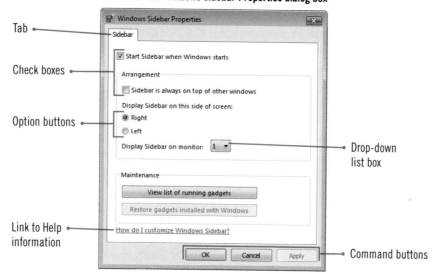

TABLE A-5: Typical elements in a dialog box

element	description
Check box	A box that turns an option on when checked or off when unchecked
Collapse button	A button that shrinks a portion of a dialog box to hide some settings
Command button	A button that completes or cancels an operation
Drop-down list button	A button that displays a list of options from which you can choose
Expand button	A button that extends a dialog box to display additional settings
Link	A shortcut for opening a Help topic or a Web site
List box	A box that displays a list of options from which you can choose (you may need to adjust your view to see additional options in the list)
Option button	A small circle you click to select only one of two or more related options
Slider	A shape you drag along a bar to select a setting that falls within a range, such as between Slow and Fast
Spin box	A text box with up and down arrows; you can type a setting in the text box or click the arrows to increase or decrease a setting
Text box	A box in which you type text (such as a password)

Using Scroll Bars

When you cannot see all of the items available in a window, list box, or drop-down list box, you must **scroll**, or adjust your view. Scrolling is similar to taking a picture with a camera. You move the camera to select a view of a landscape in front of you. If you move the camera to the right or left or up or down, you see a different part of that same landscape. When a window on your computer contains more items than it can display at once, scroll bars appear so you can adjust your view in the window. **Scroll bars** are vertical and horizontal bars that appear along the right and bottom sides of a window when there is more content than can be displayed within the window. At each end of a scroll bar are **scroll arrow buttons** for shifting your view in small increments in either direction. Within each scroll bar is a **scroll box** you can drag to display a different part of a window. You can also click in a scroll bar on either side of the scroll box to shift your view in larger increments. Instead of using a pointing device to scroll, you can also use keyboard shortcuts to scroll, which can be faster. Table A-6 summarizes different ways to scroll. 🖭🗝 For each QST tour, you work with a large variety of files. To locate your files, and to view different pages within each file, you use scroll bars. You will practice scrolling using a Windows Vista accessory called Paint—a graphics program.

STEPS

1. **Point to the Slide Show gadget on the Sidebar, then click the View button 🖭 on the Slide Show toolbar**

   An image from your Sample Pictures folder appears in the Windows Photo Gallery window.

2. **Click the Open button on the toolbar, then click Paint**

   The image opens in a Paint window for editing. Paint is one of the Windows Vista accessories.

> **TROUBLE**
> If you don't see scroll bars, drag the lower-right corner of the Paint window up and to the left until both scroll bars appear.

3. **If the Paint window fills the desktop, then click its Restore Down button 🗗**

   Because of the large size of the image, you can see only a portion of it within the window. However, Paint displays scroll bars on the right and bottom of the window so you can adjust your view. See Figure A-14. Your image and view may differ.

4. **Click the down scroll arrow in the vertical scroll bar**

   The window scrolls down to show another part of the image, and part of the image has now scrolled out of view.

5. **Drag the vertical scroll box slowly down the window to the bottom of the vertical scroll bar**

   The window view changes in larger increments, and the bottom part of the image is visible at the bottom of the window.

6. **Click the vertical scroll bar between the scroll box and the up scroll arrow**

   The view moves up approximately the height of one window.

7. **Click the right scroll arrow in the horizontal scroll bar three times**

   The window keeps scrolling right to show other views onto the image.

> **TROUBLE**
> If a dialog box opens asking if you want to save changes to the image, click Don't Save.

8. **Click the Close button 🗙 on the Paint title bar**

   The Paint window closes.

9. **Click 🗙 on the Windows Photo Gallery title bar**

   The Windows Photo Gallery window closes.

FIGURE A-14: Scroll bars

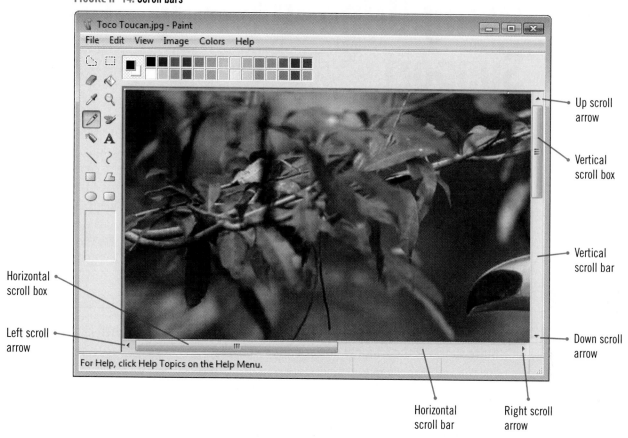

Up scroll arrow

Vertical scroll box

Vertical scroll bar

Horizontal scroll box

Left scroll arrow

Down scroll arrow

Horizontal scroll bar

Right scroll arrow

TABLE A-6: Using scroll bars

to	do this with the mouse
Move down a small increment or one line	Click the down scroll arrow at the bottom of the vertical scroll bar
Move up a small increment or one line	Click the up scroll arrow at the top of the vertical scroll bar
Move down about one window's height	Click between the scroll box and the down scroll arrow in the vertical scroll bar
Move up about one window's height	Click between the scroll box and the up scroll arrow in the vertical scroll bar
Move up a large distance	Drag the scroll box up the vertical scroll bar
Move down a large distance	Drag the scroll box down the vertical scroll bar
Move left or right a small distance	Click the left or the right scroll arrow in the horizontal scroll bar
Move to the left or right one window's width	Click between the scroll box and the left or right scroll arrow in the horizontal scroll bar
Move left or right a large distance	Drag the scroll box in the horizontal scroll bar to the left or right

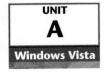
Using Windows Help and Support

When you need assistance or more information about how to use Windows, you can use Help and Support. After you open Help and Support, you can browse Help by first selecting a general category, such as "Windows Basics," then a narrower category, such as "Desktop fundamentals," and finally a specific Help topic, such as "The desktop (overview)." Or, you can select a topic from a table of contents. You can also search Help and Support using one or more descriptive words called **keywords**, such as "Windows Sidebar gadgets," to obtain a list of search results for all the Help topics that include the word or phrase. In certain places within Help and Support, you can use Windows Media Player to watch video clips called Windows Vista demos that provide an overview of Windows features and how to use them. ▨▨▨ Because you often use the Sidebar and Windows Photo Gallery as a tour guide, you decide to review the information in Windows Help and Support on these two Windows features.

STEPS

1. **Click the Start button** 🪟 **on the taskbar, click Help and Support, then click the Maximize button** 🔲 **if the window doesn't fill the desktop**

   The Windows Help and Support window opens and fills the desktop. Figure A-15 identifies the various types of Help options. Table A-7 explains the purpose of the buttons on the Help toolbar in the upper-right corner of the window.

2. **Under Find an answer, click the Windows Basics icon**

   Windows Help and Support displays categories of Help topics about basic Windows features.

3. **Under Desktop fundamentals, click Windows Sidebar and gadgets (overview)**

   The Windows Sidebar and gadgets (overview) Help topic explains what the Sidebar is, how it works, why you would use it, and how to work with gadgets—including adding, removing, and organizing gadgets.

4. **Click in the Search Help text box, type edit my digital photos, then click the Search Help button** 🔍

   A list of search results appears for the keywords you specified. As shown in Figure A-16, the 30 best results for editing digital photos are listed.

5. **Click Working with digital pictures in the list of Help topics**

   This Help topic explains how to get pictures from a camera into your computer—just what you need as a tour guide.

6. **In the second paragraph, click flash memory card (shown in green)**

   The definition of a flash memory card and how you can use this device appears.

7. **Click the Close button** ❎ **in the upper-right corner of the Windows Help and Support window**

   The Windows Help and Support window closes.

Using Windows Online Help

Windows Vista Help and Support provides answers on how to use basic and advanced Windows Vista features. You can get additional help from the Microsoft Windows Help and How-to Web site. On this Web site, you can find more information about basic and advanced Windows Vista features, view "how-to" videos, get help from other people in Windows Vista online discussion groups, read up-to-date articles on changes in Windows Vista, and get online support from Microsoft technical support staff. To open the Windows Online Help and Support Home page, click Windows Online Help in the Find an answer section of the Windows Help and Support window.

FIGURE A-15: Windows Help and Support window

Back button

Forward button

Help category

Home button

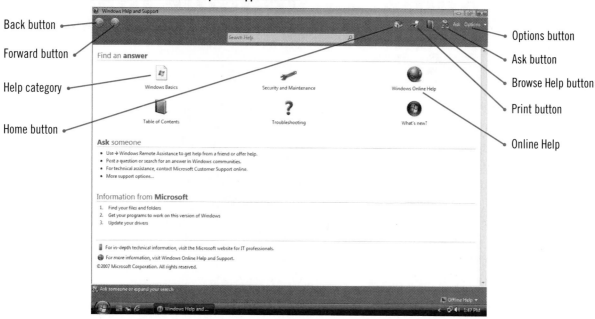

Options button

Ask button

Browse Help button

Print button

Online Help

FIGURE A-16: Search results

Search keywords

Search results

Search Help button

Search Help text box

TABLE A-7: Windows Help and Support toolbar buttons

button icon	button name	purpose
	Back	Takes you back to previous Help topic(s)
	Forward	Returns you to Help topic(s) you just left (available only after you click the Back button)
	Home	Opens the Help and Support starting page
	Print	Prints a Help topic
	Browse Help	Displays a list of Help topics to browse
	Ask	Provides additional resources and tools for finding Help information
	Options	Lists options for printing, browsing Help, adjusting the Help text size, searching a Help topic page, and changing Help settings

Ending a Windows Vista Session

When you finish working on your computer, you should save and close any open files, close any open programs, close any open windows, and shut down Windows. As shown in Table A-8, there are various options for ending your Windows sessions. Whichever option you choose, it's important to shut down your computer in an orderly manner. If you turn off the computer while Windows Vista is running, you could lose data or damage Windows Vista and your computer. If you are working in a computer lab, follow your instructor's directions and your lab's policies and guidelines for ending your Windows session. ▰▰▰▰ You have examined the basic ways in which you can use Windows Vista, so you are ready to end your Windows Vista session.

STEPS

1. **Click the Start button 🏁 on the taskbar**

   The Start menu has three buttons for ending a Windows session—the Power button, the Lock button, and the Lock menu button.

QUICK TIP

Some keyboards have Log Off and Sleep keys that you can press to perform these operations.

2. **Point to the Lock menu button ▶**

   The Lock menu lists all the shut-down options. See Figure A-17.

3. **If you are working in a computer lab, follow the instructions provided by your instructor or technical support person for ending your Windows Vista session; if you are working on your own computer, click Shut Down or the option you prefer for ending your Windows Vista session**

   After you shut down your computer, you may also need to turn off your monitor and other hardware devices, such as a printer, to conserve energy.

FIGURE A-17: Shut down Windows Vista options

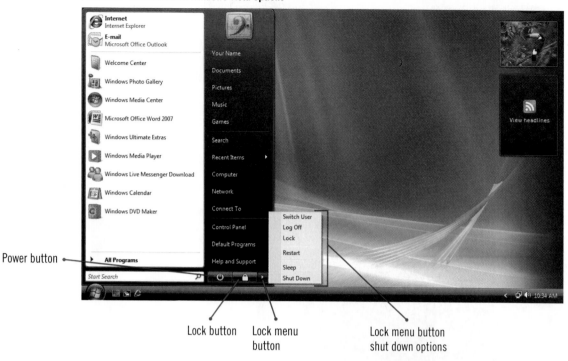

Power button

Lock button Lock menu
button

Lock menu button
shut down options

TABLE A-8: Options for ending a Windows Vista session

option	description	click
Shut Down	Completely shuts down your computer.	Start button, Lock menu button, Shut Down
Log Off	Closes all windows, programs, and documents, then displays the Welcome screen.	Start button, Lock menu button, Log Off
Restart	Shuts down your computer, then restarts it.	Start button, Lock menu button, Restart
Switch User	Locks your user account and displays the Welcome screen so another user can log on.	Start button, Lock menu button, Switch User
Lock	Locks your user account, then displays the Welcome screen.	Start button, Lock button, OR Start button, Lock menu button, Lock
Sleep	Saves your work, turns off the monitor, then reduces power consumption to all hardware components in your computer so it appears off.	Start button, Power button, OR Start button, Lock menu button, Sleep
Hibernate	Saves your work, then turns off your computer.	Start button, Lock menu button, Hibernate

Practice

▼ CONCEPTS REVIEW

Identify each of the items labeled in Figure A-18.

FIGURE A-18

Match each statement with the term it describes.

12. A desktop object that displays buttons for open programs and windows
13. A desktop object that represents a program or Windows tool
14. A type of window that opens after you select a menu command so you can specify settings for completing the operation
15. A Windows component for adjusting your view within a window
16. The workspace within which you work with a program

a. dialog box
b. taskbar
c. scroll bar
d. window
e. icon

Select the best answer from the list of choices.

17. **Operating system software is software that:**
    a. Interferes with your use of a computer.
    b. Manages the operation of a computer.
    c. Performs a single task, such as connecting to the Internet.
    d. Creates documents, such as a resume.

18. **When you right-click a pointing device such as a mouse, Windows:**
    a. Opens a Windows tool or program.
    b. Moves an object, such as a desktop icon.
    c. Opens a shortcut menu.
    d. Deletes the object.

19. What portion of a window displays the name of the program you opened?

    a. Title bar   **c.** Toolbar

    b. Menu bar   **d.** Scroll bar

20. You use the Maximize button to:

    a. Restore a window to its previous size and location.   **c.** Temporarily hide a window.

    b. Expand a window to fill the entire desktop.   **d.** Scroll through a window.

21. When you put a computer to sleep, Windows:

    a. Completely shuts down the computer.   **c.** Restarts your computer.

    b. Provides an option for switching users.   **d.** Reduces power to the computer and its hardware.

▼ SKILLS REVIEW

1. Start Windows Vista and view the desktop.

    a. Turn on your computer, select your user account or enter your user name, then enter your password (if necessary).

    b. Identify and list as many components of the Windows Vista desktop as you can without referring to the lessons.

    c. Compare your results to Figure A-1 to make sure that you have identified all the desktop objects and icons.

2. Use a pointing device.

    a. Point to the Recycle Bin icon and display its ToolTip.

    b. Double-click the Recycle Bin icon, then restore down the Recycle Bin window if it is maximized.

    c. Drag the Recycle Bin window to the upper-left corner of the desktop, then close the window.

3. Start a program.

    a. Open the Start menu.

    b. Display a list of all programs.

    c. Start Windows Calendar.

4. Move and resize windows.

    a. If the Windows Calendar window is maximized, restore down the window.

    b. Adjust the height and width of the window in one operation.

    c. Maximize, minimize, then restore the Windows Calendar window.

5. Use menus, toolbars, and keyboard shortcuts.

    a. Open the View menu on the menu bar, then choose Month to display a calendar for the current month.

    b. Use the View button on the toolbar to display a calendar for the current day.

    c. In the mini-calendar in the Navigation pane on the left, click the date for the next day to view its schedule.

    d. Use the keyboard shortcut [Alt][F4] to close Windows Calendar.

6. Use dialog boxes.

    a. If you do not see the Sidebar on the desktop, open the Start menu, display the All Programs menu, and then choose Windows Sidebar from the Accessories menu (or click the Windows Sidebar icon in the Notification area).

    b. Right-click the Clock gadget, then click Options to view settings for the Clock gadget.

    c. Under the preview of a clock, use the Next button to advance through the eight options for viewing the Clock.

    d. Use the Previous button to return to the first (default) view for the Clock gadget.

    e. Click the Cancel button to close the Clock dialog box without making any changes to the settings.

7. Use scroll bars.

    a. From the Start menu, open Windows Help and Support and maximize the window (if necessary).

    b. Open the Windows Basics Help topic.

    c. Use the down scroll arrow in the vertical scroll bar to examine other Help topics.

    d. Use the up scroll arrow in the vertical scroll bar to view previously displayed Help topics.

    e. Use the scroll box in the vertical scroll bar to view the last Windows Basics Help topic.

8. Use Windows Help and Support.

    a. Open "The Start menu (overview)" Help topic.

    b. Read the information about the Start menu in the first two paragraphs (through the bulleted list).

    c. Use the Search Help box to locate help on gadgets.

▼ SKILLS REVIEW (CONTINUED)

  d. Open the Help topic entitled "Windows Sidebar and gadgets (overview)."

  e. Under "In this article," click "Adding and removing gadgets" to jump to this Help topic.

  f. Click "To add a gadget to Sidebar" (shown in blue) to view the steps for this process, then click the "To remove a gadget from Sidebar" (shown in blue) to view the single step for this process.

  g. Close the Windows Help and Support window.

9. End a Windows Vista session.

  a. If you are working in a computer lab, follow the instructions provided by your instructor for using the Start menu to log off the computer, restart the computer, put the computer to sleep, or shut down the computer completely. If you are working on your own computer, use the Start menu to choose the shut-down option you prefer.

▼ INDEPENDENT CHALLENGE 1

You work as a teacher for ABC Computer Mentors. You need to prepare a set of handouts that provide an overview of some of the new desktop features in Windows Vista for individuals enrolled in an upcoming class on Computer Survival Skills.

  a. Open Windows Help and Support, then open the Windows Basics Help topic.

  b. Open the **Using menus, buttons, bars, and boxes** Help topic under Desktop Fundamentals.

  c. Use the vertical scroll bar to read the entire Help topic.

  d. Prepare a handwritten list of 10 new features that you learned about working with menus, buttons, bars, and boxes. Use the following title for your list: **Using Menus, Buttons, Bars, and Boxes**

  e. Close Windows Help and Support, write your name on your list, and submit it to your instructor.

▼ INDEPENDENT CHALLENGE 2

You are a freelance photographer who takes photographs for magazine covers, articles, newsletters, and Web sites. You want to evaluate how the Windows Photo Gallery can be used to make simple changes to digital photos.

  a. Open Windows Help and Support and search for tips on editing pictures in Windows Photo Gallery.

  b. After reading the Tips for editing pictures Help topic, prepare a handwritten summary with the title **Tips for Editing Pictures**, listing the recommended workflow for editing pictures in Windows Photo Gallery. (*Hint*: Use the first figure in the Help topic on the recommended workflow in Photo Gallery to identify the four steps.)

  c. Use Windows Help and Support to search for information on how to remove red eye from a picture.

  d. Add to your summary a short paragraph that describes red eye and how you can correct this problem with Windows Photo Gallery.

  e. Close Windows Help and Support, write your name on your summary, and submit it to your instructor.

▼ INDEPENDENT CHALLENGE 3

As a marketing analyst for Expert AI Systems, Ltd., in Great Britain, you contact and collaborate with employees at an Australian branch of the company. Because your colleagues live in a different time zone, you want to add another clock to your Sidebar and customize it to show the time in Australia. This way, you can quickly determine when to reach these employees at a convenient time during their workday hours.

  a. If Windows does not display the Sidebar on the desktop, use the All Programs menu or the Windows Sidebar icon in the Notification area to display the Sidebar.

  b. Use Windows Help and Support to search for information on how to customize the Windows Sidebar and how to change an individual gadget's options.

  c. Use this Help information to view the settings for the Clock gadget on the Sidebar, then try each setting.

  d. Click Cancel to close the Clock dialog box without changing the settings.

▼ INDEPENDENT CHALLENGE 3 (CONTINUED)

Advanced Challenge Exercise

- Point to the Gadgets toolbar at the top of the Sidebar, then click the Add Gadget button.
- Double-click the Clock gadget in the Add Gadgets dialog box, then close the Add Gadgets dialog box.
- Drag the new copy of the Clock gadget and place it below the last gadget on the Sidebar.
- Right-click the new Clock gadget, then click Options on the shortcut menu to view settings for the new Clock.
- Choose a different view for the clock and, in the Clock name text box, type **Australia**.
- Click the Time Zone list arrow to display a list of different time zones, then click the time zone for Canberra, Melbourne, and Sydney. (*Hint:* You want the GMT+10:00 time zone near the bottom of the list of time zones.)
- Add a check mark to the "Show the second hand" check box to enable this feature.
- Click OK to close the Clock dialog box.
- Right-click the new Clock gadget, then click Close Gadget on the shortcut menu to restore your Sidebar to its original state.

e. Prepare a handwritten summary entitled **Using Clock Gadgets** that describes what settings you examined and how you might use them in your daily life.

f. Write your name on your summary and submit it to your instructor.

▼ REAL LIFE INDEPENDENT CHALLENGE

In preparation for an upcoming convention to present new products produced by your company, Continental Saunas, Inc., you decide to prepare a slide show using the Windows Photo Gallery.

a. Open Windows Help and Support, then search for Help information on viewing your pictures as a slide show.

b. Read the Help information, studying the features of the Slide Show Controls toolbar and slide show themes.

c. Open the Photo Gallery Viewer from the Slide Show gadget on the Sidebar.

d. Use the Play Slide Show button to view a slide show of the photos in your Pictures folder.

Advanced Challenge Exercise

Note: To view the Slide Show Controls toolbar as well as certain themes and transitions, your computer must have a graphics card capable of displaying these features and special effects.

- After the slide show starts, move your pointing device to display the Slide Show Controls toolbar.
- Use the Slide Show Controls toolbar to perform the following operations during the slide show. Note the default setting for specific buttons, which options you choose, and what they do so that you can prepare a short written summary for co-workers who might use the Windows Photo Gallery for slide shows.
- Use the Themes pop-up list button to select and view other themes (or presentation formats) for slide shows. Note the default theme, try at least three other themes, then restore the default theme.
- Use the Slide Show Settings button to change the slide show speed and examine the Shuffle and Loop options, then restore the default slide show speed and Shuffle or Loop option.
- Use the Previous and Next buttons to view the previous and next image.
- Use the Exit button to end the slide show.

e. Prepare a one-page handwritten summary titled **Photo Gallery Slide Show** that describes what you have learned about the Windows Photo Gallery and how you might use it in your daily life.

f. Write your name on the summary and submit it to your instructor.

▼ VISUAL WORKSHOP

After returning from a Quest Specialty Travel tour, you want to print a copy of a digital photo to promote an upcoming trip. Use the skills you have learned in this lesson to print a copy of a digital photo:

- Use Windows Help and Support to search for information on how to print a picture using Windows Photo Gallery.
- Use the Slide Show gadget to open the Windows Photo Gallery, then choose the option to print a 4 x 6 inch copy of the image on letter-size paper, as shown in Figure A-19.
- Write your name on the printed copy and submit it to your instructor.

FIGURE A-19

Getting Started with Windows Vista

Understanding File Management

Files You Will Need:

No files needed.

You use Windows Vista to access the drives where you store your folders and files. Each **drive** on your computer is a physical location for storing files. Most people store their files on the computer's hard disk drive and keep duplicate copies on other drives, such as a USB flash drive. The **hard disk** is a built-in, high-capacity, high-speed storage medium for all the software, folders, and files on a computer. When you create a document or other types of data with a program, you save the results in a file, which consists of stored electronic data such as text, a picture, a video, or music. Each file is stored in a folder, which is a container for a group of related files such as reports, correspondence, or e-mail contacts. As a tour guide for Quest Specialty Travel (QST), you want to better understand how you can use Windows Vista to manage the files you need for proposing, planning, organizing, and documenting QST tours.

OBJECTIVES

Manage folders and files

Open the Computer window

Create and save documents

Open the Documents folder

Copy files

Open, edit, and print files

Move and rename files

Search for files

Delete and restore files

Managing Folders and Files

Most of the work you do on a computer involves using programs to create files, which you then store in folders. Over time, you create many folders and files and save them on different storage media. The process of organizing and finding your folders and files can become a challenge. It is helpful to develop a strategy for organizing your folders and files; these tasks are referred to as **file management**. Windows Vista provides a variety of file management tools to assist you in these tasks. ███ As a QST tour guide for destinations in the South Pacific, you work with many types of files. You want to review how Windows can help you track and organize your files.

DETAILS

You can use Windows Vista to:

QUICK TIP

In an office, a paper *file* refers to a manila folder that contains documents printed on paper, whereas a paper *folder* commonly refers to a hanging folder in which you place printed documents or manila folders that contain printed documents.

- ### Create folders for storing and organizing files

  Folders provide a location for your important files and help you organize them into groups of related files so that you can easily locate a file later. You give each folder you create a unique, descriptive **folder name** that identifies the files you intend to place in the folder. A folder can also contain other folders, called **subfolders**, to help organize files into smaller groups. This structure for organizing folders and files is called a **file hierarchy** because it describes the logic and layout of the folder structure on a disk. Windows Vista provides the Documents folder in which you create folders and subfolders for saving your files on your hard disk drive. Most programs automatically open and use the Documents folder when you save or open files. Figure B-1 illustrates how you might organize your tour folders and files within the Documents folder. Windows Vista provides other folders dedicated to specific types of files, such as the Pictures folder for image files; the Music folder for music or sound files; the Contacts folder for e-mail addresses and other contact information, including names, addresses, and phone numbers; and the Favorites folder for Internet shortcuts to your preferred Web sites. Figure B-2 shows the standard folders that Windows Vista creates for each user.

- ### Rename, copy, and move folders and files

  If you want to change the name of a folder or file, you can rename it. For example, you might change the name of the "French Polynesia Tour Proposal" file to "French Polynesia Tour" after your supervisor approves the tour. If you need a duplicate of a file, you can copy it. For example, you could make a copy of the "French Polynesia Tour" file, rename the copy to "Fiji Islands Tour Proposal," then modify the file's content for a new tour location. You can also move a folder or file to another folder or disk and physically change its location.

- ### Delete and restore folders and files

  Deleting folders and files you no longer need frees up storage space on your disk and helps keep your files organized. Folders and files deleted from your hard disk are moved to a Windows folder called the Recycle Bin. If you accidentally delete an important folder or file, or if you change your mind and want to restore a deleted folder or file, you can retrieve it from the Recycle Bin. Folders or files deleted from a removable disk, such as a USB flash drive, are permanently removed and cannot be retrieved with Windows.

- ### Locate folders and files quickly using Instant Search

  Instant Search helps you quickly locate a folder or file if you forget where you stored it. If you can provide part of the folder or file name—or some other fact about the item, such as the author's name—Instant Search can easily locate it and save you a lot of time and effort.

- ### Use shortcuts to access frequently used files and folders

  As your file structure becomes more complex, a file or folder you use often might be located several levels down the file hierarchy and require multiple steps to open. To save time, you can create shortcuts on your desktop to the files and folders you use frequently. A **shortcut** is a link that gives you quick access to a folder, file, or Web site. As shown in Figure B-2, Windows uses shortcuts to folders that contain sample files, such as pictures, music, and videos. Also, each program listed on the All Programs menu is a shortcut to the actual program stored elsewhere on your computer.

FIGURE B-1: Sample folder and file hierarchy

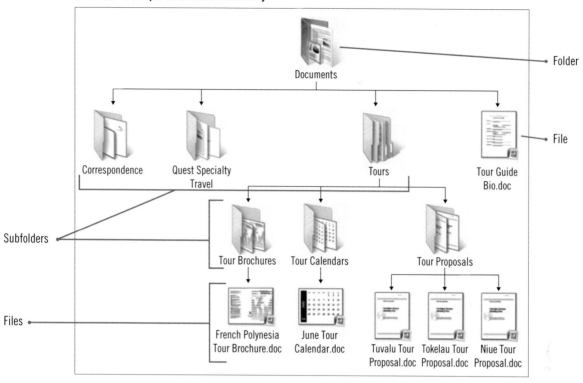

FIGURE B-2: Default user folders in Windows Vista

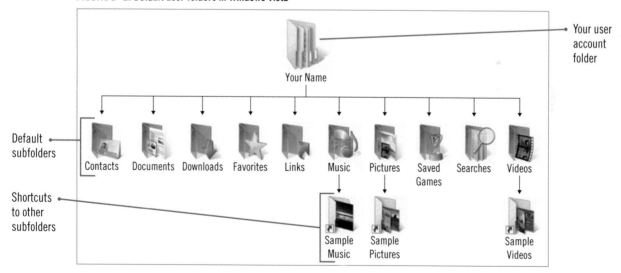

Organizing your folders and files efficiently

Good planning is essential for effective file management. First, identify the types of files you work with, such as images, music, and reports, then determine a logical system for organizing your files. The Pictures and Music folders are good places to store images and music. The Documents folder is the most common place to store all of your other files. Within each folder, use subfolders to better organize the files into smaller groups. For example, use subfolders in the Pictures folder to separate family photos from vacation photos, or to group them by year. In the Documents folder, you might group personal files in one subfolder and business files in another subfolder, then create additional subfolders to further distinguish sets of files. For example, your personal files might include subfolders for resumes, letters, and income tax returns, to name a few. Your business files might include subfolders for clients, projects, and invoices. You should periodically reevaluate your folder structure to ensure that it continues to meet your needs.

Opening the Computer Window

The **Computer window** shows the drives on your computer organized into two groups—Hard Disk Drives and Devices with Removable Storage. A **device** is a hardware component in your computer system. **Removable storage** refers to storage media that you can easily transfer from one computer to another, such as DVDs, CDs, or flash drives. **USB flash drives** (also called pen drives, jump drives, keychain drives, and thumb drives) are a popular removable storage device because of their ease of use and portability. When you attach a USB flash drive to a computer, a new drive icon appears under Devices with Removable Storage. To distinguish one drive from another, each drive has a unique **drive name** that consists of a letter followed by a colon, such as C: for the hard disk drive. Table B-1 lists examples of different drive types. Table B-2 lists commonly used terms to describe the storage capacities of different types of disks. ▓▓▓ Before you plan your next tour, you want to see what types of drives are available on your computer.

STEPS

1. **Start your computer and** Windows Vista, **logging onto your computer if necessary**

QUICK TIP

The **Navigation Pane** contains links to your personal folders, including the Documents, Pictures, and Music folders.

2. **Click the** Start button 🌐 **on the taskbar, click** Computer **on the right side of the Start menu, then click the** Maximize button 🔲 **if the Computer window does not fill the desktop**

   The Computer window opens, displaying icons for the hard disk drive and removable storage devices on your computer. Your computer may have more than one hard disk drive or other types of removable storage. You may also see icons for other types of hardware, such as a scanner or digital camera.

TROUBLE

If the Details Pane is hidden, click the Organize button on the toolbar, point to Layout, then click Details Pane.

3. **Under Hard Disk Drives, click the** your hard disk drive icon

   As shown in Figure B-3, the **Details Pane** at the bottom of the Computer window shows a friendly name for your hard disk drive (such as Local Disk), its actual drive name (C:), the total size or total storage capacity, the amount of free space, and a horizontal bar that shows the storage space already being used on the hard disk drive. When you select the hard disk drive (or some other drive), the options on the toolbar change to ones available for that drive.

4. **Click the** Close button 🔳 **on the Computer window title bar**

   The Computer window closes.

TABLE B-1: Drive names and drive icons

drive type	drive icon	friendly name	drive name	referred to as
floppy disk drive	🖫	3½ Floppy	A:	drive A
hard disk drive	🖴	Local Disk	C:	drive C
CD drive	💿	CD-RW Drive, CD-R Drive, or CD-ROM Drive	next available drive letter; for example, D:	drive D
DVD drive	📀	DVD-RW Drive, DVD-R Drive, or DVD-ROM Drive	next available drive letter; for example, E:	drive E
USB flash drive	🖴	[*varies with drive*]	next available drive letter; for example, F:	drive F

FIGURE B-3: Computer window

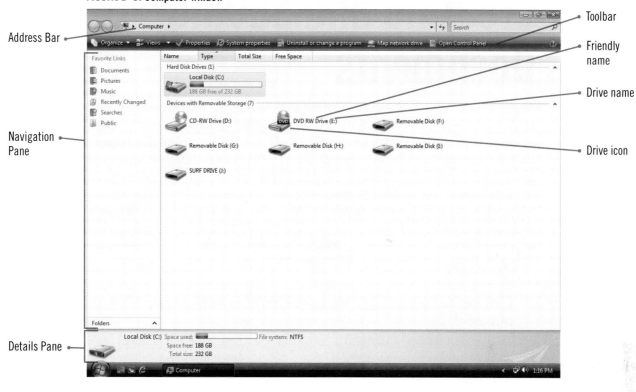

Address Bar

Navigation Pane

Details Pane

Toolbar

Friendly name

Drive name

Drive icon

TABLE B-2: Disk storage capacity terms

term	equals approximately	example	storage space
byte	one character of storage space on disk or in RAM (memory)	A simple text file with the phrase *To-Do List*	10 bytes; count all the characters in the phrase including the hyphen and the blank space between the two words (10 characters = 10 bytes of storage space)
kilobyte (KB or K)	one thousand bytes	A file with a 10-page term paper (approximately 3500 characters per page)	35 KB (approximately 35,000 bytes)
megabyte (MB or M)	one million bytes (or one thousand kilobytes)	512 MB USB flash drive	512 MB (approximately 512 million bytes)
gigabyte (GB or G)	one billion bytes (or one thousand megabytes)	350 GB hard disk	350 GB (approximately 350 billion bytes)
terabyte (TB or T)	one trillion bytes (or one thousand gigabytes)	1 TB hard disk drive	1 TB (approximately one trillion bytes)

Displaying the Computer icon on the desktop

By default, the Computer icon does not appear on the desktop. You can display the Computer icon on the desktop so you can open the Computer window in one step rather than from the Start menu, which involves several steps. To add the Computer icon to your desktop, click the Start button, right-click Computer, then click Show on Desktop. You can now quickly open the Computer window by double-clicking the Computer icon on the desktop. You can repeat these steps to remove the Computer icon from the desktop.

Creating and Saving Documents

Windows comes with easy-to-use programs called Accessories. For example, you can use the WordPad Accessory to create simple text documents such as a letter or to-do list. Any document you create with WordPad (or another program) is temporarily stored in your computer's **RAM (random access memory)**. Anything stored in RAM is lost when you turn off your computer or the power fails unexpectedly. Before you close a document or exit WordPad, you must create a permanent copy of the document by saving it as a file on a disk. You can save files in the **Documents folder** on your local hard disk drive (drive C) or on a removable storage device such as a USB flash drive. When you name a file, choose a **filename** that clearly identifies the file contents. Filenames can be no more than 255 characters, including spaces and can include letters, numbers, and certain symbols. ▓▓▓▓ You want to use WordPad to create a to-do list for your next tour, then save the file to the Documents folder. The To-Do List is shown in Figure B-4.

STEPS

1. **Click the** Start button ⊕ **on the taskbar, point to** All Programs, **click** Accessories, **then click** WordPad

    The WordPad window opens with a new, blank document. Table B-3 identifies the components of the WordPad window. In the document window, a blinking **insertion point** indicates where the next character you type will appear.

QUICK TIP

If you make a typing mistake, press [Backspace] to delete the character to the left of the insertion point.

2. **Type** To-Do List **on the first line, then press [Enter] three times**

    Each time you press [Enter], WordPad inserts a new blank line and places the insertion point at the beginning of the line.

3. **Type the text shown in Figure B-4, pressing [Enter] at the end of each line**

TROUBLE

If the Documents folder is not displayed, click Documents in the Navigation Pane.

4. **Click** File **on the menu bar, click** Save As, **then click the** Browse Folders **button in the Save As dialog box**

    The Save As dialog box expands to show the contents of the Documents folder, as shown in Figure B-5.

5. **Click** Document.rtf **in the File name text box to select it, then type** To-Do List

TROUBLE

If a Confirm Save As dialog box asks if you want to replace a file with the same name, click Yes.

6. **Click** Save **in the Save As dialog box**

    WordPad saves the document in a file named "To-Do List" in the Documents folder and closes the Save As dialog box. The title bar displays "To-Do List.rtf"—the filename you entered followed by the file extension .rtf. A **file extension** identifies the type of file. Each program assigns a file extension to files you create, so you only need to enter a name for the file. Depending on how Windows is set up, you may not see the file extensions.

7. **Click the** Close button ▓▓▓ **on the WordPad title bar**

FIGURE B-3: Components of the WordPad window

component	used to
Title bar	Display the name of the open document and program
Menu bar	Display menu names with commands for performing operations on a document and its contents and for specifying program settings
Toolbar	Display buttons for common menu commands, such as saving and printing
Format bar	Display buttons for formatting, or enhancing, the appearance of a document
Ruler	Mark a document's width in ⅛ths of an inch (also shows one-inch marks)
Document window	Display all or part of the open document
Status bar	Display simple Help information and tips

FIGURE B-4: WordPad document

Temporary filename

Program name

Insertion point

Toolbar

Format bar

Ruler

Document window

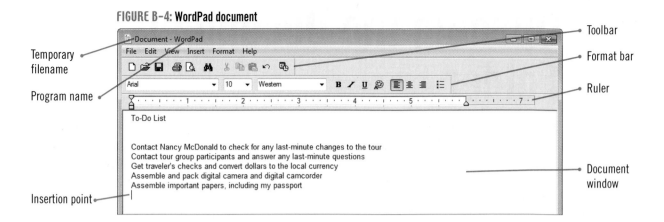

FIGURE B-5: Save As dialog box

Navigation Pane

Current folder

Folders in the current folder (yours will differ)

Temporary filename

Type of file

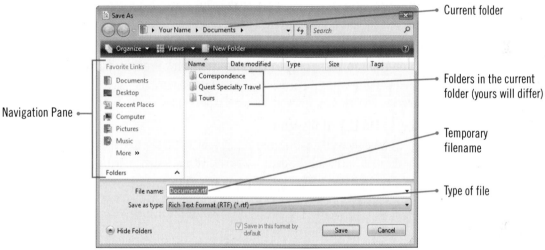

Using the Address Bar in the Save As dialog box

The **Address Bar** shows your current location in the computer's file hierarchy as a series of links separated by arrows. In Figure B-5, this series of links appears as an icon followed by "Your Name" (your user account folder name) then Documents. If you click the leftmost arrow in the Address Bar, you can use the drop-down list that opens to switch to the desktop, the Computer window, or other system folders. If you click the arrow after your user account name, you can use the list that opens to switch to any of your user account folders, such as Contacts, Music, Pictures, and Videos. If you click the arrow after Documents, you can use the list that opens to switch to a sub-folder in the Documents folder, as shown in Figure B-6.

FIGURE B-6: Address Bar drop-down menu

Address Bar

Address Bar arrow displays a drop-down list of subfolders within the Documents folder

Subfolders in the Documents folder

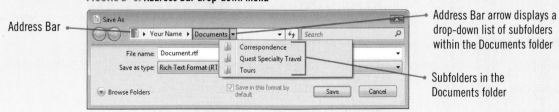

Opening the Documents Folder

The Documents folder is the most common place to store files you create or receive from others. From the Documents folder, you can examine your files, organize them into subfolders, or perform other common file management tasks such as renaming, copying, moving, or deleting a folder or file. ████████ You store all your QST tour files in the Documents folder on your computer. You want to organize the files in your Documents folder before you copy them to a USB flash drive.

STEPS

1. **Click the** Start button 🗗 **on the taskbar, then click** Documents

   The Documents window opens and displays your folders and files, including the To-Do List.rtf file. Table B-4 identifies the components of the Documents window.

TROUBLE
If your view did not change, Windows Vista is already set to Large Icons view.

2. **Click the** Views button arrow **on the toolbar, then click** Large Icons

   Like some of the other views, Large Icons view displays folder icons with different icons for the types of files (such as a text document) contained in a folder or a **live view** of the actual content in files.

QUICK TIP
The Layout option on the Organize menu controls whether to display the Details, Preview, and Navigation panes.

3. **If you do not see the Preview Pane on the right side of the window, click the** Organize button **on the toolbar, point to** Layout, **then click** Preview Pane

   The **Preview Pane** shows the actual contents of the selected file, such as the WordPad file, without starting a program. Preview may not work for some types of files.

4. **Click the** To-Do List.rtf file icon

   The Preview Pane shows the actual contents of your To-Do List file, and the Details Pane lists information about the file itself, including the dates it was created and last modified, and its size. See Figure B-7.

5. **Leave the Documents window open for the next lesson**

TABLE B-4: Components of the Documents window

component	used to
Back button	Go back to previously viewed folders
Forward button	Return to the folders you just left
Address Bar	Display the name of the current folder and navigate to a different folder
Search box	Locate files or folders in the current folder
Toolbar	Perform common tasks on a folder or its contents (such as changing the view or e-mailing a file)
Navigation Pane	Navigate to another folder
File list	Display the subfolders and files in the current folder
Details Pane	View information about the folder or file you select in the File list
Preview Pane	View the actual content within some types of files

FIGURE B-7: Documents window

Forward button

Back button

Address Bar

Navigation Pane

Files list (shows folders and files in Large Icons view)

Search box

Toolbar

Preview Pane

Details Pane

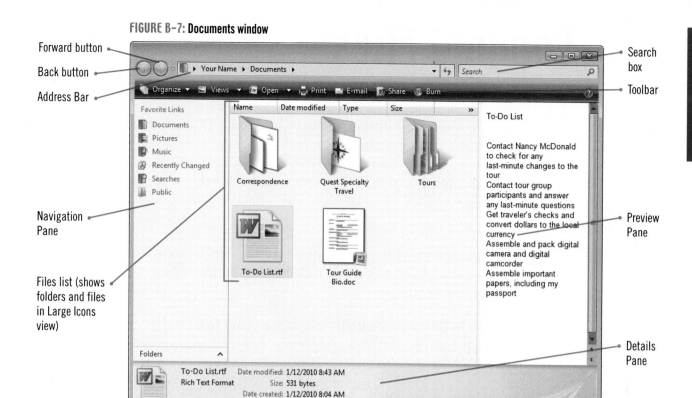

Changing views in a window

The Views button provides seven ways to display the folders and files in a window. Extra Large Icons, Large Icons, and Medium Icons views display rows of folder and file icons at different sizes, with their names displayed under the icon. Small Icons view displays rows of even smaller folder and file icons with the folder or filename to the right of the icon. List view displays columns of very small folder or filename icons with the names to the right of the icon. Tiles view is similar to Small Icons view, but displays larger icons and also lists the type of folder or file and the file size. Details view is similar to List view, but displays columns with the folder or filename, the date and time that a folder or file was modified, the type of folder or file, the size of files, and any tags assigned to a file. A **tag** is a word or phrase that reminds you of a file's content. You can use the Views button slider bar to scale icons to your preferred size between Small Icons and Extra Large Icons.

Copying Files

You can copy a file, a group of files, or a folder from one disk drive to another or from one folder to another. When you **copy** a file, the original file stays in its current location and a duplicate of the file is created in another location. This feature lets you make a backup of your important files. A **backup** is a copy of a file that is stored in another location. If you lose the original file, you can make a new working copy from your backup. You can use the Send To menu to quickly copy a file from the Documents folder to another disk drive. █████ You want to copy your To-Do List.rtf file to your USB flash drive so you can work with the file as you travel.

STEPS

TROUBLE

If you are using a different storage device, insert the appropriate disk and substitute that device whenever you see USB flash drive in the steps.

1. **Attach your USB flash drive to your computer or to a cable connected to your computer, then, if the AutoPlay dialog box opens, click the Close button** ▣
   Your USB flash drive is ready to use.

2. **Right-click the To-Do List.rtf file icon, then point to Send To on the shortcut menu**
   A list of the available drives and locations where you can copy the file appears on the shortcut menu, as shown in Figure B-8. The options on your Send To menu will differ.

QUICK TIP

If you hold down [Shift] while you click a Send To option, Windows moves the file to that disk; it does not make another copy

3. **Click the USB flash drive option**
   Windows copies the To-Do List.rtf file to your USB flash drive. There are now two copies of the same file stored in two different locations.

4. **Click the first Address Bar arrow** ▶ **on the Address Bar, as shown in Figure B-9, then click Computer**
   The contents of the Computer folder appear in the window.

5. **Double-click the USB flash drive icon**
   The contents of your USB flash drive, including the To-Do List.rtf file you copied to this disk, appear in the window. See Figure B-10.

6. **Click the Close button** ▣ **on the Removable Disk window title bar**

Using the Send To menu

You can create a shortcut on the desktop to any folder or file you use frequently with the "Desktop (create shortcut)" option on the Send To menu. The Compressed (zipped) Folder option on the Send To menu creates a new compressed file using the same filename, but with the .zip file extension. For example, compressing To-Do List.rtf creates a new file named To-Do List.zip. Before you send a file by e-mail, especially a large file, it is a good idea to **compress** it, which makes the file smaller in size.

FIGURE B-8: Send To menu

Send To
option

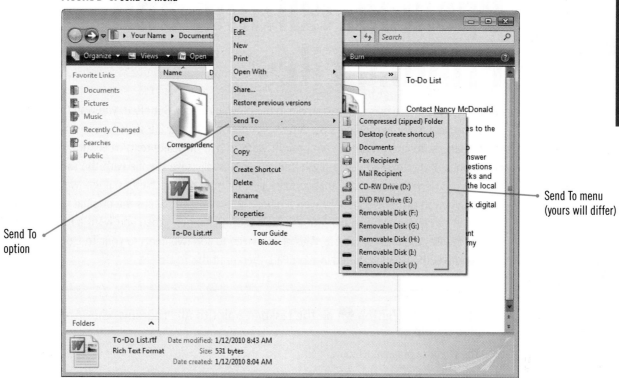

Send To menu
(yours will differ)

FIGURE B-9: Navigating with the Address Bar

Address Bar
arrow displays
a drop-down list
of locations

Switches to
the Computer
window

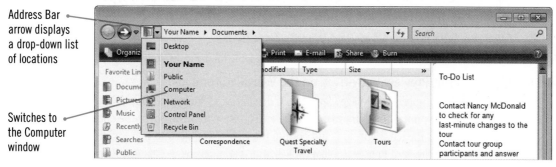

FIGURE B-10: Removable Disk window

Address Bar
arrows

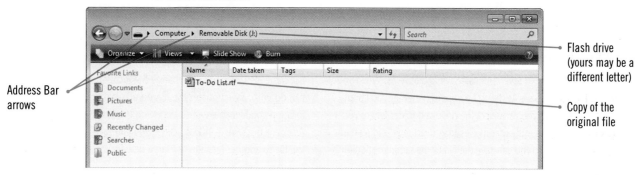

Flash drive
(yours may be a
different letter)

Copy of the
original file

Opening, Editing, and Printing Files

Sometimes you create new files, as you did in the previous lesson. But often, you want to change a file that you or someone else already created. After you open an existing file stored on a disk, you can **edit**, or make changes, to it. For example, you might want to add or delete text, or change the **formatting** or appearance of the text. After you finish editing, you usually save the file with the same filename, which replaces the file with a new copy that contains all your most recent changes. If you want to keep the original file, you can save the edited file with a different filename; this keeps the original file without the edits and creates a new copy of the file with the most recent changes. When you want a **hard copy**, or paper copy of the file, you need to print it. ▓▓▓▓▓ You need to add two items to your To-Do List, so you want to open and edit the file you created in WordPad, then print the To-Do List.

STEPS

1. **Click the Start button ⊕ on the taskbar, point to All Programs, click Accessories, then click WordPad**

   The WordPad program window opens.

2. **Click the Open button ☞ on the WordPad toolbar, click Computer in the Navigation Pane, then double-click your USB flash drive icon**

   The Open dialog box displays the contents of your USB flash drive. See Figure B-11. You may see additional files.

QUICK TIP

You can also open a file by double-clicking it in the Open dialog box.

3. **Click To-Do List.rtf in the File list, then click Open in the Open dialog box**

   The Open dialog box closes and the To-Do List.rtf file appears in the WordPad window.

4. **Click at the beginning of the last blank line in the To-Do List, then type the two additional lines shown in Figure B-12, pressing [Enter] after each line**

5. **Click the Save button 🖫 on the WordPad toolbar**

   WordPad saves the edited To-Do List.rtf file under the same filename on your USB flash drive.

QUICK TIP

You should always use Print Preview before you print to save time and effort as well as toner ink and paper.

6. **Click the Print Preview button 🔍 on the WordPad toolbar**

   Print Preview displays a full-page view of your document, as shown in Figure B-13, so you can check its layout before you print. Dotted lines separate the area on the page reserved for the document and the blank space reserved for the left, right, top, and bottom margins. If you need to make additional edits, click the Close button on the Print Preview toolbar (not the title bar), make your changes, then use Print Preview to check the document again before printing.

7. **Click the Print button on the Print Preview toolbar**

   Print Preview closes and the Print dialog box opens, so you can verify the print settings.

8. **Click Print in the Print dialog box, then retrieve your printed copy from the printer**

9. **Click the Close button ☒ on the WordPad title bar**

   WordPad closes.

Comparing Save and Save As

The File menu has two save options—Save and Save As. When you first save a file, the Save As dialog box opens (whether you choose Save or Save As) so you can select the drive and folder where you want to save the file and enter its filename. If you edit and save a previously saved file, you can save the file to the same location with the same filename, you can change the location or filename, or you can do both. Save updates the file stored on disk using the same location and filename without opening the Save As dialog box. Save As opens the Save As dialog box so you can save an updated copy of the file to another location or with a new filename.

FIGURE B-11: Open dialog box

Address Bar arrows

Navigation Pane

Current drive (yours may be a different letter)

Open this file

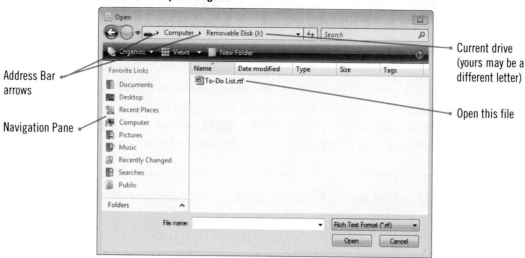

FIGURE B-12: Edited To-Do List file

Additional text

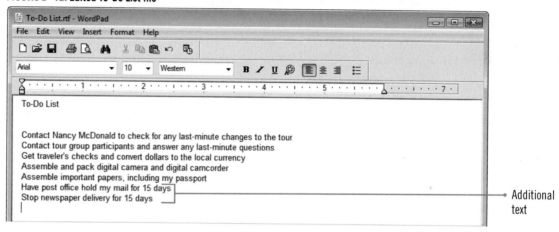

FIGURE B-13: Print Preview

Closes Print Preview, but not the document

Left margin

Closes the document and WordPad

Top margin

Right margin

Bottom margin

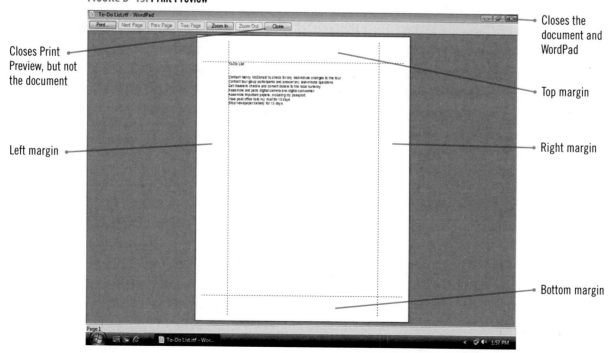

Moving and Renaming Files

You can move a file, a group of files, or a folder to another location such as a different folder on the same drive or a different drive. When you **move** a file, the original file is stored in a different location. One of the fastest ways to move a file is with **drag and drop** (which uses a pointing device to drag a file or folder to a new location). You may also need to rename a file, giving it a name that more clearly describes the file's contents and how you intend to use the file. ▰▰▰▰ You want to move the To-Do List.rtf file to a new folder and rename it so you can update the list for your next tour.

STEPS

1. **Click the** Start button ⊕ **on the taskbar, click** Computer, **then double-click your** USB flash drive icon

   The contents of your USB flash drive appear in the Computer window.

2. **Click the** Views button arrow **on the Computer window toolbar, then click** Large Icons

   The larger icons make it easier to work with folder and file icons as you move and rename files.

3. **Click the** Organize button **on the Computer window toolbar, then click** New Folder

   Windows creates a new folder named "New Folder," as shown in Figure B-14. The folder name is highlighted so you can type a more descriptive folder name.

TROUBLE
If you cannot type a name for the new folder, press [F2] (the Rename key), then repeat Step 4.

4. **Type** French Polynesia Tour **as the folder name, then press** [Enter]

   Windows changes the name of the folder.

5. **Click the** white background of the window, **point to the** To-Do List.rtf file, **press and hold the** left button **on your pointing device, drag the** To-Do List.rtf file **icon on top of the French Polynesia Tour folder, then pause**

   As shown in Figure B-15, a smaller transparent copy of the To-Do List.rtf file icon appears over the French Polynesia Tour folder and a ToolTip describes the type of operation.

6. **Release the** left button **on your pointing device**

   The To-Do List.rtf file moves into the French Polynesia Tour folder.

7. **Double-click the** French Polynesia Tour folder

   The Address Bar shows the name of the open folder, French Polynesia Tour. The To-Do List.rtf file appears in this folder.

8. **Click the** To-Do List.rtf file icon, **click the** Organize button, **then click** Rename

   The first part of the filename is highlighted so you can type a new name for the file.

9. **Type** Tour Preparation **as the new filename, then press** [Enter]

   Windows renames the file. See Figure B-16.

10. **Click the** Close button ▣ **on the title bar**

FIGURE B-14: Creating a new folder

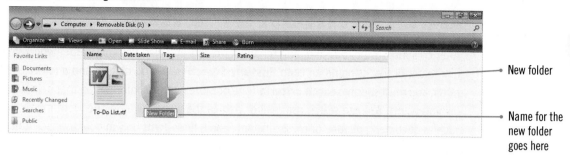

New folder

Name for the new folder goes here

FIGURE B-15: Moving a file using drag and drop

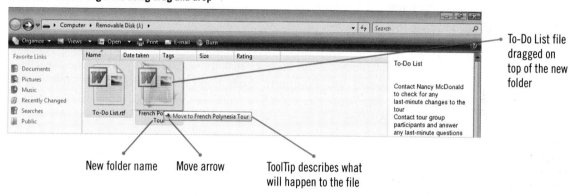

To-Do List file dragged on top of the new folder

New folder name

Move arrow

ToolTip describes what will happen to the file

FIGURE B-16: Renamed file

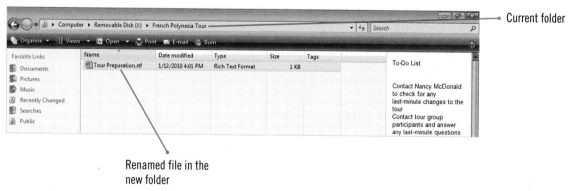

Current folder

Renamed file in the new folder

Using drag and drop to copy and move files

If you drag and drop a file to a folder on the same drive, Windows moves the file into that folder. However, if you drag and drop a file to a folder on another drive, Windows copies the file instead. If you want to move a file to another drive, hold down [Shift] while you drag and drop. If you want to copy a file to another folder on the same drive, hold down [Ctrl] while you drag and drop.

Searching for Files

After creating, saving, deleting, and renaming folders and files, you may forget where you stored a particular folder or file, its name, or both. **Instant Search** helps you quickly find a folder or file on your computer. You must specify **search criteria** (one or more pieces of information that help Windows identify the file you want). You can search using all or part of the filename, a unique word in the file, or the file type such as document, picture, or music. Instant Search finds items only in your user account, not in other user accounts on the same computer. The **Boolean filters** shown in Table B-5 allow you to specify multiple criteria so that you have a greater chance of finding what you need quickly. When you use the Boolean filters AND, OR, and NOT, you must type them in uppercase so they work properly. ░░░░ You want to quickly locate the copy of the To-Do List for your next tour.

STEPS

1. **Click the Start button ⊕ on the taskbar, then click in the Start Search box**

2. **Type To**

   The search results on the left side of the Start menu are organized by categories, as shown in Figure B-17. Your search results will differ; however, all of the search results will have the characters "To" somewhere in the name of each item in the search results. Under Files, you may see two listings for To-Do List.rtf. One is the file in your Documents folder. The other is a shortcut to the original file on the flash drive that you renamed. Windows Vista keeps a list of shortcuts to files you have used recently, even if that file no longer exists.

3. **Type -Do List after the word "To", then press [Spacebar]**

   The additional text you typed narrows the search results, as shown in Figure B-18. Now you see documents with "To," "Do," and "List" in the filename.

4. **Under Files, click To-Do List.rtf**

   The To-Do List.rtf file opens in Microsoft Word, WordPad, or another program that works with Rich Text Format files.

5. **Click the Close button ▨ in the program window's title bar**

> **QUICK TIP**
> Searches are not case sensitive, so you can use uppercase or lowercase letters when you type search criteria.

> **QUICK TIP**
> If you type "To-Do List" with quotation marks, Instant Search finds the To-Do List.rtf file and any shortcut or other files with the same name.

TABLE B-5: Boolean filters

Boolean filter	example	how it works
AND	tour AND proposal	Finds all files that contain the word *tour* and the word *proposal*; the two words may or may not be located next to each other
OR	tour OR proposal	Finds all files that contain the word *tour* or the word *proposal* (or both)
NOT	tour NOT proposal	Finds all files that contain the word *tour* but not the word *proposal*
" " (quotation marks)	"tour proposal"	Finds all files that contain the exact phrase *tour proposal*

FIGURE B-17: Search results

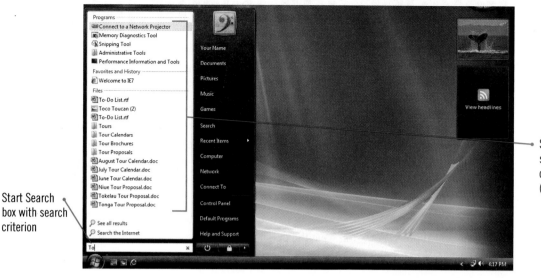

Start Search box with search criterion

Search results show items that contain "To" (yours will differ)

FIGURE B-18: Narrowed search results

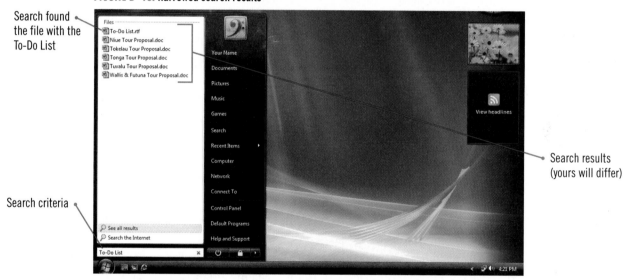

Search found the file with the To-Do List

Search criteria

Search results (yours will differ)

Performing more advanced searches

If you want to search all your personal folders for a file, use the Start Search box on the Start menu. If you want to locate a file in a specific folder and all its subfolders (such as the Documents folder), open the folder and use the Search box in the folder. If you want to locate all files that have the same file extension (such as .rtf), type the file extension as your search criteria. If you want to locate files created by a certain person, use the first name, last name, or first and last name as your search criteria. If you want to locate files created on a certain date, type the date (for example, 7/9/2010) as your search criteria. If you remember the title in a document, type the title as your search criteria. If you have created e-mail contacts in your Contacts folder, you can type the person's name to find his or her e-mail address.

Deleting and Restoring Files

If you no longer need a folder or file, you can **delete** (or remove) it. If you delete a folder, Windows removes the folder as well as everything stored in it. Windows places folders and files you delete from your hard disk drive in the Recycle Bin. If you later discover that you need a deleted file or folder, you can restore it to its original location as long as you have not yet emptied the Recycle Bin. Emptying the Recycle Bin permanently removes the deleted folders and files from your computer. By deleting files and folders you no longer need and periodically emptying the Recycle Bin, you free up valuable storage space on your hard disk drive and keep your computer uncluttered. Be aware that files and folders you delete from a removable disk drive, such as a USB flash drive, are immediately and permanently deleted and cannot be restored by Windows. If you try to delete a file or folder that is too large for the Recycle Bin, Windows asks whether you want to permanently delete the file or folder. Choose Yes to delete the file or folder, or choose No to cancel the operation. ▓▓▓▓ You have the updated copy of the To-Do List.rtf file stored on your USB flash drive, so you want to delete the copy in the Documents folder.

STEPS

1. **Click the Start button ⊕ on the taskbar, click Documents, then click the To-Do List file in the Documents folder**

   After you select a folder or file, you can delete it.

QUICK TIP

You can also quickly delete a selected folder or file by pressing [Delete] or [Del].

2. **Click the Organize button on the toolbar, then click Delete**

   The Delete File dialog box opens so you can confirm the deletion, as shown in Figure B-19.

3. **Click Yes**

   The file moves from the Documents folder into the Recycle Bin.

4. **Click the Minimize button ▭ on the Documents window title bar and examine the Recycle Bin icon**

   The Recycle Bin icon contains wads of paper if the Recycle Bin contains deleted folders and files. If the Recycle Bin icon does not contain wads of paper, then it is empty and does not contain any deleted files or folders.

5. **Double-click the Recycle Bin icon 🗑**

   The Recycle Bin window opens and displays any deleted folders and files, including the To-Do List.rtf file, as shown in Figure B-20. Your Recycle Bin's contents may differ.

QUICK TIP

Windows keeps track of the original location of deleted subfolders and files so it can restore them later, recreating the original folder structure as needed.

6. **Click the To-Do List.rtf file to select it, then click the Restore this item button on the Recycle Bin toolbar**

   The file returns its original location and no longer appears in the Recycle Bin window.

7. **Click the Close button ▨ on the Recycle Bin title bar, then click the Documents taskbar button**

   The Recycle Bin window closes, and the Documents window opens. The Documents window contains the restored file. You decide to permanently delete this previous version of the To-Do List file.

8. **Click the To-Do List file, press [Delete], then click Yes in the Delete File dialog box**

   The To-Do List moves from the Documents folder to the Recycle Bin.

9. **Click the Close button ▨ on the Documents window title bar, then end your Windows session**

FIGURE B-19: Delete File dialog box

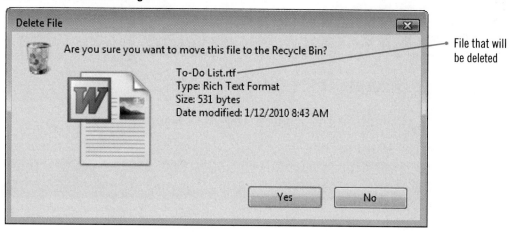

File that will be deleted

FIGURE B-20: Recycle Bin folder

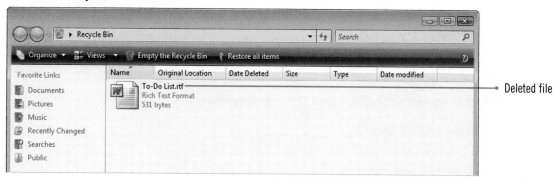

Deleted file

Emptying the Recycle Bin

If you are certain that you no longer need any of the deleted files and folders in your Recycle Bin, you can empty it. If the Recycle Bin folder is open, click the Empty the Recycle Bin button on the toolbar. If it is closed, right-click the Recycle Bin icon on the desktop, then click Empty Recycle Bin on the shortcut menu. In the Delete Multiple Items dialog box, choose Yes to confirm that you want to permanently delete all the items in the Recycle Bin, or choose No to cancel the operation.

Practice

▼ CONCEPTS REVIEW

Label each of the elements of the window shown in Figure B-21.

FIGURE B-21

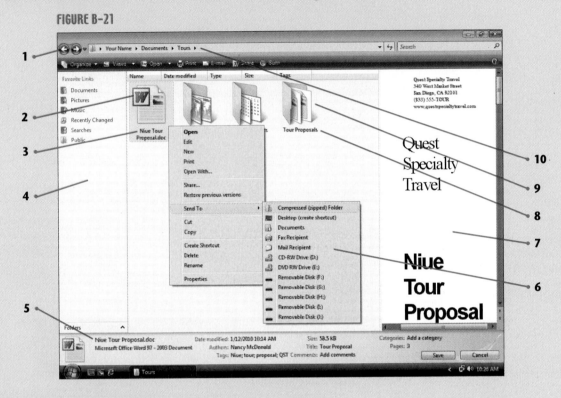

Match each statement with the term it best describes.

11. A container for related files
12. A link that provides quick access to a folder, file, or Web site
13. One or more pieces of information for locating a folder or file
14. Organizing and managing folders and files
15. The name that you assign to a file to identify its contents

a. file management
b. filename
c. folder
d. Search criteria
e. shortcut

Select the best answer from the list of choices.

16. One billion bytes of storage space on a disk is referred to as a:
   a. Kilobyte.
   b. Megabyte.
   c. Gigabyte.
   d. Terabyte.

17. To save a previously saved file with a new filename, you use the:
   a. Save command on the File menu.
   b. Save As command on the File menu.
   c. Save or Save As command on the File menu.
   d. Save button on the program's toolbar.

18. The blinking vertical bar in the WordPad application window is called the:
   a. Insertion point.
   b. Pointer.
   c. Ruler.
   d. Shortcut.

19. After you copy a file, you have:
   a. Only one copy of the file.
   b. A duplicate copy of the file in a different location.
   c. Moved the orginal file to a new location.
   d. Deleted the file.

20. After you move a file, you have:

- **a.** A backup copy of that file.
- **b.** A duplicate copy of the file in a different location.
- **c.** The orginal file in a different location.
- **d.** Deleted the file.

21. When you delete a file from your hard disk drive, Windows:

- **a.** Puts the deleted file in the Recycle Bin.
- **b.** Permanently deletes the file from the hard disk drive.
- **c.** Stores a duplicate copy of the file in the Recycle Bin..
- **d.** Moves the file to a removable disk.

▼ SKILLS REVIEW

1. Manage folders and files.

- **a.** Assume you manage a small travel agency. How would you organize your business files using a hierarchical file structure?
- **b.** What icon can you place on your desktop to quickly locate your flash drive where you store copies of important files?
- **c.** What shortcuts would you place on your desktop for easier access to your business files?

2. Open the Computer window. (If possible, use a different computer than you used for the lessons.)

- **a.** Attach your USB flash drive to your computer.
- **b.** Open the Computer window from the Start menu.
- **c.** Note the types of drives on this computer, their friendly names, and their actual drive names. Note the drive name assigned to your USB flash drive.
- **d.** Select the hard disk drive icon, then view the information in the Details Pane about the hard disk drive's total size and free space.
- **e.** Close the Computer window.

3. Create and save documents.

- **a.** Open WordPad from the All Programs menu.
- **b.** Type Oceania Tours as the title, followed by one blank line.
- **c.** Type your name, followed by two blank lines.
- **d.** Use WordPad to create the following list of current Oceania tours.

    Current Tours:

    1. French Poynesia

    2. Fiji Islands

    3. Pitcairn Islands

    4. Tonga

    5. Niue

    6. Tokelau

- **e.** Save the WordPad file with the filename Oceania Tours in the Documents folder.
- **f.** View the full filename in the WordPad title bar, then close WordPad.

4. Open the Documents folder.

- **a.** Open the Documents folder from the Start menu.
- **b.** If necessary, use the Views button to change the folder view to Large Icons.
- **c.** Click the Oceania Tours.rtf file.
- **d.** If necessary, use the Organize menu to display the Preview Pane.
- **e.** View the contents of the Oceania Tours.rtf file in the Preview Pane.

5. Copy files.

- **a.** Right-click the Oceania Tours.rft file, point to Send To on the shortcut menu, then send a copy of the WordPad file to your USB flash drive.
- **b.** Use the Address Bar to change to the Computer window, then to your USB flash drive window.
- **c.** Verify you successfully copied the Oceania Tours.rtf file to your USB flash drive, then close the USB flash drive window.

6. Open, edit, and print files.

- **a.** Open WordPad from the Start menu.
- **b.** Open the WordPad file named Oceania Tours.rtf from your USB flash drive (not from your Documents folder).

    c. Click at the beginning of the blank line after the last current tour, then add the names of two more tours on two separate lines: **Palau** and **Tuvalu**.

    d. Save the edited WordPad file.

    e. Use Print Preview to display a full-page view of the document.

    f. Print the Oceania Tours.rtf document and retrieve your printed copy from the printer, then close WordPad.

7. Move and rename files.

    a. Open a Computer window, then display the contents of your USB flash drive.

    b. If necessary, change your folder view to Large Icons.

    c. Use the Organize menu to create a new folder and name it **Oceania Tours**.

    d. Use drag and drop to move the Oceania Tours.rtf file into the new folder.

    e. Open the new folder and verify the move operation.

    f. Use the Organize menu to rename the moved WordPad file as **Current Oceania Tours**.

    g. Close the folder window.

8. Search for files.

    a. From the Start menu, enter **Oceania** in the Search box as the search criteria.

    b. Examine the Search results, then open the original Oceania Tours.rtf file.

    c. Close the program window.

9. Delete and restore files.

    a. Open the Documents folder from the Start menu.

    b. Select and delete your original WordPad file with the name **Oceania Tours.rtf**.

    c. Minimize the Documents window, then open the Recycle Bin.

    d. Select and restore the file named **Oceania Tours.rtf** that you just deleted, then close the Recycle Bin window.

    e. Use the Documents taskbar button to redisplay the Documents window.

    f. Verify Windows restored the file named Oceania Tours.rtf to the Documents folder.

    g. Select and delete this file again, then close the Documents window.

    h. Submit the printed copy of your revised WordPad document and your answers to Step 1 to your instructor.

▼ INDEPENDENT CHALLENGE 1

To meet the needs of high-tech workers in your town, you have opened an Internet café named Internet To-Go where your customers can enjoy a cup of fresh-brewed coffee and bakery goods while they check e-mail. To promote your new business, you want to develop a newspaper ad, flyers, and breakfast and lunch menus.

    a. Connect your USB flash drive to your computer, if necessary.

    b. Create a new folder named **Internet To-Go** on your USB flash drive.

    c. In the Internet To-Go folder, create three subfolders named **Advertising**, **Flyers**, and **Menus**.

    d. Use WordPad to create a short ad for your local newspaper that describes your business:

       • Use the name of the business as the title for your document.

       • Write a short paragraph about the business. Include a fictitious location, street address, and phone number.

       • After the paragraph, type your name.

    e. Save the WordPad document with the filename **Newspaper Ad** in the Advertising folder.

    f. Preview and then print your WordPad document.

▼ INDEPENDENT CHALLENGE 2

As a freelance writer for several national magazines, you depend on your computer to meet critical deadlines. Whenever you encounter a computer problem, you contact a computer consultant who helps you resolve the problem. This consultant asked you to document, or keep records of, your computer's current settings.

    a. Connect your USB flash drive to your computer, if necessary.

    b. Open the Computer window so that you can view information on your drives and other installed hardware.

▼ INDEPENDENT CHALLENGE 2 (CONTINUED)

c. Open WordPad and create a document with the title **My Hardware Documentation** and your name on separate lines.

d. List the names of the hard disk drive (or drives), devices with removable storage, and any other hardware devices, such as a digital camera, installed on the computer you are using. Also include the total size and amount of free space on your hard disk drive(s). (*Hint:* If you need to check the Computer window for this information, use the taskbar button for the Computer window to view your drives, then use the WordPad taskbar button to return to WordPad.)

e. Save the WordPad document with the filename **My Hardware Documentation** on your USB flash drive.

f. Preview your document, print your WordPad document, then close WordPad.

▼ INDEPENDENT CHALLENGE 3

As an adjunct, or part-time, instructor at Everhart College, you teach special summer classes for kids on how to use and create computer games, compose digital art, work with digital photographs, and compose digital music. You want to create a folder structure on your USB flash drive to store the files for each class.

a. Connect your USB flash drive to your computer, then open the Computer window to your USB flash drive.

b. Create a folder named **Computer Games**.

c. In the Computer Games folder, create a subfolder named **Class 1**.

Advanced Challenge Exercise

- In the Class 1 folder, create subfolders named **Class Outline** and **Hands-On Lab**.
- Rename the Class Outline folder to **Class Handouts**.
- Create a new folder named **Interactive Presentations** in the Class 1 subfolder.

d. Close the Class 1 folder window.

e. Use WordPad to create a document with the title **Photocopying** and your name on separate lines, and the following list of items that you need to photocopy for the first class:

Class 1:

Class 1 Topics & Resources

Hands-On Lab Assignment

On Your Own Exercise

Interactive Presentation Slides

f. Save the WordPad document with the filename **Photocopying** in the Class 1 folder. (*Hint:* After you switch to your USB flash drive in the Save As dialog box, open the Computer Games folder, then open the Class 1 folder before saving the file.)

g. Preview and print the Photocopying.rtf file, then close WordPad.

h. Draw a diagram of your new folder structure on the printed copy of your WordPad document.

▼ REAL LIFE INDEPENDENT CHALLENGE

This Real Life Independent Challenge requires an Internet connection. You want to open a small specialty shop for pottery, stained glass, handcrafts, and other consignments from local artists and craftspeople. First, you need to search for information on the Internet about preparing a business plan so that you can obtain financing from your local bank for the business.

a. Using the Start Search box on the Start menu, enter **Preparing a Business Plan** as the search criteria, then click the Search the Internet button in the Search Results pane.

b. From the list of Search results, locate a Web site that contains information on how to write a business plan.

c. Start WordPad and create a document in which you summarize in your own words the basic process for preparing a business plan. Include a title and your name in the document. At the bottom of your document, list the URL of the Web site or sites from which you prepared your WordPad document. (*Note:* You should not copy the exact content of a Web site, but instead summarize your findings in your own words because many sites copyright the content on their Web site. If you want to determine what content at a Web site is copyrighted and the conditions for using that content, scroll to the bottom of the Web site and click the link that covers copyright use and restrictions.)

d. Preview and print your WordPad document, then save the document on your USB flash drive.

▼ VISUAL WORKSHOP

As a technical support specialist at Advanced Robotic Systems, Ltd., in Great Britain, you need to respond to employee queries quickly and thoroughly. You decide that it is time to evaluate and reorganize the folder structure on your computer so you can quickly access the resources required for your job. Create the folder structure shown in Figure B-22 on your USB flash drive. As you work, use WordPad to prepare a simple outline of the steps you follow to create the folder structure. Include your name in the document, preview and print the document, then submit it to your instructor.

FIGURE B-22

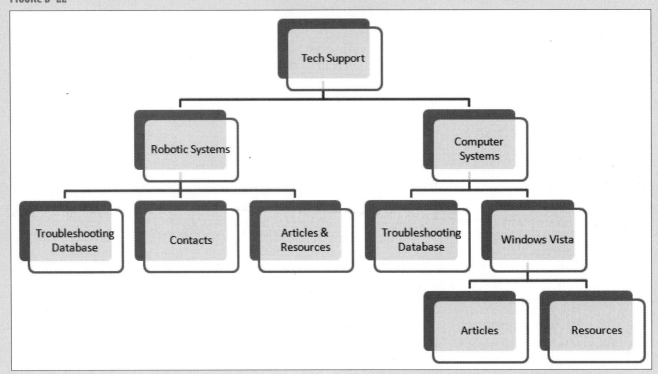

Getting Started with Microsoft Office 2007

Files You Will Need:

OFFICE A-1.xlsx

Microsoft Office 2007 is a group of software programs designed to help you create documents, collaborate with co-workers, and track and analyze information. Each program is designed so you can work quickly and efficiently to create professional-looking results. You use different Office programs to accomplish specific tasks, such as writing a letter or producing a sales presentation, yet all the programs have a similar look and feel. Once you become familiar with one program, you'll find it easy to transfer your knowledge to the others.  This unit introduces you to the most frequently used programs in Office, as well as common features they all share.

OBJECTIVES

Understand the Office 2007 Suite

Start and exit an Office program

View the Office 2007 user interface

Create and save a file

Open a file and save it with a
    new name

View and print your work

Get Help and close a file

Understanding the Office 2007 Suite

Microsoft Office 2007 features an intuitive, context-sensitive user interface, so you can get up to speed faster and use advanced features with greater ease. The programs in Office are bundled together in a group called a **suite** (although you can also purchase them separately). The Office suite is available in several configurations, but all include Word and Excel. Other configurations include PowerPoint, Access, Outlook, Publisher, and/or others.  Each program in Office is best suited for completing specific types of tasks, though there is some overlap in terms of their capabilities.

The Office programs covered in this book include:

*   **Microsoft Office Word 2007**

    When you need to create any kind of text-based document, such as memos, newsletters, or multi-page reports, Word is the program to use. You can easily make your documents look great by inserting eye-catching graphics and using formatting tools such as themes. **Themes** are predesigned combinations of color and formatting attributes you can apply, and are available in most Office programs. The Word document shown in Figure A-1 was formatted with the Solstice theme.

*   **Microsoft Office Excel 2007**

    Excel is the perfect solution when you need to work with numeric values and make calculations. It puts the power of formulas, functions, charts, and other analytical tools into the hands of every user, so you can analyze sales projections, figure out loan payments, and present your findings in style. The Excel worksheet shown in Figure A-1 tracks personal expenses. Because Excel automatically recalculates results whenever a value changes, the information is always up-to-date. A chart illustrates how the monthly expenses are broken down.

*   **Microsoft Office PowerPoint 2007**

    Using PowerPoint, it's easy to create powerful presentations complete with graphics, transitions, and even a soundtrack. Using professionally designed themes and clip art, you can quickly and easily create dynamic slideshows such as the one shown in Figure A-1.

*   **Microsoft Office Access 2007**

    Access helps you keep track of large amounts of quantitative data, such as product inventories or employee records. The form shown in Figure A-1 was created for a grocery store inventory database. Employees use the form to enter data about each item. Using Access enables employees to quickly find specific information such as price and quantity, without hunting through store shelves and stockrooms.

Microsoft Office has benefits beyond the power of each program, including:

*   **Common user interface: Improving business processes**

    Because the Office suite programs have a similar **interface**, or look and feel, your experience using one program's tools makes it easy to learn those in the other programs. Office documents are **compatible** with one another, meaning that you can easily incorporate, or **integrate**, an Excel chart into a PowerPoint slide, or an Access table into a Word document.

*   **Collaboration: Simplifying how people work together**

    Office recognizes the way people do business today, and supports the emphasis on communication and knowledge-sharing within companies and across the globe. All Office programs include the capability to incorporate feedback—called **online collaboration**—across the Internet or a company network.

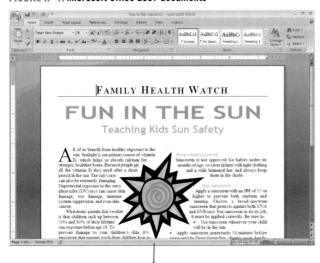

Word document

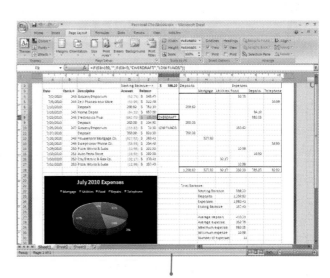

Excel worksheet

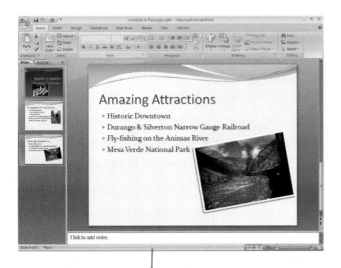

PowerPoint presentation

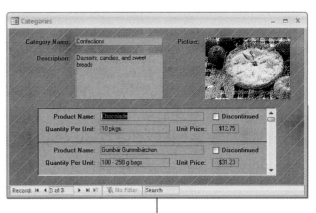

Access database form

Deciding which program to use

Every Office program includes tools that go far beyond what you might expect. For example, although Excel is primarily designed for making calculations, you can use it to create a database. So when you're planning a project, how do you decide which Office program to use? The general rule of thumb is to use the program best suited for your intended task, and make use of supporting tools in the program if you need them. Word is best for creating text-based documents, Excel is best for making mathematical calculations, PowerPoint is best for preparing presentations, and Access is best for managing quantitative data. Although the capabilities of Office are so vast that you *could* create an inventory in Excel or a budget in Word, you'll find greater flexibility and efficiency by using the program designed for the task. And remember, you can always create a file in one program, and then insert it in a document in another program when you need to, such as including sales projections (Excel) in a memo (Word).

Starting and Exiting an Office Program

The first step in using an Office program is of course to open, or **launch**, it on your computer. You have a few choices for how to launch a program, but the easiest way is to click the Start button on the Windows taskbar, or to double-click an icon on your desktop. You can have multiple programs open on your computer simultaneously, and you can move between open programs by clicking the desired program or document button on the taskbar or by using the [Alt][Tab] keyboard shortcut combination. When working, you'll often want to open multiple programs in Office, and switch among them throughout the day. Begin by launching a few Office programs now.

STEPS

QUICK TIP

You can also launch a program by double-clicking a desktop icon or clicking an entry on the Recent Items menu.

1. **Click the Start button** ⊕ **on the taskbar**

   The Start menu opens, as shown in Figure A-2. If the taskbar is hidden, you can display it by pointing to the bottom of the screen. Depending on your taskbar property settings, the taskbar may be displayed at all times, or only when you point to that area of the screen. For more information, or to change your taskbar properties, consult your instructor or technical support person.

2. **Point to All Programs, click Microsoft Office, then click Microsoft Office Word 2007**

   Microsoft Office Word 2007 starts and the program window opens on your screen.

QUICK TIP

It is not necessary to close one program before opening another.

3. **Click** ⊕ **on the taskbar, point to All Programs, click Microsoft Office, then click Microsoft Office Excel 2007**

   Microsoft Office Excel 2007 starts and the program window opens, as shown in Figure A-3. Word is no longer visible, but it remains open. The taskbar displays a button for each open program and document. Because this Excel document is **active**, or in front and available, the Microsoft Excel – Book1 button on the taskbar appears in a darker shade.

4. **Click Document1 – Microsoft Word on the taskbar**

   Clicking a button on the taskbar activates that program and document. The Word program window is now in front, and the Document1 – Microsoft Word taskbar button appears shaded.

QUICK TIP

If there isn't room on your taskbar to display the entire name of each button, you can point to any button to see the full name in a Screentip.

5. **Click** ⊕ **on the taskbar, point to All Programs, click Microsoft Office, then click Microsoft Office PowerPoint 2007**

   Microsoft Office PowerPoint 2007 starts, and becomes the active program.

6. **Click Microsoft Excel – Book1 on the taskbar**

   Excel is now the active program.

QUICK TIP

As you work in Windows, your computer adapts to your activities. You may notice that after clicking the Start button, the name of the program you want to open appears in the Start menu; if so, you can click it to start the program.

7. **Click** ⊕ **on the taskbar, point to All Programs, click Microsoft Office, then click Microsoft Office Access 2007**

   Microsoft Office Access 2007 starts, and becomes the active program.

8. **Point to the taskbar to display it, if necessary**

   Four Office programs are open simultaneously.

9. **Click the Office button** ⊕ **, then click Exit Access, as shown in Figure A-4**

   Access closes, leaving Excel active and Word and PowerPoint open.

FIGURE A-2: Start menu

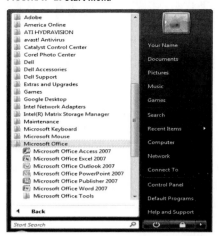

FIGURE A-3: Excel program window and Windows taskbar

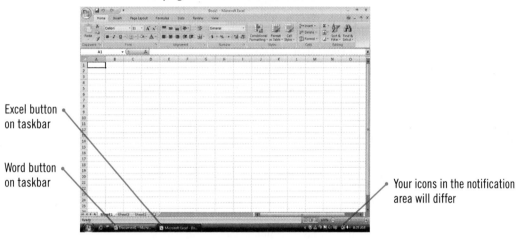

Excel button on taskbar

Word button on taskbar

Your icons in the notification area will differ

FIGURE A-4: Exiting Microsoft Office Access

Microsoft Office button

Exit Access button

Mouse pointer

Using shortcut keys to move between Office programs

As an alternative to the Windows taskbar, you can use a keyboard shortcut to move among open Office programs. The [Alt][Tab] keyboard combination lets you either switch quickly to the next open program, or choose one from a palette. To switch immediately to the next open program, press [Alt][Tab]. To choose from all open programs, press and hold [Alt], then press and release [Tab] without releasing [Alt]. A palette opens on screen, displaying the icon and filename of each open program and file. Each time you press [Tab] while holding [Alt], the selection cycles to the next open file. Release [Alt] when the program/file you want to activate is selected.

Viewing the Office 2007 User Interface

One of the benefits of using Office is that the programs have much in common, making them easy to learn and making it simple to move from one to another. Individual Office programs have always shared many features, but the innovations in the Office 2007 user interface mean even greater similarity among them all. That means you can also use your knowledge of one program to get up to speed in another. A **user interface** is a collective term for all the ways you interact with a software program. The user interface in Office 2007 includes a more intuitive way of choosing commands, working with files, and navigating in the program window. Familiarize yourself with some of the common interface elements in Office by examining the PowerPoint program window.

STEPS

1. **Click Microsoft PowerPoint – [Presentation1] on the taskbar**

   PowerPoint becomes the active program. Refer to Figure A-5 to identify common elements of the Office user interface. The **document window** occupies most of the screen. In PowerPoint, a blank slide appears in the document window, so you can build your slide show. At the top of every Office program window is a **title bar**, which displays the document and program name. Below the title bar is the **Ribbon**, which displays commands you're likely to need for the current task. Commands are organized into **tabs**. The tab names appear at the top of the Ribbon, and the active tab appears in front with its name highlighted. The Ribbon in every Office program includes tabs specific to the program, but all include a Home tab on the far left, for the most popular tasks in that program.

2. **Click the Office button**

   The Office menu opens. This menu contains commands common to most Office programs, such as opening a file, saving a file, and closing the current program. Next to the Office button is the **Quick Access toolbar**, which includes buttons for common Office commands.

3. **Click again to close it, then point to the Save button on the Quick Access toolbar, *but do not click it***

   You can point to any button in Office to see a description; this is a good way to learn the available choices.

4. **Click the Design tab on the Ribbon**

   To display a different tab, you click its name on the Ribbon. Each tab arranges related commands into **groups** to make features easy to find. The Themes group displays available themes in a **gallery**, or palette of choices you can browse. Many groups contain a **dialog box launcher**, an icon you can click to open a dialog box or task pane for the current group, which offers an alternative way to choose commands.

5. **Move the mouse pointer over the Aspect theme in the Themes group as shown in Figure A-6, *but do not click the mouse button***

   Because you have not clicked the theme, you have not actually made any changes to the slide. With the **Live Preview** feature, you can point to a choice, see the results right in the document, and then decide whether you want to make the change.

6. **Move away from the Ribbon and towards the slide**

   If you clicked the Aspect theme, it would be applied to this slide. Instead, the slide remains unchanged.

7. **Point to the Zoom slider on the status bar, then drag to the right until the Zoom percentage reads 166%**

   The slide display is enlarged. Zoom tools are located on the status bar. You can drag the slider or click the plus and minus buttons to zoom in/out on an area of interest. The percentage tells you the zoom effect.

8. **Drag the Zoom slider on the status bar to the left until the Zoom percentage reads 73%**

FIGURE A-5: PowerPoint program window

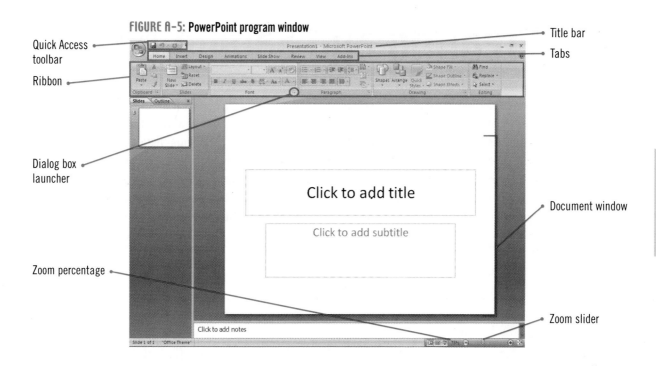

Quick Access toolbar

Ribbon

Dialog box launcher

Zoom percentage

Title bar

Tabs

Document window

Zoom slider

FIGURE A-6: Viewing a theme with Live Preview

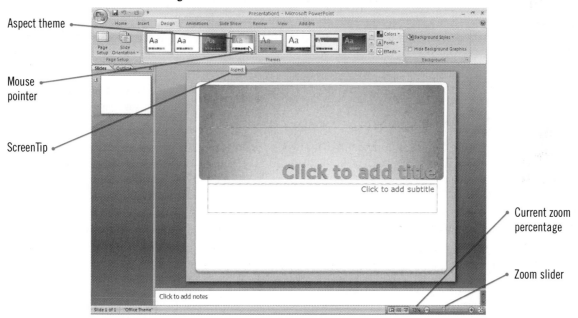

Aspect theme

Mouse pointer

ScreenTip

Current zoom percentage

Zoom slider

Customizing the Quick Access toolbar

You can customize the Quick Access toolbar to display your favorite commands. To do so, click the Customize Quick Access Toolbar button in the title bar, then click the command you want to add. If you don't see the command in the list, click More Commands to open the Customize tab of the Options dialog box. In the Options dialog box, use the Choose commands from list to choose a category, click the desired command in the list on the left, click Add to add it to the Quick Access toolbar, then click OK. To remove a button from the toolbar, click the name in the list on the right, then click Remove. To add a command to the Quick Access toolbar on the fly, simply right-click the button on the Ribbon, then click Add to Quick Access Toolbar on the shortcut menu. You can also use the Customize Quick Access Toolbar button to move the toolbar below the ribbon, by clicking Show Below the Ribbon, or to minimize the Ribbon so it takes up less space onscreen. If you click Minimize the Ribbon, the Ribbon is minimized to display only the tabs. When you click a tab, the Ribbon opens so you can choose a command; once you choose a command, the Ribbon closes again, and only the tabs are visible.

Creating and Saving a File

When working in a program, one of the first things you need to do is to create and save a file. A **file** is a stored collection of data. Saving a file enables you to work on a project now, then put it away and work on it again later. In some Office programs, including Word, Excel, and PowerPoint, a new file is automatically created when you start the program, so all you have to do is enter some data and save it. In Access, you must expressly create a file before you enter any data. You should give your files meaningful names and save them in an appropriate location, so they're easy to find. Use Microsoft Word to familiarize yourself with the process of creating and saving a document. First you'll type some notes about a possible location for a corporate meeting, then you'll save the information for later use.

STEPS

1. **Click** Document1 – Microsoft Word **on the taskbar**

2. **Type** Locations for Corporate Meeting, **then press** [Enter] **twice**
   The text appears in the document window, and a cursor blinks on a new blank line. The cursor indicates where the next typed text will appear.

3. **Type** Las Vegas, NV, **press** [Enter], **type** Orlando, FL, **press** [Enter], **type** Chicago, IL, **press** [Enter] **twice, then type your name**
   Compare your document to Figure A-7.

QUICK TIP
A filename can be up to 255 characters, including a file extension, and can include upper- or lowercase characters and spaces, but not ?, ", /, \, <, >, *, |, or :.

4. **Click the** Save button 🖫 **on the Quick Access toolbar**
   Because this is the first time you are saving this document, the Save As dialog box opens, as shown in Figure A-8. The Save As dialog box includes options for assigning a filename and storage location. Once you save a file for the first time, clicking 🖫 saves any changes to the file *without* opening the Save As dialog box, because no additional information is needed. In the Address bar, Office displays the default location for where to save the file, but you can change to any location. In the File name field, Office displays a suggested name for the document based on text in the file, but you can enter a different name.

5. **Type** Potential Corporate Meeting Locations
   The text you type replaces the highlighted text.

QUICK TIP
You can create a desktop icon that you can double-click to both launch a program and open a document, by saving it to the desktop.

6. **In the Save As dialog box, use the Address bar or Navigation pane to navigate to the drive and folder where you store your Data Files**
   Many students store files on a flash drive or Zip drive, but you can also store files on your computer, a network drive, or any storage device indicated by your instructor or technical support person.

QUICK TIP
To create a new blank file when a file is open, click the Office button, click New, then click Create.

7. **Click** Save
   The Save As dialog box closes, the new file is saved to the location you specified, then the name of the document appears in the title bar, as shown in Figure A-9. (You may or may not see a file extension.) See Table A-1 for a description of the different types of files you create in Office, and the file extensions associated with each. You can save a file in an earlier version of a program by choosing from the list of choices in the Save as type list arrow in the Save As dialog box.

TABLE A-1: Common filenames and default file extensions

File created in	is called a	and has the default extension
Excel	workbook	.xlsx
Word	document	.docx
Access	database	.accdb
PowerPoint	presentation	.pptx

FIGURE A-7: Creating a document in Word

Save button

Your name should appear here

Insertion point

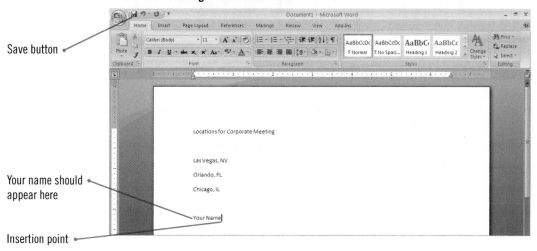

FIGURE A-8: Save As dialog box

Address bar

Navigation pane; your links and Folders setting may differ

File name field; your computer may not be set to display file extensions

Previous Locations list arrow

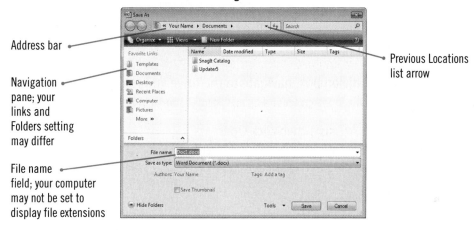

FIGURE A-9: Named Word document

Name appears in title bar

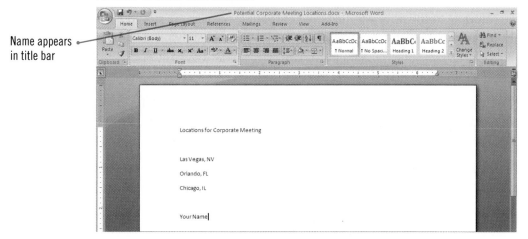

Using the Office Clipboard

You can use the Office Clipboard to cut and copy items from one Office program and paste them into others. The Clipboard can store a maximum of 24 items. To access it, open the Office Clipboard task pane by clicking the launcher in the Clipboard group in the Home tab. Each time you copy a selection, it is saved in the Office Clipboard. Each entry in the Office Clipboard includes an icon that tells you the program in which it was created. To paste an entry, click in the document where you want it to appear, then click the item in the Office Clipboard. To delete an item from the Office Clipboard, right-click the item, then click Delete.

Opening a File and Saving it with a New Name

In many cases as you work in Office, you start with a blank document, but often you need to use an existing file. It might be a file you or a co-worker created earlier as a work-in-progress, or it could be a complete document that you want to use as the basis for another. For example, you might want to create a budget for this year using the budget you created last year; you could type in all the categories and information from scratch, or you could open last year's budget, save it with a new name, and just make changes to update it for the current year. By opening the existing file and saving it with the Save As command, you create a duplicate that you can modify to your heart's content, while the original file remains intact. ▰▰▰▰ Use Excel to open an existing workbook file, and save it with a new name so the original remains unchanged.

STEPS

1. **Click Microsoft Excel – Book1 on the taskbar, click the Office button 🔵, then click Open**
   The Open dialog box opens, where you can navigate to any drive or folder location accessible to your computer to locate a file.

2. **In the Open dialog box, navigate to the drive and folder where you store your Data Files**
   The files available in the current folder are listed, as shown in Figure A-10. This folder contains one file.

3. **Click OFFICE A-1.xlsx, then click Open**
   The dialog box closes and the file opens in Excel. An Excel file is an electronic spreadsheet, so it looks different from a Word document or a PowerPoint slide.

4. **Click 🔵, then click Save As**
   The Save As dialog box opens, and the current filename is highlighted in the File name text box. Using the Save As command enables you to create a copy of the current, existing file with a new name. This action preserves the original file, and creates a new file that you can modify.

5. **Navigate to the drive and folder where your Data Files are stored if necessary, type Budget for Corporate Meeting in the File name text box, as shown in Figure A-11, then click Save**
   A copy of the existing document is created with the new name. The original file, Office A-1.xlsx, closes automatically.

6. **Click cell A19, type your name, then press [Enter], as shown in Figure A-12**
   In Excel, you enter data in cells, which are formed by the intersection of a row and a column. Cell A19 is at the intersection of column A and row 19. When you press [Enter], the cell pointer moves to cell A20.

7. **Click the Save button 💾 on the Quick Access toolbar**
   Your name appears in the worksheet, and your changes to the file are saved.

Exploring File Open options

You might have noticed that the Open button on the Open dialog box includes an arrow. In a dialog box, if a button includes an arrow you can click the button to invoke the command, or you can click the arrow to choose from a list of related commands. The Open button list arrow includes several related commands, including Open Read-Only and Open as Copy. Clicking Open Read-Only opens a file that you can only save by saving it with a new name; you cannot save changes to the original file. Clicking Open as Copy creates a copy of the file already saved and named with the word "Copy" in the title. Like the Save As command, these commands provide additional ways to use copies of existing files while ensuring that original files do not get inadvertently changed.

FIGURE A-10: Open dialog box

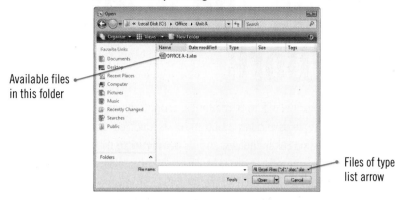

Available files
in this folder

Files of type
list arrow

FIGURE A-11: Save As dialog box

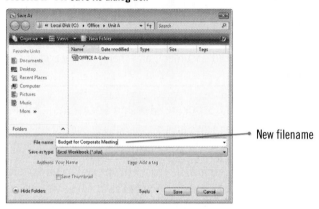

New filename

FIGURE A-12: Adding your name to the worksheet

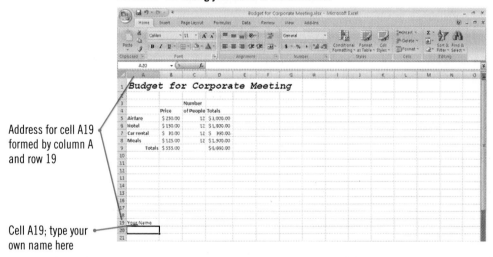

Address for cell A19
formed by column A
and row 19

Cell A19; type your
own name here

Working in Compatibility mode

Not everyone upgrades to the newest version of Office. As a general rule, new software versions are **backward-compatible**, meaning that documents saved by an older version can be read by newer software. The reverse is not always true, so Office 2007 includes a feature called Compatibility mode. When you open a file created in an earlier version of Office, "Compatibility Mode" appears in the title bar, letting you know the file was created in an earlier, but usable version of the program. If you are working with someone who may not be using the newest version of the software, you can avoid possible incompatibility problems by saving your file in another, earlier format. To do this, click the Office button, point to the Save As command, then click a choice on the Save As submenu. For example, if you're working in Excel, click Excel 97-2003 Workbook format. When the Save As dialog box opens, you'll notice that the Save as type box reads "Excel 97-2003 Workbook" instead of the default "Excel Workbook." To see more file format choices, such as Excel 97-2003 Template or Microsoft Excel 5.0/95 Workbook, click Other Formats on the Save As submenu. In the Save As dialog box, click the Save as type button, click the choice you think matches what your co-worker is using, then click Save.

Viewing and Printing Your Work

If your computer is connected to a printer or a print server, you can easily print any Office document. Printing can be as simple as clicking a button, or as involved as customizing the print job by printing only selected pages or making other choices, and/or **previewing** the document to see exactly what a document will look like when it is printed. (In order for printing and previewing to work, a printer must be installed.) In addition to using Print Preview, each Microsoft Office program lets you switch among various **views** of the document window, to show more or fewer details or a different combination of elements that make it easier to complete certain tasks, such as formatting or reading text. You can also increase or decrease your view of a document, so you can see more or less of it on the screen at once. Changing your view of a document does not affect the file in any way, it affects only the way it looks on screen. ▬▬▬ Experiment with changing your view of a Word document, and then preview and print your work.

STEPS

1. **Click Potential Corporate Meeting Locations – Microsoft Word on the taskbar**

   Word becomes the active program, and the document fills the screen.

2. **Click the View tab on the Ribbon**

   In most Office programs, the View tab on the Ribbon includes groups and commands for changing your view of the current document. You can also change views using the View buttons on the status bar.

3. **Click Web Layout button in the Document Views group on the View tab**

   The view changes to Web Layout view, as shown in Figure A-13. This view shows how the document will look if you save it as a Web page.

   > **QUICK TIP**
   > You can also use the Zoom button in the Zoom group of the View tab to enlarge or reduce a document's appearance.

4. **Click the Zoom in button ⊕ on the status bar eight times until the zoom percentage reads 180%**

   Zooming in, or choosing a higher percentage, makes a document appear bigger on screen, but less of it fits on the screen at once; **zooming out**, or choosing a lower percentage, lets you see more of the document but at a reduced size.

5. **Drag the Zoom slider 🔻 on the status bar to the center mark**

   The Zoom slider lets you zoom in and out without opening a dialog box or clicking buttons.

6. **Click the Print Layout button on the View tab**

   You return to Print Layout view, the default view in Microsoft Word.

7. **Click the Office button 🔵, point to Print, then click Print Preview**

   The Print Preview presents the most accurate view of how your document will look when printed, displaying the entire page on screen at once. Compare your screen to Figure A-14. The Ribbon in Print Preview contains a single tab, also known as a **program** tab, with commands specific to Print Preview. The commands on this tab facilitate viewing and changing overall settings such as margins and page size.

   > **QUICK TIP**
   > You can open the Print dialog box from any view by clicking the Office button, then clicking Print.

8. **Click the Print button on the Ribbon**

   The Print dialog box opens, as shown in Figure A-15. You can use this dialog box to change which pages to print, the number of printed copies, and even the number of pages you print on each page. If you have multiple printers from which to choose, you can change from one installed printer by clicking the Name list arrow, then clicking the name of the installed printer you want to use.

9. **Click OK, then click the Close Print Preview button on the Ribbon**

   A copy of the document prints, and Print Preview closes.

FIGURE A-13: Web Layout view

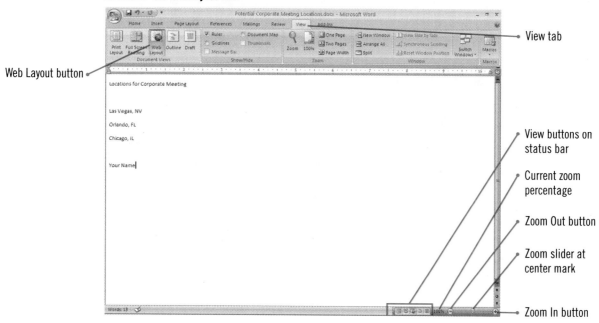

Web Layout button

View tab

View buttons on status bar

Current zoom percentage

Zoom Out button

Zoom slider at center mark

Zoom In button

FIGURE A-14: Print Preview screen

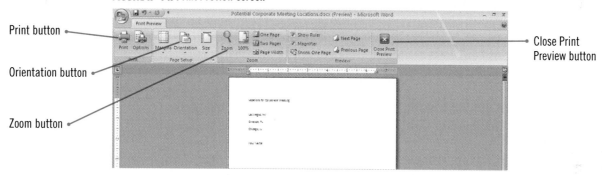

Print button

Orientation button

Zoom button

Close Print Preview button

FIGURE A-15: Print dialog box

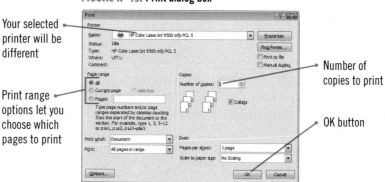

Your selected printer will be different

Print range options let you choose which pages to print

Number of copies to print

OK button

Using the Print Screen feature to create a screen capture

At some point you may want to create a screen capture. A **screen capture** is a snapshot of your screen, as if you took a picture of it with a camera. You might want to take a screen capture if an error message occurs and you want Technical Support to see exactly what's on the screen. Or perhaps your instructor wants to see what your screen looks like when you create a particular document. To create a screen capture, press [PrtScn]. (Keyboards differ, but you may find the [PrtScn] button on the Insert key in or near your keyboard's function keys. You may have to press the [F Lock] key to enable the Function keys.) Pressing this key places a digital image of your screen in the Windows temporary storage area known as the **Clipboard**. Open the document where you want the screen capture to appear, click the Home tab on the Ribbon (if necessary), then click Paste on the Home tab. The screen capture is pasted into the document.

Getting Help and Closing a File

You can get comprehensive help at any time by pressing [F1] in an Office program. You can also get help in the form of a ScreenTip by pointing to almost any icon in the program window. When you're finished working in an Office document, you have a few choices regarding ending your work session. You can close a file or exit a program by using the Office button or by clicking a button on the title bar. Closing a file leaves a program running, while exiting a program closes all the open files in that program as well as the program itself. In all cases, Office reminds you if you try to close a file or exit a program and your document contains unsaved changes. ▓▓▓▓ Explore the Help system in Microsoft Office, and then close your documents and exit any open programs.

STEPS

1. **Point to the Zoom button on the View tab of the Ribbon**

   A ScreenTip appears that describes how the Zoom button works.

2. **Press [F1]**

   The Word Help window opens, as shown in Figure A-16, displaying the home page for help in Word. Each entry is a hyperlink you can click to open a list of related topics. This window also includes a toolbar of useful Help commands and a Search field. The connection status at the bottom of the Help window indicates that the connection to Office Online is active. Office Online supplements the help content available on your computer with a wide variety of up-to-date topics, templates, and training.

3. **Click the Getting help link in the Table of Contents pane**

   The icon next to Getting help changes and its list of subtopics expands.

4. **Click the Work with the Help window link in the topics list in the left pane**

   The topic opens in the right pane, as shown in Figure A-17.

5. **Click the Hide Table of Contents button 📖 on the Help toolbar**

   The left pane closes, as shown in Figure A-18.

6. **Click the Show Table of Contents button 📄 on the Help toolbar, scroll to the bottom of the left pane, click the Accessibility link in the Table of Contents pane, click the Use the keyboard to work with Ribbon programs link, read the information in the right pane, then click the Help window Close button**

7. **Click the Office button 🔘, then click Close; if a dialog box opens asking whether you want to save your changes, click Yes**

   The Potential Corporate Meeting Locations document closes, leaving the Word program open.

8. **Click 🔘, then click Exit Word**

   Microsoft Office Word closes, and the Excel program window is active.

9. **Click 🔘, click Exit Excel, click the PowerPoint button on the taskbar if necessary, click 🔘, then click Exit PowerPoint**

   Microsoft Office Excel and Microsoft Office PowerPoint both close.

FIGURE A-16: Word Help window

Help toolbar

Search field

Hide Table of
Contents
button

The colors
of your links
may differ

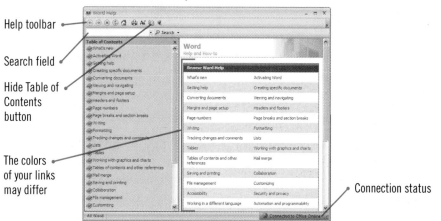

Connection status

FIGURE A-17: Work with the Help window

Print button

Icon indicates
expanded topic

Work with
the Help
window link

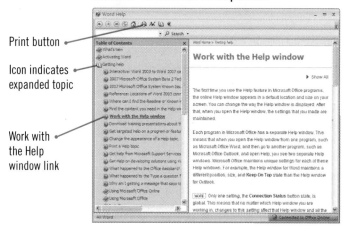

FIGURE A-18: Help window with Table of Contents closed

Show Table of
Contents button

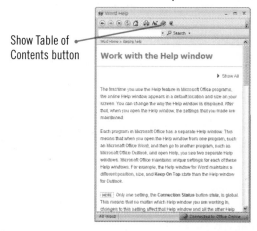

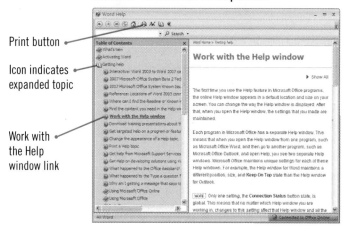

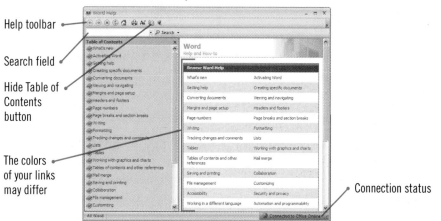

Recovering a document

Sometimes while you are using Office, you may experience a power failure or your computer may "freeze," making it impossible to continue working. If this type of interruption occurs, each Office program has a built-in recovery feature that allows you to open and save files that were open at the time of the interruption. When you restart the program(s) after an interruption, the Document Recovery task pane opens on the left side of your screen displaying both original and recovered versions of the files that were open. If you're not sure which file to open (original or recovered), it's usually better to open the recovered file because it will contain the latest information. You can, however, open and review all versions of the file that were recovered and save the best one. Each file listed in the Document Recovery task pane displays a list arrow with options that allow you to open the file, save it as is, delete it, or show repairs made to it during recovery.

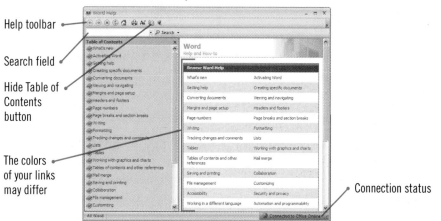

Office 2007

Practice

▼ CONCEPTS REVIEW

Label the elements of the program window shown in Figure A-19.

FIGURE A-19

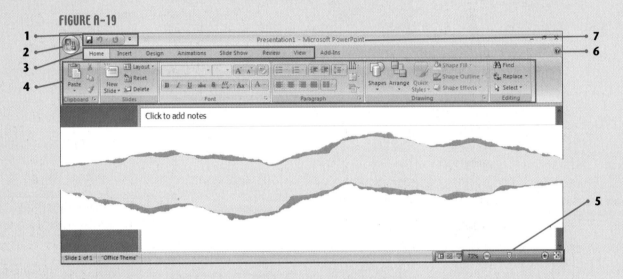

Match each project with the program for which it is best suited.

8. Microsoft Office PowerPoint

9. Microsoft Office Excel

10. Microsoft Office Word

11. Microsoft Office Access

a. Corporate expansion budget with expense projections

b. Business résumé for a job application

c. Auto parts store inventory

d. Presentation for Board of Directors meeting

▼ INDEPENDENT CHALLENGE 1

You just accepted an administrative position with a local car dealership that's recently invested in computers and is now considering purchasing Microsoft Office. You are asked to propose ways Office might help the dealership. You produce your proposal in Microsoft Word.

a. Start Word, then save the document as **Microsoft Office Proposal** in the drive and folder where you store your Data Files.

b. Type **Microsoft Office Word**, press [Enter] twice, type **Microsoft Office Excel**, press [Enter] twice, type **Microsoft Office PowerPoint**, press [Enter] twice, type **Microsoft Office Access**, press [Enter] twice, then type your name.

c. Click the line beneath each program name, type at least two tasks suited to that program, then press [Enter].

d. Save your work, then print one copy of this document.

Advanced Challenge Exercise

■ Press the [PrtScn] button to create a screen capture, then press [Ctrl][V].

■ Save and print the document.

e. Exit Word.

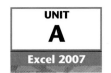

Getting Started with Excel 2007

Files You Will Need:

EX A-1.xlsx
EX A-2.xlsx
EX A-3.xlsx
EX A-4.xlsx
EX A-5.xlsx

In this unit, you will learn how spreadsheet software helps you analyze data and make business decisions, even if you aren't a math pro. You'll become familiar with the different elements of a spreadsheet and learn your way around the Excel program window. You will also work in an Excel worksheet and make simple calculations. ▰▰▰ You have been hired as an assistant at Quest Specialty Travel (QST), a company offering tours that immerse travelers in regional culture. You report to Grace Wong, the vice president of finance. As Grace's assistant, you create worksheets to analyze data from various divisions of the company, so you can help her make sound decisions on company expansion and investments.

OBJECTIVES

Understand spreadsheet software

Tour the Excel 2007 window

Understand formulas

Enter labels and values and use AutoSum

Edit cell entries

Enter and edit a simple formula

Switch worksheet views

Choose print options

Understanding Spreadsheet Software

Microsoft Excel is the electronic spreadsheet program within Microsoft Office. An **electronic spreadsheet** is an application you use to perform numeric calculations and to analyze and present numeric data. One advantage of spreadsheet programs over pencil and paper is that your calculations are updated automatically, so you can change entries without having to manually recalculate. Table A-1 shows some of the common business tasks people accomplish using Excel. In Excel, the electronic spreadsheet you work in is called a **worksheet**, and is contained in a file called a **workbook**, which has the file extension .xlsx. 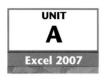 At Quest Specialty Travel, you use Excel extensively to track finances and manage corporate data.

DETAILS

When you use Excel, you have the ability to:

- **Enter data quickly and accurately**

  With Excel, you can enter information faster and more accurately than with pencil and paper. Figure A-1 shows a payroll worksheet created using pencil and paper. Figure A-2 shows the same worksheet created using Excel. Equations were added to calculate the hours and pay. You can copy the payroll deductions that don't change from quarter to quarter, then use Excel to calculate the gross and net payroll by supplying unique data and formulas for each quarter. You can also quickly create charts and other elements to help visualize how the payroll is distributed.

- **Recalculate data easily**

  Fixing typing errors or updating data is easy in Excel. In the payroll example, if you receive updated hours for an employee, you just enter the new hours and Excel recalculates the pay.

- **Perform what-if analysis**

  The ability to change data and quickly view the recalculated results gives you the power to make informed business decisions. For instance, if you're considering raising the hourly rate for an entry-level tour guide from $12.50 to $15.00, you can enter the new value in the worksheet and immediately see the impact on the overall payroll as well as on the individual employee. Any time you use a worksheet to ask the question "what if?" you are performing **what-if analysis**. Excel also includes a Scenario Manager where you can name and save different what-if versions of your worksheet.

- **Change the appearance of information**

  Excel provides powerful features for making information visually appealing and easier to understand. You can format text and numbers in different fonts, colors, and styles to make it stand out.

- **Create charts**

  Excel makes it easy to create charts based on worksheet information. Charts are updated automatically in Excel whenever data changes. The worksheet in Figure A-2 includes a 3-D pie chart.

- **Share information**

  It's easy for everyone at QST to collaborate in Excel, using the company intranet, the Internet, or a network storage device. For example, you can complete the weekly payroll that your boss, Grace Wong, started creating. You can also take advantage of collaboration tools such as shared workbooks, so that multiple people can edit a workbook simultaneously.

- **Build on previous work**

  Instead of creating a new worksheet for every project, it's easy to modify an existing Excel worksheet. When you are ready to create next week's payroll, you can open the file for last week's payroll, save it with a new filename, and modify the information as necessary. You can also use predesigned, formatted files called **templates** to create new worksheets quickly. Excel comes with many templates, that you can customize.

FIGURE A-1: Traditional paper worksheet

Quest Specialty Travel
Tour Guide Payroll Calculator

Name	Hours	O/T Hrs	Hrly Rate	Reg Pay	O/T Pay	Gross Pay
Brueghel, Pieter	40	4	15–	600–	120–	720–
Cortona, Livia	35	0	10–	350–	0–	350–
Klimt, Gustave	40	2	12⁵⁰	500–	50–	550–
Le Pen, Jean-Marie	29	0	15–	435–	0–	435–
Martinez, Juan	37	0	12⁵⁰	462.50	0–	462.50
Mioshi, Keiko	39	0	20–	780–	0–	780–
Sherwood, Burton	40	0	15–	600–	0–	600–
Strano, Riccardo	40	8	15–	600–	240–	840–
Wadsworth, Alicia	40	5	12⁵⁰	500–	125–	625–
Yamamoto, Johji	38	0	15–	570–	0–	570–

FIGURE A-2: Excel worksheet

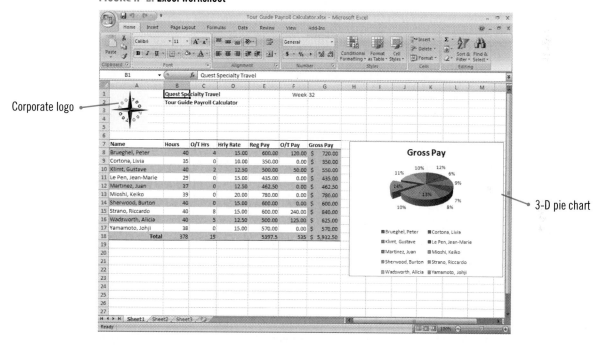

Corporate logo

3-D pie chart

TABLE A-1: Business tasks you can accomplish using Excel

you can use spreadsheets to	by
Perform calculations	Adding formulas and functions to worksheet data; for example, adding a list of sales results or calculating a car payment
Represent values graphically	Creating charts based on worksheet data; for example, creating a chart that displays expenses
Generate reports	Creating workbooks that combine information from multiple worksheets, such as summarized sales information from multiple stores
Organize data	Sorting data in ascending or descending order; for example, alphabetizing a list of products or customer names, or prioritizing orders by date
Analyze data	Creating data summaries and short lists using PivotTables or AutoFilters; for example, making a list of the top 10 customers based on spending habits
Create what-if data scenarios	Using variable values to investigate and sample different outcomes, such as changing the interest rate or payment schedule on a loan

Touring the Excel 2007 Window

To start Excel, Microsoft Windows must be running. Similar to starting any program in Office, you can use the Start button on the Windows taskbar, or you may have a shortcut on your desktop you prefer to use. If you need additional assistance, ask your instructor or technical support person. ▪▪▪▪▪ You decide to start Excel and familiarize yourself with the worksheet window.

STEPS

QUICK TIP

For more information on starting a program or opening and saving a file, see the unit "Getting Started with Microsoft Office 2007."

1. **Start Excel, click the** Microsoft Office button 🅑, **then click** Open

2. **In the Open dialog box, navigate to the drive and folder where you store your Data Files, click** EX A-1.xlsx, **then click** Open

3. **Click** 🅑, **then click** Save As

TROUBLE

If you don't see the extension .xlsx on the filenames in the Open dialog box, don't worry; Windows can be set up to display or not to display the file extensions.

4. **In the Save As dialog box, navigate to the drive and folder where you store your Data Files if necessary, type** Tour Guide Payroll Calculator **in the File name text box, then click** Save

   Using Figure A-3 as a guide, identify the following items:
   - The **Name box** displays the active cell address. "A1" appears in the Name box.
   - The **formula bar** allows you to enter or edit data in the worksheet. The worksheet window contains a grid of columns and rows. Columns are labeled alphabetically and rows are labeled numerically. The worksheet window can contain a total of 1,048,576 rows and 16,384 columns.
   - The intersection of a column and a row is called a **cell**. Cells can contain text, numbers, formulas, or a combination of all three. Every cell has its own unique location or **cell address**, which is identified by the coordinates of the intersecting column and row.
   - The **cell pointer** is a dark rectangle that outlines the cell in which you are working. This cell is called the **active cell**. In Figure A-3, the cell pointer outlines cell A1, so A1 is the active cell. The column and row headings for the active cell are highlighted, making it easier to locate.
   - **Sheet tabs** below the worksheet grid let you switch from sheet to sheet in a workbook. By default, a workbook file contains three worksheets—but you can use just one, or have as many as 255, in a workbook. The Insert Worksheet button to the right of Sheet 3 allows you to add worksheets to a workbook. **Sheet tab scrolling buttons** let you navigate to additional sheet tabs when available.
   - You can use the **scroll bars** to move around in a document that is too large to fit on the screen at once.
   - The **status bar** is located at the bottom of the Excel window. It provides a brief description of the active command or task in progress. The **mode indicator** in the bottom-left corner of the status bar provides additional information about certain tasks.

5. **Click cell** A4

   Cell A4 becomes the active cell. To activate a different cell, you can click the cell or press the arrow keys on your keyboard to move to it.

6. **Click cell** B5, **press and hold the mouse button, drag** ✛ **to cell** B14, **then release the mouse button**

   You selected a group of cells and they are highlighted, as shown in Figure A-4. A selection of two or more cells such as B5:B14 is called a **range**; you select a range when you want to perform an action on a group of cells at once, such as moving them or formatting them. When you select a range, the status bar displays the average, count (or number of items selected), and sum of the selected cells as a quick reference.

FIGURE A-3: Open workbook

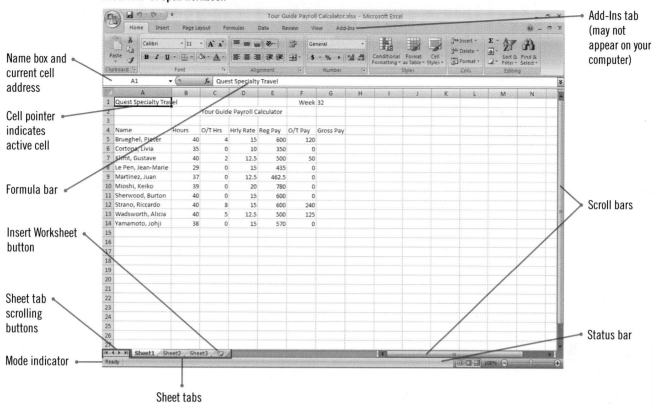

Name box and current cell address

Cell pointer indicates active cell

Formula bar

Insert Worksheet button

Sheet tab scrolling buttons

Mode indicator

Sheet tabs

Add-Ins tab (may not appear on your computer)

Scroll bars

Status bar

FIGURE A-4: Selecting a range

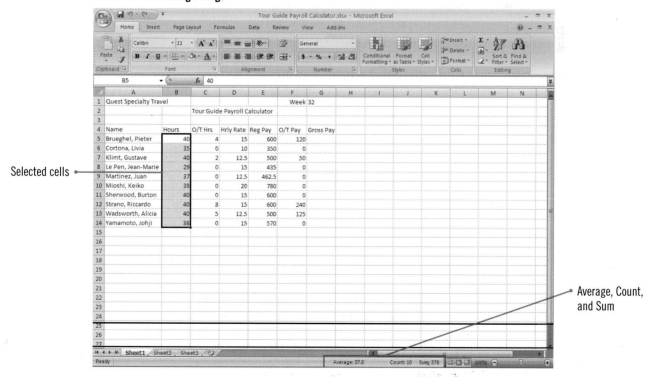

Selected cells

Average, Count, and Sum

Excel 2007

Understanding Formulas

Excel is a truly powerful program because users at every level of mathematical expertise can make calculations with accuracy. To do so, you use formulas. **Formulas** are equations in a worksheet. You use formulas to make calculations as simple as adding a column of numbers, or as complex as profit-and-loss projections for a global corporation. To tap into the power of Excel, you should understand how formulas work. Managers at QST use the Tour Guide Payroll Calculator workbook to keep track of employee hours prior to submitting them to the Payroll Department. You'll be using this workbook regularly, so you need to understand the formulas it contains and how Excel calculates the results.

STEPS

1. **Click cell E5**

   The active cell contains a formula, which appears on the formula bar. All Excel formulas begin with the equal sign (=). If you wanted a cell to show the result of adding 4 plus 2, the formula in the cell would look like this: =4+2. If you wanted a cell to show the result of multiplying two values in your worksheet, such as the values in cells B5 and D5, the formula would look like this: =B5*D5, as shown in Figure A-5.

2. **Click cell F5**

   While you're entering a formula in a cell, the cell references and arithmetic operators appear on the formula bar. See Table A-2 for a list of common Excel arithmetic operators. When you're finished entering the formula, you can either click the Enter button on the formula bar, or press [Enter]. An example of a more complex formula is the calculation of overtime pay. At QST, overtime pay is calculated at twice the regular hourly rate times the number of overtime hours. The formula used to calculate overtime pay for the employee in row 5 is:
   O/T Hrs times (2 times Hrly Rate)
   In a worksheet cell, you would enter: =C5*(2*D5), as shown in Figure A-6.

   The use of parentheses creates groups within the formula and indicates which calculations to complete first—an important consideration in complex formulas. In this formula, the hourly rate is doubled, and that value is multiplied by the number of overtime hours. Because overtime is calculated at twice the hourly rate, managers are aware that they need to closely watch this expense.

DETAILS

In creating calculations in Excel, it is important to:

- **Know where the formulas should be**

   Excel formulas are created in the cell where they are viewed. This means that the formula calculating Gross Pay for the employee in row 5 will be entered in cell G5.

- **Know exactly what cells and arithmetic operations are needed**

   Don't guess; make sure you know exactly what cells are involved before creating a formula.

- **Create formulas with care**

   Make sure you know exactly what you want a formula to accomplish before it is created. An inaccurate formula may have far-reaching effects if the formula or its results are referenced by other formulas.

- **Use cell references rather than values**

   The beauty of Excel is that whenever you change a value in a cell, any formula containing a reference to that cell is automatically updated. For this reason, it's important that you use cell references in formulas, rather than actual values whenever possible.

- **Determine what calculations will be needed**

   Sometimes it's difficult to predict what data will be needed within a worksheet, but you should try to anticipate what statistical information may be required. For example, if there are columns of numbers, chances are good that both column and row totals should be present.

FIGURE A-5: Viewing a formula

Formula appears
in formula bar

Result of formula
appears in cell

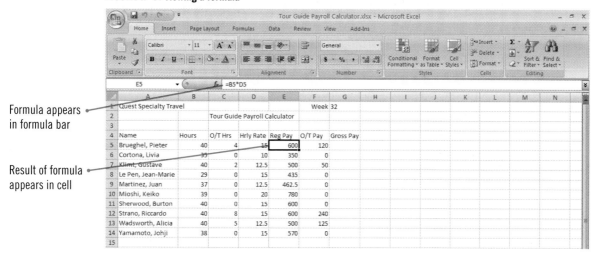

FIGURE A-6: Formula with multiple operators

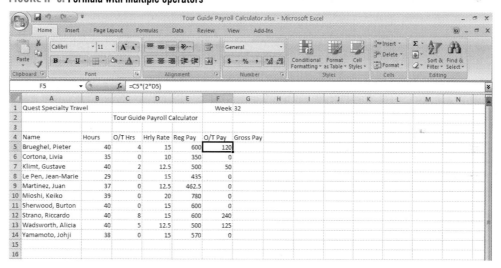

TABLE A-2: Excel arithmetic operators

operator	purpose	example
+	Addition	=A5+A7
-	Subtraction or negation	=A5-10
*	Multiplication	=A5*A7
/	Division	=A5/A7
%	Percent	=35%
^ (caret)	Exponent	=6^2 (same as 6^2)

Entering Labels and Values and Using AutoSum

To enter content in a cell, you can type on the formula bar or directly in the cell itself. When entering content in a worksheet, you should start by entering all the labels first. **Labels** are entries that contain text and numerical information not used in calculations, such as "2009 Sales" or "Travel Expenses." Labels help you identify data in worksheet rows and columns, making your worksheet easier to understand. **Values** are numbers, formulas, and functions that can be used in calculations. To enter a calculation, you type an equal sign (=) plus the formula for the calculation; some examples of an Excel calculation are "=2+2" and "=C5+C6." Functions are Excel's built-in formulas; you learn more about them in the next unit. You want to enter some information in the Tour Guide Payroll Calculator workbook, and use a very simple function to total a range of cells.

STEPS

1. **Click cell A15, then click in the formula bar**

   Notice that the **mode indicator** on the status bar now reads "Edit," indicating you are in Edit mode. You are in Edit mode any time you are entering or changing the contents of a cell.

2. **Type Totals, then click the Enter button ✓ on the formula bar**

   Clicking the Enter button accepts the entry. The new text is left-aligned. Labels are left-aligned by default, and values are right-aligned by default. Excel recognizes an entry as a value if it is a number or it begins with one of these symbols: +, -, =, @, #, or $. When a cell contains both text and numbers, Excel recognizes it as a label.

3. **Click cell B15**

   You want this cell to total the hours worked by all the tour guides. You might think you need to create a formula that looks like this: =B5+B6+B7+B8+B9+B10+B11+B12+B13+B14. However, there's an easier way to achieve this result.

4. **Click the AutoSum button Σ in the Editing group on the Home tab of the Ribbon**

   The SUM function is inserted in your formula, and a suggested range appears in parentheses, as shown in Figure A-7. A **function** is a built-in formula; it includes the **arguments** (the information necessary to calculate an answer), as well as cell references and other unique information. Clicking the AutoSum button sums the adjacent range (that is, the cells next to the active cell) above or to the left, though you can adjust the range if necessary. Using the SUM function is quicker than entering a formula, and using the range B5:B14 is more efficient than entering individual cell references.

5. **Click ✓**

   Excel calculates the total contained in cells B5:B14 and displays the result, 378, in cell B15. The cell actually contains the formula =SUM(B5:B14), and the result is displayed.

6. **Click cell C13, type 6, then press [Enter]**

   The number 6 is right-aligned, the cell pointer moves to cell C14 and the value in cell F13 changes.

7. **Click cell C18, type Average Gross Pay, then press [Enter]**

   The new label is entered in cell C18. The contents appear to spill into the empty cells to the right.

8. **Click and hold cell B15, drag the mouse pointer to cell G15, click the Fill button ⬇ in the Editing group, then click Right in the Fill menu**

   Calculated values appear in the selected range, as shown in Figure A-8. Each filled cell contains a formula that sums the range of cells above. The Fill button fills cells based on the first number sequence in the range.

9. **Save your work**

FIGURE A-7: Creating a formula using the AutoSum button

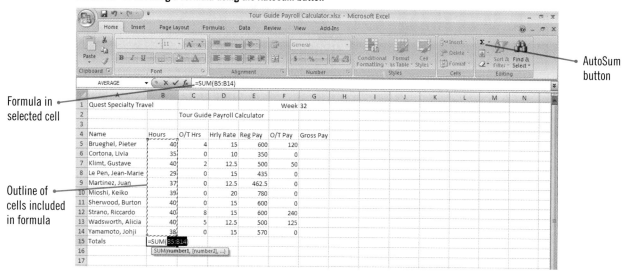

AutoSum button

Formula in selected cell

Outline of cells included in formula

FIGURE A-8: Calculated values

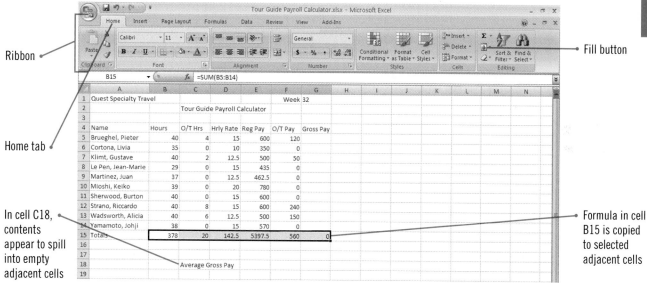

Ribbon

Home tab

In cell C18, contents appear to spill into empty adjacent cells

Fill button

Formula in cell B15 is copied to selected adjacent cells

Navigating a worksheet

With over a million cells available in a worksheet, it is important to know how to move around in, or **navigate**, a worksheet. You can use the arrow keys on the keyboard [↑], [↓], [←], or [→] to move a cell at a time, or press [Page Up] or [Page Down] to move a screen at a time. To move a screen to the left press [Alt][Page Up]; to move a screen to the right press [Alt][Page Down]. You can also use the mouse pointer to click the desired cell. If the desired cell is not visible in the worksheet window, use the scroll bars or the Go To command by clicking the Find & Select button in the Editing group on the Home tab of the Ribbon. To quickly jump to the first cell in a worksheet press [Ctrl][Home]; to jump to the last cell, press [Ctrl][End].

Editing Cell Entries

You can change, or **edit**, the contents of an active cell at any time. To do so, double-click the cell, click in the formula bar, or just start typing. Excel switches to Edit mode when you are making cell entries. Different pointers, shown in Table A-3, guide you through the editing process. You noticed some errors in the worksheet and want to make corrections. The first error is in cell A5, which contains a misspelled name.

QUICK TIP

Pressing [Enter] also accepts the cell entry, but moves the cell pointer down one cell.

1. **Click cell A5, then click to the right of P in the formula bar**

   As soon as you click in the formula bar, a blinking vertical line called the **insertion point** appears on the formula bar at the location where new text will be inserted. See Figure A-9. The mouse pointer changes to I when you point anywhere in the formula bar.

2. **Press [Delete], then click the Enter button ✓ on the formula bar**

   Clicking the Enter button accepts the edit, and the spelling of the employee's first name is corrected. You can also press [Enter] or [Tab] to accept an edit.

QUICK TIP

On some keyboards, you might need to press an "F Lock" key to enable the function keys.

3. **Click cell B6, then press [F2]**

   Excel switches to Edit mode, and the insertion point blinks in the cell. Pressing [F2] activates the cell for editing directly in the cell instead of the formula bar. Some people prefer editing right in the cell instead of using the formula bar, but it's simply a matter of preference; the results in the worksheet are the same.

QUICK TIP

The Undo button allows you to reverse up to 100 previous actions, one at a time.

4. **Press [Backspace], type 8, then press [Enter]**

   The value in the cell changes from 35 to 38, and cell B7 becomes the active cell. Did you notice that the calculations in cells B15 and E15 also changed? That's because those cells contain formulas that include cell B6 in their calculations. If you make a mistake when editing, you can click the Cancel button ✗ on the formula bar *before* pressing [Enter] to confirm the cell entry. The Enter and Cancel buttons appear only when you're in Edit mode. If you notice the mistake *after* you have confirmed the cell entry, click the Undo button ↻ on the Quick Access toolbar.

5. **Click cell A9, press [F2], press and hold [Shift], press [Home], then release [Shift]**

   Pressing and holding [Shift] lets you select text using the keyboard. Pressing [Home] moves the cursor to the beginning of the cell; pressing [End] would move the cursor to the end or the cell.

6. **Type Maez, Javier, then press [Enter]**

   When text is selected, typing deletes it and replaces it with the new text.

7. **Double-click cell C12, press [Delete], type 4, then click ✓**

   Double-clicking a cell activates it for editing directly in the cell. Compare your screen to Figure A-10.

8. **Save your work**

   Your changes to the workbook are saved.

Recovering a lost workbook file

Sometimes while you are using Excel, you may experience a power failure or your computer may "freeze," making it impossible to continue working. If this type of interruption occurs, Excel has a built-in recovery feature that allows you to open and save files that were open at the time of the interruption. When you restart Excel after an interruption, File Recovery mode automatically starts and tries to make any necessary repairs. If you need to use a corrupted workbook, you can try and repair it manually by clicking the Office button, then clicking Open. Select the workbook file you want to repair, click the Open list arrow, then click Open and Repair.

FIGURE A-9: Worksheet in Edit mode

Enter button

Active cell

Insertion point

Mode indicator

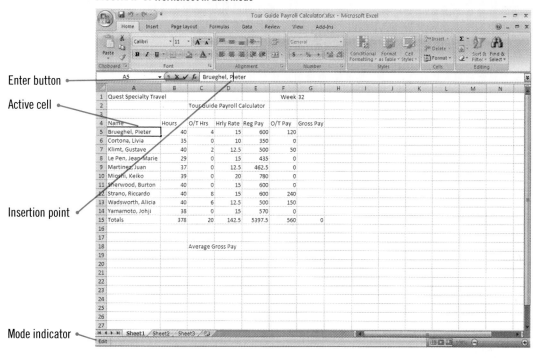

FIGURE A-10: Edited worksheet

Edited label

Edited value

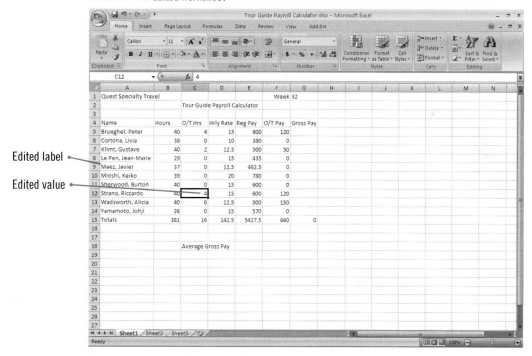

TABLE A-3: Common pointers in Excel

name	pointer	use to
Normal	⊕	Select a cell or range; indicates Ready mode
Copy	▷⁺	Create a duplicate of the selected cell(s)
Fill handle	✛	Create an alphanumeric series in a range
I-beam	I	Edit contents of formula bar
Move	✛	Change the location of the selected cell(s)

Entering and Editing a Simple Formula

You use formulas in Excel to perform calculations such as adding, multiplying, and averaging. Formulas in an Excel worksheet start with the equal sign (=), also called the **formula prefix**, followed by cell addresses, range names, and values, along with calculation operators. **Calculation operators** indicate what type of calculation you want to perform on the cells, ranges or values. They can include **arithmetic operators**, which perform mathematical calculations such as adding and subtracting, **comparison operators**, which compare values for the purpose of true/false results, **text concatenation operators**, which join strings of text in different cells, and **reference operators**, which enable you to use ranges in calculations. You want to create a formula in the worksheet that calculates gross pay for each employee.

STEPS

1. **Click cell G5**

   This is the first cell where you want to insert the formula. To calculate gross pay, you need to add regular pay and overtime pay. For employee Peter Brueghel, regular pay appears in cell E5 and overtime pay appears in cell F5.

   QUICK TIP

   You can reference a cell in a formula either by typing the cell reference or clicking the cell in the worksheet; when you click a cell to add a reference, the Mode indicator changes to "Point."

2. **Type =, click cell E5, type +, then click cell F5**

   Compare your formula bar to Figure A-11. The blue and green cell references in cell G5 correspond to the colored cell outlines. When entering a formula, it's a good idea to use cell references instead of values whenever you can. That way, if you later change a value in a cell (if, for example, Peter's regular pay changes to 615), any formula that includes this information reflects accurate, up-to-date results.

3. **Click the Enter button ☑ on the formula bar**

   The results of the formula =E5+F5, 720, appear in cell G5. This same value appears in cell G15 because cell G15 contains a formula that totals the values in cells G5:G14, and there are no other values now.

4. **Click cell F5**

   The formula in this cell calculates overtime pay by multiplying overtime hours (C5) times twice the regular hourly rate (2*D5). You want to edit this formula to reflect a new overtime pay rate.

5. **Click to the right of 2 in the formula bar, then type .5 as shown in Figure A-12**

   The formula that calculates overtime pay has been edited.

6. **Click ☑ on the formula bar**

   Compare your screen to Figure A-13. Notice that the calculated values in cells G5, F15, and G15 have all changed to reflect your edits to cell F5.

7. **Save your work**

Understanding named ranges

It can be difficult to remember the cell locations of critical information in a worksheet, but using cell names can make this task much easier. You can name a single cell or range of contiguous, or touching, cells. For example, you might name a cell that contains data on average gross pay "AVG_GP" instead of trying to remember the cell address C18. A named range must begin with a letter or an underscore. It cannot contain any spaces or be the same as a built-in name, such as a function or another object (such as a different named range) in the workbook. To name a range, select the cell(s) you want to name, click the name box in the formula bar, type the name you want to use, then press [Enter]. You can also name a range by clicking the Formulas tab, clicking the Define Name list arrow in the Defined Names group, then clicking Define Name. Type the new range name in the Name text box of the New Name dialog box, verify the selected range, then click OK. When you use a named range in a formula, the named range appears, rather than the cell address. You can also create a named range using the contents of a cell already in the range. Select the range containing the text you want to use as a name, then click Create from Selection button in the Defined Names group. The Create Names from Selection dialog box opens. Choose the location of the name you want to use, then click OK.

FIGURE A-11: Simple formula in a worksheet

Cell outline color corresponds to cell reference

Referenced cells are inserted in formula

Mode indicator changes to Point

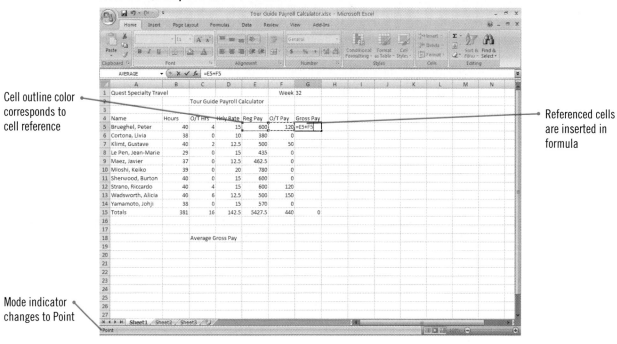

FIGURE A-12: Edited formula in a worksheet

Edited value

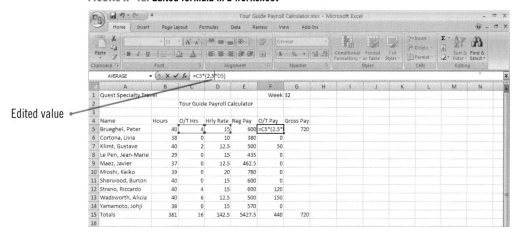

FIGURE A-13: Edited formula with changes

Edited formula results in changes to these other cells

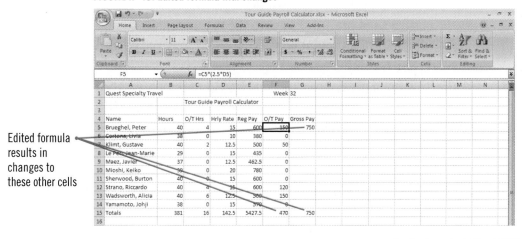

Switching Worksheet Views

You can change your view of the worksheet window at any time, using either the View tab on the Ribbon or the View buttons on the status bar. Changing your view does not affect the contents of a worksheet; it just makes it easier for you to focus on different tasks, such as entering content or preparing a worksheet for printing. The View tab includes a variety of viewing options, such as View buttons, zoom controls, and the ability to show or hide worksheet elements such as gridlines. The status bar offers fewer View options, but can be more convenient to use. ▄▄▄▄ You want to make some final adjustments to your worksheet, including adding a header so the document looks more polished.

STEPS

1. **Click the View tab on the Ribbon, then click the Page Layout View button in the Workbook Views group**

   The view switches from the default view, Normal, to Page Layout view. **Normal view** shows the worksheet without including certain details like headers and footers or tools like rulers and a page number indicator; it's great for creating and editing a worksheet, but may not be detailed enough when you want to put the finishing touches on a document. **Page Layout View** provides a more accurate view of how a worksheet will look when printed, as shown in Figure A-14. The margins of the page are displayed, along with a text box for the header. A footer text box appears at the bottom of the page, but your screen may not be large enough to view it without scrolling. Above and to the left of the page are rulers. Part of an additional page appears to the right of this page, but it is dimmed, indicating that it does not contain any data. A page number indicator on the status bar tells you the current page and the total number of pages in this worksheet.

2. **Drag the pointer ◊ over the header *without clicking***

   The header is made up of three text boxes: left, center, and right.

3. **Click the left header text box, type Quest Specialty Travel, click the center text box, type Tour Guide Payroll Calculator, click the right header text box, then type Week 32**

   The new text appears in the text boxes, as shown in Figure A-15.

4. **Select the range A1:G2, then press [Delete]**

   The duplicate information you just entered in the header is deleted from cells in the worksheet.

5. **Click the Ruler checkbox in the Show/Hide group on the View tab, then click the Gridlines checkbox**

   The rulers and the gridlines are hidden. By default, gridlines in a worksheet do not print, so hiding them gives you a more accurate image of your final document.

6. **Click the Page Break Preview button ▦ on the status bar, then click OK in the Welcome to Page Break Preview dialog box, if necessary**

   Your view changes to **Page Break Preview**, which displays a reduced view of each page of your worksheet, along with page break indicators that you can drag to include more or less information on a page.

7. **Drag the bottom page break indicator to the bottom of row 21**

   See Figure A-16. When you're working on a large worksheet with multiple pages, sometimes you need to adjust where pages break; in this worksheet, however, the information all fits comfortably on one page.

8. **Click the View tab if necessary, click Page Layout in the Workbook Views group, click the Ruler checkbox in the Show/Hide group in the View tab, then click the Gridlines checkbox**

   The rulers and gridlines are no longer hidden. You can show or hide View tab items in any view.

9. **Save your work**

FIGURE A-14: Page Layout View

Ruler checkbox

Gridlines checkbox

Workbook Views group

Header text box

Vertical ruler

Current page and total number of pages

Horizontal ruler

Additional dimmed page

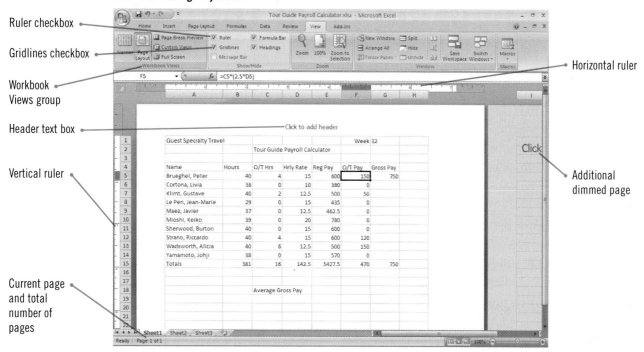

FIGURE A-15: Header boxes

Header areas

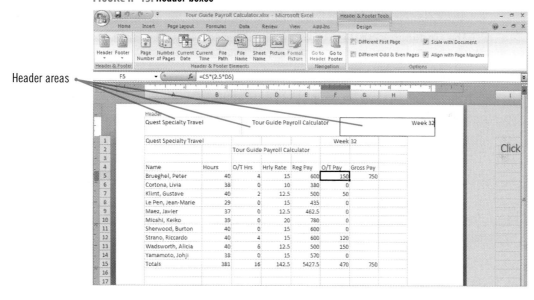

FIGURE A-16: Page Break Preview

Blue outline indicates print area

Bottom page break indicator

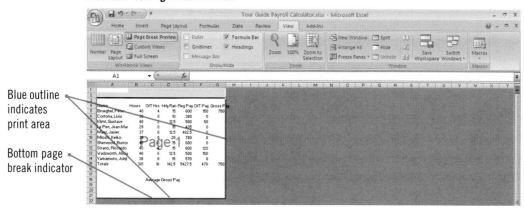

Choosing Print Options

Before printing a document, you may want to review it using the Page Layout tab and Print Preview to fine-tune your printed output. You should also review your settings in the Print dialog box, to make sure you are printing the desired number of copies and using the correct printer. Tools on the Page Layout tab include a Page Setup group, where you can adjust print orientation (the direction in which the content prints across the page), paper size, and page breaks. The Scale to Fit group makes it possible to fit a large amount of data on a single page without making changes to individual margins. In the Sheet Options group, you can turn on and off gridlines and column/row headings. Reviewing your final worksheet in Print Preview shows you exactly how the worksheet will look when printed. ▆▆▆▆ You are ready to prepare your worksheet for printing.

STEPS

1. **Click cell A21, type your name, then press [Enter]**

2. **Click the Page Layout tab on the Ribbon**
   Compare your screen to Figure A-17. The dotted line indicates the **print area**, the area to be printed.

3. **Click the Orientation button in the Page Setup group, then click Landscape** 🖾
   The paper orientation changes to **landscape**, so the contents will print across the length of the page instead of across the width.

4. **Click the Orientation button in the Page Setup group, then click Portrait** 🖺
   The orientation returns to **portrait**, so the contents will print across the width of the page.

5. **Click the Gridlines View checkbox in the Sheet Options group on the Page Layout tab, click the Gridlines Print checkbox to select it if necessary, then save your work**
   Printing gridlines makes the data easier to read, but the gridlines will not print unless the Gridlines Print checkbox is checked.

6. **Click the Office button 🔘, point to Print, then click Print Preview**
   Print Preview shows exactly how your printed copy will look. You can print from this view by clicking the Print button on the Ribbon, or close Print Preview without printing by clicking the Close Print Preview button.

7. **Click the Zoom button in the Zoom group on the Print Preview tab**
   The image of your worksheet is enlarged. Compare your screen to Figure A-18.

8. **Click the Print button in the Print group, compare your settings to Figure A-19, then click OK**
   One copy of the worksheet prints.

9. **Exit Excel**

Printing worksheet formulas

Sometimes you need to keep a record of all the formulas in a worksheet. You might want to do this to see exactly how you came up with a complex calculation, so you can explain it to others. You can do this by printing out the formulas in a worksheet rather than the results of those calculations. To do so, open the workbook containing the formulas you want to print. Click the Office button, then click Excel Options. Click Advanced in the left pane, scroll to the Display options for this worksheet section, click the list arrow and select the entire workbook or the sheet in which you want the formulas displayed, click the Show formulas in cells instead of their calculated results checkbox, then click OK.

FIGURE A-17: Worksheet with Portrait orientation

Page Layout tab

Scale field

Dotted line
surrounds
print area

Your name
appears here

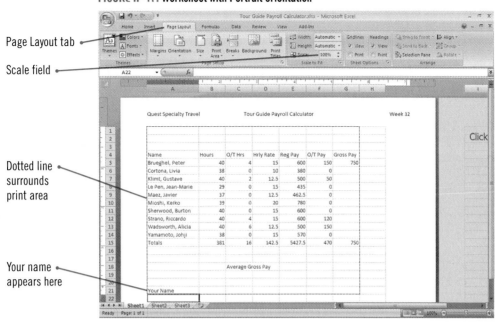

FIGURE A-18: Worksheet in Print Preview

Print button

Zoom button

Close Print
Preview button

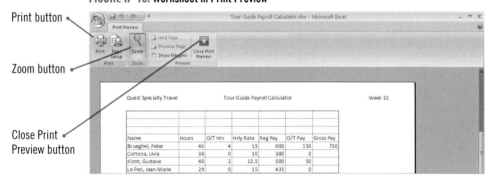

FIGURE A-19: Print dialog box

Active printer: yours
will be different

Choose which
pages to print

Number of
copies field

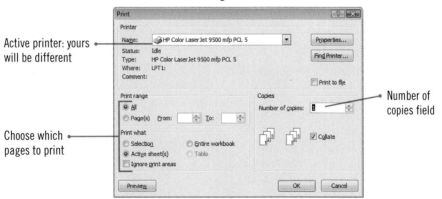

Scaling to fit

If you have a large amount of data that you want to fit to a single sheet of paper, but you don't want to spend a lot of time trying to adjust the margins and other settings, use the Fit to option in the Page Setup dialog box. Open this dialog box by clicking the launcher in the Scale to Fit group in the Page Layout tab. Make sure the Page tab is selected, then click the Fit to option button. Select the number of pages you want the worksheet to fit on, then click OK. If you're ready to print, click Print and the Print dialog box will open. Select the pages you want to print and the number of copies you want, then click OK.

Practice

If you have a SAM user profile, you may have access to hands-on instruction, practice, and assessment of the skills covered in this unit. Log in to your SAM account (http://sam2007.course.com/) to launch any assigned training activities or exams that relate to the skills covered in this unit.

▼ CONCEPTS REVIEW

Label the elements of the Excel worksheet window shown in Figure A-20.

FIGURE A-20

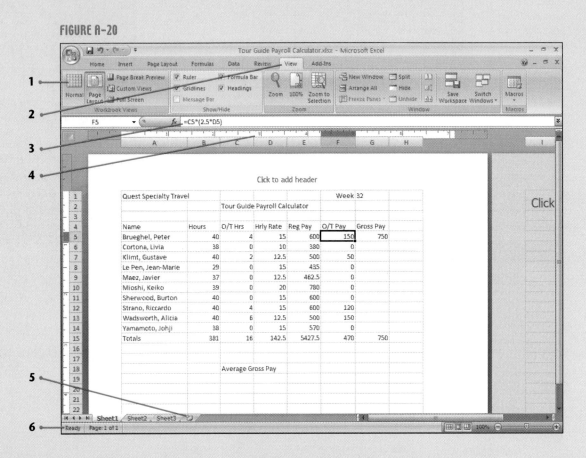

Match each term with the statement that best describes it.

7. Cell

8. Normal View

9. Workbook

10. Name Box

11. Formula prefix

12. Orientation

a. Direction in which contents of page will print

b. Equal sign preceding a formula

c. File consisting of one or more worksheets

d. Default view in Excel

e. Part of the Excel program window that displays the active cell address

f. Intersection of a column and a row

Select the best answer from the list of choices.

13. In Excel, order of precedence determines:
  a. The order in which worksheets are printed.
  b. The colors used to distinguish cell references.
  c. The order in which calculations are performed.
  d. How values are multiplied.

14. The maximum number of worksheets you can include in a workbook is:
  a. 3.
  b. 250.
  c. 255.
  d. Unlimited.

15. A selection of multiple cells is called a:
  a. Group.
  b. Range.
  c. Reference.
  d. Package.

16. Using a cell address in a formula is known as:
  a. Formularizing.
  b. Prefixing.
  c. Cell referencing.
  d. Cell mathematics.

17. Which worksheet view shows how your worksheet will look when printed?
  a. Page Layout
  b. Data
  c. Review
  d. View

18. Which button should you click if you want to print formulas in a worksheet?
  a. Save button
  b. Fill button
  c. Any button on the Quick Access Toolbar
  d. Office button

19. Clicking the launcher in the Scale to Fit group on the Page Layout tab opens which dialog box?
  a. Print
  b. Scale to Fit
  c. Width/Height
  d. Page Setup

20. In which view can you see the header and footer areas of a worksheet?
  a. Normal View
  b. Page Layout View
  c. Page Break Preview
  d. Header/Footer View

21. Which key can you press to switch to Edit mode?
  a. [F1]
  b. [F2]
  c. [F4]
  d. [F6]

▼ SKILLS REVIEW

1. Understand spreadsheet software.
  a. What is the difference between a workbook and a worksheet?
  b. Identify five common business uses for electronic spreadsheets.
  c. What is 'what-if' analysis?

2. Tour the Excel 2007 window.
  a. Start Excel.
  b. Open the file EX A-2.xlsx from the drive and folder where you store your Data Files, then save it as **Weather Statistics**.
  c. Locate the formula bar, the Sheet tabs, the mode indicator, and the cell pointer.

3. Understand formulas.
  a. What is the average high temperature of the listed cities? (*Hint*: Select the range B5:G5 and use the status bar.)
  b. What formula would you create to calculate the difference in altitude between Chicago and Phoenix?

4. Enter labels and values and use AutoSum.
  a. Click cell H7, then use the AutoSum button to calculate the total rainfall.
  b. Click cell H8, then use the AutoSum button to calculate the total snowfall.
  c. Save your changes to the file.

5. Edit cell entries.
  a. Use the [F2] key to correct the spelling of Sante Fe in a worksheet cell (the correct spelling is Santa Fe).
  b. Click cell A12, then type your name.
  c. Save your changes.

▼ SKILLS REVIEW (CONTINUED)

6. Enter and edit a simple formula.

a. Change the value 41 in cell B8 to **52**.

b. Change the value 35 in cell C7 to **35.4**.

c. Select the range B10:G10, then use the Fill button in the Editing group on the Home tab to fill the formula to the remaining cells in the selection. (*Hint*: If you see a warning icon, click it, then click Ignore Error.)

d. Save your changes.

7. Switch worksheet views.

a. Click the View tab on the Ribbon, then switch to Page Layout view.

b. Add the header **Average Annual Weather Statistics** to the center header box.

c. Add your name to the right header box.

d. Delete the contents of cell A1.

e. Delete the contents of cell A12.

f. Save your changes.

8. Choose Print options.

a. Use the Page Layout tab to change the orientation to Portrait.

b. Turn off gridlines by deselecting both the Gridlines View and Gridlines Print checkboxes in the Sheet Options group.

c. View the worksheet in Print Preview, then zoom in to enlarge the preview. Compare your screen to Figure A-21.

d. Open the Print dialog box, then print one copy of the worksheet.

e. Save your changes, then close the workbook.

FIGURE A-21

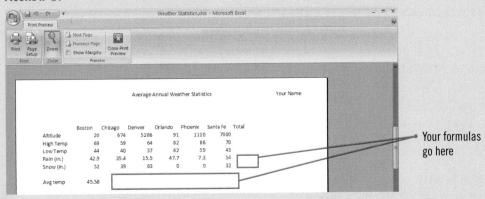

▼ INDEPENDENT CHALLENGE 1

A local real estate office has hired you to help them make the transition to using Excel in their office. They would like to list their properties in a worksheet. You've started a worksheet for this project that contains labels but no data.

a. Open the file EX A-3.xlsx from where you store your Data Files, then save it as **Real Estate Listings**.

b. Enter the data shown in Table A-4 in columns A, C, D, and E (the property address information should spill into column B).

TABLE A-4

Property Address	Price	Bedrooms	Bathrooms
1507 Cactus Lane	350000	3	2.5
32 California Lane	325000	3	4
60 Pottery Lane	475500	2	2
902 Fortunata Drive	295000	4	3
Total			

▼ INDEPENDENT CHALLENGE 1 (CONTINUED)

c. Use Page Layout View to create a header with the following components: a title in the center and your name on the right.

d. Create formulas for totals in cells C6:E6.

e. Save your changes, then preview your work and compare it to Figure A-22.

f. Print the worksheet.

g. Close the worksheet and exit Excel.

FIGURE A-22

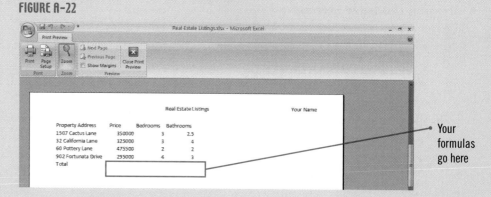

▼ INDEPENDENT CHALLENGE 2

FIGURE A-23

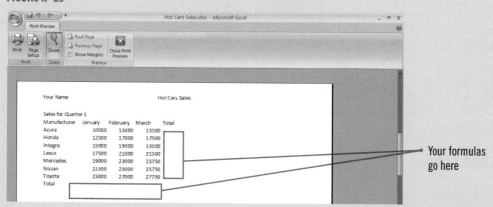

You are the General Manager for Hot Cars, a small auto parts supplier. Although the company is just three years old, it is expanding rapidly, and you are continually looking for ways to save time. You recently began using Excel to manage and maintain data on inventory and sales, which has greatly helped you to track information accurately and efficiently.

a. Start Excel.

b. Save a new workbook as **Hot Cars Sales** in the drive and folder where you store your Data Files.

c. Switch to an appropriate view, then add a header that contains your name in the left header text box and a title in the center header text box.

d. Using Figure A-23 as a guide, create labels for at least seven car manufacturers and sales for three months. Include other labels as appropriate. The car manufacturers should be in column A, and the months in columns B, C, and D. A Total row should be beneath the data, and a Total column should be in column E.

e. Enter values of your choice for the monthly sales for each manufacturer.

f. Add a formula in the Total column to calculate total monthly sales for each manufacturer. Add formulas at the bottom of each column of values to calculate the total for that column. Remember that you can use the SUM function to save time.

g. Save your changes, preview the worksheet, then print it.

▼ INDEPENDENT CHALLENGE 2 (CONTINUED)

Advanced Challenge Exercise

- Create a label two rows beneath the data in column A that says 15% increase.
- Create a formula in the row containing the 15% increase label that calculates a 15% increase in total monthly sales.
- Save the workbook.
- Display the formulas in the worksheet, then print a copy of the worksheet with formulas displayed.

h. Close the workbook(s) and exit Excel.

▼ INDEPENDENT CHALLENGE 3

FIGURE A-24

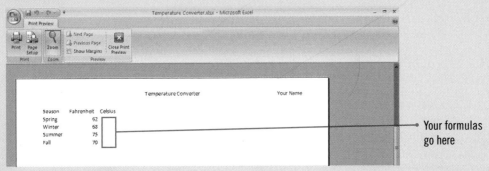

This Independent Challenge requires an Internet connection. Your office is starting a branch in Paris and you think it would be helpful to create a worksheet that can be used to convert Fahrenheit temperatures to Celsius, to help employees who are unfamiliar with this type of temperature measurement.

a. Start Excel, then save a blank workbook as **Temperature Converter** in the drive and folder where you store your Data Files.

b. Create column and row titles using Figure A-24 as a guide.

c. Create labels for each of the seasons.

d. In the appropriate cells, enter what you determine to be an ideal indoor temperature for each season.

e. Use your Web browser to find out the conversion rate for Fahrenheit to Celsius. (*Hint*: Use your favorite search engine to search on a term such as "temperature conversion.")

f. In the appropriate cells, create an equation that calculates the conversion of the Fahrenheit temperature you entered into a Celsius temperature.

g. Preview the worksheet in Page Layout View, adding your name to the header, as well as a meaningful title.

h. Save your work, then print the worksheet.

i. Close the file, then exit Excel.

$C = (F - 32) \times 5/9$

▼ REAL LIFE INDEPENDENT CHALLENGE

FIGURE A-25

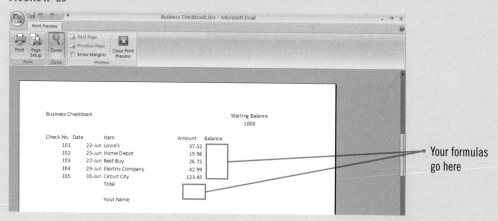

You've decided to quit your day job and turn your favorite hobby into a business. You've set up a small business selling the product or service of your choice. You want to use Excel to keep track of your many start-up costs.

a. Start Excel, open the file EX A-4.xlsx from the drive and folder where you store your Data Files, then save it as **Business Checkbook**.

b. Type check numbers (using your choice of a starting number) in cells A5 through A9.

c. Create sample data for the date, item, and amount in cells B5 through D9.

d. Save your work.

Advanced Challenge Exercise

- Use Help to find out about creating a series of numbers.
- Delete the contents of cells A5:A9.
- Create a series of numbers in cells A5:A9.
- In cell C15, type a brief description of how you created the series.
- Save the workbook.

e. Create formulas in cells E5:E9 that calculate a running balance. (*Hint*: For the first check, the running balance equals the starting balance minus a check; for the following checks, the running balance equals the previous balance value minus each check value.)

f. Create a formula in cell D10 that totals the amount of the checks.

g. Enter your name in cell C12, then compare your screen to Figure A-25.

h. Save your changes to the file, preview and print the worksheet, then exit Excel.

▼ VISUAL WORKSHOP

Open the file EX A-5.xlsx from the drive and folder where you store your Data Files, then save it as **Inventory Items**. Using the skills you learned in this unit, modify your worksheet so it matches Figure A-26. Enter formulas in cells D4 through D13 and in cells B14 and C14. Use the AutoSum button to make entering your formulas easier. Add your name in the left header text box, then print one copy of the worksheet once with the formulas not displayed, and one copy with the formulas displayed.

FIGURE A-26

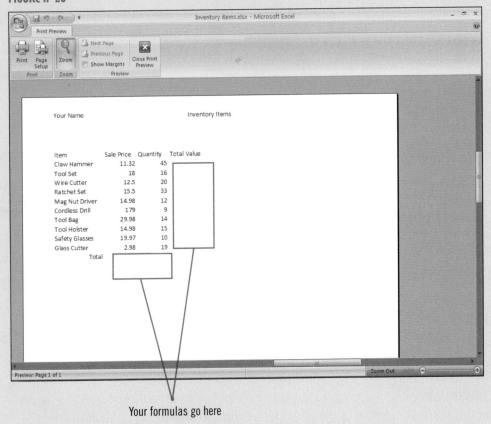

Your formulas go here

Working with Formulas and Functions

Files You Will Need:

EX B-1.xlsx
EX B-2.xlsx
EX B-3.xlsx
EX B-4.xlsx

Using your knowledge of Excel basics, you can expand your worksheets to include more complex formulas and functions. To work more efficiently, you can copy and move existing formulas into other cells instead of manually retyping the same information. When copying or moving, you can also control how cell references are handled, so that your formulas always reference the intended cells. Grace Wong, vice president of finance at Quest Specialty Travel, needs to analyze tour revenue for the current year. She has asked you to prepare a worksheet that summarizes this revenue data and includes some statistical analysis. She would also like you to perform some what-if analysis, to see what quarterly revenues would look like with various projected increases.

OBJECTIVES

Create a complex formula

Insert a function

Type a function

Copy and move cell entries

Understand relative and absolute cell references

Copy formulas with relative cell references

Copy formulas with absolute cell references

Round a value with a function

Creating a Complex Formula

A **complex formula** is one that uses more than one arithmetic operator. You might, for example, need to create a formula that uses addition and multiplication. You can use arithmetic operators to separate tasks within a complex equation. In formulas containing more than one arithmetic operator, Excel uses the standard order of precedence rules to determine which operation to perform first. You can change the order of precedence in a formula by using parentheses around the part you want to calculate first. For example, the formula =4+2*5 equals 14, because the order of precedence dictates that multiplication is performed before addition. However, the formula =(4+2)*5 equals 30, because the parentheses cause 4+2 to be calculated first. ▰▰▰▰ You want to create a formula that calculates a 20% increase in tour revenue.

STEPS

1. **Start Excel, open the file EX B-1.xlsx from the drive and folder where you store your Data Files, then save it as** Tour Revenue Analysis

QUICK TIP

When you click a cell reference, the mode indicator on the status bar reads "Point," indicating that you can click additional cell references to add them to the formula.

2. **Click cell B14, type =, click cell B12, then type +**
   In this first part of the formula, you are creating references to the total for Quarter 1.

3. **Click cell B12, then type *.2**
   The second part of this formula adds a 20% increase (B12*.2) to the original value of the cell. Compare your worksheet to Figure B-1.

4. **Click the Enter button ✓ on the formula bar**
   The result, 386122.344, appears in cell B14.

5. **Press [Tab], type =, click cell C12, type +, click cell C12, type *.2, then click ✓**
   The result, 410969.712, appears in cell C14.

6. **Drag the ✛ pointer from cell C14 to cell E14, click the Fill button ▣▾ in the Editing group on the Home tab of the Ribbon, then click Right**
   The calculated values appear in the selected range, as shown in Figure B-2.

7. **Save your work**

Reviewing the order of precedence

When you work with formulas that contain more than one operator, the order of precedence is very important because it affects the final value. For example, you might think the formula 4+2*5 equals 30, but because the order of precedence dictates that multiplication is performed before addition, the actual result is 14. If a formula contains two or more operators, such as 4+.55/4000*25, Excel performs the calculations in a particular sequence based on the following rules: Operations inside parentheses are calculated before any other operations. Reference operators (such as ranges) are calculated first. Exponents are calculated next, then any multiplication and division—progressing from left to right. Finally, addition and subtraction are calculated from left to right. In the example 4+.55/4000*25, Excel performs the arithmetic operations by first dividing 4000 into .55, then multiplying the result by 25, then adding 4. You can change the order of calculations by using parentheses. For example, in the formula (4+.55)/4000*25, Excel would first add 4 and .55, then divide that amount by 4000, then finally multiply by 25.

FIGURE B-1: Formula containing multiple arithmetic operators

Complex formula

Mode indicator

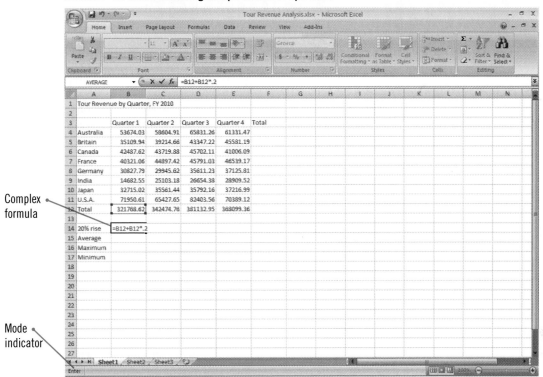

FIGURE B-2: Complex formulas in worksheet

Formula in cell C14 copied to cells D14 and E14

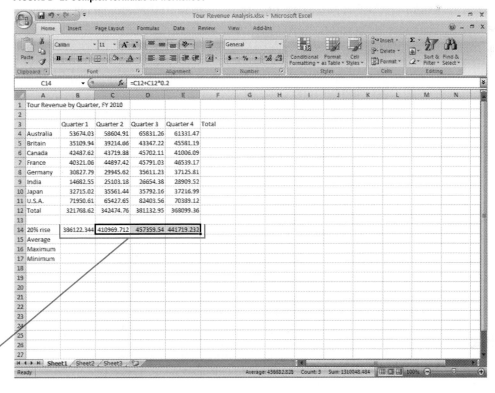

Inserting a Function

Functions are predefined worksheet formulas that enable you to perform complex calculations easily. You can use the Insert Function button on the formula bar to choose a function from a dialog box. In addition to using the AutoSum button on the Ribbon to quickly insert the SUM function, you can click the AutoSum button list arrow to enter other frequently used functions, such as Average. Functions are organized into categories, such as Financial, Date & Time, and Statistical, based on their purpose. You can insert a function on its own, or as part of another formula. For example, you have used the SUM function on its own to add a range of cells. You could also use the SUM function within a formula that adds a range of cells and then multiplies the total by a decimal. If you use a function alone, it always begins with the formula prefix = (the equal sign). You need to calculate the average sales for the first quarter of the year, and decide to use a function to do so.

STEPS

1. **Click cell B15**

   This is the cell where you want to enter the calculation that averages revenue for the first quarter. You want to use the Insert Function dialog box to enter this function.

2. **Click the Insert Function button f_x on the formula bar**

   An equal sign (=) is inserted in the active cell and in the formula bar, and the Insert Function dialog box opens, as shown in Figure B-3. In this dialog box, you specify the function you want to add by clicking it in the Select a function list. The Select a function list initially displays recently used functions. If you don't see the function you want, you can click the Or select a category list arrow to choose the desired category or, if you're not sure what category to choose, you can type the function name or a description in the Search for a function field. The AVERAGE function is a statistical function, but you don't need to open the Statistical category because this function appears in the Most Recently Used list.

3. **Click AVERAGE, if necessary, read the information that appears under the list, then click OK**

   The Function Arguments dialog box opens, where you define the range of cells you want to average.

4. **Click the Collapse button in the Number1 field of the Function Arguments dialog box, drag the ✛ pointer to select the range B4:B11, release the mouse button, then click the Expand button**

   Clicking the Collapse button minimizes the dialog box so you can select cells in the worksheet. When you click the Expand button, the dialog box is restored, as shown in Figure B-4. You can also begin dragging in the worksheet to automatically minimize the dialog box; after you select the desired range, the dialog box is restored.

5. **Click OK**

   The Function Arguments dialog box closes and the calculated value displays in cell C15. The average revenue per country for Quarter 1 is 40221.0775.

6. **Click cell C15, click the AutoSum button list arrow Σ ▾ in the Editing group on the Home tab, then click Average**

   A ScreenTip beneath cell C15 displays the arguments needed to complete the function. The text number1 is shown in boldface type, telling you that the next step is to supply the first cell in the group you want to average. You want to average a range of cells.

7. **Drag ✛ to select the range C4:C11, then click the Enter button ✓ on the formula bar**

   The average revenue per country for the second quarter appears in cell C15.

8. **Select the range C15:E15, click the Fill button ▦ ▾ in the Editing group, then click Right**

   The formula in cell C15 is copied to the rest of the selected range, as shown in Figure B-5.

9. **Save your work**

FIGURE B-3: Insert Function dialog box

Search for a function field

Your list of recently used functions may differ

Or select a category list arrow

Description of selected function

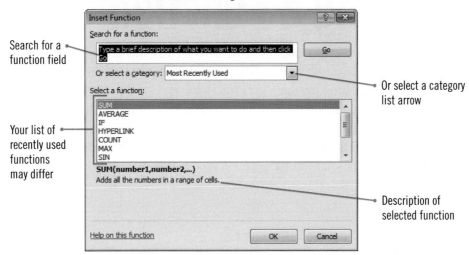

FIGURE B-4: Expanded Function Arguments dialog box

Function in formula bar

Insert Function button

Argument

Drag title bar of dialog box to move it if necessary

Description and argument format of selected function

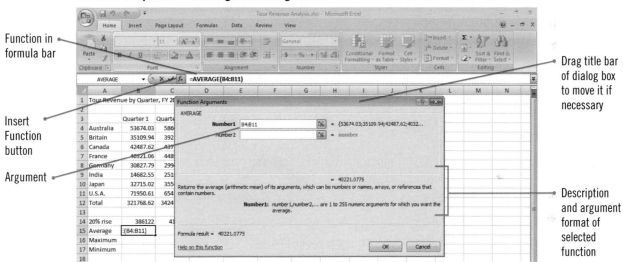

FIGURE B-5: Average function in worksheet

Completed function appears in formula bar

Formula in cell C15 copied to cells D15 and E15

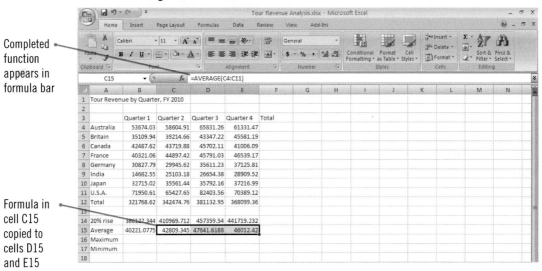

Typing a Function

In addition to entering a function using the Insert Function dialog box or the AutoSum button on the Ribbon, you can manually type the function into a cell and complete the arguments needed. This method requires that you know the name and initial characters of the function, but can be faster than opening several dialog boxes. Experienced Excel users often prefer this method, but it is only an alternative, not better or more correct than any other method. The AutoComplete feature makes it easier to enter function names because it suggests functions depending on the first letters you type. **⬛⬛⬛⬛** You want to calculate the maximum and minimum quarterly sales in your worksheet, and decide to manually enter these statistical functions.

STEPS

1. **Click cell B16, type =, then type m**

   Since you are manually typing this function, it is necessary to begin with the equal sign (=). The AutoComplete feature displays a list of function names beginning with M. Once you type an equal sign in a cell, each letter you type acts as a trigger to activate the AutoComplete feature. This feature minimizes the amount of typing you need to do to enter a function, and reduces typing and syntax errors.

   > **QUICK TIP**
   >
   > You can single-click any function in the AutoComplete list to open a Screentip describing the selected function.

2. **Click MAX in the list**

   A Screentip appears, describing the function.

3. **Double-click MAX**

   The function is added to the cell and a Screentip appears beneath the cell to help you complete the formula. See Figure B-6.

4. **Select the range B4:B11, as shown in Figure B-7, then click the Enter button ✓ on the formula bar**

   The result, 71950.61, appears in cell B16. When you completed the entry, the closing parenthesis was automatically added to the formula.

5. **Click cell B17, type =, type m, then double-click MIN**

   The argument for the MIN function appears in the cell.

6. **Select the range B4:B11, then press [Enter]**

   The result, 14682.55, appears in cell B17.

7. **Select the range B16:E17, click the Fill button list arrow 🔽 in the Editing group, then click Right**

   The maximum and minimum values for all of the quarters display in the selected range, as shown in Figure B-8.

8. **Save your work**

Using the COUNT and COUNTA functions

When you select a range, a count of cells in the range that are not blank appears in the status bar. For example, if you select the range A1:A5 and only cells A1 and A2 contain data, the status bar displays "Count: 2." To count nonblank cells more precisely, or to incorporate these calculations in a worksheet, you can use the COUNT and COUNTA functions. COUNT returns the number of cells that contain numeric data, including numbers, dates, and formulas. COUNTA returns the number of cells that contain any data at all, even text or a blank space. For example, the formula =COUNT(A1:A5) returns the number of cells in the range that contain numeric data, and the formula =COUNTA(A1:A5) returns the number of cells in the range that are not blank.

FIGURE B-6: MAX function in progress

13					
14	20% rise	386122.344	410969.712	457359.54	441719.232
15	Average	40221.0775	42809.345	47641.6188	46012.42
16	Maximum	=MAX(			
17	Minimum	MAX(**number1**, [number2], ...)			
18					

FIGURE B-7: Completing the MAX function

Closing parenthesis will be added automatically when you accept entry

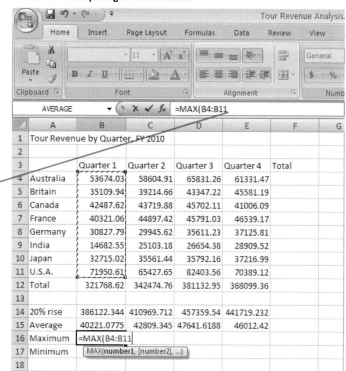

FIGURE B-8: Completed MAX and MIN functions

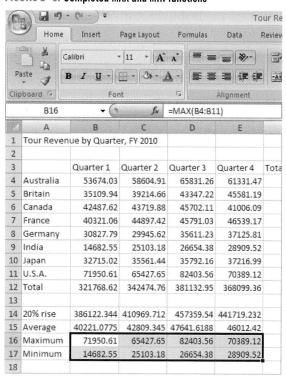

UNIT
B
Excel 2007

Copying and Moving Cell Entries

You can copy or move cells and ranges (or the contents within them) from one location to another using the Cut, Copy, and Paste buttons; the fill handle in the lower-right corner of the active cell; or the drag-and-drop feature. When you copy cells, the original data remains in the original location; when you cut or move it, the original data is deleted. You can also cut, copy, and paste cells or ranges from one worksheet to another. In addition to the 20% rise in tour revenue, you also want to show a 30% rise. Rather than retype this information, you copy and move the labels in these cells.

STEPS

QUICK TIP
To cut or copy selected contents within a cell, activate the cell and then select the characters within the cell that you want to cut or copy.

QUICK TIP
The Clipboard can hold up to 24 items. Once the clipboard is full, the oldest existing item is automatically deleted each time you add an item.

QUICK TIP
You can also close the Clipboard pane by clicking the launcher in the Clipboard group.

1. **Select the range B3:E3, then click the Copy button in the Clipboard group**
   The selected range (B3:E3) is copied to the **Office Clipboard**, a temporary storage area that holds the selections you copy or cut. A moving border surrounds the selected range until you press [Esc] or copy an additional item to the Clipboard. Notice that the information you copied remains in the selected range; if you had cut instead of copied, the information would have been deleted once it was pasted.

2. **Click the launcher in the Clipboard group, click cell B19, then click the Paste button in the Clipboard group**
   The Office Clipboard pane opens, as shown in Figure B-9. Your Clipboard may contain additional items. When pasting an item from the Clipboard into the worksheet, you only need to specify the upper-left cell of the range where you want to paste the selection.

3. **Press [Delete]**
   The selected cells are empty. You have decided to paste the cells in a different row. You can repeatedly paste an item from the Office Clipboard as many times as you like, as long as the item remains in the Clipboard.

4. **Click cell B20, click the first item in the Office Clipboard, then click the Close button on the Clipboard pane**
   Cells B20:E20 contain the copied labels.

5. **Click cell A14, press and hold [Ctrl], point to any edge of the cell until the pointer changes to , drag to cell A21, then release [Ctrl]**
   As you drag, the pointer changes to , as shown in Figure B-10.

6. **Click to the right of 2 in the formula bar, press [Backspace], type 3, then press [Enter]**

7. **Click cell B21, type =, click cell B12, type *1.3, then click on the formula bar**
   This new formula calculates a 30% increase of the revenue for Quarter 1, though using a different method from what you used previously. Anything you multiply by 1.3 returns an amount that's 130% of the original amount, or a 30% increase. Compare your screen to Figure B-11.

8. **Save your work**

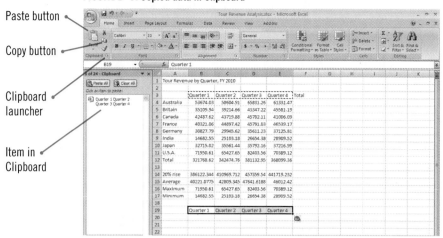

FIGURE B-9: Copied data in Clipboard

Paste button

Copy button

Clipboard launcher

Item in Clipboard

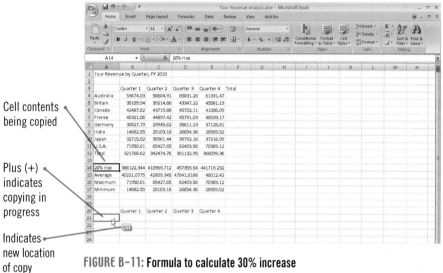

FIGURE B-10: Copying cell contents with drag-and-drop

Cell contents being copied

Plus (+) indicates copying in progress

Indicates new location of copy

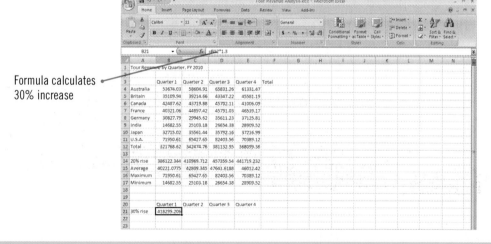

FIGURE B-11: Formula to calculate 30% increase

Formula calculates 30% increase

Excel 2007

Inserting and deleting selected cells

As you add formulas to your workbook, you may need to insert or delete cells. When you do this, Excel automatically adjusts cell references to reflect their new locations. To insert cells, click the Insert button list arrow in the Cells group on the Home tab, then click Insert Cells. The Insert dialog box opens, asking if you want to insert a cell and move the selected cell down or to the right of the new one. To delete one or more selected cells, click the Delete button list arrow in the Cells group, click Delete Cells, and in the Delete dialog box, indicate which way you want to move the adjacent cells. When using this option, be careful not to disturb row or column alignment that may be necessary to maintain the accuracy of cell references in the worksheet. Click the Insert or Delete button to add/delete a single cell.

Understanding Relative and Absolute Cell References

As you work in Excel, you may want to reuse formulas in different parts of a worksheet to reduce the amount of data you have to retype. For example, you might want to include a what-if analysis in one part of a worksheet showing a set of sales projections if sales increase by 10%, and another analysis in another part of the worksheet showing projections if sales increase by 50%; you can copy the formulas from one section to another and just change the "1" to a "5". But when you copy formulas, it is important to make sure that they refer to the correct cells. To do this, you need to understand the difference between relative and absolute cell references. ▀▀▀▀▀ You plan to reuse formulas in different parts of your worksheets, so you want to understand relative and absolute cell references.

DETAILS

- **Use relative references when you want to preserve the relationship to the formula location**

    When you create a formula that references other cells, Excel normally does not "record" the exact cell address. Instead, it looks at the relationship that cell has to the cell containing the formula. For example, in Figure B-12, cell F5 contains the formula: =SUM(B5:E5). When Excel retrieves values to calculate the formula in cell F5, it actually looks for "the cell four columns to the left of the formula," which in this case is cell B5. This way, if you copy the cell to a new location, such as cell F6, the results will reflect the new formula location, and will automatically retrieve the values in cells B6, C6, D6, and E6. These are **relative cell references**, because Excel is recording the input cells *in relation to* or *relative to* the formula cell.

    In most cases, you want to use relative cell references when copying or moving, so this is the Excel default. In Figure B-12, the formulas in F5:F12 and in B13:F13 contain relative cell references. They total the "four cells to the left of" or the "eight cells above" the formulas.

- **Use absolute cell references when you want to preserve the exact cell address in a formula**

    There are times when you want Excel to retrieve formula information from a specific cell, and you don't want the cell address in the formula to change when you copy it to a new location. For example, you might have a price in a specific cell that you want to use in all formulas, regardless of their location. If you used relative cell referencing, the formula results would be incorrect, because Excel would use a different cell every time you copied the formula. Therefore you need to use an **absolute cell reference**, a reference that does not change when you copy the formula.

    You create an absolute cell reference by placing a $ (dollar sign) in front of both the column letter and the row number of the cell address. You can either type the dollar sign when typing the cell address in a formula (for example, "=C12*$B$16"), or you can select a cell address on the formula bar and then press [F4] and the dollar signs are added automatically. Figure B-13 show formulas containing both absolute and relative references. The formulas in cells B19 to E26 use absolute cell references to refer to a potential sales increase of 50%, shown in cell B16.

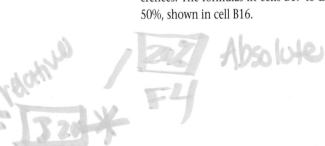

FIGURE B-12: Formulas containing relative references

Formula containing relative references

Copied formulas adjust to preserve relationship of formula to referenced cells

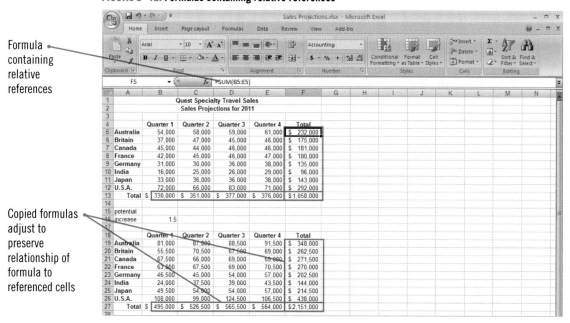

FIGURE B-13: Formulas containing absolute and relative references

Cell referenced in absolute formulas

Relative references in copied formulas adjust

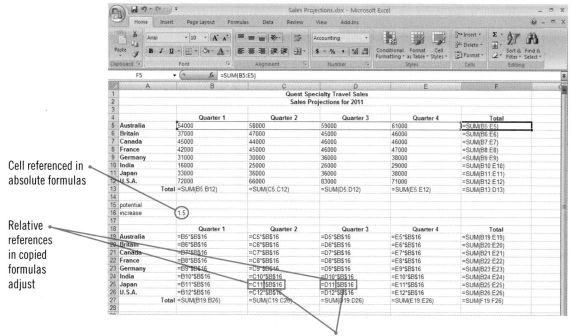

Absolute references in copied formulas do not adjust

Using a mixed reference

Sometimes when you copy a formula, you want to change the row reference, but keep the column reference the same. This type of cell referencing combines elements of both absolute and relative referencing and is called a **mixed reference**. For example, when copied, a formula containing the mixed reference C$14 would change the column letter relative to its new location, but not the row number.

In the mixed reference $C14, the column letter would not change, but the row number would be updated relative to its location. Like the absolute reference, a mixed reference can be created using the [F4] function key. With each press of the [F4] key, you cycle through all the possible combinations of relative, absolute, and mixed references ($C$14, C$14, $C14, C14).

Copying Formulas with Relative Cell References

Copying and moving a cell allows you to reuse a formula you've already created. Copying cells is usually faster than retyping the formulas in them, and helps to prevent typing errors. You can use the Copy and Paste commands or the fill handle to copy formulas. The Fill button list arrow can also be used to fill cells containing formulas going left, right, up, down, and in series. If the cells you are copying contain relative cell references and you want to maintain the relative referencing, you don't need to make any changes to the cells before copying them. ▰▰▰ You want to copy the formula in cell B21, which calculates the 30% increase in quarterly sales for quarter 1, to cells C21 through E21. You also want to create formulas to calculate total sales for each tour country.

1. **Click cell B21, if necessary, then click the Copy button 🖹 in the Clipboard group**

   The formula for calculating the 30% sales increase during Quarter 1 is copied to the Clipboard. Notice that the formula =B12*1.3 appears in the formula bar and a moving border surrounds the active cell.

   QUICK TIP

   To specify components of the copied cell or range prior to pasting, click the Paste button list arrow in the Clipboard group, then click Paste Special. You can selectively copy formulas, values, or other choices.

2. **Click cell C21, then click the Paste button in the Clipboard group**

   The formula from cell B21 is copied into cell C21, where the new result of 445217.188 appears. Notice in the formula bar that the cell references have changed, so that cell C12 is referenced in the formula. This formula contains a relative cell reference, which tells Excel to substitute new cell references within the copied formulas as necessary. This maintains the same relationship between the new cells containing the formula and the cells within the formula. In this case, Excel adjusted the formula so that cell C12—the cell reference nine rows above C21—replaced cell B12, the cell reference nine rows above B21. You can drag the fill handle in a cell to copy cells or to continue a series of data (such as Quarter 1, Quarter 2, etc.) based on previous cells. This option is called **Auto Fill**.

3. **Point to the fill handle in cell C21 until the pointer changes to ✛, press and hold the left mouse button, drag ✛ to select the range C21:E21, then release the mouse button**

   See Figure B-14. A formula similar to the one in cell C21 now appears in the range D21:E21. After you release the mouse button, the **Auto Fill Options button** appears, so you can fill the cells with only specific elements of the copied cell if you wish.

4. **Click cell F4, click the AutoSum button Σ in the Editing group, then click the Enter button ✔ on the formula bar**

   QUICK TIP

   You can use the Paste button in the Clipboard group of the Home tab to paste specific elements of a selection; click the Paste button arrow, then click an option in the list, such as Transpose (to paste column data as rows and row data as columns), No Borders (to remove any borders around pasted cells), or Paste Special (to open the Paste Special dialog box, where the complete set of paste options is available).

5. **Click 🖹 in the Clipboard group, select the range F5:F6, then click Paste**

   See Figure B-15. After you release the mouse button, the **Paste Options button** appears, so you can paste only specific elements of the copied selection if you wish. The formula for calculating quarterly revenue for tours in Britain appears in the formula bar. You would like totals to appear in cells F7:F11. The Fill command in the Editing group can be used to copy the formula into the remaining cells.

6. **Select the range F6:F11**

7. **Click the Fill button list arrow 🔽 in the Editing group, then click Down**

   The formulas are copied to each cell. Compare your worksheet to Figure B-16.

8. **Save your work**

FIGURE B-14: Copying a formula with the fill handle

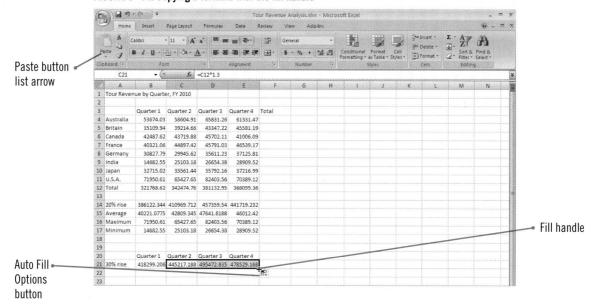

Paste button list arrow

Fill handle

Auto Fill Options button

FIGURE B-15: The results of using the Paste button

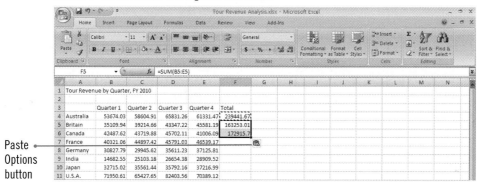

Paste Options button

FIGURE B-16: Copying cells using Fill Down

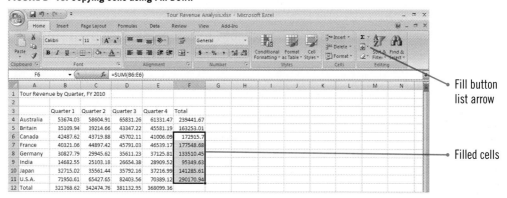

Fill button list arrow

Filled cells

Using Auto Fill options

When you use the fill handle to copy cells, the Auto Fill Options button appears. Auto Fill options differ depending on what you are copying. If you had selected cells containing a series (such as "Monday" and "Tuesday") and then used the fill handle, you would see options for continuing the series (such as "Wednesday" and "Thursday") or for simply pasting the copied cells. Clicking the Auto Fill Options button opens a list that lets you choose from the following options: Copy Cells, Fill Series (if applicable), Fill Formatting Only, or Fill Without Formatting. Choosing Copy Cells means that the cell and its formatting will be copied. The Fill Formatting Only option copies only the formatting attributes, but not the formula and its cell references. The Fill Without Formatting option copies the formula and its cell references, but no formatting attributes. Copy Cells is the default option when using the fill handle to copy a formula, so if you want to copy the cell, its references and formatting, you can ignore this button.

Copying Formulas with Absolute Cell References

When copying formulas, you might want one or more cell references in the formula to remain unchanged in relation to the formula. In such an instance, you need to apply an absolute cell reference before copying the formula, to preserve the specific cell address when the formula is copied. You create an absolute reference by placing a dollar sign ($) before the row letter and column number of the address (for example $A$1). ▰▰▰▰ You need to do some what-if analysis to see how various sales percentage increases might affect total revenues. You decide to add a column that calculates a possible increase in the total tour revenue, and then change the percentage to see various potential results.

STEPS

1. **Click cell H1, type Change, then press [→]**

2. **Type 1.1, then press [Enter]**
   You store the increase factor that will be used in the what-if analysis in this cell. The value 1.1 can be used to calculate a 10% increase; anything you multiply by 1.1 returns an amount that's 110% of the original amount, or a 10% increase.

3. **Click cell H3, type What if?, then press [Enter]**

4. **In cell H4, type =, click F4, type *, click cell I1, then click the Enter button ☑ on the formula bar**
   The result, 263385.8, appears in cell H4. This value represents the total annual revenue for Australia if there is a 10% increase. You want to perform a what-if analysis for all the tour countries.

QUICK TIP

Before you copy or move a formula, check to see if you need to use an absolute cell reference.

5. **Drag the fill handle of cell H4 to extend the selection to cell H11**
   The resulting values in the range H5:H11 are all zeros, which is not the result you wanted. See Figure B-17. Because you used relative cell addressing in cell H4, the copied formula adjusted so that the formula in cell H5 is =F5*I2. Because there is no value in cell I2, the result is 0, an error. You need to use an absolute reference in the formula to keep the formula from adjusting itself. That way, it will always reference cell I1.

6. **Click cell H4, press [F2] to change to Edit mode, then press [F4]**
   When you press [F2], the range finder outlines the arguments of the equation in blue and green. When you press [F4], dollar signs are inserted in the cell address, changing the I1 cell reference to an absolute reference.

7. **Click ☑, then drag ✚ to extend the selection to range H4:H11**
   The formula correctly contains an absolute cell reference, and the value of H4 remains unchanged. The correct values for a 10% increase appear in cells H4:H11. You now want to see a 20% increase in sales.

8. **Click cell I1, type 1.2, then click ☑**
   The values in the range H4:H11 change to reflect the 20% increase. Compare your worksheet to Figure B-18.

9. **Save your work**

FIGURE B-17: Creating an absolute reference in formula

Absolute cell reference in formula

Incorrect values from relative referencing in copied formulas

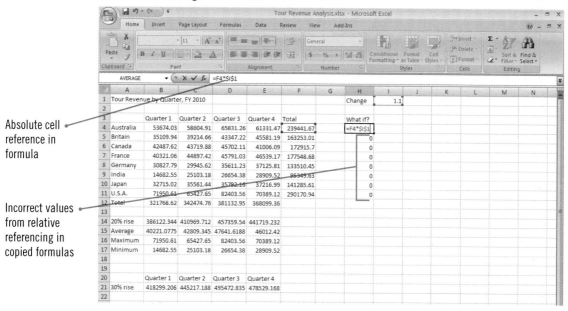

FIGURE B-18: What-if analysis with modified change factor

Modified value

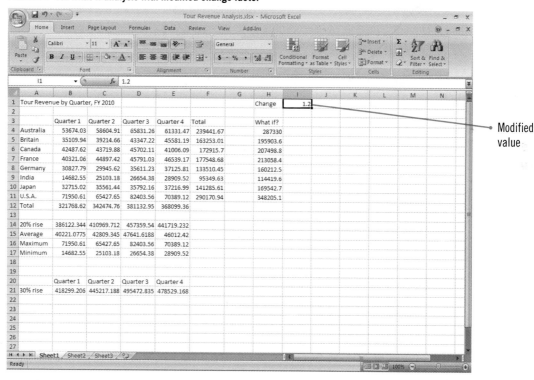

Using the fill handle for sequential text or values

Often, you need to fill cells with sequential text: months of the year, days of the week, years, or text plus a number (Quarter 1, Quarter 2,...). For example, you might want to create a worksheet that calculates data for every month of the year. Using the fill handle, you can quickly and easily create labels for the months of the year just by typing January in a cell. Drag the fill handle from the cell containing January until you have all the monthly labels you need. You can easily fill cells using sequences by dragging the fill handle. As you drag the fill handle, Excel automatically extends the existing sequence. (The content of the last filled cell appears in the ScreenTip.) Use the Fill button list arrow in the Editing group, then click Series to examine all the fill series options for the current selection.

Rounding a Value with a Function

The more you explore features and tools in Excel, the more ways you'll find to simplify your work and convey information more efficiently. For example, cells containing financial data are often easier to read if they contain fewer decimals than those that appear by default. You can achieve this result by using the ROUND function, to round down your results. In your worksheet, you'd like to round the cells showing the 20% rise in sales to show fewer digits; after all, it's not important to show cents in the projections, only whole dollars. You want Excel to round the calculated value to the nearest integer. You decide to edit cell B14 so it includes the ROUND function, and then copy the edited formula into the other formulas in this row.

STEPS

1. **Click cell B14, then click to the right of = on the formula bar**

   You want to position the function at the beginning of the formula, before any values or arguments.

2. **Type RO**

   AutoComplete displays a list of functions beginning with RO.

3. **Double-click ROUND in the AutoComplete list**

   The new function and an opening parenthesis are added to the formula, as shown in Figure B-19. A few additional modifications are needed to complete your edit of the formula. You need to indicate the number of digits to which the function should round numbers down, and you also need to add a closing parenthesis around the set of arguments that come after the ROUND function.

4. **Press [END], type ,0), then click the Enter button ✔ on the formula bar**

   The comma separates the arguments within the formula, and 0 indicates that you don't want any decimals to appear in the calculated value. When you complete the edit, the parenthesis at either end of the formula briefly become bold, indicating that the formula has the correct number of open and closed parentheses and is balanced.

5. **Click the fill handle of cell B14, then drag the ✛ pointer to cell E14**

   When you release the mouse button, the formula in cell B14 is copied to the selected range. All the values are rounded to display no decimals. Compare your worksheet to Figure B-20.

6. **Click cell A25, type your name, then click ✔ on the formula bar**

7. **Save your work, preview and print the worksheet, then exit Excel**

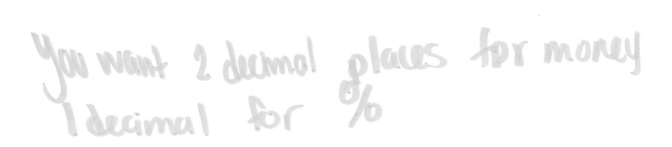
You want 2 decimal places for money
1 decimal for %

ROUND function and opening parenthesis inserted in formula

ScreenTip indicates what information is needed

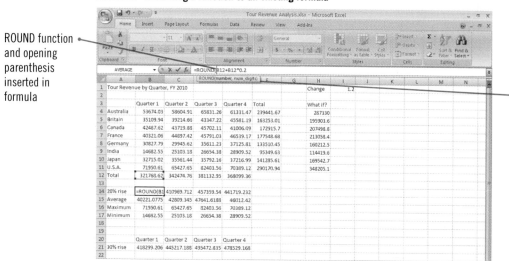

FIGURE B-20: Function added to formula

Function surrounds existing formula

Calculated values with no decimals

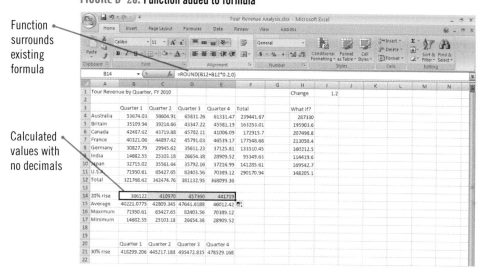

Creating a new workbook using a template

Excel **templates** are predesigned workbook files intended to save time when you create common documents such as balance sheets, expense statements, loan amortizations, sales invoices, or timecards. They contain labels, values, formulas, and formatting, so when you use a template all you have to do is customize it with your own information. Excel comes with many templates, and you can also create your own or find additional templates on the Web. Unlike a typical workbook, which has the file extension .xlsx, a template has the extension .xltx. To create a workbook using a template, click the Office button, then click New. The New Workbook dialog box opens. The Blank Workbook template is selected by default, because this is the template used to create a blank workbook with no content or special formatting. The left pane lists templates installed on your computer as well as many categories of templates available through Microsoft Office Online. Click a category, find the template you want, as shown in Figure B-21, click Download, then click Continue. A new workbook is created based on the template, so when you save the new file in the default format, it will have the regular .xlsx extension. To save a workbook of your own as a template, open the Save As dialog box, then click the Save as type list arrow and change the file type to Excel Template.

FIGURE B-21: New Workbook dialog box

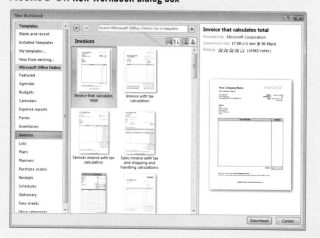

Practice

▼ CONCEPTS REVIEW

Label each element of the Excel worksheet window shown in Figure B-22.

FIGURE B-22

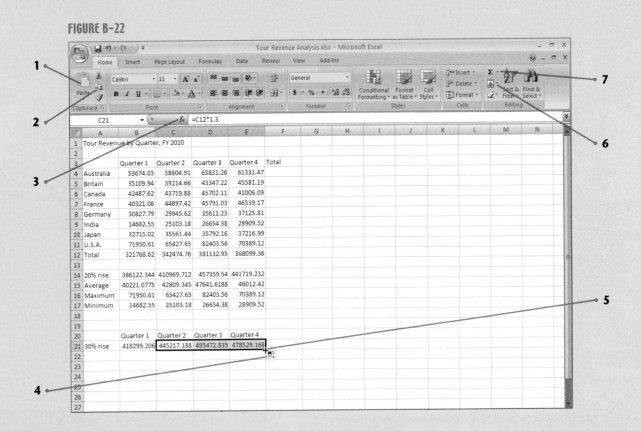

Match each term or button with the statement that best describes it.

8. **Launcher**
9. **Formula AutoComplete**
10. **Drag-and-drop**
11. **Fill handle**
12. **[Delete]**

a. Clears the contents of selected cells

b. Item on the Ribbon that opens a dialog box or task pane

c. Lets you move data from one cell to another without using the Clipboard

d. Displays an alphabetical list of functions from which you can choose

e. Lets you copy cell contents or continue a series of data into a range of selected cells

Select the best answer from the list of choices.

13. **What type of cell reference changes when it is copied?**
    a. Circular
    b. Absolute
    c. Relative
    d. Specified

14. **What type of cell reference is C$19?**
    a. Relative
    b. Absolute
    c. Mixed
    d. Certain

15. **Which key do you press to convert a relative cell reference to an absolute cell reference?**
    a. [F2]
    b. [F4]
    c. [F5]
    d. [F6]

16. **You can use any of the following features to enter a function *except*:**
    a. Insert Function button.
    b. Formula AutoComplete.
    c. AutoSum button list arrow.
    d. Clipboard.

17. **Which key do you press to copy while dragging-and-dropping selected cells?**
    a. [Alt]
    b. [Ctrl]
    c. [F2]
    d. [Tab]

▼ SKILLS REVIEW

1. **Create a complex formula.**

   a. Open the file EX B-2.xlsx from the drive and folder where you store your Data Files, then save it as **Candy Supply Company Inventory**.

   b. In cell B11, create a complex formula that calculates a 30% decrease in the total number of cases of Snickers bars.

   c. Use the Fill button to copy this formula into cell C11 through cell E11, as shown in Figure B-23.

   d. Save your work.

FIGURE B-23

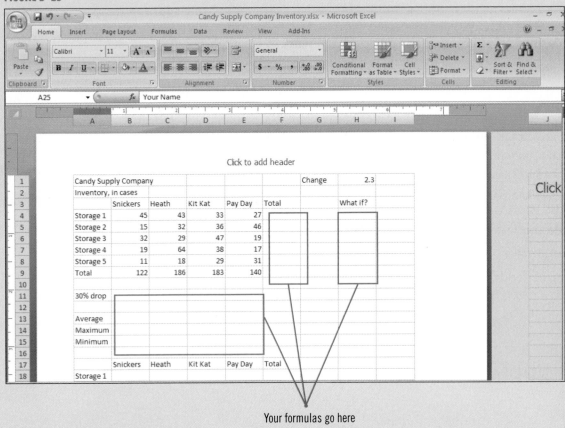

Your formulas go here

2. **Insert a function.**

   a. Use the AutoSum button to create a formula in cell B13 that averages the number of cases of Snickers bars in each storage area. (*Hint*: Click the AutoSum button list arrow to open a list of available functions.)

   b. Use the Insert Function button to create a formula in cell B14 that calculates the most cases of Snickers bars in a storage area.

   c. Use the AutoSum button to create a formula in cell B15 that calculates the minimum number of cases of Snickers bars in a storage area.

   d. Save your work.

3. **Type a function.**

   a. In cell C13, type a formula that includes a function to average the number of cases of Heath bars. (*Hint*: Use AutoComplete to enter the function.)

   b. In cell C14, type a formula that includes a function to calculate the maximum number of cases of Heath bars in a storage area.

   c. In cell C15, type a formula that includes a function to calculate the minimum number of cases of Heath bars in a storage area.

   d. Save your work.

4. Copy and move cell entries.

   a. Select the range B3:F3.

   b. Copy the selection into the Clipboard.

   c. Open the Clipboard task pane, then paste the selection into cell B17.

   d. Select the range A4:A9.

   e. Use the drag-and-drop method to copy the selection to cell A18. (*Hint*: The results should fill the range A18:A23.)

   f. Select the range H1:I1.

   g. Move the selection using the drag-and-drop method to cell G1.

   h. Save your work.

5. Understand relative and absolute cell referencess.

   a. Write a brief description of the difference between relative and absolute references.

   b. List at least three situations in which you think a business might use an absolute reference in its calculations. Examples can include calculations for different types of worksheets, such as timecards, invoices, and budgets.

6. Copy formulas with relative cell references.

   a. Select the range C13:C15.

   b. Use the fill handle to copy these cells to the range D13:E15.

   c. Calculate the total in cell F4.

   d. Use the Fill button to copy the formula in cell F4 down to cells F5:F9.

   e. Use the fill handle to copy the formula in cell E11 to cell F11.

   f. Save your work.

7. Copy formulas with absolute cell references.

   a. In cell H1, enter the value **1.575**.

   b. In cell H4, create a formula that multiplies F4 and an absolute reference to cell H1.

   c. Use the fill handle to copy the formula in cell H4 to cells H5 and H6.

   d. Use the Copy and Paste buttons to copy the formula in cell H4 to cells H7 and H8.

   e. Change the amount in cell H1 to **2.3**.

   f. Save your work.

8. Round a value with a function.

   a. Click cell H4.

   b. Edit this formula to include the ROUND function showing one digit.

   c. Use the fill handle to copy the formula in cell H4 to the range H5:H8.

   d. Enter your name in cell A25, then compare your work to Figure B-23.

   e. Save, preview, print, and close the workbook, then exit Excel.

▼ INDEPENDENT CHALLENGE 1

You are thinking of starting a small breakfast and lunch diner. Before you begin, you need to evaluate what you think your monthly expenses will be. You've started a workbook, but need to complete the entries and add formulas.

   a. Open the file EX B-3.xlsx from the drive and folder where you store your Data Files, then save it as **Estimated Diner Expenses**.

   b. Make up your own expense data and enter it in cells B4:B10. (Monthly sales are included in the worksheet.)

   c. Create a formula in cell C4 that calculates the annual rent.

   d. Copy the formula in cell C4 to the range C5:C10.

   e. Move the label in cell A15 to cell A14.

   f. Create a formula in cells B11 and C11 that totals the expenses.

   g. Create a formula in cell C13 that calculates annual sales.

   h. Create a formula in cell B14 that determines whether you will make a profit or loss, then copy the formula into cell C14.

   i. Copy the labels in cells B3:C3 to cells E3:F3.

   j. Type **Projection increase** in cell G1, then type **.2** in cell I1.

   k. Create a formula in cell E4 that calculates an increase in the monthly rent by the amount in cell I1. You will be copying this formula to other cells, so you'll need to use an absolute reference.

   l. Create a formula in cell F4 that calculates an annual increase based on the calculation in cell E4.

   m. Create formulas in cells E13 and E14 and cells F13 and F14 that calculates monthly and annual sales and profit/loss based on the increase in cell E4.

   n. Copy the formulas in cells E4:F4 in the remaining monthly and annual expenses.

   o. Change the projection increase to **.15**, then compare your work to the sample in Figure B-24.

   p. Enter your name in a cell in the worksheet.

   q. Save your work, preview and print the worksheets, then close the workbook and exit Excel.

FIGURE B-24

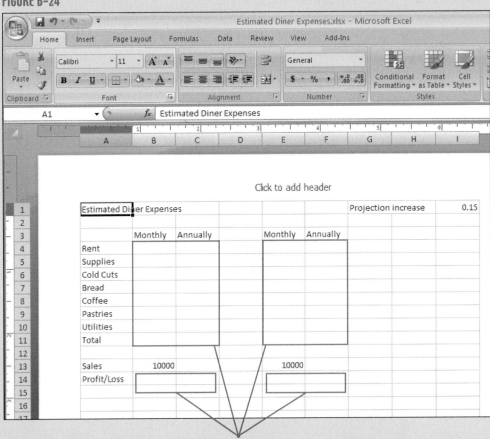

Working with Formulas and Functions

▼ INDEPENDENT CHALLENGE 2

The Pamper Yourself Salon & Day Spa is a small, growing spa that has hired you to organize its accounting records using Excel. The owners want you to track the company's expenses. Before you were hired, one of the bookkeepers began entering last year's expenses in a workbook, but the analysis was never completed.

   a. Start Excel, open the file EX B-4.xlsx from the drive and folder where you store your Data Files, then save it as **Pamper Yourself Finances**. The worksheet includes labels for functions such as the Average, Maximum, and Minimum amounts of each of the expenses in the worksheet.

   b. Think about what information would be important for the bookkeeping staff to know.

   c. Create formulas in the Total column and row using the Sum function.

   d. Create formulas in the Average, Maximum, and Minimum columns and rows using the method of your choice.

   e. Save your work, then compare your worksheet to the sample shown in Figure B-25.

Advanced Challenge Exercise

- Create the label **Expense categories** in cell B19.
- In cell A19, create a formula using the COUNT function that determines the total number of expense categories listed per quarter.
- Save the workbook.

   f. Enter your name in cell A25.

   g. Preview the worksheet, then print it.

   h. Save your work, then close the workbook and exit Excel.

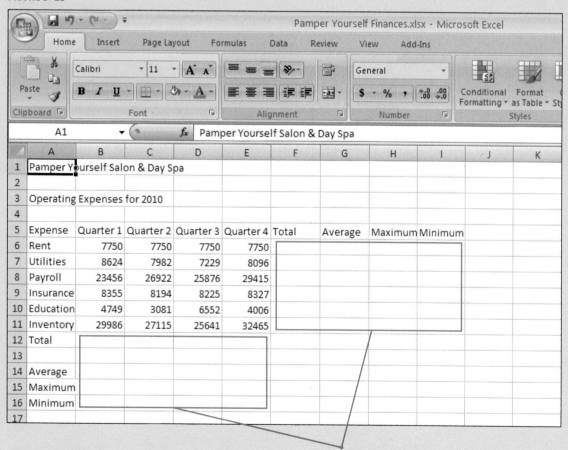

FIGURE B-25

Your formulas go here

Excel 2007

▼ INDEPENDENT CHALLENGE 3

As the accounting manager of a locally-owned clothing store, it is your responsibility to calculate and submit accrued sales tax payments on a monthly basis to the state government. You've decided to use an Excel workbook to make these calculations.

a. Start Excel, then save a new, blank workbook to the drive and folder where you store your Data Files as **Sales Tax Calculations**.

b. Decide on the layout for all columns and rows. The worksheet will contain data for four stores, which you can name by store number, neighborhood, or another method of your choice. For each store, you will calculate total sales tax based on the local sales tax rate. You'll also calculate total tax owed for all four stores.

c. Make up sales data for at least four stores.

d. Enter the rate to be used to calculate the sales tax, using your own local rate.

e. Create formulas to calculate the sales tax owed for each store. If you don't know the local tax rate, use **6.5%**.

f. Create a formula to total all the owed sales tax, then compare your work to the sample shown in Figure B-26.

Advanced Challenge Exercise

■ Use the ROUND function to eliminate any decimals in the sales tax figures for each store and the total due.

■ Save the workbook.

g. Add your name to the header.

h. Save your work, preview and print each worksheet, then close the workbook and exit Excel.

FIGURE B-26

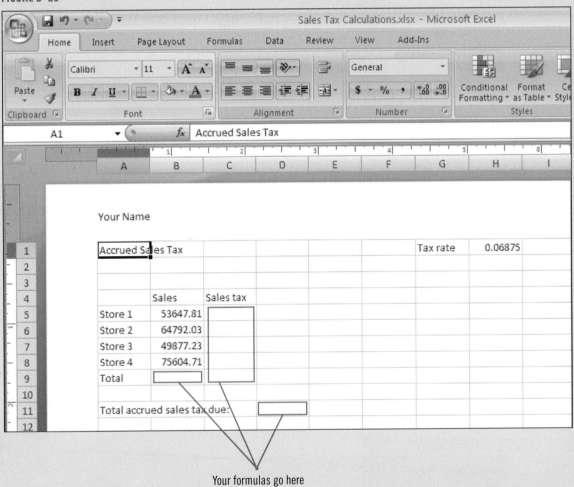

▼ REAL LIFE INDEPENDENT CHALLENGE

Many of your friends are purchasing homes, and you are thinking about taking the plunge yourself. As you begin the round of open houses and realtors' listings, you notice that there are many fees associated with buying a home. Some fees are based on a percentage of the purchase price and others are a flat fee; overall, they seem to represent a substantial amount above the purchase prices you see listed. You've seen three houses so far that interest you; one is moderately priced, one is more expensive, and the third is still more expensive. You decide to create an Excel workbook to figure out the real cost of buying each one.

a. Find out the typical cost or percentage rate of at least three fees that are usually charged when buying a home and taking out a mortgage. (*Hint*: If you have access to the Internet you can research the topic of home-buying on the Web, or you can ask friends about standard rates or percentages for items such as title insurance, credit reports, and inspection fees.)

b. Start Excel, then save a new, blank workbook to the drive and folder where you store your Data Files as **Home Purchase Fees**.

c. Create labels and enter data for three homes. If you enter this information across the columns in your worksheet, you should have one column for each house, with the purchase price in the cell below each label. Be sure to enter a different purchase price for each house.

d. Create labels for the Fees column and for an Amount or Rate column. Enter the information on the three fees you have researched.

FIGURE B-27

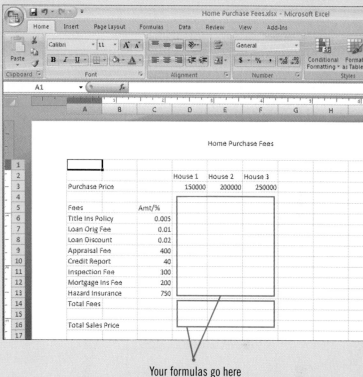

Your formulas go here

e. In each house column, enter formulas that calculate the fee for each item. The formulas (and use of absolute or relative referencing) will vary depending on whether the charges are a flat fee or based on a percentage of the purchase price.

f. Total the fees for each house, create formulas that add the total fees to the purchase price, then compare your work to the sample in Figure B-27.

g. Enter a title for the worksheet in the header.

h. Enter your name in the header, preview the worksheet, then print it.

i. Save your work, then close the file and exit Excel.

▼ VISUAL WORKSHOP

Create the worksheet shown in Figure B-28 using the skills you learned in this unit. Save the workbook as **Sales Analysis** to the drive and folder where you store your Data Files. Enter your name in the header as shown, then preview and print one copy of the worksheet. Print a second copy of the worksheet with the formulas showing.

FIGURE B-28

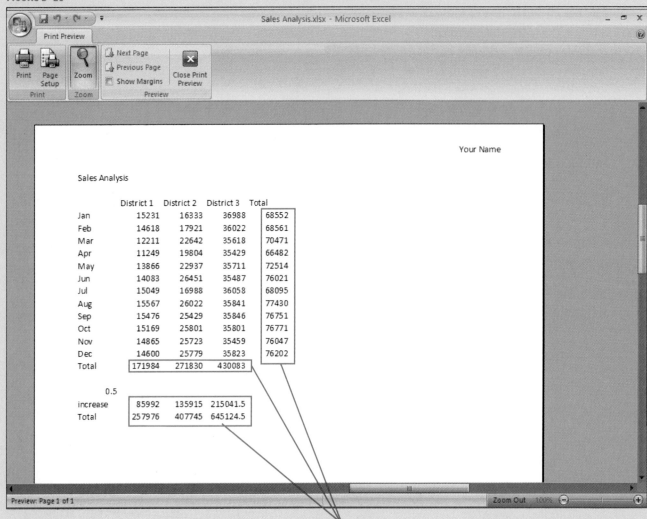

Enter formulas and not
values in these cells

Formatting a Worksheet

Files You Will Need:

EX C-1.xlsx
EX C-2.xlsx
EX C-3.xlsx
EX C-4.xlsx
EX C-5.xlsx

You can use formatting features to make a worksheet more attractive or easier to read, and to emphasize key data. You can apply different formatting attributes such as colors, font styles, and font sizes to the cell contents, you can adjust column width and row height, and you can insert or delete columns and rows. You can also apply conditional formatting so that cells meeting certain criteria are formatted differently. This makes it easy to emphasize selected information, such as sales that exceed or fall below a certain threshold. The marketing managers at QST have requested information on advertising expenses for all QST locations during the past four quarters. Grace Wong has created a worksheet listing this information. She asks you to format the worksheet to make it easier to read and to call attention to important data.

OBJECTIVES

Format values

Change font and font size

Change attributes and alignment

Adjust column width

Insert and delete rows and columns

Apply colors, patterns, and borders

Apply conditional formatting

Name and move a sheet

Check spelling

Formatting Values

The **format** of a cell determines how the labels and values look—for example, whether the contents appear boldfaced, italicized, or with dollar signs and commas. Formatting changes only the appearance of a value or label; it does not alter the actual data in any way. To format a cell or range, first you select it, then you apply the formatting using the Ribbon or a keyboard shortcut. You can apply formatting before or after you enter data in a cell or range. ▰▰▰▰ Grace has provided you with a worksheet that lists individual advertising expenses, and you're ready to improve its appearance and readability. You decide to start by formatting some of the values so they display as currency, percentages, and dates.

STEPS

1. **Start Excel, open the file EX C-1.xlsx from the drive and folder where you store your Data Files, save it as** QST Advertising Expenses, **click the** View tab **on the Ribbon, then click the** Page Layout button

   This worksheet is difficult to interpret because all the information looks the same. In some columns, the contents appear cut off because there is too much data to fit given the current column width. You decide not to widen the columns yet, because the other changes you plan to make might affect column width and row height. The first thing you want to do is format the data showing the cost of each ad.

   QUICK TIP

   You can apply a different currency format, such as Euros or British Pounds, by clicking the Accounting Number Format Button arrow, then clicking a different currency type.

2. **Select the range E4:E32, then click the** Accounting Number Format button **\$** **in the Number group on the Home tab**

   The default Accounting Number format adds dollar signs and two decimal places to the data, as shown in Figure C-1. Formatting this data in accounting format makes it easier to recognize. Excel automatically resizes the column to display the new formatting. The Accounting and Currency formats are both used for monetary values, but the Accounting format aligns currency symbols and decimal points of numbers in a column.

   QUICK TIP

   Select any range of contiguous cells by clicking the top-left cell, pressing and holding [Shift], then clicking the bottom-right cell. Add a row to the selected range by continuing to hold down [Shift] and pressing [↓]; add a column by pressing [→].

3. **Select the range G4:I32, then click the** Comma Style button **▸** **in the Number group**

   The values in columns G, H, and I display the Comma Style format, which does not include a dollar sign but can be useful for some types of accounting data.

4. **Select the range J4:J32, click the** Number Format list arrow, **click** Percentage, **then click the** Increase Decimal button **▦** **in the Number group**

   The data in the % of Total column is now formatted with a percent sign (%) and three decimal places. The Format list arrow lets you choose from popular number formats and shows an example of what the selected cell or cells would look like in each format (when multiple cells are selected, the example is based on the first cell in the range). Each time you click the Increase Decimal button, you add one decimal place; clicking the button twice would add two decimal places.

5. **Click the** Decrease Decimal button **▦** **in the Number group twice**

   Two decimal places are removed.

6. **Select the range B4:B31, click the** launcher **▣** **in the Number group**

   The Format Cells dialog box opens with the Date category already selected on the Number tab.

7. **Select the first 14-Mar-01 format in the Type list box as shown in Figure C-2, then click** OK

   The dates in column B appear in the 14-Mar-01 format. The second 14-Mar-01 format in the list displays all days in two digits (it adds a leading zero if the day is only a single-digit number), while the one you chose displays single-digit days without a leading zero. You can also open the Format Cells dialog box by right-clicking a selected range.

   QUICK TIP

   Make sure you examine formatted data to confirm that you have applied the appropriate formatting; for example, dates should not have a currency format, and monetary values should not have a date format.

8. **Select the range C4:C31, right-click the range, click** Format Cells **on the shortcut menu, click** 14-Mar **in the Type list box in the Format Cells dialog box, then click** OK

   Compare your worksheet to Figure C-3.

9. **Press [Ctrl][Home], then save your work**

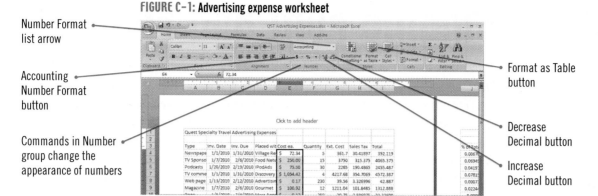

FIGURE C-1: Advertising expense worksheet

Number Format
list arrow

Accounting
Number Format
button

Commands in Number
group change the
appearance of numbers

Format as Table
button

Decrease
Decimal button

Increase
Decimal button

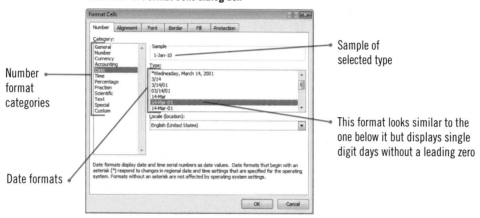

FIGURE C-2: Format Cells dialog box

Number
format
categories

Date formats

Sample of
selected type

This format looks similar to the
one below it but displays single
digit days without a leading zero

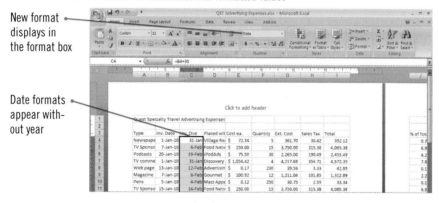

FIGURE C-3: Worksheet with formatted values

New format
displays in
the format box

Date formats
appear with-
out year

Formatting as a table

Excel includes 60 predefined table styles to make it easy to format selected worksheet cells
as a table. You can apply table styles to any range of cells that you want to format quickly,
or even to an entire worksheet, but they're especially useful for those ranges with labels in
the left column and top rows, and totals in the bottom row or right column. To apply a
table style, select the data to be formatted or click anywhere within the intended range
(Excel can automatically detect a range of cells), click the Format as Table button in the
Styles group on the Home tab, then click a style in the gallery, as shown in Figure C-4.
Table styles are organized in three categories (Light, Medium, and Dark). Once you click a
style, Excel confirms the range selection, then applies the style. Once you have formatted
a range as a table, you can use Live Preview to preview with different choices by pointing
to any style in the Table Styles gallery.

FIGURE C-4: Table Styles gallery

Changing Font and Font Size

A **font** is the name for a collection of characters (letters, numerals, symbols, and punctuation marks) with a similar, specific design. The **font size** is the physical size of the text, measured in units called points. A **point** is equal to 1/72 of an inch. The default font in Excel is 11-point Calibri. Table C-1 shows several fonts in different sizes. You can change the font and font size of any cell or range using the Ribbon, the Format Cells dialog box, or the Mini toolbar. You can open the Format Cells dialog box by clicking the launcher in the Font, Alignment, or Number group on the Home tab, or by right-clicking a selection, then clicking Format Cells in the shortcut menu. The Mini toolbar opens when you right-click a cell or range. ▰▰▰▰ You want to change the font and size of the labels and the worksheet title so that they stand out more from the data.

STEPS

QUICK TIP

To preview font and font size changes directly in selected cells, use the Font group on the Home tab; Live Preview shows font, font size, font color, and fill color when you hover the mouse pointer over selections in these lists and palettes.

1. **Right-click cell A1, click Format Cells on the shortcut menu, then click the Font tab in the Format Cells dialog box if necessary**
   See Figure C-5.

2. **Scroll down in the Font list to see an alphabetical listing of the fonts available on your computer, click Times New Roman in the Font list box, click 20 in the Size list box, preview the results in the Preview area, then click OK**
   The title appears in 20-point Times New Roman, and the Font group on the Home tab displays the new font and size information.

3. **Click the Increase Font Size button 𝐀˄ in the Font group twice**
   The size of the title increases to 24-point.

QUICK TIP

You can also format an entire row by clicking the row indicator button (or an entire column by clicking the column indicator button).

4. **Select the range A3:J3, right-click, then click the Font list arrow on the Mini toolbar**
   The Mini toolbar includes the most commonly used formatting tools, so it's great for making quick formatting changes. Notice that the font names on this font list are displayed in the font they represent.

QUICK TIP

Once you click the Font list arrow, you can quickly move to a font in the list by typing the first few characters of its name.

5. **Click Times New Roman, click the Font Size list arrow, then click 14**
   The Mini toolbar closes when you move the pointer away from the selection. Compare your worksheet to Figure C-6. Notice that some of the column headings are now too wide to appear fully in the column. Excel does not automatically adjust column widths to accommodate cell formatting; you have to adjust column widths manually. You'll learn to do this in a later lesson.

6. **Save your work**

TABLE C-1: Examples of fonts and font sizes

font	12 point	24 point
Calibri	Excel	Excel
Playbill	Excel	Excel
Comic Sans MS	Excel	Excel
Times New Roman	Excel	Excel

FIGURE C-5: Font tab in the Format Cells dialog box

Currently selected font

Available fonts might differ on your computer

Effects options

Type a custom font size or select from the list

Font style options

Preview area shows sample of selected formatting

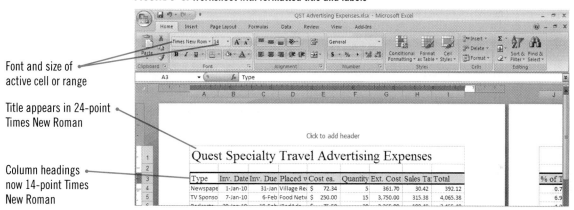

FIGURE C-6: Worksheet with formatted title and labels

Font and size of active cell or range

Title appears in 24-point Times New Roman

Column headings now 14-point Times New Roman

Inserting and adjusting clip art and other images

You can illustrate your worksheets using clip art and other images. A **clip** is an individual media file, such as art, sound, animation, or a movie. **Clip art** refers to images such as a corporate logo, a picture, or a photo. Microsoft Office comes with many clips available for your use. To add a clip to a worksheet, click Clip Art in the Illustrations group on the Insert tab. The Clip Art task pane opens. Here you can search for clips by typing one or more keywords (words related to your subject) in the Search for text box, then click Go. Clips that relate to your keywords appear in the Clip Art task pane, as shown in Figure C-7. (If you have a standard Office installation and an active Internet connection, you will see many clips available through Microsoft Office Online in addition to those on your computer.) Click the image you want, and it is inserted at the location of the active cell. You can also add your own images to a worksheet by clicking the Insert tab on the Ribbon, then clicking the Picture button. Navigate to the file you want, then click Insert Picture from File. To resize an image, drag any corner sizing handle. To move an image, point inside the clip until the pointer changes to ⟨symbol⟩, then drag it to a new location.

FIGURE C-7: Results of Clip Art search

Type keyword(s) here

Click to begin search

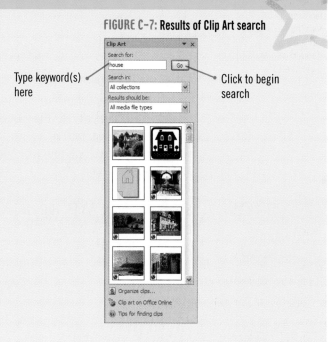

Changing Attributes and Alignment

Attributes are styling formats such as bold, italic, and underlining that you can apply to affect the way text and numbers look in a worksheet. You can "paint" or copy a cell's format into other cells by using the Format Painter button in the Clipboard group on the Home tab of the Ribbon. This is similar to using copy and paste, but instead of copying cell contents, it copies only the cell's formatting. You can also change the **alignment** of labels and values in cells to be left, right, or center. You can apply attributes and alignment options using the Home tab, the Format Cells dialog box, or the Mini toolbar. See Table C-2 for a description of common attribute and alignment buttons that are available on the Home tab of the Ribbon and the Mini toolbar. 🎨💾 You want to further enhance the worksheet's appearance by adding bold and underline formatting and centering some of the labels.

STEPS

1. **Press [Ctrl][Home], then click the Bold button** 🅱 **in the Font group**
   The title in cell A1 appears in bold.

2. **Click cell A3, then click the Underline button** 🆄 **in the Font group**
   The column heading is now underlined, though this may be difficult to see with the cell selected.

3. **Click the Italic button** 𝐼 **in the Font group, then click** 🅱
   The heading now appears in boldface, underlined, italic type. Notice that the Bold, Italic, and Underline buttons in the Font group are all selected.

4. **Click** 𝐼
   The italic attribute is removed from cell A3, but the bold and underline attributes remain.

5. **Click the Format Painter button** 🖌 **in the Clipboard group, then select the range B3:J3**
   The formatting in cell A3 is copied to the rest of the labels in the column headings. You can turn off the Format Painter by pressing [Esc] or by clicking 🖌. You decide the title would look better if it were centered over the data columns.

6. **Select the range A1:J1, then click the Merge & Center button** 🔳 **in the Alignment group**
   The Merge & Center button creates one cell out of the 10 cells across the row, then centers the text in that newly created large cell. The title "Quest Specialty Travel Advertising Expenses" is centered across the 10 columns you selected. You can change the alignment within individual cells using buttons on the Home tab; you can split merged cells into their original components by selecting the merged cells, then clicking the Merge & Center button.

7. **Select the range A3:J3, right-click, then click the Center button** 🈸 **on the Mini toolbar**
   Compare your screen to Figure C-8. Although they may be difficult to read, notice that all the headings are centered within their cells.

8. **Save your work**

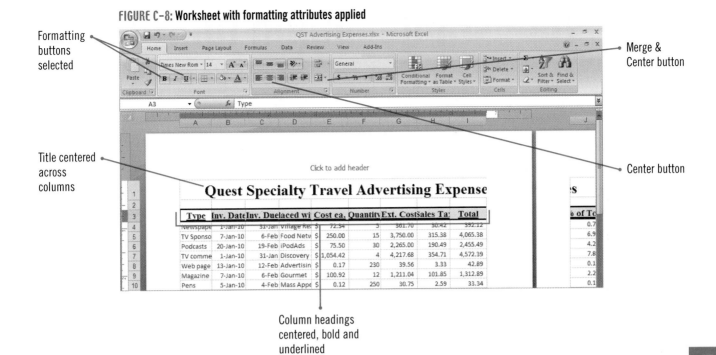

FIGURE C-8: Worksheet with formatting attributes applied

Formatting buttons selected

Merge & Center button

Title centered across columns

Center button

Column headings centered, bold and underlined

Rotating and indenting cell entries

In addition to applying fonts and formatting attributes, you can rotate or indent data within a cell to further change its appearance. You can rotate text within a cell by altering its alignment. To change alignment, select the cells you want to modify, then click the launcher in the Alignment group to open the Alignment tab of the Format Cells dialog box. Click a position in the Orientation box or type a number in the Degrees text box to change from the default horizontal alignment, then click OK. You can indent cell contents using the Increase Indent button on the Alignment group on the Home tab on the Ribbon, which moves cell contents to the right one space, or the Decrease Indent button, which moves cell contents to the left one space.

TABLE C-2: Common attribute and alignment buttons

button	description	button	description
B	Bolds text		Aligns text at the left edge of the cell
I	Italicizes text		Centers text horizontally within the cell
U	Underlines text		Aligns text at the right edge of the cell
	Adds lines or borders		Centers text across columns, and combines two or more selected, adjacent cells into one cell

UNIT
C
Excel 2007

Adjusting Column Width

As you format a worksheet, you might need to adjust the width of one or more columns to accommodate text or larger font size or style. The default column width is 8.43 characters wide, a little less than one inch. With Excel, you can adjust the width of one or more columns by using the mouse, the Ribbon, or the shortcut menu. Using the mouse, you can drag or double-click the right edge of a column heading. The Ribbon and shortcut menu include commands for making more detailed width adjustments. Table C-3 describes common column adjustment commands. You notice that some of the labels in column A don't fit in the cells. You want to adjust the widths of the columns so that the labels appear in their entirety.

STEPS

1. **Position the mouse pointer on the line between the column A and column B headings until it changes to ✛**

   See Figure C-9. The **column heading** is the box at the top of each column containing a letter. Before you can adjust column width using the mouse, you need to position the pointer on the right edge of the column you want to adjust. The entries for TV commercials are the widest in the column.

2. **Click and drag the ✛ to the right until the column displays the TV commercials entries fully**

3. **Position the pointer on the column line between columns B and C until it changes to ✛, then double-click**

   Column B automatically widens to fit the widest entry, in this case, the column label. Double-clicking activates the **AutoFit** feature, which automatically resizes a column so it accommodates the widest entry in a cell.

4. **Use AutoFit to resize columns C, D, and J**

5. **Select the range F5:I5**

   You can change the width of multiple columns at once, by first selecting either the column headings or at least one cell in each column.

6. **Click the Format button in the Cells group, then click Column Width**

   The Column Width dialog box opens. Column width measurement is based on the number of characters that will fit in the column when formatted in the Normal font and font size (in this case, 11 pt Calibri).

7. **Drag the dialog box by its title bar if its placement obscures your view of the worksheet, type .91" in the Column width text box, then click OK**

   The widths of columns F, G, H, and I change to reflect the new setting. See Figure C-10.

8. **Save your work**

QUICK TIP

To reset columns to the default width, click the column headings to select the columns, click the Format button in the Cells group, click Default Width, then click OK in the Standard Width dialog box.

QUICK TIP

If a column heading is selected, you can change the width of the column by right-clicking, then clicking Column Width in the shortcut menu.

QUICK TIP

If "#######" appears after you adjust a column of values, the column is too narrow to display the contents; increase the column width until the values appear.

Changing row height

Changing row height is as easy as changing column width. Row height is calculated in points, the same units of measure used for fonts. The row height must exceed the size of the font you are using. Normally, you don't need to adjust row heights manually, because row height adjusts automatically to accommodate other formatting changes. If you format something in a row to be a larger point size, Excel adjusts the row to fit the largest point size in the row. However, you have just as many options for changing row height as you do column width. Using the mouse, you can place the ✛ pointer on the line dividing the row heading from the heading below, and dragging to the desired height; double-clicking the line autofits the row height where necessary. You can also select one or more rows, then use the Row Height command on the shortcut menu, or the Row Height or AutoFit Row Height command on the Format button in the Cells group on the Home tab.

FIGURE C-9: Preparing to change the column width

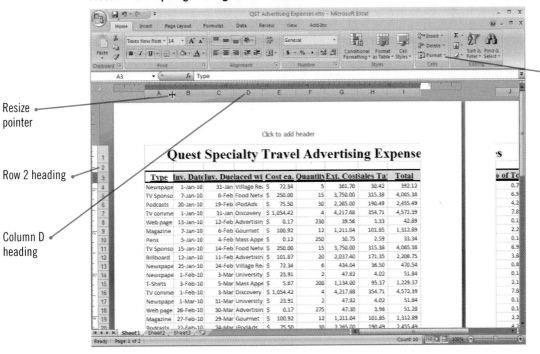

Resize pointer

Row 2 heading

Column D heading

Click to change column or row formatting

FIGURE C-10: Worksheet with column widths adjusted

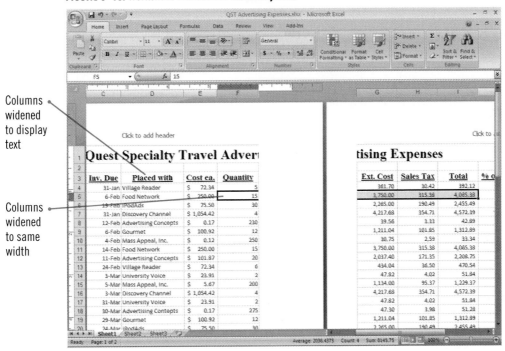

Columns widened to display text

Columns widened to same width

TABLE C-3: Common column formatting commands

command	description	available using
Column Width	Sets the width to a specific number of characters	Format button, shortcut menu
AutoFit Column Width	Fits to the widest entry in a column	Format button, mouse
Hide & Unhide	Hides or displays hidden column(s)	Format button, shortcut menu
Default Width	Changes the default column width for current worksheet	Format button

Inserting and Deleting Rows and Columns

As you modify a worksheet, you might find it necessary to insert or delete rows and columns to keep your worksheet current. For example, you might need to insert rows to accommodate new inventory products or remove a column of yearly totals that are no longer necessary. When you insert a new row, the contents of the worksheet shift down from the newly inserted row. When you insert a new column, the contents of the worksheet shift to the right from the point of the new column. Excel inserts rows above the cell pointer and inserts columns to the left of the cell pointer. To insert multiple rows, drag across row headings to select the same number of rows as you want to insert. **▓▓▓▓▓** You want to improve the overall appearance of the worksheet by inserting a row between the last row of data and the totals. Also, you have learned that row 27 and column J need to be deleted from the worksheet.

STEPS

1. **Right-click cell A32, then click Insert on the shortcut menu**

   The Insert dialog box opens. See Figure C-11. You can choose to insert a column or a row, or you can shift the data in the cells in the active column right or in the active row down. An additional row between the last row of data and the totals will visually separate the totals.

2. **Click the Entire row option button, then click OK**

   A blank row appears between the Billboard data and the totals, and the formula result in cell E33 has not changed. The Insert Options button ☑ appears beside cell A33. Pointing to the button displays a list arrow, which you can click and then choose from the following options: Format Same As Above, Format Same As Below, or Clear Formatting. You want the default formatting, Same as Above.

3. **Click the row 27 heading**

   All of row 27 is selected, as shown in Figure C-12.

4. **Click the Delete button in the Cells group; *do not click the button arrow***

   Excel deletes row 27, and all rows below this shift up one row. You must use the Delete button or the Delete command on the shortcut menu to delete a row or column; pressing [Delete] on the keyboard removes only the *contents* of a selected row or column.

5. **Click the column J heading**

   The percentage information is calculated elsewhere and is no longer necessary in this worksheet.

6. **Click the Delete button in the Cells group**

   Excel deletes column J. The remaining columns to the right shift left one column.

7. **Save your work**

QUICK TIP

To insert a single row or column, you can also right-click the row heading immediately below where you want the new row or the column heading to the right of where you want the new column, then click Insert in the shortcut menu.

QUICK TIP

If you inadvertently click the Delete list arrow instead of the button itself, click Delete Sheet Rows in the menu that opens.

QUICK TIP

After inserting or deleting rows or columns in a worksheet, be sure to proof formulas that contain relative cell references.

Hiding and unhiding columns and rows

When you don't want data in a column or row to be visible, but you don't want to delete it, you can hide the column or row. To hide a selected column, click the Format button in the Cells group, point to Hide & Unhide, then click Hide Columns. A hidden column is indicated by a dark black vertical line in its original position. This black line disappears when you click elsewhere in the worksheet. You can display a hidden column by selecting the columns on either side of the hidden column, clicking the Format button in the Cells group, pointing to Hide & Unhide, and then clicking Unhide Columns. (To hide or unhide one or more rows, substitute Hide Rows and Unhide Rows for the Hide Columns and Unhide Columns commands.)

FIGURE C-11: Insert dialog box

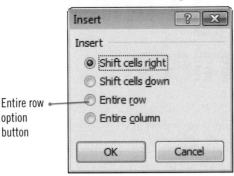

Entire row option button

FIGURE C-12: Worksheet with row 27 selected

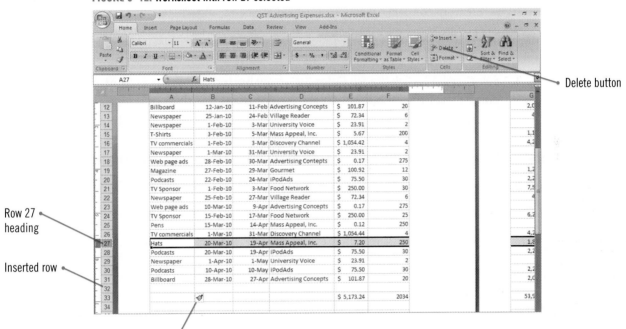

Delete button

Row 27 heading

Inserted row

On your screen, the Insert Options button might appear in a different location

Adding and editing comments

Much of your work in Excel may be in collaboration with teammates with whom you share worksheets. You can share ideas with other worksheet users by adding comments within selected cells. To include a comment in a worksheet, click the cell where you want to place the comment, click the Review tab on the Ribbon, then click the New Comment button in the Comments group. A resizable text box containing the computer user's name opens in which you can type your comments. A small, red triangle appears in the upper-right corner of a cell containing a comment. If comments are not already displayed in a workbook, other users can point to the triangle to display the comment. To see all worksheet comments, as shown in Figure C-13, click the Show All Comments button in the Comments group. To edit a comment, click the cell containing the comment, then click the Edit Comment button in the Comments group. To delete a comment, click the cell containing the comment, then click the Delete button in the Comments group.

FIGURE C-13: Comments in worksheet

18	Web page abs	28-Feb-10	30-Mar	Advertising Contepts	$	0.17
19	Magazine	27-Feb-10	29-Mar	Gourmet	$	100.92
20	Podcasts	22-Feb-10	24-Mar	iPodAds	$	75.50
21	TV Sponsor	1-Feb-10	3-Mar	Food Networ		
22	Newspaper	25-Feb-10	27-Mar	Village Reade		
23	Web page ads	10-Mar-10	9-Apr	Advertising C		
24	TV Sponsor	15-Feb-10	17-Mar	Food Networ		
25	Pens	15-Mar-10	14-Apr	Mass Appeal, Inc.	$	0.12
26	TV commercials	1-Mar-10	31-Mar	Discovery Channel		
27	Podcasts	20-Mar-10	19-Apr	iPodAds		
28	Newspaper	1-Apr-10	1-May	University Vc		
29	Podcasts	10-Apr-10	10-May	iPodAds		
30	Billboard	28-Mar-10	27-Apr	Advertising Concepts	$	101.87
31						
32					$5,166.04	
33						
34						
35						
36						
37						
38						
39						

Grace Wong: Should we continue with this market, or expand to other publications?

Grace Wong: I think this will turn out to be a very good decision.

Applying Colors, Patterns, and Borders

You can use colors, patterns, and borders to enhance the overall appearance of a worksheet and to make it easier to read. You can add these enhancements by using the Border and Fill Color buttons in the Font group on the Home tab of the Ribbon and on the Mini toolbar, or by using the Fill tab and the Border tab in the Format Cells dialog box. You can apply a color to the background of a cell or a range, or to cell contents, and you can apply a pattern to a cell or range. You can apply borders to all the cells in a worksheet or only to selected cells to call attention to selected information. To save time, you can also apply **cell styles**, predesigned combinations of formatting attributes. You want to add a pattern, a border, and color to the title of the worksheet to give the worksheet a more professional appearance.

STEPS

1. **Select cell A1, click the Fill Color list arrow button** 🔽 **in the Font group, then hover the pointer over the Turquoise, Accent 2 color (first row, sixth column from the left)**

   See Figure C-14. Live Preview shows you how the color will look *before* you apply it.

> **QUICK TIP**
>
> When you change fill or font color, the color on the Fill Color and Font Color buttons changes to the last color you selected.

2. **Click the Turquoise, Accent 2 color (first row, sixth column from the left)**

   The color is applied to the background or fill of this cell. (Remember that cell A1 spans columns A through I because the Merge and Center command was applied.)

3. **Right-click cell A1, then click Format Cells on the shortcut menu**

   The Format Cells dialog box opens. Adding a pattern to cells can add to the visual interest of your worksheet. To format an entire row or column at once, click the row heading or column heading button.

> **QUICK TIP**
>
> Use fill colors and patterns sparingly. Too many colors can be distracting or make it hard to see which information is important.

4. **Click the Fill tab, click the Pattern Style list arrow, click the 6.25% Gray style (first row, sixth column from the left), then click OK**

5. **Click the Borders list arrow** 🔳 **in the Font group, then click Thick Bottom Border**

   Unlike underlining, which is a text-formatting tool, borders extend to the width of the cell, and can appear at the bottom of the cell, at the top, or on either side. It can be difficult to see a border when the cell is selected.

> **QUICK TIP**
>
> You can also create custom cell borders. Click the Borders list arrow in the Font group, click More Borders, then click the individual border buttons to create borders or boxes.

6. **Select the range A3:I3, click the Font Color list arrow** 🔽 **in the Font group, then click the Blue, Accent 1 color (first Theme color row, fifth column from the left) on the palette**

   The new color is applied to the selected range.

7. **Select the range J1:K1, click the Cell Styles button in the Styles group, then click the Neutral button (first row, fourth column from the left) on the palette**

   The font and color change in the range, as shown in Figure C-15.

8. **Save your work**

Formatting a Worksheet

FIGURE C-14: Viewing fill color using Live Preview

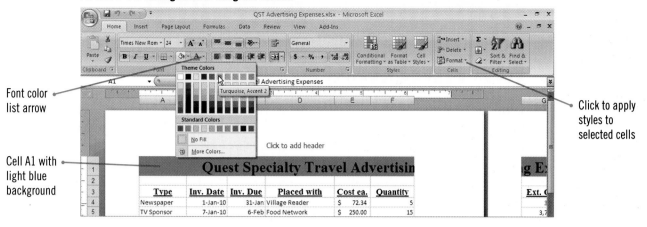

Font color
list arrow

Cell A1 with
light blue
background

Click to apply
styles to
selected cells

FIGURE C-15: Worksheet with color, patterns, border, and style applied

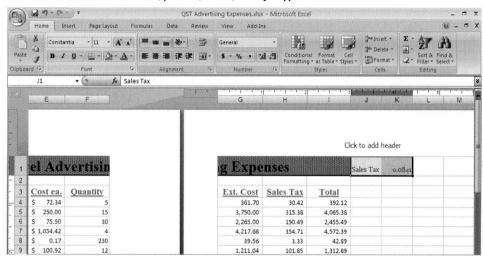

Saving time with themes and cell styles

You can save yourself time by formatting with themes and cell styles. A **theme** is a predefined set of attributes that gives your Excel worksheet a professional look. Formatting choices included in a theme are colors, fonts, and line and fill effects. A theme can be applied using the Themes button in the Themes group on the Page Layout tab on the Ribbon, as shown in Figure C-16. **Cell styles** are sets of attributes based on themes, so they are automatically updated if you change a theme. For example, if you apply the 20% - Accent1 cell style to cell A1 in a worksheet that has no theme applied, the fill color changes to light blue and the font changes to Constantia. If you change the theme of the worksheet to Metro, cell A1's fill color changes to light green and the font changes to Corbel, because these are the attributes that coordinate with the selected theme. Using themes and cell styles makes it easier to ensure that your worksheets are consistent and saves you from a lot of reformatting every time you make a change.

FIGURE C-16: Themes gallery

Applying Conditional Formatting

So far, you've used formatting to change the appearance of different types of data, such as dates, dollar amounts, worksheet titles, and column labels. But you can also use formatting to highlight important aspects of the data itself. For example, you can apply formatting that automatically changes the font color to red for any cells where ad costs exceed $100 and to green where ad costs are below $50. This type of formatting is called **conditional formatting** because Excel automatically applies different formats depending on conditions you specify. If the data meets your conditions, Excel applies the formats you specify. The formatting is updated if you change data in the worksheet. Data bars are a type of conditional formatting that visually illustrate differences among values. Grace is concerned about advertising costs exceeding yearly budget. You decide to use conditional formatting to highlight certain trends and patterns in the data, so it's easy to spot the most expensive expenditures.

STEPS

1. **Select the range I4:I30, click the Conditional Formatting button in the Styles group, point to Data Bars, then point to the Light Blue Data Bar (second row, second from left)**
   Live Preview shows how this formatting will appear in the worksheet, as shown in Figure C-17. Notice that the length of the bar in each cell reflects its value relative to other cells in the selection.

2. **Preview the Green Data Bar (first row, second from left), then click it**

3. **Select the range G4:G30, click the Conditional Formatting button in the Styles group, then point to Highlight Cells Rules**
   The Conditional Formatting menu displays choices for creating different types of formatting rules. For example, you can create a rule for values that are greater than a certain amount, less than a certain amount, or between two amounts.

   QUICK TIP
   You can apply an Icon Set to a selected range by clicking the Conditional Formatting button in the Styles group, then pointing to Icon Sets; icons appear within the cells to illustrate differences in values.

4. **Click Between**
   The Between dialog box opens. Depending on the choice you made in the Highlight Cells Rules menu (such as "Greater Than" or "Less Than"), this dialog box displays different input boxes. You can define multiple different conditions and then assign formatting attributes to each one. You define the condition first. The default setting for the first condition is "Cell Value Is" "between." The value can be a constant, formula, cell reference, or date. The formatting default format is exactly what you want: Light Red Fill with Dark Red Text.

   QUICK TIP
   You can copy conditional formats the same way you copy other formats.

5. **Type 2000 in the first text box, type 4000 in the second text box, compare your settings to Figure C-18, then click OK**
   All cells with values between 2000 and 4000 in column G appear with a light red fill and dark red text.

6. **Click cell G7, type 3975.55, then press [Enter]**
   When the value in cell G7 changes, the formatting also changes, because the new value meets the condition to apply the format. Compare your results to Figure C-19.

7. **Press [Ctrl][Home] to select cell A1, then save your work**

Managing conditional formatting rules

If you create a conditional formatting rule and then want to change the conditions to reflect a different value or format, you don't need to create a new rule; instead, you can modify the rule using the Rule Manager. Select the cell(s) containing conditional formatting, click the Conditional Formatting button in the Styles group, then click

Manage Rules. The Conditional Formatting Rules Manager dialog box opens. Select the rules you want to edit or delete, click Edit Rule, modify the settings in the Edit the Rule Description area, click OK, then click OK again to close the dialog box. The rule is modified, and the new conditions are applied to the selected cells.

FIGURE C-17: Previewing a Data Bar

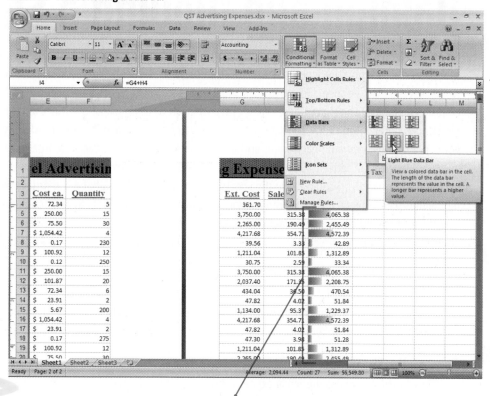

Data bars displayed
in sheet

FIGURE C-18: Setting conditions in Between dialog box

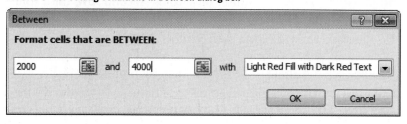

FIGURE C-19: Results of Conditional Formatting

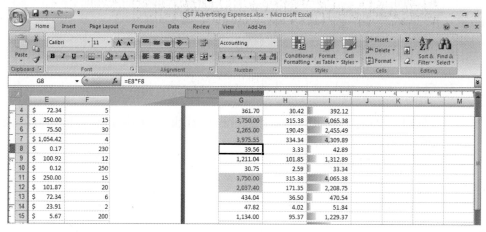

Naming and Moving a Sheet

By default, an Excel workbook initially contains three worksheets, named Sheet1, Sheet2, and Sheet3. The sheet name appears on the sheet tab at the bottom of the worksheet. When you open a workbook, the first worksheet is the active sheet. To move from sheet to sheet, you can click any sheet tab at the bottom of the worksheet window. The sheet tab scrolling buttons, located to the left of the sheet tabs, are useful when a workbook contains too many sheet tabs to display at once. To make it easier to identify the sheets in a workbook, you can rename each sheet and add color to the tabs. You can also organize them in a logical way. For instance, to better track performance goals, you could name each workbook sheet for an individual salesperson, and you could move the sheets so they appeared in alphabetical order. In the current worksheet, Sheet1 contains information on advertising expenses. Sheet2 contains an advertising budget, and Sheet3 contains no data. You want to name the two sheets in the workbook to reflect their contents, add color to a sheet tab to easily distinguish one from the other, and change their order.

STEPS

1. **Click the Sheet2 tab**

   Sheet2 becomes active, appearing in front of the Sheet1 tab; this is the worksheet that contains the budgeted expenses. See Figure C-20.

2. **Click the Sheet1 tab**

   Sheet1, which contains the actual expenses, becomes active again.

3. **Double-click the Sheet2 tab, type Budget, then press [Enter]**

   The new name for Sheet2 automatically replaces the default name on the tab. Worksheet names can have up to 31 characters, including spaces and punctuation.

4. **Right-click the Budget tab, point to Tab Color on the shortcut menu, then click the Bright Green, Accent 4, Lighter 80% color (second row, third column from the right) as shown in Figure C-21**

   The tab color changes to a bright green gradient.

5. **Double-click the Sheet1 tab, type Actual, then press [Enter]**

   Notice that the color of the Budget tab changes depending on whether it is the active tab; when the Actual tab is active, the color of the Budget tab changes to solid bright green. You decide to rearrange the order of the sheets, so that the Budget tab is to the left of the Actual tab.

6. **Click the Budget sheet tab, hold down the mouse button, drag it to the left of the Actual sheet tab, as shown in Figure C-22, then release the mouse button**

   As you drag, the pointer changes to 🡒, the sheet relocation pointer, and a small, black triangle shows its position. The first sheet in the workbook is now the Budget sheet. See Figure C-23. To see hidden sheets, click the far left tab scrolling button to display the first sheet tab; click the far right navigation button to display the last sheet tab. The left and right buttons move one sheet in their respective directions.

7. **Click the Actual sheet tab, then enter your name in the left-side header box**

8. **Click the Page Layout tab on the Ribbon, click the Orientation button in the Page Setup group, then click Landscape**

9. **Press [Ctrl][Home], then save your work**

FIGURE C-20: Sheet tabs in workbook

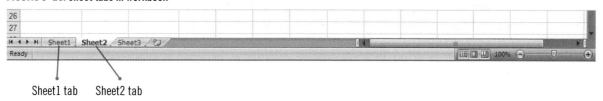

Sheet1 tab   Sheet2 tab

FIGURE C-21: Tab Color palette

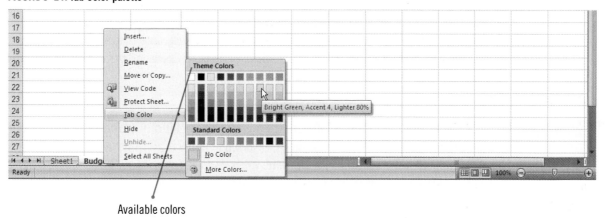

Available colors

FIGURE C-22: Sheet during move

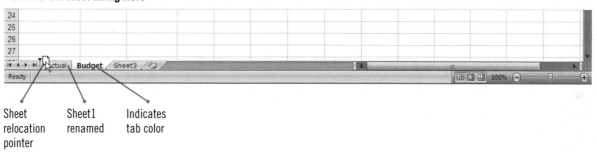

Sheet   Sheet1   Indicates
relocation   renamed   tab color
pointer

FIGURE C-23: Reordered sheets

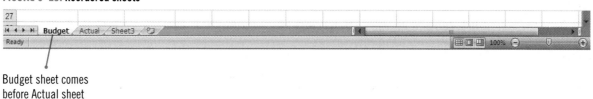

Budget sheet comes
before Actual sheet

Copying worksheets

There are times when you may want to copy a worksheet. For example, a workbook might contain a sheet with Quarter 1 expenses, and you want to use that sheet as the basis for a sheet containing Quarter 2 expenses. To copy a sheet within the same workbook, press and hold [Ctrl], drag the sheet tab to the desired tab location, release the mouse button, then release [Ctrl]. A duplicate sheet appears with the same name as the copied sheet followed by "(2)" indicating it is a copy. You can then rename the sheet to a more meaningful name. To copy a sheet to a different workbook, both the source and destination workbooks must be open. Select the sheet to copy or move, right-click the sheet tab, then click Move or Copy in the shortcut menu. Complete the information in the Move or Copy dialog box. Be sure to click the Create a copy check box if you are copying rather than moving the worksheet. Carefully check your calculation results whenever you move or copy a worksheet.

Checking Spelling

Excel includes a spelling checker to help you ensure that the words in your worksheet are spelled correctly. The spelling checker scans your worksheet, displays words it doesn't find in its built-in dictionary, and suggests replacements when they are available. To check other sheets in a multiple-sheet workbook, you need to display each sheet and run the spelling checker again. Because the built-in dictionary cannot possibly include all the words that anyone needs, you can add words to the dictionary, such as your company name, an acronym, or an unusual technical term. Once you add a word or term, the spelling checker will no longer consider that word misspelled. Any words you've added to the dictionary using Word, Access, or PowerPoint are also available in Excel. Another feature, AutoCorrect, automatically corrects some spelling errors as you type. Before you distribute this workbook to Grace and the marketing managers, you check its spelling.

STEPS

QUICK TIP

The Spelling dialog box lists the name of the language currently being used in its title bar.

1. **Click the Review tab on the Ribbon, then click the Spelling button in the Proofing group**

   The Spelling: English (U.S.) dialog box opens, as shown in Figure C-24, with "iPodAds" selected as the first misspelled word in the worksheet. For any word, you have the option to Ignore this case of the flagged word, Ignore All cases of the flagged word, or Add the word to the dictionary.

2. **Click Ignore All**

   Next, the spelling checker finds the word "Contepts" and suggests "Concepts" as an alternative.

QUICK TIP

To customize AutoCorrect to add or remove automatic corrections, click the Office button, click Excel Options, click Proofing, click AutoCorrect Options, choose options in the AutoCorrect dialog box for how you want this feature to work, then click OK.

3. **Verify that the word Concepts is selected in the Suggestions list, then click Change**

   When no more incorrect words are found, Excel displays a message indicating that all the words on the worksheet have been checked.

4. **Click OK**

5. **Click the Home tab, click Find & Select in the Editing group, then click Replace**

   The Find and Replace dialog box opens. You can use this dialog box to replace a word or phrase. It might be a misspelling that the Spelling Checker didn't recognize as wrong, such as a word that wasn't corrected with the spelling checker, or simply something you want to change. Grace has just told you that each instance of 'Billboard' in the worksheet should be changed to 'Sign'.

6. **Type Billboard in the Find what text box, press [Tab], then type Sign in the Replace with text box**

   Compare your dialog box to Figure C-25.

7. **Click Replace All, click OK to close the warning box, then click Close to close the Find and Replace dialog box**

   Excel has made two replacements.

QUICK TIP

The Fit to option button is on the Page tab of the Page Setup dialog box.

8. **Save your work, view the Actual sheet in Print Preview, click the Page Setup button on the Ribbon, fit the worksheet to one page, then return to Print Preview**

   Compare your worksheet to Figure C-26.

9. **Print one copy of the worksheet, close it, then exit Excel**

E-mailing a workbook

You can send an entire workbook from within Excel using your installed email program, such as Microsoft Office Outlook or Outlook Express. To send a workbook as an e-mail message attachment, open the workbook, click the Office button 🗔, point to

Send, then click E-mail. An email message opens with the workbook automatically attached; the filename appears in the Attached field. Complete the To and optional Cc fields, include a message if you wish, then click Send.

FIGURE C-24: Spelling: English dialog box

Misspelled word

Click to ignore all occurrences of misspelled word

Click to add word to dictionary

Suggested replacements for misspelled word

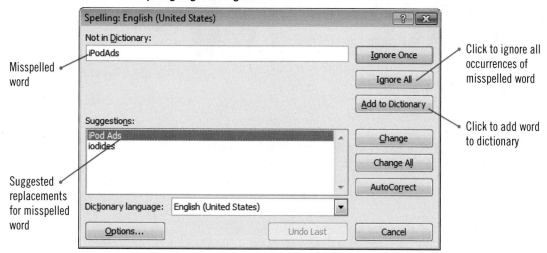

FIGURE C-25: Find and Replace dialog box

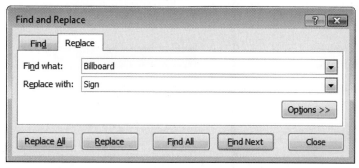

FIGURE C-26: Viewing worksheet in Print Preview

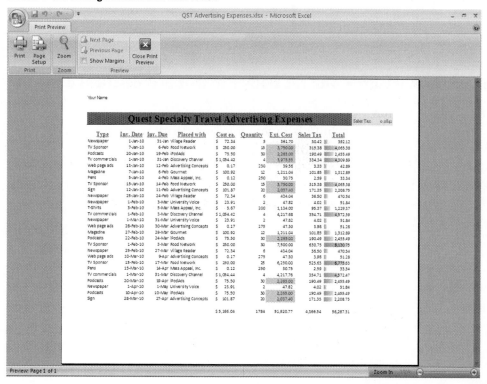

Practice

SAM — If you have a SAM user profile, you may have access to hands-on instruction, practice, and assessment of the skills covered in this unit. Log in to your SAM account (http://sam2007.course.com/) to launch any assigned training activities or exams that relate to the skills covered in this unit.

▼ CONCEPTS REVIEW

Label each element of the Excel worksheet window shown in Figure C-27.

FIGURE C-27

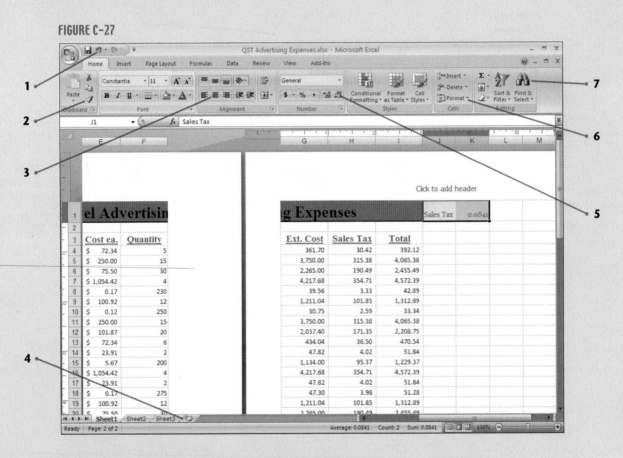

Match each command or button with the statement that best describes it.

8. Spelling & Grammar button
9. ![icon]
10. ![icon]
11. [Ctrl][Home]
12. Conditional Formatting
13. [Delete]

a. Erases the contents of a cell
b. Changes formatting of a cell based on cell contents
c. Moves cell pointer to cell A1
d. Checks for apparent misspellings in a worksheet
e. Displays options for erasing the contents of a cell
f. Centers cell contents over multiple cells

Select the best answer from the list of choices.

14. Which of the following is an example of an accounting number format?

    a. 5555
    c. 55.55%

    b. $5,555.55
    d. 5,555.55

15. What feature is used to delete a conditional formatting rule?

    a. Rule Reminder
    c. Rule Manager

    b. Conditional Rule Manager
    d. Format Manager

16. Which button removes boldface formatting from selected cells?

    a. ☐
    c. ☐

    b. ☐
    d. ☐

17. Which button opens the Format Cells dialog box?

    a. ☐
    c. ☐

    b. ☐
    d. ☐

18. What is the name of the feature used to resize a column to accommodate its widest entry?

    a. AutoFormat
    c. AutoResize

    b. AutoFit
    d. AutoRefit

19. Which button increases the number of decimal places in selected cells?

    a. ☐
    c. ☐

    b. ☐
    d. ☐

20. Which button applies multiple formatting styles to selected cells?

    a. ☐
    c. ☐

    b. ☐
    d. ☐

▼ SKILLS REVIEW

1. Format values.

    a. Start Excel, open the file EX C-2.xlsx from the drive and folder where you store your Data Files, then save it as **Health Insurance Premiums**.

    b. Enter a formula in cell B10 that totals the number of employees.

    c. Create a formula in cell C5 that calculates the monthly insurance premium for the accounting department. (*Hint*: Make sure you use the correct type of cell reference in the formula. To calculate the monthly premium, multiply the number of employees by the monthly premium.)

    d. Copy the formula in cell C5 to the range C6:C10.

    e. Format the range C5:C10 using the Accounting Number Format.

    f. Change the format of the range C6:C9 to the Comma Style.

    g. Reduce the number of decimals to 0 in cell B14, using a button in the Number group.

    h. Save your work.

2. Change fonts and font sizes.

    a. Select the range of cells containing the column labels (in row 4).

    b. Change the font of the selection to Times New Roman.

    c. Increase the font size of the selection to 12 points.

    d. Increase the font size of the label in cell A1 to 14 points.

    e. Save your changes.

3. Change attributes and alignment.

    a. Apply the bold and italic attributes to the worksheet title **QST Corporate Office**.

    b. Use the Merge & Center button to center the Health Insurance Premiums label over columns A through C.

    c. Apply the italic attribute to the Health Insurance Premiums label.

    d. Add the bold attribute to the labels in row 4.

    e. Use the Format Painter to copy the format in cell A4 to the range A5:A10.

    f. Apply the format in cell C10 to cell B14.

   g. Change the alignment of cell A10 to Align Right.

   h. Select the range of cells containing the column titles, then center them.

   i. Remove the italic attribute from the Health Insurance Premiums label, then increase the font size to 14.

   j. Move the Health Insurance Premiums label to cell A3, then add the bold and underline attributes.

   k. Add a bottom double border to the cell in the last cell in the Total column, above the calculated total value.

   l. Save your changes.

4. Adjust column width.

   a. Resize column C to a width of 10.71.

   b. Use the AutoFit feature to resize columns A and B.

   c. Clear the contents of cell A13 (do not delete the cell).

   d. Change the text in cell A14 to **Monthly Insurance Premium**, then change the width of the column to **25**.

   e. Resize any remaining columns as needed to view all the data.

   f. Save your changes.

5. Insert and delete rows and columns.

   a. Insert a new row between rows 5 and 6.

   b. Add a new department—**Humanitarian Aid**—in the newly inserted row. Enter **5** for the Employees.

   c. Copy the formula in cell C5 to C6.

   d. Add the following comment to cell A6: **New department**. Display the comment, then drag to move it out of the way, if necessary.

   e. Add a new column between the Department and Employees columns with the title **Family Coverage**, then resize the column using AutoFit.

   f. Delete the Legal row.

   g. Move the value in cell C14 to B14.

   h. Save your changes.

6. Apply colors, patterns, and borders.

   a. Add an outside border around the range A4:D10.

   b. Apply the Aqua, Accent 5, Lighter 80% fill color to the labels in the Department column (do not include the Total label).

   c. Apply the Orange, Accent 6, Lighter 60% fill color to the range A4:D4.

   d. Change the color of the font in the range A4:D4 to Red, Accent 2, Darker 25%.

   e. Add a 12.5% Gray pattern style to cell A1.

   f. Format the range A14:B14 with a pattern style of Thin Diagonal Stripes, a fill color of Dark Blue, Text 2, Lighter 40%, then apply the bold attribute.

   g. Save your changes.

7. Apply conditional formatting.

   a. Select the range D5:D9, then create a conditional format that changes cell contents to green fill with dark green text if the value is between 4000 and 7000.

   b. Select the range C5:C9, then create a conditional format that changes cell contents to red text if the number of employees exceeds 10.

   c. Select the range C5:C9, then create a blue data bar.

   d. Use the Rule Manager to modify the conditional format in cell C5 to display the cell contents in bold red text.

   e. Copy the format in cell C5 to the range in C6:C9.

   f. Merge and center the title over columns A-D.

8. Name and move a sheet.

   a. Name the Sheet 1 tab **Insurance Data**.

   b. Name the Sheet 3 tab **Employee Data**.

   c. Change the Insurance Data tab color to Red, Accent 2, Lighter 40%.

   d. Change the Employee Data tab color to Aqua, Accent 5, Lighter 40%.

▼ SKILLS REVIEW (CONTINUED)

e. Move the Employee Data sheet so it comes after (to the right of) the Insurance Data sheet.

f. Make the Insurance Data sheet active, enter your name in cell A20, then save your work.

9. Check spelling.

a. Move the cell pointer to cell A1.

b. Use the Find & Select feature to replace the Accounting label in cell A5 with Accounting/Legal.

c. Check the spelling in the worksheet using the spelling checker, and correct any spelling errors.

d. Save your changes.

e. Preview and print the Insurance Data sheet, compare your work to Figure C-28, then close the workbook and exit Excel.

FIGURE C-28

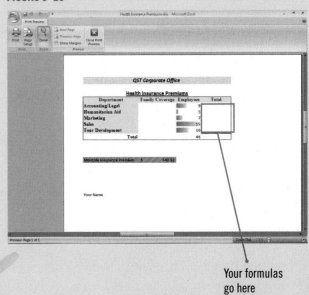

Your formulas
go here

▼ INDEPENDENT CHALLENGE 1

You run a freelance accounting business, and one of your newest clients is Lovely Locks, a small beauty salon. Now that you've converted the salon's accounting records to Excel, the manager would like you to work on an analysis of the inventory. Although more items will be added later, the worksheet has enough items for you to begin your modifications.

a. Start Excel, open the file EX C-3.xlsx from the drive and folder where you store your Data Files, then save it as **Lovely Locks Inventory**.

b. Create a formula in cell E4 that calculates the value of the on-hand inventory, based on the price paid for the item, in cell B4. Format the cell in the Comma Style.

c. Use an absolute reference to calculate the sale price of the item in cell F4, using the markup value shown in cell I1.

d. Copy the formulas created above into the range E5:F14; first convert any necessary cell references to absolute so that the formulas work correctly.

e. Add the bold attribute to the column headings, and italicize the items in column A.

f. Make sure all columns are wide enough to display the data and headings.

g. Format the Sale Price column so it displays the Accounting Number Format with two decimal places.

h. Change the Price Paid column so it displays the Comma style with two decimal places.

i. Add a row under #2 Curlers for **Nail files**, price paid **$0.31**, sold individually **(each)**, with **56** on hand.

j. Verify that all the formulas in the worksheet are correct. Adjust any items as needed, and check the spelling.

k. Use conditional formatting to call attention to items with a quantity of less than 20 on hand. Use yellow fill with dark yellow text.

l. Create an icon set for the range D4:D15 using the symbols of your choosing.

m. Add an outside border around the data in the Item column.

n. Delete the row containing the Pins item.

o. Enter your name in an empty cell below the data, then save the file.

p. Preview and print the worksheet, compare your work to the sample of page 1 shown in Figure C-29, close the workbook, then exit Excel.

FIGURE C-29

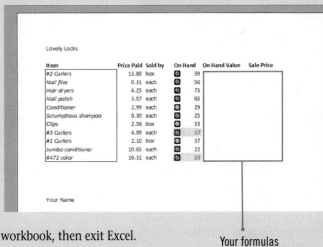

Your formulas
go here

▼ INDEPENDENT CHALLENGE 2

You volunteer several hours each week with the Assistance League of South Bend, and are in charge of maintaining the membership list. You're currently planning a mailing campaign to members in certain regions of the city. You also want to create renewal letters for members whose membership expires soon. You decide to format the list to enhance the appearance of the worksheet and make your upcoming tasks easier to plan.

a. Start Excel, open the file EX C-4.xlsx from the drive and folder where you store your Data Files, then save it as **South Bend Assistance League**.

b. Remove any blank columns.

c. Create a conditional format in the Zip Code column so that entries greater than 46649 appear in light red fill with dark red text.

d. Make all columns wide enough to fit their data and headings.

e. Use formatting enhancements, such as fonts, font sizes, and text attributes, to make the worksheet more attractive.

f. Center-align the column labels.

g. Use conditional formatting so that entries for Year of Membership Expiration that are between 2011 and 2013 appear in a bold, contrasting color.

h. Adjust any items as necessary, then check the spelling.

i. Change the name of the Sheet 1 tab to one that reflects the sheet's contents, then add a tab color of your choice.

j. Enter your name in an empty cell, then save your work.

k. Before printing, preview the worksheet, make any final changes you think necessary, then print a copy. Compare your work to the sample shown in Figure C-30.

l. Close the workbook, then exit Excel.

FIGURE C-30

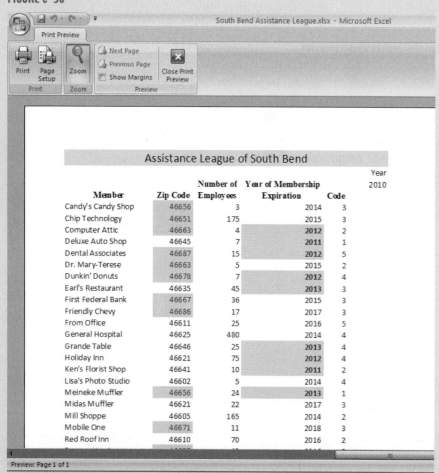

Formatting a Worksheet

▼ INDEPENDENT CHALLENGE 3

Fine Line Writing Instruments is a Chicago-based company that manufactures high-quality pens and markers. As the finance manager, one of your responsibilities is to analyze the monthly reports from your five district sales offices. Your boss, Joanne Bennington, has just asked you to prepare a quarterly sales report for an upcoming meeting. Because several top executives will be attending this meeting, Joanne reminds you that the report must look professional. In particular, she asks you to emphasize the company's surge in profits during the last month and to highlight the fact that the Northeastern district continues to outpace the other districts.

a. Plan a worksheet that shows the company's sales during the first quarter. Assume that all pens are the same price. Make sure you plan to include:

- The number of pens sold (units sold) and the associated revenues (total sales) for each of the five district sales offices. The five sales districts are: Northeastern, Midwestern, Southeastern, Southern, and Western.
- Calculations that show month-by-month totals for January, February, and March, and a three-month cumulative total.
- Calculations that show each district's share of sales (percent of Total Sales).
- Labels that reflect the month-by-month data as well as the cumulative data.
- Formatting enhancements and data bars that emphasize the recent month's sales surge and the Northeastern district's sales leadership.

b. Ask yourself the following questions about the organization and formatting of the worksheet: What worksheet title and labels do you need, and where should they appear? How can you calculate the totals? What formulas can you copy to save time and keystrokes? Do any of these formulas need to use an absolute reference? How do you show dollar amounts? What information should be shown in bold? Do you need to use more than one font? Should you use more than one point size?

c. Start Excel, then save a new, blank workbook as **Fine Line Writing Instruments** to the drive and folder where you store your Data Files.

d. Build the worksheet with your own price and sales data. Enter the titles and labels first, then enter the numbers and formulas. You can use the information in Table C-4 to get started.

e. Adjust the column widths as necessary.

f. Change the height of row 1 to 33 points.

g. Format labels and values, and change the attributes and alignment if necessary.

h. Resize columns and adjust the formatting as necessary.

i. Add data bars for the monthly Units Sold columns.

j. Add a column that calculates a 25% increase in sales dollars. Use an absolute cell reference in this calculation. (*Hint*: Make sure the current formatting is applied to the new information.)

TABLE C-4

Fine Line Writing Instruments									
1st Quarter Sales Report									
		January		February		March		Total	
Office	Price	Units Sold	Sales	Units Sold	Sales	Units Sold	Sales	Units Sold	Sales
Northeastern									
Midwestern									
Southeastern									
Southern									
Western									

▼ INDEPENDENT CHALLENGE 3 (CONTINUED)

Advanced Challenge Exercise

- Use the Format as Table feature to add a table style of your choice to the data.
- Insert a clip art image related to pens in an appropriate location, adjusting its size and position as necessary.
- Save your work.

l. Enter your name in an empty cell.

m. Check the spelling in the workbook, then save your work.

n. Preview, compare your work to Figure C-31, then print the worksheet in landscape orientation.

o. Close the workbook file, then exit Excel.

FIGURE C-31

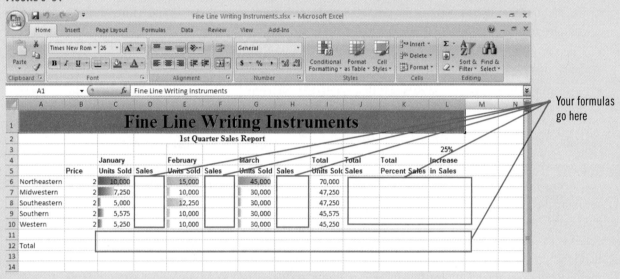

▼ REAL LIFE INDEPENDENT CHALLENGE

***Note*: This project requires an Internet connection.**

You are saving up to take an international trip you have always dreamed about. You plan to visit seven different countries over the course of two months, and budgeting an identical spending allowance in each country. To help work toward your goal, you want to create a worksheet that calculates the amount of native currency you will have in each country. You want the workbook to reflect the currency information for each country.

a. Start Excel, then save a new, blank workbook as **World Tour Budget** to the drive and folder where you store your Data Files.

b. Think of seven countries you would like to visit, then enter column and row labels for your worksheet. (*Hint*: You may wish to include row labels for each country, plus column labels for the country, the $1 equivalent in native currency, the total amount of native currency you'll have in each country, and the name of each country's monetary unit.)

c. Decide how much money you want to bring to each country (for example, $1000), and enter that in the worksheet.

d. Use your favorite search engine to find your own information sources on currency conversions for the countries you plan to visit.

e. Enter the cash equivalent to **$1** in U.S. dollars for each country in your list. Also include the name of the currency used in each country.

f. Create an equation that calculates the amount of native currency you will have in each country, using an absolute cell reference in the formula.

▼ REAL LIFE INDEPENDENT CHALLENGE (CONTINUED)

g. Format the entries in column B with three decimal places and in column C with two decimal places, using the correct currency unit for each country. (*Hint*: Use the Number tab in the Format cells dialog box; choose the appropriate currency format from the Symbol list, using two decimal places.)

h. Create a conditional format that changes the font attributes of the calculated amount in the "$1,000 US" column to bold and red if the amount exceeds **500 units** of the local currency.

i. Merge and center the title over the column headings.

j. Add any formatting attributes to the column headings, and resize the columns as necessary.

k. Add a background color to the title.

Advanced Challenge Exercise

- Modify the conditional format in the "$1,000 US" column so that entries between 1500 and 3999 display in red, boldface type, and entries above 4000 appear in blue, boldface type.
- Delete all the unused sheets in the workbook.
- Save your work as **World Tour Budget ACE** where you store your Data Files.
- If you have access to an e-mail account, e-mail this workbook to your instructor as an attachment.

l. Enter your name in the header of the worksheet.

m. Spell check, save, preview and compare your work to Figure C-32, then print the worksheet.

n. Close the workbook and exit Excel.

FIGURE C-32

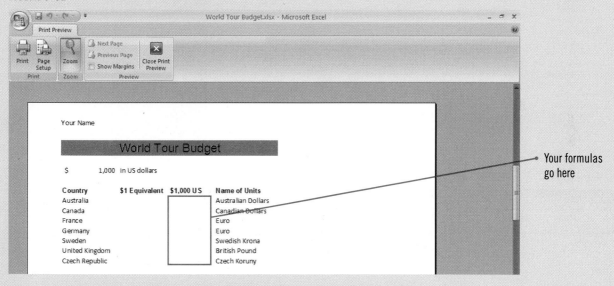

▼ VISUAL WORKSHOP

Open the file EX C-5.xlsx from the drive and folder where you store your Data Files, then save it as **Top Notch Personnel**. Use the skills you learned in this unit to format the worksheet so it looks like the one shown in Figure C-33. Create a conditional format in the Level column so that entries greater than 3 appear in red text. Create an additional conditional format in the Review Cycle column so that any value equal to 4 appears in green bold text. Replace the Accounting department label with Legal. (*Hint*: The only additional font used in this exercise is 16-point Times New Roman in row 1.) Enter your name in cell A25, check the spelling in the worksheet, then save and print your work.

FIGURE C-33

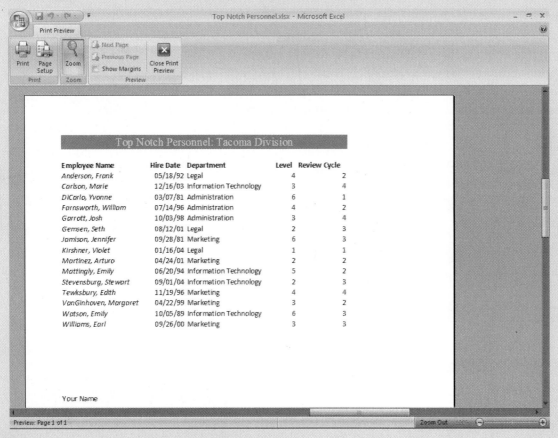

Working with Charts

Worksheets provide an effective layout for calculating and organizing data, but the grid layout is not always the best format for presenting your work to others. To display information so it's easier to interpret, you can create a chart. **Charts**, often called graphs, present information in a pictorial format, making it easier to see patterns, trends, and relationships. In this unit, you learn how to create a chart, how to edit the chart and change the chart type, how to add text annotations and arrows, and how to preview and print the chart. At the upcoming annual meeting, Grace Wong wants to emphasize a growth trend at Quest Specialty Travel. She asks you to create a chart showing the increase in company revenues over the past four quarters.

OBJECTIVES

Plan a chart

Create a chart

Move and resize a chart

Change the chart design

Change the chart layout

Format a chart

Annotate and draw on a chart

Create a pie chart

Planning a Chart

Before creating a chart, you need to plan the information you want your chart to show and how you want it to look. Planning ahead helps you to decide what type of chart to create and how to organize the data. Understanding the parts of a chart makes it easier to format it and change specific elements so that the chart best illustrates your data. ▰▰◢ In preparation for creating the chart for Grace's presentation, you identify your goals for the chart and plan it.

DETAILS

Use the following guidelines to plan the chart:

- **Determine the purpose of the chart and identify the data relationships you want to communicate graphically**

    You want to create a chart that shows quarterly revenues throughout Quest Specialty Travel. This worksheet data is shown in Figure D-1. In the first quarter, the Marketing department launched an international advertising campaign. The campaign resulted in greatly increased sales starting in the second quarter. You want to create a chart for the annual meeting that illustrates the increase and compares sales across the quarters for each location.

- **Determine the results you want to see, and decide which chart type is most appropriate**

    Different chart types display data in distinctive ways. For example, a pie chart compares parts to the whole, so it's useful for showing what proportion of a budget amount was spent on print ads relative to what was spent on direct mail or radio commercials. A line chart, in contrast, is best for showing trends over time. To choose the best chart type for your data, you should first decide how you want your data displayed and interpreted. Table D-1 describes several different types of charts you can create in Excel and their corresponding buttons on the Insert tab of the Ribbon. Because you want to compare QST revenues in multiple locations over a period of four quarters, you decide to use a column chart.

- **Identify the worksheet data you want the chart to illustrate**

    Sometimes you use all the data in a worksheet to create a chart, while at other times you may need to select a range within the sheet. The worksheet from which you are creating your chart contains revenue data for the past year. You will need to use all the quarterly data contained in the worksheet.

- **Understand the elements of a chart**

    The chart shown in Figure D-2 contains basic elements of a chart. In the figure, QST locations are on the horizontal axis (also called the **x-axis**) and monthly sales are on the vertical axis (also called the **y-axis**). The horizontal axis is also called the **category axis** because it often contains the names of data groups, such as locations, months, or years. The vertical axis is also called the **value axis** because it often contains numerical values that help you interpret the size of chart elements. (3-D charts also contain a **z-axis**, for comparing data across both categories and values.) The area inside the horizontal and vertical axes is the **plot area**. The **tick marks** at the left edge of the vertical axis and **gridlines** (extending across the plot area) create a scale of measure for each value. Each value in a cell you select for your chart is a **data point**. In any chart, a **data marker** visually represents each data point, which in this case is a column. A collection of related data points is a **data series**. In this chart, there are four data series (Quarter 1, Quarter 2, Quarter 3, and Quarter 4), so you include a **legend** to make it easy to identify them.

FIGURE D-1: Worksheet containing revenue data

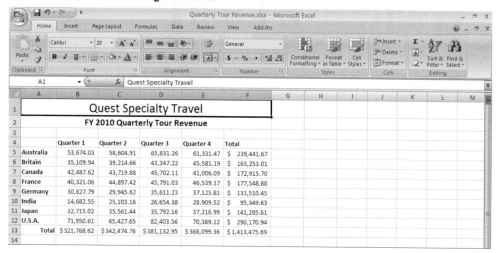

FIGURE D-2: Chart elements

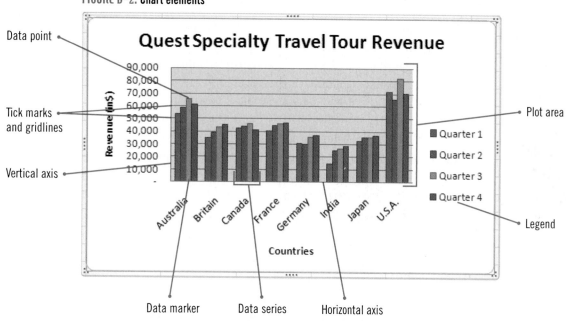

TABLE D-1: Common chart types

type	button	description
Column		Compares distinct object levels using a vertical format; the Excel default; sometimes referred to as a bar chart in other spreadsheet programs
Line		Compares trends over even time intervals; looks similar to an area chart, but does not emphasize total
Pie		Compares sizes of pieces as part of a whole; used for a single series of numbers
Bar		Compares distinct object levels using a horizontal format; sometimes referred to as a horizontal bar chart in other spreadsheet programs
Area		Shows how individual volume changes over time in relation to total volume
Scatter		Compares trends over uneven time or measurement intervals; used in scientific and engineering disciplines for trend spotting and extrapolation

Creating a Chart

To create a chart in Excel, you first select the range in a worksheet containing the data you want to chart. Once you've selected a range, you can use buttons on the Insert tab of the Ribbon to create and modify a chart. Using the worksheet containing the quarterly revenue data, you create a chart that shows the growth trend that occurred.

STEPS

1. **Start Excel, open the file EX D-1.xlsx from the drive and folder where you store your Data Files, then save it as** Quarterly Tour Revenue

   You want the chart to include the quarterly tour revenue figures, as well as quarter and country labels. You don't include the Total column and row because the quarterly figures make up the totals, and these figures would skew the chart.

2. **Select the range A4:E12, then click the** Insert tab **on the Ribbon**

   The Insert tab contains groups for inserting various types of objects, including charts. The Charts group includes buttons for each major chart type, plus an Other Charts button for additional chart types, such as stock charts for charting stock market data.

3. **Click the** Column chart button, **then click the** Clustered Column button **on the Column palette, as shown in Figure D-3**

   The chart is inserted in the center of the worksheet, and three contextual Chart Tools tabs open on the Ribbon: Design, Layout, and Format. On the Design tab, which is currently in front, you can quickly change the chart type, chart layout, and chart format and you can swap the data between the columns and rows. Currently, the countries are charted along the horizontal axis, with the quarterly revenues charted along the y-axis. This lets you easily compare quarterly revenues for each country.

4. **Click the** Switch Row/Column button **in the Data group on the Chart Tools Design tab**

   Clicking this button switches the data in the columns and rows, as shown in Figure D-4, so that the quarterly revenues are charted along the horizontal axis and the countries are plotted as the data points.

5. **Click the** Undo button **on the Quick Access toolbar**

   The chart returns to its original configuration.

6. **Click the** Chart Tools Layout tab, **click the** Chart Title button **in the Labels group, then click** Above Chart **on the palette**

   A title placeholder appears above the chart.

7. **Click anywhere in the** Chart Title **text box, press [Ctrl][A] to select the text, type** Quarterly Tour Revenue, **then click anywhere in the chart to deselect the title**

   Adding a title helps identify the chart. This chart is known as an **embedded** chart because it's inserted directly in the current worksheet. The **sizing handles**, the small series of dots at the corners and sides of the chart's border, indicate that the chart is selected. See Figure D-5. Your chart might be in a different location on the worksheet and may look slightly different; you will move and resize it in the next lesson. Any time a chart is selected, as it is now, a blue border surrounds the worksheet data range, a purple border surrounds the row labels, and a green border surrounds the column labels. Embedding a chart in the current sheet is the default selection when creating a chart, but you can also place a chart on a different sheet in the workbook, or on a newly created chart sheet. A **chart sheet** is a sheet in a workbook that contains only a chart, which is linked to the workbook data.

8. **Save your work**

FIGURE D-3: Column chart palette

Clustered Column chart type

Column chart types

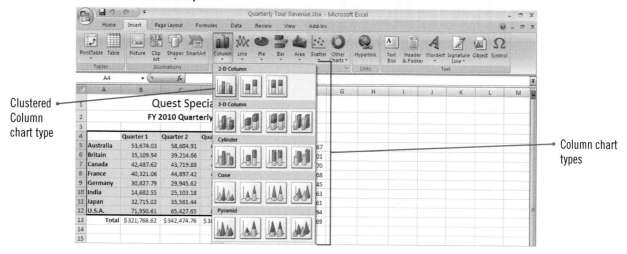

FIGURE D-4: Clustered Column chart with rows and columns switched

Undo button

Switch Row/Column button

Column labels

Row labels

Data range

Selected chart object

Chart Tools tabs

Legend

Quarter labels on horizontal axis

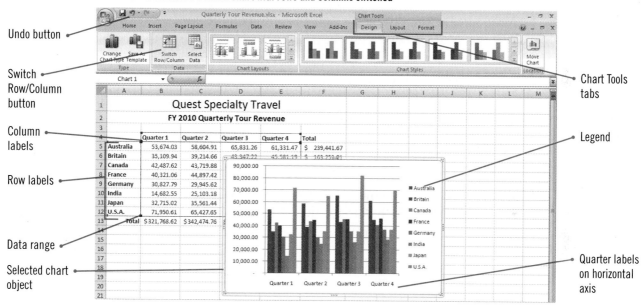

FIGURE D-5: Chart with rows and columns restored and title added

Title

Sizing handles

Country labels on horizontal axis

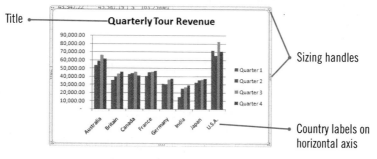

Using the contextual Chart Tools tabs

When a chart is selected, the three contextual Chart Tools tabs (Design, Layout, and Format) appear on the Ribbon. These tabs help guide you through developing and perfecting your chart. Using the Design tab, you can change overall color schemes and positioning of objects within the chart as well as the data range and configuration used for the chart. The Layout tab is used to add and modify chart elements, such as titles and labels, and for adding graphics,

such as pictures, shapes, and text boxes. The Format tab lets you format objects such as shapes and text, arrange multiple objects so they are layered attractively, and resize any object to exact specifications. While these tabs organize chart tools in a logical order, it is not necessary to use them in the order in which they appear. In other words, you can jump from the Design tab to the Format tab, back to Design, then to Layout, if you wish.

Moving and Resizing a Chart

Charts are graphics, or drawn objects, and are not located in a specific cell or at a specific range address. An **object** is an independent element on a worksheet. You can select an object by clicking within its borders; sizing handles around the object indicate it is selected. You can move a selected chart object anywhere on a worksheet without affecting formulas or data in the worksheet. However, any data changed in the worksheet is automatically updated in the chart. You can resize a chart to improve its appearance by dragging its sizing handles. You can even move a chart to a different sheet, and it will still reflect the original data. Chart objects contain other objects, such as a title and legend, which you can move and resize. In addition to repositioning chart elements to set locations using commands on the Layout tab, you can freely move any object using the mouse. Simply select it, then drag it or cut and paste it to a new location. When the mouse pointer hovers over any chart object, the name of the selected object appears on screen as a ScreenTip. ▓▓▓▓ You want to resize the chart, position it below the worksheet data, and move the legend.

STEPS

> **QUICK TIP**
> If you want to delete a chart, select it, then press [Delete].

1. **Make sure the chart is still selected, then position the pointer over the chart**

   The pointer shape ⬚ indicates that you can move the chart object or use a sizing handle to resize it. For a table of commonly used graphic object pointers, refer to Table D-2.

> **TROUBLE**
> If you do not drag a blank area on the chart, you might inadvertently move a chart element instead of the whole chart; if this happens, undo the action and try again.

2. **Position ⬚ on a blank area near the top left edge of the chart, press and hold the left mouse button, drag the chart until its upper left corner is at the upper left corner of cell A16, then release the mouse button**

   As you drag the chart, you can see an outline representing the chart's perimeter. The chart appears in the new location.

3. **Position the pointer on the right-middle sizing handle until it changes to ⟷, then drag the right edge of the chart to the right edge of column G**

   The chart is widened. See Figure D-6.

> **QUICK TIP**
> To resize a chart object to exact specification, select the object, click the Chart Tools Format tab on the Ribbon, then enter the desired height and width in the Size group.

4. **Position the pointer over the upper-middle sizing handle until it changes to ↕, then drag it to the top edge of row 15**

5. **Scroll down if necessary so row 26 is visible, position the pointer over the lower-middle sizing handle until it changes to ↕, then drag the bottom border of the chart to the bottom border of row 26**

   You can move any object on a chart. You want to align the top of the legend with the top of the plot area.

> **QUICK TIP**
> Although the sizing handles on objects within a chart look different from the sizing handles that surround a chart, they function the same way.

6. **Click the legend to select it, press and hold [Shift], drag the legend up using ⬚ so the dotted outline is approximately ¼" above the top of the plot area, then release [Shift]**

   When you click the legend, sizing handles appear around it and "Legend" appears as a ScreenTip when the pointer hovers over the object. As you drag, a dotted outline of the legend border appears. Pressing and holding the [Shift] key holds the horizontal position of the legend as you move it vertically.

7. **Click cell A12, type United States, click the Enter button ✓ on the formula bar, use AutoFit to resize column A, then press [Ctrl][Home]**

   The axis label changes to reflect the updated cell contents, as shown in Figure D-7. Changing any data in the worksheet modifies corresponding text or values in the chart. Because the chart is no longer selected, the Chart Tools tabs no longer appear on the Ribbon.

8. **Save your work**

FIGURE D-6: Moved and resized chart

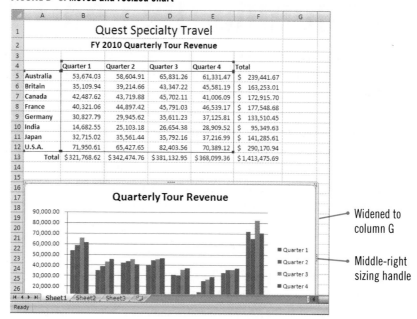

FIGURE D-7: Worksheet with modified legend and label

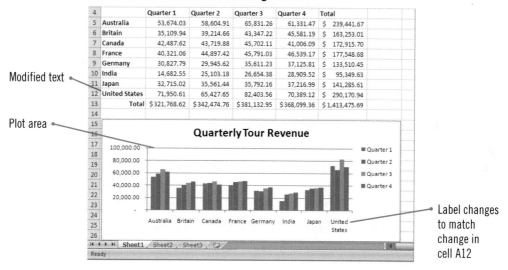

TABLE D-2: Common graphic object pointers

name	pointer	use	name	pointer	use
Diagonal resizing	⤡ or ⤢	Change chart shape	I-beam	I	Edit chart text from corners
Draw	+	Create shapes	Move chart	⇭	Change chart location
Horizontal resizing	⟺	Change chart shape from left to right	Vertical resizing	↕	Change chart shape from top to bottom

Moving an embedded chart to a sheet

Suppose you have created an embedded chart that you decide would look better on a chart sheet. You can make this change without recreating the entire chart. To do so, first select the chart, click the Chart Tools Design tab, then click the Move Chart button in the Location group. The Move Chart dialog box opens. If the chart is embedded, click the New sheet option button, then click OK. If the chart is on its own sheet, click the Object in option button, then click OK.

Changing the Chart Design

Once you've created a chart, it's easy to modify the design. You can change data values in the worksheet, and the chart is automatically updated to reflect the new data. Each of the Chart Tools tabs can be used to make specific changes in a chart. Using the Chart Tools Design tab, you can change the chart type in the Type group, modify the data range and configuration in the Data group, change the layout of objects in the Chart Layouts group, choose from coordinating color schemes in the Chart Styles group, and move the location of the chart in the Location group. The layouts in the Chart Styles group offer preconfigured arrangements of objects in your chart, such as a legend, title, or gridlines; these layouts offer an alternative to manually making formatting and design changes. ██████ You look over your worksheet and realize the data for the United States in Quarter 2 and Quarter 4 is incorrect. After you correct this data, you want to see how the same data looks using different chart layouts and types.

STEPS

1. **Click cell C12, type 75432.29, press [Tab] twice, type 84295.27, then press [Enter]**
   In the worksheet, the United States entries for Quarter 2 and Quarter 4 reflect the increased sales figures. See Figure D-8. The totals in column F and row 13 are also updated.

> **QUICK TIP**
> You can see more layout choices by clicking the More button in the Chart Layouts group.

2. **Select the chart by clicking a blank area within the chart border, click the Chart Tools Design tab on the Ribbon, then click the Layout 3 button in the Chart Layouts group**
   The legend moves to the bottom of the chart. You prefer the original layout.

3. **Click the Undo button on the Quick Access toolbar, then click the Change Chart Type button in the Type group**
   The Change Chart Type dialog box opens, as shown in Figure D-9, where you can choose from all available chart type categories and types. The left pane lists the available categories, and the right pane shows the individual chart types. An orange border surrounds the currently selected chart type.

> **QUICK TIP**
> If you plan to print a chart on a black-and-white printer, you may wish to change to a black-and-white chart style, so you can see how the output will look as you work.

4. **Click Bar in the left pane of the Change Chart Type dialog box, confirm that the Clustered Bar chart type is selected, then click OK**
   The column chart changes to a clustered bar chart. See Figure D-10. You look at the bar chart, then decide to see if the large increase in sales is more apparent if you use a three-dimensional column chart.

5. **Click the Change Chart Type button in the Type group, click Column in the left pane of the Change Chart Type dialog box, click 3-D Clustered Column (fourth from the left in the first row), then click OK**
   A three-dimensional column chart appears. You notice that the three-dimensional column format is more crowded than the two-dimensional format, but it gives you a sense of volume.

> **QUICK TIP**
> You can also use the Undo button on the Quick Access toolbar to return to a previous chart type.

6. **Click the Change Chart Type button in the Type group, click the Clustered Column button (first from the left, first row), then click OK**

7. **Click the Style 3 button in the Chart Styles group**
   The columns change to shades of blue. You prefer the previous color scheme.

8. **Click in the Quick Access toolbar, then save your work**

Creating a Combination Chart

You can apply a chart type to an existing data series in a chart, to create a combination chart. In the existing chart, select the data series that you want plotted on a secondary axis, then open the Format dialog box (use the shortcut menu, or click Format Selection in the Current Selection group of the Format tab on the Ribbon). In the Format dialog box, click Series Options, if necessary, click the Secondary Axis option button under Plot Series On, then click Close. Click the Layout tab on the Ribbon, click Axes in the Axes group, then click the type of secondary axis you want and where you want it to appear. To finish, click the Change Chart Type button in the Type group on the Design tab, then select a chart type for the secondary axis.

FIGURE D-8: Worksheet with modified data

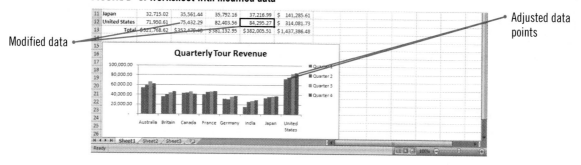

Modified data

Adjusted data points

FIGURE D-9: Change Chart Type dialog box

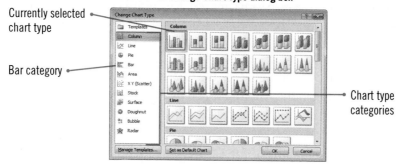

Currently selected chart type

Bar category

Chart type categories

FIGURE D-10: Column chart changed to bar chart

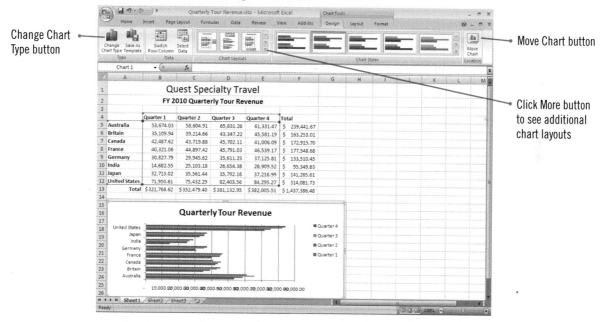

Change Chart Type button

Move Chart button

Click More button to see additional chart layouts

Working with a 3-D chart

Excel includes true 3-D chart types as well as chart types formatted in 3-D. In a true 3-D chart, a third axis, called the **z-axis**, lets you compare data points across both categories and values. The z-axis runs along the depth of the chart, so it appears to advance from the back of the chart. To create a true 3-D chart, look for chart subtypes that begin with "3-D," such as 3-D Column. Charts that are formatted in 3-D contain only two axes but their graphics give the illusion of three-dimensionality. For example, the Clustered Column in 3-D chart displays columns in a 3-D format, but does not include a z-axis that you can modify. To create a chart that is only formatted in 3-D, look for chart subtypes that end with "in 3-D." In a 3-D chart, other

data series in the same chart can sometimes obscure columns or bars, but you can rotate the chart to obtain a better view. Right-click the chart, then click 3-D Rotation. The Format Chart Area dialog box opens, with the 3-D Rotation category active. This dialog box can also be used to modify fill, line, line style, shadow, and 3-D format. The 3-D Rotation options let you choose the orientation and perspective of the chart area, plot area, walls, and floor for a 3-D chart. You can use these rotation options to improve the appearance of plotted data within a chart. The 3-D Format options let you choose what three-dimensional effects you would like to apply to select chart elements. (Not all 3-D Format options are available on all charts.)

Excel 2007

Changing the Chart Layout

Changing chart layout involves adding, removing, and modifying individual chart elements such as the chart title, plot area, gridlines, and data series. While the Chart Tools Design tab includes preconfigured chart layouts you can apply, the Chart Tools Layout tab makes it easy to create and modify individual chart objects. Using buttons on this tab, you can also add shapes and additional text to a chart, add and modify labels, change the display of axes, and modify the fill behind the plot area. You can also eliminate or change the look of gridlines. **Gridlines** are the horizontal and vertical lines in the chart that enable the eye to follow the value on an axis. You can create titles for the horizontal and vertical axes, add graphics, or add background color. You can even format the text you use in a chart. █████ ████ You want to make some layout changes in the chart, to make sure it's easy to interpret and improve its general appearance.

STEPS

1. **With the chart still selected, click the Chart Tools Layout tab on the Ribbon, click the Gridlines button in the Axes group, point to Primary Horizontal Gridlines, then click None**

   The gridlines that extend from the value axis tick marks across the chart's plot area are removed from the chart, as shown in Figure D-11.

2. **Click the Gridlines button in the Axes group, point to Primary Horizontal Gridlines, then click Major & Minor Gridlines**

   Both major and minor gridlines now appear in the chart. **Minor gridlines** show the values between the tick marks. You can change the color of the columns to better distinguish the data series.

3. **Click the Axis Titles button in the Labels group, point to Primary Horizontal Axis Title, click Title Below Axis, triple-click the axis title, then type Tour Countries**

   Descriptive text on the category axis helps readers understand the chart.

4. **Click the Axis Titles button in the Labels group, point to Primary Vertical Axis Title, then click Rotated Title**

   A placeholder for the vertical axis title is added to the left of the vertical axis.

5. **Triple-click the vertical axis title, then type Revenue (in $)**

   The text "Revenue (in $)" appears to the left of the vertical axis, as shown in Figure D-12.

6. **Right-click the horizontal axis labels ("Australia", "Britain", etc.), click the Font list on the Mini toolbar, click Times New Roman, click the Font Size list on the Mini toolbar, then click 8**

   The font of the horizontal axis text changes to Times New Roman, and the font size decreases, making more of the plot area visible.

7. **Right-click the vertical axis labels, click the Font list on the Mini toolbar, click Times New Roman, click the Font Size list on the Mini toolbar, then click 8**

8. **Right-click the chart title ("Quarterly Tour Revenue"), click Format Chart Title on the shortcut menu, click Border Color in the left pane, then click the Solid line option button in the right pane**

   Adding a solid border is the first step to creating a shadow box that surrounds the title. You can only add a shadow to a text box that has a border.

9. **Click Shadow in the left pane, click the Presets list arrow, click the Offset Diagonal Bottom Right (first row, first from the left) style in the Outer group, click Close, then save your work**

   A border with a drop shadow surrounds the title. Compare your work to Figure D-13.

FIGURE D-11: Gridlines removed from chart

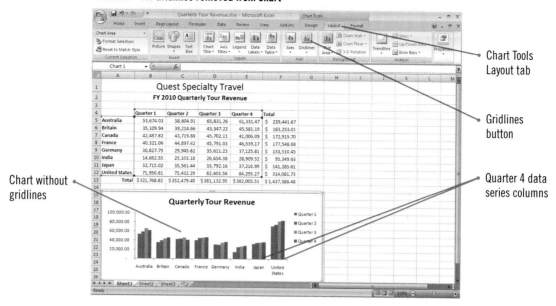

Chart Tools
Layout tab

Gridlines
button

Chart without
gridlines

Quarter 4 data
series columns

FIGURE D-12: Axes titles added to chart

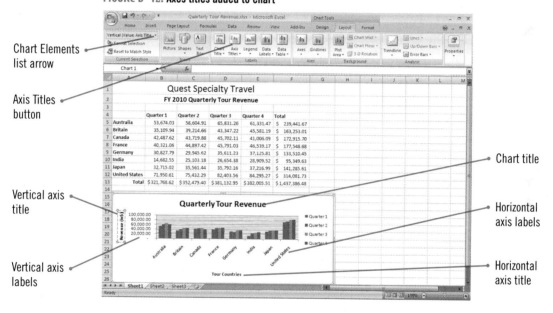

Chart Elements
list arrow

Axis Titles
button

Vertical axis
title

Vertical axis
labels

Chart title

Horizontal
axis labels

Horizontal
axis title

FIGURE D-13: Enhanced chart

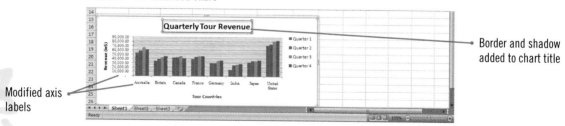

Border and shadow
added to chart title

Modified axis
labels

Adding data labels to a chart

There are times when your audience might benefit by seeing data labels on a chart. These labels can indicate the series name, category name, and/or the value of one or more data points. Once your chart is selected, you can add this information to your chart by clicking the Data Labels button in the Labels group in the Chart Tools Layout tab on the Ribbon. Once you have added the data labels, you can apply formatting to them or delete individual data labels. Delete individual data labels by clicking them until handles surround the set you want to delete, then press [Delete].

Formatting a Chart

Formatting a chart can make it easier to read and understand. Many formatting enhancements can be made using the Chart Tools Format tab. You can change colors in a specific data series or you can apply a style to a series using the Shape Styles group. Styles make it possible to apply multiple formats, such as an outline, fill color, and text color, all with a single click. You can also make individual selections of fill color, outline, and other effects using the Shape Styles group. WordArt, which lets you create curved or stylized text, can be created using the WordArt Styles group. ▓▓▓▓▓ You want to improve the appearance of the chart by creating titles for the horizontal and vertical axes and adding a drop shadow to the chart title.

STEPS

1. **With the chart selected, click the** Chart Tools Format tab **on the Ribbon, then click any column in the Quarter 4 data series**

   The Chart Tools Format tab opens, and handles surround each column in the Quarter 4 data series, indicating that the entire series is selected.

2. **Click the** Format Selection button **in the Current Selection group**

3. **Click** Fill **in the left pane of the Format Data Series dialog box, then click the** Solid fill option button

4. **Click the** Color list arrow ▨ ▾**, click** Orange, Accent 6 **(first row, tenth from the left) as shown in Figure D-14, then click** Close

   All the columns for the series become orange, and the legend changes to match the new color. You can also change the color of selected objects by applying a shape style.

5. **Click any** column **in the Quarter 3 data series**

   Handles surround each column in the Quarter 3 data series.

6. **Click the** More button ▾ **on the Shape Styles gallery, then hover the pointer over the** Moderate Effect – Accent 3 button **(fifth row, fourth from the left) as shown in Figure D-15**

7. **Click the** Subtle Effect – Accent 3 button **(fourth row, fourth from the left) in the palette**

   The color for the data series changes, as shown in Figure D-16.

8. **Save your work**

Changing alignment in axis text and titles

The buttons on the Chart Tools Layout tab provide a few options for aligning axis text and titles, but you can customize the position and rotation to exact specifications using the Format dialog box. You can modify the alignment of axis text to make it fit better within the plot area. With a chart selected, right-click the axis text you want to modify, then click Format Axis on the shortcut menu. The Format Axis

dialog box opens for the selected element. Click Alignment, then select the appropriate option. You can create a custom angle by clicking the Text direction list arrow, clicking Horizontal, then selecting the number of degrees from the Custom angle text box. When you have made the desired changes, click Close.

FIGURE D-14: Format Data Series dialog box

Click Border Color to control line display

Click Shadow to control shadow settings

Orange, Accent 6

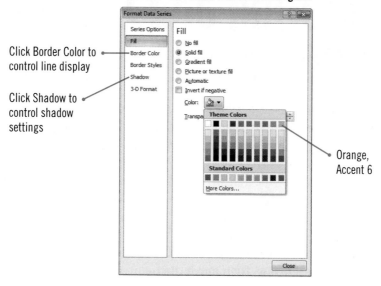

FIGURE D-15: Chart with formatted data series

Subtle Effect – Accent 3

Moderate Effect – Accent 3

In Step 6, point to this style

Live Preview of current style

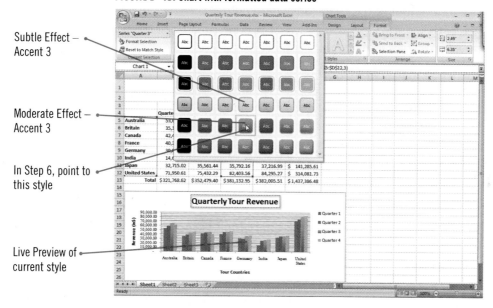

FIGURE D-16: Color of data series changed

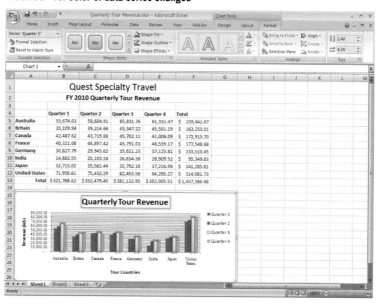

Annotating and Drawing on a Chart

You can add text annotations and graphics to a chart to point out critical information. **Text annotations** are labels that further describe your data. You can also draw lines and arrows that point to the exact locations you want to emphasize. Shapes such as arrows and boxes can be added from the Illustrations group on the Insert tab or from the Insert group on the Chart Tools Layout group on the Ribbon. These groups are also used to Insert pictures and clip art. You want to call attention to the India tour revenue increases, so you decide to add a text annotation and an arrow to this information in the chart.

STEPS

1. **Make sure the chart is selected, click the Chart Tools Layout tab, click the Text Box button in the Insert group, then move the pointer over the worksheet**

   The pointer changes to ↓, indicating that you can begin typing text by clicking.

QUICK TIP

You can also insert text by clicking the Text Box button in the Text group in the Insert tab.

2. **Click to the right of the chart (anywhere *outside* the chart boundary)**

   A text box is added to the worksheet, and the Drawing Tools Format tab opens, so that you can format the new object. First you need to type the text.

3. **Type Great improvement**

   The text appears in a selected text box on the worksheet and the chart is no longer selected, as shown in Figure D-17. Your text box may be in a different location; this is not important, because you'll move the annotation in the next step.

4. **Point to an edge of the text box so that the pointer changes to ⌖, drag the text box into the chart to the left of the chart title, as shown in Figure D-18, then release the mouse button**

   You want to add a simple arrow shape in the chart.

QUICK TIP

To annotate a chart, you can also use the Callouts category of the Shapes palette in either the Illustrations group on the Insert tab or the Insert group on the Chart Tools Layout tab.

5. **Click the chart to select it, click the Chart Tools Layout tab, click the Shapes button in the Insert group, click the Arrow shape in the Lines category, then move the pointer over the chart**

   The pointer changes to ┼, and the status bar displays "Click and drag to insert an AutoShape." When you draw an arrow, the point farthest from where you start has the arrowhead. When ┼ is near the text box handles, the handles turn red. The red handles act as an anchor for the arrow.

6. **Position ┼ at the red square to the right of the t in the word "improvement" (in the text box), press and hold the left mouse button, drag the line to the Quarter 2 column in the India series, then release the mouse button**

   An arrow points to India's second quarter revenue, and the Drawing Tools Format tab displays options for working with this new object. You can resize, format, or delete it just like any other object in a chart.

7. **Click the Shape Outline list arrow in the Shape Styles group, point to Weight, then click 1½ pt**

   Compare your finished chart to Figure D-19.

8. **Save your work**

FIGURE D-17: Text box added

Drawing Tools
Format tab

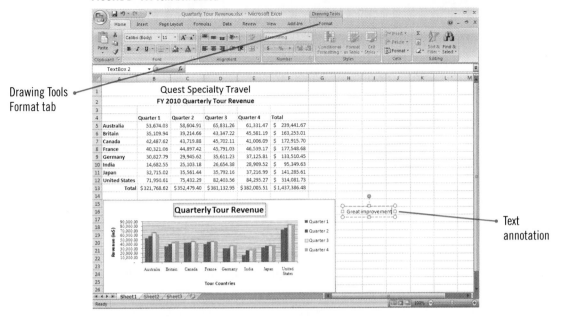

Text
annotation

FIGURE D-18: Text annotation on chart

Text annotation

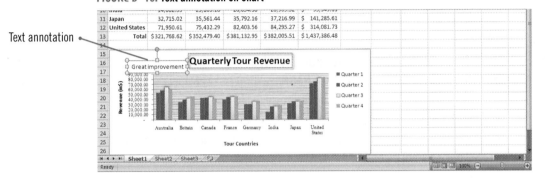

FIGURE D-19: Drawn object added to chart

Arrow added and
formatted

Adding SmartArt graphics

In addition to charts, annotations, and drawn objects, you can create a variety of diagrams using SmartArt. Diagram types include List, Process, Cycle, Hierarchy, Relationship, Matrix, and Pyramid. To insert SmartArt, click the SmartArt button in the Illustrations group on the Insert tab on the Ribbon. Click the category of SmartArt you want to create from the left panel, then click the style from the center panel. The right panel shows a sample of the selection you've chosen, as shown in Figure D-20. The diagram appears on the worksheet as an embedded object with sizing handles. An additional window opens where you can enter the diagram text.

FIGURE D-20: Choose a SmartArt Graphic dialog box

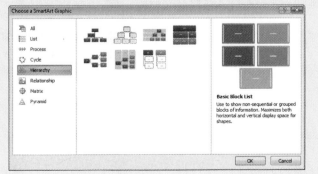

Creating a Pie Chart

You can create multiple charts based on the same worksheet data. While a column chart may illustrate certain important aspects of your worksheet data, you may find you want to create an additional chart to emphasize a different point. Depending on the type of chart you create, you have additional options for calling attention to trends and patterns. For example, if you create a pie chart, you can emphasize one data point by **exploding**, or pulling that slice away from, the pie chart. When you're ready to print a chart, you can preview it just as you do a worksheet, to check the output before committing it to paper. You can print a chart by itself or as part of the worksheet. ▓▓▓▓▓ At an upcoming meeting, Grace plans to discuss the total tour revenue and which countries need improvement. You want to create a pie chart she can use to illustrate total revenue. Finally, you want to print the worksheet and the charts.

STEPS

1. **Select the range A5:A12, press and hold [Ctrl], select the range F5:F12, click the Insert tab, click the Pie button in the Charts group, then click the Pie in 3-D button in the gallery**

   The new chart appears in the center of the worksheet. You can move the chart and quickly format it using a Chart Layout.

2. **Drag the chart so its top left corner is at the top left corner of cell G1, then click the Layout 2 button in the Chart Layouts group**

3. **Click the slice for the India data point, click again so it is the only data point selected, right-click, then click Format Data Point**

   The Format Data Point dialog box opens, as shown in Figure D-21. You can use the Point Explosion slider to control the distance a pie slice moves or you can type a value in the Point Explosion text box.

4. **Double-click 0 in the Point Explosion text box, type 40, then click Close**

   Compare your chart to Figure D-22. You decide to preview the chart and data before you print.

5. **Drag the bottom edge of the chart so it is close to the top of row 15, if necessary**

6. **Click cell A1, switch to Page Layout view, type Your Name in the left-hand header box, then click cell A1**

   You decide the chart and data would fit better on the page if they were printed in **landscape** orientation— that is, with the text running the long way on the page.

7. **Click the Page Layout tab, click the Orientation button in the Page Setup group, then click Landscape**

8. **Open the Print Preview window, click the Page Setup button on the Print Preview tab, click the Fit to option button, make sure the contents are set to fit to 1 page wide by 1 page tall, then click OK**

   The data and chart are positioned horizontally on a single page. See Figure D-23. The printer you have selected may affect the appearance of your preview screen, and if you do not have a color printer installed, the image will appear in black & white.

9. **Click the Print button on the Print Preview tab, print one copy of the page, save and close the workbook, then exit Excel**

FIGURE D-21: Format Data Point dialog box

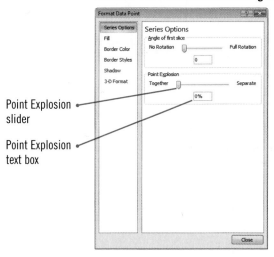

Point Explosion slider

Point Explosion text box

FIGURE D-22: Exploded pie slice

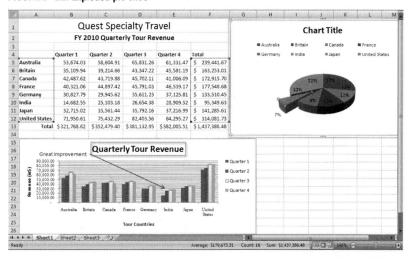

FIGURE D-23: Landscape view of completed charts

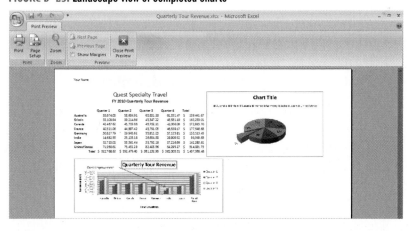

Using the Page Setup dialog box for a chart

When a chart is selected (or a chart sheet is active) and the Print Preview window is open, you can make modifications by clicking Page Setup in the Print group on the Print Preview tab. The Page Setup dialog box does not display all the options normally available. For example, the Center on page options (in the Margins tab) are not always available, and the Scaling options (in the Page tab) are grayed out.

You can also use the Show Margins checkbox in the Preview group of the Print Preview tab to accurately position a chart on the page. Margin lines appear on the screen and show you exactly how the margins appear on the page. The exact placement appears in the status bar when you press and hold the mouse button on the margin line. You can drag the lines to the exact settings you want.

Practice

▼ CONCEPTS REVIEW

Label each element of the Excel chart shown in Figure D-24.

FIGURE D-24

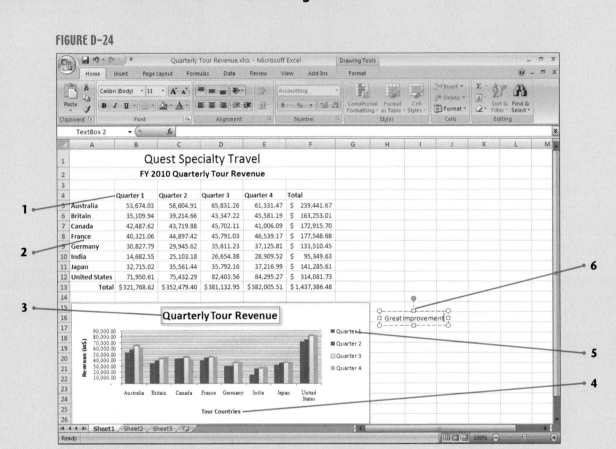

Match each chart type with the statement that best describes it.

7. Line   **a.** Compares trends over even time intervals

8. Pie   **b.** Shows how volume changes over time

9. Area   **c.** Compares data over time the Excel default

10. Column   **d.** Displays a column and line chart using different scales of measurement

11. Combination   **e.** Compares data as parts of a whole

Select the best answer from the list of choices.

12. **Which tab on the Ribbon do you use to create a chart?**
    a. Design
    b. Insert
    c. Page Layout
    d. Format

13. **Which tab appears only when a chart is selected?**
    a. Insert
    b. Chart Tools Format
    c. Review
    d. Page Layout

14. **Which pointer do you use to resize a chart object?**
    a. +
    b. I
    c. ↓
    d. ↕

15. **How do you move an embedded chart to a chart sheet?**
    a. Click a button on the Chart Tools Design tab.
    b. Drag the chart to the sheet tab.
    c. Delete the chart, switch to a different sheet, then create a new chart.
    d. Use the Copy and Paste buttons on the Ribbon.

16. **The object in a chart that identifies patterns used for each data series is a(n):**
    a. Data marker.
    b. Data point.
    c. Organizer
    d. Legend.

17. **A collection of related data points in a chart is called a:**
    a. Data series.
    b. Data tick.
    c. Cell address.
    d. Value title.

▼ SKILLS REVIEW

1. **Plan a chart.**
    a. Start Excel, open the Data File EX D-2.xlsx from the drive and folder where you store your Data Files, then save it as **Departmental Software Usage**.
    b. Describe the type of chart you would use to plot this data.
    c. What chart type would you use to compare total company expenses by department?
    d. What term is used to describe each value in a worksheet range selected for a chart?

2. **Create a chart.**
    a. In the worksheet, select the range containing all the data and headings.
    b. Click the Insert tab, if necessary.
    c. Create a clustered column chart, then add the chart title **Software Usage, by Department** above the chart.
    d. Save your work.

3. **Move and resize a chart.**
    a. Make sure the chart is still selected.
    b. Move the chart beneath the data.
    c. Resize the chart so it extends to the left edge of column I.
    d. Use the Chart Tools Layout tab to move the legend below the charted data.
    e. Resize the chart so its bottom edge is at the top of row 25.
    f. Save your work.

4. **Change the chart design.**
    a. Change the value in cell B3 to **25**. Observe the change in the chart.
    b. Select the chart.
    c. Use the Chart Layouts group on the Chart Tools Design tab to change to Layout 7, then undo the change.
    d. Use the Change Chart Type button on the Chart Tools Design tab to change the chart to a clustered bar chart.
    e. Change the chart to a 3-D clustered column chart , then change it back to a clustered column chart.
    f. Save your work.

5. Change the chart layout.

    a. Use the Layout tab to turn off the displayed gridlines in the chart.

    b. Change the font used in the horizontal and vertical axes labels to Times New Roman.

    c. Turn on the major gridlines for both the horizontal and vertical axes.

    d. Change the chart title's font to Times New Roman, with a font size of 20.

    e. Enter **Departments** as the horizontal axis title.

    f. Enter **Number of Users** as the vertical axis title. (*Hint*: Use a rotated title)

    g. Change the font size of the horizontal axis to 10, if necessary, and the font to Times New Roman.

    h. Change the font size of the vertical axis labels to 10, if necessary, and the font to Times New Roman.

    i. Change Personnel in the column heading to **Human Resources**. (*Hint*: Change the label in the worksheet, then resize the column.)

    j. Change the font size of the legend to 14.

    k. Add an offset diagonal bottom-right outer drop shadow to the chart title. (*Hint*: Use a solid line border in the default color.)

    l. Save your work.

6. Format a chart.

    a. Make sure the chart is selected, then select the Format tab, if necessary.

    b. Change the color of the Excel data series to Olive Green, Accent 3 Darker 50%.

    c. Change the shape effect of the Excel data series to Bevel – Circle.

    d. Save your work.

7. Annotate and draw on a chart.

    a. Make sure the chart is selected, then create the text annotation **Needs more users**.

    b. Position the text annotation so the 'N' in 'Needs' is positioned approximately below the 't' in 'Software'.

    c. Use the Shapes group on the Insert tab to create a 1½ pt weight arrow that points to the Excel users in the Design Department.

    d. Deselect the chart.

    e. Save your work.

8. Create a pie chart.

    a. Select the range A1:F2, then create a 3-D pie chart.

    b. Drag the 3-D pie chart beneath the existing chart.

    c. Change the chart title to **Excel Users**.

    d. Apply Chart Style 26 to the chart.

    e. Explode the Human Resources slice from the pie chart at 25%.

    f. In the worksheet, enter your name in the left section of the header.

▼ SKILLS REVIEW (CONTINUED)

g. View the worksheet and charts in the Print Preview window, make sure all the contents fit on one page, then compare your work to Figure D-25.

h. Save your work.

i. Close the workbook, then exit Excel.

FIGURE D-25

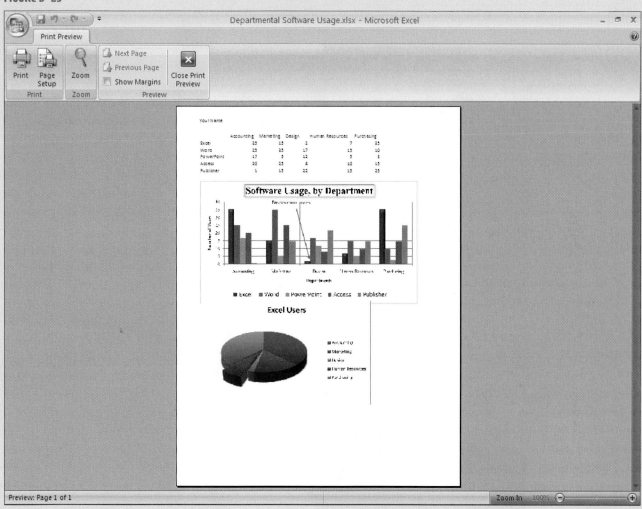

▼ INDEPENDENT CHALLENGE 1

You are the operations manager for the Springfield Theater Group in Massachusetts. Each year the group applies to various state and federal agencies for matching funds. For this year's funding proposal, you need to create charts to document the number of productions in previous years.

a. Start Excel, open the file EX D-3.xlsx from the drive and folder where you store your Data Files, then save it as **Springfield Theater Group**.

b. Take some time to plan your charts. Which type of chart or charts might best illustrate the information you need to display? What kind of chart enhancements do you want to use? Will a 3-D effect make your chart easier to understand?

c. Create a clustered column chart for the data.

d. If you wish, change at least one of the colors used in a data series.

e. Make the appropriate modifications to the chart to make it easy to read and understand, and visually attractive. Include chart titles, legends, and value and category axis titles, using the suggestions in Table D-3.

TABLE D-3

suggested chart enhancements for a column chart	
Title	Types and Number of Plays
Legend	Year 1, Year 2, Year 3, Year 4
Vertical axis title	Number of Plays
Horizontal axis title	Play Types

f. Create at least two additional charts for the same data to show how different chart types display the same data. Place each new chart on its own sheet in the workbook, and name the sheet according to the type of chart you created. One of the additional charts should be a pie chart; the other is up to you. Modify each new chart as necessary to improve its appearance and effectiveness. Compare your chart to the sample in Figure D-26.

FIGURE D-26

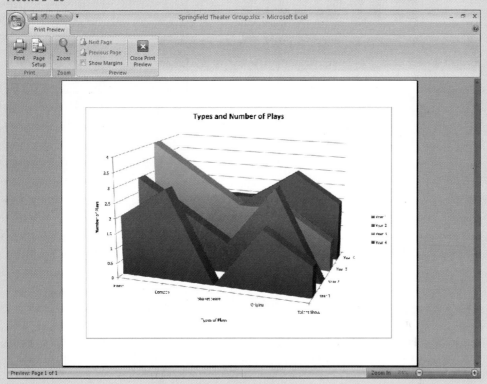

g. Enter your name in the worksheet header.

h. Save your work. Before printing, preview the workbook in Print Preview, then adjust any items as necessary.

i. Print the worksheet (charts and data).

j. Close the workbook, then exit Excel.

▼ INDEPENDENT CHALLENGE 2

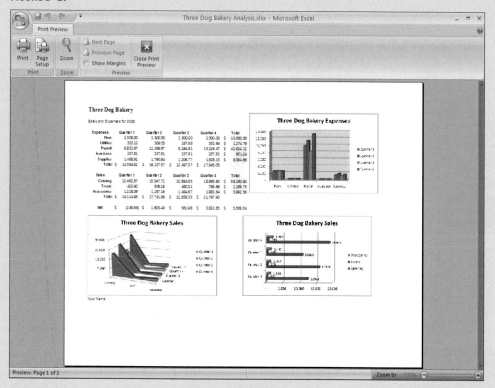

You work at Three Dog Bakery, a locally-owned bakery for dogs. One of your responsibilities at the bakery is to manage the company's sales and expenses using Excel. Another is to convince the current staff that Excel can help them make daily operating decisions more easily and efficiently. To do this, you've decided to create charts using the previous year's operating expenses, including rent, utilities, and payroll. The manager will use these charts at the next monthly meeting.

a. Start Excel, open the Data File EX D-4.xlsx from the drive and folder where you store your Data Files, then save it as **Three Dog Bakery Analysis**.

b. Decide which data in the worksheet should be charted. What type of chart or charts are best suited for the information you need to show? What kinds of chart enhancements are necessary?

c. Create a 3-D column chart (with the data series in rows) on the worksheet, showing the expense data for all four quarters. (*Hint*: Do not include the totals.)

d. Change the scale of the vertical axis (Expense data) so no decimals are displayed. (*Hint*: Right-click the scale you want to modify, click Format Axis, click Number category, change the number of decimal places, then click Close.)

e. Using the sales data, create two charts on this worksheet that illustrate trends in the data. (*Hint*: Move each chart to a new location on the worksheet, then deselect it before creating the next one.)

f. In one chart of the sales data, add data labels, then add chart titles as you see fit.

g. Make any necessary formatting changes to make the charts look more attractive, then enter your name in a worksheet cell.

h. Save your work.

i. Before printing, preview each chart, and adjust any items as needed. Fit the charts to a single page, then print one copy. Compare your work to the sample in Figure D-27.

j. Close the workbook, then exit Excel.

▼ INDEPENDENT CHALLENGE 3

FIGURE D-28

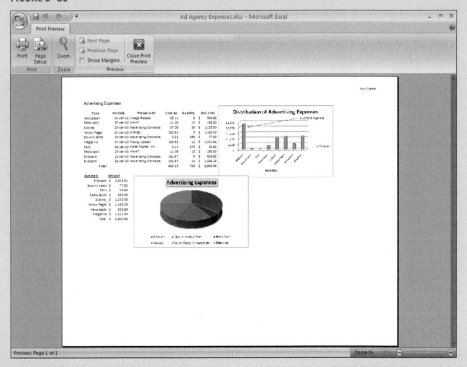

You are working as an account representative at the Inspiration Ad Agency. You have been examining the expenses charged to clients of the firm. The board of directors wants to examine certain advertising expenses and has asked you to prepare charts that can be used in this evaluation. In particular, you want to see how dollar amounts compare among the different expenses, and you also want to see how expenses compare with each other proportional to the total budget.

a. Start Excel, open the Data File EX D-5.xlsx from the drive and folder where you store your Data Files, then save it as **Ad Agency Expenses**.

b. Choose three types of charts that seem best suited to illustrate the data in the range A16:B24. What kinds of chart enhancements are necessary?

c. Create at least two different types of charts that show the distribution of advertising expenses. (*Hint*: Move each chart to a new location on the same worksheet.) One of the charts should be a 3-D pie chart.

d. Add annotated text and arrows highlighting important data, such as the largest expense.

e. Change the color of at least one data series in at least one of the charts.

f. Add chart titles and category and value axis titles where appropriate. Format the titles with a font of your choice. Place a drop shadow around the chart title in at least one chart.

g. Add your name to a section of the header, then save your work.

h. View the file in Print Preview. Adjust any items as needed. Be sure the charts are all visible on the page. Compare your work to the sample in Figure D-28.

Advanced Challenge Exercise

- Explode a slice from the 3-D pie chart.
- Add a data label to the exploded pie slice.
- Change the number format of labels in the non-pie charts so no decimals are displayed.
- Modify the scale of the vertical axis in one of the charts. (*Hint*: Right-click the vertical axis, click Format Axis, then click Axis Options.)
- Save your work, then view it in Print Preview.

i. Print the charts, close the workbook, then exit Excel.

▼ REAL LIFE INDEPENDENT CHALLENGE

FIGURE D-29

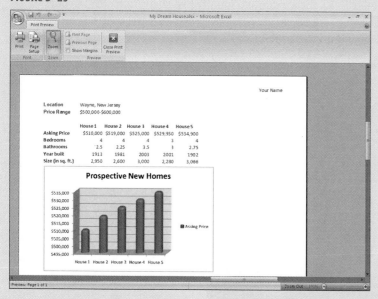

Note: This project requires an Internet connection.

A cash inheritance from a distant relative has finally been deposited in your bank account, and you have decided to quit your job and relocate to the town of your dreams. You have a good idea where you'd like to live and decide to use the Web to see what sort of houses are currently available.

a. Start Excel, then save a new, blank workbook as **My Dream House** to the drive and folder where you save your Data Files.

b. Decide on where you would like to live, and use your favorite search engine to find information sources on homes for sale in that area.

c. Determine a price range and features within the home. Find data for at least five homes that meet your location and price requirements, and enter them in the worksheet. See Table D-4 below for suggested data layout.

d. Format the data so it looks attractive and professional.

e. Create any type of column chart, using only the House and Asking Price data. Place it on the same worksheet as the data. Include a descriptive title.

f. Change the colors in the chart, using the Chart Style of your choice.

g. Enter your name in a section of the header.

TABLE D-4

location					
price range					
	House 1	House 2	House 3	House 4	House 5
Asking price					
Bedrooms					
Bathrooms					
Year built					
Size (in sq. ft.)					

h. Save the workbook. Preview the chart(s) and change margins and/or orientation as necessary. Compare your work to the sample chart shown in Figure D-29.

i. Print your worksheet(s), including the data and chart(s), making setup modifications as necessary.

Advanced Challenge Exercise

- Change the chart type to a Clustered Column chart.
- Create a combination chart that plots the asking price on one axis and the size of the home on the other axis. (*Hint*: Use Help to get tips on how to chart with a secondary axis.)

j. Close the workbook, then exit Excel.

▼ VISUAL WORKSHOP

Open the Data File EX D-6.xlsx from the drive and folder where you store your Data Files, then save it as **Projected Project Revenue**. Modify the worksheet data so it looks like Figure D-30, then create and modify two charts to match the ones shown in the figure. You will need to make formatting, layout, and design changes once you create the charts. Enter your name in the left section of the header, then save, preview, and print your results.

FIGURE D-30

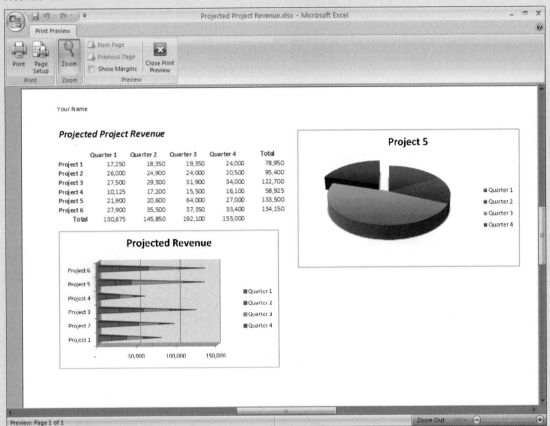

Analyzing Data Using Formulas

Files You Will Need:

EX E-1.xlsx
EX E-2.xlsx
EX E-3.xlsx
EX E-4.xlsx
EX E-5.xlsx
EX E-6.xlsx
EX E-7.xlsx

As you have learned, formulas and functions help you to analyze worksheet data. As you learn how to use different types of formulas and functions, you will discover more valuable uses for Excel. In this unit, you will gain a deeper understanding of Excel formulas and learn how to use several Excel functions. Kate Morgan, QST's vice president of sales, uses Excel formulas and functions to analyze sales data for the U.S. region and to consolidate sales data from several worksheets. Because management is considering adding a new regional branch, Kate asks you to estimate the loan costs for a new office facility and to compare tour sales in the existing U.S. offices.

MIDTE

OBJECTIVES

Format data using text functions

Sum a data range based on conditions

Consolidate data using a formula

Check formulas for errors

Construct formulas using named ranges

Build a logical formula with the IF function

Build a logical formula with the AND function

Calculate payments with the PMT function

Formatting Data Using Text Functions

Often, data you import needs restructuring or reformatting to be understandable and attractive, or to match the formatting of other data in your worksheet. Instead of handling these tasks manually in each cell, you can use Excel conversion tools and text functions to perform these tasks automatically for a range of cell data. The Convert Text to Columns feature breaks data fields in one column into separate columns. Your data elements should be separated by a **delimiter**, or separator, such as a space, comma, or semicolon. The text function PROPER capitalizes (converts to a proper noun) the first letter in a string of text as well as any text following a space. For example, if cell A1 contains the text string marketing department, then =PROPER(A1) would display Marketing Department. The CONCATENATE function is used to join two or more strings into one text string. ▰▰▰▰ Kate has received the U.S. sales representatives' data from the human resources department. She asks you to use text formulas to format the data into a more useful layout.

STEPS

1. **Start Excel, open the file EX E-1.xlsx from the drive and folder where you store your Data Files, then save it as Sales Data**

2. **On the Sales Reps sheet, select the range A4:A15, click the Data tab, then click the Text to Columns button in the Data Tools group**

   The Convert Text to Columns Wizard opens, as shown in Figure E-1. The data fields on your worksheet are separated by commas, which will act as delimiters.

3. **If necessary, click the Delimited option button to select it, click Next, in the Delimiters area of the dialog box click the Comma check box to select it if necessary, click any other selected check boxes to deselect them, then click Next**

   You instructed Excel to separate your data at the comma delimiter.

QUICK TIP

You can move the Function Arguments dialog box if it overlaps a cell or range that you need to click. You can also click the Collapse Dialog Box button ▦, select the cell or range, then click the Expand Dialog box button ▦ to return to the Function Arguments dialog box.

4. **Click the Text option button in the Column data format area, click the General column to select it in the Data preview area, click the Text option button in the Column data format area, then click Finish**

   The data are separated into three columns of text. You want to format the letters to the correct cases.

5. **Click cell D4, click the Formulas tab, click the Text button in the Function Library group, click PROPER, with the insertion point in the Text text box, click cell A4, then click OK**

   The name is copied from cell A4 to cell D4 with the correct uppercase letters for proper names. The remaining names and the cities are still in lowercase letters.

6. **Drag the fill handle to copy the formula in cell D4 to cell E4, then copy the formulas in cells D4:E4 into the range D5:E15**

   You want to format the years data to be more descriptive.

QUICK TIP

Excel automatically inserts quotation marks to enclose the space and the Years text.

7. **Click cell F4, click the Text button in the Function Library group, click CONCATENATE, with the insertion point in the Text1 text box, click cell C4, press [Tab], with the insertion point in the Text2 text box, press [Spacebar], type Years, then click OK**

8. **Copy the formula in cell F4 into the range F5:F15, click the Insert tab, click the Header & Footer button in the Text group, click the Go to Footer button in the Navigation group, enter your name in the center text box, click cell A1, then click the Normal button ▦ in the status bar**

9. **Save your file, then print the worksheet and compare your work to Figure E-2**

FIGURE E-1: Convert Text to Columns dialog box

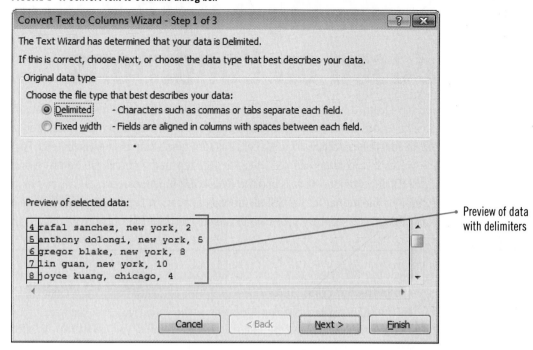

Preview of data with delimiters

FIGURE E-2: Worksheet with data formatted in columns

			United States Sales Representatives		
			Name	Office	Years of Service
rafal sanchez	new york	2	Rafal Sanchez	New York	2 Years
anthony dolongi	new york	5	Anthony Dolongi	New York	5 Years
gregor blake	new york	8	Gregor Blake	New York	8 Years
lin guan	new york	10	Lin Guan	New York	10 Years
joyce kuang	chicago	4	Joyce Kuang	Chicago	4 Years
garrin cunha	chicago	7	Garrin Cunha	Chicago	7 Years
cathy jaques	chicago	5	Cathy Jaques	Chicago	5 Years
alyssa maztta	chicago	4	Alyssa Maztta	Chicago	4 Years
april radka	miami	6	April Radka	Miami	6 Years
jose costello	miami	7	Jose Costello	Miami	7 Years
joyce haddad	miami	4	Joyce Haddad	Miami	4 Years
summer zola	miami	7	Summer Zola	Miami	7 Years

Using text functions

Other commonly used text functions include UPPER, LOWER, and SUBSTITUTE. The UPPER function converts text to all uppercase letters, the LOWER function converts text to all lowercase letters, and SUBSTITUTE replaces text in a text string. For example, if cell A1 contains the text string Today is Wednesday, then =LOWER(A1) would produce today is wednesday, =UPPER(A1) would produce

TODAY IS WEDNESDAY, and =SUBSTITUTE(A1, "Wednesday", "Tuesday") would result in Today is Tuesday.

If you want to copy and paste data formatted using text functions, you need to select Values Only from the Paste Options drop-down list to paste the cell values rather than the text formulas.

Summing a Data Range Based on Conditions

You have learned how to use the SUM, COUNT, and AVERAGE functions for data ranges. You can also use Excel functions to sum, count, and average data in a range based on criteria, or conditions, you set. The SUMIF function conditionally totals cells in a sum range that meet given criteria. For example, you can total the values in a column of sales where a sales rep name equals Joe Smith (the criterion). Similarly, the COUNTIF function counts cells and the AVERAGEIF function averages cells in a range based on a specified condition. The format for the SUMIF function appears in Figure E-3. ▓▓▓▓ Kate asks you to analyze the New York branch's January sales data to provide her with information about each tour.

STEPS

1. **Click the NY sheet tab, click cell G7, click the Formulas tab, click the More Functions button in the Function Library group, point to Statistical, then click COUNTIF**

   The Function Arguments dialog box opens, as shown in Figure E-4. You want to count the number of times Pacific Odyssey appears in the Tour column. The formula you use will say, in effect, "Examine the range I specify, then count the number of cells in that range that contain "Pacific Odyssey." You will specify absolute addresses for the range so you can copy the formula.

2. **With the insertion point in the Range text box, select the range A6:A25, press [F4], press [Tab], with the insertion point in the Criteria text box, click cell F7, then click OK**

   The number of Pacific Odyssey tours, 4, appears in cell G7. You want to calculate the total sales revenue for the Pacific Odyssey tours.

QUICK TIP
You can also sum, count, and average ranges with multiple criteria using the functions SUMIFS, COUNTIFS, and AVERAGEIFS

3. **Click cell H7, click the Math & Trig button in the Function Library group, scroll down the list of functions, then click SUMIF**

   The Function Arguments dialog box opens. You want to enter two ranges and a criterion; the first range is the one where you want Excel to search for the criteria entered. The second range contains the corresponding cells that will be totaled when the criterion you want Excel to search for in the first range is met.

4. **With the insertion point in the Range text box, select the range A6:A25, press [F4], press [Tab], with the insertion point in the Criteria text box, click cell F7, press [Tab], with the insertion point in the Sum_range text box, select the range B6:B25, press [F4], then click OK**

   Your formula asks Excel to search the range A6:A25, and where it finds the value shown in cell F7 (that is, when it finds the value Pacific Odyssey), add the corresponding amounts from column B. The revenue for the Pacific Odyssey tours, 12403, appears in cell H7. You want to calculate the average price paid for the Pacific Odyssey tours.

5. **Click cell I7, click the More Functions button in the Function Library group, point to Statistical, then click AVERAGEIF**

6. **With the insertion point in the Range text box, select the range A6:A25, press [F4], press [Tab], with the insertion point in the Criteria text box, click cell F7, press [Tab], with the insertion point in the Average_range text box, select the range B6:B25, press [F4], then click OK**

   The average price paid for the Pacific Odyssey tours, 3101, appears in cell I7.

7. **Select the range G7:I7, then drag the fill handle to fill the range G8:I10**

   Compare your results with those in Figure E-5.

8. **Add your name to the center of the footer, save the workbook, then preview and print the worksheet**

FIGURE E-3: Format of SUMIF function

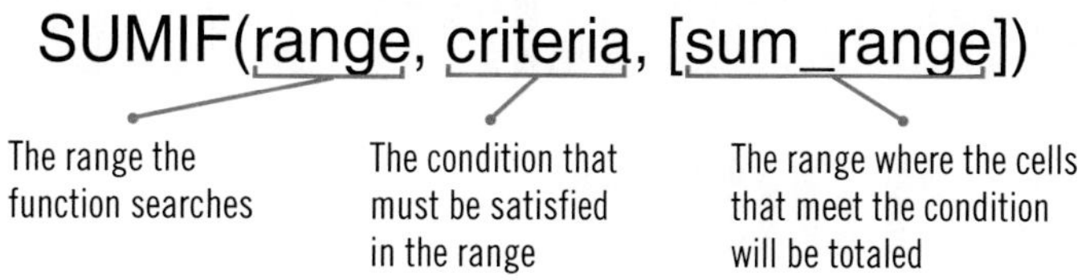

SUMIF(range, criteria, [sum_range])
The range the function searches
The condition that must be satisfied in the range
The range where the cells that meet the condition will be totaled

FIGURE E-4: COUNTIF function in the Function Arguments dialog box

Function Arguments
COUNTIF
Range
= reference
Criteria
= any
=
Counts the number of cells within a range that meet the given condition.
Range is the range of cells from which you want to count nonblank cells.
Formula result =
Help on this function
OK
Cancel

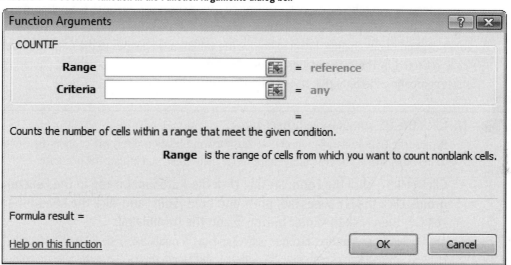

FIGURE E-5: Worksheet with conditional statistics

	A	B	C	D	E	F	G	H	I
4									
5	Tour	Price	Sale Date	Sales Representative					
6	Pacific Odyssey	$ 3,105	1/3/2010	Rafal Sanchez		Tour	Tours Sold	Revenue	Average Price
7	Essential India	$ 3,933	1/4/2010	Anthony Dolongi		Pacific Odyssey	4	12403	3101
8	Old Japan	$ 2,100	1/4/2010	Gregor Blake		Old Japan	5	10505	2101
9	Essential India	$ 3,955	1/6/2010	Lin Guan		Down Under Exodus	5	14016	2803
10	Pacific Odyssey	$ 3,090	1/8/2010	Anthony Dolongi		Essential India	6	23583	3931
11	Down Under Exodus	$ 2,800	1/10/2010	Anthony Dolongi					
12	Old Japan	$ 2,099	1/12/2010	Gregor Blake					
13	Down Under Exodus	$ 2,804	1/13/2010	Rafal Sanchez					
14	Old Japan	$ 2,103	1/14/2010	Rafal Sanchez					
15	Down Under Exodus	$ 2,810	1/16/2010	Lin Guan					
16	Pacific Odyssey	$ 3,110	1/17/2010	Anthony Dolongi					
17	Essential India	$ 3,920	1/17/2010	Lin Guan					
18	Old Japan	$ 2,108	1/18/2010	Gregor Blake					
19	Down Under Exodus	$ 2,798	1/19/2010	Lin Guan					
20	Essential India	$ 3,875	1/19/2010	Lin Guan					
21	Old Japan	$ 2,095	1/21/2010	Gregor Blake					
22	Essential India	$ 3,945	1/23/2010	Rafal Sanchez					
23	Down Under Exodus	$ 2,804	1/27/2010	Gregor Blake					
24	Pacific Odyssey	$ 3,098	1/27/2010	Lin Guan					
25	Essential India	$ 3,955	1/29/2010	Rafal Sanchez					

Conditional statistics

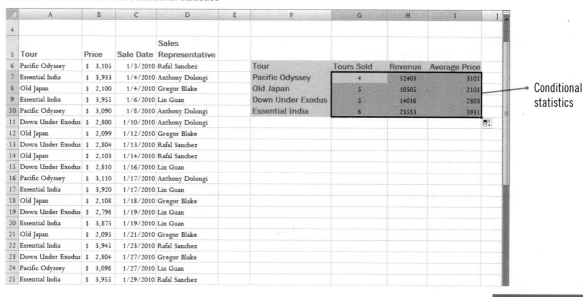

Consolidating Data Using a Formula

When you want to summarize similar data that exists in different sheets or workbooks, you can **consolidate**, or combine and display, the data in one sheet. For example, you might have entered departmental sales figures on four different store sheets that you want to consolidate on one summary sheet, showing total departmental sales for all stores. The best way to consolidate data is to use cell references to the various sheets on a consolidation, or summary, sheet. Because they reference other sheets that are usually behind the summary sheet, such references effectively create another dimension in the workbook and are called **3-D references**, as shown in Figure E-6. You can reference, or **link** to, data in other sheets and in other workbooks. Linking to a worksheet or workbook is a better method than retyping calculated results from the worksheet or workbook because the data values on which calculated totals depend might change. If you reference the values, any changes to the original values are automatically reflected in the consolidation sheet. ▰▰▰ Kate asks you to prepare a January sales summary sheet comparing the total U.S. revenue for the tours sold in the month.

STEPS

QUICK TIP

You can also consolidate data using named ranges. For example, you might have entered team sales figures using the names team1, team2, and team3 on different sheets that you want to consolidate on one summary sheet. As you enter the summary formula you can click the Formulas tab, click the Use in Formula button in the Defined Names group, and select the range name.

1. **Click the US Summary Jan sheet tab**

   Because the US Summary Jan sheet (which is the consolidation sheet) will contain the reference to the data in the other sheets, the cell pointer must reside there when you initiate the reference.

2. **Click cell B7, click the Formulas tab, click the AutoSum button in the Function Library group, click the NY sheet tab, press and hold [Shift] and click the Miami sheet tab, click cell G7, then click the Enter button ✓ on the formula bar**

   The US Summary Jan sheet becomes active, and the formula bar reads =SUM(NY:Miami!G7), as shown in Figure E-7. NY:Miami references the NY, Chicago, and Miami sheets. The ! (exclamation point) is an **external reference indicator**, meaning that the cells referenced are outside the active sheet; G7 is the actual cell reference you want to total in the external sheets. The result, 12, appears in cell B7 of the US Summary Jan sheet; it is the sum of the number of Pacific Odyssey tours sold and referenced in cell G7 of the NY, Chicago, and Miami sheets. Because the Revenue data is in the column to the right of the Tours Sold column on the NY, Chicago, and Miami sheets, you can copy the tours sold summary formula, with its relative addresses, into the cell that holds the revenue summary information.

3. **Drag the fill handle to copy the formula in cell B7 to cell C7**

   The result, 37405, appears in cell C7 of the US Summary Jan sheet, showing the sum of the Pacific Odyssey tour revenue referenced in cell H7 of the NY, Chicago, and Miami sheets.

QUICK TIP

You can also use a summary worksheet to consolidate yearly sales figures. Place data for each quarter on a separate sheet. On a summary sheet, use a row for each quarter that references each quarter's sales. Then sum the quarterly information to display total yearly sales.

4. **In the US Summary Jan sheet, with the range B7:C7 selected, drag the fill handle to fill the range B8:C10**

   You can test a consolidation reference by changing one cell value on which the formula is based and seeing if the formula result changes.

5. **Click the Chicago sheet tab, edit cell A6 to read Pacific Odyssey, then click the US Summary Jan sheet tab**

   The number of Pacific Odyssey tours sold is automatically updated to 13 and the revenue is increased to 40280, as shown in Figure E-8.

6. **Click the Insert tab, click the Header & Footer button in the Text group, click the Go to Footer button, enter your name in the center text box, click cell A1, then click the Normal button ▦ in the status bar**

FIGURE E-6: Consolidating data from three worksheets

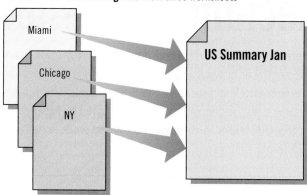

FIGURE E-7: Worksheet showing total Pacific Odyssey tours sold

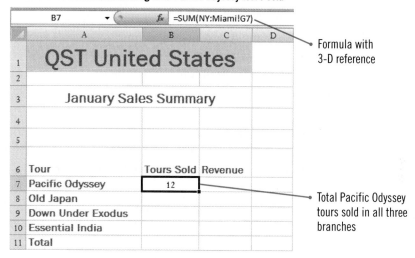

Formula with 3-D reference

Total Pacific Odyssey tours sold in all three branches

FIGURE E-8: US Summary Jan worksheet with updated totals

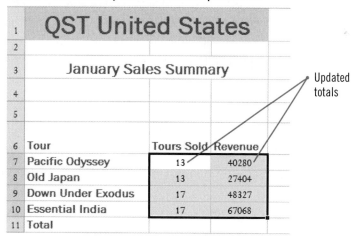

Updated totals

Linking data between workbooks

Just as you can link data between cells in a worksheet and between sheets in a workbook, you can link workbooks so that changes made in referenced cells in one workbook are reflected in the consolidation sheet in the other workbook. To link a single cell between workbooks, open both workbooks, select the cell to receive the linked data, type = (the equal sign), select the cell in the other workbook containing the data to be linked, then press [Enter]. Excel automatically inserts the name of the referenced workbook in the cell reference. For example, if the linked data is contained in cell C7 of worksheet New in the Products workbook, the cell entry reads ='[Product.xlsx]New'!$C$7. To perform calculations, enter formulas on the consolidation sheet using cells in the supporting sheets. If you are linking more than one cell, you can copy the linked data to the Clipboard, select the upper left cell in the workbook to receive the link, click the Home tab, click the Paste list arrow, then click Paste Link.

Checking Formulas for Errors

When formulas result in errors, Excel displays an error value based on the error type. See Table E-1 for a description of the error types and error codes that might appear in worksheets. The IFERROR function simplifies the error-checking process for your worksheets. This function displays a message or value that you specify, rather than the one automatically generated by Excel, if there is an error in a formula. ▆▆▆▆ Kate asks you to use formulas to compare the tour revenues for January. You will use the IFERROR function to help catch formula errors.

STEPS

1. **Click cell B11, click the Formulas tab, click the AutoSum button in the Function Library group, then click the Enter button ☑ on the formula bar**

   The number of tours sold, 60, appears in cell B11.

2. **Drag the fill handle to copy the formula in cell B11 into cell C11**

   The tour revenue total of 183079 appears in cell C11. You decide to enter a formula to calculate the percentage of revenue the Pacific Odyssey tour represents by dividing the individual tour revenue figures by the total revenue figure. To help with error checking, you decide to enter the formula using the IFERROR function.

3. **Click cell B14, click the Logical button in the Function Library group, click IFERROR, with the insertion point in the Value text box, click cell C7, type /, click cell C11, press [Tab], in the Value_if_error text box, type ERROR, then click OK**

   The percentage of Pacific Odyssey tour revenue of 22.00% appears in cell B14. You want to be sure that your error message will display properly, so you decide to test it by intentionally creating an error. You copy and paste the formula—which has a relative address in the denominator, where an absolute address should be used.

4. **Drag the fill handle to copy the formula in cell B14 into the range B15:B17**

   The ERROR value appears in cells B15:B17, as shown in Figure E-9. The errors are a result of the relative address for C11 in the denominator of the copied formula. Changing the relative address of C11 in the copied formula to an absolute address of $C$11 will correct the errors.

QUICK TIP
You can also check formulas for errors using the buttons in the Formula Auditing group on the Formulas tab.

5. **Double-click cell B14, select C11 in the formula, press [F4], then click ☑ on the formula bar**

   The formula now contains an absolute reference to cell C11.

6. **Copy the corrected formula in cell B14 into the range B15:B17**

   The tour revenue percentages now appear in all four cells, without error messages, as shown in Figure E-10.

7. **Save the workbook, print the worksheet, then close the workbook**

Correcting circular references

A cell with a circular reference contains a formula that refers to its own cell location. If you accidentally enter a formula with a circular reference, a warning box opens, alerting you to the problem. Click OK to open a Help window explaining how to find the circular reference. In simple formulas, a circular reference is easy to spot. To correct it, edit the formula to remove any reference to the cell where the formula is located.

FIGURE E-9: Worksheet with error codes

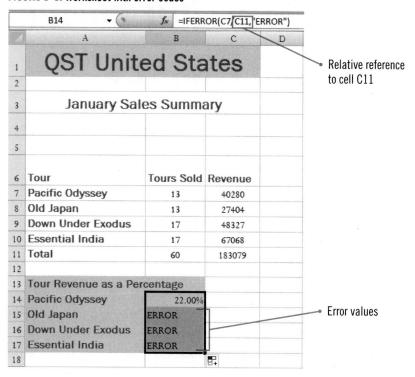

Relative reference
to cell C11

Error values

FIGURE E-10: Worksheet with tour percentages

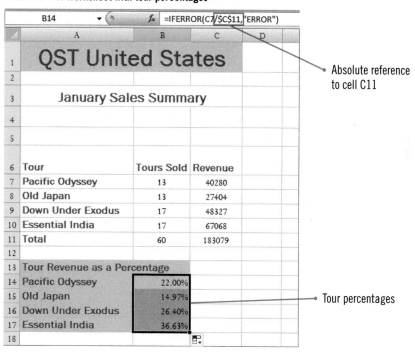

Absolute reference
to cell C11

Tour percentages

TABLE E-1: Understanding error values

error value	cause of error	error value	cause of error
#DIV/0!	A number is divided by 0	#NAME?	Formula contains text error
#NA	A value in a formula is not available	#NULL!	Invalid intersection of areas
#NUM!	Invalid use of a number in a formula	#REF!	Invalid cell reference
#VALUE!	Wrong type of formula argument or operand	#####	Column is not wide enough to display data

Constructing Formulas Using Named Ranges

To make your worksheet easier to follow, you can assign names to cells and ranges. You can also use names in formulas to make them easier to build and to reduce formula errors. For example, a formula named revenue-cost is easier to understand than the formula A5-A8. Names can use uppercase or lowercase letters as well as digits, but cannot have spaces. After you name a cell or range, you can define its **scope**, or the worksheets where it can be used. When defining a name's scope, you can limit its use to a worksheet or make it available to the entire workbook. If you move a named cell or range, its name moves with it, and if you add or remove rows or column to the worksheet the ranges are adjusted to their new position in the worksheet. When used in formulas, names become absolute cell references by default. ▓▓▓▓ Kate asks you to calculate the number of days before each tour departs. You will use range names to construct the formula.

STEPS

1. **Open the file** EX E-2.xlsx **from the drive and folder where you store your Data Files, then save it as** Tours

2. **Click cell** B4, **click the** Formulas tab **if necessary, click the** Define Name button **in the Defined Names group**

   The New Name dialog box opens, as shown in Figure E-11. You can name ranges containing dates to make formulas that perform date calculations easier to build.

3. **Type** current_date **in the Name text box, click the** Scope list arrow, **click** April Tours, **then click** OK

   The name assigned to cell B4, current_date, appears in the Name box. Because its scope is the April Tours worksheet, the range name current_date will appear on the name list on that worksheet only. You can also name ranges that contain dates.

4. **Select the range** B7:B13, **click the** Define Name button **in the Defined Names group, enter** tour_date **in the Name text box, click the** Scope list arrow, **click** April Tours, **then click** OK

   Now you can use the named range and named cell in a formula. The formula =tour_date–current_date is easier to understand than =B7-$B$4.

5. **Click cell** C7, **type** =, **click the** Use in Formula button **in the Defined Names group, click** tour_date, **type** –, **click the** Use in Formula button, **click** current_date, **then click the** Enter button ☑ **on the formula bar**

   The number of days before the Pacific Odyssey tour departs, 10, appears in cell C7. You can use the same formula to calculate the number of days before the other tours depart.

6. **Drag the fill handle to copy the formula in cell** C7 **into the range** C8:C13, **then compare your formula results with those in Figure E-12**

7. **Save the workbook**

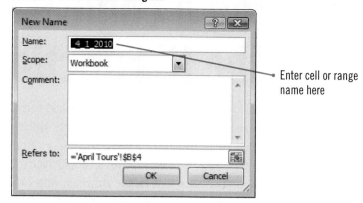

FIGURE E-11: New Name dialog box

Enter cell or range name here

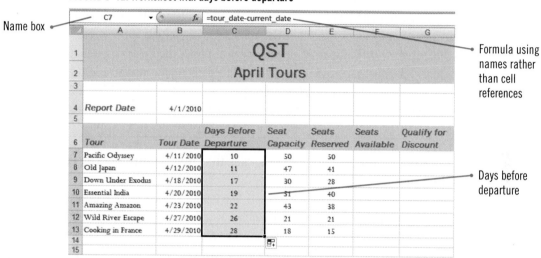

FIGURE E-12: Worksheet with days before departure

Name box

Formula using names rather than cell references

Days before departure

Managing workbook names

You can use the Name Manager to create, delete, and edit names in a workbook. Click the Name Manager button in the Defined Names group on the Formulas tab to open the Name Manager dialog box, as shown in Figure E-13. Click the New button to create a new named cell or range, click Edit to change a highlighted cell name, and click Delete to remove a highlighted name. Click Filter to see options for displaying specific criteria for displaying names.

FIGURE E-13: Name Manager dialog box

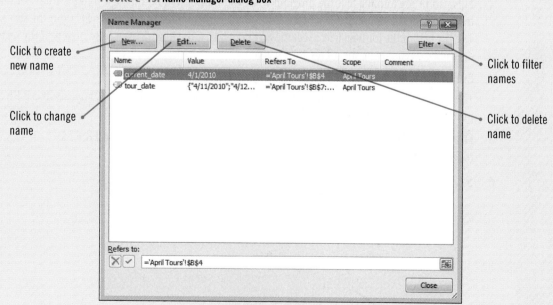

Click to create new name

Click to change name

Click to filter names

Click to delete name

Building a Logical Formula with the IF Function

You can build a logical formula using an IF function. A **logical formula** makes calculations based on criteria that you create, called **stated conditions**. For example, you can build a formula to calculate bonuses based on a person's performance rating. If a person is rated a 5 (the stated condition) on a scale of 1 to 5, with 5 being the highest rating, he or she receives an additional 10% of his or her salary as a bonus; otherwise, there is no bonus. A condition that can be answered with a true or false response is called a **logical test**. The IF function has three parts, separated by commas: a condition or logical test, an action to take if the logical test or condition is true, and an action to take if the logical test or condition is false. Another way of expressing this is: IF(test_cond,do_this,else_this). Translated into an Excel IF function, the formula to calculate bonuses might look like this: IF(Rating=5,Salary*0.10,0). In other words, if the rating equals 5, multiply the salary by 0.10 (the decimal equivalent of 10%), then place the result in the selected cell; if the rating does not equal 5, place a 0 in the cell. When entering the logical test portion of an IF statement, you typically use some combination of the comparison operators listed in Table E-2. ⬛⬛⬛ Kate asks you to use an IF function to calculate the number of seats available for each tour in April.

STEPS

1. **Click cell F7, on the Formulas tab, click the Logical button in the Function Library group, then click IF**

   The Function Arguments dialog box opens. You want the function to calculate the seats available as follows: If the seat capacity is greater than the number of seats reserved, calculate the number of seats that are available (capacity–number reserved), and place the result in cell F7; otherwise, place the text "None" in the cell.

2. **With the insertion point in the Logical_test text box, click cell D7, type >, click cell E7, then press [Tab]**

   The symbol (>) represents "greater than." So far, the formula reads "If the seating capacity is greater than the number of reserved seats,". The next part of the function tells Excel the action to take if the capacity exceeds the reserved number of seats.

3. **With the insertion point in the Value_if_true text box, click cell D7, type –, click cell E7 , then press [Tab]**

   This part of the formula tells the program what you want it to do if the logical test is true. Continuing the translation of the formula, this part means "Subtract the number of reserved seats from the seat capacity." The last part of the formula tells Excel the action to take if the logical test is false (that is, if the seat capacity does not exceed the number of reserved seats).

4. **Enter None in the Value_if_false text box, then click OK**

   The function is complete, and the result, None (the number of available seats), appears in cell F7, as shown in Figure E-14.

5. **Drag the fill handle to copy the formula in cell F7 into the range F8:F13**

   Compare your results with Figure E-15.

6. **Save the workbook**

Analyzing Data Using Formulas

FIGURE E-14: Worksheet with IF function

	A	B	C	D	E	F	G
	F7 ▼ f_x =IF(D7>E7,D7-E7,"None")						
1			QST				
2			April Tours				
3							
4	*Report Date*	4/1/2010					
5							
6	*Tour*	*Tour Date*	*Days Before Departure*	*Seat Capacity*	*Seats Reserved*	*Seats Available*	*Qualify for Discount*
7	Pacific Odyssey	4/11/2010	10	50	50	None	
8	Old Japan	4/12/2010	11	47	41		
9	Down Under Exodus	4/18/2010	17	30	28		
10	Essential India	4/20/2010	19	51	40		
11	Amazing Amazon	4/23/2010	22	43	38		
12	Wild River Escape	4/27/2010	26	21	21		
13	Cooking in France	4/29/2010	28	18	15		
14							

IF function   Seats available

FIGURE E-15: Worksheet showing seats available

	A	B	C	D	E	F	G
	F7 ▼ f_x =IF(D7>E7,D7-E7,"None")						
1			QST				
2			April Tours				
3							
4	*Report Date*	4/1/2010					
5							
6	*Tour*	*Tour Date*	*Days Before Departure*	*Seat Capacity*	*Seats Reserved*	*Seats Available*	*Qualify for Discount*
7	Pacific Odyssey	4/11/2010	10	50	50	None	
8	Old Japan	4/12/2010	11	47	41	6	
9	Down Under Exodus	4/18/2010	17	30	28	2	
10	Essential India	4/20/2010	19	51	40	11	
11	Amazing Amazon	4/23/2010	22	43	38	5	
12	Wild River Escape	4/27/2010	26	21	21	None	
13	Cooking in France	4/29/2010	28	18	15	3	
14							

Seats available

TABLE E-2: Comparison operators

operator	meaning	operator	meaning
<	Less than	<=	Less than or equal to
>	Greater than	>=	Greater than or equal to
=	Equal to	<>	Not equal to

Building a Logical Formula with the AND Function

You can also build a logical function using the AND function. The AND function evaluates all of its arguments and **returns**, or displays, TRUE if every logical test in the formula is true. The AND function returns a value of FALSE if one or more of its logical tests is false. The AND function arguments can include text, numbers, or cell references. ▞▞▞ Kate wants you to analyze the tour data to find tours that qualify for discounting. You will use the AND function to check for tours with seats available and that depart within 21 days.

STEPS

1. **Click cell G7, click the Logical button in the Function Library group, then click AND**

   The Function Arguments dialog box opens. You want the function to evaluate the discount qualification as follows: There must be seats available and the tour must depart within 21 days.

TROUBLE
If you get a formula error, check to be sure that you typed the quotation marks around None.

2. **With the insertion point in the Logical1 text box, click cell F7, type < >, type "None", then press [Tab]**

   The symbol (<>) represents "not equal to ." So far, the formula reads "If the number of seats available is not equal to None,"—in other words, if it is an integer. The next logical test checks the number of days before the tour departs.

3. **With the insertion point in the Logical2 text box, click cell C7, type <21, then click OK**

   The function is complete, and the result, FALSE, appears in cell G7, as shown in Figure E-16.

4. **Drag the fill handle to copy the formula in cell G7 into the range G8:G13**

   Compare your results with Figure E-17.

5. **Click the Insert tab, click the Header & Footer button in the Text group, click the Go to Footer button, enter your name in the center text box, click cell A1, then click the Normal button ▦ in the status bar**

6. **Save the workbook, then preview and print the worksheet**

Using the OR and NOT logical functions

The OR logical function has the same syntax as the AND function, but rather than returning TRUE if every argument is true, the OR function will return TRUE if any of its arguments are TRUE. It will only return FALSE if all of its arguments are FALSE. The NOT logical function reverses the value of its argument. For example NOT(TRUE) reverses its argument of TRUE and returns FALSE. This can be used in a worksheet to ensure that a cell is not equal to a particular value. See Table E-3 for examples of the AND, OR, and NOT functions.

TABLE E-3: Examples of AND, OR, and NOT functions with cell values A1=10 and B1=20

function	formula	result
AND	=AND(A1>5,B1>25)	FALSE
OR	=OR(A1>5,B1>25)	TRUE
NOT	=NOT(A1=0)	TRUE

FIGURE E-16: Worksheet with AND function

	A	B	C	D	E	F	G	
	G7	▾	f_x	=AND(F7<>"None",C7<21)				
1				QST				
2				April Tours				
3								
4	Report Date	4/1/2010						
5								
6	Tour	Tour Date	Days Before Departure	Seat Capacity	Seats Reserved	Seats Available	Qualify for Discount	
7	Pacific Odyssey	4/11/2010	10	50	50	None	FALSE	
8	Old Japan	4/12/2010	11	47	41	6		
9	Down Under Exodus	4/18/2010	17	30	28	2		
10	Essential India	4/20/2010	19	51	40	11		
11	Amazing Amazon	4/23/2010	22	43	38	5		
12	Wild River Escape	4/27/2010	26	21	21	None		
13	Cooking in France	4/29/2010	28	18	15	3		
14								

AND function   Result of AND function

FIGURE E-17: Worksheet with discount status evaluated

	A	B	C	D	E	F	G	
	G7	▾	f_x	=AND(F7<>"None",C7<21)				
1				QST				
2				April Tours				
3								
4	Report Date	4/1/2010						
5								
6	Tour	Tour Date	Days Before Departure	Seat Capacity	Seats Reserved	Seats Available	Qualify for Discount	
7	Pacific Odyssey	4/11/2010	10	50	50	None	FALSE	
8	Old Japan	4/12/2010	11	47	41	6	TRUE	
9	Down Under Exodus	4/18/2010	17	30	28	2	TRUE	
10	Essential India	4/20/2010	19	51	40	11	TRUE	
11	Amazing Amazon	4/23/2010	22	43	38	5	FALSE	
12	Wild River Escape	4/27/2010	26	21	21	None	FALSE	
13	Cooking in France	4/29/2010	28	18	15	3	FALSE	
14								

Calculating Payments with the PMT Function

PMT is a financial function that calculates the periodic payment amount for money borrowed. For example, if you want to borrow money to buy a car, and you know the principal amount, interest rate, and loan term, the PMT function can calculate your monthly payment. Say you want to borrow $20,000 at 6.5% interest and pay the loan off in five years. The Excel PMT function can tell you that your monthly payment will be $391.32. The main parts of the PMT function are: PMT(rate, nper, pv). See Figure E-18 for an illustration of a PMT function that calculates the monthly payment in the car loan example. ▰▰▰▰ For several months, QST's United States region has been discussing opening a new branch in San Francisco. Kate has obtained quotes from three different lenders on borrowing $259,000 to begin the expansion. She obtained loan quotes from a commercial bank, a venture capitalist, and an investment banker. She wants you to summarize the information using the Excel PMT function.

STEPS

1. **Click the Loan sheet tab, click cell F5, click the Formulas tab, click the Financial button in the Function Library group, scroll down the list of functions, then click PMT**

2. **With the insertion point in the Rate text box, click cell D5 on the worksheet, type /12, then press [Tab]**
   You must divide the annual interest by 12 because you are calculating monthly, not annual, payments.

3. **With the insertion point in the Nper text box, click cell E5; click the Pv text box, click cell B5, then click OK**
   The payment of (5445.81) in cell F5 appears in red, indicating that it is a negative amount. Excel displays the result of a PMT function as a negative value to reflect the negative cash flow the loan represents to the borrower. To show the monthly payment as a positive number, you can place a minus sign in front of the Pv cell reference in the function. The Fv and Type arguments are optional: The argument Fv is the future value, or the total amount you want to obtain after all payments. If you omit it, Excel assumes the Fv is 0. The Type argument indicates when the payments are made; 0 is the end of the period, and 1 is the beginning of the period. The default is the end of the period.

4. **Double-click cell F5 and edit it so it reads =PMT(D5/12,E5,-B5), then click the Enter button ☑ on the formula bar**
   A positive value of $5,445.81 now appears in cell F5, as shown in Figure E-19. You can use the same formula to generate the monthly payments for the other loans.

5. **With cell F5 selected, drag the fill handle to fill the range F6:F7**
   A monthly payment of $8,266.30 for the venture capitalist loan appears in cell F6. A monthly payment of $11,826.41 for the investment banker loan appears in cell F7. The loans with shorter terms have much higher payments. You will not know the entire financial picture until you calculate the total payments and total interest for each lender.

6. **Click cell G5, type =, click cell E5, type *, click cell F5, then press [Tab], in cell H5, type =, click cell G5, type –, click cell B5, then click ☑**

7. **Copy the formulas in cells G5:H5 into the range G6:H7, then click cell A1**
   Your worksheet appears as shown in Figure E-20. You can experiment with different interest rates, loan amounts, or terms for any one of the lenders; the PMT function generates a new set of values automatically.

8. **Add your name to the center section of the footer, save the workbook, preview and print the worksheet, then close the workbook and exit Excel**

FIGURE E-18: Example of PMT function for car loan

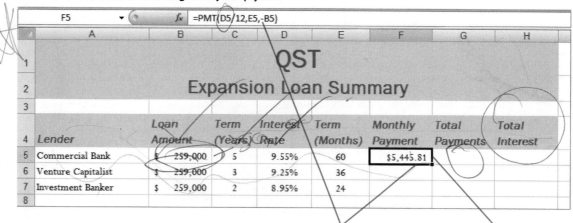

$$PMT(0.065/12, 60, 20000) = \$391.32$$

Interest rate per period (rate)
Number of payments (nper)
Present value of loan amount (pv)
Monthly payment calculated

FIGURE E-19: PMT function calculating monthly loan payment

F5		fx	=PMT(D5/12,E5,-B5)

QST

Expansion Loan Summary

Lender	Loan Amount	Term (Years)	Interest Rate	Term (Months)	Monthly Payment	Total Payments	Total Interest
Commercial Bank	$ 259,000	5	9.55%	60	$5,445.81		
Venture Capitalist	$ 259,000	3	9.25%	36			
Investment Banker	$ 259,000	2	8.95%	24			

Minus sign before present value displays payment as a positive amount

Monthly payment calculated

FIGURE E-20: Completed worksheet

QST

Expansion Loan Summary

Lender	Loan Amount	Term (Years)	Interest Rate	Term (Months)	Monthly Payment	Total Payments	Total Interest
Commercial Bank	$ 259,000	5	9.55%	60	$5,445.81	$ 326,748.77	$ 67,748.77
Venture Capitalist	$ 259,000	3	9.25%	36	$8,266.30	$ 297,586.78	$ 38,586.78
Investment Banker	$ 259,000	2	8.95%	24	$11,826.41	$ 283,833.78	$ 24,833.78

Copied formula calculates total payments and interest for remaining two loan options

Calculating future value with the FV function

You can use the FV (Future Value) function to determine the amount of money a given monthly investment will amount to, at a given interest rate, after a given number of payment periods. The syntax is similar to that of the PMT function: FV(rate,nper,pmt,pv,type). The rate is the interest paid by the financial institution, the nper is the number of periods, and the pmt is the amount that you deposit. For example, suppose you want to invest $1000 every month for the next 12 months into an account that pays 12% a year, and you want to know how much you will have at the end of 12 months (that is, its future value). You enter the function FV(.01,12,-1000), and Excel returns the value $12,682.50 as the future value of your investment. As with the PMT function, the units for the rate and nper must be consistent. If you made monthly payments on a three-year loan at 6% annual interest, you use the rate .06/12 and 36 periods (12*3). The arguments pv and type are optional; pv is the present value, or the total amount the series of payments is worth now. If you omit it, Excel assumes the pv is 0. The "type" argument indicates when the payments are made; 0 is the end of the period, and 1 is the beginning of the period. The default is the end of the period.

Practice

▼ CONCEPTS REVIEW

FIGURE E-21

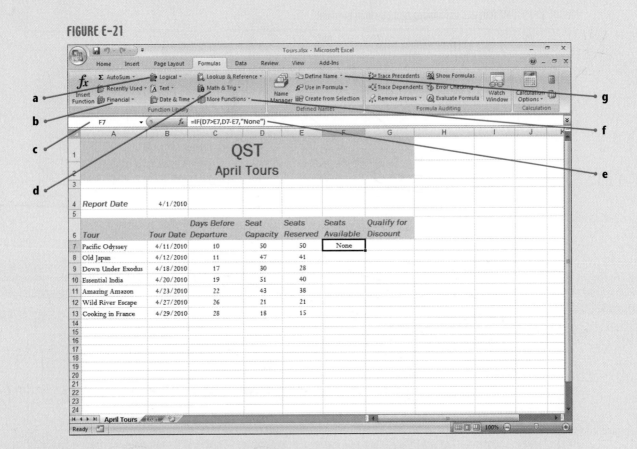

1. Which element points to the area where the name of a selected cell or range is displayed?
2. Which element points to a logical formula?
3. Which element do you click to add a statistical function to a worksheet?
4. Which element do you click to name a cell or range?
5. Which element do you click to insert an IF function into a worksheet?
6. Which element do you click to add a PMT function to a worksheet?
7. Which element do you click to add a SUMIF function to a worksheet?

Match each term with the statement that best describes it.

8. SUMIF
9. PROPER
10. test_cond
11. FV
12. PV

a. Function used to change the first letter of a string to uppercase
b. Function used to determine the future amount of an investment
c. Part of the PMT function that represents the loan amount
d. Part of the IF function in which the conditions are stated
e. Function used to conditionally total cells

Select the best answer from the list of choices.

13. **When you enter the rate and nper arguments in a PMT function, you must:**
    - **a.** Use monthly units instead of annual units.
    - **b.** Multiply both units by 12.
    - **c.** Divide both values by 12.
    - **d.** Be consistent in the units used.

14. **To express conditions such as less than or equal to, you can use a(n):**
    - **a.** Statistical function.
    - **b.** PMT function.
    - **c.** Text formula.
    - **d.** Comparison operator.

15. **Which of the following statements is false?**
    - **a.** If you move a named cell or range, its name moves with it.
    - **b.** Named ranges make formulas easier to build.
    - **c.** Names cannot contain spaces.
    - **d.** When used in formulas, names become relative cell references by default.

16. **Which of the following is an external reference indicator in a formula?**
    - **a.** :
    - **b.** &
    - **c.** !
    - **d.** =

▼ SKILLS REVIEW

1. **Format data using text functions.**
   - **a.** Start Excel, open the file EX E-3.xlsx from the drive and folder where you store your Data Files, then save it as **Reviews**.
   - **b.** On the Managers worksheet, select the range A2:A9 and, using the Text to Columns button on the Data tab, separate the names into two text columns. (*Hint*: The delimiter is a space.)
   - **c.** In cell D2, enter the text formula to convert the first letter of the department in cell C2 to uppercase, then copy the formula in cell D2 into the range D3:D9.
   - **d.** In cell E2, enter the text formula to convert all letters of the department in cell C2 to uppercase, then copy the formula in cell E2 into the range E3:E9.
   - **e.** In cell F2, use the text formula to convert all letters of the department in cell C2 to lowercase, then copy the formula in cell F2 into the range F3:F9.
   - **f.** In cell G2, use the text formula to substitute "Human Resources" for "hr" in cell F2. (*Hint*: In the Function Arguments dialog box, Text is F2, Old_text is hr, and New_text is Human Resources.) Copy the formula in cell G2 into the range G3:G9 to change the other cells containing hr to Human Resources. (Note that the marketing and sales entries will not change because the formula searches for the text hr).
   - **g.** Save your work, then enter your name in the worksheet footer. Compare your screen to Figure E-22.
   - **h.** Display the formulas in the worksheet, then print the worksheet.
   - **i.** Redisplay the formula results.

   FIGURE E-22

	A	B	C	D	E	F	G
1	Name		Department	PROPER	UPPER	LOWER	SUBSTITUTE
2	Paul	Keys	hR	Hr	HR	hr	Human Resources
3	Shimada	Story	hR	Hr	HR	hr	Human Resources
4	Kim	Hadley	MarKeting	Marketing	MARKETING	marketing	marketing
5	Albert	Ny	MarKeting	Marketing	MARKETING	marketing	marketing
6	Reggie	Delgado	saLEs	Sales	SALES	sales	sales
7	Harry	DePaul	saLEs	Sales	SALES	sales	sales
8	Mel	Abbott	hR	Hr	HR	hr	Human Resources
9	Jody	Wallace	MarKeting	Marketing	MARKETING	marketing	marketing
10							

2. **Sum a range of data conditionally.**
   - **a.** Make the HR sheet active.
   - **b.** In cell B20, use the COUNTIF function to count the number of employees with a rating of 5.
   - **c.** In cell B21, use the AVERAGEIF function to average the salaries of employees with a rating of 5.
   - **d.** In cell B22, enter the SUMIF function that totals the salaries of employees with a rating of 5.
   - **e.** Format cells B21 and B22 with the Number format using commas and no decimals. Save your work.

3. Consolidate data using a formula.

a. Make the Summary sheet active.

b. In cell B4, use the AutoSum function to total cell F15 on the HR and Accounting sheets.

c. Format cell B4 with the Accounting number format.

d. Enter your name in the worksheet footer, then save your work. Compare your screen to Figure E-23.

e. Display the formula in the worksheet, then print the worksheet.

f. Redisplay the formula results in the worksheet.

FIGURE E-23

	A	B
1	**Payroll Summary**	
2		
3		**Salary**
4	**TOTAL**	$ 565,787.00
5		
6		

4. Check formulas for errors.

a. Make the HR sheet active.

b. In cell I6, use the IFERROR function to display "ERROR" in the event that the formula F6/F15 results in a formula error. (*Note*: This formula will generate an intentional error, which you will correct in a moment.)

c. Copy the formula in cell I6 into the range I7:I14.

d. Correct the formula in cell I6 by making the denominator, F15, an absolute address.

e. Copy the new formula in cell I6 into the range I7:I14.

f. Format the range I6:I14 as percentage with two decimal places.

g. Save your work.

5. Construct formulas using named ranges.

a. On the HR sheet, name the range C6:C14 **review_date** and limit the scope of the name to the HR worksheet.

b. In cell E6, enter the formula **=review_date+183**, using the Use in Formula button to enter the cell name.

c. Copy the formula in cell E6 into the range E7:E14.

d. Use the Name Manager to add a comment of "Date of last review" to the review_date name. (*Hint*: In the Name Manager dialog box, click the review_date name, then click Edit to enter the comment.)

e. Save your work.

6. Build a logical formula with the IF function.

a. In cell G6, use the Function Arguments dialog box to enter the formula **=IF(D6=5,F6*0.05,0)**

b. Copy the formula in cell G6 into the range G7:G14.

c. In cell G15, use AutoSum to total the range G6:G14.

d. Format the range G6:G15 with the Currency number format, using the $ symbol and no decimal places.

e. Save your work.

7. Build a logical formula with the AND function.

a. In cell H6, use the Function Arguments dialog box to enter the formula **=AND(G6>0,B6>5)**.

b. Copy the formula in cell H6 into the range H7:H14.

c. Enter your name in the worksheet footer, save your work, compare your worksheet to Figure E-24, then print the worksheet.

d. Make the Accounting sheet active.

e. In cell H6, indicate if the employee needs more development hours to reach the minimum of 5: Use the Function Arguments dialog box for the NOT function to enter **B6>5** in the Logical text box. Copy the formula in cell H6 into the range H7:H14.

f. In cell I6, indicate if the employee needs to enroll in a quality class, as indicated by a rating less than 5 and having less than 5 development hours: Use the Function Arguments dialog box for the OR function to enter **D6<>5** in the Logical1 text box and **B6<=5** in the Logical2 text box. Copy the formula in cell I6 into the range I7:I14.

FIGURE E-24

	A	B	C	D	E	F	G	H	I
1			**Human Resources Department**						
2			**Merit Pay**						
3									
4									
5	Last Name	Professional Development Hours	Review Date	Rating	Next Review	Salary	Bonus	Pay Bonus	Percentage of Total
6	Barry	5	2/1/2010	4	8/3/2010	19,840	$0	FALSE	7.21%
7	Gray	8	3/1/2010	5	8/31/2010	26,700	$1,335	TRUE	9.71%
8	Greenwood	1	7/1/2010	3	12/31/2010	33,200	$0	FALSE	12.07%
9	Hemsley	3	4/1/2010	5	10/1/2010	25,500	$1,275	FALSE	9.27%
10	Kim	9	3/1/2010	3	8/31/2010	37,500	$0	FALSE	13.63%
11	Manchevski	8	5/1/2010	5	10/31/2010	36,500	$1,825	TRUE	13.27%
12	Marley	10	6/1/2010	4	12/1/2010	37,500	$0	FALSE	13.63%
13	Smith	6	1/1/2010	3	7/3/2010	28,600	$0	FALSE	10.40%
14	Storey	1	9/1/2010	5	3/3/2011	29,700	$1,485	FALSE	10.80%
15					Total	$ 275,040	$5,920		
16									
17									
18	**Department Statistics**								
19		**Rating of 5**							
20	Number	4							
21	Average Salary	29,600							
22	Total Salary	118,400							
23									

g. Enter your name in the worksheet footer, save your work, compare your screen to Figure E-25, then print the worksheet.

8. Calculate payments with the PMT function.

a. Make the Loan sheet active.

b. In cell B9, determine the monthly payment using the loan information shown: Use the Function Arguments dialog box to enter the formula **=PMT(B5/12,B6,-B4)**.

c. In cell B10, enter the formula **=B9*B6**.

d. In cell B11, enter the formula **=B10-B4**, then compare your screen to Figure E-26.

e. Enter your name in the worksheet footer, save the workbook, then print the worksheet.

f. Close the workbook, then exit Excel.

FIGURE E-25

Last Name	Professional Development Hours	Review Date	Rating	Next Review	Salary	Bonus	Hours Required	Enroll in Quality Class
		Accounting Department						
		Merit Pay						
Adams	8	3/10/2010	2	9/9/2010	21,647	$0	FALSE	TRUE
Greenwood	2	5/1/2010	5	10/31/2010	28,600	$1,430	TRUE	TRUE
LaMonte	6	8/1/2010	3	1/31/2011	33,200	$0	FALSE	TRUE
Healy	7	6/1/2010	4	12/1/2010	35,500	$0	FALSE	TRUE
Gosselin	9	3/8/2010	5	9/7/2010	39,500	$1,975	FALSE	FALSE
Ramerez	6	5/1/2010	5	10/31/2010	36,500	$1,825	FALSE	FALSE
Martin	10	6/1/2010	4	12/1/2010	36,500	$0	FALSE	TRUE
Small	6	1/1/2010	5	7/3/2010	29,600	$1,480	FALSE	FALSE
Zigler	6	9/15/2010	1	3/17/2011	29,700	$0	FALSE	TRUE
				Total	$ 290,747	$6,710		

FIGURE E-26

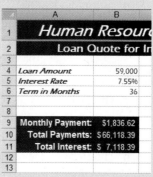

	A	B
1	*Human Resour*	
2	Loan Quote for In	
3		
4	*Loan Amount*	59,000
5	*Interest Rate*	7.55%
6	*Term in Months*	36
7		
8		
9	**Monthly Payment:**	$1,836.62
10	**Total Payments:**	$66,118.39
11	**Total Interest:**	$ 7,118.39
12		
13		

▼ INDEPENDENT CHALLENGE 1

As the accounting manager of Travel Well, a travel insurance company, you are reviewing the accounts payable information for your advertising accounts and prioritizing the overdue invoices for your collections service. You will analyze the invoices and use logical functions to emphasize priority accounts.

a. Start Excel, open the file EX E-4.xlsx from the drive and folder where you store your Data Files, then save it as **Ad Accounts**.

b. Name the range B7:B13 **invoice_date** and give the name a scope of the accounts payable worksheet.

c. Name the cell B4 **current_date** and give the name a scope of the accounts payable worksheet.

d. Enter a formula using the named range invoice_date in cell E7 that calculates the invoice due date by adding 30 to the invoice date.

e. Copy the formula in cell E7 to the range E8:E13.

f. In cell F7, enter a formula using the named range invoice_date and the named cell current_date that calculates the invoice age by subtracting the invoice date from the current date.

g. Copy the formula in cell F7 to the range F8:F13.

h. In cell G7, enter an IF function that calculates the number of days an invoice is overdue, assuming that an invoice must be paid in 30 days. (*Hint*: The Logical_test should check to see if the age of the invoice is greater than 30, the Value_if_true should calculate the current date minus the invoice due date, and the Value_if_false should be 0). Copy the IF function into the range G8:G13.

i. In cell H7, enter an AND function to prioritize the overdue invoices that are more than $1000 for collection services. (*Hint:* The Logical1 condition should check to see if the number of days overdue is more than 0 and the Logical2 condition should check if the amount is more than 1000). Copy the AND function into the range H8:H13.

j. Enter your name in the worksheet footer, then save, preview, and print the worksheet.

k. Close the workbook, then exit Excel.

Advanced Challenge Exercise

■ Use the "Refers to:" text box in the Name Manager dialog box to verify that the names in the worksheet refer to the correct ranges.

■ Use the filter in the Name Manager dialog box to verify that your names are scoped to the worksheet and not the workbook.

■ Use the filter in the Name Manager dialog box to verify that your names are defined, free of errors, and not part of a table.

▼ INDEPENDENT CHALLENGE 2

You are an auditor with a certified public accounting firm. Goals, a manufacturer of ice skating products based in Quebec, has contacted you to audit its first-quarter sales records. The management at Goals is considering opening a branch in Great Britain and needs its sales records audited to prepare the business plan. Specifically, they want to show what percent of annual sales each category represents. You will use a formula on a summary worksheet to summarize the sales for January, February, and March and to calculate the overall first-quarter percentage of the sales categories.

a. Start Excel, open the file EX E-5.xlsx from the drive and folder where you store your Data Files, then save it as **Goals Sales**.

b. In cell B10 of the Jan, Feb, and Mar sheets, enter the formulas to calculate the sales totals for the month.

c. For each month, in cell C5, create a formula calculating the percent of sales for the Sticks sales category. Use a function to display "ERROR" if there is a mistake in the formula. Verify that the percent appears with two decimal places. Copy this formula as necessary to complete the % of Sales data for all sales categories on all sheets. If any cells display "ERROR", fix the formulas in those cells.

d. In column B of the Summary sheet, use formulas to total the sales categories for the Jan, Feb, and Mar worksheets.

e. Locate the first-quarter sales total in cell B10 of the Summary sheet. Calculate the percent of each sales category on the Summary sheet. Use a function to display "ERROR" if there is a mistake in the formula. Copy this formula as necessary. If any cells display "ERROR", fix the formulas in those cells.

f. Enter your name in the Summary worksheet footer, then save, preview, and print the worksheet.

g. On the Products sheet, separate the product list in cell A1 into separate columns of text data. (*Hint*: The products are delimited with commas.) Widen the columns as necessary. Use the second row to display the products with the first letter of each word in uppercase, as shown in Figure E-27.

h. Enter your name in the Products worksheet footer, then save, preview, and print the worksheet.

i. Close the workbook, then exit Excel.

FIGURE E-27

	A	B	C	D	E	F
1	sticks	ice skates	apparel	pads	equipment bags	
2	Sticks	Ice Skates	Apparel	Pads	Equipment Bags	
3						

▼ INDEPENDENT CHALLENGE 3

As the owner of Best Dressed, a clothing boutique with a growing clientele, you are planning to expand your business into a neighboring city. Because you will have to purchase additional inventory and renovate your new rental space, you decide to take out a $20,000 loan to finance your expansion expenses. You check three loan sources: the Small Business Administration (SBA), your local bank, and a consortium of investors. The SBA will lend you the money at 7.5% interest, but you have to pay it off in three years. The local bank offers you the loan at 8.25% interest over four years. The consortium offers you a 7% loan, but they require you to pay it back in two years. To analyze all three loan options, you decide to build a loan summary worksheet. Using the loan terms provided, build a worksheet summarizing your options.

a. Start Excel, open a new workbook, then save it as **Dress Shop Loan**.

b. Using Figure E-28 as a guide, enter labels and worksheet data for the three loan sources. (*Hint*: The Aspect theme is used with Orange Accent 1 as the fill color in the first two rows and Orange, Accent 1, Darker 25% as the text color in the calculation area.)

c. Enter the monthly payment formula for your first loan source (making sure to show the payment as a positive amount), copy the formula as appropriate, then name the range containing the monthly payment formulas **Monthly_Payment** with a scope of the workbook.

FIGURE E-28

	A	B	C	D	E	F	G
1				Best Dressed			
2				Loan Options			
3							
4	Loan Source	Loan Amount	Interest Rate	# Payments	Monthly Payment	Total Payments	Total Interest
5	SBA	20,000	7.50%	36			
6	Bank	20,000	8.25%	48			
7	Investors	20,000	7.00%	24			
8							

Analyzing Data Using Formulas

▼ INDEPENDENT CHALLENGE 3 (CONTINUED)

d. Name the cell range containing the number of payments **Number_Payments** with the scope of the workbook.

e. Enter the formula for total payments for your first loan source using the named ranges Monthly_Payment and Number_Payments, then copy the formula as necessary.

f. Name the cell range containing the formulas for Total payments **Total_Payments**. Name the cell range containing the loan amounts **Loan_Amount**.

g. Enter the formula for total interest for your first loan source using the named ranges Total_Payments and Loan_Amount, then copy the formula as necessary.

h. Format the worksheet using formatting appropriate to the worksheet purpose, then enter your name in the worksheet footer.

i. Save, preview, and print the worksheet in landscape orientation, on a single page.

Advanced Challenge Exercise

- Turn on the print gridlines option for the worksheet.
- Turn on the printing of row and column headings.
- Print the worksheet formulas with the worksheet gridlines and headings on one page.
- Display the worksheet values.

j. Close the workbook then exit Excel.

▼ REAL LIFE INDEPENDENT CHALLENGE

You decide to create a weekly log of your daily aerobic exercise. As part of this log, you record your aerobic activity along with the number of minutes spent working out. If you do more than one activity in a day, for example, if you bike and walk, record each as a separate event. Along with each activity, you record the location where you exercise. For example, you may walk in the gym or outdoors. You will use the log to analyze the amount of time that you spend on each type of exercise.

a. Start Excel, open the file EX E-6.xlsx from the drive and folder where you store your Data Files, then save it as **Workout**.

b. Use the structure of the worksheet to record your aerobic exercise activities. Change the data in columns A, B, C, D, and F to reflect your activities, locations, and times. If you do not have any data to enter, use the provided worksheet data.

c. Use a SUMIF function in the column G cells to calculate the total minutes spent on each activity.

d. Enter an AVERAGEIF function in the column H cells to average the number of minutes spent on each activity.

e. Enter a COUNTIF function in the column I cells to calculate the number of sessions spent on each activity.

Advanced Challenge Exercise

- Enter one of your activities with a specific location, such as Walk Outdoors, in a column F cell, then enter the SUMIFS function in the adjacent column G cell that calculates the total number of minutes spent on that activity in the specific location (such as walking ...outdoors).
- Enter the AVERAGEIFS function in the corresponding column H cell that calculates the average number of minutes spent on the activity in the specified location.
- Enter the COUNTIFS function in the corresponding column I cell that calculates the number of days spent on the activity in the specific location.

f. Enter your name in the worksheet footer, then save, preview, and print the worksheet.

g. Close the workbook, then exit Excel.

▼ VISUAL WORKSHOP

Open the file EX E-7.xlsx from the drive and folder where you store your Data Files, then save it as **Quarterly Sales Summary**. Create the worksheet shown in Figure E-29 using the data in columns B, C, and D. (*Hints:* Use AND formulas to determine if a person is eligible for a bonus, and use IF formulas to enter the bonus amounts. An employee with a performance rating of seven or higher and who meets the sales quota receives a bonus of one percent of the sales. If the rating is less than seven, or if the sales amounts are less than the quota, no bonus is awarded.) Enter your name in the worksheet footer, then preview and print the worksheet.

FIGURE E-29

	A	B	C	D	E	F
1	Bonus Pay Summary					
2						
3	Last Name	Quota	Sales	Performance Rating	Eligible	Bonus Amount
4	Allen	$100,000	$125,400	7	TRUE	$1,254
5	Gray	$80,000	$75,420	3	FALSE	$0
6	Greenwood	$90,000	$83,540	9	FALSE	$0
7	Hanson	$120,000	$132,980	5	FALSE	$0
8	Kerns	$150,000	$147,650	8	FALSE	$0
9	Maloney	$140,000	$149,800	5	FALSE	$0
10	Martin	$135,000	$132,200	7	FALSE	$0
11	Smith	$100,000	$98,650	3	FALSE	$0
12	Storey	$90,000	$96,700	9	TRUE	$967
13						

Analyzing Data Using Formulas

Managing Workbook Data

Files You Will Need:

EX F-1.xlsx

EX F-2.xlsx

EX F-3.gif

EX F-4.xlsx

EX F-5.xlsx

EX F-6.xlsx

EX F-7.gif

Classifications.xlsx

Expenses.xlsx

Hardware.xlsx

Logo.gif

Price Information.xlsx

Toronto Sales.xlsx

As you analyze data using Excel, you will find that your worksheets and workbooks become more complex. In this unit, you will learn several Excel features to help you manage workbook data. In addition, you will want to share workbooks with coworkers, but you need to ensure that they can view your data while preventing unwarranted changes. You will learn how to save workbooks in different formats and how to prepare workbooks for distribution. Kate Morgan, the vice president of sales at Quest Specialty Travel, asks for your help in analyzing yearly sales data from the Canadian branches. When the analysis is complete, she will distribute the workbook for branch managers to review.

OBJECTIVES

View and arrange worksheets

Protect worksheets and workbooks

Save custom views of a worksheet

Add a worksheet background

Prepare a workbook for distribution

Insert hyperlinks

Save a workbook for distribution

Group worksheets

Viewing and Arranging Worksheets

As you work with workbooks made up of multiple worksheets, you may need to compare data in the various sheets. To do this, you can view each worksheet in its own workbook window, called an **instance**, and display the windows in an arrangement that makes it easy to compare data. When you work with worksheets in separate windows, you are working with different views of the same worksheet; the data itself remains in one file. ▦▦▦ Kate asks you to compare the monthly store sales totals for the Toronto and Vancouver branches. Because the sales totals are on different worksheets, you want to arrange the worksheets side by side in separate windows.

STEPS

1. **Start Excel, open the file EX F-1.xlsx from the drive and folder where you store your Data Files, then save it as Store Sales**

2. **With the Toronto sheet active, click the View tab, then click the New Window button in the Window group**

   There are now two instances of the Store Sales workbook on the task bar: Store Sales.xlsx:1 and Store Sales.xlsx:2. The Store Sales.xlsx:2 window is active—you can see its button selected on the taskbar, and the filename in the title bar has :2 after it.

3. **Click the Vancouver sheet tab, click the Switch Windows button in the Window group, then click Store Sales.xlsx:1**

   The Store Sales.xlsx:1 instance is active. The Toronto sheet is active in the Store Sales.xlsx:1 workbook and the Vancouver sheet is active in the Store Sales.xlsx:2 workbook.

4. **Click the Arrange All button in the Window group**

   The Arrange Windows dialog box, shown in Figure F-1, provides configurations for displaying the worksheets. You want to view the workbooks vertically.

▶ 5. **Click the Vertical option button to select it, then click OK**

   The windows are arranged vertically, as shown in Figure F-2. You can activate a workbook by clicking one of its cells. You can also view only one of the workbooks by hiding the one you do not wish to see.

6. **Scroll horizontally to view the data in the Store Sales.xlsx:1 workbook, click anywhere in the Store Sales.xlsx:2 workbook, scroll horizontally to view the data in the Store Sales.xlsx:2 workbook, then click the Hide button in the Window group**

   When you hide the second instance, only the Store Sales.xlsx:1 workbook is visible.

7. **Click the Unhide button in the Window group; click Store Sales.xlsx:2, if necessary, in the Unhide dialog box; then click OK**

   The Store Sales.xlsx:2 book appears.

8. **Close the Store Sales.xlsx:2 instance, then maximize the Toronto worksheet in the Store Sales.xlsx workbook**

   Closing the Store Sales.xlsx:2 instance leaves only the first instance open, which is now named Store Sales.xlsx in the title bar.

FIGURE F-1: Arrange Windows dialog box

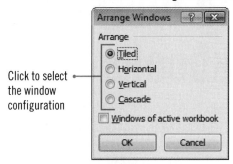

Click to select the window configuration

FIGURE F-2: Windows displayed vertically

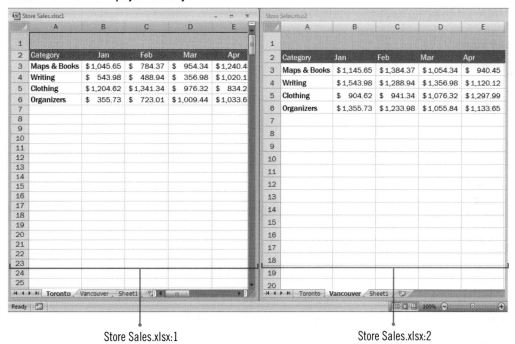

Store Sales.xlsx:1   Store Sales.xlsx:2

Splitting the worksheet into multiple panes

Excel lets you split the worksheet area into vertical and/or horizontal panes, so that you can click inside any one pane and scroll to locate information in that pane while the other panes remain in place, as shown in Figure F-3. To split a worksheet area into multiple panes, drag a split box (the small box at the top of the vertical scroll bar or at the right end of the horizontal scroll bar) in the direction you want the split to appear. To remove the split, move the pointer over the split until the pointer changes to a double-headed arrow, then double-click.

FIGURE F-3: Worksheet split into two horizontal and two vertical panes

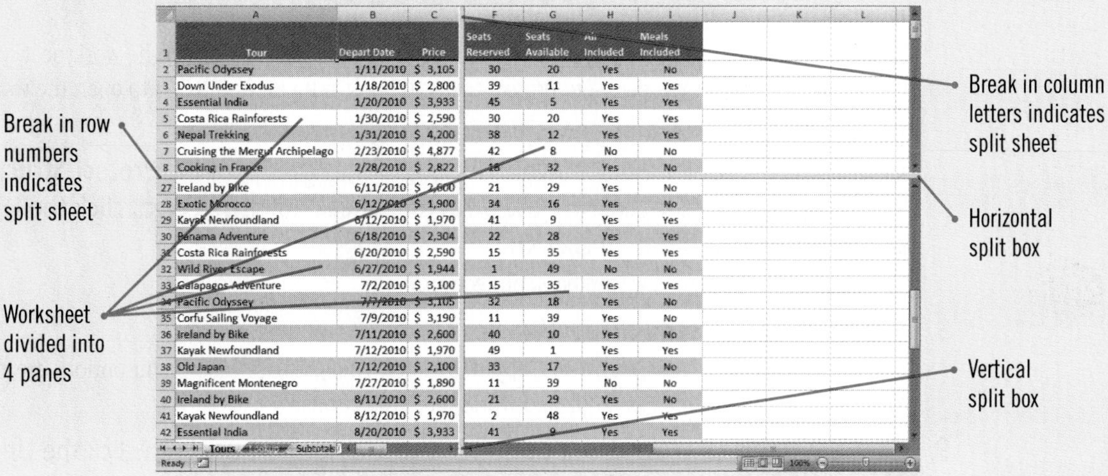

Break in column letters indicates split sheet

Break in row numbers indicates split sheet

Horizontal split box

Worksheet divided into 4 panes

Vertical split box

Protecting Worksheets and Workbooks

To protect sensitive information, Excel allows you to **lock** selected cells so that other people are able to view the data (values, numbers, labels, formulas, etc.) in those cells, but not change it. Excel locks all cells by default, but this protection does not take effect until you activate the Excel protection feature. A common worksheet protection strategy is to unlock cells in which data will be changed, sometimes referred to as the **data entry area**, and to lock cells in which the data should not be changed. Then, when you protect the worksheet, the unlocked areas can still be changed. ▰▰▰ Because the Toronto sales figures for January through March have been confirmed as final, Kate asks you to protect that area of the worksheet so the figures cannot be altered.

STEPS

1. **On the Toronto sheet, select the range E3:M6, click the Home tab, click the Format button in the Cells group, click Format Cells, then in the Format Cells dialog box click the Protection tab**

   The Locked check box in the Protection tab is already checked, as shown in Figure F-4. This check box is selected by default, meaning that all the cells in a new workbook start out locked. However, cell locking is not applied unless the protection feature is also activated. The protection feature is inactive by default. Because the April through December sales figures have not yet been confirmed as final and may need to be changed, you do not want those cells to be locked when the protection feature is activated.

QUICK TIP

To hide any formulas that you don't want to be visible, select the cells that contain formulas that you want to hide, then click the Hidden check box on the Protection tab to select it. The formula will be hidden after the worksheet is protected.

2. **Click the Locked check box to deselect it, then click OK**

   The data remains unlocked until you set the protection in the next step.

3. **Click the Review tab, then click the Protect Sheet button in the Changes group**

   The Protect Sheet dialog box opens, as shown in Figure F-5. In the "Allow users of this worksheet to" list, you can select the actions that you want your worksheet users to be able to perform. The default options protect the worksheet while allowing users to select locked or unlocked cells only. You choose not to use a password.

4. **Verify that Protect worksheet and contents of locked cells is checked and that Select locked cells and Select unlocked cells are checked, then click OK**

   You are ready to test the new worksheet protection.

5. **In cell B3, type 1 to confirm that locked cells cannot be changed, then click OK**

   When you attempt to change a locked cell, a dialog box, shown in Figure F-6, reminds you of the protected cell's read-only status. **Read-only format** means that users can view but not change the data.

6. **Click cell F3, type 1, and notice that Excel allows you to begin the entry, press [Esc] to cancel the entry, then save the workbook**

   Because you unlocked the cells in columns E through M before you protected the worksheet, you can make changes to these cells. You decide to protect the workbook, but you want users to open the workbook without typing a password first.

7. **Click the Protect Workbook button in the Changes group, in the Protect Structure and Windows dialog box make sure the Structure check box is selected, click the Windows check box to select it, then click OK**

   You are ready to test the new workbook protection.

8. **Right-click the Toronto sheet tab**

   The Insert, Delete, Rename, Move or Copy, Tab Color, Hide, and Unhide menu options are not available. You decide to remove the workbook and worksheet protections.

9. **Click the Unprotect Workbook button in the Changes group, then click the Unprotect Sheet button to remove the worksheet protection**

FIGURE F-4: Protection tab in Format Cells dialog box

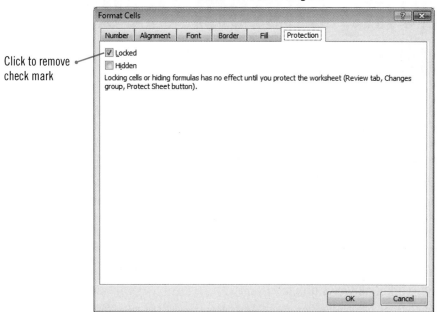

Click to remove
check mark

FIGURE F-5: Protect Sheet dialog box

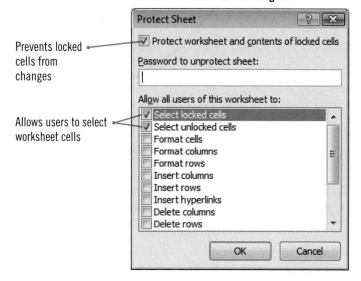

Prevents locked
cells from
changes

Allows users to select
worksheet cells

FIGURE F-6: Reminder of protected cell's read-only status

Freezing rows and columns

As the rows and columns of a worksheet fill up with data, you might need to scroll through the worksheet to add, delete, modify, and view information. You can temporarily freeze columns and rows so you can keep labeling information in view as you scroll. **Panes** are the columns and rows that **freeze**, or remain in place, while you scroll through your worksheet. To freeze panes you need to click the View tab, click the Freeze Panes button in the Window group then click Freeze Panes. Excel freezes the columns to the left and the rows above the selected cell. You can also select Freeze Top Row or Freeze First Column to freeze the top row or left worksheet column.

Saving Custom Views of a Worksheet

A **view** is a set of display and/or print settings that you can name and save, then access at a later time. By using the Excel Custom Views feature, you can create several different views of a worksheet without having to create separate sheets. For example, if you often hide columns in a worksheet, you can create two views, one that displays all of the columns and another with the columns hidden. You set the worksheet display first, then name the view. ▨▨▨ Because Kate wants to generate a sales report from the final sales data for January through March, she asks you to save the first-quarter sales data as a custom view. You begin by creating a view showing all of the worksheet data.

STEPS

1. **With the Toronto sheet active, click the View tab, then click the Custom Views button in the Workbook Views group**

   The Custom Views dialog box opens. Any previously defined views for the active worksheet appear in the Views box. No views are defined for the Toronto worksheet. You decide to add a named view that shows all the worksheet columns.

   QUICK TIP

   To delete views from the active work-sheet, select the view in the Custom Views dialog box, then click Delete.

2. **Click Add**

   The Add View dialog box opens, as shown in Figure F-7. Here, you enter a name for the view and decide whether to include print settings and hidden rows, columns, and filter settings. You want to include the selected options.

3. **In the Name box, type Year Sales, then click OK**

   You have created a view called Year Sales that shows all the worksheet columns. You want to set up another view that will hide the April through December columns.

4. **Select columns E through M, right-click the selected area, then click Hide on the shortcut menu**

   You are ready to create a custom view of the January through March sales data.

5. **Click cell A1, click the Custom Views button in the Workbook Views group, click Add, in the Name box type First Quarter, then click OK**

   You are ready to test the two custom views.

   TROUBLE

   If you receive the message "Some view settings could not be applied," turn off worksheet protec-tion by clicking the Unprotect Sheet button in the Changes group of the Review tab.

6. **Click the Custom Views button in the Workbook Views group, click Year Sales in the Views list, then click Show**

   The Year Sales custom view displays all of the months' sales data. Now you are ready to test the First Quarter custom view.

7. **Click the Custom Views button in the Workbook Views group, then with First Quarter in the Custom Views dialog box selected, click Show**

   Only the January through March sales figures appear on the screen, as shown in Figure F-8.

8. **Return to the Year Sales view, then save your work**

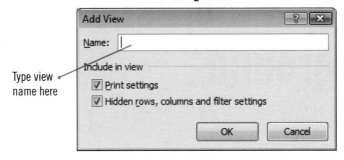

Type view
name here

January –
March sales
figures

Break in column
letters indicates
hidden columns

Excel 2007

Using Page Break Preview

The vertical and horizontal dashed lines in the Normal view of worksheets represent page breaks. Excel automatically inserts a page break when your worksheet data doesn't fit on one page. These page breaks are **dynamic**, which means they adjust automatically when you insert or delete rows and columns and when you change column widths or row heights. Everything to the left of the first vertical dashed line and above the first horizontal dashed line is printed on the first page. You can manually add or remove page breaks by clicking the Page Layout tab, clicking the Breaks button in the Page

Setup group, then clicking the appropriate command. You can also view and change page breaks manually by clicking the View tab, then clicking the Page Break Preview button in the Workbook Views group, or by clicking the Page Break Preview button on the status bar, then clicking OK. You can drag the blue page break lines to the desired location, as shown in Figure F-9. If you drag a page break to the right to include more data on a page, Excel shrinks the type to fit the data on that page. To exit Page Break Preview, click the Normal button in the Workbook Views group.

FIGURE F-9: **Page Break Preview window**

	A	B	C	D	E	F	G	H	I	J	K	L	M
1							QST Toronto						
2	Category	Jan	Feb	Mar	Apr	May	Jun	Jul	Aug	Sep	Oct	Nov	Dec
3	Maps & Books	$ 1,045.65	$ 784.37	$ 954.34	$ 1,240.45	$ 567.76	$ 1,240.76	$ 1,240.43	$ 1,240.34	$ 675.54	$ 1,240.54	$ 1,240.34	$ 1,240.34
4	Writing	$ 543.98	$ 488.94	$ 356.98	$ 1,020.12	$ 378.23	$ 392.41	$ 934.62	$ 145.89	$ 345.98	$ 435.78	$ 359.76	$ 289.88
5	Clothing	$ 1,204.62	$ 1,341.34	$ 976.32	$ 834.23	$ 1,022.35	$ 634.22	$ 1,309.22	$ 749.33	$ 1,209.04	$ 1,383.11	$ 1,456.21	$ 1,341.47
6	Organizers	$ 355.73	$ 723.01	$ 1,009.44	$ 1,033.65	$ 998.98	$ 1,003.48	$ 1,006.23	$ 942.56	$ 1,097.99	$ 865.11	$ 898.99	$ 1,012.75

Drag blue page
break lines to
change page
breaks

Adding a Worksheet Background

In addition to using a theme's font colors and fills, you can make your Excel data more attractive to view by adding a picture to the worksheet background. Companies often use their logo as a worksheet background. A worksheet background will display on the screen but will not print with the worksheet. If you want to add a worksheet background that appears on printouts, you can add a **watermark**, a translucent background design that prints behind your data. To add a watermark, you add the image to the worksheet header or footer.  Kate asks you to add the Quest logo to the printed background of the Toronto worksheet. You will begin by adding the logo as a worksheet background.

STEPS

1. **With the Toronto sheet active, click the** Page Layout tab, **then click the** Background button **in the Page Setup group**

   The Sheet Background dialog box opens.

2. **Navigate to the drive and folder where you store your Data Files, click** Logo.gif, **then click** Insert

   The Quest logo is tiled behind the worksheet data. It appears twice because the graphic is **tiled**, or repeated, to fill the background.

3. **Preview the Toronto worksheet, then click the** Close Print Preview button

   Because the logo is only for display purposes, it will not print with the worksheet, so is not visible in Print Preview. You want the logo to print with the worksheet, so you decide to remove the background and add the logo to the worksheet header.

4. **Click the** Delete Background button **in the Page Setup group, click the** Insert tab, **then click the** Header & Footer button **in the Text group**

   The Design tab of the Header & Footer Tools appears, as shown in Figure F-10. The Header & Footer group buttons add preformatted headers and footers to a worksheet. The Header & Footer Elements buttons allow you to add page numbers, the date, the time, pictures, and names to the header or footer. The Navigation group buttons move the insertion point from the header to the footer and back. The Options group buttons specify special circumstances for the worksheet's headers and footers. You want to add a picture to the header.

5. **With the insertion point in the center section of the header, click the** Picture button **in the Header & Footer Elements group, navigate to the drive and folder where you store your Data Files, click** Logo.gif, **then click** Insert

   A code representing a picture, &[Picture], appears in the center of the header.

6. **Click cell A1, then click the** Normal button ▦ **on the Status Bar**

   You want to scale the worksheet data to print on one page.

7. **Click the** Page Layout tab, **click the** Width list arrow **in the Scale to Fit group, click 1 page, click the** Height list arrow **in the Scale to Fit group, click 1 page, then preview the worksheet**

   Your worksheet should look like Figure F-11.

8. **Click the** Close Print Preview button, **then save the workbook**

Managing Workbook Data

FIGURE F-10: Design tab of the Header & Footer tools

Click these buttons to customize the header and footer

Header & Footer Tools Design tab

Some cells may temporarily display ######### while header is added

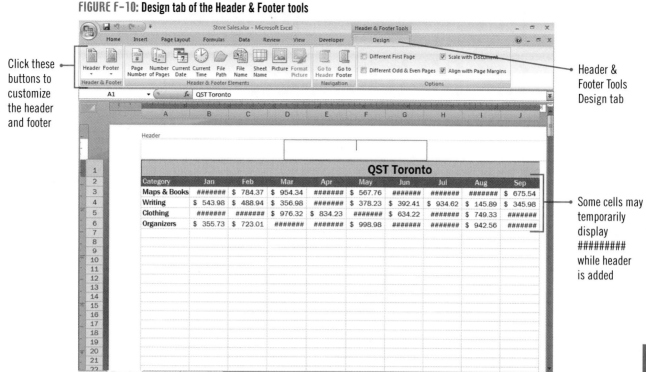

FIGURE F-11: Preview of Toronto worksheet with logo in the background

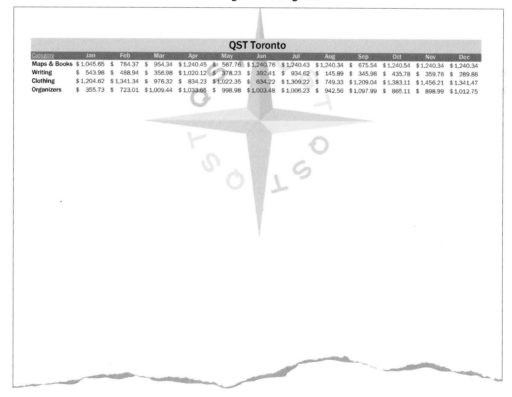

Excel 2007

Preparing a Workbook for Distribution

If you are collaborating with others and want to share a workbook with them, you might want to remove sensitive information, such as headers, footers, or hidden elements, before distributing the file. You can use the Document Inspector feature to find and remove hidden data and personal information in your workbooks. On the other hand, you might want to add helpful information, called **properties**, to a file to help others identify, understand, and locate it, such as keywords, the author's name, a title, the status, and comments. **Keywords** are terms users can search for that will help them locate your workbook. Properties are a form of **metadata**, information that describe data and are used in Microsoft Windows document searches. You enter properties in the Document Properties Panel. In addition, to insure that others do not make unauthorized changes to your workbook, you can mark a file as final, which changes it to a read-only file, which others can open but not alter. ▰▰▰ To protect the workbook and prepare it for distribution to the sales managers, Kate asks you to remove sensitive information, add document properties, and mark the workbook as final.

STEPS

1. **Click the** Office button ⬤**, point to** Prepare**, then click** Inspect Document

   The Document Inspector dialog box opens, as shown in Figure F-12. It lists items that you can have Excel evaluate for personal information. All the components are selected by default.

2. **Click** Inspect

   After inspecting your document, the inspector displays the inspection results. Areas with personal information have a ! in front of them. Headers and footers are also flagged. You want to keep the file's header and footer and remove personal information.

3. ▶ **Click** Remove All **next to Document Properties and Personal Information, then click** Close

   You decide to add keywords to help the sales managers find the worksheet using the search words Toronto or Vancouver.

4. **Click** ⬤**, point to** Prepare**, then click** Properties

   The Document Properties Panel appears at the top of the worksheet, as shown in Figure F-13. You decide to add a title, status, keywords, and comments.

5. ▶ **In the Title text box type** Store Sales**, in the Keywords text box type** Toronto Vancouver store sales**, in the Status text box type** DRAFT**, then in the Comments text box type** The first-quarter figures are final.**, then click the** Close button **on the Document Properties Panel**

   You are ready to mark the workbook as final.

6. **Click** ⬤**, point to** Prepare**, click** Mark as Final**, click** OK**, then click** OK **again**

   The workbook is saved as a read-only file. [Read-Only] appears in the title bar.

7. **Click cell** B3**, then type** 1 **to confirm that the cell cannot be changed**

   Marking a workbook as final prevents accidental changes to the workbook. However, it is not a strong form of workbook protection because a workbook recipient can remove this Final status and edit the document. You decide to remove the read-only status from the workbook so that it is again editable.

8. **Click** ⬤**, point to** Prepare**, then click** Mark as Final

   The title bar no longer displays [Read-Only] after the workbook title, indicating that you can now edit the workbook.

FIGURE F-12: Document Inspector dialog box

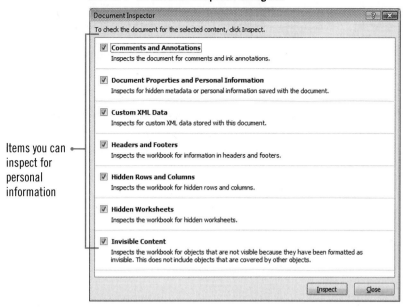

Items you can inspect for personal information

FIGURE F-13: Document Properties Panel

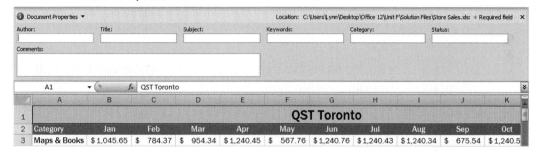

Adding a digital signature to a workbook

You can digitally sign a workbook to establish its validity and prevent it from being changed. You must obtain a valid certificate from a certificate authority to authenticate the workbook. To add a signature line in a workbook, click the Insert tab, click the Signature Line button in the Text group, then click OK. In the Signature Setup dialog box, enter information about the signer of the worksheet and then click OK. To add a signature, double-click the signature line, click OK, if prompted with a Get a Digital ID dialog box, click the Create your own digital ID option button, save your file if prompted, in the Sign dialog box click Select Image next to the sign box, browse to the location where your signature is saved, click Sign, then click OK. To add the certificate authenticating the workbook, click the Office button, point to Prepare, click Add a Digital Signature, then click OK. In the Sign dialog box click Sign, then click OK. The workbook will be saved as read-only and it will not be able to be changed by other users.

Sharing a workbook

You can make an Excel file a **shared workbook** so that several users can open and modify it at the same time. Click the Review tab, click the Share Workbook button in the Changes group, then on the Editing tab of the Share Workbook dialog box click "Allow changes by more than one user at the same time. This also allows workbook merging." If you get an error that the workbook cannot be shared because privacy is enabled, click the Office button, click Excel Options, click the Trust Center category on the left side of the dialog box, click Trust Center Settings, click Privacy Options in the list on the left, click the "Remove personal information from file properties on save" check box to deselect it, then click OK twice. When you share workbooks, it is often helpful to **track** modifications, or identify who made which changes. You can track all changes to a workbook by clicking the Track Changes button in the Changes group, and then clicking Highlight Changes. To resolve the tracked changes in a workbook, click the Track Changes button, then click Accept/Reject Changes. The changes are displayed one by one. You can accept the change or, if you disagree with any of the changes, you can reject them.

Inserting Hyperlinks

As you manage the content and appearance of your workbooks, you may want the workbook user to view information in another location. It might be nonessential information or data that is too detailed to place in the workbook itself. In these cases, you can create a hyperlink. A **hyperlink** is an object (a filename, word, phrase, or graphic) in a worksheet that, when you click it, displays, or "jumps to," another location, called the **target**. The target can also be a worksheet, another document, or a site on the World Wide Web. For example, in a worksheet that lists customer invoices, at each customer's name, you might create a hyperlink to an Excel file containing payment terms for each customer. Kate wants managers who view the Store Sales workbook to be able to view the item totals for each sales category in the Toronto sheet. She asks you to create a hyperlink at the Category heading so that users can click the hyperlink to view the items for each category.

STEPS

1. **Click cell A2 on the Toronto worksheet**

2. **Click the Insert tab if necessary, then click the Hyperlink button in the Links group**
    The Insert Hyperlink dialog box opens, as shown in Figure F-14. The icons under "Link to" on the left side of the dialog box let you specify the type of location you want the link to jump to: an existing file or Web page, a place in the same document, a new document, or an e-mail address. Because you want the link to dis-play an already-existing document, the selected first icon, Existing File or Web Page, is correct, so you won't have to change it.

3. **Click the Look in list arrow, navigate to the location where you store your Data Files if necessary, then click Toronto Sales.xlsx in the file list**
    The filename you selected and its path appear in the Address text box. This is the document users will see when they click the hyperlink. You can also specify the ScreenTip that users see when they hold the pointer over the hyperlink.

4. **Click ScreenTip, type Items in each category, click OK, then click OK again**
    Cell A2 now contains underlined red text, indicating that it is a hyperlink. The color of a hyperlink depends on the worksheet theme colors. You need to change the text color of the hyperlink text so it is visible on the dark background. After you create a hyperlink, you should check it to make sure that it jumps to the correct destination.

5. **Click the Home tab, click the Font Color list arrow** ![A] **in the Font group, click the White, Background 1 color (first color in the Theme Colors), move the pointer over the Category text, view the ScreenTip, then click once**
    After you click, the Toronto Sales workbook opens, displaying the Sales sheet, as shown in Figure F-15.

6. **Close the Toronto Sales workbook, then save the Store Sales workbook**

Returning to your document

After you click a hyperlink and view the destination document, you will often want to return to your original document that contains the hyperlink. To do this, you can add the Back button to the Quick Access Toolbar. However, the Back button does not appear in the Quick Access toolbar by default; you need to customize the toolbar. (If you are using a computer in a lab, check with your system administrator to see if you have permission to do this.) To cus-tomize the Quick Access toolbar, click the Office button, click Excel Options, click Customize in the Excel Options dialog box, click the "Choose Commands from" list arrow, select All Commands, click the Back button, click Add>>, then click OK.

FIGURE F-14: Insert Hyperlink dialog box

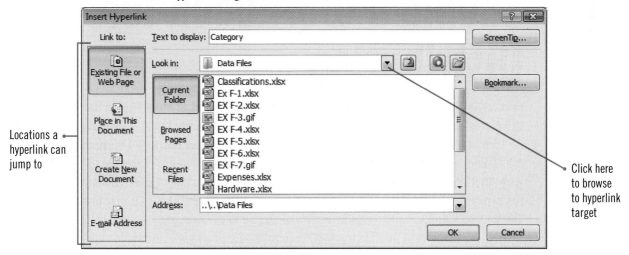

Locations a hyperlink can jump to

Click here to browse to hyperlink target

FIGURE F-15: Target document

	A	B	C	D
1	QST Toronto			
2				
3	Travel Store Sales			
4				
5	Item	Total Sales	Category	
6	PopOut Maps	$ 2,619.82	Maps & Books	
7	Smart Packing Books	$ 3,934.77	Maps & Books	
8	Airport Guides	$ 4,941.62	Maps & Books	
9	Pack It Guides	$ 1,214.65	Maps & Books	
10	Travel Pens	$ 2,855.65	Writing	
11	Jounals	$ 2,836.92	Writing	
12	Plane Slippers	$ 2,099.15	Clothing	
13	Travel Socks	$ 1,108.26	Clothing	
14	Men's Sandals	$ 2,103.14	Clothing	
15	Women's Sandals	$ 1,954.29	Clothing	
16	Hats	$ 975.44	Clothing	
17	Men's T-Shirts	$ 3,112.76	Clothing	
18	Women's T-Shirts	$ 2,108.42	Clothing	
19	Cosmetics Folders	$ 2,798.53	Organizers	
20	Jewelry Cases	$ 2,108.42	Organizers	
21	Travel Cases	$ 2,095.75	Organizers	
22	Passport holders	$ 3,945.22	Organizers	

Sales ⟋ Sheet2 ⟋ Sheet3

Ready

Using research tools

You can access resources online and locally on your computer using the Research task pane. To open the Research task pane, click the Review tab, then click the Research button in the Proofing group. You can click the Thesaurus button in the Proofing group for help with synonyms. You can click the Translate button in the Proofing group to translate your text into a selected language. The Search for text box in the Research pane allows you to specify a research topic. The Research pane has a drop-down list of the resources available to search for your topic.

Saving a Workbook for Distribution

One way to share Excel data is to place, or **publish**, the data on a network or on the Web so that others can access it using their Web browsers. To publish an Excel document to an **intranet** (a company's internal Web site) or the Web, you can save it in an **HTML (Hypertext Markup Language)** format, which is the coding format used for all Web documents. You can also save your Excel file as a **single file Web page** that integrates all of the worksheets and graphical elements from the workbook into a single file. This file format is called MHTML. In addition to distributing files on the Web, you may need to distribute your files to people working with an earlier version of Excel. You can save your files as Excel 97-2003 workbooks. Excel workbooks can be saved in many other formats to support wide distribution and to make them load faster. The most popular formats are listed in Table F-1. Kate asks you to create a workbook version that managers running an earlier version of Excel can open and modify. She also asks you to save the Store Sales workbook in MHT format so she can publish it on the Quest intranet for their sales managers to view.

STEPS

QUICK TIP

You can check your files for unsupported features before saving them by clicking the Office button, pointing to Prepare, then clicking Run Compatibility Checker.

1. **Click the Office button, point to Save As, click Excel 97-2003 Workbook, in the Save As dialog box, navigate to the drive and folder where you store your Data Files, then click Save**
   The Compatibility Checker appears on the screen, alerting you to the features that will be lost by saving in the earlier format. Some Excel 2007 features are not available in earlier versions of Excel.

2. **Click Continue, close the workbook, then reopen the Store Sales.xls workbook**
   [Compatibility Mode] appears in the title bar, as shown in Figure F-16. Compatibility mode prevents you from including Excel features in your workbook that are not supported in Excel 97-2003 workbooks. To exit compatibility mode, you need to save your file in one of the Excel 2007 formats and reopen the file.

3. **Click, point to Save As, click Excel Workbook, if necessary navigate to the drive and folder where you store your Data Files, click Save, then click Yes when you are asked if you want to replace the existing file**
   [Compatibility Mode] remains displayed in the title bar. You decide to close the file and reopen it to exit compatibility mode.

4. **Close the workbook, then reopen the Store Sales.xlsx workbook**
   The title bar no longer displays [Compatibility mode]. You decide to save the file for Web distribution.

QUICK TIP

To ensure that your workbook displays the same way on different computer platforms and screen settings, you can publish it in PDF format. You need to download an Add-in to save files in this format. The PDF format preserves all of the workbook's formatting so that it appears on the Web exactly as it was created.

5. **Click, click Save As, in the Save As dialog box, navigate to the drive and folder where you store your Data Files, change the filename to sales, then click the Save as type list arrow and click Single File Web Page (*.mht, *.mhtml)**
   The Save as type list box indicates that the workbook is to be saved as a Single File Web Page, which is in mhtml or mht format. To avoid problems when publishing your pages to a Web server, it is best to use lowercase characters, omit special characters and spaces, and limit your filename to eight characters with an additional three-character extension.

6. **Click Save, then click Yes**
   The dialog box indicated that some features may not be retained in the Web page file. Excel saves the workbook as an MHT file in the folder location you specified in the Save As dialog box. The MHT file is open on your screen, as shown in Figure F-17. It's a good idea to open an mht file in your browser to see how it will look to viewers.

7. **Close the sales.mht file in Excel, open Windows Explorer, open the sales.mht file, click the Vancouver sheet tab, then close your browser window**

FIGURE F-16: Workbook in compatibility mode

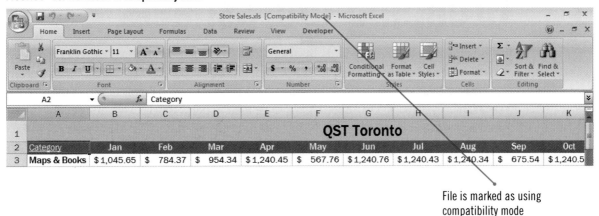

File is marked as using
compatibility mode

FIGURE F-17: Workbook saved as a single file web page

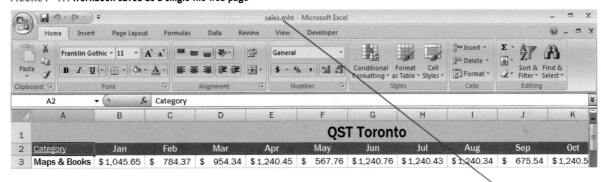

Web file with new name

TABLE F-1: Workbook formats

type of file	file extension(s)	Used for
Macro-enabled workbook	xlsm	Files that contain macros
Excel 97-2003 workbook	xls	Working with people using older versions of Excel
Single file Web page	mht, mhtml	Web sites with multiple pages and graphics
Web page	htm, html	Simple single-page Web sites
Excel template	xltx	Excel files that will be reused with small changes
Excel macro-enabled template	xltm	Excel files that will be used again and contain macros
Portable document format	pdf	Files with formatting that needs to be preserved
XML paper specification	xps	Files with formatting that needs to be preserved and files that need to be shared

Understanding Excel file formats

The default file format for Excel 2007 files is the Office Open XML format, which supports all Excel features. This format stores Excel files in small XML components which are zipped for compression. This default format has different types of files with their own extensions that are also often called formats themselves. The most often used format, xlsx , does not support macros. Macros, programmed instructions that perform tasks, can be a security risk. If your worksheet contains macros, you need to save it with an extension of xlsm so the macros will function in the workbook. If you use a workbook's text and formats repeatedly, you may want to save it as a template with the extension xltx. If your template contains macros, you need to save it with the xltm extension.

Grouping Worksheets

You can group worksheets to work on them as a collection so that data entered into one worksheet is automatically entered into all of the selected worksheets. This is useful for data that is common to every sheet of a workbook, such as headers and footers, or for column headings that will apply to all monthly worksheets in a yearly summary. Grouping worksheets can also be used to print multiple worksheets at one time. Kate asks you to add the text Quest to the footer of both the Toronto and Vancouver worksheets. You will also add one-inch margins to the left and right sides of both worksheets.

STEPS

1. **Open the Store Sales.xlsx file from the drive and folder where you store your Data Files**

2. **With the Toronto sheet active, press and hold [Shift], click the Vancouver sheet, then release [Shift]**

   Both sheet tabs are selected, and the title bar now contains [Group], indicating that the worksheets are grouped together, so any changes you make to the Toronto sheet will also be made to the Vancouver sheet.

3. **Click the Insert tab, then click the Header & Footer button in the Text group**

4. **On the Header & Footer Tools Design tab, click the Go to Footer button in the Navigation group, type Quest in the center section of the footer, enter your name in the left section of the footer, click cell A1, then click the Normal button ▦ on the Status Bar**

   You decide to check the footers in Print Preview.

5. **With the worksheets still grouped, click the Office button ⊙, point to Print, click Print Preview, then click the Next Page button in the Preview group**

   Because the worksheets are grouped, both pages contain the footer with Quest and your name. The worksheets would look better with a wider top margin.

6. **Click the Close Print Preview button, click the Page Layout tab, click the Margins button in the Page Setup group, click Custom Margins, in the Top text box type 1, then click OK**

7. **Preview and print the worksheets**

   The Toronto worksheet is shown in Figure F-18; the Vancouver worksheet is shown in Figure F-19. You decide to ungroup the worksheets.

8. **Right-click the Toronto worksheet sheet tab, then click Ungroup Sheets**

9. **Save the workbook, then close it and exit Excel**

Creating a workspace

If you work with several workbooks at a time, you can group them so that you can open them in one step by creating a **workspace**, a file with an .xlw extension. Then, instead of opening each workbook individually, you can open the workspace. To create a workspace, open the workbooks you wish to group, then position and size them as you would like them to appear. Click the View tab, click the Save Workspace button in the Window group, type a name for the workspace file, navigate to the location where you want to store it, then click Save. Remember, however, that the workspace file does not contain the workbooks themselves, so you still have to save any changes you make to the original workbook files. If you work at another computer, you need to have the workspace file and all of the workbooks that are part of the workspace.

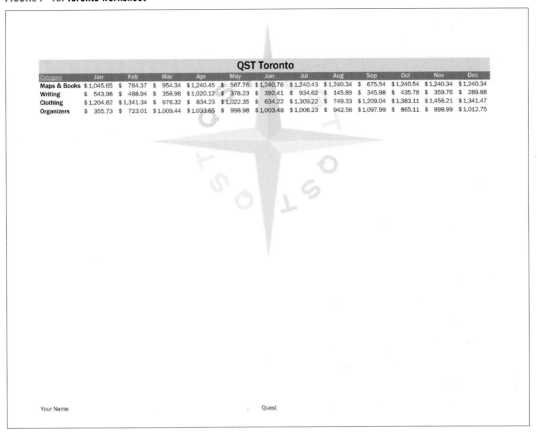

QST Toronto

Category	Jan	Feb	Mar	Apr	May	Jun	Jul	Aug	Sep	Oct	Nov	Dec
Maps & Books	$1,045.65	$ 784.37	$ 954.34	$1,240.45	$ 567.76	$1,240.76	$1,240.43	$1,240.34	$ 675.54	$1,240.54	$1,240.34	$1,240.34
Writing	$ 543.98	$ 488.94	$ 356.98	$1,020.12	$ 378.23	$ 392.41	$ 934.62	$ 145.89	$ 345.98	$ 435.78	$ 359.76	$ 289.88
Clothing	$1,204.62	$1,341.34	$ 976.32	$ 834.23	$1,022.35	$ 634.22	$1,309.22	$ 749.33	$1,209.04	$1,383.11	$1,456.21	$1,341.47
Organizers	$ 355.73	$ 723.01	$1,009.44	$1,033.65	$ 998.98	$1,003.48	$1,006.23	$ 942.56	$1,097.99	$ 865.11	$ 898.99	$1,012.75

Your Name   Quest

FIGURE F-19: Vancouver worksheet

QST Vancouver

Category	Jan	Feb	Mar	Apr	May	Jun	Jul	Aug	Sep	Oct	Nov	Dec
Maps & Books	$1,145.65	$1,384.37	$1,054.34	$ 940.45	$1,567.76	$1,040.76	$ 940.43	$1,140.34	$1,275.54	$ 940.54	$1,040.34	$1,040.34
Writing	$1,543.98	$1,288.94	$1,356.98	$1,120.12	$1,311.22	$1,392.41	$1,134.62	$1,145.89	$1,194.86	$ 835.78	$ 859.76	$ 889.88
Clothing	$ 904.62	$ 941.34	$1,076.32	$1,297.99	$ 922.35	$1,234.22	$1,509.22	$1,049.33	$1,009.04	$1,283.11	$1,126.21	$1,141.47
Organizers	$1,355.73	$1,233.98	$1,055.84	$1,133.65	$1,298.98	$1,303.48	$1,106.23	$ 842.56	$1,197.99	$ 965.11	$ 988.99	$1,112.75

Your Name   Quest

Practice

If you have a SAM user profile, you may have access to hands-on instruction, practice, and assessment of the skills covered in this unit. Log in to your SAM account (http://sam2007.course.com/) to launch any assigned training activities or exams that relate to the skills covered in this unit.

▼ CONCEPTS REVIEW

FIGURE F-20

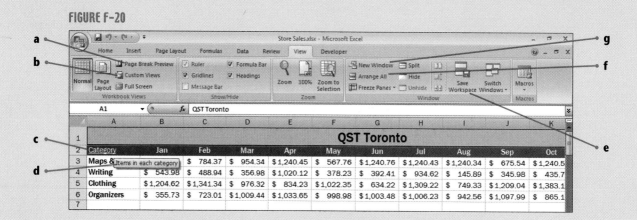

1. Which element do you click to organize windows in a specific configuration?
2. Which element points to a ScreenTip for a hyperlink?
3. Which element points to a hyperlink?
4. Which element do you click to open the active worksheet in a new window?
5. Which element do you click to name and save a set of display and/or print settings?
6. Which element do you click to group workbooks so that they open together as a unit?
7. Which element do you click to view and change the way worksheet data is distributed on printed pages?

Match each term with the statement that best describes it.

8. Data entry area
9. Hyperlink
10. Watermark
11. HTML
12. Dynamic page breaks

a. Web page format
b. Portion of a worksheet that can be changed
c. Translucent background design on a printed worksheet
d. An object that when clicked displays another worksheet or a Web page
e. Adjusted automatically when rows and columns are inserted or deleted

Select the best answer from the list of choices.

13. You can establish the validity of a workbook by adding a _____.
    a. Keyword
    b. Custom Views
    c. Digital signature
    d. Template

14. You can group several workbooks in a _____ so they can be opened together rather than individually.
    a. Workgroup
    b. Consolidated workbook
    c. Workspace
    d. Work unit

15. Which of the following formats means that users can view but not change data in a workbook?

   a. Macro   **c.** Read-only

   b. PDF   **d.** Template

16. You can group noncontiguous worksheets by pressing and holding _____ while clicking the sheet tabs that you want to group.

   a. [Ctrl]   **c.** [Alt]

   b. [Spacebar]   **d.** [F6]

▼ SKILLS REVIEW

1. View and arrange worksheets.

   a. Start Excel, open the file EX F-2.xlsx from the drive and folder where you store your Data Files, then save it as **Chicago Budget**.

   b. Activate the 2010 sheet if necessary, then open the 2011 sheet in a new window.

   c. Activate the 2010 sheet in the Chicago Budget.xlsx:1 workbook. Activate the 2011 sheet in the Chicago Budget.xlsx:2 workbook.

   d. View the Chicago Budget.xlsx:1 and Chicago Budget.xlsx:2 workbooks tiled horizontally. View the workbooks in a vertical arrangement.

   e. Hide the Chicago Budget.xlsx:2 instance, then unhide the instance. Close the Chicago Budget.xlsx:2 instance and maximize the Chicago Budget.xlsx workbook.

   f. Split the 2010 sheet into two horizontal panes. (*Hint*: Drag the Horizontal split box.) Remove the split by double-clicking it, then save your work.

2. Protect worksheets and workbooks.

   a. On the 2010 sheet, unlock the expense data in the range C9:F17.

   b. Protect the sheet without using a password.

   c. To make sure the other cells are locked, attempt to make an entry in cell D4. You should see the error message displayed in Figure F-21.

   d. Change the first-quarter mortgage expense to 4500.

FIGURE F-21

   e. Protect the workbook's structure and windows without applying a password. Right-click the 2010 and 2011 worksheets to verify that you cannot insert, delete, rename, move, copy, hide, or unhide the sheets, or change their tab color.

   f. Unprotect the workbook. Unprotect the 2010 worksheet.

   g. Save the workbook.

3. Save custom views of a worksheet

   a. Using the 2010 sheet, create a view of the entire worksheet called **Entire 2010 Budget**.

   b. Hide rows 8 through 19, then make a new view called **Income** showing only the income data.

   c. Use the Custom Views dialog box to display all of the data on the 2010 worksheet.

   d. Use the Custom Views dialog box to display only the income data on the 2010 worksheet.

   e. Use the Custom Views dialog box to return to the Entire 2010 Budget view.

   f. Save the workbook.

4. Add a worksheet background.

   a. Use EX F-3.gif as a worksheet background for the 2010 sheet.

   b. Delete the background image on the 2010 sheet.

   c. Add EX F-3.gif to the 2010 header.

   d. Preview the 2010 worksheet to verify that the background will print, then exit Print Preview and save the workbook.

   e. Add your name to the center section of the 2010 worksheet footer, then print the worksheet.

5. Prepare a workbook for distribution.

   a. Inspect the workbook and remove any document properties, personal information, and header and footer information.

   b. Use the Document Properties Panel to add a title of Quarterly Budget and the keywords café and Chicago.(*Hint*: Separate the keywords with a space.) If you are using your own computer, add your name in the Author text box.

   c. Mark the workbook as final and verify that [Read-Only] is in the title bar.

   d. Remove the final status of the workbook.

   e. Save the workbook.

6. Insert hyperlinks.

   a. On the 2010 worksheet, make cell A8 a hyperlink to the file **Expenses.xlsx** in your Data Files folder.

   b. Test the link, then print Sheet 1 of the Expenses workbook.

   c. Return to the Chicago Budget workbook, edit the hyperlink in cell A8, adding a ScreenTip that reads **Expense Details**, then verify that the ScreenTip appears.

   d. On the 2011 worksheet, enter the text **Based on 2010 budget** in cell A21.

   e. Make the text in cell A21 a hyperlink to cell A1 in the 2010 worksheet. (*Hint*: Use the Place in This Document button and note the cell reference in the Type the cell reference text box.)

   f. Test the hyperlink.

   g. Remove the hyperlink in cell A8 of the 2010 worksheet.

   h. Save the workbook.

7. Save a workbook for distribution.

   a. Save the Chicago Budget workbook as a single file Web page with the name chicago.mht. Close the chicago.mht file in Excel, then open the chicago.mht file in your Web browser. Close your browser window and reopen the Chicago Budget.xlsx file.

   b. If you have the PDF Add-in installed on your computer, save the Chicago Budget workbook as a PDF file.

   c. Save the Chicago Budget workbook as an Excel 97-2003 workbook and review the results of the Compatibility Checker.

   d. Close the Chicago Budget.xls file and reopen the Chicago Budget.xlsx file.

   e. Save the file as a macro-enabled template in the drive and folder where you store your Data Files. (*Hint*: Select the type Excel Macro-Enabled template xltm in the Save as type list.)

   f. Close the template file, then reopen the Chicago Budget.xlsx file.

8. Grouping worksheets.

   a. Group the 2010 and 2011 worksheets.

   b. Add your name to the center footer section of the worksheets.

   c. Save the workbook, then preview both sheets.

   d. Print both sheets, compare your sheets to Figure F-22, then ungroup the sheets.

   e. Close all open files and exit Excel.

FIGURE F-22

Chicago 2010 Quarterly Café Budget

			1st QTR	2nd QTR	3rd QTR	4th QTR	TOTAL	% OF TOTAL
Income		Description						
		Coffee	$ 8,500	$ 8,700	$ 7,500	$ 8,100	$ 32,800	34.02%
		Tea	$ 7,500	$ 6,800	$ 5,700	$ 6,800	$ 26,800	27.80%
		Pastries	$ 9,100	$ 9,100	$ 8,700	$ 9,900	$ 36,800	38.17%
		TOTAL	$ 25,100	$ 24,600	$ 21,900	$ 24,800	$ 96,400	100.00%
Expenses								
		Mortgage	$ 4,500	$ 4,300	$ 4,300	$ 4,300	$ 17,400	32.67%
		Payroll	$ 5,500	$ 5,500	$ 5,500	$ 5,800	$ 22,300	41.87%
		Pastries	$ 1,150	$ 1,150	$ 1,180	$ 1,150	$ 4,630	8.69%
		Utilities	$ 580	$ 580	$ 580	$ 580	$ 2,320	4.36%
		Phone	$ 490	$ 490	$ 490	$ 450	$ 1,920	3.60%
		Coffee	$ 580	$ 580	$ 590	$ 580	$ 2,330	4.37%
		Tea	$ 370	$ 370	$ 330	$ 370	$ 1,440	2.70%
		Advertising	$ 230	$ 230	$ 230	$ 230	$ 920	1.73%
		TOTAL	$ 13,400	$ 13,200	$ 13,200	$ 13,460	$ 53,260	100.00%
Cash Flow			$ 11,700	$ 11,400	$ 8,700	$ 11,340	$ 43,140	

Chicago 2011 Quarterly Café Budget

			1st QTR	2nd QTR	3rd QTR	4th QTR	TOTAL	% OF TOTAL
Income		Description						
		Coffee	$ 8,800	$ 8,500	$ 7,500	$ 8,100	$ 32,900	33.64%
		Tea	$ 7,700	$ 6,900	$ 5,700	$ 6,800	$ 27,100	27.71%
		Pastries	$ 9,900	$ 9,300	$ 8,700	$ 9,900	$ 37,800	38.65%
		TOTAL	$ 26,400	$ 24,700	$ 21,900	$ 24,800	$ 97,800	100.00%
Expenses								
		Mortgage	$ 4,300	$ 4,300	$ 4,300	$ 4,300	$ 4,300	31.85%
		Payroll	$ 5,600	$ 5,600	$ 5,600	$ 5,600	$ 5,600	41.48%
		Pastries	$ 1,250	$ 1,250	$ 1,250	$ 1,250	$ 1,250	9.26%
		Utilities	$ 590	$ 590	$ 590	$ 590	$ 590	4.37%
		Phone	$ 500	$ 500	$ 500	$ 500	$ 500	3.70%
		Coffee	$ 590	$ 590	$ 590	$ 590	$ 590	4.37%
		Tea	$ 390	$ 390	$ 390	$ 390	$ 390	2.89%
		Advertising	$ 280	$ 280	$ 280	$ 280	$ 280	2.07%
		TOTAL	$ 13,500	$ 13,500	$ 13,500	$ 13,500	$ 13,500	100.00%
Cash Flow			$ 12,900	$ 11,200	$ 8,400	$ 11,300	$ 84,300	
Based on 2010 Budget								

▼ INDEPENDENT CHALLENGE 1

You manage Old City Photo, a photo supply company located in Montreal, Canada. You are organizing your first-quarter sales in an Excel worksheet. Because the sheet for the month of January includes the same type of information you need for February and March, you decide to enter the headings for all of the first-quarter months at the same time. You use a separate worksheet for each month and create data for three months.

a. Start Excel, create a new workbook, then save it as **Photo Sales.xlsx** in the drive and folder where you store your Data Files.

b. Name the first sheet January, name the second sheet February, and name the third sheet March.

c. Group the worksheets.

d. With the worksheets grouped, use Table F-2 as a guide to enter the row and column labels that need to appear on each of the three sheets. Add the headings in rows one and two. Center the first row across columns A and B. Enter the labels with the data in the range B3:B9 and the Total label in cell A10.

TABLE F-2

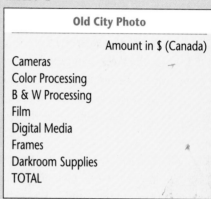

Old City Photo	
	Amount in $ (Canada)
Cameras	
Color Processing	
B & W Processing	
Film	
Digital Media	
Frames	
Darkroom Supplies	
TOTAL	

e. Enter the formula to sum the Amount column in cell B10. Ungroup the worksheets and enter your own data for each of the sales categories in the January, February, and March sheets.

f. Display each worksheet in its own window, then arrange the three sheets vertically.

g. Hide the window displaying the March sheet. Unhide the March sheet window.

h. Split the March window into two panes, the upper pane displaying rows one through five and the lower pane displaying rows six through ten. Scroll through the data in each pane, then remove the split.

i. Close the windows displaying Photo Sales.xlsx:2 and Photo Sales.xlsx:3, then maximize the Photo Sales.xlsx workbook.

j. Add the keywords **photo supplies** to your workbook, using the Document Properties Panel.

k. Group the worksheets again.

l. Add headers that include your name in the left section to all three worksheets.

m. With the worksheets still grouped, format the worksheets appropriately.

n. Ungroup the worksheets, then mark the workbook status as final.

o. Save the workbook, preview and print the three worksheets, then exit Excel.

▼ INDEPENDENT CHALLENGE 2

As the payroll manager at Media Communications, an advertising firm, you decide to organize the weekly timecard data using Excel worksheets. You use a separate worksheet for each week and track the hours for employees with different job classifications. A hyperlink in the worksheet provides pay rates for each classification and custom views limit the information that is displayed.

a. Start Excel, open the file EX F-4.xlsx from the drive and folder where you store your Data Files, then save it as **Timesheets**.

b. Compare the data in the workbook by arranging the Week 1, Week 2, and Week 3 sheets horizontally.

c. Maximize the Week 1 window. Unlock the hours data in the Week 1 sheet and protect the worksheet. Verify that the employee names, numbers, and classifications cannot be changed. Verify that the total hours data can be changed, but do not change the data.

d. Unprotect the Week 1 sheet and create a custom view called **Complete Worksheet** that displays all of the worksheet data.

e. Hide column E and create a custom view of the data in the range A1:D22. Give the view a name of **Employee Classifications**. Display each view, then return to the Complete Worksheet view.

▼ INDEPENDENT CHALLENGE 2 (CONTINUED)

f. Add a page break between columns D and E so that the Total Hours data prints on a second page. Preview the worksheet, then remove the page break. (*Hint:* Use the Breaks button on the Page Layout tab.)

g. Add a hyperlink to the Classification heading in cell D1 that links to the file Classifications.xlsx. Add a ScreenTip that reads Pay rates, then test the hyperlink. Compare your screen to Figure F-23.

h. Save the workbook as an Excel 97-2003 workbook, reviewing the Compatibility Checker information. Close the Timesheets.xls file, then reopen the Timesheets.xlsx workbook.

i. Group the three worksheets and add your name to the center section of the footer.

j. Save the workbook, then preview the grouped worksheets.

k. Ungroup the worksheets and add two-inch top and left margins to the Week 1 worksheet.

l. Hide the Week 2 and Week 3 worksheets.

m. Inspect the file and remove all document properties, personal information, headers, footers, and hidden worksheets.

n. Add the keyword hours to the workbook, save the workbook, then mark it as final.

FIGURE F-23

	A	B
1	**Media Communications**	
2	**Classifications**	**Pay Rate**
3	**Associate**	**$37**
4	**Sr. Associate**	**$45**
5	**Assistant**	**$22**
6	**Sr. Assistant**	**$30**
7		

Advanced Challenge Exercise

- Remove the final status from the workbook.
- If you have Windows Rights Management Services client software installed on your computer, restrict the permissions to the workbook by granting only yourself permission to change the workbook.
- If you have a valid certificate authority, add a digital signature to the workbook.
- Delete the hours data in the worksheet and save the workbook as an Excel Template.

o. Add your name to the center footer section, save the workbook, print the Week 1 worksheet, close the workbook and exit Excel.

▼ INDEPENDENT CHALLENGE 3

One of your responsibilities as the office manager at your technology training company is to order paper supplies for the office. You decide to create a spreadsheet to track these orders, placing each month's orders on its own sheet. You create custom views that will focus on the categories of supplies. A hyperlink will provide the supplier's contact information.

a. Start Excel, open the file EX F-5.xlsx from the drive and folder where you store your Data Files, then save it as **Supplies**.

b. Arrange the sheets for the three months horizontally to compare supply expenses, then close the extra workbook windows and maximize the remaining window.

c. Create a custom view of the entire January worksheet named **All Supplies**. Hide the paper, pens, and miscellaneous supply data and create a custom view displaying only the hardware supplies. Call the view **Hardware**.

d. Display the All Supplies view, group the worksheets, and create totals for the total costs in cell D28 on each month's sheet.

e. With the sheets grouped, add the sheet name to the center section of each sheet's header and your name to the center section of each sheet's footer.

f. Use the compatibility checker to view the unsupported features in earlier Excel formats.

g. Add a hyperlink in cell A1 of the January sheet that opens the file Hardware.xlsx. Add a ScreenTip of **Hardware Supplier**. Test the link, viewing the ScreenTip, then return to the Supplies workbook.

h. Create a workspace that includes the workbooks Supplies.xlsx and Hardware.xlsx in the tiled layout. Name the workspace **Office Supplies**. (*Hint:* Save Workspace is a button on the View tab in the Window group.)

i. Hide the Hardware.xlsx workbook.

j. Unhide the Hardware.xlsx workbook.

▼ INDEPENDENT CHALLENGE 3 (CONTINUED)

k. Close the Hardware.xlsx file and maximize the Supplies.xlsx worksheet.

l. Save the Supplies workbook as a macro-enabled workbook.

m. Print the January worksheet, close the workbook, and exit Excel.

▼ REAL LIFE INDEPENDENT CHALLENGE

Excel can be a useful tool in planning vacations. Whether you are planning a trip soon or in the distant future, you can use Excel to organize your travel budget. Use the table below as a guide in organizing your travel expenses. After your data is entered, you create custom views of the data, add a hyperlink and keywords, and save the file in an earlier version of Excel.

a. Start Excel, create a new workbook, then save it as **Travel Budget** in the drive and folder where you store your Data Files.

b. Enter your travel budget data using the relevant items from the Table F-3.

c. Add a hyperlink to your accommodations label that links to a Web page with information about the hotel, campground, B & B, or inn that you will stay at on your trip.

d. Create a custom view called **Entire Budget** that displays all of the budget information. Create a custom view named **Transportation** that displays only the transportation data. Check each view, then display the entire budget.

e. Add appropriate keywords to the workbook.

f. Add a footer that includes your name on the left side of the printout.

g. Unlock the price information in the worksheet. Protect the worksheet without using a password.

h. Save the workbook, then print the worksheet.

i. Save the workbook in Excel 97-2003 format.

j. Close the Travel Budget.xls file.

TABLE F-3

	Amount
Transportation	
Air	
Auto	
Train	
Cab	
Bus	
Accommodations	
Hotel	
Campground fees	
Bed & Breakfast	
Inn	
Meals	
Food	
Beverage	
Miscellaneous	
Admissions fees	
Souvenirs	

Advanced Challenge Exercise

- Open the Travel Budget.xlsx file and unprotect the worksheet.
- Enable the workbook to be changed by multiple people simultaneously.
- Set up the shared workbook so that all future changes will be tracked.
- Change the data for two of your dollar amounts.
- Review the tracked changes and accept the first change and reject the second change
- Save the workbook.

k. Exit Excel.

▼ VISUAL WORKSHOP

Start Excel, open the file EX F-6.xlsx from the drive and folder where you store your Data Files, then save it as **Summer Rentals**. Create the worksheet shown in Figure F-24. Enter your name in the footer, then print the worksheet. The text in cell A18 is a hyperlink to the Price Information workbook; the worksheet background is the Data File EX F-7.gif, and the picture in the header is the file EX F-7.gif.

FIGURE F-24

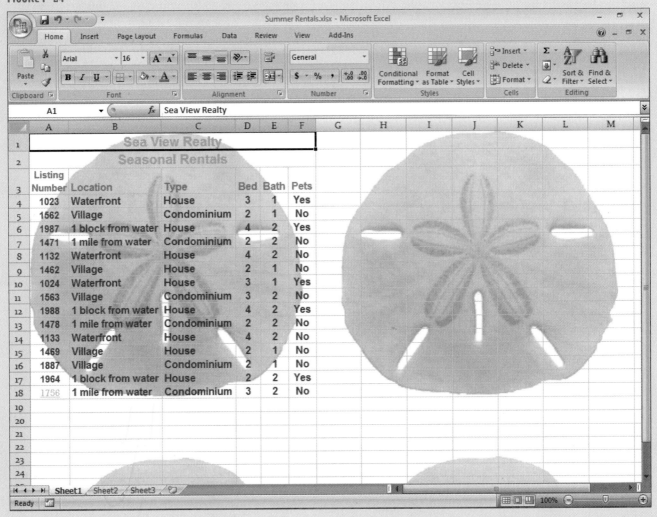

Using Tables

Files You Will Need:

EX G-1.xlsx
EX G-2.xlsx
EX G-3.xlsx
EX G-4.xlsx
EX G-5.xlsx

In addition to using Excel spreadsheet features, you can analyze and manipulate data in a table structure. An Excel **table** is an organized collection of rows and columns of similarly structured data in a worksheet. For example, a table might contain customer, sales, or inventory information. When you designate a particular range of worksheet data as a table, its formatting is extended when you add data and all table formulas are updated to include the new data. Without a table, you would have to manually adjust formatting and formulas every time data is added to a range. In this unit, you'll learn how to plan and create a table; add, change, find, and delete information in a table; and then sort, perform table calculations, and print a table. Quest uses tables to analyze tour data. The vice president of sales, Kate Morgan, asks you to help her build and manage a table of 2010 tour information.

OBJECTIVES

Plan a table

Create a table

Add table data

Find and replace table data

Delete table data

Sort table data

Use formulas in a table

Print a table

Planning a Table

When planning a table, consider what information you want your table to contain and how you want to work with the data, now and in the future. As you plan a table, you should understand its most important components. A table is organized into rows called records. A **record** contains data about an object, person, or other type of table item. Records are composed of fields. **Fields** are columns in the table; each field describes a characteristic of the record, such as a customer's last name or street address. Each field has a **field name**, which is a column label, such as "Address," that describes its contents. Tables usually have a **header row** as the first row that contains the field names. To plan your table, use the steps below. See Table G-1 for additional planning guidelines. Kate asks you to compile a table of the 2010 tours. Before entering the tour data into an Excel worksheet, you plan the table contents.

As you plan your table, use the following guidelines:

- **Identify the purpose of the table**

  Determine the kind of information the table should contain. You want to use the tours table to quickly find all departure dates of a particular tour. You also want to display the tours in order of departure date.

- **Plan the structure of the table**

  Determine the fields that are necessary to achieve the table's purpose. You have worked with the sales department to determine the type of information that they need to obtain about each tour. Figure G-1 shows a layout sketch for the table. Each row will contain one tour record. The columns represent fields that contain pieces of descriptive information you will enter for each tour, such as the name, departure date, and duration.

- **Document the table design**

  In addition to your table sketch, you should make a list of the field names that documents the type of data and any special number formatting required for each field. Field names should be as short as possible while still accurately describing the column info. When naming fields it is important to use text rather than numbers because numbers may be interpreted as parts of formulas. Your field names should be unique and not easily confused with cell addresses, such as the name D2. Your Tours table will contain eight field names, each one corresponding to the major characteristics of the 2010 tours. Table G-2 shows the documentation of the field names in your table.

TABLE G-1: Guidelines for planning a table

worksheet structure guidelines	row and column content guidelines
Tables can be created from any contiguous range of cells on your worksheet	Plan and design your table so that all rows have similar items in the same column
A table should not have any blank rows or columns	Do not insert extra spaces at the beginning of a cell because this can affect sorting and searching
Data in your table can be used independently of data outside of the table on the worksheet	Instead of blank rows or columns between your labels and your data, use formatting to make column labels stand out from the data
Data can be organized on a worksheet using multiple tables to define sets of related data	Use the same format for all cells below the field name in a column

Tour	Depart Date	Number of Days	Seat Capacity	Seats Reserved	Price	Air Included	Meals Included

Header row will contain field names

Each tour will be placed in a table row

TABLE G-2: **Table documentation**

field name	type of data	description of data
Tour	Text	Name of tour
Depart Date	Date	Date tour departs
Number of Days	Number with 0 decimal places	Duration of the tour
Seat Capacity	Number with 0 decimal places	Maximum number of people the tour can accommodate
Seats Reserved	Number with 0 decimal places	Number of reservations for the tour
Price	Accounting with 0 decimal places and $ symbol	Tour price (This price is not guaranteed until a 30% deposit is received)
Air Included	Text	Yes: Airfare is included in the price No: Airfare is not included in the price
Meals Included	Text	Yes: Breakfast and dinner included in the price No: Meals are not included in the price

Creating a Table

Once you have planned the table structure, the sequence of fields, and appropriate data types, you are ready to create the table in Excel. After you create a table, a Table Tools Design tab appears, containing a gallery of table styles. **Table styles** allow you to easily add formatting to your table by using preset formatting combinations that define fill color, borders, and type style and color. ▒▒▒▒ Kate asks you to build a table with the 2010 tour data. You begin by entering the field names. Then you enter the tour data that corresponds to each field name, create the table, and format the data using a table style.

STEPS

1. **Start Excel, open the file EX G-1.xlsx from the drive and folder where you store your Data Files, then save it as 2010 Tours**

TROUBLE
Don't worry if your field names are wider than the cells; you will fix this later.

2. **Beginning in cell A1 of the Practice sheet, enter each field name in a separate column, as shown in Figure G-2**
   Field names are usually entered in the first row of the table.

3. **Enter the information from Figure G-3 in the rows immediately below the field names, leaving no blank rows**
   The data appears in columns organized by field name.

4. **Select the range A1:H4, click the Format button in the Cells group, click AutoFit Column Width, then click cell A1**
   Resizing the column widths this way is faster than double-clicking the column divider lines.

5. **With cell A1 selected, click the Insert tab, then click the Table button in the Tables group, in the Create Table dialog box verify that your table data is in the range $A$1:$H$4 and make sure My table has headers is checked, then click OK**
   Filter list arrows, which let you display portions of your data, appear next to each column header. When you create a table, Excel automatically applies a default table style. The Table Tools Design tab appears and the Table Styles group displays a gallery of table formatting options. You decide to use a different table style from the gallery.

6. **Click the Table Styles More button ▼, scroll to view all of the table styles, then move the mouse pointer over several styles without clicking**
   As you point to each table style, Live Preview shows you what your table will look like with the style applied. However, you only see a preview of each style; you need to click a style to apply it.

7. **Click the Table Style Medium 7 to apply it to your table, then click cell A1**
   Compare your table to Figure G-4.

Coordinating table styles with your document

The Table Styles gallery on the Table Tools Design tab has three style categories: Light, Medium, and Dark. Each category has numerous design types; for example, in some of the designs, the header row and total row are darker and the rows alternate colors. The available table designs use the current workbook theme colors so the table coordinates with your existing workbook content. If you select a different workbook theme and color scheme in the Themes group on the Page Layout tab, the Table Styles gallery uses those colors. You can modify gallery styles further by using the options in the Table Style Options group on the Table Tools Design tab; for example, if you select Header Row, the table styles in the gallery will all display distinctive header rows.

FIGURE G-2: Field names entered in row 1

	A	B	C	D	E	F	G	H	I
1	Tour	Depart Date	Number of Days	Seat Capacity	Seats Reserved	Price	Air Included	Meals Included	
2									

FIGURE G-3: Three records entered in the worksheet

	A	B	C	D	E	F	G	H	I
1	Tour	Depart Date	Number of Days	Seat Capacity	Seats Reserved	Price	Air Included	Meals Included	
2	Pacific Odyssey	1/11/2010	14	50	50	3105	Yes	No	
3	Old Japan	1/12/2010	21	47	41	2100	Yes	No	
4	Down Under Exodus	1/18/2010	10	30	28	2800	Yes	Yes	
5									

FIGURE G-4: Formatted table with three records

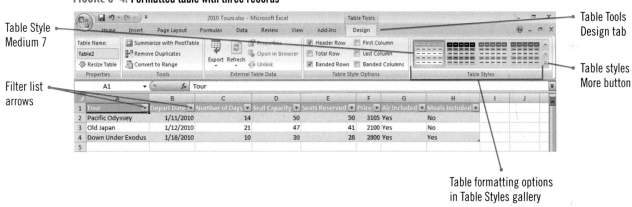

Table Style Medium 7

Filter list arrows

Table Tools Design tab

Table styles More button

Table formatting options in Table Styles gallery

Changing table style options

You can modify a table's appearance by using the check boxes in the Table Styles Options group on the Table Tools Design tab. For example, you can turn on or turn off the following options: **banding**, which creates different formatting for adjacent rows and columns; special formatting for first and last columns; Total Row, which calculates totals for each column; and Header Row, which displays or hides the header row. Use these options to modify a table's appearance either before or after applying a Table Style. For example, if your table has banded rows, you can select the Banded Columns check box to change the table to display with banded columns. Also, you may want to deselect the Header Row check box to hide a table's header row if a table will be included in a presentation. Figure G-5 shows the available table style options.

You can also create your own table style by clicking the Table Styles More button, then at the bottom of the Table Styles Gallery, clicking New Table Style. In the New Table Quick Style dialog box, name the style in the Name text box, click a table element, then

format selected table elements by clicking Format. You can also set a custom style as the default style for your tables by checking the Set as default table quick style for this document check box. You can click Clear at the bottom of the Table Styles gallery if you want to clear a table style.

FIGURE G-5: Table Styles Options

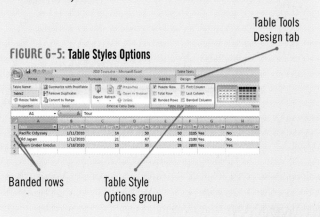

Table Tools Design tab

Banded rows

Table Style Options group

Adding Table Data

You can add records to a table by typing data directly below the last row of the table. After you press [Enter], the new row is added to the table and the table formatting is extended to the new data. When the active cell is the last cell of a table, you can add a new row by pressing [Tab]. You can add rows in any table location. If you decide you need additional data fields, you can add new columns to a table. Another way to expand a table is to drag the sizing handle in a table's lower-right corner; drag down to add rows and drag to the right to add columns. After entering all of the 2010 tour data, Kate decides to offer two additional tours. She also wants the table to display the number of available seats for each tour and whether visas are required for the destination.

STEPS

1. Activate the 2010 Tours sheet

The sheet contains the 2010 tour data.

2. Click cell A65 in the table, enter the data for the new Costa Rica Rainforest tour, as shown in Figure G-6, then press [Enter]

The new Costa Rica tour is part of the table. You want to enter a record about a new January tour above row 6.

QUICK TIP

You can select a table column by clicking the top edge of the field name. Be careful not to click a column letter or row number, however, because this selects the entire worksheet column or row. You can select the table data by clicking the upper-left corner of the first table cell. Clicking a second time will include the table header in the selection.

3. Click the inside left edge of cell A6 to select the table row data, click the Insert list arrow in the Cells group, then click Insert Table Rows Above

Clicking the left edge of the first cell in a table row selects the entire table row. A new blank row 6 is available to enter the new record.

4. Click cell A6, then enter the Nepal Trekking record, as shown in Figure G-7

The new Nepal tour is part of the table. You want to add a new field that displays the number of available seats for each tour.

5. Click cell I1, enter the field name Seats Available, then press [Enter]

The new field becomes part of the table and the header formatting extends to the new field. The AutoCorrect menu allows you to undo or stop the automatic table expansion, but in this case, you decide to leave this feature on. You want to add another new field to the table to display tours that require visas, but this time you will add the new field by resizing the table.

QUICK TIP

You can also resize a table by clicking the Table Tools Design tab, clicking the Resize Table button in the Properties group, selecting the new data range for the table, then clicking OK.

6. Scroll down until cell I66 is visible, drag the sizing handle in the table's lower-right corner one column to the right to add column J to the table, as shown in Figure G-8.

The table range is now A1:J66 and the new field name is Column1.

7. Click cell J1, enter Visa Required, then press [Enter]

8. Click the Insert tab, click the Header & Footer button in the Text group, enter your name in the center header text box, click cell A1, click the Normal button ▦ in the status bar, then save the workbook

FIGURE G-6: New record in row 65

61	Galapagos Adventure	12/20/2010	14	15	1	$ 3,100	Yes	Yes
62	Pacific Odyssey	12/21/2010	14	50	10	$ 3,105	Yes	No
63	Essential India	12/30/2010	18	51	15	$ 3,933	Yes	Yes
64	Old Japan	12/31/2010	21	47	4	$ 2,100	Yes	No
65	Costa Rica Rainforests	1/30/2010	7	20	0	$ 2,590	Yes	Yes
66								

New record
in row 65

FIGURE G-7: New record in row 6

	A	B	C	D	E	F	G	H
1	Tour	Depart Date	Number of Days	Seat Capacity	Seats Reserved	Price	Air Included	Meals Included
2	Pacific Odyssey	1/11/2010	14	50	50	$ 3,105	Yes	No
3	Old Japan	1/12/2010	21	47	41	$ 2,100	Yes	No
4	Down Under Exodus	1/18/2010	10	30	28	$ 2,800	Yes	Yes
5	Essential India	1/20/2010	18	51	40	$ 3,933	Yes	Yes
6	Nepal Trekking	1/31/2010	14	18	0	$ 4,200	Yes	Yes
7	Amazing Amazon	2/23/2010	14	43	38	$ 2,877	No	No
8	Cooking in France	2/28/2010	7	18	15	$ 2,822	Yes	No
9	Pearls of the Orient	3/12/2010	14	50	15	$ 3,400	Yes	No
10	Silk Road Travels	3/18/2010	18	25	19	$ 2,190	Yes	Yes

New record
in row 6

FIGURE G-8: Resizing a table using the resizing handles

60	Panama Adventure	12/18/2010	10	50	21	$ 2,304	Yes	Yes
61	Galapagos Adventure	12/20/2010	14	15	1	$ 3,100	Yes	Yes
62	Galapagos Adventure	12/20/2010	14	15	1	$ 3,100	Yes	Yes
63	Pacific Odyssey	12/21/2010	14	50	10	$ 3,105	Yes	No
64	Essential India	12/30/2010	18	51	15	$ 3,933	Yes	Yes
65	Old Japan	12/31/2010	21	47	4	$ 2,100	Yes	No
66	Costa Rica Rainforests	1/30/2010	7	20	0	$ 2,590	Yes	Yes
67								
68								
69								

Drag sizing handle
to add column J

Finding and Replacing Table Data

From time to time, you need to locate specific records in your table. You can use the Excel Find feature to search your table for a particular record. You can also use the Replace feature to locate and replace existing entries or portions of entries with information you specify. If you don't know the exact spelling of the text you are searching for, you can use wildcards to help locate the records. **Wildcards** are special symbols that substitute for unknown characters. ▨▧▦ In response to feedback from the sales representatives about customers' lack of familiarity of Istria, Kate wants to replace "Istria" with "Croatia" in all of the tour names. She also wants to know how many Pacific Odyssey tours are scheduled for the year. You begin by searching for records with the text "Pacific Odyssey".

STEPS

1. **Click cell A1 if necessary, click the Home tab, click the Find & Select button in the Editing group, then click Find**

   The Find and Replace dialog box opens, as shown in Figure G-9. In this dialog box, you enter criteria that specify the records you want to find in the Find what text box. You want to search for records whose Tour field contains the label "Pacific Odyssey".

2. **Type Pacific Odyssey in the Find what text box, then click Find Next**

   A2 is the active cell because it is the first instance of Pacific Odyssey in the table.

3. **Click Find Next and examine the record for each found Pacific Odyssey tour until no more matching cells are found in the table and the active cell is A2 again, then click Close**

   There are four Pacific Odyssey tours.

4. **Return to cell A1, click the Find & Select button in the Editing group, then click Replace**

   The Find and Replace dialog box opens with the Replace tab selected and the insertion point in the Replace with text box, as shown in Figure G-10. You will search for entries containing "Istria" and replace them with "Croatia". You are not sure of the spelling of Istria, so you will use the * wildcard to help you locate the records containing the correct tour name.

5. **Delete any text in the Find what text box, type Is* in the Find what text box, click the Replace with text box, then type Croatia**

   The asterisk (*) wildcard stands for one or more characters, meaning that the search text Is* will find words such as "Is", "Isn't", and "Islington". Because you notice that there are other table entries containing the text "is" with a lowercase "i" (in the Visa Required column heading), you need to make sure that only capitalized instances of the letter I are replaced.

6. **Click Options >>, click the Match case check box to select it, click Options <<, then click Find Next**

   Excel moves the cell pointer to the first occurrence of "Istria".

7. **Click Replace All, click OK, then click Close**

   The dialog box closes. Excel made two replacements, in cells A22 and A51. The Visa Required field heading remains unchanged because the "is" in "Visa" is lowercase.

8. **Save the workbook**

FIGURE G-9: Find and Replace dialog box

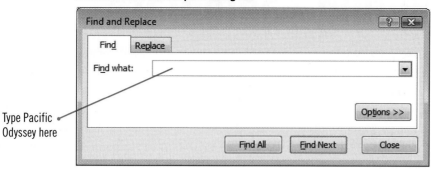

Type Pacific
Odyssey here

FIGURE G-10: The Replace tab in the Find and Replace dialog box

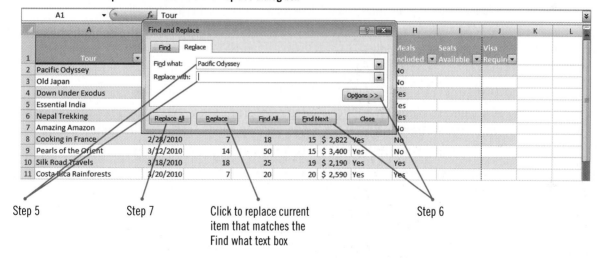

Step 5   Step 7   Click to replace current   Step 6
                                item that matches the
                                Find what text box

Using Find and Select features

You can also use the Find feature to navigate to a specific place in a workbook by clicking the Find & Select button in the Editing group, clicking Go To, typing a cell address, then clicking OK. Clicking the Find & Select button also allows you to find comments and conditional formatting in a worksheet by clicking Go to Special. You can use the Go to Special dialog box to select cells that contain different types of formulas, objects, or data validation. Some Go to Special commands also appear on the Find & Select menu. Using this menu, you can also change the mouse pointer shape to the Select Objects pointer ⬚ so you can quickly select drawing objects when necessary. To return to the standard Excel pointer, press [Esc].

Deleting Table Data

In order to keep a table up to date, you need to be able to periodically remove records. You may even need to remove fields if the information stored in a field becomes unnecessary. You can delete table data using the Delete button or by dragging the sizing handle at the table's lower right corner. You can also easily delete duplicate records from a table. ▰▰▰▰▰ Kate is canceling the Old Japan tour that departs on 1/12/2010 and asks you to delete the record from the table. You will also remove any duplicate records from the table. Because the visa requirements are difficult to keep up with, Kate asks you to delete the field with visa information.

STEPS

1. **Click the left edge of cell A3 to select the table row data, click the Delete button list arrow in the Cells group, then click Delete Table Rows**

   The Old Japan tour is deleted and the Down Under Exodus tour moves up to row 3, as shown in Figure G-11. You can also delete a table row or a column using the Resize Table button in the Properties group of the Table Tools Design tab, or by right-clicking the row or column, pointing to Delete on the shortcut menu, then clicking Table Columns or Table Rows. You decide to check the table for duplicate records.

2. **Click the Table Tools Design tab, then click the Remove Duplicates button in the Tools group**

   The Remove Duplicates dialog box opens, as shown in Figure G-12. You need to select the columns that the program should use to evaluate duplicates. Because you don't want to delete tours with the same destination but different departure dates, you will look for duplicate data in all of the columns.

> **QUICK TIP**
> You can also remove duplicates from worksheet data by clicking the Data tab, then clicking the Remove Duplicates button in the Data Tools group.

3. **Make sure that "My data has headers" is checked and that all the columns headers are checked, then click OK**

   Two duplicate records are found and removed, leaving 63 rows in the table, including the header row. You want to remove the last column, which contains space for visa information.

4. **Click OK, scroll down until cell J63 is visible, drag the sizing handle of the table's lower-right corner one column to the left to remove column J from the table**

   The table range is now A1:I63 and the Visa Required field no longer appears in the table.

5. **Delete the contents of cell J1, return to cell A1, then save the workbook**

FIGURE G-11: Table with row deleted

	Tour	Depart Date	Number of Days	Seat Capacity	Seats Reserved	Price	Air Included	Meals Included	Seats Available	Visa Required
2	Pacific Odyssey	1/11/2010	14	50	50	$ 3,105	Yes	No		
3	Down Under Exodus	1/18/2010	10	30	28	$ 2,800	Yes	Yes		
4	Essential India	1/20/2010	18	51	40	$ 3,933	Yes	Yes		
5	Nepal Trekking	1/31/2010	14	18	0	$ 4,200	Yes	Yes		
6	Amazing Amazon	2/23/2010	14	43	38	$ 2,877	No	No		
7	Cooking in France	2/28/2010	7	18	15	$ 2,822	Yes	No		
8	Pearls of the Orient	3/12/2010	14	50	15	$ 3,400	Yes	No		
9	Silk Road Travels	3/18/2010	18	25	19	$ 2,190	Yes	Yes		
10	Costa Rica Rainforests	3/20/2010	7	20	20	$ 2,590	Yes	Yes		
11	Green Adventures in Ecuador	3/23/2010	18	25	22	$ 2,450	No	No		
12	African National Parks	4/7/2010	30	12	10	$ 4,870	Yes	Yes		
13	Experience Cambodia	4/10/2010	12	40	21	$ 2,908	Yes	No		
14	Old Japan	4/14/2010	21	47	30	$ 2,100	Yes	No		
15	Down Under Exodus	4/18/2010	10	30	20	$ 2,800	Yes	Yes		
16	Essential India	4/20/2010	18	51	31	$ 3,933	Yes	Yes		
17	Amazing Amazon	4/23/2010	14	43	30	$ 2,877	No	No		
18	Catalonia Adventure	5/9/2010	14	51	30	$ 3,100	Yes	No		
19	Treasures of Ethiopia	5/18/2010	10	41	15	$ 3,200	Yes	Yes		
20	Monasteries of Bulgaria	5/20/2010	7	19	11	$ 2,103	Yes	Yes		
21	Cooking in Croatia	5/23/2010	7	12	10	$ 2,110	No	No		
22	Magnificent Montenegro	5/27/2010	10	48	4	$ 1,890	No	No		
23	Catalonia Adventure	6/9/2010	14	51	15	$ 3,100	Yes	No		
24	Nepal Trekking	6/9/2010	14	18	18	$ 4,200	Yes	Yes		
25	Corfu Sailing Voyage	6/10/2010	21	12	10	$ 3,190	Yes	No		
26	Ireland by Bike	6/11/2010	10	15	10	$ 2,600	Yes	No		

Practice **2010 Tours** Sheet2

Ready   Average: 8612.8   Count: 8   Sum: 43064   100%

Row is deleted and tours move up one row

FIGURE G-12: Remove Duplicates dialog box

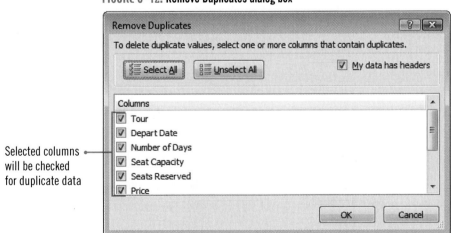

Selected columns will be checked for duplicate data

Sorting Table Data

Usually, you enter table records in the order in which you receive information, rather than in alphabetical or numerical order. When you add records to a table, you usually enter them at the end of the table. You can change the order of the records any time using the Excel **sort** feature. You can sort a table in ascending or descending order on one field using the filter list arrows next to the field name. In **ascending order**, the lowest value (the beginning of the alphabet or the earliest date) appears at the top of the table. In a field containing labels and numbers, numbers appear first in the sorted list. In **descending order**, the highest value (the end of the alphabet or the latest date) appears at the top of the table. In a field containing labels and numbers, labels appear first. Table G-3 provides examples of ascending and descending sorts. Because the data is structured as a table, Excel changes the order of the records while keeping each record, or row of information, together. ▓▓▓▓ Kate wants the tour data sorted by departure date, displaying tours that depart the soonest at the top of the table.

STEPS

QUICK TIP

Before you sort records, consider making a backup copy of your table or create a field that numbers the records so you can return them to their original order, if necessary.

1. **Click the** Depart Date filter list arrow, **then click** Sort Oldest to Newest

   Excel rearranges the records in ascending order by depart date, as shown in Figure G-13. The Depart Date filter list arrow has an upward pointing arrow indicating the ascending sort in the field. You can also sort the table on one field using the Sort & Filter button.

2. **Click the** Home tab, **click any cell in the** Price **column, click the** Sort & Filter **button in the Editing group, then click** Sort Largest to Smallest

   Excel sorts the table, placing those records with the higher price at the top. The Price filter list arrow now has a downward pointing arrow next to the filter list arrow, indicating the descending sort order. You can also rearrange the table data using a **multilevel sort**. This type of sort rearranges the table data using different levels. If you use two sort levels, the data is sorted by the first field and the second field is sorted within each grouping of the first field. Since you have many groups of tours with different departure dates, you want to use a multilevel sort to arrange the table data by tours and then by departure dates within each tour.

QUICK TIP

You can also add a multilevel sort by clicking the Data tab and then clicking the Sort button in the Sort & Filter group.

3. **Click the** Sort & Filter **button in the Editing group, then click** Custom Sort

   The Sort dialog box opens, as shown in Figure G-14.

QUICK TIP

You can include capitalization as a sort criterion by clicking Options in the Sort dialog box, then selecting the Case sensitive box. When you choose this option, lowercase entries precede uppercase entries.

4. **Click the** Sort by **list arrow, click** Tour, **click the** Order **list arrow, click** A to Z, **click** Add Level, **click the** Then by **list arrow, click** Depart Date, **click the second** Order **list arrow, click** Oldest to Newest **if necessary, then click** OK

   Figure G-15 shows the table sorted alphabetically in ascending order (A-Z) by Tour and, within each tour, in ascending order by the Depart Date.

5. **Save the workbook**

Sorting a table using conditional formatting

If conditional formats have been applied to a table, you can sort the table using conditional formatting to arrange the rows. For example, if cells are conditionally formatted with color, you can sort a field on Cell Color, using the color with the order of On Top or On Bottom in the Sort dialog box.

TABLE G-3: Sort order options and examples

option	alphabetic	numeric	date	alphanumeric
Ascending	A, B, C	7, 8, 9	1/1, 2/1, 3/1	12A, 99B, DX8, QT7
Descending	C, B, A	9, 8, 7	3/1, 2/1, 1/1	QT7, DX8, 99B, 12A

FIGURE G-13: Table sorted by depature date

Up arrow indicates ascending sort in the field

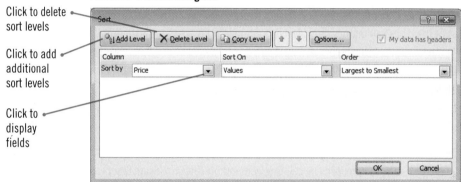

	A	B	C	D	E	F	G	H	I
1	Tour	Depart Date	Number of Days	Seat Capacity	Seats Reserved	Price	Air Included	Meals Included	Seats Available
2	Pacific Odyssey	1/11/2010	14	50	50	$ 3,105	Yes	No	
3	Down Under Exodus	1/18/2010	10	30	28	$ 2,800	Yes	Yes	
4	Essential India	1/20/2010	18	51	40	$ 3,933	Yes	Yes	
5	Costa Rica Rainforests	1/30/2010	7	20	0	$ 2,590	Yes	Yes	
6	Nepal Trekking	1/31/2010	14	18	0	$ 4,200	Yes	Yes	
7	Amazing Amazon	2/23/2010	14	43	38	$ 2,877	No	No	
8	Cooking in France	2/28/2010	7	18	15	$ 2,822	Yes	No	
9	Pearls of the Orient	3/12/2010	14	50	15	$ 3,400	Yes	No	
10	Silk Road Travels	3/18/2010	18	25	19	$ 2,190	Yes	Yes	
11	Costa Rica Rainforests	3/20/2010	7	20	20	$ 2,590	Yes	Yes	
12	Green Adventures in Ecuador	3/23/2010	18	25	22	$ 2,450	No	No	
13	African National Parks	4/7/2010	30	12	10	$ 4,870	Yes	Yes	
14	Experience Cambodia	4/10/2010	12	40	21	$ 2,908	Yes	No	
15	Old Japan	4/14/2010	21	47	30	$ 2,100	Yes	No	
16	Down Under Exodus	4/18/2010	10	30	20	$ 2,800	Yes	Yes	
17	Essential India	4/20/2010	18	51	31	$ 3,933	Yes	Yes	
18	Amazing Amazon	4/23/2010	14	43	30	$ 2,877	No	No	
19	Catalonia Adventure	5/9/2010	14	51	30	$ 3,100	Yes	No	
20	Treasures of Ethiopia	5/18/2010	10	41	15	$ 3,200	Yes	Yes	
21	Monasteries of Bulgaria	5/20/2010	7	19	11	$ 2,103	Yes	No	
22	Cooking in Croatia	5/23/2010	7	12	10	$ 2,110	No	No	
23	Magnificent Montenegro	5/27/2010	10	48	4	$ 1,890	No	No	
24	Catalonia Adventure	6/9/2010	14	51	15	$ 3,100	Yes	No	
25	Nepal Trekking	6/9/2010	14	18	18	$ 4,200	Yes	Yes	

FIGURE G-14: Sort dialog box

Click to delete sort levels

Click to add additional sort levels

Click to display fields

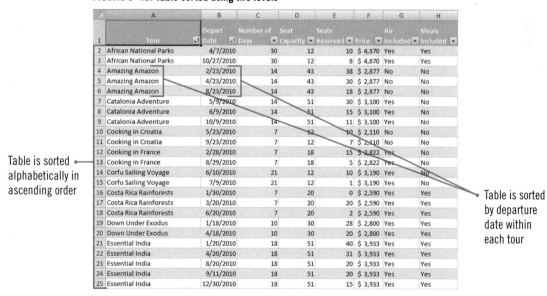

FIGURE G-15: Table sorted using two levels

	A	B	C	D	E	F	G	H
1	Tour	Depart Date	Number of Days	Seat Capacity	Seats Reserved	Price	Air Included	Meals Included
2	African National Parks	4/7/2010	30	12	10	$ 4,870	Yes	Yes
3	African National Parks	10/27/2010	30	12	8	$ 4,870	Yes	Yes
4	Amazing Amazon	2/23/2010	14	43	38	$ 2,877	No	No
5	Amazing Amazon	4/23/2010	14	43	30	$ 2,877	No	No
6	Amazing Amazon	8/23/2010	14	43	18	$ 2,877	No	No
7	Catalonia Adventure	5/9/2010	14	51	30	$ 3,100	Yes	No
8	Catalonia Adventure	6/9/2010	14	51	15	$ 3,100	Yes	No
9	Catalonia Adventure	10/9/2010	14	51	11	$ 3,100	Yes	No
10	Cooking in Croatia	5/23/2010	7	12	10	$ 2,110	No	No
11	Cooking in Croatia	9/23/2010	7	12	7	$ 2,110	No	No
12	Cooking in France	2/28/2010	7	18	15	$ 2,822	Yes	No
13	Cooking in France	8/29/2010	7	18	5	$ 2,822	Yes	No
14	Corfu Sailing Voyage	6/10/2010	21	12	10	$ 3,190	Yes	No
15	Corfu Sailing Voyage	7/9/2010	21	12	1	$ 3,190	Yes	No
16	Costa Rica Rainforests	1/30/2010	7	20	0	$ 2,590	Yes	Yes
17	Costa Rica Rainforests	3/20/2010	7	20	20	$ 2,590	Yes	Yes
18	Costa Rica Rainforests	6/20/2010	7	20	2	$ 2,590	Yes	Yes
19	Down Under Exodus	1/18/2010	10	30	28	$ 2,800	Yes	Yes
20	Down Under Exodus	4/18/2010	10	30	20	$ 2,800	Yes	Yes
21	Essential India	1/20/2010	18	51	40	$ 3,933	Yes	Yes
22	Essential India	4/20/2010	18	51	31	$ 3,933	Yes	Yes
23	Essential India	8/20/2010	18	51	20	$ 3,933	Yes	Yes
24	Essential India	9/11/2010	18	51	20	$ 3,933	Yes	Yes
25	Essential India	12/30/2010	18	51	15	$ 3,933	Yes	Yes

Table is sorted alphabetically in ascending order

Table is sorted by departure date within each tour

Specifying a custom sort order

You can identify a custom sort order for the field selected in the Sort by box. Click the Order list arrow in the Sort dialog box, click Custom List, then click the desired custom order. Commonly used custom sort orders are days of the week (Sun, Mon, Tues, Wed, etc.) and months (Jan, Feb, Mar, etc.); alphabetic sorts do not sort these items properly.

Using Formulas in a Table

Many tables are large, making it difficult to know from viewing them the "story" the table tells. The Excel table calculation features help you summarize table data so you can see important trends. After you enter a single formula into a table cell, the **calculated columns** feature fills in the remaining cells with the formula's results. The column continues to fill with the formula results as you enter rows in the table. This makes it easy to update your formulas because you only need to edit the formula once, and the change will fill in to the other column cells. The **structured reference** feature allows your formulas to refer to table columns by names that are automatically generated when you create the table. These names automatically adjust as you add or delete table fields. An example of a table reference is =[Sales]–[Costs], where Sales and Costs are field names in the table. Tables also have a specific area at the bottom called the **table total row** for calculations using the data in the table columns. The cells in this row contain a dropdown list of functions that can be used for the column calculation. The table total row adapts to any changes in the table size. ▓▓▓▓▓ Kate wants you to use a formula to calculate the number of available seats for each tour. You will also add summary information to the end of the table.

STEPS

1. **Click cell I2, then type =[**

   A list of the table field names is displayed, as shown in Figure G-16. Structured referencing allows you to use the names that Excel created when you defined your table to reference fields in a formula. You can choose a field by clicking it and pressing [TAB] or by double-clicking the field name.

2. **Click [Seat Capacity], press [Tab], then type]**

   Excel begins the formula, placing [Seat Capacity] in the cell in blue and framing the Seat Capacity data in a blue border.

3. **Type -[, double-click [Seats Reserved], then type]**

   Excel places [Seats Reserved] in the cell in green and outlines the Seats Reserved data in a green border.

4. **Press [Enter]**

   The formula result, 2, is displayed in cell I2. The table column also fills with the formula displaying the number of available seats for each tour.

5. **Click the AutoCorrect Options list arrow** ⚡▾

   Because the calculated columns option saves time, you decide to leave the feature on. You want to display the total number of available seats on all of the tours.

6. **Click any cell inside the table, click the Table Tools Design tab, then click the Total Row check box in the Table Style Options group to select it**

   A total row appears at the bottom of the table and the sum of the available seats, 1035, is displayed in cell I64. You can select other formulas in the total row.

7. **Click cell C64, then click the cell list arrow on the right side of the cell**

   The list of available functions appears, as shown in Figure G-17. You want to find the average tour length.

8. **Click Average, then save your workbook**

   The average tour length, 13 days, appears in cell C64.

> **QUICK TIP**
> You can undo the calculated column results by clicking Undo Calculated Column in the AutoCorrect Options list. You can turn off the Calculated Columns feature by clicking Stop Automatically Creating Calculated Columns in the AutoCorrect Options list.

	A	B	C	D	E	F	G	H	I	J
1	Tour	Depart Date	Number of Days	Seat Capacity	Seats Reserved	Price	Air Included	Meals Included	Seats Available	
2	African National Parks	4/7/2010	30	12	10	$ 4,870	Yes	Yes	=[	
3	African National Parks	10/27/2010	30	12	8	$ 4,870	Yes	Yes		
4	Amazing Amazon	2/23/2010	14	43	38	$ 2,877	No	No		
5	Amazing Amazon	4/23/2010	14	43	30	$ 2,877	No	No		
6	Amazing Amazon	8/23/2010	14	43	18	$ 2,877	No	No		
7	Catalonia Adventure	5/9/2010	14	51	30	$ 3,100	Yes	No		
8	Catalonia Adventure	6/9/2010	14	51	15	$ 3,100	Yes	No		
9	Catalonia Adventure	10/9/2010	14	51	11	$ 3,100	Yes	No		
10	Cooking in Croatia	5/23/2010	7	12	10	$ 2,110	No	No		
11	Cooking in Croatia	9/23/2010	7	12	7	$ 2,110	No	No		
12	Cooking in France	2/28/2010	7	18	15	$ 2,822	Yes	No		

Dropdown list: Tour, Depart Date, Number of Days, Seat Capacity, Seats Reserved, Price, Air Included, Meals Included, Seats Available

Table field names

	Tour	Depart Date	Number of Days	Seat Capacity	Seats Reserved	Price	Air Included	Meals Included	Seats Available	J
51	Pacific Odyssey	7/7/2010	14	50	35	$ 3,105	Yes	No	15	
52	Pacific Odyssey	9/14/2010	14	50	20	$ 3,105	Yes	No	30	
53	Pacific Odyssey	12/21/2010	14	50	10	$ 3,105	Yes	No	40	
54	Panama Adventure	6/18/2010	10	50	29	$ 2,304	Yes	Yes	21	
55	Panama Adventure	12/18/2010	10	50	21	$ 2,304	Yes	Yes	29	
56	Pearls of the Orient	3/12/2010	14	50	15	$ 3,400	Yes	No	35	
57	Pearls of the Orient	9/12/2010	14	50	11	$ 3,400	Yes	No	39	
58	Silk Road Travels	3/18/2010	18	25	19	$ 2,190	Yes	Yes	6	
59	Silk Road Travels	9/18/2010	18	25	9	$ 2,190	Yes	Yes	16	
60	Treasures of Ethiopia	5/18/2010	10	41	15	$ 3,200	Yes	Yes	26	
61	Treasures of Ethiopia	11/18/2010	10	41	12	$ 3,200	Yes	Yes	29	
62	Wild River Escape	6/27/2010	10	21	21	$ 1,944	No	No	0	
63	Wild River Escape	8/27/2010	10	21	11	$ 1,944	No	No	10	
64	Total								1035	
65										
66										
67										
68										
69										
70										
71										
72										

Dropdown list: None, Average, Count, Count Numbers, Max, Min, Sum, StdDev, Var, More Functions...

Functions available in
the Total Row

Using structured references

Structured references make it easier to work with formulas that use table data. You can reference all of the table, columns in the table, or specific data. What makes structured references helpful to use in formulas is that they automatically adjust as data ranges change in a table, so you don't need to edit formulas. When you create a table from worksheet data, Excel creates a default table name such as Table1. This references all of the table data but not the header row or any total rows. To refer to a table such as Table1 with its header row, you need to use the reference =Table1[#All]. Excel also names each column of a table which can be referenced in formulas. For example, in Table 1, the formula =Table1[Sales] references the data in the Sales field.

Printing a Table

You can determine the way a table will print using the Page Layout tab. Because tables often have more rows than can fit on a page, you can define the first row of the table (containing the field names) as the **print title**, which prints at the top of every page. You can also scale the table to print more or fewer rows on each page. Most tables do not have any descriptive information above the field names on the worksheet, so to augment the field name information, you can use headers and footers to add identifying text, such as the table title or the report date. ░░░░ Kate asks you for a printout of the tour information. You begin by previewing the table.

STEPS

1. **Click the Office button ⊙, point to Print, then click Print Preview**
   The status bar reads Preview: Page 1 of 3. All of the field names in the table fit across the width of the page.

2. **In the Print Preview window, click the Next Page button in the Preview group to view the second page, then click Next Page again to view the third page**
   The third page contains only one record and the total row, so you will scale the table to print on two pages.

3. **Click the Close Print Preview button, click the Page Layout tab, click the Width list arrow in the Scale to Fit group, click 1 page, click the Height list arrow, then click 2 pages**
   You decide to preview the table again to view the changes in scale.

4. **Click the Office button, point to Print, click Print Preview, then click the Next Page button in the Preview group**
   The records are scaled to fit on two pages. The status bar reads Preview: Page 2 of 2. Because the records on page 2 appear without column headings, you want to set up the first row of the table, which contains the field names, as a repeating print title.

5. **Click the Close Print Preview button, click the Print Titles button in the Page Setup group, click inside the Rows to repeat at top text box under Print titles, click any cell in row 1 on the table, then compare your Page Setup dialog box to Figure G-18**
   When you select row 1 as a print title, Excel automatically inserts an absolute reference to the row that will repeat at the top of each page.

6. **Click Print Preview, click the Next Page button to view the second page, then click the Close Print Preview button**
   Setting up a print title to repeat row 1 causes the field names to appear at the top of each printed page. The printout would be more informative with a header to identify the table information.

7. **Click the Insert tab, click the Header & Footer button in the Text group, click the left header section text box, then type 2010 Tours**

8. **Select the left header section information, click the Home tab, click the Increase Font Size button A˙ in the Font group twice to change the font size to 14, click the Bold button B in the Font group, click any cell in the table, then click the Normal button ▦ in the status bar**

9. **Save the table, preview then print it, close the workbook, then exit Excel**
   Compare your printed table with Figure G-19.

FIGURE G-18: Page Setup dialog box

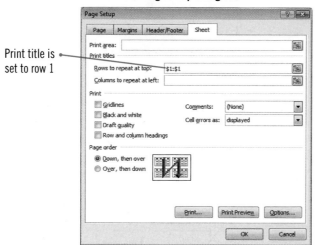

Print title is
set to row 1

FIGURE G-19: Completed table

2010 Tours   Your Name

Tour	Depart Date	Number of Days	Seat Capacity	Seats Reserved	Price	Air Included	Meals Included	Seats Available
African National Parks	4/7/2010	30	12	10	$ 4,870	Yes	Yes	2
African National Parks	10/27/2010	30	12	8	$ 4,870	Yes	Yes	4
Amazing Amazon	2/23/2010	14	43	38	$ 2,877	No	No	5
Amazing Amazon	4/23/2010	14	43	30	$ 2,877	No	No	13
Amazing Amazon	8/23/2010	14	43	18	$ 2,877	No	No	25
Catalonia Adventure	5/9/2010	14	51	30	$ 3,100	Yes	No	21
Catalonia Adventure	6/9/2010	14	51	15	$ 3,100	Yes	No	36
Catalonia Adventure	10/9/2010	14	51	11	$ 3,100	Yes	No	40
Cooking in Croatia	5/23/2010	7	12	10	$ 2,110	No	No	2
Cooking in Croatia	9/23/2010	7	12	7	$ 2,110	No	No	5
Cooking in France	2/28/2010	7	18	15	$ 2,822	Yes	No	3
Cooking in France	8/29/2010	7	18	5	$ 2,822	Yes	No	13
Corfu Sailing Voyage	6/10/2010	21	12	10	$ 3,190	Yes	No	2
Corfu Sailing Voyage	7/9/2010	21	12	1	$ 3,190	Yes	No	11
Costa Rica Rainforests	1/30/2010	7	20	0	$ 2,590	Yes	Yes	20
Costa Rica Rainforests	3/20/2010	7	20	20	$ 2,590	Yes	Yes	0
Costa Rica Rainforests	6/20/2010	7	20	2	$ 2,590	Yes	Yes	18
Down Under Exodus	1/18/2010	10	30	28	$ 2,800	Yes	Yes	2
Down Under Exodus	4/18/2010	10	30	20	$ 2,800	Yes	Yes	10
Essential India	1/20/2010	18	51	40	$ 3,933	Yes	Yes	11
Essential India	4/20/2010	18	51	31	$ 3,933	Yes	Yes	20
Essential India	8/20/2010	18	51	20	$ 3,933	Yes	Yes	31
Essential India	9/11/2010	18	51	20	$ 3,933	Yes	Yes	31
Essential India	12/30/2010	18	51	15	$ 3,933	Yes	Yes	36
Exotic Morocco	6/12/2010	7	38	25	$ 1,900	Yes	No	13
Exotic Morocco	10/31/2010	7	38	15	$ 1,900	No	No	23
Experience Cambodia	4/10/2010	12	40	21	$ 2,908	Yes	No	19
Experience Cambodia	10/31/2010	12	40	2	$ 2,908	Yes	No	38
Galapagos Adventure	7/2/2010	14	15	12	$ 3,100	Yes	Yes	3
Galapagos Adventure	12/20/2010	14	15	1	$ 3,100	Yes	Yes	14
Green Adventures in Ecuador	3/23/2010	18	25	22	$ 2,450	No	No	3
Green Adventures in Ecuador	10/23/2010	18	25	12	$ 2,450	No	No	13
Ireland by Bike	6/11/2010	10	15	10	$ 2,600	Yes	No	5

		Seats Reserved	Price	Air Included	Meals Included	Seats Available
		9	$ 2,600	Yes	No	6
		6	$ 2,600	Yes	No	9
		15	$ 1,970	Yes	Yes	5
		15	$ 1,970	Yes	Yes	5
		12	$ 1,970	Yes	Yes	8
		4	$ 1,890	No	No	44
		0	$ 1,890	No	No	48
		11	$ 2,103	Yes	Yes	8
		9	$ 2,103	Yes	Yes	10
		0	$ 4,200	Yes	Yes	18
		18	$ 4,200	Yes	Yes	0
		8	$ 4,200	Yes	Yes	10
		30	$ 2,100	Yes	No	17
		31	$ 2,100	Yes	No	16
		4	$ 2,100	Yes	No	43
		50	$ 3,105	Yes	No	0
		35	$ 3,105	Yes	No	15
		20	$ 3,105	Yes	No	30
		10	$ 3,105	Yes	No	40
		29	$ 2,304	Yes	Yes	21
		21	$ 2,304	Yes	Yes	29
		15	$ 3,400	Yes	No	35
		11	$ 3,400	No	No	39
		19	$ 2,190	Yes	Yes	6
		9	$ 2,190	Yes	Yes	16
		15	$ 3,200	Yes	Yes	26
		12	$ 3,200	Yes	Yes	29

Tour	Depart Date	Number of Days	Seats Reserved	Price	Air Included	Meals Included	Seats Available
Wild River Escape	6/27/2010	10	21	$ 1,944	No	No	0
Wild River Escape	8/27/2010	10	21	$ 1,944	No	No	10
Total		**13**					**1035**

Setting a print area

Sometimes you will want to print only part of a worksheet. To do this, select any worksheet range, click the Office button [icon], click Print, in the Print dialog box choose Selection under Print what, then click OK. If you want to print a selected area repeatedly, it's best to define a **print area**, which prints when you use the Quick Print feature. To set a print area, click the Page Layout tab, click the Print Area button in the Page Setup group, then click Set Print Area. You can extend the print area by selecting a range, clicking the Print Area button, then clicking Add to Print Area. If you want to print the table rather than a print area, click the Ignore print areas check box in the Print what section of the Print dialog box. To clear a print area, click the Print Area button, then click Clear Print Area.

Practice

▼ CONCEPTS REVIEW

FIGURE G-20

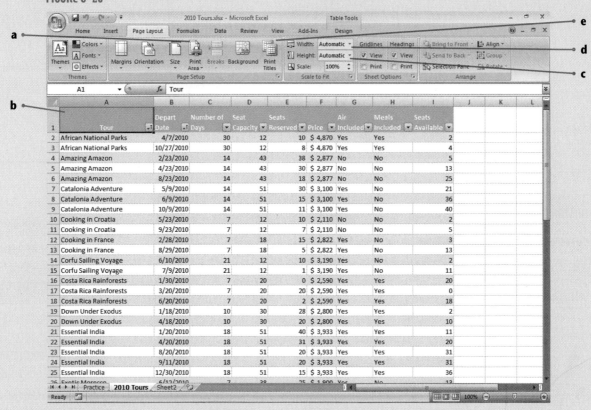

1. Which element points to a field that has been sorted in ascending order?
2. Which element do you click to adjust the number of rows printed on a page?
3. Which element do you click to adjust the number of fields printed on a page?
4. Which element do you click to print field names at the top of every page?
5. Which element do you click to set a range in a table that will print using Quick Print?

Match each term with the statement that best describes it.

6. **Header row**	**a.** Organized collection of related information in Excel
7. **Record**	**b.** Arrange records in a particular sequence
8. **Table**	**c.** Column in an Excel table
9. **Field**	**d.** First row of a table containing field names
10. **Sort**	**e.** Row in an Excel table

Select the best answer from the list of choices.

11. **Which of the following Excel sorting options do you use to sort a table of employee names in order from Z to A?**

    a. Absolute
    b. Ascending
    c. Alphabetic
    d. Descending

12. **Which of the following series appears in descending order?**

    a. 4, 5, 6, A, B, C
    b. 8, 6, 4, C, B, A
    c. 8, 7, 6, 5, 6, 7
    d. C, B, A, 6, 5, 4

13. **You can easily add formatting to a table by using:**

    a. Table styles.
    b. Print titles.
    c. Print areas.
    d. Calculated columns.

14. **When printing a table on multiple pages, you can define a print title to:**

    a. Include appropriate fields in the printout.
    b. Include the sheet name in table reports.
    c. Include field names at the top of each printed page.
    d. Exclude from the printout all rows under the first row.

▼ SKILLS REVIEW

1. **Create a table.**

    a. Start Excel, open the file EX G-2.xlsx from the drive and folder where you store your data files, then save it as **Employees**.
    b. Using the Practice sheet, enter the field names in the first row and the first two records in rows two and three, as shown in Table G-4. Create a table using the data you entered.

TABLE G-4

Last Name	First Name	Years Employed	Position	Full/Part Time	Training Completed
Leone	Sally	5	Book Sales	F	Y
Mello	Donato	3	Video Sales	P	N

    c. Create a table with a header row using the data on the Staff sheet. Adjust the column widths, if necessary, to display the field names.
    d. Apply a table style of Light 12 to the table and adjust the columns widths if necessary.
    e. Enter your name in the center section of the worksheet footer, then save the workbook.

2. **Add table data.**

    a. Add a new record in row seven for **Hank Worthen**, a five-year employee in book sales. Hank works full time and has completed training. Adjust the height of the new row to match the other table rows.
    b. Insert a row above Jay Kherian's record and add a new record for **Stacy Atkins**. Stacy works full time, has worked at the company for two years in video sales, and has not completed training.
    c. Insert a new data field in cell G1 with a label **Weeks Vacation**. Adjust the column width and wrap the label in the cell to display the field name with Weeks above Vacation.
    d. Add a new column to the table by dragging the table's sizing handle and give the new field a label of **Employee #**.
    e. Save the file.

3. **Find and replace table data.**

    a. Return to cell A1.
    b. Open the Find and Replace dialog box and if necessary uncheck the Match Case option. Find the first record that contains the text **Book Sales**.
    c. Find the second record that contains the text **Book Sales**.
    d. Replace all Video text in the table with **Movie**.
    e. Save the file.

4. Delete table data.

    a. Go to cell A1.

    b. Delete the record for **Sally Leone**.

    c. Use the Remove Duplicates button to confirm that the table does not have any duplicate records.

    d. Delete the **Employee #** column from the table, then delete its column header.

    e. Save the file.

5. Sort table data.

    a. Sort the table by years employed in largest to smallest order.

    b. Sort the table by last name in A to Z order.

    c. Sort the table first by Full/Part Time in A to Z order and then by last name in A to Z order.

    d. Check the table to make sure the records appear in the correct order.

    e. Save the file.

6. Use formulas in a table.

    a. In cell G2, enter the formula that calculates an employee's vacation time; base the formula on the company policy that employees working at the company less than three years have two weeks of vacation. At three years of employment and longer, an employee has three weeks of vacation time. Use the table's field names where appropriate. (*Hint:* The formula is: **=IF([Years Employed]<3,2,3)**)

    b. Check the table to make sure the formula filled into the cells in column G and that the correct vacation time is calculated for all cells in the column.

    c. Add a Total Row and verify the accuracy of the total number of vacation weeks.

    d. Change the function in the Total Row to display the average number of vacation weeks.

    e. Compare your table to Figure G-21, then save the workbook.

FIGURE G-21

	Last Name	First Name	Years Employed	Position	Full/Part Time	Training Completed	Weeks Vacation
2	Atkins	Stacy	2	Movie Sales	F	N	2
3	Guan	Joyce	1	Book Sales	F	N	2
4	Kherian	Jay	1	Book Sales	F	Y	2
5	Worthen	Hank	5	Book Sales	F	Y	3
6	Mello	Donato	3	Movie Sales	P	N	3
7	Rabin	Mimi	1	Movie Sales	P	Y	2
8	Total						2.333333333

7. Print a table.

    a. Add a header that reads **Employees** in the center section, then format the header in bold with a font size of 16.

    b. Add column A as a print title that repeats at the left of each printed page.

    c. Preview your table to check that the last names appear on both pages.

    d. Change the page orientation to landscape, save the workbook, then print the Staff sheet.

    e. Close the workbook, then exit Excel.

▼ INDEPENDENT CHALLENGE 1

You are the marketing director for a national sporting goods store. Your assistants have created an Excel worksheet with customer data including the results of an advertising survey. You will create a table using the customer data and analyze the survey results to help focus the company's advertising expenses in the most successful areas.

    a. Start Excel, open the file EX G-3.xlsx from the drive and folder where you store your Data Files, then save it as **Customers**.

    b. Create a table from the worksheet data and apply Table Style Light 20. Widen the columns as necessary to display the table data.

▼ INDEPENDENT CHALLENGE 1 (CONTINUED)

c. Use the data below to add the two records shown in Table G-5 to the table:

TABLE G-5

Last Name	First Name	Street Address	City	State	Zip	Area Code	Ad Source	Comments
Ross	Cathy	92 Arrow St.	Seattle	WA	98101	206	Yellow Pages	found ad informative
Janis	Steve	402 9th St.	Seattle	WA	98001	206	Newspaper	found in restaurant section

d. Find, then delete the record for Mary Ryder.

e. Click cell A1 and replace all instances of TV with WWIN TV, making sure the case is properly matched. Compare your table to Figure G-22.

f. Remove duplicate records where all fields are identical.

g. Sort the list by Last Name in A to Z order.

h. Sort the list again by Area Code in Smallest to Largest order.

i. Sort the table first by State in A to Z order, then within the state, by Zip in Smallest to Largest order.

FIGURE G-22

	Last Name	First Name	Street Address	City	State	Zip	Area Code	Ad Source	Comments
2	Kim	Kathy	19 North St.	San Francisco	CA	94177	415	Newspaper	favorite with friends
3	Jacobs	Martha	Hamilton Park St.	San Francisco	CA	94107	415	Newspaper	no comments
4	Majors	Kathy	1 Spring St.	San Luis	CA	94018	510	Radio	loved ad voice
5	Wong	Sandy	2120 Central St.	San Francisco	CA	93772	415	Newspaper	graphics caught eye
6	Hesh	Gayle	1192 Dome St.	San Diego	CA	93303	619	Newspaper	great ads
7	Chavez	Jane	11 Northern St.	San Diego	CA	92208	619	WWIN TV	interesting ad
8	Chelly	Yvonne	900 Sola St.	San Diego	CA	92106	619	Newspaper	likes description of products
9	Smith	Carolyn	921 Lopez St.	San Diego	CA	92104	619	Newspaper	likes ad prose
10	Owen	Scott	72 Yankee St.	Brookfield	CT	06830	203	Newspaper	no comments
11	Wallace	Salvatore	100 Westside St.	Chicago	IL	60620	312	Newspaper	likes graphics
12	Roberts	Bob	56 Water St.	Chicago	IL	60618	771	Newspaper	likes ad graphic
13	Miller	Hope	111 Stratton St.	Chicago	IL	60614	773	Newspaper	likes ad in local newspaper
14	Duran	Maria	Galvin St.	Chicago	IL	60614	773	Subway	no comments
15	Roberts	Bob	56 Water St.	Chicago	IL	60614	312	Newspaper	liked photo
16	Graham	Shelley	989 26th St.	Chicago	IL	60611	773	Yellow Pages	great store description
17	Kim	Janie	9 First St.	San Francisco	CA	94177	415	Newspaper	great ads
18	Kim	Janie	9 First St.	San Francisco	CA	94177	415	Newspaper	great ads
19	Williams	Tasha	1 Spring St.	Reading	MA	03882	413	Newspaper	likes font we use
20	Julio	Manuel	544 Cameo St.	Belmont	MA	02483	617	Newspaper	no comments
21	Masters	Latrice	88 Las Puntas Rd.	Boston	MA	02205	617	Yellow Pages	likes clear store location
22	Kooper	Peter	671 Main St.	Cambridge	MA	02138	617	WWIN TV	no comments
23	Kelly	Shawn	22 Kendall St.	Cambridge	MA	02138	617	Yellow Pages	found under "cafés"
24	Rodriguez	Virginia	123 Main St.	Boston	MA	02007	617	Radio	loves radio personality
25	Frei	Carol	123 Elm St.	Salem	MA	01970	978	Newspaper	no comments
26	Stevens	Crystal	14 Waterford St.	Salem	MA	01970	508	Radio	does not like radio personality
27	Ichikawa	Pam	232 Shore Rd.	Boston	MA	01801	617	Newspaper	told friends
28	Paxton	Gail	100 Main St.	Woburn	MA	01801	508	Newspaper	no comments
29	Spencer	Robin	293 Serenity Dr.	Concord	MA	01742	508	Radio	loved radio personality
30	Lopez	Luis	1212 City St.	Kansas City	MO	64105	816	WWIN TV	liked characters
31	Nelson	Michael	229 Rally Rd.	Kansas City	MO	64105	816	Yellow Pages	found under "Compact Discs"
32	Lee	Ginny	3 Way St.	Kansas City	MO	64102	816	Radio	intrigued by announcer

j. Scale the table width to 1 page and the height to 2 pages.

k. Enter your name in the center section of the worksheet footer.

l. Add a centered header that reads **Customer Survey Data** in bold with a font size of 16.

m. Add print titles to repeat the first row at the top of printed pages.

n. Save the workbook, preview it, then print the table on two pages.

Advanced Challenge Exercise

- Create a print area that prints only the first six columns of the table.
- Print the print area.
- Clear the print area

o. Save the workbook, close the workbook, then exit Excel.

▼ INDEPENDENT CHALLENGE 2

You own Around the World, a travel bookstore located in New Zealand. The store sells travel-related items such as maps, travel books, journals, and DVDs of travel destinations. Your customers are primarily tour guides who purchase items in quantities of ten or more for their tour customers. You decide to plan and build a table of sales information with eight records using the items sold.

a. Prepare a plan for a table that states your goal, outlines the data you need, and identifies the table elements.

b. Sketch a sample table on a piece of paper, indicating how the table should be built. Create a table documenting the table design including the field names, type of data, and description of the data.

▼ INDEPENDENT CHALLENGE 2 (CONTINUED)

TABLE G-6

c. Start Excel, create a new workbook, then save it as **Store Items** in the drive and folder where you store your Data Files. Enter the field names from Table G-6 in the designated cells.

d. Enter eight data records using your own data.

e. Create a table using the data in the range A1:E9. Adjust the column widths as necessary.

f. Apply the Table Style Light 4 to the table.

g. Add the following fields to the table: **Subtotal** in cell F1, and **Total** in cell G1.

h. Add the label **Tax** in cell H1 and click the first option in the AutoCorrect Options to undo the table AutoExpansion. Enter **.125** in cell I1 (the 12.5% Goods and Services tax).

Cell	Field name
A1	Customer Last
B1	Customer First
C1	Item
D1	Quantity
E1	Cost

i. Enter formulas to calculate the subtotal (Quantity*Cost) in cell F2 and the total (including tax) in cell G2. Check that the formulas were filled down both of the columns. (*Hint:* Remember to use an absolute reference to the tax rate cell.)

j. Format the Cost, Subtotal, and Total columns using the Accounting number format with two decimal places and the symbol $ English (New Zealand). Adjust the column widths as necessary.

k. Add a new record to your table in row 10. Add another record above row 4.

l. Sort the table in ascending order by Item.

m. Enter your name in the worksheet footer, then save the workbook.

n. Preview the worksheet, use the Scale to Fit width option to scale the worksheet to print on one page.

o. Print the worksheet, close the workbook, then exit Excel.

▼ INDEPENDENT CHALLENGE 3

You are the project manager at a local advertising firm. You are managing your accounts using an Excel worksheet and have decided that a table will provide additional features to help you keep track of the accounts. You will use the table sorting features and table formulas to analyze your account data.

a. Start Excel, open the file EX G-4.xlsx from the drive and folder where you store your Data Files, then save it as **Accounts**.

b. Create a table with the worksheet data and apply Table Style Light 3.

c. Sort the table on the Budget field using the Smallest to Largest order. Compare your table to Figure G-23.

d. Sort the table using two fields, by Contact in A to Z order, then by Budget in Smallest to Largest order.

e. Add the new field label **Balance** in cell G1 and adjust the column width as necessary. Format the Budget, Expenses, and Balance columns using the Accounting format with no decimal places.

FIGURE G-23

	A	B	C	D	E	F	G
1	Project	Deadline	Code	Budget	Expenses	Contact	
2	Kelly	2/1/2010	AA1	100000	30000	Connie Blake	
3	Vincent	1/15/2010	C43	100000	150000	Jane Smith	
4	Jaffrey	3/15/2010	A3A	200000	210000	Kate Jeung	
5	Karim	4/30/2010	C43	200000	170000	Connie Blake	
6	Landry	11/15/2010	V53	200000	210000	Jane Smith	
7	Kaplan	9/30/2010	V51	300000	320000	Jane Smith	
8	Graham	7/10/2010	V13	390000	400000	Charlie Katter	
9	Lannou	10/10/2010	C21	450000	400000	Connie Blake	
10	Mason	6/1/2010	AA5	500000	430210	Jane Smith	
11	Melon	12/15/2010	B12	810000	700000	Nelly Atli	
12							

f. Enter a formula in cell G2 that uses structured references to table fields to calculate the balance on an account as the Budget minus the Expenses.

g. Add a new record for a project named **Franklin** with a deadline of **2/15/2010**, a code of **AB2**, a budget of **200000**, expenses of **150000**, and a contact of **Connie Blake**.

h. Verify that the formula accurately calculated the balance for the new record.

i. Replace all of the Jane Smith data with **Jane Jacobson** and adjust the column width as necessary.

j. Enter your name in the center section of the worksheet footer, add a center section header of **Accounts** using formatting of your choice, then save the workbook.

▼ INDEPENDENT CHALLENGE 3 (CONTINUED)

Advanced Challenge Exercise

- Sort the table on the Balance field using the smallest to largest order.
- Use conditional formatting to format the cells of the table containing negative balances with a dark green text on a green fill.
- Sort the table using the order of no cell color on top.
- Format the table to emphasize the Balance column and turn off the banded rows. (*Hint*: Use the Table Style Options on the Table Tools Design tab.)
- Compare your table with Figure G-24.

k. Save the workbook, print the table, close the workbook, then exit Excel.

FIGURE G-24

Goal Sales

	A	B	C	D	E	F	G	H
1	Project	Deadline	Code	Budget	Expenses	Contact	Balance	
2	Karim	4/30/2010	C43	$ 200,000	$ 170,000	Connie Blake	$ 30,000	
3	Lannou	10/10/2010	C21	$ 450,000	$ 400,000	Connie Blake	$ 50,000	
4	Franklin	2/15/2010	AB2	$ 200,000	$ 150,000	Connie Blake	$ 50,000	
5	Mason	6/1/2010	AA5	$ 500,000	$ 430,210	Jane Jacobson	$ 69,790	
6	Kelly	2/1/2010	AA1	$ 100,000	$ 30,000	Connie Blake	$ 70,000	
7	Melon	12/15/2010	B12	$ 810,000	$ 700,000	Nelly Atli	$ 110,000	
8	Vincent	1/15/2010	C43	$ 100,000	$ 150,000	Jane Jacobson	$ (50,000)	
9	Kaplan	9/30/2010	V51	$ 300,000	$ 320,000	Jane Jacobson	$ (20,000)	
10	Graham	7/10/2010	V13	$ 390,000	$ 400,000	Charlie Katter	$ (10,000)	
11	Landry	11/15/2010	V53	$ 200,000	$ 210,000	Jane Jacobson	$ (10,000)	
12	Jaffrey	3/15/2010	A3A	$ 200,000	$ 210,000	Kate Jeung	$ (10,000)	
13								
14								

▼ REAL LIFE INDEPENDENT CHALLENGE

You have decided to organize your recording collection using a table in Excel. This will enable you to easily find songs in your music library. You will add records as you purchase new music and delete records if you discard a recording.

a. Use the fields Title, Artist, Genre, and Format and prepare a diagram of your table structure.

b. Document the table design by detailing the type of data that will be in each field and a description of the data. For example, in the Format field you may have mp3, aac, wma, or other formats.

c. Start Excel, create a new workbook, then save it as **Music Titles** in the drive and folder where you store your Data Files.

d. Enter the field names into the worksheet, enter the records for seven of your music recordings, then save the workbook.

e. Create a table that contains your music information. Resize the columns as necessary.

f. Choose a Table Style and apply it to your table.

g. Add a new field with a label of Comments. Enter information in the new table column describing the setting in which you listen to the title, such as driving, exercising, entertaining, or relaxing.

h. Sort the records by the Format field using A to Z order.

i. Add a record to the table for the next recording you will purchase.

j. Add a Total row to your table and verify that the Count function accurately calculated the number of your recordings.

k. Enter your name in the worksheet footer, then save the workbook.

l. Print the table, close the workbook, then exit Excel.

Start Excel, open the file EX G-5.xlsx from the drive and folder where you store your Data Files, then save it as **Products**. Sort the data as shown in Figure G-25. The table is formatted using Table Style Light 3. Add a header with the file name that is centered and formatted in bold with a size of 18. Enter your name in the worksheet footer. Save the workbook, preview and print the table, close the workbook, then exit Excel.

FIGURE G-25

Products.xlsx

Order Number	Order date	Amount	Shipping	Sales Rep
1134	4/30/2010	$ 200,000	Air	Edward Callegy
1465	11/15/2010	$ 210,000	Air	Edward Callegy
7733	3/15/2010	$ 230,000	Air	Edward Callegy
2889	2/15/2010	$ 300,000	Air	Edward Callegy
1532	10/10/2010	$ 450,000	Air	Edward Callegy
9345	1/15/2010	$ 100,000	Ground	Gary Clarkson
5623	2/1/2010	$ 130,000	Air	Gary Clarkson
1112	9/30/2010	$ 300,000	Ground	Gary Clarkson
2156	6/1/2010	$ 500,000	Ground	Gary Clarkson
2134	7/10/2010	$ 390,000	Ground	Ned Blair
2144	12/15/2010	$ 810,000	Ground	Ned Blair

Analyzing Table Data

Excel data tables let you manipulate and analyze data in many ways. One way is to filter a table so that it displays only the rows that meet certain criteria. In this unit, you will display selected records using the filter feature, create a custom filter, and filter a table using an Advanced Filter. In addition, you will learn to insert automatic subtotals, use lookup functions to locate table entries, and apply database functions to summarize table data that meet specific criteria. You'll also learn how to restrict entries in a column by using data validation. The vice president of sales, Kate Morgan, asks you to extract information from a table of the 2010 scheduled tours to help the sales representatives with customer inquiries. She also asks you to prepare summaries of the tour sales for a presentation at the international sales meeting.

OBJECTIVES

Filter a table

Create a custom filter

Filter a table with Advanced Filter

Extract table data

Look up values in a table

Summarize table data

Validate table data

Create subtotals

Filtering a Table

When you create a table, arrows automatically appear next to each column header. These arrows are called **filter list arrows**, or **list arrows**, and you can use them to **filter** a table to display only the records that meet criteria you specify, temporarily hiding records that do not meet those criteria. For example, you can use the filter list arrow next to the Tour field header to display only records that contain Nepal Trekking in the Tour field. Once you filter data, you can copy, chart, and print the displayed records. You can easily clear a filter to redisplay all the records. Kate asks you to display only the records for the Pacific Odyssey tours. She also asks for information about the tours that sell the most seats and the tours that depart in March.

STEPS

1. **Start Excel, open the file EX H-1.xlsx from the drive and folder where you save your Data Files, then save it as Tours**

2. **Click the Tour list arrow**

   Sort options appear at the top of the menu, advanced filtering options appear in the middle, and at the bottom is a list of the tour data from column A, as shown in Figure H-1. Because you want to display data for only the Pacific Odyssey tours, your **search criterion** (the text you are searching for) is Pacific Odyssey. You can select one of the Tour data options in the menu, which acts as your search criterion.

3. **In the list of tours for the Tour field, click Select All to clear the checks from the tours, scroll down the list of tours, click the Pacific Odyssey check box, then click OK**

   Only those records containing Pacific Odyssey in the Tour field appear, as shown in Figure H-2. The row numbers for the matching records change to blue, and the list arrow for the filtered field has a filter icon. Both indicate that there is a filter in effect and that some of the records are temporarily hidden.

4. **Move the pointer over the Tour list arrow**

   The ScreenTip (Tour: Equals "Pacific Odyssey") describes the filter for the field, meaning that only the Pacific Odyssey records appear. You decide to remove the filter to redisplay all of the table data.

5. **Click the Tour list arrow, then click Clear Filter From "Tour"**

   You have cleared the Pacific Odyssey filter, and all the records reappear. You want to display the most popular tours, those that are in the top five percent of seats reserved.

6. **Click the Seats Reserved list arrow, point to Number Filters, click Top 10, select 10 in the middle box, type 5, click the Items list arrow, click Percent, then click OK**

   Excel displays the records for the top five percent in the number of Seats Reserved field, as shown in Figure H-3. You decide to clear the filter to redisplay all the records.

7. **Click the Home tab, click the Sort & Filter button in the Editing group, then click Clear**

   You have cleared the filter and all the records reappear. You want to find all of the tours that depart in March.

8. **Click the Depart Date list arrow, point to Date Filters, point to All Dates in the Period, then click March**

   Excel displays the records for the four tours that leave in March. You decide to clear the filter and display all of the records.

9. **Click Sort & Filter button in the Editing group, click Clear, then save the workbook**

FIGURE H-1: Worksheet showing filter options

Tour filter list arrow

Sort Options

Advanced filtering options

List of tours

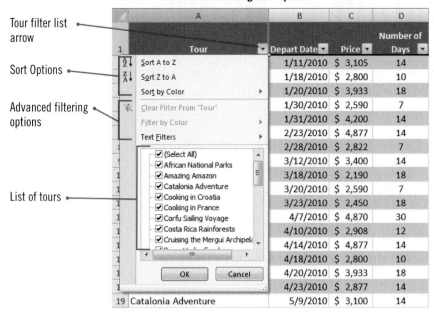

	A	B	C	D
1	Tour	Depart Date	Price	Number of Days
		1/11/2010	$ 3,105	14
		1/18/2010	$ 2,800	10
		1/20/2010	$ 3,933	18
		1/30/2010	$ 2,590	7
		1/31/2010	$ 4,200	14
		2/23/2010	$ 4,877	14
		2/28/2010	$ 2,822	7
		3/12/2010	$ 3,400	14
		3/18/2010	$ 2,190	18
		3/20/2010	$ 2,590	7
		3/23/2010	$ 2,450	18
		4/7/2010	$ 4,870	30
		4/10/2010	$ 2,908	12
		4/14/2010	$ 4,877	14
		4/18/2010	$ 2,800	10
		4/20/2010	$ 3,933	18
		4/23/2010	$ 2,877	14
19	Catalonia Adventure	5/9/2010	$ 3,100	14

Filter dialog options: Sort A to Z, Sort Z to A, Sort by Color, Clear Filter From "Tour", Filter by Color, Text Filters, (Select All), African National Parks, Amazing Amazon, Catalonia Adventure, Cooking in Croatia, Cooking in France, Corfu Sailing Voyage, Costa Rica Rainforests, Cruising the Mergui Archipela... OK Cancel

FIGURE H-2: Table filtered to show Pacific Odyssey tours

	A	B	C	D	E	F	G	H	I
1	Tour	Depart Date	Price	Number of Days	Seat Capacity	Seats Reserved	Seats Available	Air Included	Meals Included
2	Pacific Odyssey	1/11/2010	$ 3,105	14	50	30	20	Yes	No
34	Pacific Odyssey	7/7/2010	$ 3,105	14	50	32	18	Yes	No
48	Pacific Odyssey	9/14/2010	$ 3,105	14	50	26	24	Yes	No
61	Pacific Odyssey	12/21/2010	$ 3,105	14	50	50	0	Yes	No
64									

Matching row numbers are blue and sequence indicates that not all rows appear

Filter displays only Pacific Odyssey tours

Filter icon

FIGURE H-3: Table filtered with top 5% of Seats Reserved

	A	B	C	D	E	F	G	H	I
1	Tour	Depart Date	Price	Number of Days	Seat Capacity	Seats Reserved	Seats Available	Air Included	Meals Included
18	Amazing Amazon	4/23/2010	$ 2,877	14	50	48	2	No	No
37	Kayak Newfoundland	7/12/2010	$ 1,970	7	50	49	1	Yes	Yes
45	Cooking in France	8/29/2010	$ 2,822	7	50	48	2	Yes	No
61	Pacific Odyssey	12/21/2010	$ 3,105	14	50	50	0	Yes	No
64									

Table filtered with top 5% in this field

Creating a Custom Filter

So far, you have filtered rows based on an entry in a single column. You can perform more complex filters by using options in the Custom Filter dialog box. For example, your criteria can contain comparison operators such as "greater than" or "less than" that let you display values above or below a certain amount. You can also use **logical conditions** like And and Or to narrow a search even further. You can have Excel display records that meet a criterion in a field *and* another criterion in that same field. This is often used to find records between two values. For example, by specifying an And logical condition, you can display records for customers with incomes between $40,000 *and* $70,000. You can also have Excel display records that meet either criterion in a field by specifying an Or condition. The Or condition is used to find records that satisfy either of two values. For example, in a table of book data you can use the Or condition to find records that contain either Beginning *or* Introduction in the title name. ▰▰▰▰ Kate wants to locate water tours for customers who like boating adventures. She also wants to find tours that depart between February 15, 2010 and April 15, 2010. She asks you to create custom filters to find the tours satisfying these criteria.

STEPS

1. **Click the Tour list arrow, point to Text Filters, then click Contains**

   The Custom AutoFilter dialog box opens. You enter your criteria in the text boxes. The left text box on the first line currently displays "contains." You want to display tours that contain the word sailing in their names.

2. **Type sailing in the right text box on the first line**

   You want to see entries that contain either sailing or cruising.

   QUICK TIP

   When specifying criteria in the Custom AutoFilter dialog box, you can use the ? wildcard to represent any single character and the * wildcard to represent any series of characters.

3. **Click the Or option button to select it, click the left text box list arrow on the second line, select contains, then type cruising in the right text box on the second line**

   Your completed Custom AutoFilter dialog box should match Figure H-4.

4. **Click OK**

   The dialog box closes, and only those records having sailing or cruising in the Tour field appear in the worksheet. You want to find all tours that depart between February 15, 2010 and April 15, 2010.

5. **Click the Tour list arrow, click Clear Filter From "Tour", click the Depart Date list arrow, point to Date Filters, then click Custom Filter**

   The Custom AutoFilter dialog box opens. The word "equals" appears in the left text box on the first line. You want to find the departure dates that are between February 15, 2010 and April 15, 2010 (that is, after February 15th *and* before April 15th).

6. **Click the left text box list arrow on the first line, click is after, then type 2/15/2010 in the right text box on the first line**

   The And condition is selected, which is correct.

7. **Click the left text box list arrow on the second line, select is before, type 4/15/2010 in the right text box on the second line, then click OK**

   The records displayed have departing dates between February 15, 2010 and April 15, 2010. Compare your records to those shown in Figure H-5.

8. **Add your name to the center section of the footer, scale the page width to one page, then preview and print the filtered table**

   The worksheet prints using the existing landscape orientation, on one page with your name in the footer.

9. **Click the Depart Date list arrow, then click Clear Filter From "Depart Date"**

   You have cleared the filter, and all the tour records reappear.

FIGURE H-4: Custom AutoFilter dialog box

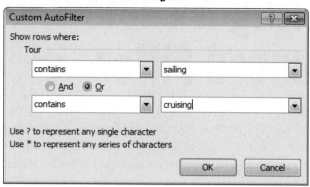

FIGURE H-5: Results of custom filter

	A	B	C	D	E	F	G	H	I
1	Tour	Depart Date	Price	Number of Days	Seat Capacity	Seats Reserved	Seats Available	Air Included	Meals Included
7	Cruising the Mergui Archipelago	2/23/2010	$ 4,877	14	50	42	8	No	No
8	Cooking in France	2/28/2010	$ 2,822	7	50	18	32	Yes	No
9	Pearls of the Orient	3/12/2010	$ 3,400	14	50	22	28	Yes	No
10	Silk Road Travels	3/18/2010	$ 2,190	18	50	44	6	Yes	Yes
11	Costa Rica Rainforests	3/20/2010	$ 2,590	7	50	32	18	Yes	Yes
12	Green Adventures in Ecuador	3/23/2010	$ 2,450	18	50	45	5	No	No
13	African National Parks	4/7/2010	$ 4,870	30	50	18	32	Yes	Yes
14	Experience Cambodia	4/10/2010	$ 2,908	12	50	29	21	Yes	No
15	Cruising the Mergui Archipelago	4/14/2010	$ 4,877	14	50	20	30	No	No
64									

Depature dates are
between 2/15 and 4/15

Using more than one rule when conditionally formatting data

You can apply conditional formatting to table cells in the same way that you can format a range of worksheet data. You can add multiple rules by clicking the Home tab, clicking the Conditional Formatting button in the Styles group, then clicking New Rule for each additional rule that you want to apply. You can also add rules using the Conditional Formatting Rules Manager, which displays all of the rules for a data range. To use the Rules Manager, click the Home tab, click the Conditional Formatting button in the Styles group, click Manage Rules, then click New Rule for each rule that you want to apply to the data range.

Filtering a Table with Advanced Filter

The Advanced Filter command lets you search for data that matches criteria in more than one column, using And and Or conditions. For example, you can use Advanced Filter to find Tours that leave before a certain date *and* have meals included. To use advanced filtering, you must create a criteria range. A **criteria range** is a cell range containing one row of labels (usually a copy of the column labels) and at least one additional row underneath the row of labels that contains the criteria you want to match. Placing the criteria in the same row indicates that the records you are searching for must match both criteria; that is, it specifies an **And condition**. Placing the criteria in the different rows indicates that the records you are searching for must match only one of the criterion; that is, it specifies an **Or condition**. Kate wants to identify tours that depart after 6/1/2010 and that cost less than $2000. She asks you to use the Advanced Filter to retrieve these records. You begin by defining the criteria range.

STEPS

1. **Select table rows 1 through 6, click the Insert list arrow in the Cells group, click Insert Sheet Rows; click cell A1, type Criteria Range, then click the Enter button ✓ on the Formula bar**

    Six blank rows are added above the table. Excel does not require the label Criteria Range, but it is useful in organizing the worksheet. It is also helpful to see the column labels.

2. **Select the range A7:I7, click the Copy button in the Clipboard group, click cell A2, click the Paste button in the Clipboard group, then press [Esc]**

    Next, you want to list records for only those tours that depart after June 1, 2010 and that cost under $2000.

3. **Click cell B3, type >6/1/2010, click cell C3, type <2000, then click ✓**

    You have entered the criteria in the cells directly beneath the Criteria Range labels, as shown in Figure H-6.

4. **Click any cell in the table, click the Data tab, then click the Advanced button in the Sort & Filter group**

    The Advanced Filter dialog box opens, with the table range already entered. The default setting under Action is to filter the table in its current location ("in-place") rather than copy it to another location.

TROUBLE
If your filtered records don't match Figure H-7, make sure there are no spaces between the > symbol and the 6 in cell B3 and the < symbol and the 2 in cell C3.

5. **Click the Criteria range text box, select range A2:I3 in the worksheet, then click OK**

    You have specified the criteria range and performed the filter. The filtered table contains eight records that match both criteria—the departure date is after 6/1/2010 and the price is less than $2000, as shown in Figure H-7. You'll filter this table even further in the next lesson.

FIGURE H-6: Criteria in the same row

	A	B	C	D	E	F	G	H	I
1	Criteria Range								
2	Tour	Depart Date	Price	Number of Days	Seat Capacity	Seats Reserved	Seats Available	Air Included	Meals Included
3		>6/1/2010	<2000						
4									
5									
6									
7	Tour	Depart Date	Price	Number of Days	Seat Capacity	Seats Reserved	Seats Available	Air Included	Meals Included
8	Pacific Odyssey	1/11/2010	$ 3,105	14	50	30	20	Yes	No
9	Down Under Exodus	1/18/2010	$ 2,800	10	50	39	11	Yes	Yes

Filtered records will
match these criteria

FIGURE H-7: Filtered table

	A	B	C	D	E	F	G	H	I
1	Criteria Range								
2	Tour	Depart Date	Price	Number of Days	Seat Capacity	Seats Reserved	Seats Available	Air Included	Meals Included
3		>6/1/2010	<2000						
4									
5									
6									
7	Tour	Depart Date	Price	Number of Days	Seat Capacity	Seats Reserved	Seats Available	Air Included	Meals Included
34	Exotic Morocco	6/12/2010	$ 1,900	7	50	34	16	Yes	No
35	Kayak Newfoundland	6/12/2010	$ 1,970	7	50	41	9	Yes	Yes
38	Wild River Escape	6/27/2010	$ 1,944	10	50	1	49	No	No
43	Kayak Newfoundland	7/12/2010	$ 1,970	7	50	49	1	Yes	Yes
45	Magnificent Montenegro	7/27/2010	$ 1,890	10	50	11	39	No	No
47	Kayak Newfoundland	8/12/2010	$ 1,970	7	50	2	48	Yes	Yes
50	Wild River Escape	8/27/2010	$ 1,944	10	50	18	32	No	No
62	Exotic Morocco	10/31/2010	$ 1,900	7	50	18	32	Yes	No
70									

Dates are after
6/1/2010

Prices are less
than $2,000

Using advanced conditional formatting options

You can emphasize top or bottom ranked values in a field using conditional formatting. To highlight the top or bottom values in a field, select the field data, click the Conditional Formatting button on the Home tab, point to Top/Bottom Rules, select a Top or Bottom rule, if necessary enter the percentage or number of cells in the selected range that you want to format, select the format for the cells that meet the top or bottom criteria, then click OK. You can also format your worksheet or table data using icon sets and color scales based on the cell values. A **color scale** uses a set of two, three, or four fill colors to convey relative values. For example, red could fill cells to indicate they have higher values and green could signify lower values. To add a color scale, select a data range, click the Home tab, click the Conditional Formatting button in the Styles group, then point to Color Scales. On the submenu, you can select preformatted color sets or click More Rules to create your own color sets. **Icon sets** let you visually communicate relative cell values by adding icons to cells based on the values they contain. An upward-pointing green arrow might represent the highest values, and downward-pointing red arrows could represent lower values. To add an icon set to a data range, select a data range, click the Conditional Formatting button in the Styles group, then point to Icon Sets. You can customize the values that are used as thresholds for color scales and icon sets by clicking the Conditional Formatting button in the Styles group, clicking Manage Rules, clicking the rule in the Conditional Formatting Rules Manager dialog box, then clicking Edit Rule.

Extracting Table Data

Whenever you take the time to specify a complicated set of search criteria, it's a good idea to extract the matching records, rather than filtering it in-place. When you **extract** data, you place a copy of a filtered table in a range that you specify in the Advanced Filter dialog box. This way, you won't accidentally clear the filter or lose track of the records you spent time compiling. To extract data, you use an advanced filter and enter the criteria beneath the copied field names, as you did in the previous lesson. ▰▰▰▰▰ Kate needs to filter the table one step further to reflect only the Exotic Morocco or Kayak Newfoundland tours in the current filtered table. She asks you to complete this filter by specifying an Or condition, which you will do by entering two sets of criteria in two separate rows. You decide to save the filtered records by extracting them to a different location in the worksheet.

STEPS

1. **In cell A3, enter** Exotic Morocco, **then in cell A4, enter** Kayak Newfoundland

   The new sets of criteria need to appear in two separate rows, so you need to copy the previous filter criteria to the second row.

2. **Copy the criteria in B3:C3 to** B4:C4

   The criteria are shown in Figure H-8. When you perform the advanced filter this time, you indicate that you want to copy the filtered table to a range beginning in cell A75, so that Kate can easily refer to the data, even if you perform more filters later.

3. **Click the** Data tab **if necessary, then click** Advanced **in the Sort & Filter group**

4. **Under Action, click the** Copy to another location **option button to select it, click the** Copy to **text box, then type** A75

   The last time you filtered the table, the criteria range included only rows 2 and 3, and now you have criteria in row 4.

TROUBLE
Make sure the criteria range in the Advanced Filter dialog box includes the field names and the number of rows underneath the names that contain criteria. If you leave a blank row in the criteria range, Excel filters nothing and shows all records.

5. **Edit the contents of the** Criteria range text box **to show the range** $A$2:$I$4, **click** OK, **then if necessary scroll down until row 75 is visible**

   The matching records appear in the range beginning in cell A75, as shown in Figure H-9. The original table, starting in cell A7, contains the records filtered in the previous lesson.

6. **Select the range** A75:I80, **click the** Office button ⊕, **click** Print, **under Print what click the** Selection **option button, click** Preview, **then click** Print

   The selected area prints.

7. **Press [Ctrl][Home], then click the** Clear button **in the Sort & Filter group**

   The original table is displayed starting in cell A7, and the extracted table remains in A75:I80.

8. **Save the workbook**

FIGURE H-8: Criteria in separate rows

	A	B	C	D	E	F	G	H	I
1	Criteria Range								
2	Tour	Depart Date	Price	Number of Days	Seat Capacity	Seats Reserved	Seats Available	Air Included	Meals Included
3	Exotic Morocco	>6/1/2010	<2000						
4	Kayak Newfoundland	>6/1/2010	<2000						
5									

Two sets of criteria on
separate lines indicates
an OR condition

FIGURE H-9: Extracted data records

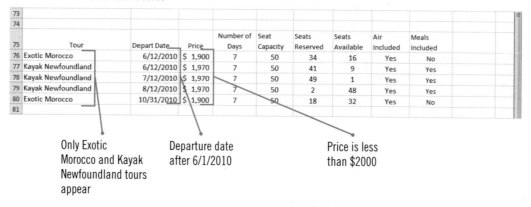

	Tour	Depart Date	Price	Number of Days	Seat Capacity	Seats Reserved	Seats Available	Air Included	Meals Included
73									
74									
75	Tour	Depart Date	Price	Number of Days	Seat Capacity	Seats Reserved	Seats Available	Air Included	Meals Included
76	Exotic Morocco	6/12/2010	$ 1,900	7	50	34	16	Yes	No
77	Kayak Newfoundland	6/12/2010	$ 1,970	7	50	41	9	Yes	Yes
78	Kayak Newfoundland	7/12/2010	$ 1,970	7	50	49	1	Yes	Yes
79	Kayak Newfoundland	8/12/2010	$ 1,970	7	50	2	48	Yes	Yes
80	Exotic Morocco	10/31/2010	$ 1,900	7	50	18	32	Yes	No
81									

Only Exotic
Morocco and Kayak
Newfoundland tours
appear

Departure date
after 6/1/2010

Price is less
than $2000

Understanding the criteria range and the copy-to location

When you define the criteria range and the copy-to location in the Advanced Filter dialog box, Excel automatically creates the names Criteria and Extract for these ranges in the worksheet. The criteria range includes the field names and any criteria rows underneath them. The extract range includes just the field names above the extracted table. You can select these ranges by clicking the Name box list arrow, then clicking the range name. If you click the Name Manager button in the Defined Names group on the Formulas tab, you will see these new names and the ranges associated with the names.

Looking Up Values in a Table

The Excel VLOOKUP function helps you locate specific values in a table. VLOOKUP searches vertically (V) down the far left column of a table, then reads across the row to find the value in the column you specify, much as you might look up a number in a phone book: You locate a person's name, then read across the row to find the phone number you want. Kate wants to be able to find a tour destination by entering the tour code. You will use the VLOOKUP function to accomplish this task. You begin by viewing the table name so you can refer to it in a Lookup function.

STEPS

QUICK TIP

You can change table names to better represent their content so they are easier to use in formulas. Click the table in the list of names in the Name Manager text box, click Edit, type the new table name in the Name text box, then click OK.

1. **Click the Lookup sheet tab, click the Formulas tab, then click the Name Manager button in the Defined Names group**

   The named ranges for the workbook appear in the Name Manager dialog box, as shown in Figure H-10. The Criteria and Extract ranges appear at the top of the range name list. At the bottom of the list is information about the three tables in the workbook. Table1 refers to the table on the Tours sheet, Table2 refers to the table on the Lookup sheet, and Table3 refers to the table on the Subtotals worksheet. These table names were automatically generated when the table was created by the Excel structured reference feature.

2. **Click Close**

   You want to find the tour represented by the code 675Y. The VLOOKUP function lets you find the tour name for any trip code. You will enter a trip code in cell L2 and a VLOOKUP function in cell M2.

3. **Click cell L2, enter 675Y, click cell M2, click the Lookup & Reference button in the Function Library group, then click VLOOKUP**

   The Function Arguments dialog box opens, with boxes for each of the VLOOKUP arguments. Because the value you want to find is in cell L2, L2 is the Lookup_value. The table you want to search is the table on the Lookup sheet, so its assigned name, Table2, is the Table_array.

QUICK TIP

If you want to find only the closest match for a value, enter TRUE in the Range_lookup text box. However, this can give misleading results if you are looking for an exact match. If you use FALSE and Excel can't find the value, you see an error message.

4. **With the insertion point in the Lookup_value text box, click cell L2, click the Table_array text box, then type Table2**

   The column containing the information that you want to find and display in cell M2 is the second column from the left in the table range, so the Col_index_num is 2. Because you want to find an exact match for the value in cell L1, the Range_lookup argument is FALSE.

5. **Click the Col_index_num text box, type 2, click the Range_lookup text box, then enter FALSE**

   Your completed Function Arguments dialog box should match Figure H-11.

6. **Click OK**

   Excel searches down the leftmost column of the table until it finds a value matching the one in cell L2. It finds the tour for that record, Catalonia Adventure, then displays it in cell M2. You use this function to determine the tour for one other trip code.

7. **Click cell L2, type 439U, then click the Enter button ☑ on the formula bar**

   The VLOOKUP function returns the value of Cooking in France in cell M2.

8. **Press [Ctrl][Home], then save the workbook**

Finding records using the DGET function

You can also use the DGET function to find a record in a table that matches specified criteria. For example, you could use the criteria of L1:L2 in the DGET function. When using DGET, you need to include [#All] after your table name in the formula to include the column labels that are used for the criteria range.

FIGURE H-10: Named ranges in the workbook

Created by
Advanced
Filter

Tables in the
workbook

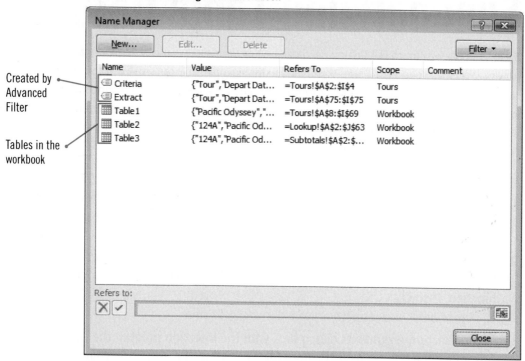

FIGURE H-11: Completed Function Arguments dialog box for **VLOOKUP**

Range name of
table to search

Finds exact
match

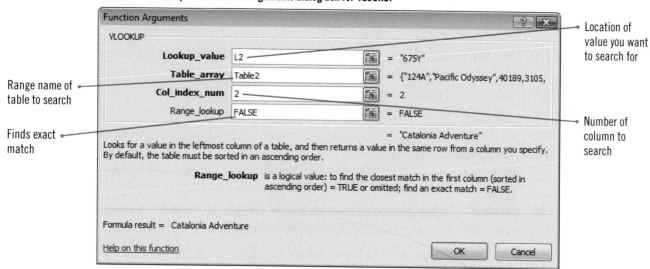

Location of
value you want
to search for

Number of
column to
search

Using the HLOOKUP and MATCH functions

The VLOOKUP (Vertical Lookup) function is useful when your data is arranged vertically, in columns. The HLOOKUP (Horizontal Lookup) function is useful when your data is arranged horizontally, in rows. HLOOKUP searches horizontally across the upper row of a table until it finds the matching value, then looks down the number of rows you specify. The arguments for this function are identical to those for the VLOOKUP function, with one exception. Instead of a Col_index_number, HLOOKUP uses a Row_index_number, which indicates the location of the row you want to search. For example, if you want to search the fourth row from the top, the Row_index_number should be 4. You can use the MATCH function when you want the position of an item in a range. The MATCH function uses the syntax: MATCH (lookup_value,lookup_array,match_ type) where lookup_value is the value you want to match in the lookup_array range. The match_type can be 0 for an exact match, 1 for matching the largest value that is less than or equal to lookup_value, or –1 for matching the smallest value that is greater than or equal to lookup_value.

Summarizing Table Data

Because a table acts much like a database, database functions allow you to summarize table data in a variety of ways. When working with a sales activity table, for example, you can use Excel to count the number of client contacts by sales representative or to total the amount sold to specific accounts by month. Table H-1 lists database functions commonly used to summarize table data. Kate is considering adding tours for the 2010 schedule. She needs your help in evaluating the number of seats available for scheduled tours.

STEPS

1. **Review the criteria range for the Pacific Odyssey tour in the range** L6:L7

   The criteria range in L6:L7 tells Excel to summarize records with the entry Pacific Odyssey in the Tour column. The functions will be in cells N6 and N7. You use this criteria range in a DSUM function to sum the seats available for only the Pacific Odyssey tours.

2. **Click cell** N6, **click the** Insert Function button **in the Function Library group, in the Search for a function text box type** database, **click** Go, **click** DSUM **under Select a function, then click** OK

   The first argument of the DSUM function is the table, or database.

QUICK TIP

Because the DSUM formula uses the column headings to locate and sum the table data, the header row needs to be included in the database range.

3. **In the Function Arguments dialog box, with the insertion point in the Database text box, move the pointer over the upper-left corner of the Trip Code column header until the pointer becomes ↘, click once, then click again**

   The first click selects the table's data range and the second click selects the entire table, including the header row. The second argument of the DSUM function is the label for the column that you want to sum. You want to total the number of available seats. The last argument for the DSUM function is the criteria that will be used to determine which values to total.

TROUBLE

If your Function Arguments dialog box does not match Figure H-12, click Cancel and repeat steps 2 – 4.

4. **Click the** Field text box, **then click cell** H1, **Seats Available; click the** Criteria text box **and select the range** L6:L7

   Your completed Function Arguments dialog box should match Figure H-12.

5. **Click** OK

   The result in cell N6 is 62. Excel totaled the information in the column Seats Available for those records that meet the criterion of Tour equals Pacific Odyssey. The DCOUNT and the DCOUNTA functions can help you determine the number of records meeting specified criteria in a database field. DCOUNTA counts the number of nonblank cells. You will use DCOUNTA to determine the number of tours scheduled

6. **Click cell** N7, **click** *fx* **on the formula bar, in the Search for a function text box type** database, **click** Go, **select** DCOUNTA **from the Select a function list, then click** OK

7. **With the insertion point in the Database text box, move the pointer over the upper-left corner of the Trip Code column header until the pointer becomes ↘, click once, click again to, click the** Field text box **and click cell** B1, **click the** Criteria text box **and select the range** L6:L7, **then click** OK

   The result in cell N7 is 4, meaning that there are four Pacific Odyssey tours scheduled for the year. You also want to display the number of seats available for the Cooking in France tours.

8. **Click cell** L7, **type** Cooking in France, **then click the** Enter button ☑ **on the formula bar**

   Figure H-13 shows that only three seats are available in the Cooking in France tours.

FIGURE H-12: Completed Function Arguments dialog box for DSUM

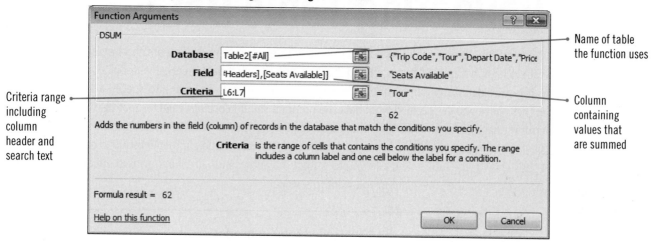

Criteria range including column header and search text

Name of table the function uses

Column containing values that are summed

FIGURE H-13: Result generated by database functions

	D	E	F	G	H	I	J	K	L	M	N
1	Price	Number of Days	Seat Capacity	Seats Reserved	Seats Available	Air Included	Meals Included		Trip Code	Tour	
2	$ 3,105	14	50	30	20	Yes	No		439U	Cooking in France	
3	$ 2,800	10	50	39	11	Yes	Yes				
4	$ 3,933	18	50	45	5	Yes	Yes				
5	$ 2,590	7	50	30	20	Yes	Yes		Criteria		
6	$ 4,200	14	50	38	12	Yes	Yes		Tour	Seats Available	3
7	$ 4,877	14	50	42	8	No	No		Cooking in France	Number of tours scheduled	2
8	$ 2,822	7	50	48	2	Yes	No				

TABLE H-1: Common database functions

function	result
DGET	Extracts a single record from a table that matches criteria you specify
DSUM	Totals numbers in a given table column that match criteria you specify
DAVERAGE	Averages numbers in a given table column that match criteria you specify
DCOUNT	Counts the cells that contain numbers in a given table column that match criteria you specify
DCOUNTA	Counts the cells that contain nonblank data in a given table column that match criteria you specify

Validating Table Data

When setting up data tables, you want to help ensure accuracy when you or others enter data. The Excel data validation feature allows you to do this by specifying what data users can enter in a range of cells. You can restrict data to whole numbers, decimal numbers, or text. You can also specify a list of acceptable entries. Once you've specified what data the program should consider valid for that cell, Excel displays an error message when invalid data is entered and can prevent users from entering any other data that it considers to be invalid. Kate wants to make sure that information in the Air Included column is entered consistently in the future. She asks you to restrict the entries in that column to two options: Yes and No. First, you select the table column you want to restrict.

STEPS

QUICK TIP

To specify a long list of valid entries, type the list in a column elsewhere in the worksheet, then type the list range in the Source text box.

1. **Click the top edge of the Air Included column header**

   The column data is selected.

2. **Click the Data tab, click the Data Validation button in the Data Tools group, click the Settings tab if necessary, click the Allow list arrow, then click List**

   Selecting the List option lets you type a list of specific options.

3. **Click the Source text box, then type Yes, No**

   You have entered the list of acceptable entries, separated by commas, as shown in Figure H-14. You want the data entry person to be able to select a valid entry from a drop-down list.

TROUBLE

If you get an invalid data error, make sure that cell I1 is not included in the selection. If I1 is included, open the Data Validation dialog box, click Clear All, click OK, then begin with step 1 again.

4. **Click the In-cell dropdown check box to select it if necessary, then click OK**

   The dialog box closes, and you return to the worksheet.

5. **Click the Home tab, click any cell in the last table row, click the Insert list arrow in the Cells group, click Insert Table Row Below, click cell I64, then click the list arrow to display the list of valid entries**

   The dropdown list is shown in Figure H-15. You could click an item in the list to have it entered in the cell, but you want to test the data restriction by entering an invalid entry.

6. **Click the list arrow to close the list, type Maybe, then press [Enter]**

   A warning dialog box appears to prevent you from entering the invalid data, as shown in Figure H-16.

7. **Click Cancel, click the list arrow, then click Yes**

   The cell accepts the valid entry. The data restriction ensures that records contain only one of the two correct entries in the Air Included column. The table is ready for future data entry.

8. **Delete the last table row, then save the workbook**

9. **Add your name to the center section of the footer, select the range L1:N7, click the Office button 🪟, click Print, under Print what, click the Selection option button, click Preview, then click Print**

Restricting cell values and data length

In addition to providing an in-cell drop-down list for data entry, you can use data validation to restrict the values that are entered into cells. For example, if you want to restrict cells to values less than a certain number, date, or time, click the Data tab, click the Data Validation button in the Data Tools group, and on the Settings tab, click the Allow list arrow, select Whole number, Decimal, Date, or Time, click the Data list arrow, select less than, then in the bottom text box, enter the maximum value. You can also limit the length of data entered into cells by choosing Text length in the Allow list, clicking the Data list arrow and selecting less than, then entering the maximum length in the Maximum text box.

FIGURE H-14: Creating data restrictions

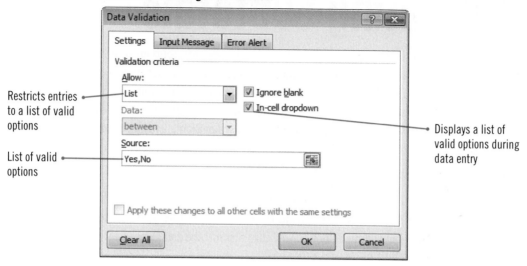

Restricts entries to a list of valid options

List of valid options

Displays a list of valid options during data entry

FIGURE H-15: Entering data in restricted cells

61	307R	Pacific Odyssey	12/21/2010	$ 3,105	14	50	50	0	Yes	No
62	927F	Essential India	12/30/2010	$ 3,933	18	50	31	19	Yes	Yes
63	448G	Old Japan	12/31/2010	$ 2,100	21	50	44	6	Yes	No
64								0		
65									Yes	
66									No	

Dropdown list

FIGURE H-16: Invalid data warning

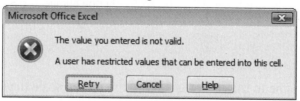

Adding input messages and error alerts

You can customize the way data validation works by using the two other tabs in the Data Validation dialog box: Input Message and Error Alert. The Input Message tab lets you set a message that appears when the user selects that cell; for example, the message might contain instructions about what type of data to enter. On the Input Message tab, enter a message title and message, then click OK. The Error Alert tab lets you set one of three alert levels if a user enters invalid data. The Information level displays your message with the information icon but allows the user to proceed with data entry. The Warning level displays your information with the warning icon and gives the user the option to proceed with data entry or not. The Stop level, which you used in this lesson, displays your message and only lets the user retry or cancel data entry for that cell.

Creating Subtotals

The Excel Subtotals feature provides a quick, easy way to group and summarize a range of data. Usually, you create subtotals with the SUM function, but you can also summarize data groups with functions such as COUNT, AVERAGE, MAX, and MIN. Subtotals cannot be used in a table structure. Before you can add subtotals to a table, you must first convert the data to a range and sort it. Kate wants you to group data by tours, with subtotals for the number of seats available and the number of seats reserved. You begin by converting the table to a range.

STEPS

1. **Click the** Subtotals sheet tab, **click any cell inside the table, click the** Table Tools Design **tab, click the** Convert to Range button **in the Tools group, then click** Yes

    Before you can add the subtotals, you must first sort the data. You decide to sort it in ascending order, first by tour and then by departure date.

2. **Click the** Data tab, **click the** Sort button **in the Sort & Filter group, in the Sort dialog box click the** Sort by list arrow, **click** Tour, **then click the** Add Level button, **click the** Then by list arrow, **click** Depart Date, **verify that the order is** Oldest to Newest, **then click** OK

    You have sorted the range in ascending order, first by tour, then by departure date.

3. **Click any cell in the data range, then click the** Subtotal button **in the Outline group**

    The Subtotal dialog box opens. Here you specify the items you want subtotaled, the function you want to apply to the values, and the fields you want to summarize.

4. **Click the** At each change in list arrow, **click** Tour, **click the** Use function list arrow, **click** Sum; **in the Add subtotal to list, click the** Seats Reserved and Seats Available check boxes **to select them, if necessary, then click the** Meals Included check box **to deselect it**

5. **If necessary, click the** Replace current subtotals and Summary below data check boxes **to select them**

    Your completed Subtotal dialog box should match Figure H-17.

6. **Click** OK, **then scroll down so row 90 is visible**

    The subtotaled data appears, showing the calculated subtotals and grand total in columns G and H, as shown in Figure H-18. Notice that Excel displays an outline to the left of the worksheet, with outline buttons to control the level of detail that appears. The button number corresponds to the detail level that is displayed. You want to show the second level of detail, the subtotals and the grand total.

7. **Click the** outline symbol 2

    The subtotals and the grand totals appear.

8. **Add your name to the center section of the footer, scale the worksheet width to print on one page, save, preview the worksheet, then print it**

9. **Close the workbook and exit Excel**

FIGURE H-17: Completed Subtotal dialog box

Field to use in grouping data

Function to apply to groups

Subtotal these fields

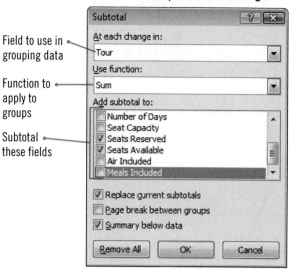

FIGURE H-18: Portion of subtotaled table

Outline symbols

1 2 3		A	B	C	D	E	F	G	H	I	J
	66		**Nepal Trekking Total**					94	56		
	67	622V	Old Japan	7/12/2010	$ 2,100	21	50	33	17	Yes	No
	68	448G	Old Japan	12/31/2010	$ 2,100	21	50	44	6	Yes	No
	69		**Old Japan Total**					77	23		
	70	124A	Pacific Odyssey	1/11/2010	$ 3,105	14	50	30	20	Yes	No
	71	133E	Pacific Odyssey	7/7/2010	$ 3,105	14	50	32	18	Yes	No
	72	698N	Pacific Odyssey	9/14/2010	$ 3,105	14	50	26	24	Yes	No
	73	307R	Pacific Odyssey	12/21/2010	$ 3,105	14	50	50	0	Yes	No
	74		**Pacific Odyssey Total**					138	62		
	75	4678	Panama Adventure	6/18/2010	$ 2,304	10	50	22	28	Yes	Yes
	76	793T	Panama Adventure	12/18/2010	$ 2,304	10	50	30	20	Yes	Yes
	77		**Panama Adventure Total**					52	48		
	78	966W	Pearls of the Orient	3/12/2010	$ 3,400	14	50	22	28	Yes	No
	79	572D	Pearls of the Orient	9/12/2010	$ 3,400	14	50	19	31	Yes	No
	80		**Pearls of the Orient Total**					41	59		
	81	653S	Silk Road Travels	3/18/2010	$ 2,190	18	50	44	6	Yes	Yes
	82	724D	Silk Road Travels	9/18/2010	$ 2,190	18	50	18	32	Yes	Yes
	83		**Silk Road Travels Total**					62	38		
	84	544T	Treasures of Ethiopia	5/18/2010	$ 3,200	10	50	18	32	Yes	Yes
	85	621R	Treasures of Ethiopia	11/18/2010	$ 3,200	10	50	46	4	Yes	Yes
	86		**Treasures of Ethiopia Total**					64	36		
	87	558B	Wild River Escape	6/27/2010	$ 1,944	10	50	1	49	No	No
	88	923Q	Wild River Escape	8/27/2010	$ 1,944	10	50	18	32	No	No
	89		**Wild River Escape Total**					19	81		
	90		**Grand Total**					1817	1283		

Subtotals

Grand totals

Practice

▼ CONCEPTS REVIEW

FIGURE H-19

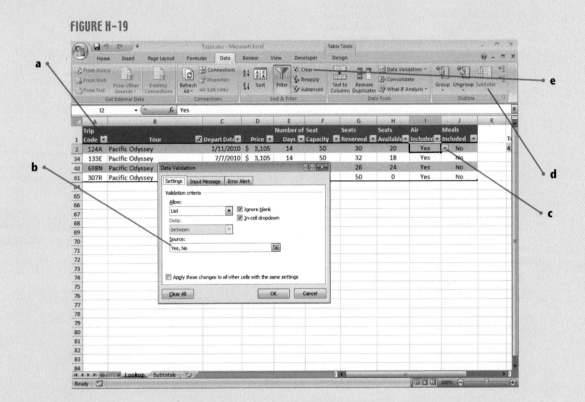

1. Which element do you click to specify acceptable data entries for a table?
2. Which element points to a field's list arrow?
3. Which element do you click to group data and summarize data in a table?
4. Which element would you click to remove a filter?
5. Which element points to an In-cell dropdown list arrow?

Match each term with the statement that best describes it.

6. DSUM
7. Data validation
8. Criteria range
9. Extracted table
10. Table_array

a. Cell range when Advanced Filter results are copied to another location
b. Range in which search conditions are set
c. Restricts table entries to specified options
d. Name of the table searched in a VLOOKUP function
e. Function used to total table values that meet specified criteria

Select the best answer from the list of choices.

11. The _____ logical condition finds records matching both listed criteria.
   a. Or
   b. And
   c. True
   d. False

12. What does it mean when you select the Or option when creating a custom filter?
   a. Both criteria must be true to find a match.
   b. Neither criterion has to be 100% true.
   c. Either criterion can be true to find a match.
   d. A custom filter requires a criteria range.

13. **What must a data range have before subtotals can be inserted?**
    - **a.** Enough records to show multiple subtotals
    - **b.** Grand totals
    - **c.** Formatted cells
    - **d.** Sorted data
14. **Which function finds the position of an item in a table?**
    - **a.** MATCH
    - **b.** VLOOKUP
    - **c.** DGET
    - **d.** HLOOKUP

▼ SKILLS REVIEW

1. **Filter a table.**
    - **a.** Start Excel, open the file EX H-2.xlsx from the drive and folder where you store your Data Files, then save it as **Salary Summary**.
    - **b.** With the Compensation sheet active, filter the table to list only records for employees in the Boston branch.
    - **c.** Clear the filter, then add a filter that displays the records for employees in the Boston and Philadelphia branches.
    - **d.** Redisplay all employees, then use a filter to show the three employees with the highest annual salary.
    - **e.** Redisplay all the records, then save the workbook.
2. **Create a custom filter.**
    - **a.** Create a custom filter showing employees hired before 1/1/2007 or after 12/31/2007.
    - **b.** Create a custom filter showing employees hired between 1/1/2007 and 12/31/2007.
    - **c.** Enter your name in the worksheet footer, save the workbook, then preview and print the filtered worksheet.
    - **d.** Redisplay all records.
    - **e.** Save the workbook.
3. **Filter and extract a table with Advanced Filter.**
    - **a.** You want to retrieve a list of employees who were hired before 1/1/2008 and who have an annual salary of more than $80,000 a year. Define a criteria range by inserting six new rows above the table on the worksheet and copying the field names into the first row.
    - **b.** In cell D2, enter the criterion **<1/1/2008**, then in cell G2 enter **>80000**.
    - **c.** Click any cell in the table.
    - **d.** Open the Advanced Filter dialog box.
    - **e.** Indicate that you want to copy to another location, enter the criteria range **A1:J2**, verify that the List range is $A$7:$J$17, then indicate that you want to place the extracted list in the range starting at cell **A20**.
    - **f.** Confirm that the retrieved list meets the criteria as shown in Figure H-20.
    - **g.** Save the workbook, then preview and print the worksheet.

FIGURE H-20

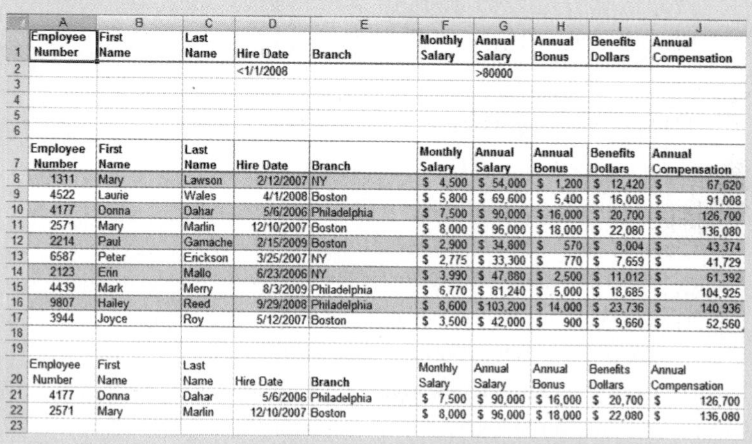

	A	B	C	D	E	F	G	H	I	J
1	Employee Number	First Name	Last Name	Hire Date	Branch	Monthly Salary	Annual Salary	Annual Bonus	Benefits Dollars	Annual Compensation
2				<1/1/2008			>80000			
3										
4										
5										
6										
7	Employee Number	First Name	Last Name	Hire Date	Branch	Monthly Salary	Annual Salary	Annual Bonus	Benefits Dollars	Annual Compensation
8	1311	Mary	Lawson	2/12/2007	NY	$ 4,500	$ 54,000	$ 1,200	$ 12,420	$ 67,620
9	4522	Laurie	Wales	4/1/2008	Boston	$ 5,800	$ 69,600	$ 5,400	$ 16,008	$ 91,008
10	4177	Donna	Dahar	5/6/2006	Philadelphia	$ 7,500	$ 90,000	$ 16,000	$ 20,700	$ 126,700
11	2571	Mary	Marlin	12/10/2007	Boston	$ 8,000	$ 96,000	$ 18,000	$ 22,080	$ 136,080
12	2214	Paul	Gamache	2/15/2009	Boston	$ 2,900	$ 34,800	$ 570	$ 8,004	$ 43,374
13	6587	Peter	Erickson	3/25/2007	NY	$ 2,775	$ 33,300	$ 770	$ 7,659	$ 41,729
14	2123	Erin	Mallo	6/23/2006	NY	$ 3,990	$ 47,880	$ 2,500	$ 11,012	$ 61,392
15	4439	Mark	Merry	8/3/2009	Philadelphia	$ 6,770	$ 81,240	$ 5,000	$ 18,685	$ 104,925
16	9807	Hailey	Reed	9/29/2008	Philadelphia	$ 8,600	$103,200	$ 14,000	$ 23,736	$ 140,936
17	3944	Joyce	Roy	5/12/2007	Boston	$ 3,500	$ 42,000	$ 900	$ 9,660	$ 52,560
18										
19										
20	Employee Number	First Name	Last Name	Hire Date	Branch	Monthly Salary	Annual Salary	Annual Bonus	Benefits Dollars	Annual Compensation
21	4177	Donna	Dahar	5/6/2006	Philadelphia	$ 7,500	$ 90,000	$ 16,000	$ 20,700	$ 126,700
22	2571	Mary	Marlin	12/10/2007	Boston	$ 8,000	$ 96,000	$ 18,000	$ 22,080	$ 136,080
23										

4. **Look up values in a table.**
    - **a.** Click the Summary sheet tab. Use the Name Manager to view the table names in the workbook, then close the dialog box.
    - **b.** You will use a lookup function to locate an employee's annual compensation; enter the Employee Number **2214** in cell A17.
    - **c.** In cell B17, use the VLOOKUP function and enter **A17** as the Lookup_value, **Table2** as the Table_array, **10** as the Col_index_num, and **FALSE** as the Range_lookup; observe the compensation displayed for that employee number, then check it against the table to make sure it is correct.
    - **d.** Enter another Employee Number, **4177**, in cell A17 and view the annual compensation for that employee.
    - **e.** Format cell B17 with the Accounting format with no decimal places and the $ symbol.
    - **f.** Save the workbook.

▼ SKILLS REVIEW (CONTINUED)

5. Summarize table data.

a. You want to enter a database function to average the annual salaries by branch, using the NY branch as the initial criterion. In cell E17, use the DAVERAGE function and click the top left corner of cell A1 twice to select the table and its header row as the Database, select cell G1 for the Field and select the range D16:D17 for the Criteria.

b. Test the function further by entering the text **Philadelphia** in cell D17. When the criterion is entered, cell E17 should display 91480.

c. Format cell E17 in Accounting format with no decimal places and the $ symbol.

d. Save the workbook.

6. Validation table data.

a. Select the data in column E of the table and set a validation criterion specifying that you want to allow a list of valid options.

b. Enter a list of valid options that restricts the entries to **NY**, **Boston**, and **Philadelphia**. Remember to use a comma between each item in the list.

c. Indicate that you want the options to appear in an in-cell dropdown list, then close the dialog box.

d. Add a row to the table. Go to cell E12, then select Boston in the dropdown list.

e. Select column F in the table and indicate that you want to restrict the data entered to only whole numbers. In the Minimum text box, enter **1000**; in the Maximum text box, enter **20000**. Close the dialog box.

f. Click cell F12, enter **25000**, then press [Enter]. You should get an error message.

g. Click Cancel, then enter **17000**.

h. Complete the new record by adding an Employee Number of 1112, a First Name of Caroline, a Last Name of Dow, a Hire Date of 2/1/2010, and an Annual Bonus of $1000. Format the range F12:J12 as Accounting with no decimal places and using the $ symbol. Compare your screen to Figure H-21.

i. Add your name to the center section of the footer, save, preview the worksheet and fit it to one page if necessary, then print it.

FIGURE H-21

	A	B	C	D	E	F	G	H	I	J
1	Employee Number	First Name	Last Name	Hire Date	Branch	Monthly Salary	Annual Salary	Annual Bonus	Benefits Dollars	Annual Compensation
2	1311	Mary	Lawson	2/12/2007	NY	$ 4,500	$ 54,000	$ 1,200	$ 12,420	$ 67,620
3	4522	Laurie	Wales	4/1/2008	Boston	$ 5,800	$ 69,600	$ 5,400	$ 16,008	$ 91,008
4	4177	Donna	Dahar	5/6/2006	Philadelphia	$ 7,500	$ 90,000	$ 16,000	$ 20,700	$ 126,700
5	2571	Mary	Marlin	12/10/2007	Boston	$ 8,000	$ 96,000	$ 18,000	$ 22,080	$ 136,080
6	2214	Paul	Gamache	2/15/2009	Boston	$ 2,900	$ 34,800	$ 570	$ 8,004	$ 43,374
7	6587	Peter	Erickson	3/25/2007	NY	$ 2,775	$ 33,300	$ 770	$ 7,659	$ 41,729
8	2123	Erin	Mallo	6/23/2006	NY	$ 3,990	$ 47,880	$ 2,500	$ 11,012	$ 61,392
9	4439	Mark	Merry	8/3/2009	Philadelphia	$ 6,770	$ 81,240	$ 5,000	$ 18,685	$ 104,925
10	9807	Hailey	Reed	9/29/2008	Philadelphia	$ 8,600	$ 103,200	$ 14,000	$ 23,736	$ 140,936
11	3944	Joyce	Roy	5/12/2007	Boston	$ 3,500	$ 42,000	$ 900	$ 9,660	$ 52,560
12	1112	Caroline	Dow	2/1/2010	Boston	$ 17,000	$ 204,000	$ 1,000	$ 46,920	$ 251,920
13										
14										
15										
16	Employee Number	Annual Compensation		Branch	Average Annual Salary					
17	4177	$ 126,700		Philadelphia	$ 91,480					

7. Create subtotals using grouping and outlines.

a. Click the Subtotals sheet tab.

b. Use the Department field list arrow to sort the table in ascending order by department.

c. Convert the table to a range.

d. Group and create subtotals by department, using the SUM function, then click the AnnualCompensation checkbox if necessary in the Add Subtotal to list.

e. Click the 2 outline button on the outline to display only the subtotals and the grand total. Compare your screen to Figure H-22.

f. Enter your name in the worksheet footer, save the workbook, preview, then print the subtotals and grand total.

g. Save the workbook, close the workbook, then exit Excel.

FIGURE H-22

	A	B	C	D	E	F	G	H	I	J
1	Employee Number	First Name	Last Name	Hire Date	Department	Monthly Salary	Annual Salary	Annual Bonus	Benefits Dollars	Annual Compensation
6					Boston Total					$ 323,022
10					NY Total					$ 170,741
14					Philadelphia Total					$ 372,561
15					Grand Total					$ 866,325
16										

▼ INDEPENDENT CHALLENGE 1

As the owner of Preserves, a gourmet food store located in Dublin, Ireland, you spend a lot of time managing your inventory. To help with this task, you have created an Excel table of your jam inventory. You want to filter the table and add subtotals and a grand total to the table. You also need to add data validation and summary information to the table.

▼ INDEPENDENT CHALLENGE 1 (CONTINUED)

a. Start Excel, open the file EX H-3.xlsx from the drive and folder where you store your Data Files, then save it as Jams.

b. Using the table data on the Inventory sheet, create a filter to generate a list of rhubarb jams. Enter your name in the worksheet footer, save the workbook, then preview and print the table. Clear the filter.

c. Use a Custom Filter to generate a list of jams with a quantity greater than 20. Preview, then print the table. Clear the filter.

d. Copy the labels in cells A1:F1 into A16:F16. Type **Gooseberry** in cell B17 and type **Small** in cell C17. Use the Advanced Filter with a criteria range of A16:F17 to extract a table of small gooseberry jams to the range of cells beginning in cell A20. Save the workbook, preview, then print the table with the extracted information.

e. Click the Summary sheet tab, select the table data in column B. Open the Data Validation dialog box, then indicate you want to use a validation list with the acceptable entries of **Gooseberry, Blackberry, Rhubarb**. Make sure the In-cell dropdown check box is selected.

f. Test the data validation by trying to change a cell in column B of the table to Strawberry.

FIGURE H-23

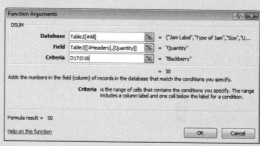

g. Using Figure H-23 as a guide, enter a function in cell G18 that calculates the total quantity of blackberry jam in your store. Enter your name in the worksheet footer, save the workbook, then preview and print the worksheet.

h. Use the filter list arrow for the Type of Jam field to sort the table in ascending order by type of jam. Convert the table to a range. Insert subtotals by type of jam using the SUM function, then select Quantity in the Add Subtotal to table box. Use the appropriate button on the outline to display only the subtotals and grand total. (Note that the number of Blackberry Jams calculated in cell G22 is incorrect after subtotals are added because the subtotals are included in the database calculation.) Save the workbook, preview, then print the range containing the subtotals and grand total.

FIGURE H-24

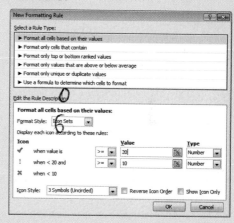

Advanced Challenge Exercise

- Clear the subtotals from the worksheet.
- Use conditional formatting to add icons to the quantity field using the following criteria: quantities greater than or equal to 20 are formatted with a green check mark, quantities greater than or equal to 10 but less than 20 are formatted with a yellow exclamation point, and quantities less than 10 are formatted with a red x. Use Figure H-24 as a guide to adding the formatting rule, then compare your Quantity values to Figure H-25. (*Hint*: You may need to click in the top Value text box for the correct value to display for the red x.)
- Save the workbook, preview then print the worksheet.

i. Close the workbook, then exit Excel.

FIGURE H-25

	A	B	C	D	E	F
1	Jam Label	Type of Jam	Size	Unit Price	Quantity	Total
2	Tipperary Ranch	Blackberry	Medium	6.00	11	66.00
3	Galway Estate	Blackberry	Small	5.25	12	63.00
4	Wexford Hills	Blackberry	Medium	5.75	15	86.25
5	Kerry Lane	Blackberry	Small	6.55	12	78.60
6	Tipperary Ranch	Gooseberry	Small	5.75	6	34.50
7	Cork Estate	Gooseberry	Small	5.75	8	46.00
8	Wexford Hills	Gooseberry	Small	5.75	21	120.75
9	Kerry Lane	Gooseberry	Medium	7.25	18	130.50
10	Tipperary Ranch	Rhubarb	Small	6.50	5	32.50
11	Galway Estate	Rhubarb	Small	6.25	11	68.75
12	Wexford Hills	Rhubarb	Small	5.25	31	162.75
13	Kerry Lane	Rhubarb	Medium	7.55	24	181.20
14						

▼ INDEPENDENT CHALLENGE 2

You recently started a personalized pet tag business, called Paw Tags. The business sells engraved cat and dog tags. Customers order tags for their cat or dog and provide you with the name of the pet and whether they want engraving on one or both sides of the tag. You have put together an invoice table to track sales for the month of October. Now that you have this table, you would like to manipulate it in several ways. First, you want to filter the table to retrieve only tags retailing for more than a particular price and ordered during a particular part of the month. You also want to subtotal the unit price and total cost columns by tag and restrict entries in the Order Date column. Finally, you would like to add database and lookup functions to your worksheet to efficiently retrieve data from the table.

Excel 2007

▼ INDEPENDENT CHALLENGE 2 (CONTINUED)

a. Start Excel, open the file EX H-4.xlsx from the drive and folder where you store your Data Files, then save it as **Paw Tags**.

b. Use the Advanced Filter to show tags with a price of $12.99 ordered before 10/15/2010, using cells A27:B28 to enter your criteria and filtering the table in place. (*Hint*: You don't need to specify an entire row as the criteria range.) Enter your name in the worksheet footer, save the workbook, then print the filtered table. Clear the filter, then save your work again.

c. Use the Data Validation dialog box to restrict entries to those with order dates on or after 10/1/2010 and before or on 10/31/2010. Test the data restrictions by attempting to enter an invalid date in cell D25.

d. Enter **23721** in cell F28. Enter a VLOOKUP function in cell G28 to retrieve the total based on the invoice number entered in cell F28. Make sure you have an exact match with the invoice number. Test the function with the invoice number 23718.

e. Enter the date **10/1/2010** in cell I28. Use the database function, DCOUNT, in cell J28 to count the number of invoices for the date in cell I28. Save the workbook.

f. Sort the table in ascending order by Tag, then convert the table to a range. Create subtotals showing the number of cat and dog tags in the Invoice Number column. Save your subtotaled data, then preview and print the Invoice worksheet.

Advanced Challenge Exercise

- Clear the subtotals and create a table using the data in the range A1:J25. Change the font color of the column headers to white. If the font headers are not visible, change the font color to one that contrasts with the fill color of your headers.
- Use the filtering feature to display only the Cat tags, then add a total row to display the number of cat tags in cell E26. Change the font color in cells A26 and E26 to white. If the contents of cells A26 and E26 are not visible, change the font color to one that contrasts with the fill color for those cells. Delete the total in cell J26.
- Use conditional formatting to format the cells where the Total is greater than $12.00 with light red fill and dark red text.
- Using the Total Filter arrow, sort the table by color to display the totals exceeding $12.00 on top. Filter the table by color to display only the rows with totals greater than $12.00.

g. Save the workbook, print the Invoice worksheet, close the workbook, then exit Excel.

▼ INDEPENDENT CHALLENGE 3

You are the manager of Green Mountain, a gift shop in Burlington, Vermont. You have created an Excel table that contains your order data, along with the amounts for each item ordered and the date the order was placed. You would like to manipulate this table to display product categories and ordered items meeting specific criteria. You would also like to add subtotals to the table and add database functions to total orders. Finally, you want to restrict entries in the Category column.

a. Start Excel, open the file EX H-5.xlsx from the drive and folder where you store your Data Files, then save it as **Gifts**.

b. Using the table data, create an advanced filter that retrieves, to its current location, records with dates before 9/10/2010 and whose orders were greater than $1000, using cells A37:E38 to enter your criteria for the filter. Clear the filter.

c. Create an advanced filter that extracts records with the following criteria to cell A42: orders greater than $1000 having dates either before 9/10/2010 or after 9/24/2010. (*Hint*: Recall that when you want records to meet one criterion or another, you need to place the criteria on separate lines.) Enter your name in the worksheet footer, then preview and print the worksheet.

d. Use the DSUM function in cell H2 to let worksheet users find the total order amounts for the category entered in cell G2. Format the cell containing the total order using the Accounting format with the $ symbol and no decimals. Test the DSUM function using the Food category name. (The sum for the Food category should be $5,998.) Print the worksheet.

e. Use data validation to create an in-cell drop-down that restricts category entries to Food, Clothing, Book, Personal. Use the Error Alert tab of the Data Validation dialog box to set the alert level to the Warning style with the message "Data is not valid." Test the validation in the table with valid and invalid entries.

▼ INDEPENDENT CHALLENGE 3 (CONTINUED)

f. Sort the table by category in ascending order. Add Subtotals to the order amounts by category. The total order amount in cell H2 will be incorrect after adding subtotals because the subtotals will be included in the database calculation.

g. Use the outline to display only category names with subtotals and the grand total.

Advanced Challenge Exercise

- Clear the subtotals from the worksheet.
- Conditionally format the 1-Month Order data using Top/Bottom Rules to emphasize the cells containing the top 10 percent with yellow fill and dark yellow text.
- Add another rule to format the bottom 10 percent in the 1-Month Order column with a light blue fill.

h. Save the workbook, preview, then print the worksheet.

i. Close the workbook, then exit Excel.

▼ REAL LIFE INDEPENDENT CHALLENGE

You decide to organize your business and personal contacts using the Excel table format. You want to use the table to look up cell, home, and work phone numbers. You also want to include addresses and a field documenting whether the contact relationship is personal or business. You enter your contact information in an Excel worksheet that you will convert to a table so you can easily filter the data. You also use lookup functions to locate phone numbers when you provide a last name in your table. Finally, you restrict the entries in one of the fields to values in drop-down lists to simplify future data entry and reduce errors.

a. Start Excel, open a new workbook, then save it as **Contacts** in the drive and folder where you store your Data Files.

b. Use the structure of Table H-2 to enter at least six of your personal and business contacts into a worksheet. (*Hint*: You will need to format the Zip column using the Zip Code type of the Special category.) In the Relationship field, enter either Business or Personal. If you don't have phone numbers for all the phone fields, leave them blank.

TABLE H-2

Last name	First name	Cell phone	Home phone	Work phone	Street address	City	State	Zip	Relationship

c. Use the worksheet information to create a table. Use the Name Manager dialog box to edit the table name to Contacts.

d. Create a filter that retrieves records of personal contacts. Clear the filter.

e. Create a filter that retrieves records of business contacts. Clear the filter.

f. Restrict the Relationship field entries to Business or Personal. Provide an in-cell drop-down list allowing the selection of these two options. Add an input message of **Select from the dropdown list**. Add an Information level error message of **Choose Business or Personal**. Test the validation by adding a new record to your table.

g. Below your table, create a phone lookup area with the following labels in adjacent cells: **Last name**, **Cell phone**, **Home phone**, **Work phone**.

h. Enter one of the last names from your table under the label Last Name in your phone lookup area.

i. In the phone lookup area, enter lookup functions to locate the cell phone, home phone, and work phone numbers for the contact last name that you entered in the previous step. Make sure you match the last name exactly.

j. Enter your name in the center section of the worksheet footer, save the workbook, preview, then print the worksheet on one page.

k. Close the workbook, then exit Excel.

▼ VISUAL WORKSHOP

Open the file EX H-6.xlsx from the drive and folder where you save your Data Files, then save it as **Schedule**. Complete the worksheet as shown in Figure H-26. Cells B18:E18 contain lookup functions that find the instructor, day, time, and room for the course entered in cell A18. Use HIS101 in cell A18 to test your lookup functions. The range A22:G27 is extracted from the table using the criteria in cells A20:A21. Add your name to the worksheet footer, save the workbook, then preview and print the worksheet.

FIGURE H-26

	A	B	C	D	E	F	G
1			Spring 2011 Schedule of History Classes				
2							
3	Course number	ID #	Time	Day	Room	Credits	Instructor
4	HIS100	1245	8:00 - 9:00	M,W,F	126	3	Walsh
5	HIS101	1356	8:00 - 9:30	T,TH	136	3	Guan
6	HIS102	1567	9:00 - 10:00	M,W,F	150	3	Marshall
7	HIS103	1897	10:00 - 11:30	T,TH	226	3	Benson
8	HIS104	3456	2:00 - 3:30	M,W,F	129	4	Paulson
9	HIS200	4678	12:00 - 1:30	T,TH	156	3	Dash
10	HIS300	7562	3:00 - 4:30	M,W,F	228	4	Christopher
11	HIS400	9823	11:00 - 12:00	M,W,F	103	3	Robbinson
12	HIS500	7123	3:00 - 4:30	T,TH	214	3	Matthews
13							
14							
15							
16							
17	Course Number	Instructor	Day	Time	Room		
18	HIS101	Guan	T,TH	8:00 - 9:30	136		
19							
20	Day						
21	M,W,F						
22	Course number	ID #	Time	Day	Room	Credits	Instructor
23	HIS100	1245	8:00 - 9:00	M,W,F	126	3	Walsh
24	HIS102	1567	9:00 - 10:00	M,W,F	150	3	Marshall
25	HIS104	3456	2:00 - 3:30	M,W,F	129	4	Paulson
26	HIS300	7562	3:00 - 4:30	M,W,F	228	4	Christopher
27	HIS400	9823	11:00 - 12:00	M,W,F	103	3	Robbinson
28							

Automating Worksheet Tasks

Files You Will Need:

EX I-1.xlsx

A **macro** is a set of instructions that performs tasks in the order you specify. You create macros to automate Excel tasks that you perform frequently. Because they perform tasks rapidly, macros can save you a great deal of time. For example, if you usually enter your name and date in a worksheet footer, you can record the keystrokes in an Excel macro that enters the text and inserts the current date automatically when you run the macro. In this unit, you will plan and design a simple macro, then record and run it. You will then edit the macro and explore ways to make it more easily available as you work. Kate Morgan, the vice president of sales at Quest, wants you to create a macro for the sales division. The macro needs to automatically insert text that identifies the worksheet as a sales division document.

OBJECTIVES

Plan a macro

Enable a macro

Record a macro

Run a macro

Edit a macro

Use shortcut keys with macros

Use the Personal Macro Workbook

Assign a macro to a button

Planning a Macro

You create macros for Excel tasks that you perform frequently. For example, you can create a macro to enter and format text or to save and print a worksheet. To create a macro, you record the series of actions or write the instructions in a special programming language. Because the sequence of actions is important, you need to plan the macro carefully before you record it.  Kate wants you to create a macro for the sales division that inserts the text "Sales Division" in the upper-left corner of any worksheet. You work with her to plan the macro.

DETAILS

To plan a macro, use the following guidelines:

- **Assign the macro a descriptive name**

  The first character of a macro name must be a letter; the remaining characters can be letters, numbers, or underscores. Letters can be uppercase or lowercase. Spaces are not allowed in macro names; use underscores in place of spaces. (Press [Shift][-] to enter an underscore character.) Kate wants you to name the macro "DivStamp". See Table I-1 for a list of macros that could be created to automate other tasks at Quest.

- **Write out the steps the macro will perform**

  This planning helps eliminate careless errors. Kate writes a description of the macro she wants, as shown in Figure I-1.

- **Decide how you will perform the actions you want to record**

  You can use the mouse, the keyboard, or a combination of the two. Kate wants you to use both the mouse and the keyboard.

- **Practice the steps you want Excel to record, and write them down**

  Kate has written down the sequence of actions she wants you to include in the macro.

- **Decide where to store the description of the macro and the macro itself**

  Macros can be stored in an active workbook, in a new workbook, or in the **Personal Macro Workbook**, a special workbook used only for macro storage. Kate asks you to store the macro in a new workbook.

FIGURE I-1: Paper description of planned macro

Macro to create stamp with the division name

Name:	DivStamp
Description:	Adds a stamp to the top left of the worksheet, identifying it as a sales division worksheet
Steps:	1. Position the cell pointer in cell A1.
	2. Type Sales Division, then click the Enter button.
	3. Click the Format button, then click Format Cells.
	4. Click the Font tab, under Font style, click Bold; under Underline; click Single; under Color; click Red; then click OK.

Excel 2007

TABLE I-1: Possible macros and their descriptive names

description of macro	descriptive name
Enter a frequently used proper name, such as Kate Morgan	KateMorgan
Enter a frequently used company name, such as Quest	Company_Name
Print the active worksheet on a single page, in landscape orientation	FitToLand
Add a footer to a worksheet	FooterStamp
Show a generic view of a worksheet using the default print and display settings	GenericView

Enabling a Macro

Because a macro may contain a virus—destructive software that can damage your computer files—the default security setting in Excel disables macros from running. Although a workbook containing a macro will open, if macros are disabled, they will not function. You can manually change the Excel security setting to allow macros to run if you know a macro came from a trusted source. When saving a workbook with a macro, you need to save it as a macro-enabled workbook with the extension xlsm. Kate asks you to change the security level to enable all macros. You will change the security level back to the default setting after you create and run your macros.

STEPS

1. **Start Excel, click the** Save button 🔲 **on the Quick Access Toolbar, in the Save As dialog box click the** Save as type list arrow, **click** Excel Macro-Enabled Workbook (*.xlsm), **then in the File name text box type** Macro Workbook

2. **Navigate to the drive and folder where you store your Data Files, then click** Save
   The security settings that enable macros are available on the Developer tab.

QUICK TIP
If the Developer tab is displayed on your Ribbon, skip steps three and four.

3. **Click the** Microsoft Office button 🔵, **then click the** Excel Options button **at the bottom of the menu**
   The Excel Options dialog box opens, as shown in Figure I-2.

4. **If necessary, click** Popular **in the category list, click the** Show Developer tab in the Ribbon check box **to select it if necessary, then click** OK
   The Developer tab appears on the Ribbon. You are ready to change the security settings.

5. **Click the** Developer tab, **then click the** Macro Security button **in the Code group**
   The Trust Center dialog box opens, as shown in Figure I-3.

6. **Click** Macro Settings **if necessary, click the** Enable all macros (not recommended; potentially dangerous code can run) option button **to select it, then click** OK
   The dialog box closes. Macros remain enabled until you disable them by deselecting the Enable all macros option. As you work with Excel, you should disable macros when you are not working with them.

FIGURE I-2: Excel Options dialog box

Select to display
the Developer tab

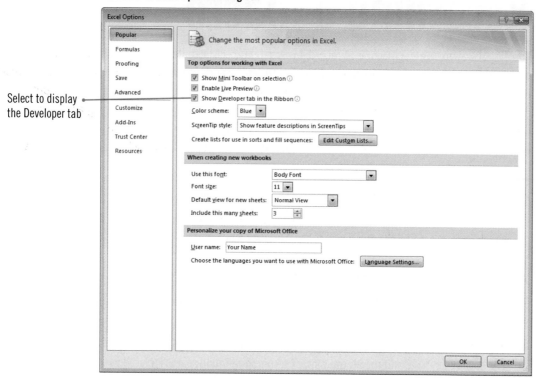

FIGURE I-3: Trust Center dialog box

Click to enable
all macros

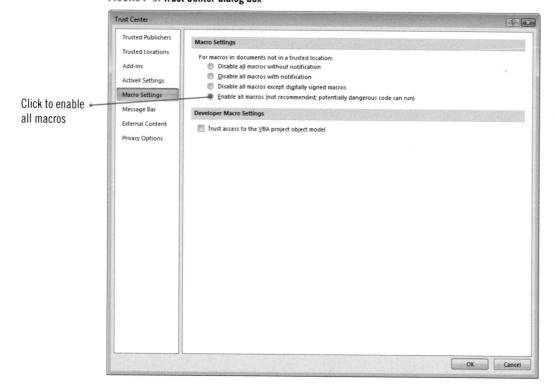

Disabling macros

To prevent viruses from running on your computer, you should disable all macros when you are not working with them. To disable macros, click the Developer tab, then click the Macro Security button in the Code group. Clicking any of the first three options will disable macros. The first option will disable all macros without notifying you. The second option will notify you when macros are disabled, and the third option will allow only digitally signed macros to run.

Recording a Macro

The easiest way to create a macro is to record it using the Excel Macro Recorder. You turn the Macro Recorder on, name the macro, enter the keystrokes and select the commands you want the macro to perform, then stop the recorder. As you record the macro, Excel automatically translates each action into program code that you can later view and modify. You can take as long as you want to record the macro; a recorded macro contains only your actions, not the amount of time you took to record it. ▓▓▓▓ Kate wants you to create a macro that enters a division "stamp" in cell A1 of the active worksheet. You create this macro by recording your actions.

STEPS

QUICK TIP

You can also click the Record Macro button in the Code group on the Developer tab to record a new macro.

1. **Click the Record Macro button** 🔲 **on the left side of the status bar**

   The Record Macro dialog box opens, as shown in Figure I-4. The default name Macro1 is selected. You can either assign this name or enter a new name. This dialog box also lets you assign a shortcut key for running the macro and assign a storage location for the macro.

2. **Type DivStamp in the Macro name text box**

3. **If the Store macro in list box does not display This Workbook, click the list arrow and select This Workbook**

4. **Type your name in the Description text box, then click OK**

   The dialog box closes and the Record Macro button on the status bar is replaced with a Stop Recording button. Take your time performing the steps below. Excel records every keystroke, menu selection, and mouse action that you make.

5. **Press [Ctrl][Home]**

   When you begin an Excel session, macros record absolute cell references. By beginning the recording in cell A1, you ensure that the macro includes the instruction to select cell A1 as the first step, in cases where A1 is not already selected.

QUICK TIP

You can press [Ctrl][Enter] instead of clicking the Enter button.

6. **Type Sales Division in cell A1, then click the Enter button** ✅ **on the Formula Bar**

7. **Click the Home tab, click the Format button in the Cells group, then click Format Cells**

8. **Click the Font tab, in the Font style list box click Bold, click the Underline list arrow and click Single, click the Color list arrow and click the Red, Accent 2 Theme color (first row, sixth color from the left), then compare your dialog box to Figure I-5**

QUICK TIP

You can also click the Stop Recording button in the Code group on the Developer tab to stop recording a macro.

9. **Click OK, click the Stop Recording button** 🔲 **on the left side of the status bar, click cell D1 to deselect cell A1, then save the workbook**

   Figure I-6 shows the result of recording the macro.

FIGURE I-4: Record Macro dialog box

Type macro name here

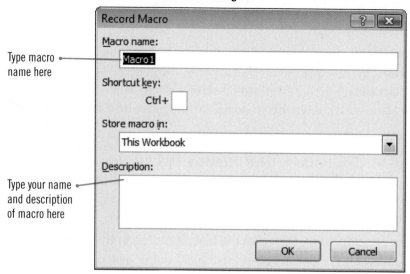

Type your name and description of macro here

FIGURE I-5: Font tab of the Format Cells dialog box

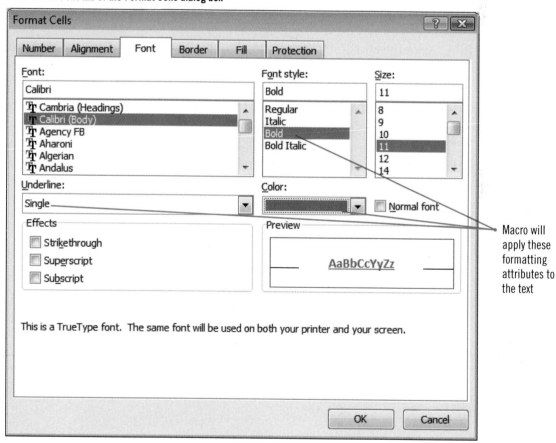

Macro will apply these formatting attributes to the text

FIGURE I-6: Sales Division stamp

	A	B	C
1	Sales Division		
2			
3			
4			

Running a Macro

Once you record a macro, you should test it to make sure that the actions it performs are correct. To test a macro, you **run** (play) it. You can run a macro using the Macros button in the Code group of the Developer tab. 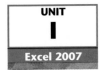 Kate asks you to clear the contents of cell A1 and then test the DivStamp macro. After you run the macro in the Macro workbook, she asks you to test the macro once more from a newly opened workbook.

STEPS

1. **Click cell A1, click the Home tab if necessary, click the Clear button ❷˅ in the Editing group, click Clear All, then click any other cell to deselect cell A1**

   When you delete only the contents of a cell, any formatting still remains in the cell. By using the Clear All option you can be sure that the cell is free of contents and formatting.

2. **Click the Developer tab, then click the Macros button in the Code group**

   The Macro dialog box, shown in Figure I-7, lists all the macros contained in the open workbooks. If other people have used your computer, other macros may be listed.

3. **Make sure DivStamp is selected, as you watch cell A1, click Run, then deselect cell A1**

   The macro quickly plays back the steps you recorded in the previous lesson. When the macro is finished, your screen should look like Figure I-8. As long as the workbook containing the macro remains open, you can run the macro in any open workbook.

4. **Click the Microsoft Office button ●, click New, then in the New Workbook dialog box click Create**

   Because the Macro Workbook.xlsm is still open, you can use its macros.

5. **Deselect cell A1, click the Macros button in the Code group, make sure 'Macro Workbook.xlsm'!DivStamp is selected, click Run, then deselect cell A1**

   When multiple workbooks are open, the macro name in the Macro dialog box includes the workbook name between single quotation marks, followed by an exclamation point, indicating that the macro is outside the active workbook. Because you only used this workbook to test the macro, you don't need to save it.

6. **Close Book2.xlsx without saving changes**

   The Macro Workbook.xlsm workbook remains open.

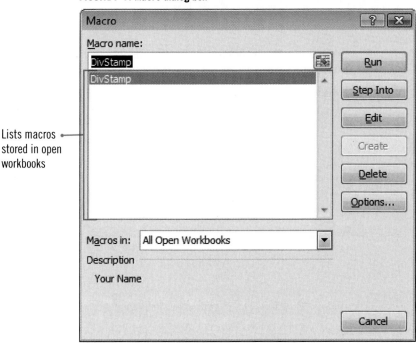

FIGURE I-7: Macro dialog box

Lists macros stored in open workbooks

FIGURE I-8: Result of running DivStamp macro

Formatted text inserted into cell A1

	A	B	C
1	**Sales Division**		
2			
3			
4			

Running a macro automatically

You can create a macro that automatically performs certain tasks when the workbook it is saved in is opened. This is useful for actions you want to do every time you open a workbook. For example, you may import data from an external data source into the workbook or format the worksheet data in a certain way. To create a macro that will automatically run when the workbook is opened, you need to name the macro Auto_Open and save it in the workbook.

Editing a Macro

When you use the Macro Recorder to create a macro, the program instructions, called **program code**, are recorded automatically in the **Visual Basic for Applications (VBA)** programming language. Each macro is stored as a **module**, or program code container, attached to the workbook. After you record a macro, you might need to change it. If you have a lot of changes to make, it might be best to record the macro again. But if you need to make only minor adjustments, you can edit the macro code directly using the **Visual Basic Editor**, a program that lets you display and edit your macro code. Kate wants you to modify the DivStamp macro to change the point size of the department stamp to 14.

STEPS

1. **Make sure the Macro Workbook.xlsm workbook is open, click the Macros button in the Code group, make sure DivStamp is selected, then click Edit**

   The Visual Basic Editor starts, showing three windows: the Project Explorer window, the Properties window, and the Code window, as shown in Figure I-9.

TROUBLE

If the Properties window does not appear in the lower-left portion of your screen, click the Properties Window button [icon] in the Visual Basic Standard Toolbar, then resize it as shown in the figure if necessary.

2. **Click Module 1 in the Project Explorer window if it's not already selected, then examine the steps in the macro, comparing your screen to Figure I-9**

   The name of the macro and your name appear at the top of the module window. Below this area, Excel has translated your keystrokes and commands into macro code. When you open and make selections in a dialog box during macro recording, Excel automatically stores all the dialog box settings in the macro code. For example, the line `.FontStyle = "Bold"` was generated when you clicked Bold in the Format Cells dialog box. You also see lines of code that you didn't generate directly while recording the DivStamp macro, for example, `.Name = "Calibri"`.

3. **In the line `.Size = 11`, double-click 11 to select it, then type 14**

   Because Module1 is attached to the workbook and not stored as a separate file, any changes to the module are saved automatically when you save the workbook.

QUICK TIP

You can return to Excel without closing the module by clicking the View Microsoft Excel button [icon] on the Visual Basic Editor toolbar.

4. **Click File on the Visual Basic Editor menu bar, click Print, click OK to print the module, then review the printout**

5. **Click File on the menu bar, then click Close and Return to Microsoft Excel**

   You want to rerun the DivStamp macro to make sure the macro reflects the change you made using the Visual Basic Editor. You begin by clearing the division name from cell A1.

6. **Click cell A1, click the Home tab, click the Clear button [icon] in the Editing group, then click Clear All**

QUICK TIP

Another way to start the Visual Basic Editor is to click the Developer tab, then click the Visual Basic button in the Code group.

7. **Click any other cell to deselect cell A1, click the Developer tab, click the Macros button in the Code group, make sure DivStamp is selected, click Run, then deselect cell A1**

   The department stamp is now in 14-point type, as shown in Figure I-10.

8. **Save the workbook**

FIGURE I-9: Visual Basic Editor showing Module1

Comments appear in green

Project Explorer window with Module1 selected

Properties window showing properties for Module1

Properties window button

Code window

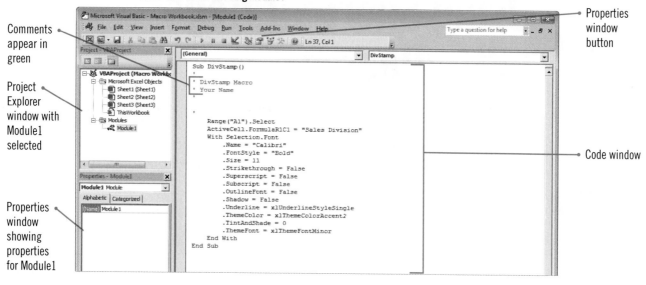

```
Sub DivStamp()
'
' DivStamp Macro
' Your Name
'

    Range("A1").Select
    ActiveCell.FormulaR1C1 = "Sales Division"
    With Selection.Font
        .Name = "Calibri"
        .FontStyle = "Bold"
        .Size = 11
        .Strikethrough = False
        .Superscript = False
        .Subscript = False
        .OutlineFont = False
        .Shadow = False
        .Underline = xlUnderlineStyleSingle
        .ThemeColor = xlThemeColorAccent2
        .TintAndShade = 0
        .ThemeFont = xlThemeFontMinor
    End With
End Sub
```

FIGURE I-10: Result of running edited DivStamp macro

Font size is enlarged to 14-point

	A	B	C
1	Sales Division		
2			
3			
4			

Adding comments to Visual Basic code

With practice, you will be able to interpret the lines of macro code. Others who use your macro, however, might want to know the function of a particular line. You can explain the code by adding comments to the macro. **Comments** are explanatory text added to the lines of code. When you enter a comment, you must type an apostrophe (') before the comment text. Otherwise, the program tries to interpret it as a command. On the screen, comments appear in green after you press [Enter], as shown in Figure I-9. You can also insert blank lines as comments in the macro code to make the code more readable. To do this, type an apostrophe, then press [Enter].

Using Shortcut Keys with Macros

In addition to running a macro from the Macro dialog box, you can run a macro by using a shortcut key combination that you assign to the macro. Using shortcut keys saves you time by reducing the number of actions you need to take to run a macro. You assign shortcut key combinations in the Record Macro dialog box. **≋≋≋≋** Kate also wants you to create a macro called CompanyName to enter the company name into a worksheet. You assign a shortcut key combination to run the macro.

STEPS

1. **Click cell B2**

   You want to record the macro in cell B2, but you want the macro to enter the company name anywhere in a worksheet. Therefore, you do not begin the macro with an instruction to position the cell pointer, as you did in the DivStamp macro.

2. **Click the Record Macro button 🖾 on the status bar**

   The Record Macro dialog box opens. Notice the option Shortcut key: Ctrl+ followed by a blank box. You can type a letter (A-Z) in the Shortcut key text box to assign the key combination of [Ctrl] plus that letter to run the macro. Because some common Excel shortcuts use the [Ctrl][letter] combination, such as [Ctrl][C] for Copy, you decide to use the key combination [Ctrl][Shift] plus a letter to avoid overriding any of these shortcut key combinations.

3. **With the default macro name selected, type CompanyName, click the Shortcut key text box, press and hold [Shift], type C, then in the Description box type your name**

   You have assigned the shortcut key combination [Ctrl][Shift][C] to the CompanyName macro. After you create the macro, you will use this shortcut key combination to run it. Compare your screen with Figure I-11. You are ready to record the CompanyName macro.

4. **Click OK to close the dialog box**

5. **Type Quest in cell B2, click the Enter button ✔ on the formula bar, press [Ctrl][I] to italicize the text, click the Stop Recording button ⬛ on the status bar, then deselect cell B2**

   Quest appears in italics in cell B2. You are ready to run the macro in cell A5 using the shortcut key combination.

6. **Click cell A5, press and hold [Ctrl][Shift], type C, then deselect the cell**

   The company name appears in cell A5, as shown in Figure I-12. The macro played back in the selected cell (A5) instead of the cell where it was recorded (B2) because you did not begin recording the macro by clicking cell B2.

FIGURE I-11: Record Macro dialog box with shortcut key assigned

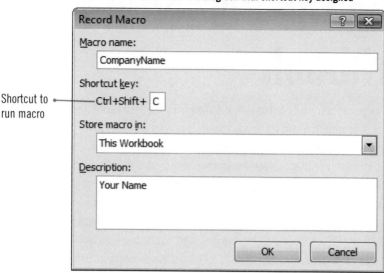

Shortcut to run macro → Ctrl+Shift+ C

FIGURE I-12: Result of running the CompanyName macro

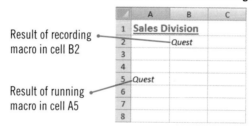

Result of recording macro in cell B2

Result of running macro in cell A5

Using Relative Referencing when creating a macro

By default, Excel records absolute cell references in macros. You can record a macro's actions based on the relative position of the active cell by clicking the Use Relative References button in the Code group prior to recording the action. For example, when you create a macro using the default setting of absolute referencing, bolding the range A1:D1 will always bold that range when the macro is run. However, if you click the Use Relative References button when recording the macro before bolding the range, then running the macro will not necessarily result in bolding the range A1:D1. The range that will be bolded will depend on the location of the active cell when the macro is run. If the active cell is A4, then the range A4:D4 will be bolded. Selecting the Use Relative References button highlights the button

name, indicating it is active, as shown in Figure I-13. The button remains active until you click it again to deselect it. This is called a **toggle**, meaning that it acts like an off/on switch: it retains the relative reference setting until you click it again to turn it off or you exit Excel.

FIGURE I-13: Use Relative References button selected

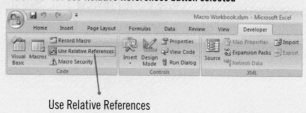

Use Relative References button selected

Using the Personal Macro Workbook

When you create a macro, it is automatically stored in the workbook in which you created it. But if you wanted to use that macro in another workbook, you would have to copy the macro to that workbook. Instead, it's easier to store commonly used macros in a Personal Macro Workbook. The **Personal Macro Workbook** is an Excel file that is always available, unless you specify otherwise, and gives you access to all the macros it contains, regardless of which workbooks are open. The Personal Macro Workbook file is automatically created the first time you choose to store a macro in it, and is named PERSONAL.XLSB. You can add additional macros to the Personal Macro Workbook by saving them in the workbook. By default, the PERSONAL.XLSB workbook opens each time you start Excel, but you don't see it because Excel designates it as a hidden file. Kate often likes to print her worksheets in landscape orientation with one-inch left, right, top, and bottom margins. She wants you to create a macro that automatically formats a worksheet for printing this way. Because she wants to use this macro in future workbooks, she asks you to store the macro in the Personal Macro Workbook.

STEPS

1. **Click the Record New Macro button ⊞ on the status bar**
   The Record Macro dialog box opens.

2. **Type FormatPrint in the Macro name text box, click the Shortcut key text box, press and hold [Shift], type F, then click the Store macro in list arrow**
   You have named the macro FormatPrint and assigned it the shortcut combination [Ctrl][Shift][F]. Notice that This Workbook is selected by default, indicating that Excel automatically stores macros in the active workbook, as shown in Figure I-14. You also can choose to store the macro in a new workbook or in the Personal Macro Workbook.

   > **TROUBLE**
   > If a dialog box appears saying that a macro is already assigned to this shortcut combination choose another letter for a keyboard shortcut. If a dialog box appears with the message that a macro named FormatPrint already exists, click Yes to replace it.

3. **Click Personal Macro Workbook, in the Description text box enter your name, then click OK**
   The recorder is on, and you are ready to record the macro keystrokes.

4. **Click the Page Layout tab, click the Orientation button in the Page Setup group, click Landscape, click the Margins button in the Page Setup group, click Custom Margins, then enter 1 in the Top, Left, Bottom, and Right text boxes**
   Compare your margin settings to Figure I-15.

5. **Click OK, then click the Stop Recording button ⊞ on the status bar**
   You want to test the macro.

   > **TROUBLE**
   > You may have to wait a few moments for the macro to finish. If you are using a different letter for the shortcut key combination, type that letter instead of the letter F.

6. **Activate Sheet2, in cell A1 type Macro Test, press [Enter], press and hold [Ctrl][Shift], then type F**
   The FormatPrint macro plays back the sequence of commands.

7. **Preview Sheet2 and verify that the orientation is landscape and the margins are one inch on the left, right, top, and bottom**

8. **Close Print Preview and save the workbook**

FIGURE I-14: Record Macro dialog box showing macro storage options

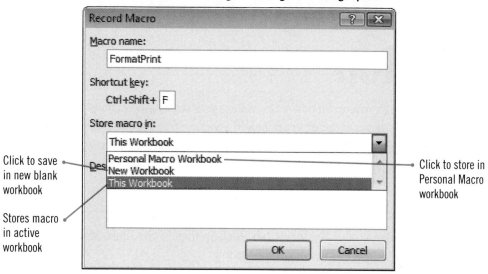

Click to save in new blank workbook

Stores macro in active workbook

Click to store in Personal Macro workbook

FIGURE I-15: Margin settings for the FormatPrint macro

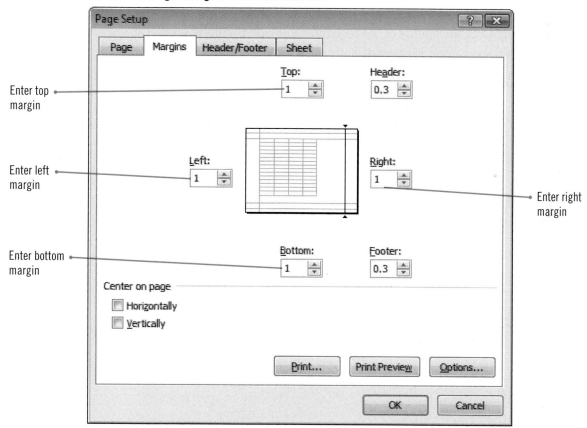

Enter top margin

Enter left margin

Enter bottom margin

Enter right margin

Working with the Personal Macro Workbook

Once you use the Personal Macro Workbook, it opens automatically each time you start Excel so you can add macros to it. By default, the Personal Macro Workbook is hidden in Excel as a precautionary measure so you don't accidentally delete anything from it. If you need to delete a macro from the Personal Macro Workbook, click the View tab, click Unhide in the Window group, click PERSONAL.XLSB, then click OK. To hide the Personal Macro Workbook, make it the active workbook, click the View tab, then click Hide in the Window group.

Assigning a Macro to a Button

When you create macros for others who will use your workbook, you might want to make the macros more visible so they're easier to use. In addition to using shortcut keys, you can run a macro by assigning it to a button on your worksheet. Then when you click the button the macro will run. To make it easier for people in the sales division to run the DivStamp macro, Kate asks you to assign it to a button on the workbook. You begin by creating the button.

STEPS

1. **Click** Sheet3, **click the** Insert tab, **click** Shapes **in the Illustrations group, then click the** first rectangle **in the Rectangles group**

   The mouse pointer changes to a + symbol.

2. **Click at the top-left corner of cell** A8 **and drag the pointer to the lower-right corner of cell** B9

   Compare your screen to Figure I-16.

QUICK TIP

When you print a worksheet with a macro button, the button will print, just like any worksheet object.

3. **Click the middle of the rectangle and type** Division Macro

   Now that you have created the button, you are ready to assign the macro to it.

4. **Right-click the** new button, **then on the shortcut menu click** Assign Macro

   The Assign Macro dialog box opens.

5. **Click** DivStamp **under Macro name, then click** OK

   You have assigned the DivStamp macro to the button.

6. **Click any cell to deselect the button, then click the button**

   The DivStamp macro plays and the text Sales Division appears in cell A1, as shown in Figure I-17.

7. **Save the workbook, print Sheet3, close the workbook, then exit Excel clicking** No **when asked to save changes to the Personal Macro Workbook**

FIGURE I-16: **Button shape**

Rectangle shape
will become
button

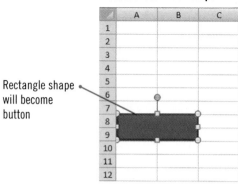

FIGURE I-17: **Sheet3 with the Sales Division text**

Result of running
macro using
the button

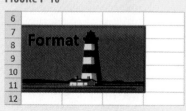

	A	B	C
1	Sales Division		
2			
3			
4			
5			
6			
7			
8	Division Macro		
9			
10			
11			
12			

Formatting a macro button

You can format macro buttons using 3-D effects, clip art, photographs, fills, and shadows. To format a button, right-click it and select Format Shape from the shortcut menu. In the Format Shape dialog box you can select the Fill, Line Color, Line Style, Shadow, 3-D Format, 3-D Rotation, Picture, or Text Box. To add an image to the button, click Fill, then click the Picture or texture fill option button. To insert a picture from a file, click the File button, select a picture, then click Insert. To insert a clip art picture, click Clip Art, select a picture, then click OK. You may need to resize your button to fully display a picture. You may also want to move the text on the button if it overlaps the image. Figure I-18 shows a button formatted with clip art.

FIGURE I-18

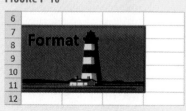

Practice

▼ CONCEPTS REVIEW

FIGURE I-19

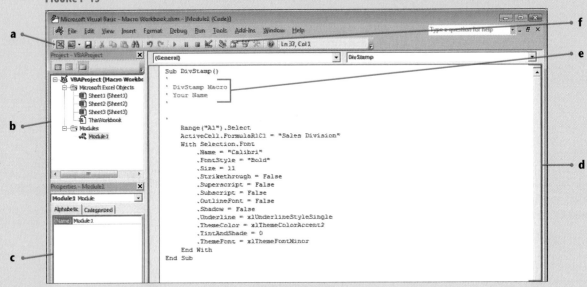

1. Which element points to the Properties window?
2. Which element points to the Code window?
3. Which element points to the Properties Window button?
4. Which element do you click to return to Excel without closing the module?
5. Which element points to a comment?
6. Which element points to the Project Explorer window?

Match each term or button with the statement that best describes it.

7. Visual Basic Editor
8. Comments
9. Personal Macro Workbook
10. Virus
11. Macro

a. Set of instructions that perform a task in a specified order
b. Statements that appear in green explaining the macro
c. Destructive software that can damage computer files
d. Used to make changes to macro code
e. Used to store commonly used macros

Select the best answer from the list of choices.

12. **Which of the following is the best candidate for a macro?**
    a. Often-used sequences of commands or actions
    b. Nonsequential tasks
    c. Seldom-used commands or tasks
    d. One-button or one-keystroke commands

13. **You can open the Visual Basic Editor by clicking the _____ button in the Macro dialog box.**
    a. Programs
    b. Visual Basic Editor
    c. Modules
    d. Edit

14. **A Macro named _____ will automatically run when the workbook it is saved in opens.**
    a. Macro1
    b. Default
    c. Auto_Open
    d. Open_Macro

15. **Which of the following is NOT true about editing a macro?**
    a. You edit macros using the Visual Basic Editor.
    b. A macro cannot be edited and must be recorded again.
    c. You can type changes directly in the existing program code.
    d. You can make more than one editing change in a macro.

16. **Why is it important to plan a macro?**
    a. Planning helps prevent careless errors from being introduced into the macro.
    b. Macros can't be deleted.
    c. It is impossible to edit a macro.
    d. Macros won't be stored if they contain errors.

17. **Macros are recorded with relative references:**
    a. Only if the Use Relative References button is selected.
    b. In all cases.
    c. By default.
    d. Only if the Use Absolute References button is not selected.

18. **You can run macros:**
    a. From the Macro dialog box.
    b. From shortcut key combinations.
    c. From a button on the worksheet.
    d. Using all of the above.

19. **Macro security settings can be changed using the _____ tab.**
    a. Security
    b. Home
    c. Developer
    d. Review

▼ SKILLS REVIEW

1. **Plan and enable a macro.**
    a. You need to plan a macro that enters and formats your name and e-mail address in a worksheet.
    b. Write out the steps the macro will perform.
    c. Write out how the macro could be used in a workbook.
    d. Start Excel, open a new workbook, then save it as a Macro-Enabled workbook named **Macros** in the drive and folder where you store your Data Files. (*Hint*: The file will have the file extension xlsm.)
    e. Use the Excel Options feature to display the Developer tab if it is not showing in the Ribbon.
    f. Using the Trust Center dialog box, enable all macros.

2. **Record a macro.**
    a. You want to record a macro that enters and formats your name and e-mail address in a worksheet using the steps below.
    b. Name the macro **MyEmail**, store it in the current workbook, and make sure your name appears as the person who recorded the macro.
    c. Record the macro, entering your name in cell A1 and your email address in cell A2.
    d. Resize column A to fit the information entirely in that column.
    e. Add an outside border around the range A1:A2 and format the font using purple from the Standard Colors.
    f. Add bold formatting to the text in the range A1:A2.
    g. Stop the recorder and save the workbook.

3. Run a macro.

  a. Clear cell entries and formats in the range affected by the macro, then resize the width of column A to 8.43.

  b. Run the MyEmail macro to place your name and e-mail information in the range A1:A2.

  c. On the worksheet, clear all the cell entries and formats generated by running the MyEmail macro. Resize the width of column A to 8.43.

  d. Save the workbook.

4. Edit a macro.

  a. Open the MyEmail macro in the Visual Basic Editor.

  b. Change the line of code above the last line from Selection.Font.Bold = True to Selection.Font.Bold = False.

  c. Use the Close and Return to Microsoft Excel option on the File menu to return to Excel.

  d. Test the macro on Sheet1 and compare your worksheet to Figure I-20 verifying that the text is not bold.

  e. Save the workbook.

FIGURE I-20

	A	B
1	Your Name	
2	yourname@yourschool.edu	
3		
4		
5		

5. Use shortcut keys with macros.

  a. You want to record a macro that enters your e-mail address in italics with a font color of red in the selected cell of a worksheet, using the steps below.

  b. Record the macro called **EmailStamp** in the current workbook, assigning your macro the shortcut key combination [Ctrl][Shift][E], storing it in the current workbook, with your name in the description.

  c. After you record the macro, clear the contents and formats from the cell containing your e-mail address that you used to record the macro.

  d. Use the shortcut key combination to run the EmailStamp macro in a cell other than the one it was recorded in. Compare your macro result to Figure I-21. Your email address may appear in a different cell.

  e. Save the workbook.

FIGURE I-21

B	C	D	E	F
	yourname@yourschool.edu			

6. Use the Personal Macro Workbook.

  a. Using Sheet1, record a new macro called **FitToLand** and store it in the Personal Macro workbook with your name in the Description text box. If you already have a macro named FitToLand replace that macro. The macro should set the print orientation to landscape.

  b. After you record the macro, activate Sheet2, and enter **Test data for FitToLand macro** in cell A1.

  c. Verify that the orientation for Sheet2 is set to portrait.

  d. Run the macro. (You may have to wait a few moments.)

  e. Preview Sheet2 and verify that it is now in Landscape orientation.

  f. Save the workbook.

7. Assign a macro to a button.

  a. Enter **Button Test** in cell A1 of Sheet3.

  b. Using the rectangle shape, draw a rectangle in the range A7:B8.

  c. Label the button with the text **Landscape**.

  d. Assign the macro PERSONAL.XLSB!FitToLand to the button.

  e. Verify that the orientation of Sheet3 is set to portrait.

  f. Run the FitToLand macro using the button.

  g. Preview the worksheet and verify that it is in landscape view.

  h. Add your name to the Sheet3 footer, save the workbook, then print Sheet3.

  i. Compare your printed worksheet to Figure I-22, close the workbook then exit Excel without saving the FitToLand macro in the Personal Macro Workbook.

FIGURE I-22

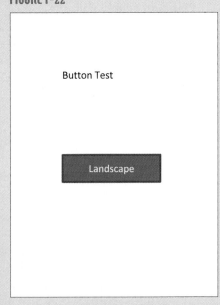

Button Test

Landscape

Automating Worksheet Tasks

▼ INDEPENDENT CHALLENGE 1

As a computer-support employee of Portland Marketing Group, you need to develop ways to help your fellow employees work more efficiently. Employees have asked for Excel macros that can do the following:

- Adjust the column widths to display all column data in a worksheet.
- Place the department name of Marketing in red font in cell A1 (the width of A1 should be increased if necessary).

a. Plan and write the steps necessary for each macro.

b. Start Excel, open the Data file EX I-1.xlsx from the drive and folder where you store your Data Files, then save it as a macro-enabled workbook called **Marketing Macros**.

c. Check your macro security on the Developer tab to be sure that macros are enabled.

d. Create a macro named **ColumnFit**, save it in the Marketing Macros.xlsm workbook, assign the ColumnFit macro a shortcut key combination of [Ctrl][Shift][C], and add your name in the description area for the macro. Record the macro using the following steps.

e. Record the ColumnFit macro to adjust a worksheet's column widths to display all data. (*Hint*: Select the entire sheet, click the Home tab, click the Format button in the Cells group, then select AutoFit Column Width.) End the macro recording.

f. Format the widths of columns A through G to 8.43, then test the ColumnFit macro with the shortcut key combination [Ctrl][Shift][C].

g. Using Sheet2, create a macro named **DepartmentName** and save it in the Marketing Macros.xlsm workbook. Assign the macro a shortcut key combination of [Ctrl][Shift][D], and add your name in the description area for the macro.

h. Record the DepartmentName macro. The macro should do the following:

- Place Marketing in a red font in cell A1 of a worksheet
- Change the font size of Marketing in cell A1 to 14-point
- Increase the width of column A to fit the Marketing label

i. Clear the text and formats from cell A1 and reformat the width of column A to 8.43. Test the DepartmentName macro using the shortcut key combination [Ctrl][Shift][D].

j. Edit the DepartmentName macro in the Visual Basic Editor to change the font to 13-point. Close the Visual Basic Editor and return to Excel.

k. Add a rectangle button to the Sheet2 in the range A6:B7. Label the button with the text **Department Name**.

l. Assign the DepartmentName macro to the button.

m. Clear the text and formats from cell A1 and reformat the width of column A to 8.43. Use the button to run the DepartmentName macro. Check the font to be sure it is 13-point. Compare your screen to Figure I-23.

FIGURE I-23

Advanced Challenge Exercise

- Format the button using the fill color of your choice. (*Hint*: Right-click the button and select Format Shape from the shortcut menu.)
- Format the button to add the 3-D effect of your choice.
- Add a shadow in the color of your choice to the button.

n. Save the workbook, print the module containing the program code for both macros, then close the workbook and exit Excel.

▼ INDEPENDENT CHALLENGE 2

You are an administrative assistant at the Toronto branch of Rare Books, a provider of out-of-print books. As part of your work, you create spreadsheets with sales projections for different titles. You frequently have to change the print settings so that workbooks print in landscape orientation with custom margins of one inch on the top and bottom. You have decided that it's time to create a macro to streamline this process.

   a. Plan and write the steps necessary to create the macro.

   b. Check your macro security settings to confirm that macros are enabled.

   c. Start Excel, create a new workbook, then save it as a macro-enabled file named **Books Macro** in the drive and folder where you store your Data Files.

   d. Create a macro that changes the page orientation to landscape and adds custom margins of one inch on the top and bottom of the page. Name the macro **Format**, add your name in the description, assign it the shortcut key combination [Ctrl][Shift][Z], and store it in the current workbook.

   e. Go to Sheet2 and enter the text **Macro Test** in cell A1. Test the macro using the shortcut key combination of [Ctrl][Shift][Z].

   f. Enter the text **Macro Test** in cell A1 of Sheet 3, add a rectangular button with the text Format to run the Format macro, then test the macro using the button.

   g. Print the module for the macro.

   h. Save and close the workbook, then exit Excel.

▼ INDEPENDENT CHALLENGE 3

You are the eastern region sales manager of Confetti, a national party supplies store. You manage the Boston, New York, and Philadelphia stores and frequently create workbooks with data from the three locations. It's tedious to change the tab names and colors every time you open a new workbook, so you decide to create a macro that will add the store locations and colors to your three default worksheet tabs, as shown in Figure I-24.

   a. Plan and write the steps to create the macro described above.

   b. Start Excel and open a new workbook.

   c. Create the macro using the plan from step a, name it **SheetFormat**, assign it the shortcut key combination [Ctrl][Shift][Z], store it in the Personal Macro Workbook, and add your name in the description area.

   d. After recording the macro, close the workbook without saving it.

   e. Open a new workbook, then save it as a macro-enabled workbook named **Store Test** in the drive and folder where you store your Data Files. Use the shortcut key combination of [Ctrl][Shift][Z] to test the macro in the new workbook.

   f. Unhide the PERSONAL.XLSB workbook. (*Hint*: Click the View tab, click the Unhide button in the Window group, then click PERSONAL.XLSB.)

   g. Edit the SheetFormat macro using Figure I-25 as a guide, changing the Sheet3 name from Philadelphia to Phil. (*Hint*: There are three instances of Philadelphia that need to be changed.)

   h. Open a new workbook, then save it as a macro-enabled workbook named **Store Test New** in the drive and folder where you store your data files. Test the edited macro using the shortcut key combination of [Ctrl][Shift][Z].

   i. Save the workbook, print the module for the macro, then close the module and return to Excel.

FIGURE I-24

FIGURE I-25

```
Sub SheetFormat()
'
' SheetFormat Macro
' Your Name
'
' Keyboard Shortcut: Ctrl+Shift+Z
'
    Sheets("Sheet1").Select
    Sheets("Sheet1").Name = "Boston"
    Sheets("Sheet2").Select
    Sheets("Sheet2").Name = "NY"
    Sheets("Sheet3").Select
    Sheets("Sheet3").Name = "Phil"
    Sheets("Boston").Select
    With ActiveWorkbook.Sheets("Boston").Tab
        .Color = 255
        .TintAndShade = 0
    End With
    Sheets("NY").Select
    With ActiveWorkbook.Sheets("NY").Tab
        .Color = 5287936
        .TintAndShade = 0
    End With
    Sheets("Phil").Select
    With ActiveWorkbook.Sheets("Phil").Tab
        .Color = 65535
        .TintAndShade = 0
    End With
End Sub
```

▼ INDEPENDENT CHALLENGE 3 (CONTINUED)

j. Hide the PERSONAL.XLSB workbook. (*Hint*: With the PERSONAL.XLSB workbook active, click the View tab, then click the Hide button in the Window group.)

k. Close the workbook, click No to save the PERSONAL.XLSB changes, then exit Excel.

▼ REAL LIFE INDEPENDENT CHALLENGE

Excel can be a helpful tool in keeping track of hours worked at a job or on a project. A macro can speed up the repetitive process of entering a formula to total your hours each week.

a. Start Excel, create a new workbook, then save it as **Hours** in the drive and folder where you store your data files. Be sure to save it as a macro-enabled file.

b. If necessary, change your security settings to enable macros.

c. Use Table I-2 as a guide in entering labels and hours into a worksheet tracking your work or project effort.

d. Create a macro named **TotalHours** in the cell adjacent to the Total label that can be activated by the [Ctrl][Shift][T] key combination. Save the macro in the Hours workbook and add your name in the description area.

e. The TotalHours macro should do the following:
- Total the hours for the week.
- Boldface the Total amount and the Total label to its left.

f. Test the macro using the key combination [Ctrl][Shift][T].

g. Add a button to the range A11:B12 with the label Total.

h. Assign the TotalHours macro to the Total button.

i. Test the macro using the button.

j. Enter your name in the footer, save your workbook, then print the results of the macro.

k. Open the macro in the Visual Basic Editor, then print the macro code.

TABLE I-2

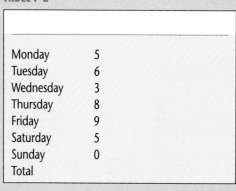

Monday	5
Tuesday	6
Wednesday	3
Thursday	8
Friday	9
Saturday	5
Sunday	0
Total	

Advanced Challenge Exercise

- Edit the macro code to add a comment with a description of your work or project.
- Add another comment with your email address.
- Above the keyboard comment enter the comment "Macro can be run using the Total button."
- Print the macro code.

l. Return to Excel, save and close the workbook, then exit Excel.

▼ VISUAL WORKSHOP

Start Excel, create a new workbook, then save it as a macro-enabled workbook with the name **Yearly Data** in the drive and folder where you save your Data Files. Create a macro with the name **Quarters** in the Yearly Data workbook that enters labels for the first, second, third, and fourth quarters. Use the macro recorder to create the macro, using the code shown in Figure I-26 as a guide for the placement and font style of the labels, and the shortcut key combination to run the macro. The code also specifies the column width format for the labels. Test the macro, edit the macro code as necessary, then print the module.

FIGURE I-26

```
Sub Quarters()
'
' Quarters Macro
' Your Name
'
' Keyboard Shortcut: Ctrl+Shift+Q
'
    Range("A1").Select
    ActiveCell.FormulaR1C1 = "First Quarter"
    Range("B1").Select
    ActiveCell.FormulaR1C1 = "Second Quarter"
    Range("C1").Select
    ActiveCell.FormulaR1C1 = "Third Quarter"
    Range("D1").Select
    ActiveCell.FormulaR1C1 = "Fourth Quarter"
    Columns("A:D").Select
    Selection.Columns.AutoFit
    Range("A1:D1").Select
    Selection.Font.Bold = True
End Sub
```

Enhancing Charts

Although Excel offers a variety of eye-catching chart types, you can customize your charts by adjusting data and chart features and by adding special formatting and graphics so that your data presentation has greater impact. In this unit, you learn to enhance your charts by manipulating chart data, formatting axes, and rotating the chart. You clarify your data display by adding a data table, special text effects, a picture, and trendlines. As you enhance your charts, keep in mind that too much customization can be distracting; your goal in enhancing charts should be to communicate your data more clearly and accurately.  Quest's vice president of sales, Kate Morgan, has requested charts comparing sales in the Quest regions over the first two quarters. You will produce these charts and enhance them to improve their appearance and make the worksheet data more accessible.

OBJECTIVES

Customize a data series

Change a data source and add data labels

Format the axes of a chart

Add a data table to a chart

Rotate a chart

Enhance a chart with WordArt

Add a picture to a chart

Identify data trends

Customizing a Data Series

A **data series** is the sequence of values that Excel uses to **plot**, or create, a chart. You can format the data series in a chart to make the chart more attractive and easier to read. As with other Excel elements, you can change the borders, patterns, or colors of a data series. Kate wants you to create a chart showing the sales for each region in January and February. You begin by creating a column chart, which you will customize to make it easier to compare the sales for each region.

STEPS

1. **Start Excel, open the file EX J-1.xlsx from the drive and folder where you store your Data Files, then save it as Region Sales**

   Kate wants to see how each region performed over January and February before adding the March data. The first step is to select the data you want to appear in the chart. In this case, you want the row labels in cells A3:A6 and the data for January and February in cells B2:C6, including the column labels.

2. **Select the range A2:C6**

TROUBLE

If your chart overlaps the worksheet data, you can drag it to move it below row 6.

3. **Click the Insert tab, click the Column button in the Charts group, then click the 3-D Clustered Column chart (the first chart in the 3-D Column group)**

   The column graph compares the January and February sales for each branch, as shown in Figure J-1. You decide to display the data so that it is easier to compare the monthly sales for each branch.

4. **Click the Switch Row/Column button in the Data group**

   The legend now contains the region data, and the horizontal axis groups the bars by month. Kate can now easily compare the branch sales for each month. The graph will be easier to read if the U.S. and Canada data series are plotted in colors that are easier to distinguish.

QUICK TIP

You can also format a data series by clicking the data series on the chart, clicking the Chart Tools Layout tab, then clicking the Format Selection button.

5. **Right-click the Jan U.S. data series bar (the leftmost bar on the graph), click Format Data Series from the shortcut menu, click Fill in the left pane of the Format Data Series dialog box, click the Solid fill option button, click the Color list arrow, select Lime, Accent 6 in the Theme Colors group, then click Close**

   Now the U.S. data series is easy to distinguish from the Canada data series.

6. **Select the Chart Area, then drag the chart to place its upper-left corner in cell A8**

   You can resize a chart by dragging its corner sizing handles. When a chart is resized this way, all of the elements are resized to maintain its appearance.

7. **Drag the chart's lower-right sizing handle to fit the chart in the range A8:H23, then compare your chart to Figure J-2**

8. **Save the workbook**

Adding width and depth to data series

You can change the gap depth and the gap width in 3-D bar or column charts by right-clicking one of the data series of the chart then clicking Format Data Series from the shortcut menu. With Series Option selected in the left pane of the Format Data Series dialog box you can move the Gap Depth and Gap Width sliders from No Gap or 0% to Large Gap or 500%. Increasing the gap width adds space between each set of data on the chart by increasing the width of chart's data series. Increasing the gap depth adds depth to all categories of data.

FIGURE J-1: Chart comparing January and February sales for each region

Chart data

3-D clustered column chart

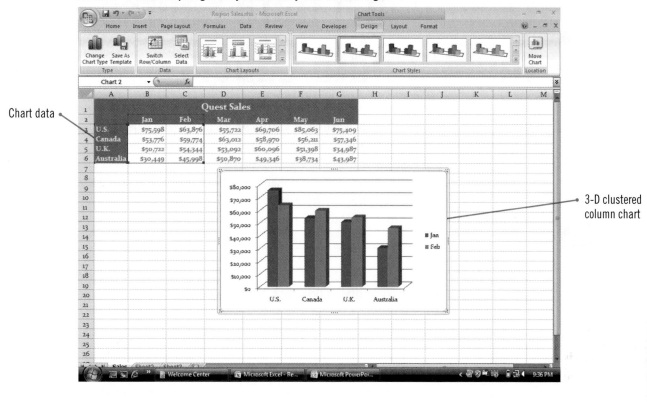

FIGURE J-2: Chart comparing region sales in January and February

Customized U.S. data series

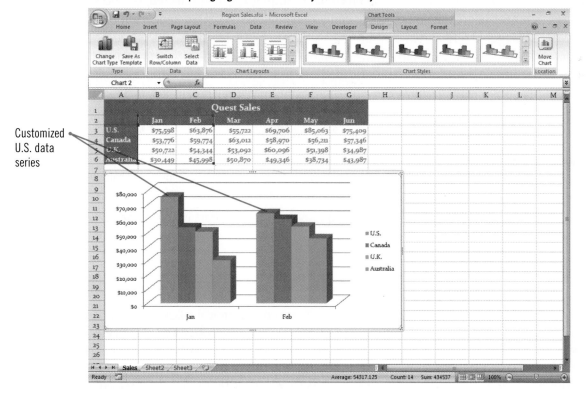

Changing a Data Source and Adding Data Labels

As you update your workbooks with new data, you may also need to add data series to (or delete them from) a chart. Excel makes it easy to revise a chart's data source and to rearrange chart data. To communicate chart data more clearly, you can add descriptive text, called a **data label**, which appears above a data marker in a chart.  Kate wants you to create a chart showing the branch sales for the first quarter. You need to add the March data to your chart so that it reflects the first-quarter sales. Kate asks you to add data labels to clarify the charted data and to make the chart more attractive. It will be easier to compare the branch sales in a 3-D column chart that is not clustered.

STEPS

1. **Click the Chart Tools Design tab, click the Change Chart Type button in the Type group, in the Change Chart Type dialog box click 3-D Column (the last chart in the first row), then click OK**

   The chart bars are no longer clustered. You want to change the data view to compare branch sales for each month in the new chart type.

2. **Click the Switch Row/Column button in the Data group**

   The labels that were in the legend are now on the horizontal axis. You want to add the March data to the chart.

3. **Click the Select Data button in the Data group**

   The Select Data Source dialog box opens.

   > **QUICK TIP**
   > You can also add data to a chart by selecting the chart and dragging the corner of the data border to the right to include the new worksheet data.

4. **Verify that the range in the Chart data range text box is selected, on the Sales worksheet select the range A2:D6, verify that =Sales!$A$2:$D$6 appears in the Chart data range text box, then click OK**

   The March data series appears on the chart, as shown in Figure J-3. You want to change all of the column colors to make them more attractive and decide to use one of the preformatted chart styles.

5. **Click the More button ⬇ in the Chart Styles group, then click Style 26**

   The bars are now three shades of blue with gradients. You can quickly add data labels to your chart using one of the predefined chart layouts in the Chart Layouts gallery.

   > **QUICK TIP**
   > You can also add or delete data labels using the Data Labels button in the Labels group on the Chart Tools Layout tab.

6. **Click the More button ⬇ in the Chart Layouts group, then click Layout 4**

   Data labels showing the exact value of each data point now appear above each bar. The data labels are crowded together. You decide to resize the chart so that the data labels are easier to read.

7. **Drag the chart's lower-right sizing handle to fit the chart in the range A8:J27, then compare your chart to Figure J-4**

Representing proportional relationships

Pie charts are often used to show the relative sizes of items in a data series by displaying the proportional relationships of entities in a data series to the sum. Pie charts represent the contribution of each value to a total in either a 2-D or 3-D format. For example if you want to show the part of a budget a department uses in an organization, you can create a pie chart and display the data labels as percentages. The percentages represent the parts of the whole pie for each of the departments.

To annotate a pie chart so it displays the percentage share of each item in a data series, select the chart, click the Chart Tools Layout tab, click the Data Labels button in the Labels group, select the position for the data labels, click the Data Labels button again, click More Data Label Options, click the Percentage check box to select it, deselect the Value check box, then click Close. Some of the layouts in the Chart Layouts group of the Chart Tools Design tab also feature percentage labels.

FIGURE J-3: Chart with March data series added

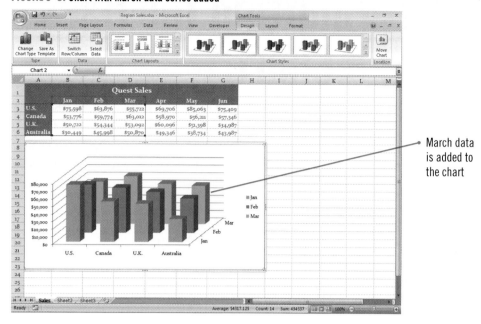

March data is added to the chart

FIGURE J-4: Chart with data labels

U.S. data labels

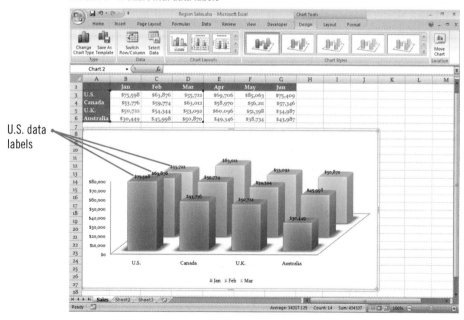

Moving, removing, and formatting legends

To change the position of a legend or to remove it, click the Chart Tools Layout tab, click the Legend button in the Labels group, then select the desired legend position or select None to remove the legend. To format a legend's position, fill, border color and style, or shadows, click More Legend Options at the bottom of the Legend menu. You can add textured fills or pictures and customize the border and shadow characteristics. If you position the Format Legend dialog box next to the legend, you can use the Excel Live Preview feature to try out different effects, such as those shown in Figure J-5. To change a legend's font size, right-click the legend text, click Font on the shortcut menu, then adjust the font size in the Font dialog box. You can also drag a legend to the location of your choice.

FIGURE J-5: Formatted legend

Formatting the Axes of a Chart

Excel plots and formats chart data and places the chart axes within the chart's **plot area**. Data values in two-dimensional charts are plotted on the vertical y-axis (often called the **value axis** because it usually shows value levels). Categories are plotted on the horizontal x-axis (often called the **category axis** because it usually shows data categories). Excel creates a scale for the value (y) axis based on the highest and lowest values in the series and places intervals along the scale. A three-dimensional (3-D) chart, like the one in Figure J-6, has three axes; the x-axis remains the category axis, but the z-axis becomes the value axis and the y-axis becomes the measure for the chart's depth and is not visible. In 3-D charts, the value (z) axis usually contains the scale. For a summary of the axes Excel uses to plot data, see Table J-1. You can override the Excel default formats for chart axes at any time by using the Format Axis dialog box. Kate asks you to increase the maximum number on the value axis and change the axis number format. She would also like you to add axes titles to explain the plotted data.

STEPS

1. **Click the chart to select it if necessary, click the** Chart Tools Layout tab, **click the** Axes **button in the Axes group, point to** Primary Vertical Axis, **then click** More Primary Vertical Axis Options

   The Format Axis dialog box opens. The minimum, maximum, and unit Axis Options are set to Auto, and the default scale settings appear in the text boxes on the right. You can override any of these settings by clicking the Fixed option buttons and entering new values.

2. **With Axis Options selected in the list on the left, click the** Fixed option button **in the Maximum line, press [Tab], in the Fixed text box type** 90000, **then click** Close

   Now 90,000 appears as the maximum value on the value axis, and the chart bar heights adjust to reflect the new value. Next, you want the vertical axis values to appear without zeroes to make the chart data easier to read.

3. **Click the** Axes button **in the Axes group, point to** Primary Vertical Axis, **then click** Show Axis in Thousands

   The values are reduced to two digits and the word "Thousands" appears in a text box to the left of the values. You decide that vertical and horizontal axis titles would improve the clarity of the chart information.

4. **Click the** Axis Titles button **in the Labels group, point to** Primary Vertical Axis Title, **then click** Rotated Title

   A text box containing the text Axis Title appears on the vertical axis, next to Thousands.

5. **Type** Sales, **then click outside the text box to deselect it**

   The word Sales appears in the Vertical axis label. You decide to label the horizontal axis.

6. **Click the** Axis Titles button **in the Labels group, point to** Primary Horizontal Axis Title, **click** Title Below Axis, **type** Regions, **then click outside the text box to deselect it**

7. **Drag the** Thousands text box **on the vertical axis lower in the Chart Area to match Figure J-7, then deselect it**

FIGURE J-6: Chart elements in a 3-D chart

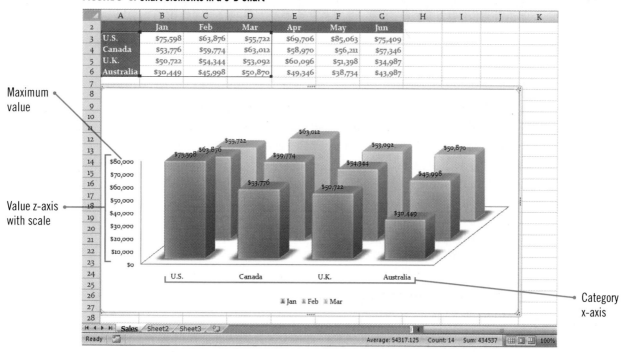

Maximum value

Value z-axis with scale

Category x-axis

FIGURE J-7: Chart with formatted axes

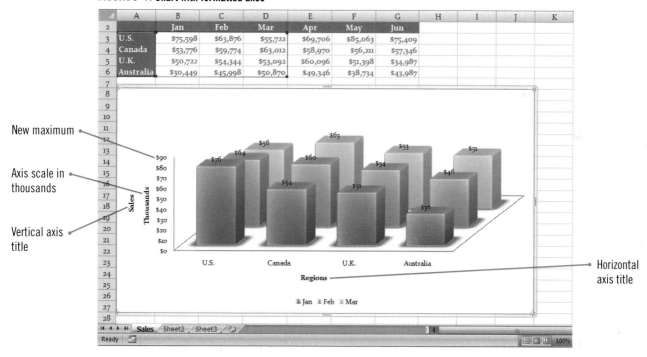

New maximum

Axis scale in thousands

Vertical axis title

Horizontal axis title

TABLE J-1: Axes used by Excel for chart formatting

axes in a two-dimensional chart	axes in a three-dimensional chart
Category (x) axis (horizontal)	Category (x) axis (horizontal)
Value (y) axis (vertical)	Series (y) axis (depth)
	Value (z) axis (vertical)

Adding a Data Table to a Chart

A **data table** is a grid containing the chart data, attached to the bottom of a chart. Data tables are useful because they display—directly on the chart itself—the data you used to generate a chart. You can display data tables in line, area, column, and bar charts, and print them automatically along with a chart. It's good practice to add data tables to charts that are stored separately from worksheet data.  Kate wants you to move the chart to its own worksheet and add a data table to emphasize the chart's first-quarter data.

STEPS

1. **Click the chart object to select it if necessary, click the Chart Tools Design tab, then click the Move Chart button in the Location group**

   The Move Chart dialog box opens. You want to place the chart on a new sheet named First-Quarter Chart.

2. **Click the New sheet option button, type First Quarter Chart in the New sheet text box, then click OK**

3. **Click the Chart Tools Layout tab, click the Data Table button in the Labels group, then click Show Data Table with Legend Keys**

   A data table with the first-quarter data and a key to the legend appears at the bottom of the chart, as shown in Figure J-8. The data table would stand out more if it were formatted.

   > **QUICK TIP**
   > You can also add a data table by selecting a chart with a data table from the Chart Layouts gallery.

4. **Click the Data Table button, then click More Data Table Options**

   The Format Data Table dialog box opens.

5. **Click Border Color in the left pane, click the Solid line option button to select it, click the Color list arrow, click the Lime, Accent 6 color (first row, last color) in the Theme Colors section, click Close, then click the chart area to deselect the data table.**

   The data table appears with green lines, as shown in Figure J-9.

   > **QUICK TIP**
   > To hide a data table, click the Data Table button in the Labels group, then click None.

6. **Save the workbook**

Using the Modeless Format dialog box

Many of the buttons on the Chart Tools Layout tab have a "More ...Options " command at the bottom of the menu that appears when you click them. For example, clicking the Data Table button allows you to click More Data Table Options. The Format dialog box that opens when you click it allows you to format the selected data table. But while the dialog box is open, you can also click and format other elements. The Format dialog boxes are **modeless**, which means when they are open, you can click on other chart elements and then change their formatting in the same dialog box, whose options adjust to reflect the selected element. You are not restricted to changing only one object—i.e., you are not in a single **mode**, or limited set of possible choices. For example if the Format Data Table dialog box is open and you click a data label, the dialog box changes to Format Data Labels. If you click the legend, the dialog box becomes the Format Legend dialog box, allowing you to modify the legend characteristics.

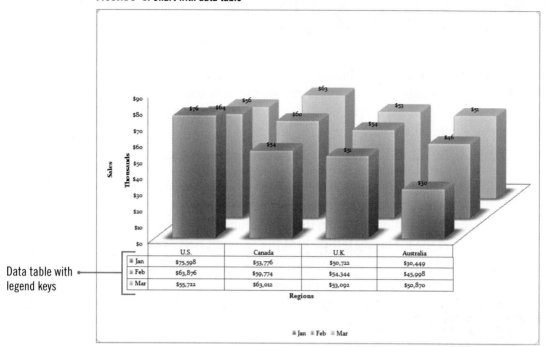

	U.S.	Canada	U.K.	Australia
▓ Jan	$75,598	$53,776	$50,722	$30,449
▓ Feb	$63,876	$59,774	$54,344	$45,998
▓ Mar	$55,722	$63,012	$53,092	$50,870

Data table with legend keys

FIGURE J-9: **Chart with formatted data table**

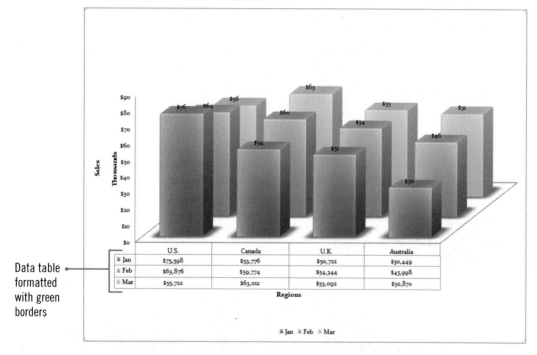

	U.S.	Canada	U.K.	Australia
▓ Jan	$75,598	$53,776	$50,722	$30,449
▓ Feb	$63,876	$59,774	$54,344	$45,998
▓ Mar	$55,722	$63,012	$53,092	$50,870

Data table formatted with green borders

Rotating a Chart

Three-dimensional (3-D) charts do not always display data in the most effective way. In many cases, one or more of a chart's data points can obscure the view of other data points, making the chart difficult to read. By rotating and/or changing the chart's depth, you can make the data easier to see. Kate wants you to rotate the chart and increase the depth. You will begin by hiding the data table so it doesn't overlap the view of the data.

STEPS

1. **Click the chart to select it if necessary, click the** Chart Tools Layout tab, **click the** Data Table button **in the Labels group, then click** None

2. **Click the** 3-D Rotation button **in the Background group, then if necessary click** 3-D Rotation **in the list on the left pane of the Format Chart Area dialog box**

   The 3-D rotation options are shown in Figure J-10.

3. **In the Chart Scale section, click the** Right Angle Axes check box **to deselect it, double-click the** X: text box **in the Rotation section, then enter** 25

   The X: Rotation setting rotates the chart to the left and right. You can also click the Left and Right buttons to rotate the chart.

4. **Double-click the** Y: text box, **then enter** 20

   The Y: Rotation setting rotates the chart up and down. You decide to change the depth of the columns.

5. **Double-click the** Depth (% of base) text box **in the Chart Scale section, then enter** 200

6. **Click** Close, **then compare your chart to Figure J-11**

   The chart columns now appear deeper and less crowded, making the chart easier to read.

7. **Save the workbook**

Making 3-D charts easier to read

In addition to rotating a chart there are other ways to view smaller data points that may be obscured by larger data markers in the front of a 3-D chart. To reverse the order that the data series are charted you can click the Axes button in the Axes group of the Chart Tools Layout tab, point to Depth Axis, click More Depth Axis Options, click the Series in reverse order check box in the Format Axis dialog box to select it, then click Close. Another way to see smaller data series in the back of a 3-D chart is to add transparency to the large data markers in the front of the chart. To do this you can right-click the data series that you want to make transparent, click Format Data Series in the shortcut menu, click Fill in the Format Data Series dialog box, click either the Solid fill or Gradient fill option buttons, move the slider on the Transparency bar to a percentage that allows you to see the other data series on the chart, then click Close. If you have a picture on the chart's back wall, adding transparency to the series in front of it makes more of the picture visible.

FIGURE J-10: 3-D rotation options

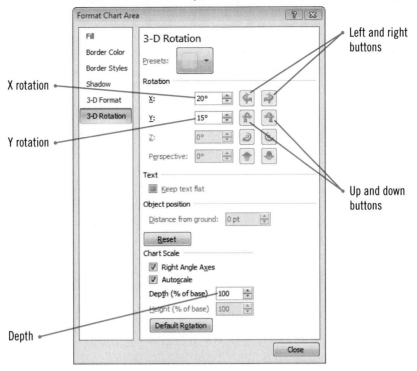

X rotation

Y rotation

Depth

Left and right buttons

Up and down buttons

FIGURE J-11: Chart with increased depth and rotation

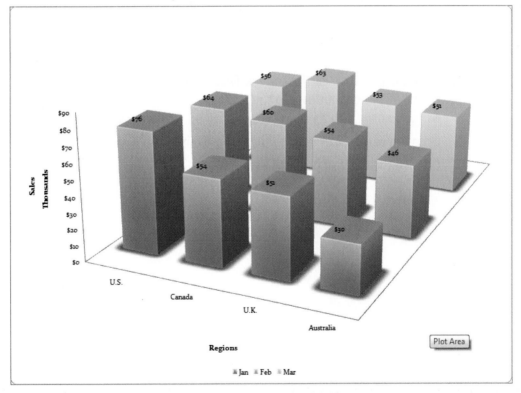

Charting data accurately

The purpose of a chart is to help viewers to interpret the worksheet data. When creating charts, you need to make sure that your chart accurately portrays your data. Charts can sometimes misrepresent data and thus mislead people. For example, you can change the y-axis units or its starting value to make charted sales values appear larger than they are. Even though you may have correctly labeled the sales values on the chart, the height of the data points will lead people viewing the chart to think the sales are higher than the labeled values. So use caution when you modify charts to make sure you accurately represent your data.

Enhancing a Chart with WordArt

You can enhance your chart or worksheet titles using **WordArt**, which is preformatted text. Once you've added WordArt text to your worksheet or chart, you can edit or format it by adding 3-D effects and shadows. WordArt text is a shape rather than text. This means that you cannot treat WordArt objects as if they were labels entered in a cell; that is, you cannot sort, use the spelling checker, or use their cell references in formulas. Kate wants you to add a WordArt title to the first-quarter chart. You will begin by adding a title to the chart.

STEPS

QUICK TIP
To delete a chart title, right-click it, then select Delete from the shortcut menu. You can also select the chart title and press [Delete].

1. **Click the chart to select it if necessary, click the Chart Tools Layout tab, click the Chart Title button in the Labels group, then click Above Chart**

   A chart title text box appears above the chart.

2. **Select the Chart Title text in the text box, then type First Quarter Sales**

3. **Drag to select the chart title text if necessary, click the Chart Tools Format tab, then click the More button ▼ in the WordArt Styles group**

   The WordArt Gallery opens, as shown in Figure J-12. This is where you select the style for your text.

4. **Click Gradient Fill - Accent 4, Reflection (the last style in the fourth row), then click outside the chart title to deselect it**

   The title text becomes formatted with capital letters with a gradient turquoise fill, a white background, and a light shadow. You decide the chart title would look better if it were closer to the chart.

5. **Place the pointer over the edge of First Quarter Sales (the WordArt title), drag First Quarter Sales down closer to the chart**

   Adding the title caused the vertical axis label and the vertical axis title to overlap.

6. **Drag the vertical axis label to the right, as shown in Figure J-13**

7. **Click on the chart to deselect any items**

Adding WordArt to a worksheet

You can use WordArt to add interest to the text on a worksheet. To insert WordArt, click the Insert tab, click the WordArt button in the Text group, choose a WordArt Style from the gallery, then replace the WordArt text "Your Text Here" with your text. After selecting the text, you can use the Text Fill list arrow in the WordArt Styles group to add a solid, picture, gradient, or texture fill to your text. The Text

Outline list arrow in the WordArt Styles group allows you to add color, weight, and dashes to the text outline. You can use the Text Effects button in the WordArt Styles group to add shadows, reflections, glows, bevels, 3-D rotations, and transformations to the WordArt text.

FIGURE J-12: WordArt Styles gallery

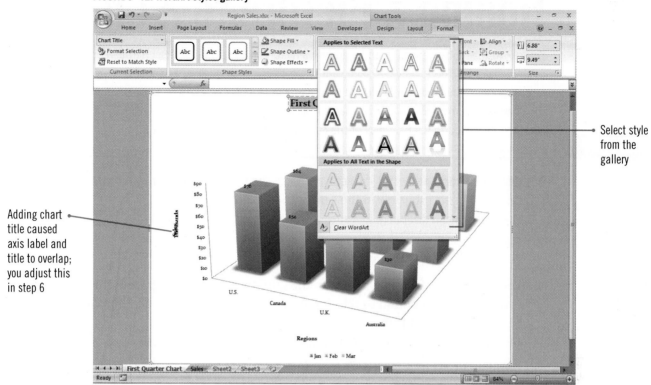

Adding chart title caused axis label and title to overlap; you adjust this in step 6

Select style from the gallery

FIGURE J-13: Chart with WordArt title

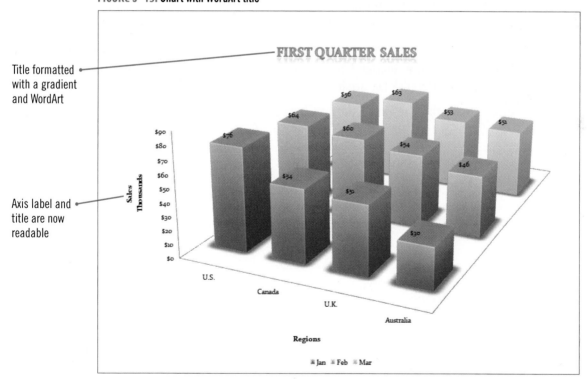

Title formatted with a gradient and WordArt

Axis label and title are now readable

Rotating chart labels

You can rotate the category labels on a chart so that longer labels won't appear crowded. Select the Category Axis on the chart, click the Chart Tools Format tab, click the Format Selection button in the Current Selection group, click Alignment in the left pane of the dialog box, click the Text direction list arrow, then select the rotation option for the labels. In a two-dimensional chart, you can also select a custom angle for the axis labels.

Adding a Picture to a Chart

You can further enhance your chart by adding a picture to the data markers, chart area, plot area, legend, or chart walls and floors. However, you want to keep your chart as clean and simple as possible, so use pictures sparingly. When you add a picture to a chart element, its purpose should be to enhance the message the chart data communicates, rather than to call attention to the image itself. ▰▰▰ Kate wants you to add the Quest logo to the back wall of the chart to identify the company data.

STEPS

1. **Click the chart to select it if necessary, click the** Chart Tools Format tab, **then click the** Chart Elements list arrow **in the Current Selection group**

   The chart elements that can be formatted are displayed as shown in Figure J-14.

2. **Click** Back Wall

   The back wall of the chart is selected, as shown by the four small circles on its corners.

3. **Click the** Format Selection button **in the Current Selection group, click the** Picture or texture fill option button **to select it in the Format Wall dialog box, then click the** File button **under Insert from**

   The Insert Picture dialog box opens, allowing you to navigate to the logo image.

4. **Navigate to the location where you store your Data Files, click the** chartlogo.gif **file, click** Insert, **then click** Close

   The Quest logo appears on the back wall of the chart.

5. **Move the chart title if necessary to view the top of the logo, then compare your chart to Figure J-15**

6. **Click the** Insert tab, **click the** Header & Footer button **in the Text group, click the** Custom Footer button **on the Header/Footer tab, enter your name in the center section text box, click** OK, **then click** OK **again**

7. **Preview then print the First-Quarter Chart sheet**

Creating a chart template

After you create a custom chart with specific formatting, you can save it as a chart template. Chart templates can be opened and reused later, and the applied formatting will be available. Chart templates have the file extension crtx. If you use a custom chart frequently, you can save the template as the default chart type. To save a chart as a chart template, click the Chart Tools Design tab, click Save As Template in the Type group, enter a filename in the Save Chart Template dialog box, then click Save. Your chart template will be saved in the Templates\Charts folder. When you want to format a chart like a chart template, you need to apply the template. Select your chart, click the Insert tab, click a chart type in the Charts group, click All Chart Types, click the Templates folder in the Change Chart Type dialog box, select a template in the My Templates area, then click OK.

FIGURE J-14: Chart elements list

Chart Elements list arrow

Click to select a chart element

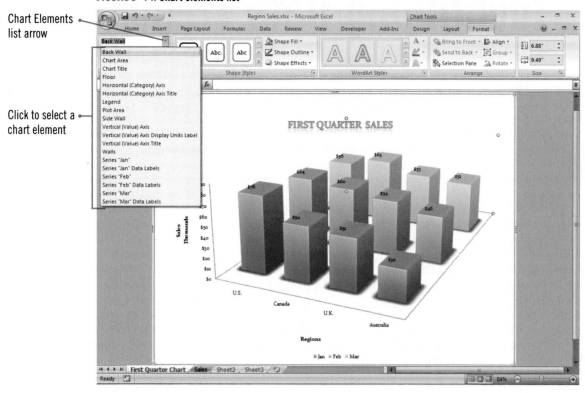

FIGURE J-15: First Quarter chart with picture inserted

Logo inserted on back wall of chart

Identifying Data Trends

You often use charts to visually represent data over a period of time. To emphasize patterns in data, you can add trendlines to your charts. A **trendline** is a series of data points on a line that shows data values representing the general direction in a data series. In some business situations, you can use trendlines to predict future data based on past trends.  Kate wants you to compare the U.S. and U.K. sales performance over the first two quarters and to project sales for each region in the following three months, assuming past trends. You begin by charting the six months sales data in a 2-D Column chart.

STEPS

1. Click the Sales sheet tab, scroll to the top of the worksheet if necessary, select the range A2:G6, click the Insert tab, click the Column button in the Charts group, then click the Clustered Column button (First chart in the 2-D Column group)

2. Drag the chart left until its upper-left corner is at the upper left corner of cell A8, drag the middle-right sizing handle right to the border between column G and column H

   You are ready to add a trendline for the U.S. data series.

3. Click the U.S. January data point (the leftmost column in the chart) to select the U.S. data series, click the Chart Tools Layout tab, click the Trendline button in the Analysis group, then click Linear Trendline

   A linear trendline identifying U.S. sales trends in the first six months is added to the chart, along with an entry in the legend identifying the line. You need to compare the U.S. sales trend with the U.K. sales trend.

4. Click the U.K. January data point (the third column in the chart) to select the U.K. data series, click the Trendline button, then click Linear Trendline

   The chart now has two trendlines, making it easy to compare the sales trends of the U.S. and the U.K. branches. Now you want to project the next three months sales for the U.S. and U.K. sales branches based on the past six months trends.

5. Click the U.S. data series trendline, click the Trendline button, then click More Trendline Options

   The Format Trendline dialog box opens, as shown in Figure J-16.

   > **TROUBLE**
   > If you have trouble selecting the trendline you can click the Layout tab, click the Chart Elements list arrow in the Current Selection group, then select Series "U.S." Trendline1.

6. In the Forecast section, enter 3 in the Forward text box, click Close, click the U.K. data series trendline, click the Trendline button, click More Trendline Options, enter 3 in the Forward text box, then click Close

   The trendlines project three additional months, predicting the future sales trends for the U.S. and U.K. regions. The two trendlines look identical, so you decide to format them.

7. Click the U.S. data series trendline, click the Trendline button, click More Trendline Options, click the Custom option button in the Trendline name section, then type U.S. Trends in the Custom text box

8. Click Line Color in the left pane of the dialog box, click the Solid line option button, click the Color list arrow, select Red in the Standard colors section, click Line Style in the left pane, click the Dash type list arrow, select the Dash option, then click Close

   The U.S. data series trendline is now a red dashed line and is clearly identified in the legend.

9. Select the U.K. data series trendline, repeat steps 7 and 8 but using the name U.K. Trends and a Green dashed line, then click outside the chart and go to cell A1

10. Compare your chart to Figure J-17, enter your name in the center section of the Sales sheet footer, save the workbook, preview and print the Sales sheet, then exit Excel

FIGURE J-16: Format Trendline dialog box

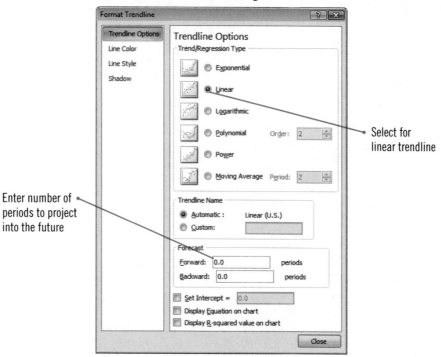

Select for linear trendline

Enter number of periods to project into the future

FIGURE J-17: Sales chart with trendlines for U.S. and U.K. data

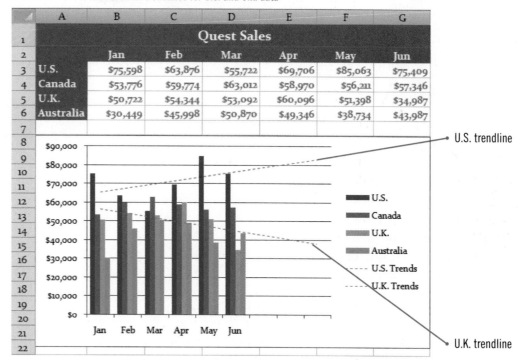

U.S. trendline

U.K. trendline

Choosing the right trendline for your chart

Trendlines can help you forecast where your data is headed and understand its past values. This type of data analysis is called **regression analysis** in mathematics. You can choose from four types of trendlines: Linear, Exponential, Linear Forecast, and Two Period Moving Average. A **linear trendline** is used for data series with data points that have the pattern of a line. An exponential trendline is a curved line that is used when data values increase or decrease quickly. You cannot use an exponential trendline if your data contains negative values. A linear forecast trendline is a linear trendline with a two-period forecast. A two-period moving average smoothes out fluctuations in data by averaging the data points.

Practice

▼ CONCEPTS REVIEW

FIGURE J-18

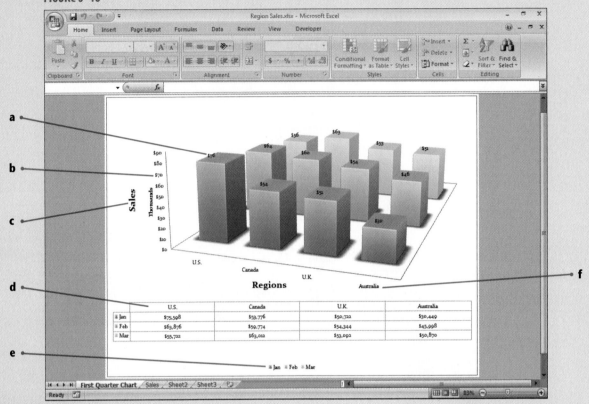

1. Which element points to the chart legend?
2. Which element points to a data table?
3. Which element points to a data label?
4. Which element points to a vertical axis title?
5. Which element points to the value axis?
6. Which element points to the category axis?

Match each term with the statement that best describes it.

7. Data series
8. Plot area
9. x-axis
10. y-axis
11. z-axis

a. Category axis
b. Depth in a 3-D chart
c. Vertical axis in a 3-D chart
d. Sequence of values plotted on a chart
e. Location holding data charted on the axes

Select the best answer from the list of choices.

12. Which of the following is true regarding WordArt?

   a. Spelling errors in WordArt can be detected by the spell checker.

   b. Cell references to WordArt can be used in formulas.

   c. Cells containing WordArt can be sorted.

   d. WordArt is a shape.

13. In 2-dimensional charts, the y-axis is the:

   a. Category axis.   **c.** 2-D axis.

   b. Depth axis.   **d.** Value axis.

14. A chart's scale:

   a. Always appears on the z-axis.   **c.** Always appears on the x-axis.

   b. Can be adjusted.   **d.** Always appears on the y-axis.

15. Which Chart Tools tab is used to format the axes of a chart?

   a. Layout   **c.** Format

   b. Design   **d.** Insert

16. What is a data table?

   a. The data used to create a chart, displayed in a grid

   b. A customized data series

   c. A grid with chart data displayed above a chart

   d. A three-dimensional arrangement of data on the y-axis

17. A chart template is saved with the extension:

   a. crtx   **c.** xlsx

   b. tem   **d.** xlsm

18. Which of the following is false regarding trendlines?

   a. Trendlines visually represent patterns in past data.

   b. Trendlines are used to predict future data.

   c. Six types of trendlines can be added to a chart.

   d. Trendlines can be formatted to stand out on a chart.

▼ SKILLS REVIEW

1. Customize a data series.

   a. Start Excel, open the file EX J-2.xlsx from the drive and folder where you save your Data Files, then save it as **Pastry Sales**.

   b. With the Sales sheet active, select the range A2:D6.

   c. Create a 3-D column chart using the selected data. (*Hint*: Do not choose the 3-D clustered column chart.)

   d. Move and resize the chart to fit in the range A8:G20.

   e. Change the color of the January data series to a light blue color in the Standard Colors group.

   f. Save the workbook.

2. Change a data source and add data labels.

   a. Add the April, May, and June data to the chart.

   b. Change the chart view by exchanging the row and column data.

   c. Resize the chart to fill the range A8:J28 to display the new data.

   d. Change the chart view back to show the months in the legend by exchanging the row and column data. Apply Chart Layout 4 to add data labels to your chart. Delete the data labels for all but the June series. (*Hint*: Click one of the data labels in the series, then press [Delete].) Move any June data labels that are difficult to view.

   e. Save the workbook.

3. Format the axes of a chart.

   a. Change the display of the vertical axis values to thousands.

   b. Move the thousands label lower along the axis so it appears between $3 and $5.

    c. Set the value axis maximum to 7000.

    d. Add a horizontal axis title below the chart. Label the axis **Products**.

    e. Move the horizontal axis title so it appears between Cookies and Brownies.

    f. Save the workbook.

4. Add a data table to a chart.

    a. Move the chart to its own sheet named **Sales Chart**.

    b. Add a data table with legend keys.

    c. Move the horizontal axis title up to a location above the data table between Cookies and Brownies. Move the vertical thousands label to the right so that it is closer to the chart.

    d. Format the data table to change the border color to the standard color purple.

    e. Enter your name in the center section of the Sales Chart footer. Preview, then print the chart.

    f. Save the workbook, then compare your screen to Figure J-19.

FIGURE J-19

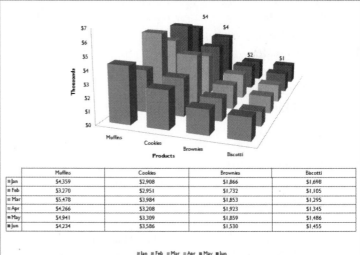

5. Rotate a chart.

    a. Apply Chart Layout 1. (*Hint*: This will remove the data table, the data labels, and the horizontal title.)

    b. Set the X: rotation to 70 degrees.

    c. Set the Y: rotation to 20 degrees.

    d. Change the depth to 180% of the base.

    e. Move the thousands label to the left of the vertical axis, then save the workbook.

6. Enhance a chart with WordArt.

    a. Add a chart title of **Pastry Sales** to the top of the chart. Format the chart title with WordArt Gradient Fill – Accent 1.

    b. Add a linear gradient fill to the title, with a transparency of 90%. (*Hint*: On the Chart Tools Layout tab, use the Chart Title button in the Labels group.)

FIGURE J-20

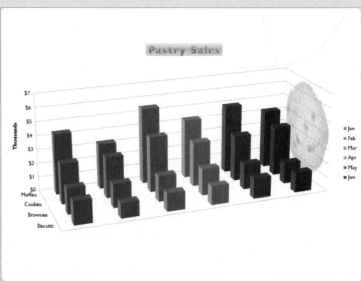

    c. Position the new title approximately half way across the top of the chart and closer to the chart.

    d. Save the workbook.

7. Add a picture to a chart.

    a. Select the back chart wall.

    b. Format the back wall fill with the picture cookie.gif from the drive and folder where you store your Data Files.

    c. Save the workbook.

    d. Preview the worksheet.

    e. Print the worksheet, then compare your printout to Figure J-20.

▼ SKILLS REVIEW (CONTINUED)

8. Identify data trends.

a. Activate the Sales sheet and scroll to the top of the worksheet.

b. Create a 2-D line chart using the data in the range A2:G6, then move and resize the chart to fit in the range A8:G20.

c. Add a linear trendline to the Muffins data series.

d. Change the trendline color to red and the line style to dash.

e. Set the forward option to six periods to view the future trend, then compare your screen to Figure J-21.

f. Add your name to the center footer section, save the workbook, then preview and print the worksheet.

g. Exit Excel.

FIGURE J-21

	A	B	C	D	E	F	G
1				Nancy's Pastry			
2		Jan	Feb	Mar	Apr	May	Jun
3	Muffins	$4,359	$3,270	$5,478	$4,266	$4,941	$4,234
4	Cookies	$2,908	$2,951	$3,984	$3,208	$3,309	$3,586
5	Brownies	$1,866	$1,732	$1,853	$1,923	$1,859	$1,530
6	Biscotti	$1,698	$1,105	$1,295	$1,345	$1,486	$1,455

▼ INDEPENDENT CHALLENGE 1

You are the assistant to the vice president of marketing at the Metro-West Philharmonic located outside of Boston. The vice president has asked you to chart some information from a recent survey of the Philharmonic's customers. Your administrative assistant has entered the survey data in an Excel worksheet, which you will use to create two charts.

a. Start Excel, open the file titled EX J-3.xlsx from the drive and folder where you store your Data Files, then save it as **Customer Survey**.

b. Using the data in A2:B7 of the Education data worksheet, create a 3-D pie chart (the first chart in the 3-D Pie group) on the worksheet.

c. Add a title of **Education Data** above the chart. Format the title using Word Art Gradient Fill - Accent 6, Inner Shadow.

d. Move the chart to a separate sheet named **Education Chart**. Format the chart using chart Style 13. Add data labels to the outside end of the data points. Format the legend text in 14-point bold. (*Hint*: Use the font options on the Home tab or the Mini toolbar.)

e. Select the Bachelor's degree pie slice by clicking the chart, then clicking the Bachelor's degree slice. Change the slice color to the standard color of purple. (*Hint*: On the Chart Tools Format tab, click the Format Selection button in the Current Selection group and use the Format Data Point dialog box.) Compare your chart to Figure J-22

f. On the Family data worksheet, use the data in A2:B6 to create a standard clustered column (The first chart in the 2-D Column group) chart.

g. Delete the legend. (*Hint*: Select the legend and press [Delete].)

h. Place the chart on a new sheet named **Family Chart**. Format the chart using chart Style 5.

i. Add a chart title of **Family Data** above the chart and format the title using WordArt Style Gradient Fill - Black, Outline - White, Outer Shadow.

j. Title the category axis **Number of Children**. Format the category axis title in 14-point bold. (*Hint*: Use the font options on the Home tab or use the Mini toolbar.)

k. Enter your name in the center sections of the footers of the Family Chart and Education Chart sheets.

l. Save the workbook, then preview and print the Family Chart and the Education Chart sheets.

m. Close the workbook and exit Excel.

FIGURE J-22

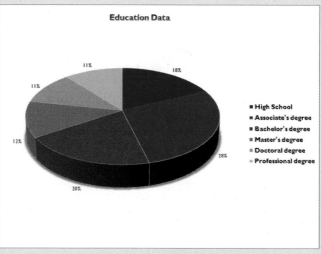

Education Data

- High School
- Associate's degree
- Bachelor's degree
- Master's degree
- Doctoral degree
- Professional degree

▼ INDEPENDENT CHALLENGE 2

You were voted employee of the month for January at Careers, an employment agency. Your manager has asked you to assemble a brief presentation on your placements during January to show to the newly hired staff. You decide to include a chart showing your placements in each of three job categories: technical, business, and medical.

a. Start Excel and save a new workbook as **Careers** in the drive and folder where you store your Data Files.

b. Enter worksheet labels and your own data on a worksheet named **January Placements**. Use Table J-2 as a guide for the worksheet layout.

c. Create a clustered bar chart (the first chart in the 2-D Bar group) on the worksheet, showing your placements. Format the chart using Chart Style 11. Make sure the Office theme is selected.

d. Display data values using Chart Layout 4.

e. Add a chart title of **January Placements** above the chart and format it using WordArt Style Fill - None, Outline - Accent 2.

f. Delete the chart legend.

g. Add new data to the worksheet for the Academic job category.

h. Add the new data to the chart.

i. Move the chart to a sheet named **January Chart**.

j. Add a horizontal axis title of **Number of Placements** and format the title in 14-point bold font.

k. Change the value scale if necessary to fit your sales data and improve its readability.

l. Add a data table to the chart. Format the data table lines to display in red.

TABLE J-2

Job Category	Number of Placements
Technical	
Business	
Medical	

Advanced Challenge Exercise

- Change the name of the chart's data series name in the legend to **Placements**. (*Hint*: On the Chart Tools Design tab, use the Select Data button and use the editing features in the Select Data Source dialog box. Change the existing Series name to Placements.)
- Use the Format Data Series dialog box to add a shadow with a format of your choice to the bars in the chart.
- Add a bevel with a format of your choice to the bars in the chart.
- Change the fill color for the bars to one of the theme colors.

m. Enter your name in the center section of the January Chart sheet footer, save the workbook, then preview and print the sheet.

n. Close the workbook and exit Excel.

▼ INDEPENDENT CHALLENGE 3

You manage the Pine Hills Pro Shop. You meet twice a year with the store owner to discuss store sales trends. You decide to use a chart to represent the sales trends for the department's product categories. You begin by charting the sales for the first five months of the year. Then you add data to the chart and analyze the sales trend using a trendline. Lastly, you enhance the chart by adding a data table, titles, and a picture.

a. Start Excel, open the file EX J-4.xlsx from the drive and folder where you store your Data Files, then save the workbook as **Golf Sales**.

b. Create a 2-D line chart on the worksheet showing the January through May sales information. Move the chart and resize it if necessary.

c. Format the Clubs data series and the Cart rentals data series using colors of your choice.

d. Add the June data from Table J-3 to the worksheet. Add the June data series to the chart.

e. Move the chart to its own sheet named **Jan - June** and add a data table without legend keys. Format the data table line color using the color of your choice.

f. Add a chart title of **January - June Sales** using the Centered Overlay position. Format the chart title using the WordArt Style of your choice.

TABLE J-3

Jun
$3,409
$5,187
$3,450
$3,709

▼ INDEPENDENT CHALLENGE 3 (CONTINUED)

g. Add a rotated title of **Sales** in 20-point bold to the vertical axis.

h. Add a linear trendline to the Clubs data series.

i. Change the color of the trendline to red and format the width in 2-pt dash style.

j. Insert the golfball.gif picture from the drive and folder where your Data Files are stored into the legend area of the chart.

Advanced Challenge Exercise

- Move the legend to the left side of the chart. Move the vertical axis title to the right if necessary.
- Remove the horizontal chart gridlines.
- Change the value axis scale to increment by 500.
- Add a gradient fill of your choice to the plot area.
- Drag the legend to the plot area and add a clip art background. Adjust the transparency of the legend background and the font color, if necessary, so that the legend text is readable.

k. Enter your name in the center footer section of the chart sheet, save the workbook, then preview and print the chart.

l. Close the workbook and exit Excel.

▼ REAL LIFE INDEPENDENT CHALLENGE

This Independent Challenge requires a Web connection.

Stock charts are used to graph a stock's high, low, and closing prices. You will create a stock chart using four weeks of high, low, and close prices for a stock that you are interested in tracking.

a. Start Excel, save a new workbook as **Stock Chart** in the drive and folder where you store your Data Files.

b. Use the search engine of your choice to research the high, low, and close prices for a stock over the past four weeks.

c. Create a worksheet with the data from your chart. Use Table J-4 as a guide for the worksheet structure. Apply a document theme of your choice.

d. Create a High-Low-Close stock chart using your worksheet data. (*Hint*: To find the stock charts, click the Other Charts button.)

e. Format the horizontal axis to change the major unit to seven days.

f. Change the color of the high-low lines to the standard color of dark red.

TABLE J-4

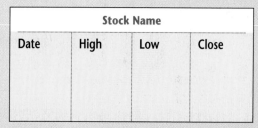

Stock Name			
Date	High	Low	Close

g. Add a rotated vertical axis title of **Stock Price**. Format the title in 14-point bold.

h. Delete the chart legend.

i. Add a chart title with your stock name. Format the title with a WordArt style of your choice from the WordArt Styles gallery.

j. Add data labels above the data series. (*Hint*: Use the Data Labels button on the Layout tab.) Delete the High and Low labels but keep the Close data labels. Add a line to the chart title with the text **Closing Prices**.

k. Format the chart area using a gradient and transparency of your choice. Format the plot area with a clip art fill related to the company or its product. Adjust the clip art transparency as necessary to view the chart.

l. Enter your name in the center footer section of the worksheet, save the workbook, then preview and print the sheet in landscape orientation on one page.

m. Close the workbook and exit Excel.

▼ VISUAL WORKSHOP

Open the file EX J-5.xlsx from the drive and folder where you store your Data Files, and create the custom chart shown in Figure J-23. Save the workbook as **Tea Sales**. Study the chart and worksheet carefully to make sure you select the displayed chart type with all the enhancements shown. Enter your name in the center section of the worksheet footer, then preview and print the worksheet in landscape orientation on one page.

FIGURE J-23

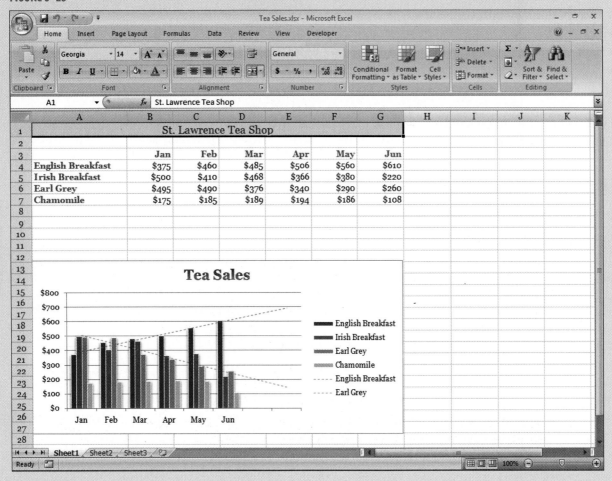

Using What-if Analysis

Each time you use a worksheet to explore different outcomes for Excel formulas, you are performing a **what-if analysis**. For example, what would happen to a firm's overall expense budget if company travel expenses decreased by 30%? Using Excel, you can perform a what-if analysis in many ways. In this unit, you will learn to track what-if scenarios and generate summary reports using the Excel Scenario Manager. You will design and manipulate data tables to project outcomes. Also, you will use the Goal Seek feature to solve a what-if analysis. Finally, you will use Solver to perform a complex what-if analysis involving multiple variables and use the Analysis ToolPak to generate descriptive statistics about your data. Kate Morgan, the vice president of sales at Quest, is meeting with the U.S. region manager to discuss sales projections for the first half of the year. Kate asks you to help analyze the U.S. sales data in preparation for her meeting.

OBJECTIVES

Define a what-if analysis

Track a what-if analysis with Scenario Manager

Generate a scenario summary

Project figures using a data table

Use Goal Seek

Set up a complex what-if analysis with Solver

Run Solver and summarize results

Analyze data using the Analysis ToolPak

Defining a What-if Analysis

By performing a what-if analysis in a worksheet, you can get immediate answers to questions such as "What happens to profits if we sell 25% more of a certain product?" or "What happens to monthly payments if interest rates rise or fall?" A worksheet you use to produce a what-if analysis is often called a **model** because it acts as the basis for multiple outcomes, or sets of results. To perform a what-if analysis in a worksheet, you change the value in one or more **input cells** (cells that contain data rather than formulas), then observe the effects on dependent cells. A **dependent cell** usually contains a formula whose resulting value changes depending on the values in the input cells. A dependent cell can be located either in the same worksheet as the changing input value or in another worksheet. Kate Morgan has created a worksheet model to perform an initial what-if analysis of projected sales totals and percentages using the projected data submitted by the regional managers, as shown in Figure K-1. She thinks the U.S. sales projections for the months of February, March, and April should be higher. You first review the guidelines for performing what-if analysis.

DETAILS

When performing a what-if analysis, use the following guidelines:

- **Understand and state the purpose of the worksheet model**

  Identify what you want to accomplish with the model. What problem are you trying to solve? What questions do you want the model to answer for you? Kate's Quest worksheet model is designed to total Quest sales projections for the first half of the year and to calculate the percentage of total sales for each Quest region. It also calculates the totals and percentages of total sales for each month.

- **Determine the data input value(s) that, if changed, affect the dependent cell results**

  In what-if analysis, changes in the content of the data input cells produces varying results in the output cells. You will use the model to work with three data input values: the February, March, and April values for the U.S. region, in cells C3, D3, and E3, respectively.

- **Identify the dependent cell(s) that will contain results**

  The dependent cells usually contain formulas, and the formula results adjust as you enter different values in the input cells. The results of two dependent cell formulas (labeled Total and Percent of Total Sales) appear in cells H3 and I3, respectively. The totals for the months of February, March, and April in cells C7, D7, and E7 are also dependent cells, as are the percentages for these months in cells C8, D8, and E8.

- **Formulate questions you want the what-if analysis to answer**

  It is important that you know the questions you want your model to answer. In the Quest model, you want to answer the following questions: (1) What happens to the U.S. regional percentage if the sales for the months of February, March, and April are each increased by $5000? (2) What happens to the U.S. regional percentage if the sales for the months of February, March, and April are each increased by $10,000?

- **Perform the what-if analysis**

  When you perform the what-if analysis, you explore the relationships between the input values and the dependent cell formulas. In the Quest worksheet model, you want to see what effect a $5000 increase in sales for February, March, and April has on the dependent cell formulas containing totals and percentages. Because the sales amounts for these months are located in cells C3, D3, and E3, any formula that references the cells is directly affected by a change in these sales amounts—in this case, the total formulas in cells H3, C7, D7, and E7. Because the formula in cell I3 references cell H3, a change in the sales amounts affects this cell as well. A change will also be seen in the percentage formulas in cells C8, D8, and E8 because they reference the total formulas in cells C7, D7, and E7. Figure K-2 shows the result of the what-if analysis described in this example.

FIGURE K-1: Worksheet model for a what-if analysis

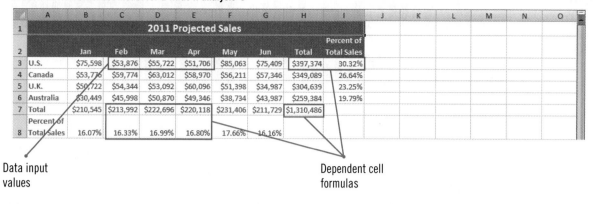

Data input values

Dependent cell formulas

FIGURE K-2: Changed input values and dependent formula results

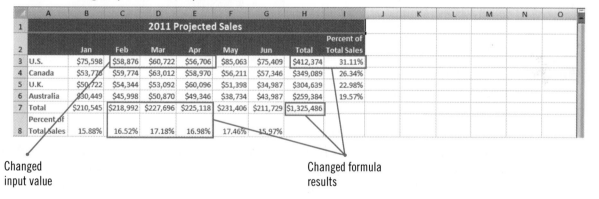

Changed input value

Changed formula results

Tracking a What-if Analysis with Scenario Manager

A **scenario** is a set of values you use to observe different worksheet results. For example, you might plan to sell 100 of a particular item, at a price of $5 per item, producing sales results of $500. But what if you reduced the price to $4 or increased it to $6? Each of these price scenarios would produce different sales results. A changing value, such as the price in this example, is called a **variable**. The Excel Scenario Manager simplifies the process of what-if analysis by allowing you to name and save scenarios with variable values in a worksheet. ██████ Kate asks you to use Scenario Manager to create scenarios showing the change in the U.S. sales percentage if the region can increase sales over these three months.

STEPS

1. **Start Excel, open the file EX K-1.xlsx from the drive and folder where you store your Data Files, then save it as US Sales**

   The first step in defining a scenario is choosing the cells that will vary in the different scenarios; in Excel, these are called **changing cells**.

2. **With the Projected Sales sheet active, select range C3:E3, click the Data tab, click the What-If Analysis button in the Data Tools group, then click Scenario Manager**

   The Scenario Manager dialog box opens with the following message: "No Scenarios defined. Choose Add to add scenarios."

   > **QUICK TIP**
   >
   > It is important to create a scenario with the original worksheet data so that you can restore these values after viewing other scenarios.

3. **Click Add, drag the Add Scenario dialog box to the right if necessary until columns A and B are visible, then type Original Sales Figures in the Scenario name text box**

   The range in the Changing cells box shows the range you selected, as shown in Figure K-3.

4. **Click OK to confirm the scenario range**

   The Scenario Values dialog box opens, as shown in Figure K-4. The existing values appear in the changing cell boxes.

   > **QUICK TIP**
   >
   > You can delete a scenario by selecting it in the Scenario Manager dialog box and clicking Delete.

5. **Click OK**

   The Scenario Manager dialog box reappears with the new scenario, named Original Sales Figures, listed in the Scenarios box. You want to create a second scenario.

6. **Click Add; in the Scenario name text box type Increase Feb, Mar, Apr by 5000; verify that the Changing cells text box reads C3:E3, then click OK; in the Scenario Values dialog box, change the value in the $C$3 text box to 58876, change the value in the $D$3 text box to 60722, change the value in the $E$3 text box to 56706, then click Add**

7. **In the Scenario name text box, type Increase Feb, Mar, Apr by 10000 and click OK; in the Scenario Values dialog box, change the value in the $C$3 text box to 63876, change the value in the $D$3 text box to 65722, change the value in the $E$3 text box to 61706, then click OK**

   The Scenario Manager dialog box reappears, as shown in Figure K-5.

   > **QUICK TIP**
   >
   > To edit a scenario, select it in the Scenario Manager dialog box, click the Edit button, then edit the Scenario. Use the Prevent changes checkbox to prevent others from changing your scenarios.

8. **Make sure the Increase Feb, Mar, Apr by 10000 scenario is still selected, click Show, notice that the percent of U.S. sales in cell I3 changes from 30.32% to 31.88%; click Increase Feb, Mar, Apr by 5000, click Show, notice that the U.S. sales percent is now 31.11%; click Original Sales Figures, click Show to return to the original values, then click Close**

9. **Save the workbook**

FIGURE K-3: Add Scenario dialog box

Cell range to be changed

Your user name and date will be different

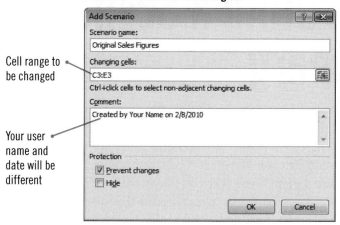

FIGURE K-4: Scenario Values dialog box

Changing cell boxes with original values

FIGURE K-5: Scenario Manager dialog box with three scenarios listed

Scenarios

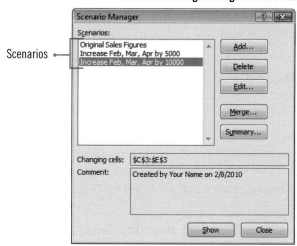

Merging scenarios

Excel stores scenarios in the workbook and on the worksheet in which you created them. To apply scenarios from another worksheet or workbook into the current worksheet, click the Merge button in the Scenario Manager dialog box. The Merge Scenarios dialog box opens, letting you select scenarios from other locations. When you click a sheet name in the sheet list, the text under the sheet list tells you how many scenarios exist on that sheet. To merge scenarios from another workbook, such as those sent to you in a workbook by a coworker, open the other workbook file, click the Book list arrow in the Merge Scenarios dialog box, then click the workbook name. If a merged scenario has the same name as an existing scenario, such as Higher Sales, Excel will add a date, the name of the creator, or a number after it, to distinguish it from the original. When you merge workbook scenarios, it's best if the workbooks have the same structure, so that there is no confusion of cell values.

Generating a Scenario Summary

Although it may be useful to display the different scenario outcomes when analyzing data, it can be difficult to keep track of them. In most cases, you will want to refer to a single report that summarizes the results of all the scenarios in a worksheet. A **scenario summary** is an Excel table that compiles data from the changing cells and corresponding result cells for each scenario. For example, you might use a scenario summary to illustrate the best, worst, and most likely scenarios for a particular set of circumstances. Using cell naming makes the summary easier to read because the names, not the cell references, appear in the report. ▩▩▩ Now that you have defined Kate's scenarios, she needs you to generate and print a scenario summary report. You begin by creating names for the cells in row 2 based on the labels in row 1, so that the report will be easier to read.

STEPS

1. **Select the range B2:I3, click the Formulas tab, click the Create from Selection button in the Defined Names group, click the Top row check box to select it if necessary, then click OK**

   Excel creates the names based on the labels in row 1.

2. **Click the Name Manager button in the Defined Names group**

   The eight labels appear, along with other workbook names, in the Name Manager dialog box, confirming that they were created, as shown in Figure K-6. Now you are ready to generate the scenario summary report.

3. **Click Close to close the Name Manager dialog box, click the Data tab, click the What-If Analysis button in the Data Tools group, click Scenario Manager, then click Summary in the Scenario Manager dialog box**

   Excel needs to know the location of the cells that contain the formula results.

4. **With the Result cells text box selected, click cell H3 on the worksheet, type , (a comma), click cell I3, type , (a comma), then click cell H7**

   With the report type and result cells specified, as shown in Figure K-7, you are now ready to generate the report.

5. **Click OK**

   A summary of the worksheet's scenarios appears on a new sheet titled Scenario Summary. The report shows outline buttons to the left of and above the worksheet so that you can hide or show report details. Because the Current Values column shows the same values as the Original Sales Figures column, you decide to delete column D.

6. **Right-click the column D heading, then click Delete in the shortcut menu**

   Next, you notice that the notes at the bottom of the report refer to the column that no longer exists. You want to make the report title and labels for the result cells more descriptive.

7. **Select the range B13:B15, press [Delete], select cell B2, edit its contents to read Scenario Summary for U.S. Sales, click cell C10, then edit its contents to read Total U.S. Sales**

8. **Click cell C11, edit its contents to read Percent U.S. Sales, click cell C12, edit its contents to read Total Quest Sales, then click cell A1**

   The completed scenario summary is shown in Figure K-8.

9. **Add your name to the center section of the Summary sheet footer, save the workbook, then preview and print the report in landscape orientation**

FIGURE K-6: Name Manager dialog box displaying new names

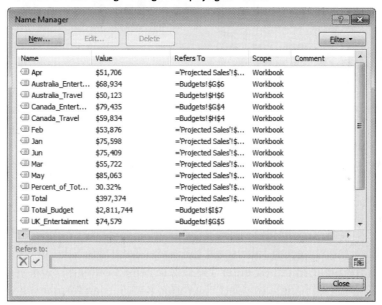

FIGURE K-7: Scenario Summary dialog box

Default report type •

Cells to be • recalculated when a new scenario is applied

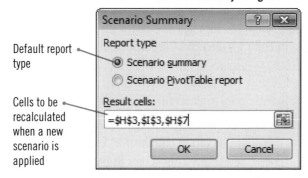

FIGURE K-8: Completed Scenario Summary report

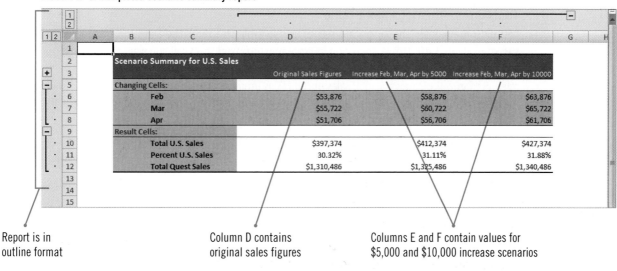

Report is in outline format

Column D contains original sales figures

Columns E and F contain values for $5,000 and $10,000 increase scenarios

Projecting Figures Using a Data Table

Another way to answer what-if questions in a worksheet is by using a data table. A **data table** is a range of cells that simultaneously shows the varying resulting values when one or more input values is changed in a formula. For example, you could use a data table to display your monthly mortgage payment based on several different interest rates. A **one-input data table** is a table that shows the result of varying one input value, such as the interest rate. ▓▓▓▓ Now that you have completed Kate's analysis, she wants you to find out how the U.S. sales percentage would change as U.S. total sales increased.

STEPS

1. **Click the Projected Sales sheet tab, enter Total U.S. Sales in cell K1, widen column K to fit the label, in cell K2 enter 397374, in cell K3 enter 447374, select the range K2:K3, drag the fill handle to select the range K4:K6, then format the values using the Accounting number format with zero decimal places**

   You begin setting up your data table by entering the total U.S. sales from cell H3 and then increasing the amount by increments of $50,000. These are the **input values** in the data table. With the varying input values listed in column K, you enter a formula reference to cell I3 that you want Excel to use in calculating the resulting percentages (the **output values**) in column L, based on the possible sales levels in column K.

QUICK TIP
You cannot delete individual output values in a data table; you must delete all output values.

2. **Click cell L1, type =, click cell I3, click the Enter button ✓ on the formula bar, then format the value in cell L1 using the Percentage format with two decimal places**

   The value in cell I3, 30.32%, appears in cell L1, and the cell name =Percent_of_Total_Sales appears in formula bar, as shown in Figure K-9. Because it isn't necessary for users of the data table to see the value in cell L1, you want to hide the cell's contents from view.

3. **With cell L1 selected, click the Home tab, click the Format button in the Cells group, click Format Cells, click the Number tab in the Format Cells dialog box if necessary, click Custom under Category, select any characters in the Type box, type ;;; (three semicolons), then click OK**

   The three semicolons hide the values in a cell. With the table structure in place, you can now generate the data table showing percentages for the varying sales amounts.

4. **Select the range K1:L6, click the Data tab, click the What-If Analysis button in the Data Tools group, then click Data Table**

   You have highlighted the range that makes up the table structure. The Data Table dialog box opens, as shown in Figure K-10. This is where you indicate in which worksheet cell you want the varying input values (the sales figures in column K) to be substituted. Because the percentage formula in cell I3 (which you just referenced in cell L1) uses the total sales in cell H3 as input, you enter a reference to cell H3. You place this reference in the Column input cell text box, rather than in the Row input cell text box, because the varying input values are arranged in a column in your data table structure.

TROUBLE
If you receive the message "Selection not valid," repeat Step 4, taking care to select the entire range K1:L6.

5. **Click the Column input cell text box, click cell H3, then click OK**

   Excel completes the data table by calculating percentages for each sales amount.

6. **Format the range L2:L6 with the Percent Style with two decimal places, then click cell A1**

   The formatted data table is shown in Figure K-11. It shows the sales percentages for each of the possible levels of U.S. sales. By looking at the data table, Kate determines that if she can increase total U.S. sales to about $600,000, the U.S. division will then comprise about 40% of total QST sales for the first half of 2011.

7. **Add your name to the center section of the worksheet footer, change the worksheet orientation to landscape, save the workbook, then preview and print the worksheet**

FIGURE K-9: One-input data table structure

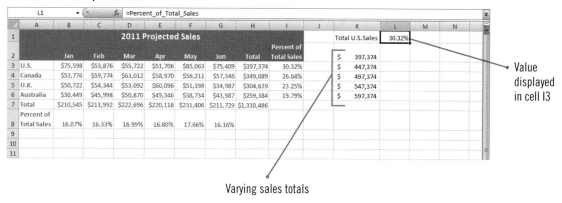

Varying sales totals

Value displayed in cell I3

FIGURE K-10: Data Table dialog box

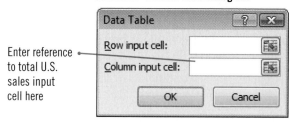

Enter reference to total U.S. sales input cell here

FIGURE K-11: Completed data table with resulting values

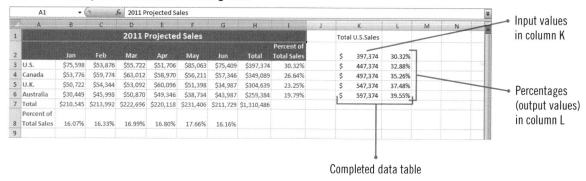

Input values in column K

Percentages (output values) in column L

Completed data table

Creating a Two-input Data Table

A **two-input data table** shows the resulting values when two different input values are varied in a formula. You could, for example, use a two-input data table to calculate your monthly mortgage payment based on varying interest rates and varying loan terms, as shown in Figure K-12. In a two-input data table, different values of one input cell appear across the top row of the table, while different values of the second input cell are listed down the left column of the table. You create a two-input data table the same way that you created a one-input data table, except you enter both a row and a column input cell.

FIGURE K-12: Two-input data table

	Term	
	180	360
5.85%	$1,671.55	$1,179.88
6.10%	$1,698.54	$1,211.99
6.35%	$1,725.76	$1,244.47
6.60%	$1,753.23	$1,277.32
6.85%	$1,780.93	$1,310.52
7.10%	$1,808.86	$1,344.06
7.35%	$1,837.02	$1,377.94
7.60%	$1,865.41	$1,412.15
7.85%	$1,894.03	$1,446.67
8.10%	$1,922.87	$1,481.50
8.35%	$1,951.93	$1,516.62
8.60%	$1,981.22	$1,552.02

Monthly Mortgage Payment for $200,000 Loan

Using Goal Seek

You can think of goal seeking as a what-if analysis in reverse. In a what-if analysis, you might try many sets of values to achieve a certain solution. To **goal seek**, you specify a solution, then find the input value that produces the answer you want. "Backing into" a solution in this way, sometimes referred to as **backsolving**, can save a significant amount of time. For example, you can use Goal Seek to determine how many units must be sold to reach a particular sales goal or to determine what expense levels are necessary to meet a budget target. After reviewing her data table, Kate has a follow-up question: What January U.S. sales target is required to bring the January Quest sales percentage to 17%, assuming the sales for the other regions don't change? You use Goal Seek to answer her question.

STEPS

1. **Click cell B8**

   The first step in using Goal Seek is to select a goal cell. A **goal cell** contains a formula in which you can substitute values to find a specific value, or goal. You use cell B8 as the goal cell because it contains the percent formula.

2. **Click the Data tab, click the What-If Analysis button in the Data Tools group, then click Goal Seek**

   The Goal Seek dialog box opens. The Set cell text box contains a reference to cell B8, the percent formula cell you selected in Step 1. You need to indicate that the figure in cell B8 should equal 17%.

3. **Click the To value text box, then type 17%**

   The value 17% represents the desired solution you want to reach by substituting different values in the By changing cell.

4. **Click the By changing cell text box, then click cell B3**

   You have specified that you want cell B3, the U.S. January amount, to change to reach the 17% solution, as shown in Figure K-13.

5. **Click OK**

   The Goal Seek Status dialog box opens with the following message: "Goal Seeking with Cell B8 found a solution." By changing the sales amount in cell B3 to $90,274, Goal Seek achieves a January percentage of 17.

   > **QUICK TIP**
   > Before you select another command, you can return the worksheet to its status prior to the Goal Seek by pressing [Ctrl][Z].

6. **Click OK, then click cell A1**

   Changing the sales amount in cell B3 changes the other dependent values in the worksheet (B7, H3, I3, and H7) as shown in Figure K-14.

7. **Save the workbook, then preview and print the worksheet**

FIGURE K-13: **Completed Goal Seek dialog box**

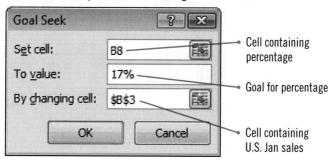

Cell containing percentage

Goal for percentage

Cell containing U.S. Jan sales

FIGURE K-14: **Worksheet with new dependent values**

	A	B	C	D	E	F	G	H	I
1	2011 Projected Sales								
2		Jan	Feb	Mar	Apr	May	Jun	Total	Percent of Total Sales
3	U.S.	$90,274	$53,876	$55,722	$51,706	$85,063	$75,409	$412,050	31.09%
4	Canada	$53,776	$59,774	$63,012	$58,970	$56,211	$57,346	$349,089	26.34%
5	U.K.	$50,722	$54,344	$53,092	$60,096	$51,398	$34,987	$304,639	22.99%
6	Australia	$30,449	$45,998	$50,870	$49,346	$38,734	$43,987	$259,384	19.57%
7	Total	$225,221	$213,992	$222,696	$220,118	$231,406	$211,729	$1,325,162	
8	Percent of Total Sales	17.00%	16.15%	16.81%	16.61%	17.46%	15.98%		
9									
10									
11									

New target values calculated by Goal Seek

New dependent values

Setting up a Complex What-if Analysis with Solver

The Excel Solver is an **add-in** program that provides optional features. It must be installed before you can use it. Solver finds the best solution to a problem that has several inputs. The cell containing the formula is called the **target cell**. As you learned earlier, cells containing the values that vary are called "changing cells." Solver is helpful when you need to perform a complex what-if analysis involving multiple input values or when the input values must conform to specific limitations or restrictions called **constraints**. For example, if you are calculating the best ordering combination from several vendors, you may want to restrict the total ordered from a specific company to a certain amount. ▰▰▰▰ Kate decides to fund each region with the same amount, $750,000, to cover expenses. Realizing that many of the budget items are fixed expenses, Kate adjusts the travel and entertainment allocations to keep expenditures to the allocated amount of $750,000. You use Solver to help Kate find the best possible allocation.

STEPS

1. **Click the Budgets sheet tab**

   This worksheet is designed to calculate the travel and entertainment budget for each region. It assumes fixed costs for communications, equipment, advertising, salaries, and rent. You use Solver to change the entertainment and travel amounts in cells G3:H6 (the changing cells) to achieve your target of a total budget of $3,000,000 in cell I7 (the target cell). You want your solution to include a constraint on cells G3:H6 specifying that each region is equally funded at $750,000. Based on past budgets, you know there are two other constraints: the travel budgets must include at least $80,000 and the entertainment budgets must include at least $93,000. It is a good idea to enter constraints on the worksheet for documentation purposes, as shown in Figure K-15.

2. **Click the Data Tab, then click the Solver button in the Analysis group**

   The Solver Parameters dialog box opens. This is where you indicate the target cell, the changing cells, and the constraints under which you want Solver to work. You begin by changing the value in the target cell.

3. **With the insertion point in the Set Target Cell text box, click cell I7 in the worksheet, click the Value of option button, double-click the Value of text box, then type 3,000,000**

   You have specified a target value of $3,000,000 for the total budget. In typing the total budget figure, be sure to type the commas.

4. **Click the By Changing Cells text box, then select cells G3:H6 on the worksheet**

   You have told Excel which cells to vary to reach the goal of $3,000,000 total budget. You need to specify the constraints on the worksheet values to restrict the Solver's answer to realistic values.

5. **Click Add, with the insertion point in the Cell Reference text box in the Add Constraint dialog box select range I3:I6 in the worksheet, click the list arrow in the dialog box, select =, with the insertion point in the Constraint text box click cell C9**

   As shown in Figure K-16, the Add Constraint dialog box specifies that cells in the range I3:I6, the total region budget amounts, should equal $750,000. Next, you need to add the constraint that the budgeted entertainment amounts should be at least $93,000.

6. **Click Add, with the insertion point in the Cell Reference text box select range G3:G6 in the worksheet, click the list arrow, select >=, with the insertion point in the Constraint text box click cell C11**

   Next, you need to specify that the budgeted travel amounts should be greater than or equal to $80,000.

7. **Click Add, with the insertion point in the Cell Reference box select cells H3:H6, select >=, with the insertion point in the Constraint text box click cell C10, then click OK**

   The Solver Parameters dialog box opens with the constraints listed, as shown in Figure K-17. In the next lesson, you run Solver and generate solutions to the budget constraints.

Using What-if Analysis

FIGURE K-15: Worksheet set up for a complex what-if analysis

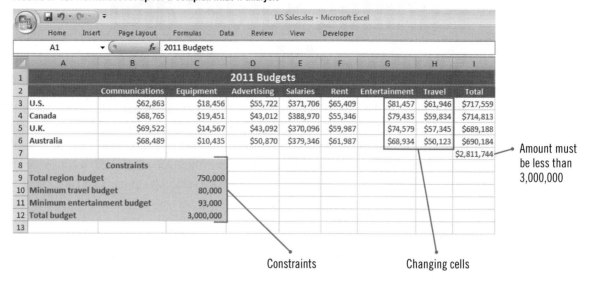

Amount must be less than 3,000,000

Constraints

Changing cells

FIGURE K-16: Adding constraints

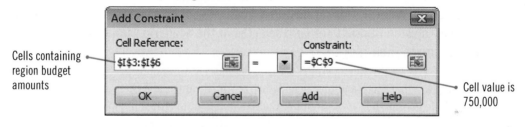

Cells containing region budget amounts

Cell value is 750,000

FIGURE K-17: Completed Solver Parameters dialog box

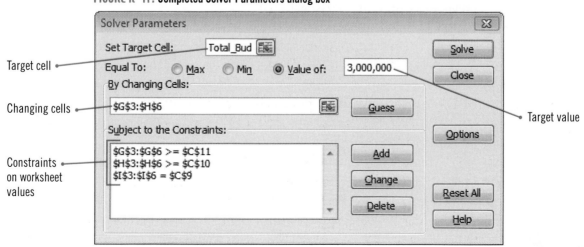

Target cell

Changing cells

Constraints on worksheet values

Target value

Running Solver and Summarizing Results

After entering all the parameters in the Solver Parameters dialog box, you can run Solver to find a solution. In some cases, Solver may not be able to find a solution that meets all of your constraints; then you would need to enter new constraints and try again. Once Solver finds a solution, you can choose to create a summary of the solution or a special report displaying the solution. ▓▓▓▓▓ You have finished entering the parameters in the Solver Parameters dialog box. Kate wants you to run Solver and create a summary of the solution on a separate worksheet.

STEPS

1. **Make sure your Solver Parameters dialog box matches Figure K-17 in the previous lesson**

2. **Click Solve**

   The Solver Results dialog box opens, indicating that Solver has found a solution, as shown in Figure K-18. The solution values appear in the worksheet, but you decide to save the solution values in a summary worksheet and display the original values in the worksheet.

3. **Click the Restore Original Values option button, click Save Scenario, enter Adjusted Budgets in the Scenario Name text box, then click OK twice**

   The Solver Results dialog box closes, and the original values appear in the worksheet. You will display the Solver solution values on a separate sheet.

4. **Click the What-If Analysis button in the Data Tools group, click Scenario Manager, with the Adjusted Budgets scenario selected in the Scenario Manager dialog box click Summary, then click OK**

   The Solver results appear on the Scenario Summary 2 worksheet, as shown in Figure K-19. To keep the budget at $3,000,000 and equally fund each region, the travel and entertainment budget allocations are calculated in column E labeled Adjusted Budgets. You want to format the solution values on the worksheet.

5. **Select the range B16:B18, press [Del], right-click the Scenario Summary 2 worksheet tab, click Rename on the shortcut menu, type Adjusted Budgets, then press [Enter]**

6. **Select the range B2:E3, click the Home tab, click the Fill Color list arrow, click Red, Accent 2, select the range B5:E15, click the Fill Color list arrow, click Red Accent 2, Lighter 80%, select cell B2, enter Solver Solution then click cell A1**

   The formatted Solver solution is shown in Figure K-20.

7. **Enter your name in the center section of the worksheet footer, save the workbook, then preview and print the worksheet**

   You have successfully found the best budget allocations using Solver.

FIGURE K-18: Solver Results dialog box

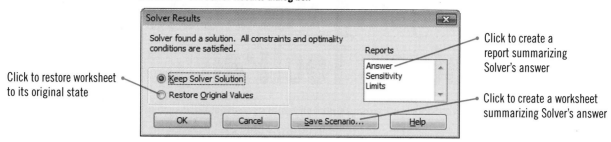

Click to restore worksheet to its original state

Click to create a report summarizing Solver's answer

Click to create a worksheet summarizing Solver's answer

FIGURE K-19: Solver Answer Report

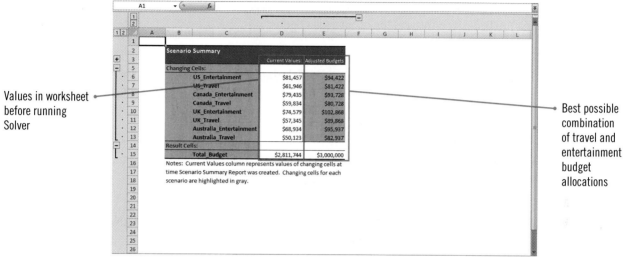

Values in worksheet before running Solver

Best possible combination of travel and entertainment budget allocations

FIGURE K-20: Completed Answer Report

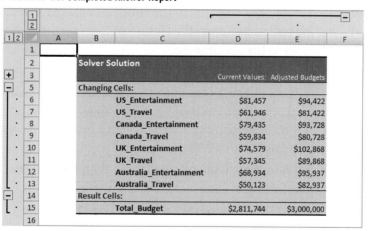

Understanding Answer Reports

Instead of saving Solver results as a scenario, you can select from three types of answer reports in the Solver Results window. One of the most useful is the Answer Report, which compares the original values with the Solver's final values. The report has three sections. The top section has the target cell information; it compares the original value of the target cell with the final value. The middle section of the report contains information about the adjustable cells. It lists the original and final values for all cells that were changed to reach the target value. The last report section has information about the constraints. Each constraint that was added into Solver is listed in the Formula column along with the cell address and a description of the cell data. The Cell Value column contains the Solver solution values for the cells. These values will be different from your worksheet values if you restored the original values to your worksheet rather than keeping Solver's solution. The Status column contains information on whether the constraints were binding or not binding in reaching the solution. If a solution is not binding, the slack—or how far the result is from the constraint value—is provided. Frequently, the answer report shows equality constraints as nonbinding with a slack of zero.

Analyzing Data Using the Analysis ToolPak

The Analysis ToolPak is an Excel add-in that contains many statistical analysis tools. The Descriptive Analysis tool in the Data Analysis dialog box generates a statistical report including mean, median, mode, minimum, maximum, and sum for an input range you specify on your worksheet. ███████ After reviewing the projected sales figures for the Quest regions, Kate decides to statistically analyze the projected regional sales totals submitted by the managers. You use the Analysis ToolPak to help her generate the sales statistics. You begin by displaying the original sales figures.

STEPS

1. **Click the Projected Sales sheet tab, click the Data tab, click the What-if Analysis button in the Data Tools group, click Scenario Manager, with the Original Sales Figures scenario selected click Show, then click Close**

2. **Click the Data Analysis button in the Analysis group**
   The Data Analysis dialog box opens, listing the available analysis tools.

3. **Click Descriptive Statistics, then click OK**
   The Descriptive Statistics dialog box opens, as shown in Figure K-21.

4. **With the insertion point in the Input Range text box, select cells H3:H6 on the worksheet**
   You have told Excel to use the total projected sales cells in the statistical analysis. You need to specify that the data is grouped in a column and the results should be placed on a new worksheet named Region Statistics.

5. **Click the Columns option button in the Grouped By: area if necessary, click the New Worksheet Ply option button in the Output options section if necessary, then type Region Statistics in the text box**
   Next, you need to add the summary statistics to the new worksheet.

6. **Click the Summary statistics check box to select it, then click OK**
   The statistics are generated and placed on the new worksheet named Region Statistics. Table K-1 describes some of the statistical values provided in the worksheet. Column A is not wide enough to view the labels, and the worksheet needs a descriptive title.

7. **Widen column A to display the column labels, then edit the contents of cell A1 to read Total Projected Sales Jan - Jun**
   Figure K-22 shows statistical values for the total projected sales.

8. **Enter your name in the center section of the Region Statistics footer, save the workbook, then preview and print the report**

9. **Close the workbook and exit Excel**

Choosing the right tool for your data analysis

The Analysis ToolPak offers 19 options for data analysis. ANOVA, or the analysis of variance, can be applied to one or more samples of data. The regression option creates a table of statistics from a least-squares regression. The correlation choice measures how strong of a linear relationship exists between two random variables. A moving average is often calculated for stock prices or any other data that is time sensitive. Moving averages display long-term trends by smoothing out short-term changes. The Random Number Generation creates a set of random numbers between values that you specify. The Rank and Percentile option creates a report of the ranking and percentile distribution.

FIGURE K-21: Descriptive Statistics dialog box

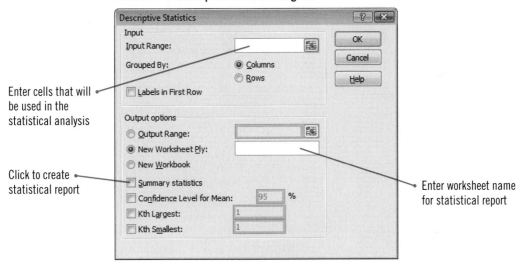

Enter cells that will be used in the statistical analysis

Click to create statistical report

Enter worksheet name for statistical report

FIGURE K-22: Region Statistics worksheet

New title

	A	B	C
1	Total Projected Sale	Jan - Jun	
2			
3	Mean	331290.6	
4	Standard Error	32557.35	
5	Median	326864	
6	Mode	#N/A	
7	Standard Deviation	65114.7	
8	Sample Variance	4.24E+09	
9	Kurtosis	-0.5431	
10	Skewness	0.342015	
11	Range	152666.3	
12	Minimum	259384	
13	Maximum	412050.3	
14	Sum	1325162	
15	Count	4	
16			

TABLE K-1: Descriptive Statistics

Mean	The average of a set of numbers
Median	The middle value of a set of numbers
Mode	The most common value in a set of numbers
Standard Deviation	The measure of how widely spread the values in a set of numbers are. If the values are all close to the mean, the standard deviation is close to zero.
Range	The difference between the largest and smallest values in a set of numbers
Minimum	The smallest value in a set of numbers
Maximum	The largest value in a set of numbers
Sum	The total of the values in a set of numbers
Count	The number of values in a set of numbers
Skewness	The measure of the asymmetry of the values in a set of numbers
Sample Variance	The measure of how scattered the values in a set of numbers are from an expected value
Kurtosis	The measure of the peakedness or flatness of a distribution of data

Practice

▼ CONCEPTS REVIEW

FIGURE K-23

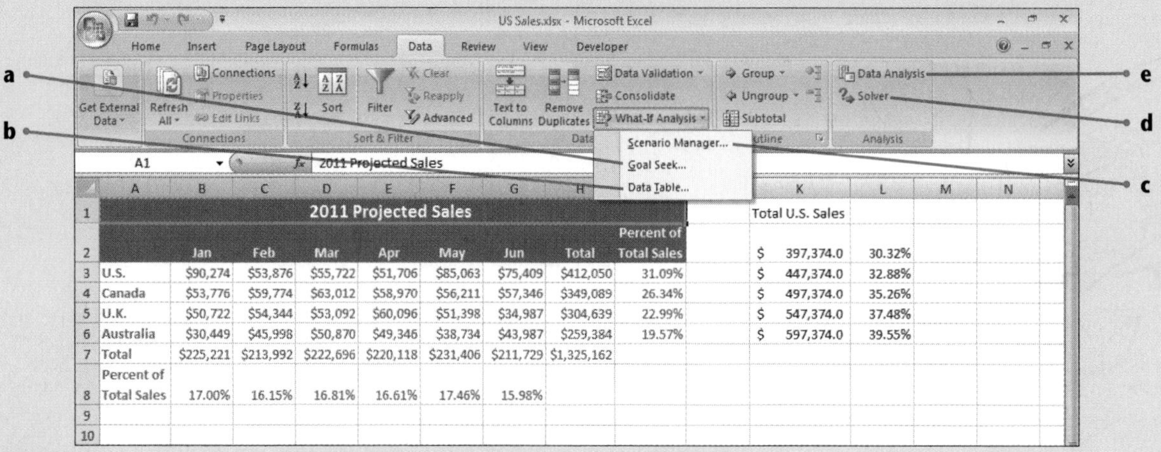

![Excel screenshot of US Sales.xlsx showing the Data tab ribbon with labels a through e pointing to various elements, and a worksheet titled "2011 Projected Sales"]

The worksheet shows:

	A	B	C	D	E	F	G	H		K	L
1				2011 Projected Sales						Total U.S. Sales	
2		Jan	Feb	Mar	Apr	May	Jun	Total	Percent of Total Sales	$ 397,374.0	30.32%
3	U.S.	$90,274	$53,876	$55,722	$51,706	$85,063	$75,409	$412,050	31.09%	$ 447,374.0	32.88%
4	Canada	$53,776	$59,774	$63,012	$58,970	$56,211	$57,346	$349,089	26.34%	$ 497,374.0	35.26%
5	U.K.	$50,722	$54,344	$53,092	$60,096	$51,398	$34,987	$304,639	22.99%	$ 547,374.0	37.48%
6	Australia	$30,449	$45,998	$50,870	$49,346	$38,734	$43,987	$259,384	19.57%	$ 597,374.0	39.55%
7	Total	$225,221	$213,992	$222,696	$220,118	$231,406	$211,729	$1,325,162			
8	Percent of Total Sales	17.00%	16.15%	16.81%	16.61%	17.46%	15.98%				

1. **Which element do you click to find the input values that produce a specified result?**
2. **Which element do you click to name and save different sets of values to forecast worksheet results?**
3. **Which element do you click to perform a what-if analysis involving multiple input values with constraints?**
4. **Which element do you click to perform a statistical analysis on worksheet data?**
5. **Which element do you click to create a range of cells showing the resulting values with varied formula input?**

Match each term with the statement that best describes it.

6. Two-input data table
7. Scenario summary
8. Goal Seek
9. One-input data table
10. Solver

a. Add-in that helps you solve complex what-if scenarios with multiple input values

b. Separate sheet with results from the worksheet's scenarios

c. Generates values resulting from varying two sets of changing values in a formula

d. Helps you backsolve what-if scenarios

e. Generates values resulting from varying one set of changing values in a formula

Select the best answer from the list of choices.

11. **To hide the contents of a cell from view, you can use the custom number format:**
    - **a.** " "
    - **b.** —
    - **c.** Blank
    - **d.** ;;;
12. **The _____ button in the Scenario Manager dialog box allows you to bring scenarios from another workbook into the current workbook.**
    - **a.** Combine
    - **b.** Add
    - **c.** Merge
    - **d.** Import

13. **When you use Goal Seek, you specify a** _____**, then find the values that produce it.**

   a. Row input cell   **c.** Solution

   b. Column input cell   **d.** Changing value

14. **In Solver, the cell containing the formula is called the:**

   a. Changing cell   **c.** Input cell

   b. Output cell   **d.** Target cell

15. **Which of the following Excel Add-Ins can be used to generate a statistical summary of worksheet data?**

   a. Solver   **c.** Conditional Sum Wizard

   b. Lookup Wizard   **d.** Analysis ToolPak

▼ SKILLS REVIEW

1. Define a what-if analysis.

   a. Start Excel, open the file EX K-2.xlsx from the drive and folder where you store your Data Files, then save it as **Capital Equipment**.

   b. Examine the Lawn Mower Repair worksheet and determine the purpose of the worksheet model. Use Sheet 3 to enter your answer.

   c. Locate the data input cells. Use Sheet 3 of the workbook to enter your answer.

   d. Locate any dependent cells. Use Sheet 3 of the workbook to enter your answer.

   e. Write three questions that could be answered by this what-if analysis model. Use Sheet 3 of the workbook to enter your answer.

2. Track a what-if analysis with Scenario Manager.

   a. On the Lawn Mower Repair worksheet, select the range B3:B5, then use the Scenario Manager to set up a scenario called **Most Likely** with the current data input values.

   b. Add a scenario called **Best Case** using the same changing cells, but change the Labor cost per hour in the $B$3 text box to **75**, change the Parts cost per job in the $B$4 text box to **65**, then change the Hours per job value in cell $B$5 to **1.5**.

   c. Add a scenario called **Worst Case**. For this scenario, change the Labor cost per hr. in the $B$3 text box to **95**, change the Parts cost per job in the $B$4 text box to **80**, then change the Hrs. per job in the $B$5 text box to **3**.

   d. If necessary, drag the Scenario Manager dialog box to the right until columns A and B are visible.

   e. Show the Worst Case scenario results, and view the total job cost.

   f. Show the Best Case scenario results, and observe the job cost. Finally, display the Most Likely scenario results.

   g. Close the Scenario Manager dialog box.

   h. Save the workbook.

3. Generate a scenario summary.

   a. Create names for the input value cells and the dependent cell using the range A3:B7.

   b. Verify that the names were created.

   c. Create a scenario summary report, using the Cost to complete job value in cell B7 as the result cell.

   d. Edit the title of the Summary report in cell B2 to read **Scenario Summary for Lawn Mower Repair**.

   e. Delete the Current Values column.

FIGURE K-24

   f. Delete the notes beginning in cell B11. Compare your worksheet to Figure K-24.

   g. Return to cell A1, enter your name in the center section of the Scenario Summary sheet footer, save the workbook, then preview and print the Scenario Summary sheet.

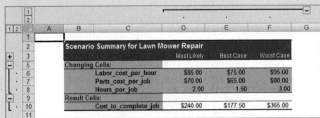

4. Project figures using a data table.

   a. Click the Lawn Mower Repair sheet tab.

   b. Enter the label **Labor $** in cell D3.

c. Format the label so that it is boldfaced and right-aligned.

d. In cell D4, enter **75**; then in cell D5, enter **80**.

e. Select range D4:D5, then use the fill handle to extend the series to cell D8.

f. In cell E3, reference the job cost formula by entering **=B7**.

g. Format the contents of cell E3 as hidden, using the ;;; Custom formatting type on the Number tab of the Format Cells dialog box.

h. Generate the new job costs based on the varying labor costs: Select range D3:E8 and create a data table. In the Data Table dialog box, make cell B3 (the labor cost) the column input cell.

i. Format range E4:E8 as currency with two decimal places. Compare your worksheet to Figure K-25.

j. Enter your name in the center section of the worksheet footer, save the workbook, then preview and print the worksheet.

FIGURE K-25

	A	B	C	D	E	F
1	**Lawn Mower Repair Model**					
2						
3	Labor cost per hour	$85.00		Labor $		
4	Parts cost per job	$70.00		75	$220.00	
5	Hours per job	2.00		80	$230.00	
6				85	$240.00	
7	Cost to complete job:	$240.00		90	$250.00	
8				95	$260.00	
9						

5. Use Goal Seek.

a. Click cell B7, and open the Goal Seek dialog box.

b. Assuming the labor rate and the hours remain the same, determine what the parts would have to cost so that the cost to complete the job is $180. (*Hint*: Enter a job cost of **180** as the To value, and enter **B4** (the Parts cost) as the By changing cell. Write down the parts cost that Goal Seek finds.

c. Click OK, then use **[Ctrl][Z]** to reset the parts cost to its original value.

d. Enter the cost of the parts in cell A14.

e. Assuming the parts cost and hours remain the same, determine what the labor would have to cost so that the cost to complete the job is $175. Use **[Ctrl][Z]** to reset the labor cost to its original value. Enter the labor cost in cell A15.

f. Add your name to the center section of the worksheet footer, save the workbook, then preview and print the worksheet.

6. Perform a complex what-if analysis with Solver and generate an Answer Report.

a. With the Vehicle Repair sheet active, open the Solver dialog box.

b. Make B14 (the total repair costs) the target cell, with a target value of 15,000.

c. Use cells B6:D6 (the number of scheduled repairs) as the changing cells.

d. Specify that cells B6:D6 must be integers. (*Hint*: Select int in the Add Constraint dialog box.)

e. Specify a constraint that cells B6:D6 must be greater than or equal to 10.

f. Use Solver to find a solution.

g. Save the solution as a scenario named Repair Solution and restore the original values to the worksheet.

h. Create a scenario summary using the Repair Solution scenario, delete the notes at the bottom of the solution, and rename the worksheet Repair Solution. Compare your worksheet to Figure K-26.

i. Enter your name in the center section of the worksheet footer, save the workbook, then preview and print the worksheet.

FIGURE K-26

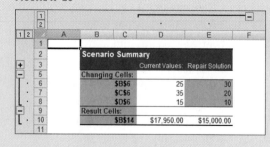

7. Analyze data using the Analysis ToolPak.

a. With the Vehicle Repair sheet active, generate summary descriptive statistics for the repair cost per model, using cells B10:D10 as the input range. (*Hint*: The input is grouped in a row.) Place the new statistics on a worksheet named Repair Cost Statistics.

b. Widen columns as necessary to view the statistics.

▼ SKILLS REVIEW (CONTINUED)

	A	B	C
1	Repair Cost Per Model		
2			
3	Mean	5983.333	
4	Standard Error	1626.239	
5	Median	7125	
6	Mode	#N/A	
7	Standard Deviation	2816.728	
8	Sample Variance	7933958	
9	Skewness	-1.52429	
10	Range	5275	
11	Minimum	2775	
12	Maximum	8050	
13	Sum	17950	
14	Count	3	
15			

c. Change the contents of cell A1 to **Repair Cost Per Model**. Delete row 9 containing the kurtosis error information. (This was generated because you only have three data values.) Compare your worksheet to Figure K-27.

d. Add your name to the center section of the worksheet footer, then preview and print the worksheet.

e. Save and close the workbook, then exit Excel.

▼ INDEPENDENT CHALLENGE 1

You are the manager for Image Pro, a graphic design firm based in Chicago. You are planning a computer hardware upgrade for the graphic designers in the company. Your manager has asked you to research the monthly cost for a $100,000 equipment loan to purchase the new computers. You will create a worksheet model to determine the monthly payments based on several different interest rates and loan terms, using data from the company's bank. Using Scenario Manager, you will create the following three scenarios: a four-year loan at 6.0%; a three-year loan at 5.75%; and a two-year loan at 5.5%. You will also prepare a scenario summary report outlining the payment details for your manager.

a. Start Excel, open the file EX K-3.xlsx from the drive and folder where you store your Data Files, then save it as **Hardware Payment Model**.

b. Create cell names for the cells B4:B11 based on the labels in cells A4:A11, using the Create Names from Selection dialog box.

c. Use Scenario Manager to create scenarios that calculate the monthly payment on a $100,000 loan under the three sets of loan possibilities listed below. (*Hint*: Create three scenarios using cells B5:B6 as the changing cells.)

Scenario Name	Interest Rate	Term
6.0% 4 Yr	.06	48
5.75% 3 Yr	.0575	36
5.5% 2 Yr	.055	24

d. Show each scenario to make sure it performs as intended, then display the 6.0% 4 Yr scenario.

e. Generate a scenario summary titled **Scenario Summary for $100,000 Hardware Purchase**. Use cells B9:B11 as the Result cells.

f. Delete the Current Values column in the report, and delete the notes at the bottom of the report.

g. Enter your name in the center section of the Scenario Summary sheet footer. Save the workbook, then preview and print the scenario summary.

Advanced Challenge Exercise

- Create a copy of the Loan sheet. Name the new sheet **My Loan**.
- Create a new scenario in the copied sheet called **Local**, using an interest rate and term available at a local lending institution.
- Merge the scenario from the My Loan sheet into the Loan sheet. (*Hint*: Use the Merge option in the Scenario Manager dialog box.)
- Verify that the Local scenario displays in the Scenario Manager dialog box of the Loan sheet, then generate a scenario summary titled **Advanced Scenario Summary**, using cells B9:B11 as the Result cells. Delete the Current Values column in the report and the notes at the bottom.
- Enter your name in the center section of the Scenario Summary 2 sheet footer, save the workbook, then preview and print the Advanced Scenario Summary in landscape orientation.

h. Close the workbook, then exit Excel.

▼ INDEPENDENT CHALLENGE 2

You are a VP at Soft Solutions, a software development company based in Dublin. The company president has asked you to pre-pare a loan summary report for a business expansion. You need to develop a model to show what the monthly payments would be for a €1,000,000 loan with a range of interest rates. You will create a one-input data table that shows the results of varying interest rates in 0.25% increments, then you will use Goal Seek to specify a total payment amount for this loan application.

a. Start Excel, open the file EX K-4.xlsx from the drive and folder where you store your Data Files, then save it as **Capital Loan Payment Model**.

b. Reference the monthly payment amount from cell B9 in cell E4, and format the contents of cell E4 as hidden.

FIGURE K-28

	A	B	C	D	E
1	Soft Solutions				
2					
3					
4	Loan Amount	€1,000,000.00		Interest Rate	
5	Annual Interest Rate	6.00%		6.00%	
6	Term in Months	60		6.25%	
7				6.50%	
8				6.75%	
9	Monthly Payment:	€19,332.80		7.00%	
10	Total Payments:	€1,159,968.09		7.25%	
11	Total Interest:	€159,968.09		7.50%	
12				7.75%	
13				8.00%	
14					

c. Using cells D4:E13, create a one-input data table structure with varying interest rates for a 5-year loan. Use cells D5:D13 for the interest rates, with 6% as the lowest possible rate and 8% as the highest. Vary the rates in between by 0.25%. Use Figure K-28 as a guide.

d. Generate the data table that shows the effect of varying interest rates on the monthly payments. Use cell B5, the Annual Interest Rate, as the column input cell. Format cells E5:E13 as currency with the €English (Ireland) symbol and two decimal places.

e. Select cell B10 and use Goal Seek to find the interest rate necessary for a total payment amount of €1,110,000. Use cell B5, the Annual Interest Rate, as the By changing cell. Accept the solution found by Goal Seek.

Advanced Challenge Exercise

- Reference the monthly payment amount from cell B9 in cell A13, and format the contents of cell A13 as hidden.
- Using cells A13:C22, create a two-input data table struc-ture with varying interest rates for 10- and 15-year terms. Use Figure K-29 as a guide.
- Generate the data table that shows the effect of varying interest rates and loan terms on the monthly payments. (*Hint*: Use cell B6, Term in Months, as the row input cell, and cell B5, the Annual Interest Rate, as the column input cell).
- Format cells B14:C22 as currency with the €English (Ireland) symbol and two decimal places.

FIGURE K-29

	A	B	C	D	E	F
1	Soft Solutions					
2						
3						
4	Loan Amount	€1,000,000.00		Interest Rate		
5	Annual Interest Rate	4.18%		6.00%	€19,332.80	
6	Term in Months	60		6.25%	€19,449.26	
7				6.50%	€19,566.15	
8				6.75%	€19,683.46	
9	Monthly Payment:	€18,500.00		7.00%	€19,801.20	
10	Total Payments:	€1,110,000.00		7.25%	€19,919.36	
11	Total Interest:	€110,000.00		7.50%	€20,037.95	
12				7.75%	€20,156.96	
13			120	180	8.00%	€20,276.39	
14		6.00%				
15		6.25%				
16		6.50%				
17		6.75%				
18		7.00%				
19		7.25%				
20		7.50%				
21		7.75%				
22		8.00%				
23						

f. Enter your name in the center section of the worksheet footer, save the workbook, then preview and print the worksheet.

g. Close the workbook, then exit Excel.

▼ INDEPENDENT CHALLENGE 3

You are the owner of Poppies, a florist based in Boston. You are considering adding local delivery service to your business. You decide on a plan to purchase a combination of vans, sedans, and compact cars that can deliver a total of 90 floral orders. You want to first look at how the interest rate affects the monthly payments for each vehicle type you are considering purchasing. To do this, you use Goal Seek. You need to keep the total monthly payments for all of the vehicles at or below $4000. You use Solver to help find the best possible combination of vehicles. You produce a worksheet summarizing your analysis.

a. Start Excel, open the file EX K-5.xlsx from the drive and folder where you store your Data Files, then save it as **Vehicle Purchase**.

▼ INDEPENDENT CHALLENGE 3 (CONTINUED)

b. Use Goal Seek to find the interest rate that produces a monthly payment for the van purchase of $1,400, and write down the interest rate that Goal Seek finds. Record the interest rate in cell A19, enter **Interest rate for $1400 van payment** in cell B19, then reset the interest rate to its original value.

c. Use Goal Seek to find the interest rate that produces a monthly payment for the sedan purchase of $990. Record the interest rate in cell A20, enter **Interest rate for $990 sedan payment** in cell B20, then reset the interest rate to its original value.

d. Use Goal Seek to find the interest rate that produces a monthly payment for the compact purchase of $790. Record the interest rate in cell A21, enter **Interest rate for $790 compact payment** in cell B21, then reset the interest rate to its original value.

e. Name cell B8 **Quantity_Van**, name cell C8 **Quantity_Sedan**, name cell D8 **Quantity_Compact**, and name cell B15 **Total_Monthly_Payments**. Use Solver to set the total delivery capacity of all vehicles to 90. Use the quantity to purchase, cells B8:D8, as the changing cells. Specify that cells B8:D8 must be integers that are greater than or equal to 0. Make sure that the total monthly payments amount in cell B15 is less than or equal to $4000.

f. Generate a scenario named Delivery Solution with the Solver values and restore the original values in the worksheet. Create a scenario summary using the Delivery Solution scenario, delete the notes at the bottom of the solution, and edit cell B2 to contain **Solver Solution**.

g. Enter your name in the center footer section of each worksheet. Save the workbook, then preview and print each sheet.

h. Close the workbook, then exit Excel.

▼ REAL LIFE INDEPENDENT CHALLENGE

You decide to take out a loan for a new car. You haven't decided whether to finance the car for three, four, or five years. You will create scenarios for car loans with the different terms, using interest rates at your local lending institution. You will summarize the scenarios to make them easy to compare.

a. Start Excel, open the file EX K-6.xlsx from the drive and folder where you store your Data Files, then save it as **Car Payment**.

b. Research the interest rates for 3-year, 4-year, and 5-year auto loans at your local lending institution. Record your 48-month interest rate in cell B5 of the worksheet. Change the data in cell B4 to the price of a car you would like to purchase, then widen columns as necessary.

c. Create cell names for the cells B4:B11 based on the labels in cells A4:A11.

d. Create a scenario named **48 months** to calculate the monthly payment for your loan amount, using the 48-month term and the corresponding interest rate at your lending institution.

e. Create a scenario named **36 months** to calculate the monthly payment for your loan amount, using the 36-month term and the corresponding interest rate at your lending institution.

f. Create a scenario named **60 months** to calculate the monthly payment for your loan amount, using the 60-month term and the corresponding interest rate at your lending institution.

g. Generate a scenario summary titled **Scenario Summary for Car Purchase** that summarizes the payment information in cells B9:B11 for the varying interest rates and terms. Delete the Current Values column in the report and the notes at the bottom of the report.

h. Enter your name in the center section of the scenario summary footer, save the workbook, then preview and print the scenario summary.

i. Create a two-input data table on the Loan sheet using the terms 36, 48, and 60. Use 12 rates, beginning with the lowest rate and incrementing by the difference between the lowest and second lowest rates. Use Figure K-30 as a guide.

j. Enter your name in the center section of the Loan sheet footer, change the page orientation to landscape, save the workbook, then preview and print the Loan sheet.

k. Close the workbook, then exit Excel.

FIGURE K-30

	Term		
	36	**48**	**60**
6.86%	$ 616.26	$ 477.63	$ 394.70
6.93%	$ 616.90	$ 478.28	$ 395.36
7.00%	$ 617.54	$ 478.92	$ 396.02
7.07%	$ 618.18	$ 479.57	$ 396.68
7.14%	$ 618.82	$ 480.23	$ 397.35
7.21%	$ 619.46	$ 480.88	$ 398.01
7.28%	$ 620.11	$ 481.53	$ 398.67
7.35%	$ 620.75	$ 482.18	$ 399.33
7.42%	$ 621.39	$ 482.83	$ 400.00
7.49%	$ 622.03	$ 483.48	$ 400.66
7.56%	$ 622.68	$ 484.14	$ 401.33
7.63%	$ 623.32	$ 484.79	$ 402.00

▼ VISUAL WORKSHOP

Open the file EX K-7.xlsx from the drive and folder where you save your Data Files, then save it as **Custom Bookcases**. Create the worksheet shown in Figure K-31. (*Hint*: Use Goal Seek to find the Hourly labor cost to reach the total profit in cell H11 and accept the solution.) Then generate descriptive statistics for the model's profits, as shown in Figure K-32. Add your name to the center footer section of each sheet, change the orientation of the Profit sheet to landscape, then preview and print both worksheets.

FIGURE K-31

	A	B	C	D	E	F	G	H	I
1				Custom Bookcases					
2									
3	Hourly labor cost	$43.94							
4	Component cost	$55.00							
5									
6		Hours per Unit	Components per Unit	Cost to Produce	Retail Price	Unit Profit	Units Produced	Total Profit	
7	Model A	8.00	6	$ 681.51	$1,695.00	$1,013.49	51	$ 51,688.13	
8	Model B	10.00	9	$ 934.38	$2,200.00	$1,265.62	73	$ 92,389.97	
9	Model C	15.00	12	$1,319.08	$2,900.00	$1,580.92	67	$105,921.90	
10	Model D	17.00	14	$1,516.95	$3,100.00	$1,583.05	55	$ 87,067.59	
11	Total Profit							$250,000.00	
12									

FIGURE K-32

	A	B	C
1	Profit Statistics		
2			
3	Mean	84266.9	
4	Standard Error	11561.95	
5	Median	89728.78	
6	Mode	#N/A	
7	Standard Deviation	23123.89	
8	Sample Variance	5.35E+08	
9	Kurtosis	2.248468	
10	Skewness	-1.28676	
11	Range	54233.77	
12	Minimum	51688.13	
13	Maximum	105921.9	
14	Sum	337067.6	
15	Count	4	
16			

Analyzing Data with PivotTables

Files You Will Need:

EX L-1.xlsx
EX L-2.xlsx
EX L-3.xlsx
EX L-4.xlsx
EX L-5.xlsx
EX L-6.xlsx
EX L-7.xlsx

The Excel **PivotTable** feature lets you summarize selected worksheet data in an interactive table format. You can freely rearrange, or "pivot," parts of the table structure around the data to summarize any data values within the table by category. You can also view data three-dimensionally, with data for each category arranged in a stack of pages. Excel includes two PivotTable features: PivotTable reports and PivotChart reports. In this unit, you plan, design, create, update, and change the layout and format of a PivotTable report. You also add a report filter to a PivotTable report and create a PivotChart report. Kate Morgan, the vice president of sales at Quest, is preparing for the annual meeting for the United States region. She decides to develop an analysis of products sold in Quest's Chicago, New York, and Miami branches over the past year. Kate asks you to create a PivotTable to summarize the 2010 sales data by quarter, product, and branch.

OBJECTIVES

Plan and design a PivotTable report

Create a PivotTable report

Change a PivotTable's summary function and design

Filter and sort PivotTable data

Update a PivotTable report

Change the structure and format of a PivotTable report

Create a PivotChart report

Use the GETPIVOTDATA function

Planning and Designing a PivotTable Report

Creating a **PivotTable report** (often called a PivotTable) involves only a few steps. Before you begin, however, you need to review the data and consider how a PivotTable can best summarize it. 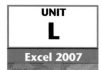 Kate asks you to design a PivotTable to display Quest's sales information for its branches in the United States. You begin by reviewing guidelines for creating PivotTables.

Before you create a PivotTable, think about the following guidelines:

- **Review the source data**

  Before you can effectively summarize data in a PivotTable, you need to understand the source data's scope and structure. The source data does not have to be defined as a table, but should be in a table-like format. That is, it should not have any blank rows or columns, and should have the same type of data in each column. In order to create a meaningful PivotTable, make sure that one or more of the fields has repeated information so that the PivotTable can effectively group it. Numeric data that can be totaled for each group must also be included. The data columns represent categories of data, which are called fields, just as in a table. You are working with sales information that Kate received from Quest's U.S. branch managers, shown in Figure L-1. Information is repeated in the Product ID, Category, Branch, and Quarter columns, and numeric information is displayed in the Sales column, so you will be able to summarize this data effectively in a PivotTable.

- **Determine the purpose of the PivotTable and write the names of the fields you want to include**

  The purpose of your PivotTable is to summarize sales information by quarter across various branches. You will include the following fields in the PivotTable: Product ID, Category, Branch, Quarter, and Sales.

- **Determine which field contains the data you want to summarize and which summary function you want to use**

  You want to summarize sales information by summing the Sales field for each product in a branch by quarter. You'll do this by using the Excel SUM function.

- **Decide how you want to arrange the data**

  The layout of a PivotTable is crucial in delivering its intended message. Product ID will appear in the PivotTable columns, Branch and Quarter will appear in rows, and the PivotTable will summarize Sales figures, as shown in Figure L-2.

- **Determine the location of the PivotTable**

  You can place a PivotTable in any worksheet of any workbook. Placing a PivotTable on a separate worksheet makes it easier to locate and prevents you from accidentally overwriting parts of an existing sheet. You decide to create the PivotTable as a new worksheet in the current workbook.

FIGURE L-1: Sales worksheet

	A	B	C	D	E	F
1		United States Sales				
2	Product ID	Category	Branch	Quarter	Sales	
3	250	Travel Accessory	Chicago	1	$ 2,300.56	
4	250	Travel Accessory	Chicago	2	$ 5,767.76	
5	250	Travel Accessory	Chicago	3	$ 4,883.65	
6	250	Travel Accessory	Chicago	4	$ 5,697.45	
7	100	Travel Insurance	Chicago	1	$ 980.65	
8	100	Travel Insurance	Chicago	2	$ 2,634.69	
9	100	Travel Insurance	Chicago	3	$ 2,500.74	
10	100	Travel Insurance	Chicago	4	$ 3,612.93	
11	350	Tour	Chicago	1	$ 8,995.43	
12	350	Tour	Chicago	2	$ 7,976.43	
13	350	Tour	Chicago	3	$ 8,232.65	
14	350	Tour	Chicago	4	$ 8,631.98	
15	780	Travel Accessory	Chicago	1	$ 999.65	
16	780	Travel Accessory	Chicago	2	$ 2,334.56	
17	780	Travel Accessory	Chicago	3	$ 2,210.32	
18	780	Travel Accessory	Chicago	4	$ 1,245.67	
19	640	Travel Insurance	Chicago	1	$ 1,289.65	
20	640	Travel Insurance	Chicago	2	$ 6,434.56	
21	640	Travel Insurance	Chicago	3	$ 6,100.32	
22	640	Travel Insurance	Chicago	4	$ 6,345.67	
23	510	Tour	Chicago	1	$ 999.43	
24	510	Tour	Chicago	2	$ 1,954.43	
25	510	Tour	Chicago	3	$ 2,412.65	
26	510	Tour	Chicago	4	$ 2,661.98	
27	250	Travel Accessory	Miami	1	$ 1,394.32	
28	250	Travel Accessory	Miami	2	$ 3,231.80	
29	250	Travel Accessory	Miami	3	$ 3,511.65	
30	250	Travel Accessory	Miami	4	$ 2,687.95	
31	100	Travel Insurance	Miami	1	$ 6,634.43	

FIGURE L-2: Example of PivotTable report

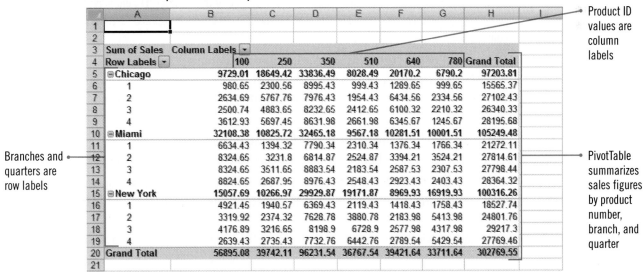

Product ID values are column labels

Branches and quarters are row labels

PivotTable summarizes sales figures by product number, branch, and quarter

	A	B	C	D	E	F	G	H	I
1									
2									
3	Sum of Sales	Column Labels							
4	Row Labels	100	250	350	510	640	780	Grand Total	
5	⊟Chicago	9729.01	18649.42	33836.49	8028.49	20170.2	6790.2	97203.81	
6	1	980.65	2300.56	8995.43	999.43	1289.65	999.65	15565.37	
7	2	2634.69	5767.76	7976.43	1954.43	6434.56	2334.56	27102.43	
8	3	2500.74	4883.65	8232.65	2412.65	6100.32	2210.32	26340.33	
9	4	3612.93	5697.45	8631.98	2661.98	6345.67	1245.67	28195.68	
10	⊟Miami	32108.38	10825.72	32465.18	9567.18	10281.51	10001.51	105249.48	
11	1	6634.43	1394.32	7790.34	2310.34	1376.34	1766.34	21272.11	
12	2	8324.65	3231.8	6814.87	2524.87	3394.21	3524.21	27814.61	
13	3	8324.65	3511.65	8883.54	2183.54	2587.53	2307.53	27798.44	
14	4	8824.65	2687.95	8976.43	2548.43	2923.43	2403.43	28364.32	
15	⊟New York	15057.69	10266.97	29929.87	19171.87	8969.93	16919.93	100316.26	
16	1	4921.45	1940.57	6369.43	2119.43	1418.43	1758.43	18527.74	
17	2	3319.92	2374.32	7628.78	3880.78	2183.98	5413.98	24801.76	
18	3	4176.89	3216.65	8198.9	6728.9	2577.98	4317.98	29217.3	
19	4	2639.43	2735.43	7732.76	6442.76	2789.54	5429.54	27769.46	
20	Grand Total	56895.08	39742.11	96231.54	36767.54	39421.64	33711.64	302769.55	
21									

Creating a PivotTable Report

Once you've planned and designed your PivotTable report, you can create it. After you create the PivotTable, you populate it by adding fields to areas in the PivotTable. A PivotTable has four areas: the Report Filter, which is the field the PivotTable will be filtered by; the Row Labels, which contain the fields whose labels will describe the values in the rows; the Column Labels, which appear above the PivotTable values describing the columns; and the Values, which contain the field that is summarized. ▓▓▓ With the planning and design stage complete, you are ready to create a PivotTable that summarizes sales information. Kate will use the information in her presentation to the branch managers in the Chicago, New York, and Miami offices.

STEPS

1. **Start Excel if necessary, open the file EX L-1.xlsx from the drive and folder where you store your Data Files, then save it as US Sales**

   This worksheet contains the year's sales information for Quest's branches in the United States, including Product ID, Category, Branch, Quarter, and Sales. The records are sorted by branch.

2. **Click the Insert tab, then click the PivotTable button in the Tables group**

   The Create PivotTable dialog box opens, as shown in Figure L-3. This is where you specify the type of data source you want to use for your PivotTable: an Excel Table/Range or an external data source such as a database file. You also specify where you want to place the PivotTable.

3. **Make sure the Select a table or range option button is selected and the range Sales!$A$2:$E$74 appears in the Table/Range text box, make sure the New Worksheet option button is selected, then click OK**

   The PivotTable appears on the left side of the worksheet and the PivotTable Field List pane appears on the right, as shown in Figure L-4. You add the fields in the field list that you want summarized in the PivotTable by clicking their check boxes. The diagram area at the bottom of the Field List task pane represents the main PivotTable areas and helps you track field locations as you populate the PivotTable.

QUICK TIP

You can also add fields from the Field list to the PivotTable by dragging them to the desired area in the diagram area at the bottom of the PivotTable Field List pane.

4. **Click the Product ID check box**

   The Product ID field name appears in the Values area in the diagram area, and the Product ID information is automatically added to the PivotTable. Because the data type of the Product ID field is numeric, the field is added to the Values area of the PivotTable and the Product ID values are summed. You want the Product IDs as column headers in the PivotTable.

5. **Click the Sum of Product ID list arrow in the Values area at the bottom of the PivotTable Field List, then choose Move to Column Labels**

   The Product ID field becomes a column label, causing the Product ID values to appear in the PivotTable as column headers.

QUICK TIP

To remove a field from a PivotTable, click the field's check box to uncheck it.

6. **Click the Branch field check box in the PivotTable Field List**

   The Branch field is added to the Row Labels area. If a field is nonnumeric, it is added to the Row Labels area.

7. **Drag the Quarter field from the top of the PivotTable Field List and drop it below the Branch field in the Row Labels area at the bottom, then select the Sales field check box in the PivotTable Field List**

   You have created a PivotTable that totals U.S. sales, with the Product IDs as column headers and Branches and Quarters as row labels. Adding the Quarter field as a row label below the Branches field displays the quarters below each branch in the Row Labels area of the PivotTable. Because the data in the Sales field is numeric, the Sales field is added to the Values area. SUM is the Excel default function for data fields containing numbers, so Excel automatically calculates the sum of the sales in the PivotTable. The PivotTable tells you that Miami sales of Product #100 were twice the New York sales level and more than three times the Chicago sales level. Product #350 was the best selling product overall, as shown in the Grand Total row. See Figure L-5.

QUICK TIP

You can click the Hide Details button ▬ next to the branch names to collapse the outline. You can click the Show Details button ➕ next to any field name on a PivotTable to expand an outline.

8. **Save the workbook**

FIGURE L-3: Create PivotTable dialog box

Data source for PivotTable

Location for PivotTable

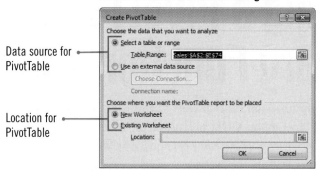

FIGURE L-4: New PivotTable ready to receive field data

PivotTable

Click to add field to the PivotTable

Diagram of the PivotTable areas

PivotTable Field List pane

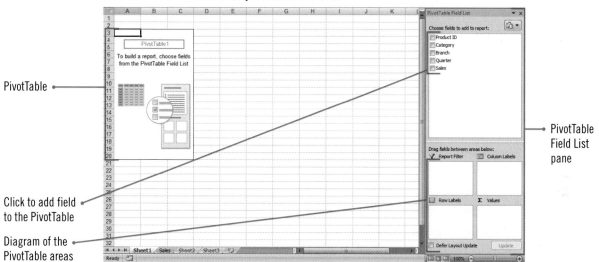

FIGURE L-5: New PivotTable with fields in place

Miami sales for this product are twice as high as New York and three times Chicago's sales

Product 350 shows highest sales overall

Product ID in Column area

Sum of Sales in Values area

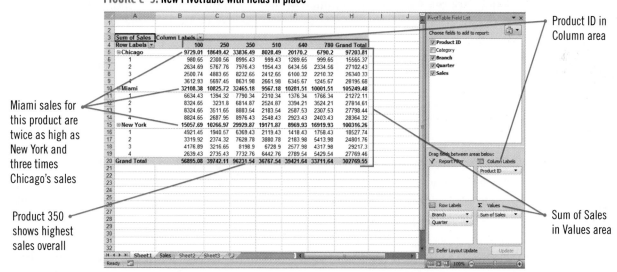

Changing the PivotTable layout

The default layout for PivotTables is the compact form; the row labels are displayed in a single column and the second-level field items (such as the quarters in the US Sales example) are indented to easily tell them apart. You can change the layout of your PivotTable by clicking the PivotTable Tools Design tab, clicking the Report Layout button in the Layout group, then clicking either Show in Outline Form or Show in Tabular Form. The tabular form and the outline form show each row label in its own column. The outline form places subtotals at the top of every column. The tabular and outline layouts take up more space on a worksheet than the compact layout.

Changing a PivotTable's Summary Function and Design

A PivotTable's **summary function** controls what calculation is used to summarize the table data. Unless you specify otherwise, Excel applies the SUM function to numeric data and the COUNT function to data fields containing text. However, you can easily change the SUM function to a different summary function, such as AVERAGE, which calculates the average of all values in the field. ▓▓▓▓▓ Kate wants you to calculate the average sales for the U.S. branches using the AVERAGE function. She also asks you to improve the appearance of the PivotTable for her presentation.

STEPS

1. **Right-click cell A3, then point to** Summarize Data By **in the shortcut menu**

   The menu shows that the Sum function is selected by default, as shown in Figure L-6.

2. **Click** Average

   The data area of the PivotTable shows the average sales for each product by branch and quarter, and cell A3 now contains Average of Sales, as shown in Figure L-7. You want to view the PivotTable data without the subtotals.

3. **Click the** PivotTable Tools Design tab, **click the** Subtotals button **in the Layout group, then click** Do Not Show Subtotals

   After reviewing the data, you decide that it would be more useful to sum the sales information than to average it. You also want to display the subtotals.

4. **Right-click cell A3, point to** Summarize Data By **in the shortcut menu, then click** Sum

   Excel recalculates the PivotTable—in this case, summing the sales data instead of averaging it.

5. **Click the** Subtotals button **in the Layout group, then click** Show all Subtotals at Top of Group

   In the same way that tables have styles available to quickly format them, PivotTables have a gallery of styles to choose from. You decide to add a PivotTable style to the PivotTable to improve its appearance.

6. **Click the** More button ▾ **in the PivotTable Styles gallery, then click** Pivot Style Medium 11

   You decide to give the PivotTable sheet a more descriptive name. When you name a PivotTable sheet, it is best to avoid using spaces in the name. If a PivotTable name contains a space, you must put single quotes around the name if you refer to it in a function.

7. **Rename Sheet1** PivotTable, **add your name to the worksheet footer, save the workbook, then print the worksheet**

FIGURE L-6: Shortcut menu showing Sum function selected

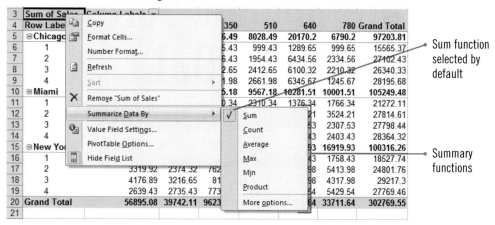

Sum function selected by default

Summary functions

FIGURE L-7: PivotTable showing averages

Summary function is Average

Average of Sales	Column Labels						
Row Labels	100	250	350	510	640	780	Grand Total
⊟Chicago	2432.2525	4662.355	8459.1225	2007.1225	5042.55	1697.55	4050.15875
1	980.65	2300.56	8995.43	999.43	1289.65	999.65	2594.228333
2	2634.69	5767.76	7976.43	1954.43	6434.56	2334.56	4517.071667
3	2500.74	4883.65	8232.65	2412.65	6100.32	2210.32	4390.055
4	3612.93	5697.45	8631.98	2661.98	6345.67	1245.67	4699.28
⊟Miami	8027.095	2706.43	8116.295	2391.795	2570.3775	2500.3775	4385.395
1	6634.43	1394.32	7790.34	2310.34	1376.34	1766.34	3545.351667
2	8324.65	3231.8	6814.87	2524.87	3394.21	3524.21	4635.768333
3	8324.65	3511.65	8883.54	2183.54	2587.53	2307.53	4633.073333
4	8824.65	2687.95	8976.43	2548.43	2923.43	2403.43	4727.386667
⊟New York	3764.4225	2566.7425	7482.4675	4792.9675	2242.4825	4229.9825	4179.844167
1	4921.45	1940.57	6369.43	2119.43	1418.43	1758.43	3087.956667
2	3319.92	2374.32	7628.78	3880.78	2183.98	5413.98	4133.626667
3	4176.89	3216.65	8198.9	6728.9	2577.98	4317.98	4869.55
4	2639.43	2735.43	7732.76	6442.76	2789.54	5429.54	4628.243333
Grand Total	4741.256667	3311.8425	8019.295	3063.961667	3285.136667	2809.303333	4205.132639

⊢ ◀ ▶ ▶⊢ \ Sheet1 ╱ Sales ╱ Sheet2 ╱ Sheet3 ╱ ⁁ ╱

Using the Show/Hide buttons

To display and hide PivotTable elements, you can use the buttons in the Show/Hide group on the PivotTable Tools Options tab. For example, the Field List button will hide or display the PivotTable Field List pane. The +/– Buttons button will hide or display the Hide and Show Details buttons, and the Field Headers button will hide or display the Row and Column Label headers on the PivotTable.

Analyzing Data with PivotTables

Filtering and Sorting PivotTable Data

When you worked with Excel tables, you used filters to hide and display table data. You can filter a PivotTable using a **report filter**, which lets you filter data so that the PivotTable summarizes data based on one or more field values. For example, if you add a field with monthly data to the Report Filter area, you can filter a PivotTable so that only data representing the sum of sales in January appears in the PivotTable. Moving a field to the Report Filter area of a PivotTable filters the report data by that field. You can also sort PivotTable row and column data to organize it in ascending or descending order. ▆▆▆▆▆ Kate wants you to filter the PivotTable so that only one quarter's data is visible at one time. She also wants you to sort the fourth quarter Chicago data by sales values and format the sales value cells in the PivotTable as U.S. currency.

STEPS

1. **In the PivotTable Field List, click the Quarter field list arrow in the Row Labels area, then select Move to Report Filter**

   The Quarter field moves up to cell A1, and a list arrow and the word (All) appear in cell B1. The list arrow allows you to filter the data in the PivotTable by Quarter. (All) indicates that the PivotTable currently shows data for all quarters. You decide to filter the data so it displays the data for only the first quarter.

2. **In the PivotTable cell B1, click the Quarter list arrow**

   Each quarter is listed in addition to an option to show All quarters, as shown in Figure L-8.

3. **Click 1, then click OK**

   > **QUICK TIP**
   > To display each quarter on a separate worksheet, click the PivotTable Tools Options tab, click the Options list arrow in the PivotTable group, click Show Report Filter Pages, select the appropriate filter field, then click OK.

   The PivotTable filters the sales data to display the first quarter only, as shown in Figure L-9. The Quarter field list arrow changes to a filter symbol. A filter symbol also appears to the right of the Quarter field in the PivotTable Field List pane, indicating that the PivotTable is filtered and summarizes only a portion of the PivotTable data.

4. **Click the Quarter filter arrow, click 4, then click OK**

   The sales for the fourth quarter appear. You want to display the columns in ascending order by fourth quarter Chicago sales. You begin by clicking a Chicago sales value so you can make Chicago sales the basis for the sort.

5. **Click cell B5, click the PivotTable Tools Options tab, then click the Sort button in the Sort group**

   The Sort By Value dialog box opens. As you select options in the dialog box, the Summary information at the bottom of the dialog box changes to describe the sort results using your field names.

   > **QUICK TIP**
   > If you click the Top to Bottom button in the Sort direction section, the branches will be sorted by the sales values in the column.

6. **Make sure the Smallest to Largest option button is selected in the Sort options section, click the Left to Right option button in the Sort direction section, review the sort description in the Summary section of the dialog box, then click OK**

   The columns are arranged in the PivotTable in increasing order from left to right. The data would be more readable if it were in currency format.

7. **Click any sales value in the PivotTable, click the Field Settings button in the Active Field group, click Show values as tab in the Value Field Settings dialog box, click Number Format, select Currency in the Category list, make sure Decimal places is 2 and Symbol is $, click OK, then click OK again**

   > **QUICK TIP**
   > You can also sort and filter the row and column labels by clicking their list arrows and selecting a sort option.

8. **Save the workbook**

FIGURE L-8: PivotTable with Quarter as a report filter

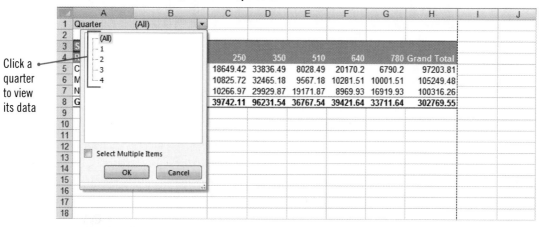

Click a quarter to view its data

	A	B	C	D	E	F	G	H	I	J
1	Quarter	(All)								
2										
3										
4			250	350	510	640		780 Grand Total		
5			18649.42	33836.49	8028.49	20170.2	6790.2	97203.81		
6			10825.72	32465.18	9567.18	10281.51	10001.51	105249.48		
7			10266.97	29929.87	19171.87	8969.93	16919.93	100316.26		
8			39742.11	96231.54	36767.54	39421.64	33711.64	302769.55		
9										

Dialog list: (All), 1, 2, 3, 4 — Select Multiple Items — OK — Cancel

FIGURE L-9: Filtered PivotTable

List arrow now includes filter symbol

PivotTable is filtered to show only first quarter sales

	A	B	C	D	E	F	G	H	I	J	K
1	Quarter	1									
2											
3	Sum of Sales	Column Labels									
4	Row Labels	100	250	350	510	640		780 Grand Total			
5	Chicago	980.65	2300.56	8995.43	999.43	1289.65	999.65	15565.37			
6	Miami	6634.43	1394.32	7790.34	2310.34	1376.34	1766.34	21272.11			
7	New York	4921.45	1940.57	6369.43	2119.43	1418.43	1758.43	18527.74			
8	Grand Total	12536.53	5635.45	23155.2	5429.2	4084.42	4524.42	55365.22			
9											

Filtering PivotTables using multiple values

You can select multiple values when filtering a PivotTable report using a report filter. After clicking a field's report filter list arrow in the top section of the PivotTable Field List or in cell B1 on the PivotTable itself, click the Select Multiple Items check box at the bottom of the filter selections. This allows you to select multiple values for the filter. For example, selecting 1 and 2 as the report filter in a PivotTable with quarters would display all of the data for the first two quarters. You can also select multiple values for the row and column labels by clicking the Row Label list arrow or the Column Label list arrow in cells A4 and B3 on the PivotTable and selecting the data items that you want to display.

Updating a PivotTable Report

The data in a PivotTable report looks like typical worksheet data. Because the PivotTable data is linked to a **data source** (the data you used to create the PivotTable), however, the values and results in the PivotTable are read-only values. That means you cannot move or modify a part of a PivotTable by inserting or deleting rows, editing results, or moving cells. To change PivotTable data, you must edit the items directly in the data source, then update, or **refresh**, the PivotTable to reflect the changes. ▰▰▰▰ Kate just learned that sales information for a custom group tour sold in New York during the fourth quarter was never entered into the Sales worksheet. Kate asks you to add information about this tour to the data source and PivotTable. You start by inserting a row for the new information in the Sales worksheet.

STEPS

1. **Click the Sales sheet tab**

   By inserting the new row in the correct position by branch, you will not need to sort the data again.

QUICK TIP

If you want to change the source data range for your PivotTable, click the PivotTable Tools Options tab, then click the Change Data Source button in the Data group.

2. **Right-click the row 51 heading, then click Insert on the shortcut menu**

   A blank row appears as the new row 51, and the data in the old row 51 moves down to row 52. You now have room for the tour data.

3. **Enter the data for the new tour in row 51 using the following information**

Product ID	490
Category	Tour
Branch	New York
Quarter	4
Sales	2910.04

   The PivotTable does not yet reflect the additional data.

4. **Click the PivotTable sheet tab, then verify that the Quarter 4 data appears**

   The fourth quarter list does not currently include the new tour information, and the grand total is $84,329.46. Before you refresh the PivotTable data, you need to make sure that the cell pointer is located within the PivotTable range.

QUICK TIP

If you want Excel to refresh your PivotTable report automatically when you open the workbook in which it is contained, click the Options button in the PivotTable group of the PivotTable Tools Options tab, click the Data tab in the PivotTable Options dialog box, click the Refresh data when opening the file check box, then click OK.

5. **Click anywhere within the PivotTable if necessary, click the PivotTable Tools Options tab, then click the Refresh button in the Data group**

   The PivotTable now contains a column for the new product ID, which includes the new tour information in column B, and the grand total has increased by the amount of the tour's sales (2,910.04) to $87,239.50, as shown in Figure L-10.

6. **Save the workbook**

FIGURE L-10: Updated PivotTable report

New data is added

Totals are updated to include the new data

	A	B	C	D	E	F	G	H	I
1	Quarter	4							
2									
3	Sum of Sales	Column Labels							
4	Row Labels	490	780	510	100	250	640	350	Grand Total
5	Chicago		$1,245.67	$2,661.98	$3,612.93	$5,697.45	$6,345.67	$8,631.98	$28,195.68
6	Miami		$2,403.43	$2,548.43	$8,824.65	$2,687.95	$2,923.43	$8,976.43	$28,364.32
7	New York	$2,910.04	$5,429.54	$6,442.76	$2,639.43	$2,735.43	$2,789.54	$7,732.76	$30,679.50
8	Grand Total	$2,910.04	$9,078.64	$11,653.17	$15,077.01	$11,120.83	$12,058.64	$25,341.17	$87,239.50
9									

Adding a calculated field to a PivotTable

You can use formulas to analyze PivotTable data in a field by adding a calculated field. A calculated field appears in the PivotTable Field List pane and can be manipulated like other PivotTable fields. To add a calculated field, click any cell in the PivotTable, click the PivotTable Tools Options tab, click the Formulas button in the Tools group, then click Calculated Field. The Insert Calculated Field dialog box opens, as shown in Figure L-11. Enter the field name in the Name text box, click in the Formula text box, click a field name in the Fields list that you want to use in the formula and click Insert Field. Use standard arithmetic operators to enter the formula you want to use. Click Add, then click OK. The new field with the formula results appears in the PivotTable, and the field will be added to the PivotTable Field List.

FIGURE L-11: Insert Calculated Field dialog box

Enter the new field name here

Enter formula here

Click fields that will be used in the formula here

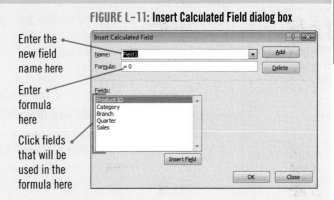

Grouping PivotTable data

You can group PivotTable data to analyze specific values in a field as a unit. For example, you may want to group sales data for quarters one and two to analyze sales for the first half of the year. To group PivotTable data, you need to first select the rows and columns that you want to group, click the PivotTable Tools Options tab, then click the Group Selection button in the Group group. After you group data you can summarize it by clicking the Field Settings button in the Active Field group, clicking the Custom button in the Field Settings dialog box, selecting the function that you want to use to summarize the data, then clicking OK. To ungroup data, select the Group name in the PivotTable, then click the Ungroup button in the Group group.

Changing the Structure and Format of a PivotTable Report

What makes a PivotTable such a powerful analysis tool is the ability to change the way data is organized in the report. You can easily change the structure of a PivotTable by adding fields or by moving fields to new positions in the PivotTable. ▄▄▄▄ Kate asks you to include category information in the sales report. She is also interested in viewing the PivotTable in different arrangements to find the best organization of data for her presentation.

STEPS

1. **Make sure that the PivotTable sheet is active, that the active cell is located anywhere inside the PivotTable, and that the PivotTable Field List is visible**

2. **Click the Category check box in the PivotTable Field List**

Because the category data is nonnumeric, it is added to the Row Labels area. The PivotTable displays the category sales information for each branch. When you have two row labels, the data is organized by the values in the outer field and then by the data in the inner field. The inner field values are indented to make them easy to distinguish from the outer field. You can move fields within an area of a PivotTable by dragging and dropping them to the desired location. When you drag a field, the pointer appears with a PivotTable outline attached to its lower-right corner.

3. **In the diagram section of the PivotTable Field List, locate the Row Labels area, then drag the Category field up and drop it above the Branch field**

The category field is now the outer or upper field, and the branch field is the inner or lower field. The PivotTable is restructured to display the sales data by the category values and then the branch values within the category field. The subtotals now reflect the sum of the categories, as shown in Figure L-12. You can also move fields to new areas in the PivotTable.

4. **In the diagram area of the PivotTable Field List, drag the Category field from the Row Labels area to the Column Labels area, then drag the Product ID field from the Column Labels area to the Row Labels area below the Branch field**

The PivotTable is restructured to display the sales data with the category values in the columns and then the product IDs grouped by branches. The product ID values are indented below the branches because the Product ID field is the inner row label.

5. **In the diagram area of the PivotTable Field List, drag the Category field from the Column Labels area to the Report Filter area above the Quarter field, then drag the Product ID field from the Row Labels area to the Column Labels area**

The PivotTable now has two filters. The upper filter, Category, summarizes data using all of the categories. Kate asks you to display the tour sales information for all quarters.

6. **Click the Category list arrow in cell B1 of the PivotTable, click Tour, click OK, click the Quarter filter list arrow, click All, then click OK**

The PivotTable displays sales totals for the Tour category for all quarters. Kate asks you to provide the sales information for all categories.

7. **Click the Category filter arrow, click All, then click OK**

The completed PivotTable appears as shown in Figure L-13.

8. **Save the workbook, then preview and print the PivotTable in landscape orientation**

FIGURE L-12: PivotTable structured by branches within categories

Category is outer field →

Branch is inner field and values are indented →

	A	B	C	D	E	F	G	H	I	J
1	Quarter	4								
2										
3	Sum of Sales	Column Labels								
4	Row Labels		100	250	350	510	640	780	490 Grand Total	
5	Tour			$25,341.17	$11,653.17				$2,910.04	$39,904.38
6	Chicago			$8,631.98	$2,661.98					$11,293.96
7	Miami			$8,976.43	$2,548.43					$11,524.86
8	New York			$7,732.76	$6,442.76				$2,910.04	$17,085.56
9	Travel Accessory		$11,120.83				$9,078.64			$20,199.47
10	Chicago		$5,697.45				$1,245.67			$6,943.12
11	Miami		$2,687.95				$2,403.43			$5,091.38
12	New York		$2,735.43				$5,429.54			$8,164.97
13	Travel Insurance	$15,077.01				$12,058.64				$27,135.65
14	Chicago	$3,612.93				$6,345.67				$9,958.60
15	Miami	$8,824.65				$2,923.43				$11,748.08
16	New York	$2,639.43				$2,789.54				$5,428.97
17	Grand Total	$15,077.01	$11,120.83	$25,341.17	$11,653.17	$12,058.64	$9,078.64	$2,910.04		$87,239.50
18										

FIGURE L-13: Completed PivotTable report

	A	B	C	D	E	F	G	H	I
1	Category	(All)							
2	Quarter	(All)							
3									
4	Sum of Sales	Column Labels							
5	Row Labels	100	250	350	510	640	780	490	Grand Total
6	Chicago	$9,729.01	$18,649.42	$33,836.49	$8,028.49	$20,170.20	$6,790.20		$97,203.81
7	Miami	$32,108.38	$10,825.72	$32,465.18	$9,567.18	$10,281.51	$10,001.51		$105,249.48
8	New York	$15,057.69	$10,266.97	$29,929.87	$19,171.87	$8,969.93	$16,919.93	$2,910.04	$103,226.30
9	Grand Total	$56,895.08	$39,742.11	$96,231.54	$36,767.54	$39,421.64	$33,711.64	$2,910.04	$305,679.59
10									

Adding conditional formatting to a PivotTable

You can add conditional formatting to a PivotTable to make it easier to compare the data values. The conditional formatting is applied to cells in a PivotTable the same way as it is to non-PivotTable data. The conditional formatting rules will follow the PivotTable cells when you move fields to different areas of the PivotTable.

Creating a PivotChart Report

A **PivotChart report** is a chart that you create from data or from a PivotTable report. Table L-1 describes how the elements in a PivotTable report correspond to the elements in a PivotChart report. When you create a PivotChart directly from data, Excel automatically creates a corresponding PivotTable report. If you change a PivotChart report by filtering or sorting the charted elements, Excel updates the corresponding PivotTable report to show the new data values. You can move the fields of a PivotChart using the PivotTable Field List window; the new layout will be reflected in the PivotTable. Kate wants you to chart the fourth quarter tour sales and the yearly tour sales average for her presentation. You create the PivotChart report from the PivotTable data.

STEPS

1. **Click the Category list arrow in cell B1, click Tour, click OK, click the Quarter list arrow, click 4, then click OK**

   The fourth quarter tour sales information appears in the PivotTable. You want to create the PivotChart from the PivotTable information you have displayed.

2. **Click any cell in the PivotTable, click the PivotTable Tools Options tab, then click the PivotChart button in the Tools group**

   The Insert Chart dialog box opens and shows a gallery of chart types.

> **TROUBLE**
> If you don't see the PivotChart Filter Pane, click inside the PivotChart.

3. **Click the Clustered Column chart if necessary, then click OK**

   The PivotChart appears on the worksheet, along with the PivotChart Filter Pane, as shown in Figure L-14. This pane enables you to filter and sort a PivotChart in the same way that you do a PivotTable. It will be easier to view the PivotChart if it is on its own sheet.

4. **Click the Move Chart button in the Location group, click the New sheet option button, type PivotChart in the text box, click OK, then resize the PivotChart and move the PivotChart Filter pane, the PivotTable Field List pane, and the chart legend to match Figure L-15**

   The chart represents the fourth quarter tour sales. Kate asks you to change the chart to show the average sales for all quarters.

> **QUICK TIP**
> You can sort and filter the axis and legend fields by clicking their list arrows in the PivotChart Filter Pane and selecting a sort or filter option.

5. **Click the Quarter filter arrow in the PivotChart Filter Pane, click All, then click OK**

   The chart now represents the sum of tour sales for the year. You can change a PivotChart's summary function to display averages instead of totals.

> **QUICK TIP**
> If the PivotTable Field List is not visible, click the "Active Fields on the PivotChart" button to display it.

6. **Click the Sum of Sales list arrow in the Values area of the PivotTable Field List, click Value Field Settings, click Average on the Summarize by tab, then click OK**

   The PivotChart report recalculates to display averages. The chart would be easier to understand if it had a title.

7. **Click the PivotChart Tools Layout tab, click the Chart Title button in the Labels group, click Above Chart, then replace Chart Title in the text box with Average Tour Sales**

8. **Drag the chart title border to center the title over the columns if necessary, enter your name in the PivotChart sheet footer, save the workbook, then preview and print the PivotChart report**

   The final PivotChart report displaying the average tour sales for the year is shown in Figure L-16.

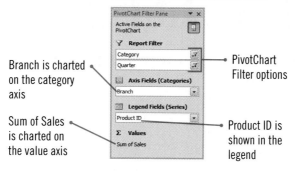

FIGURE L-14: PivotChart Filter Pane

Branch is charted on the category axis

Sum of Sales is charted on the value axis

PivotChart Filter options

Product ID is shown in the legend

FIGURE L-15: New chart sheet displaying fourth quarter tour sales

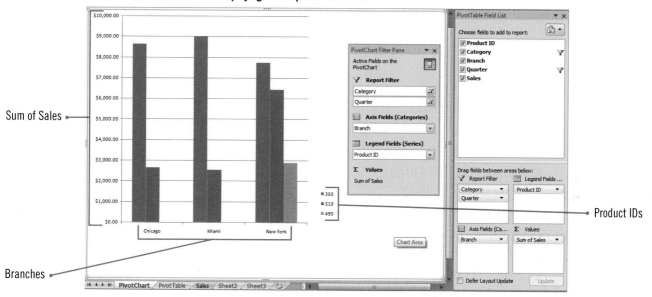

Sum of Sales

Branches

Product IDs

FIGURE L-16: Completed PivotChart report

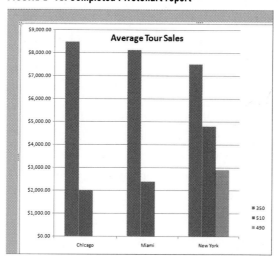

TABLE L-1: PivotTable and PivotChart elements

PivotTable items	PivotChart items
row labels	axis fields (categories)
column labels	legend fields (series)
report filters	report filters

Excel 2007

Using the GETPIVOTDATA Function

Because you can rearrange a PivotTable so easily, you can't use an ordinary cell reference when you want to reference a PivotTable cell in another worksheet. The reason is that if you change the way data is displayed in a PivotTable, the data moves, rendering an ordinary cell reference incorrect. Instead, to retrieve summary data from a PivotTable, you need to use the Excel GETPIVOTDATA function. See Figure L-17 for the GETPIVOTDATA function format.  Kate wants to include the yearly sales total for the Chicago branch in the Sales sheet. She asks you to retrieve this information from the PivotTable and place it in the Sales sheet. You use the GETPIVOTDATA function to retrieve this information.

STEPS

1. **Click the PivotTable sheet tab**

   The sales figures in the PivotTable are average values for tours. You decide to show sales information for all categories and change the summary information back to Sum.

2. **Click the Category filter arrow in cell B1, click All, then click OK**

   The PivotChart report displays sales information for all categories.

3. **Right-click cell A4 on the PivotTable, point to Summarize Data By on the shortcut menu, then click Sum**

   The PivotChart report is recalculated to display sales totals. Next, you want to include the total for sales for the Chicago branch in the Sales sheet by retrieving it from the PivotTable.

4. **Click the Sales sheet tab, click cell G1, type Total Chicago Sales:, click the Enter button ✓ on the Formula Bar, click the Home tab, click the Align Text Right button ≡ in the Alignment group, click the Bold button B in the Font group, then adjust the width of column G to display the label in cell G1**

   You want the GETPIVOTDATA function to retrieve the total Chicago sales from the PivotTable. Cell I6 on the PivotTable contains the data you want to return to the Sales sheet.

5. **Click cell G2, type =, click the PivotTable sheet tab, click cell I6 on the PivotTable, then click ✓**

   The GETPIVOTDATA function along with its arguments is inserted into cell G2 of the Sales sheet, as shown in Figure L-18.

6. **Click the Accounting Number Format button $ in the Number group**

   The current sales total for the Chicago branch is $97,203.81, as shown in Figure L-19. This is the same value displayed in cell I6 of the PivotTable.

7. **Enter your name in the Sales sheet footer, save the workbook, then preview and print the first page of the Sales worksheet**

8. **Close the file and exit Excel**

Analyzing Data with PivotTables

FIGURE L-17: Format of GETPIVOTDATA function

=GETPIVOTDATA("Sales",PivotTable!$A$4,"Branch","Chicago")

Field where data is extracted from

PivotTable name and cell in the report that contains the data you want to retrieve

Field and value pair that describe the data you want to retrieve

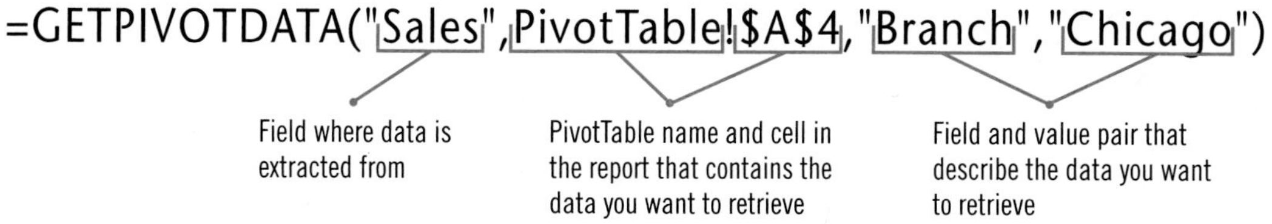

FIGURE L-18: GETPIVOTDATA function in the Sales sheet

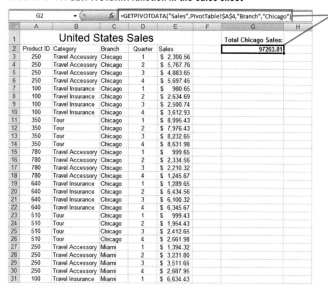

Function is entered into the formula bar and the result is placed in the cell

FIGURE L-19: Completed Sales worksheet showing total Chicago sales

Total Chicago sales

Working with PivotTable versions

PivotTables created using Excel 2007 have a version of 12, which is the technical version number of the 2007 version of Microsoft Office. PivotTables created using Excel 2002 and Excel 2003 have a version of 10. If you are working in Compatibility Mode in Excel 2007 by saving a workbook in an earlier Excel format, any PivotTable that you create will have a version of 10, but if you save the file it is contained in as an .xlsx file and reopen it, the PivotTable will be upgraded to version 12 when it is refreshed. However, when a file containing a version 12 PivotTable is saved as an .xls file, you will not be able to refresh the PivotTable using Excel 2002 or Excel 2003. If you are working with someone using an earlier version of Excel you should create an .xls file, save it, reopen the file, then create your PivotTables using the compatibility mode. This will ensure that people using your PivotTable will be able to refresh it.

Practice

If you have a SAM user profile, you may have access to hands-on instruction, practice, and assessment of the skills covered in this unit. Log in to your SAM account (http://sam2007.course.com/) to launch any assigned training activities or exams that relate to the skills covered in this unit.

▼ CONCEPTS REVIEW

FIGURE L-20

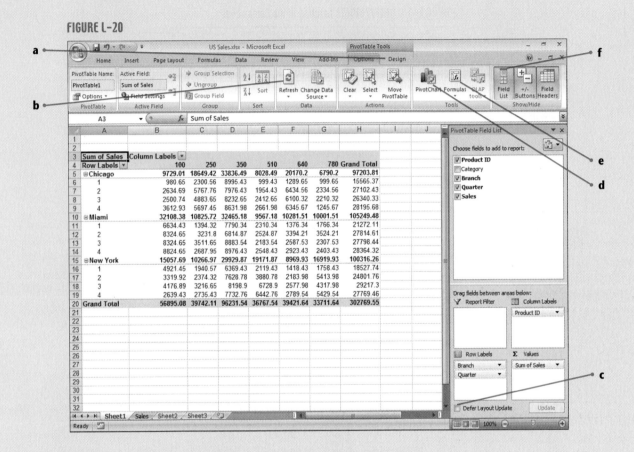

1. Which element do you click to display or hide the PivotTable Field List pane?
2. Which element do you click to update a PivotTable?
3. Which element do you click to display a gallery of PivotTable Styles?
4. Which element do you click to create a chart based on the data in a PivotTable?
5. Which element do you click to create a calculated field in a PivotTable?
6. Which element do you click to control when PivotTable changes will occur?

Match each term with the statement that best describes it.

7. GETPIVOTDATA function	a. Retrieves information from a PivotTable
8. Compact form	b. Default layout for a PivotTable
9. Summary function	c. Format of values in a PivotTable
10. Read-only	d. PivotChart axis field
11. PivotTable Row Label	e. Determines if data is summed or averaged

Select the best answer from the list of choices.

12. **When a numeric field is added to a PivotTable, it is placed in the _____ area.**
    a. Values
    b. Row Labels
    c. Column Labels
    d. Report Filter

13. **Which PivotTable report area allows you to average values?**
    a. Report Filter
    b. Column Labels
    c. Row Labels
    d. Values

14. **To make changes to PivotTable data, you must:**
    a. Edit cells in the source list and then refresh the PivotTable.
    b. Create a page field.
    c. Drag a column header to the column area.
    d. Edit cells in the PivotTable and refresh the source list.

15. **When a nonnumeric field is added to a PivotTable, it is placed in the _____ area.**
    a. Values
    b. Row Labels
    c. Column Labels
    d. Report Filter

16. **The default summary function for data fields containing numbers in an Excel PivotTable is:**
    a. Count
    b. Max
    c. Average
    d. Sum

17. **When a PivotTable has two row labels, the inner field values are _____ to make them easy to distinguish from the outer field values.**
    a. Bolded
    b. Highlighted
    c. Underlined
    d. Indented

18. **Pre-formatted PivotTables that are arranged in a gallery are called:**
    a. PivotTable Styles
    b. PivotTable Formats
    c. Format Paragraphs
    d. PivotCharts

19. **Which of the following allows you to filter and sort a PivotChart?**
    a. PivotTable Filter Pane
    b. PivotChart Filter Pane
    c. PivotTable Sort Wizard
    d. PivotChart Sort Wizard

20. **The default summary function for data fields containing text in an Excel PivotTable is:**
    a. Min
    b. Max
    c. Count
    d. CountA

▼ SKILLS REVIEW

1. **Plan and design a PivotTable report.**
    a. Start Excel, open the file titled EX L-2.xlsx from the drive and folder where you store your Data Files, then save it as **July Videos**.
    b. You will create a PivotTable to show the sum of sales across regions and stores. Study the worksheet data, then list the field names you think should be included in the PivotTable.
    c. Determine which fields you think should be column labels, row labels, and values.
    d. Sketch a draft PivotTable.

2. **Create a PivotTable report.**
    a. Create a PivotTable report on a new worksheet using the Sales worksheet data in the range A1:E25.
    b. Add the Product field in the PivotTable Field List pane to the Column Labels area.
    c. Add the Sales field in the PivotTable Field List pane to the Values Area.
    d. Add the Store field in the PivotTable Field List pane to the Row Labels area.
    e. Add the Sales Rep field in the PivotTable Field List pane to the Row Labels area below the Store field.

3. **Change the summary function of a PivotTable report.**
    a. Change the PivotTable summary function to Average.
    b. Rename the new sheet **July PivotTable**.

   c. Change the PivotTable Style to Pivot Style Medium 13.

   d. Enter your name in the center section of the PivotTable report footer, then save the workbook.

   e. Print the PivotTable report, then change the Summary function back to Sum.

4. Filter and sort PivotTable data.

   a. Add the Region field to the Report Filter area in the PivotTable Field List pane.

   b. Display sales for only the West region in the PivotTable.

   c. Display sales for all regions, then display sales for only the East region.

   d. Format the sales values in the PivotTable as Currency with a $ symbol and no decimal places.

   e. Sort the DC sales values from smallest to largest running left to right.

   f. Save the workbook, then print the worksheet.

5. Update a PivotTable report.

   a. With the July PivotTable sheet active, note the NY total for DVDs.

   b. Activate the Sales sheet and change K. Lyons's sales of DVDs in cell D6 to **$10,750**.

   c. Refresh the PivotTable so it reflects the new sales figure.

   d. Note the NY total for DVDs in the East and verify that it increased by $1000.

   e. Save the workbook, then preview and print the PivotTable.

6. Change the structure and format of a PivotTable report.

   a. With the July PivotTable active, redisplay data for all regions.

   b. In the PivotTable Field List, drag the Product field from the Column Labels area to the Row Labels area.

   c. Drag the Sales Rep field from the Row Labels area to the Column Labels area.

   d. Drag the Store field from the Row Labels area to the Report Filter area.

   e. Drag the Product field back to the Column Labels area.

   f. Drag the Store field back to the Row Labels area.

   g. Remove the Sales Rep field from the PivotTable.

   h. Compare your completed PivotTable to Figure L-21, save the workbook, then preview and print the PivotTable.

FIGURE L-21

	A	B	C	D	E	F
1						
2	Region	(All)				
3						
4	Sum of Sales	Column Labels				
5	Row Labels	DVD	Game	VHS	Grand Total	
6	DC	$26,925	$18,750	$24,639	$70,314	
7	Houston	$31,050	$23,898	$20,890	$75,838	
8	LA	$23,362	$15,589	$22,289	$61,240	
9	NY	$21,250	$20,389	$17,077	$58,716	
10	Grand Total	$102,587	$78,626	$84,895	$266,108	
11						

7. Create a PivotChart report.

   a. Use the existing PivotTable data to create a line PivotChart report.

   b. Move the PivotChart to a new worksheet and name the sheet **PivotChart**.

   c. Change the chart to display average sales.

   d. Add the title **Average Sales** above the chart .

   e. Add your name to the center section of the PivotChart sheet footer.

   f. Compare your PivotChart to Figure L-22, save the workbook, then preview and print the chart.

8. Use the GETPIVOTDATA function.

   a. Change the summary function on the PivotTable report to Sum.

   b. In cell D27 of the Sales sheet enter = , click the July PivotTable sheet, click the cell that contains the grand total for LA, then press [Enter].

   c. Review the GETPIVOTDATA function that was entered in cell D27.

FIGURE L-22

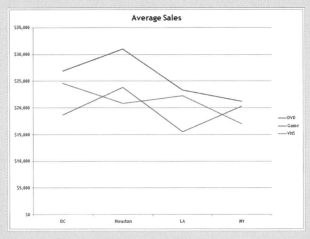

FIGURE L-23

	A	B	C	D	E	F
1	**Product**	**Region**	**Store**	**Sales**	**Sales Rep**	
2	Game	West	LA	$10,934	H. Jeung	
3	DVD	West	LA	$16,512	H. Jeung	
4	VHS	West	LA	$18,511	H. Jeung	
5	Game	East	NY	$11,989	K. Lyons	
6	DVD	East	NY	$10,750	K. Lyons	
7	VHS	East	NY	$8,843	K. Lyons	
8	Game	West	Houston	$13,998	M. Holak	
9	DVD	West	Houston	$20,550	M. Holak	
10	VHS	West	Houston	$15,690	M. Holak	
11	Game	East	DC	$10,850	J. Forum	
12	DVD	East	DC	$16,225	J. Forum	
13	VHS	East	DC	$19,331	J. Forum	
14	Game	West	LA	$4,655	D. Janes	
15	DVD	West	LA	$6,850	D. Janes	
16	VHS	West	LA	$3,778	D. Janes	
17	Game	East	NY	$8,400	L. Sorrento	
18	DVD	East	NY	$10,500	L. Sorrento	
19	VHS	East	NY	$8,234	L. Sorrento	
20	Game	West	Houston	$9,900	T. Leni	
21	DVD	West	Houston	$10,500	T. Leni	
22	VHS	West	Houston	$5,200	T. Leni	
23	Game	East	DC	$7,900	M. Gregoire	
24	DVD	East	DC	$10,700	M. Gregoire	
25	VHS	East	DC	$5,308	M. Gregoire	
26						
27			**LA Sales for July:**	$61,240		
28						
29						

d. Enter your name in the Sales sheet footer, compare your Sales sheet to Figure L-23, save the workbook, then preview and print the worksheet.

e. Close the workbook and exit Excel.

▼ INDEPENDENT CHALLENGE 1

You are the accountant for Appliance Depot, an appliance repair company that employs three technicians. Until recently, the owner had been tracking the technicians' hours manually in a log. You have created an Excel worksheet to track the following basic information: service date, technician name, job #, job category, hours, and warranty information. The owner has asked you to analyze the billing data to give him information about the number of hours being spent on installations versus the time spent with repairs. He also wants to find out how much of the technicians' work is covered by manufacturer's warranties. You will create a PivotTable that sums the hours by category and technician. Once the table is completed, you will create a column chart representing the billing information.

FIGURE L-24

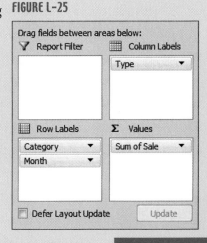

a. Start Excel, open the file titled EX L-3.xlsx from the drive and folder where you store your Data Files, then save it as **Appliances**.

b. Create a PivotTable on a separate worksheet that sums hours by technician and category. Use Figure L-24 as a guide.

c. Name the new sheet **PivotTable** and apply the Pivot Style Medium 6.

d. Add the Warranty field to the Report Filter area of the PivotTable. Display only the PivotTable data for jobs covered by warranties.

e. Create a clustered column PivotChart that shows the warranty hours. Move the PivotChart to a new sheet named **PivotChart**.

f. Add the title **Warranty Hours** above the chart .

g. Change the PivotChart filter to display hours where the work was not covered by a warranty. Edit the chart title to read **Nonwarranty Hours**.

h. Add your name to the center section of the PivotTable and PivotChart footers, then save the workbook. Preview and print both the PivotTable and the PivotChart.

i. Close the workbook and exit Excel.

▼ INDEPENDENT CHALLENGE 2

You are the owner of an art supply store called Portfolio based in Vancouver. You sell products at the store as well as online. You also take orders by phone from your catalog customers. You have been using Excel to maintain a sales summary for the second quarter sales of paint, brushes, and paper. You want to create a PivotTable to analyze and graph the sales in each category by month and type of order.

FIGURE L-25

a. Start Excel, open the file titled EX L-4.xlsx from the drive and folder where you store your Data Files, then save it as **Portfolio Sales**.

b. Create a PivotTable on a new worksheet named **PivotTable** that sums the sales amount for each category across the rows and each type of sale down the columns. Add the month field as an inner row label. Use Figure L-25 as a guide.

c. Move the month field to the Report Filter location. Display the sum of sales data for the month of April.

▼ INDEPENDENT CHALLENGE 2 (CONTINUED)

d. Turn off the grand totals for the columns. (*Hint*: Use the Grand Totals button on the Design tab and choose On for Rows Only.)

e. Change the summary function in the PivotTable to Average.

f. Format the sales values using the Currency format with no decimal places and the $ English (Canada) symbol.

g. Format the PivotTable using the Pivot Style Dark 7.

h. On the Sales worksheet, change the April online paint sales in cell D2 to $53,225. Update the PivotTable to reflect this increase in sales.

i. Sort the average sales of brushes from smallest to largest values.(*Hint*: Be sure to select the Left to Right option button in the Sort by Value dialog box.)

j. Create a stacked column PivotChart report for the average April sales data for all three types of sales.

k. Change the PivotChart to display the June sales data.

l. Move the PivotChart to a new sheet and name the chart sheet **PivotChart**.

m. Add the title **Average June Sales** above your chart .

Advanced Challenge Exercise

- Filter the PivotTable to display both the April and May sales data.
- Remove the Row Labels and Column Labels headers in cells A4 and B3 using the Field Headers button.
- Check the PivotChart to be sure that the new data has been added, and change the chart title to describe the charted sales.

n. Add your name to the center section of the PivotTable and PivotChart worksheet footers, save the workbook, then print the PivotTable and the PivotChart.

o. Close the workbook and exit Excel.

▼ INDEPENDENT CHALLENGE 3

You manage Motivation Travel, a national travel agency that specializes in incentive travel for North American corporations with offices in the United States and Canada. Management has asked you to provide a summary table showing information on your sales staff, including their locations, status, and titles. You have been using Excel to keep track of the staff in the San Francisco, Los Angeles, Chicago, Minneapolis, Toronto, Montreal, Vancouver, Boston, and New York offices. Now you will create a PivotTable and PivotChart summarizing this information.

a. Start Excel, open the file titled EX L-5.xlsx from the drive and folder where you store your Data Files, then save it as **Travel Employees**.

b. On a new worksheet, create a PivotTable that lists the number of employees in each city, with the names of the cities listed across the columns, the titles listed down the rows, and the status indented below the titles. (*Hint*: Remember that the default summary function for cells containing text is Count.) Use Figure L-26 as a guide. Rename the new sheet **PivotTable**.

c. Change the structure of the PivotTable to display the data as shown in Figure L-27.

d. Add a report filter using the region field. Display only the U.S. employees.

FIGURE L-26

3	Count of Last Name	Column Labels										
4	Row Labels	Boston	Chicago	Los Angeles	Minneapolis	Montreal	New York	San Francisco	Toronto	Vancouver	Grand Total
5	⊟ Sales Manager		1	2	1	2	1	2	3	3	1	16
6	Full-time			2	1	1	1	2	2	2	1	12
7	Part-time	1			1			1	1		4
8	⊟ Sales Representative	4	2	5	2	4	7	7	3	3	37
9	Full-time	3	1	4	1	3	5	5	2	2	26
10	Part-time	1	1	1	1	1	2	2	1	1	11
11	Grand Total	5	4	6	4	5	9	10	6	4	53

FIGURE L-27

3	Count of Last Name	Column Labels		
4	Row Labels	Full-time	Part-time	Grand Total
5	⊟ Sales Manager	12	4	16
6	Boston		1	1
7	Chicago	2		2
8	Los Angeles	1		1
9	Minneapolis	1	1	2
10	Montreal	1		1
11	New York	2		2
12	San Francisco	2	1	3
13	Toronto	2	1	3
14	Vancouver	1		1
15	⊟ Sales Representative	26	11	37
16	Boston	3	1	4
17	Chicago	1	1	2
18	Los Angeles	4	1	5
19	Minneapolis	1	1	2
20	Montreal	3	1	4
21	New York	5	2	7
22	San Francisco	5	2	7
23	Toronto	2	1	3
24	Vancouver	2	1	3
25	Grand Total	38	15	53

▼ INDEPENDENT CHALLENGE 3 (CONTINUED)

e. Rearrange the fields on the PivotTable to create the PivotChart shown in Figure L-28. Move the chart to its own sheet named **PivotChart**.

FIGURE L-28

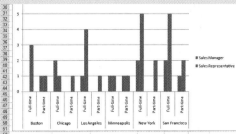

f. Add the title **U.S. Sales Staff** above the chart .

g. Add the Pivot Style Light 14 format to the PivotTable.

h. Insert a new row in the Employees worksheet above row 7. In the new row, add information reflecting the recent hiring of Cathy Crosby, a full-time sales manager at the Boston office. Update the PivotTable to display the new employee information.

i. Add the label **Total San Francisco Staff** in cell G1 of the Employees sheet. Widen column G to fit the label.

j. Enter a function in cell H1 that retrieves the total number of employees located in San Francisco from the PivotTable. Change the page orientation of the Employees sheet to landscape.

Advanced Challenge Exercise

- Filter the Row Labels of the PivotTable to display only the cities of Boston and San Francisco.
- Filter the Column Labels of the PivotTable to display only the sales representatives.
- Verify that the number of San Francisco employees on the Employees sheet is now seven.

k. Add your name to the center section of all three worksheet footers, save the workbook, then print the PivotTable, the first page of the Employee worksheet, and the PivotChart. Close the workbook and exit Excel.

▼ REAL LIFE INDEPENDENT CHALLENGE

PivotTables can be effective tools for analyzing your personal investments. You will use a PivotTable and a PivotChart to represent the market trends for four stocks by summarizing the performance of the stocks over five business days. You will use a PivotTable function to display each stock's weekly high, and you will use a PivotChart to represent each stock's five-day performance.

a. Start Excel, open the file EX L-6.xlsx , then save it as **My Stocks** in the drive and folder where you save your Data Files.

b. If you have stock information available you can replace the data in the file with your own data.

c. Create a PivotTable on a new worksheet that sums the stock prices for each stock across the rows and for each day down the columns. Rename the PivotTable sheet **PivotTable**.

d. Format the sales figures as Currency with two decimal places and apply the Pivot Style Light 18 format.

e. Turn off the grand totals for both the rows and columns.

f. Add the Exchange field to the Report Filter area of the PivotTable. Display only the NASDAQ data, then redisplay the data from both exchanges.

g. Create a clustered column PivotChart report from your data. Move the PivotChart to its own sheet named **PivotChart**. Change the column chart to a clustered bar chart. (*Hint*: Use the Change Chart Type button).

h. Add grand totals for the rows of the PivotTable. Change the summary function to MAX, then change the label in cell G4 from Grand Total to **Highest Price**. Widen column G to fit the label.

i. Enter the label **Highest Price** in cell F1 of the Stocks sheet. Widen column F to fit the label. Enter the VZ stock symbol in cell F2. If you are using your own data, enter one of your stock symbols in cell F2.

j. Enter a function in cell G2 that retrieves the highest price for the stock in cell F2 over the past five days from the PivotTable.

k. Display grand totals for both the rows and columns of the PivotTable. (*Hint*: Click the Grand Totals button, then click On for Rows and Columns.)

l. Change the structure of the PivotTable, moving the Day field to the Row (Labels) Area and Stock to the Column (Labels) Area. Verify that the highest price for the VZ stock (or your own stock if you are using personal data) is still correct on the Stocks worksheet.

m. Change the PivotChart type to a line.

n. Add your name to the center section of each worksheet footer, save the workbook, then print the PivotTable, the Stocks sheet, and the PivotChart. Close the workbook and exit Excel.

▼ VISUAL WORKSHOP

Open the file EX L-7.xlsx from the drive and folder where you store your Data Files, then save it as **Mortgages**. Using the data in the workbook, create the PivotTable shown in Figure L-29. (*Hint*: The PivotTable has been formatted using the Pivot Style Medium 6.) Add your name to the PivotTable sheet footer, then preview and print the PivotTable. Save the workbook, then close the workbook and exit Excel.

FIGURE L-29

	Sum of Sales	Column Labels ▼			
3	Sum of Sales	Column Labels ▼			
4	Row Labels ▼	Jan	Feb	Mar	Grand Total
5	⊟ NY				
6	Home Equity	$39,027,554	$28,011,550	$77,020,776	$144,059,880
7	Mortgage	$70,518,444	$50,027,452	$40,025,444	$160,571,340
8	Refinance	$8,018,009	$3,015,222	$11,025,664	$22,058,895
9	⊟ Miami				
10	Home Equity	$21,045,444	$19,002,445	$40,048,442	$80,096,331
11	Mortgage	$25,043,225	$80,489,557	$19,045,454	$124,578,236
12	Refinance	$2,742,221	$9,030,458	$9,049,554	$20,822,233
13	⊟ DC				
14	Home Equity	$15,505,377	$67,508,511	$62,504,845	$145,518,733
15	Mortgage	$17,505,645	$30,503,133	$38,515,452	$86,524,230
16	Refinance	$4,511,899	$6,505,556	$8,504,845	$19,522,300
17	Grand Total	$203,917,818	$294,093,884	$305,740,476	$803,752,178
18					

Exchanging Data with Other Programs

In a Windows environment, you can freely exchange data among Excel and most other Windows programs, a process known as **integration**. In this unit, you plan a data exchange between Excel and other Microsoft Office programs. Quest's upper management has asked Kate Morgan, the vice president of sales, to research the possible purchase of Culinary Adventures, a small travel company specializing in culinary tours for corporate clients, small businesses, and individual customers. Kate is reviewing the broker's files and developing a presentation on the feasibility of acquiring the company. To complete this project, Kate asks you to help set up the exchange of data between Excel and other programs.

OBJECTIVES

Plan a data exchange

Import a text file

Import a database table

Insert a graphic file in a worksheet

Embed a workbook in a Word document

Link a workbook to a Word document

Link an Excel chart to a PowerPoint slide

Import a table into Access

Planning a Data Exchange

Because the tools available in Microsoft Office programs are designed to be compatible, exchanging data between Excel and other programs is easy. The first step involves planning what you want to accomplish with each data exchange. Kate asks you to use the following guidelines to plan data exchanges between Excel and other programs in order to complete the business analysis project.

DETAILS

To plan an exchange of data:

QUICK TIP

For more information on importable file formats, see the Help topics "File formats that are supported in Excel," "Data sources that you can access," and "Connect to (Import) external data."

- **Identify the data you want to exchange, its file type, and, if possible, the program used to create it**

  Whether the data you want to exchange is a graphics file, a database file, a worksheet, or consists only of text, it is important to identify the data's **source program** (the program used to create it) and the file type. Once you identify the source program, you can determine options for exchanging the data with Excel. Kate needs to analyze a text file containing the Culinary Adventures tour sales. Although she does not know the source program, Kate knows that the file contains unformatted text. A file that consists of text but no formatting is sometimes called an **ASCII** or **text** file. Because ASCII is a universally accepted file format, Kate can easily import an ASCII file into Excel. See Table M-1 for a partial list of other file formats that Excel can import. Excel can also import older file formats as well as templates, backup files, and workspace files that are easily accessible in Excel.

- **Determine the program with which you want to exchange data**

  Besides knowing which program created the data you want to exchange, you must also identify which program will receive the data, called the **destination program**. This determines the procedure you use to perform the exchange. You might want to insert a graphic object into an Excel worksheet or add a spreadsheet to a Word document. Kate received a database table of Culinary Adventures' corporate customers created with the Access database program. After determining that Excel can import Access tables and reviewing the import procedure, she imports the database file into Excel so she can analyze it using Excel tools.

- **Determine the goal of your data exchange**

  Windows offers two ways to transfer data within and between programs that allow you to retain some connection with the source program. These data transfer methods use a Windows feature known as **object linking and embedding**, or **OLE**. The data to be exchanged, called an **object**, may consist of text, a worksheet, or any other type of data. You use **embedding** to insert a copy of the original object in the destination document and, if necessary, to subsequently edit this data separately from the source document. This process is illustrated in Figure M-1. You use **linking** when you want the information you inserted to be updated automatically if the data in the source document changes. This process is illustrated in Figure M-2. Embedding and linking are discussed in more detail later in this unit. Kate has determined that she needs to use both object embedding and object linking for her analysis and presentation project.

- **Set up the data exchange**

  When you exchange data between two programs, it is often best to start both programs prior to starting the exchange. You might also want to tile the program windows on the screen either horizontally or vertically so that you can see both during the exchange. You will work with Excel, Word, Access, and PowerPoint when exchanging data for this project.

- **Execute the data exchange**

  The steps you use will vary, depending on the type of data you want to exchange. Kate is ready to have you start the data exchanges for the business analysis of Culinary Adventures.

FIGURE M-1: Embedded object

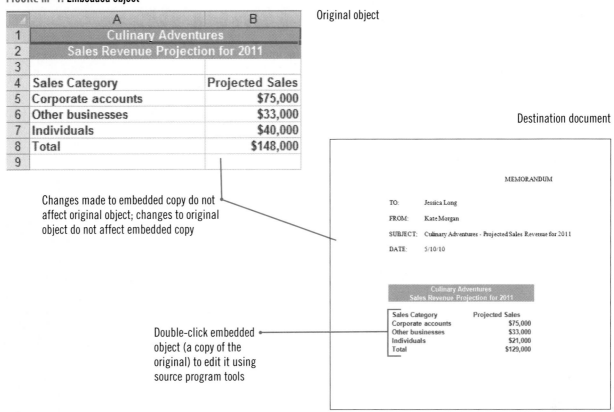

Original object

Destination document

Changes made to embedded copy do not affect original object; changes to original object do not affect embedded copy

Double-click embedded object (a copy of the original) to edit it using source program tools

FIGURE M-2: Linked object

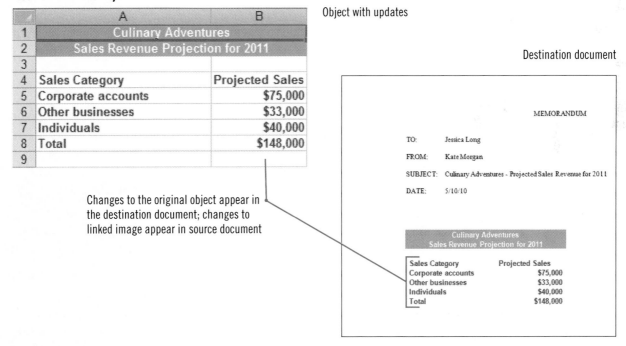

Object with updates

Destination document

Changes to the original object appear in the destination document; changes to linked image appear in source document

TABLE M-1: Importable file formats and extensions

file format	file extension(s)	file format	file extension(s)
Access	.mdb, .accdb	All Data Sources	.odc, .udl, .dsn
Text	.txt, .prn, .csv, .dif, .sylk	Quattro/Quattro Pro	.wb1, .wb3
Query	.iqy, .dqy, .oqy, .rqy	XML	.xml
Web page	.htm, .html .mht, .mhtml	dBASE	.dbf

Importing a Text File

You can import data created in other programs into Excel by opening the file, as long as Excel can read the file type. After importing the file, you use the Save As command on the Office menu to save the data in Excel format. Text files use a tab or space as the **delimiter**, or column separator, to separate columns of data. When you import a text file into Excel, the Text Import Wizard automatically opens and describes how text is separated in the imported file. Now that Kate has planned the data exchange, she wants you to import a tab-delimited text file containing region and profit data from Culinary Adventures.

STEPS

1. **Start Excel if necessary, click the Office button , click Open, then navigate to the folder containing your Data Files**

   The Open dialog box shows only those files that match the file types listed in the Files of type box—usually Microsoft Excel files. In this case, however, you're importing a text file.

2. **Click All Excel Files, click Text Files (*.prn; *.txt, *.csv), click EX M-1.txt, then click Open**

   The first Text Import Wizard dialog box opens, as shown in Figure M-3. Under Original data type, the Delimited option button is selected. In the Preview of file box, line 1 indicates that the file contains two columns of data: Region and Profit. No changes are necessary in this dialog box.

3. **Click Next**

   The second Text Import Wizard dialog box opens. Under Delimiters, Tab is selected as the delimiter, indicating that tabs separate the columns of incoming data. The Data preview box contains lines showing where the tab delimiters divide the data into columns.

4. **Click Next**

   The third Text Import Wizard dialog box opens with options for formatting the two columns of data. Under Column data format, the General option button is selected. This is the best formatting option for text mixed with numbers.

5. **Click Finish**

   Excel imports the text file into the blank worksheet as two columns of data: Region and Profit.

6. **Maximize the Excel window if necessary, click , point to Save As, click Excel workbook, in the Save As dialog box navigate to the folder containing your Data Files, change the filename to Culinary Adventures, then click Save**

   The file is saved as an Excel workbook, and the new name appears in the title bar. The sheet tab automatically changes to the name of the imported file, EX M-1. The worksheet information would be easier to read if it were formatted and if it showed the total profit for all regions.

7. **Double-click the border between the headers in Columns A and B, click cell A8, type Total Profit, click cell B8, click the Sum button Σ in the Editing group, then click the Enter button ✓ on the Formula Bar**

8. **Rename the sheet tab Profit Information, center the column labels, apply bold formatting to them, format the data in column B using the Currency style with the $ symbol and no decimal places, then click cell A1**

   Figure M-4 shows the completed worksheet, which analyzes the text file data you imported into Excel.

9. **Add your name to the center section of the worksheet footer, save the workbook, preview and print the worksheet, then close the workbook**

FIGURE M-3: First Text Import Wizard dialog box

Original data
is delimited

Two column
headings

Preview of
file data

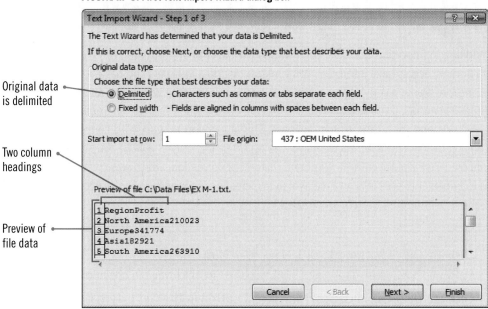

FIGURE M-4: Completed worksheet with imported text file

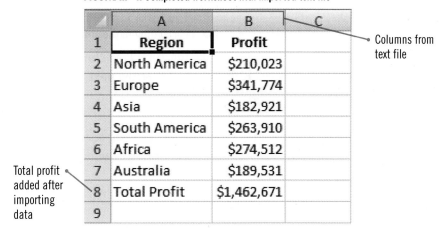

Columns from
text file

Total profit
added after
importing
data

Importing files using other methods

Another way to open the Text Import Wizard to import a text file into Excel is to click the Data tab, click the Get External Data button, click From Text, select a data source in the Import Text File dialog box, then click Import. You can also drag the icon representing a text file on the Windows desktop into a blank worksheet window ; Excel will create a worksheet from the data without using the Wizard.

Importing a Database Table

In addition to importing text files, you can also use Excel to import data from database tables. To import data from an Access table into Excel, you can copy the data in Access and paste it into an Excel worksheet. This method places a copy of the Access data into Excel; the data will not be refreshed in Excel if changes are made in Access. If you need the data in Excel to update when changes are made to it in Access, you create a connection, or a **link**, to the database. This allows you to work with current data in Excel without recopying the data from Access whenever the Access data changes. ▰▰▰▰▰ Kate received a database table containing Culinary Adventures' corporate customer information, which was created with Access. She asks you to import this table into an Excel workbook, creating a connection to the Access data. She would also like the data formatted, sorted, and totaled.

STEPS

1. **Click the Office button ⊙, click New, then click Create**
   A new workbook opens, displaying a blank worksheet to which you can import the Access data.

2. **Click the Data tab, click the From Access button in the Get External Data group, then navigate to the folder containing your Data Files**

3. **Click EX M-2.accdb, click Open, then click OK in the Import Data dialog box**
   Excel inserts the Access data into the worksheet as a table with the table style Medium 9 format applied, as shown in Figure M-5.

4. **Rename the sheet tab Customer Information, then format the data in columns F and G with the Number format, using commas and no decimal places**
   You are ready to sort the data using the values in column G.

5. **Click cell G1, click the Data tab, then click the Sort A to Z button ⿻ in the Sort & Filter group**
   The records are reorganized in ascending order according to the amount of the 2010 orders.

6. **Click the Table Tools Design tab, click the Total Row check box in the Table Style Options group to select it, click cell F19, click the list arrow next to cell F19, select Sum from the drop-down list of functions, then click cell A1**
   Your completed worksheet should match Figure M-6.

7. **Add your name to the center section of the worksheet footer, save the workbook as Customer Information, then preview and print the worksheet in landscape orientation**

FIGURE M-5: Imported Access table

	A	B	C	D	E	F	G	H
1	COMPANY NAME	CITY	STATE	CONTACT	PHONE	2009 ORDER	2010 ORDER	
2	Accutec	Jacksonville	FL	Lee Jones	904-334-4388	8500	9021	
3	Computer City	Pensacola	FL	Maria Lopez	850-335-9934	7250	5893	
4	Safety Insurance	Sarasota	FL	Sam Winston	941-334-4421	3212	4544	
5	Cornerstone Security	Naples	FL	Jack Wilcox	239-356-9943	1395	1544	
6	Jones & Jones Law	Clearwater	FL	Amy Fong	813-356-4595	1100	1311	
7	Miami Mutual Mortgage	Miami	FL	Nick Albert	305-332-3393	1499	1633	
8	Symphonic Equipment	Tampa	FL	Jenny Garcia	813-434-2232	2350	2543	
9	Vista Minerals	Orlando	FL	Priscilla Gomez	321-538-7789	1839	1922	
10	Northern Bank	Orlando	FL	Alex Hart	321-733-9877	1534	1699	
11	Recycle Paper	Jacksonville	FL	Mary Tyler	904-733-9987	1100	1234	
12	South Shore Pools	Pensacola	NM	Corey Olsen	850-233-4432	3254	3523	
13	First Investments	Naples	FL	Jeff Punatar	239-233-9939	2456	2588	
14	Gulf Art	Tampa	FL	Gilbert Hahn	813-334-2203	7234	7409	
15	Organic Foods	Orlando	FL	Lisa Sanchez	321-434-4432	8193	8233	
16	Toddler Toys	Miami	FL	Harry Yang	305-356-9987	6190	6433	
17	International Office	Sarasota	FL	Pam Miller	941-334-6785	5334	5511	
18	Turners Nurseries	Tampa	UT	Willy McFee	813-538-4493	3180	3688	
19								

FIGURE M-6: Completed worksheet containing imported data

	A	B	C	D	E	F	G	H
1	COMPANY NAME	CITY	STATE	CONTACT	PHONE	2009 ORDER	2010 ORDER	
2	Recycle Paper	Jacksonville	FL	Mary Tyler	904-733-9987	1,100	1,234	
3	Jones & Jones Law	Clearwater	FL	Amy Fong	813-356-4595	1,100	1,311	
4	Cornerstone Security	Naples	FL	Jack Wilcox	239-356-9943	1,395	1,544	
5	Miami Mutual Mortgage	Miami	FL	Nick Albert	305-332-3393	1,499	1,633	
6	Northern Bank	Orlando	FL	Alex Hart	321-733-9877	1,534	1,699	
7	Vista Minerals	Orlando	FL	Priscilla Gomez	321-538-7789	1,839	1,922	
8	Symphonic Equipment	Tampa	FL	Jenny Garcia	813-434-2232	2,350	2,543	
9	First Investments	Naples	FL	Jeff Punatar	239-233-9939	2,456	2,588	
10	South Shore Pools	Pensacola	NM	Corey Olsen	850-233-4432	3,254	3,523	
11	Turners Nurseries	Tampa	UT	Willy McFee	813-538-4493	3,180	3,688	
12	Safety Insurance	Sarasota	FL	Sam Winston	941-334-4421	3,212	4,544	
13	International Office	Sarasota	FL	Pam Miller	941-334-6785	5,334	5,511	
14	Computer City	Pensacola	FL	Maria Lopez	850-335-9934	7,250	5,893	
15	Toddler Toys	Miami	FL	Harry Yang	305-356-9987	6,190	6,433	
16	Gulf Art	Tampa	FL	Gilbert Hahn	813-334-2203	7,234	7,409	
17	Organic Foods	Orlando	FL	Lisa Sanchez	321-434-4432	8,193	8,233	
18	Accutec	Jacksonville	FL	Lee Jones	904-334-4388	8,500	9,021	
19	Total					65,620	68,729	
20								

Data is sorted in ascending order for 2010 values

Order Totals

Inserting a Graphic File in a Worksheet

A graphic object (such as a drawing, logo, or photograph) can greatly enhance a worksheet's visual impact. You can insert a picture into a worksheet and then format it using the options on the Format tab. Kate wants you to insert the Quest logo at the top of the customer worksheet. The company's graphic designer has created the graphic and saved it in JPG format. You insert and format the image on the worksheet. You start by creating a space for the logo on the worksheet.

1. **Select rows 1 through 5, click the Home tab, then click the Insert button in the Cells group**
   Five blank rows appear above the header row, leaving space to insert the picture.

2. **Click cell A1, click the Insert tab, then click Picture in the Illustrations group**
   The Insert Picture dialog box opens. You want to insert a picture that already exists in a file. The file you will insert has a .jpg file extension, so it is called a "jay-peg" file. JPEG files can be viewed in a Web browser.

3. **Navigate to the folder containing your Data Files, click EX M-3.jpg, then click Insert**
   Excel inserts the image and activates the Format tab. The small circles around the picture's border are sizing handles. Sizing handles appear when a picture is selected; you use them to change the size of a picture.

4. **Position the pointer over the sizing handle in the logo's lower-right corner, then click and drag the corner up and to the left so that the logo's outline fits within rows 1 through 5**
   Compare your screen to Figure M-7. You decide to remove the logo's white background.

5. **With the image selected, click the Recolor button in the Adjust group, click Set Transparent Color, then click the white background on the logo**
   You decide that the logo will be more visually interesting with a frame and a border color.

6. **With the image selected, click the More button ⬒ in the Picture Styles group, preview the picture with the different styles, click the Beveled Oval, Black style (the fourth from the left in the second row), click the Picture Border button in the Picture Styles group, then click Blue, Accent 1, Darker 25% in the Theme Colors group**
   You decide to add a glow to the image.

7. **Click the Picture Effects button in the Picture Styles group, point to Glow, point to More Glow Colors, click Blue, Accent 1, Lighter 80% in the Theme Colors group, then resize the logo as necessary to fit it in rows 1 through 5**
   Compare your worksheet to Figure M-8.

8. **Save the workbook, preview and print the worksheet, close the workbook, then exit Excel**

FIGURE M-7: Logo resized

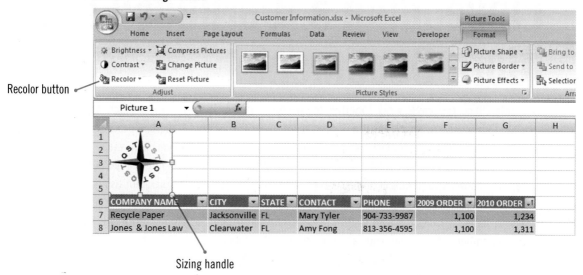

Recolor button

Sizing handle

FIGURE M-8: Worksheet with formatted picture

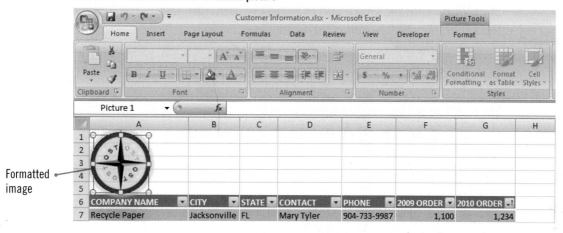

Formatted image

Formatting SmartArt graphics

SmartArt graphics provide another way to visually communicate information on a worksheet. Excel offers various layout templates that provide different ways to display your content. These layouts are easy to change, allowing you to see your graphic information in many different formats. To insert a SmartArt graphic into a worksheet, click the Insert tab, then click the SmartArt button in the Illustrations group. The Choose a SmartArt Graphic dialog box allows you to choose a layout from seven categories: List, Process, Cycle, Hierarchy, Relationship, Matrix, and Pyramid. The SmartArt dialog box also provides descriptions of the type of information that is appropriate for each layout. After you choose a layout, a graphic template appears along with a text entry area on the left side. As you enter text in the text entry area, the graphic automatically resizes to fit the text. If you decide to change your graphic to a different layout, the SmartArt Tools Design tab allows you to select a new layout from the Layouts group. You can easily see what your graphic will look like in another format by using Live Preview. The SmartArt Tools Design tab also

allows you to choose from a selection of SmartArt styles and to change the graphic's colors in SmartArt Styles group. You can add effects to SmartArt graphics by clicking the SmartArt Tools Format tab, clicking the Shape Effects button in the Shape Styles group, and selecting Shadow, Reflection, Glow, Soft Edges, Bevel, or 3-D Rotation. Figure M-9 shows examples of two SmartArt graphics.

FIGURE M-9: SmartArt graphics

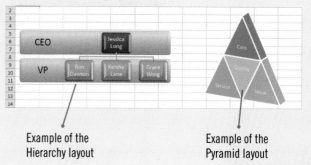

Example of the Hierarchy layout

Example of the Pyramid layout

Embedding a Workbook in a Word Document

Microsoft Office programs work together to make it easy to copy an object (such as text, data, or a graphic) in a source program and then insert it into a document in a different program (the destination program). If you insert the object using a simple Paste command, however, you retain no connection to the source program. That's why it is often more useful to embed objects rather than simply paste them. Embedding allows you to edit an Excel workbook from within a different program using Excel commands and tools. If you send a Word document with an embedded workbook to another person, you do not need to send a separate Excel file with it. All the necessary information is embedded in the Word document. When you embed information, you can either display the data itself or an icon representing the data; users double-click the icon to view the embedded data. ▓▓▓▓ Kate decides to update Jessica Long, the CEO of Quest, on the project status. She asks you to prepare a Word memo that includes the projected sales workbook embedded as an icon. You begin by starting the Word program and opening the memo.

STEPS

1. **Start Word, click the Office button 🔘, click Open, navigate to the folder containing your Data Files, click EX M-4.docx, then click Open**

   The memo opens in Word.

2. **Click 🔘, click Save As, navigate to the folder containing your Data Files, change the file name to Culinary Adventures Sales Memo, then click Save**

   You want to embed the workbook below the last line of the document.

3. **Press [Ctrl][End], click the Insert tab, click Object in the Text group, then click the Create from File tab**

   Figure M-10 shows the Create from File tab in the Object dialog box. You need to indicate the file you want to embed.

4. **Click Browse, navigate to the folder containing your Data Files, click EX M-5.xlsx, click Insert, select the Display as icon check box**

   You will change the icon label to a more descriptive name.

5. **Click Change Icon, select the text in the Caption textbox, type Projected Sales, then click OK twice**

   The memo contains an embedded copy of the sales projection data, displayed as an icon, as shown in Figure M-11.

6. **Double-click the Projected Sales icon on the Word memo, then maximize the Excel window and the worksheet window if necessary**

   The Excel program starts and displays the embedded worksheet, with its location displayed in the title bar, as shown in Figure M-12. Any changes you make to the embedded object using Excel tools are not reflected in the source document. Similarly, if you open the source document in the source program, changes you make are not reflected in the embedded copy.

7. **Click 🔘, click Close & Return to Culinary Adventures Sales Memo.docx, exit Excel, click 🔘, then click Save to save the memo**

FIGURE M-10: Object dialog box

Click this tab to embed an existing file

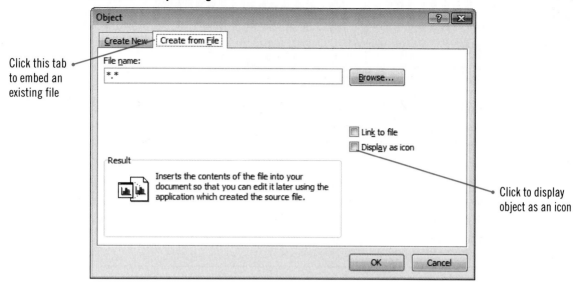

Click to display object as an icon

FIGURE M-11: Memo with embedded workbook

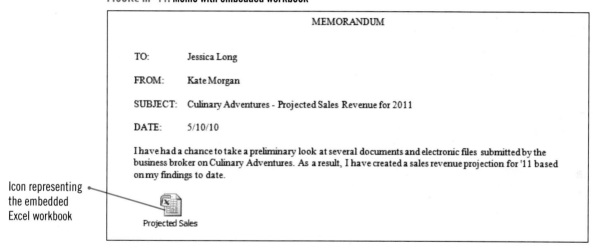

Icon representing the embedded Excel workbook

FIGURE M-12: Embedded worksheet opened in Excel

Location of the embedded worksheet

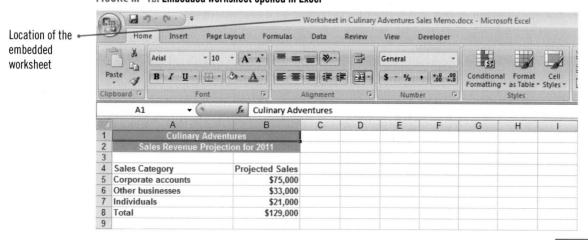

Linking a Workbook to a Word Document

Linking a workbook to another file retains a connection with the original document as well as the original program. When you link a workbook to another program, the link contains a connection to the source document so that, when you double-click it, the source document opens for editing. Once you link a workbook to another program, any changes you make to the original workbook (the source document) are reflected in the linked object. ▰▰▱▱ Kate realizes she may be making some changes to the workbook she embedded in the memo to Jessica. To ensure that these changes will be reflected in the memo, she feels you should use linking instead of embedding. She asks you to delete the embedded worksheet icon and replace it with a linked version of the same workbook.

STEPS

QUICK TIP

If you want to link part of an existing worksheet to another file, you can copy the worksheet information that you want to link, go to the destination document, click the Paste button list arrow in the Clipboard group, click Paste Special, then click Paste link to paste the link as a Microsoft Office Excel Worksheet Object in the Paste Special dialog box.

1. **With the Word memo still open, click the** Projected Sales Worksheet icon **to select it if necessary, then press** [Delete]

   The embedded workbook is removed. The linking process is similar to embedding.

2. **Make sure the insertion point is below the last line of the memo, click the** Insert tab**, click** Object **in the Text group, then click the** Create from File tab **in the Object dialog box**

3. **Click** Browse**, navigate to the folder containing your Data Files, click** EX M-5.xlsx**, click** Insert**, select the** Link to file check box**, then click** OK

   The memo now displays a linked copy of the sales projection data, as shown in Figure M-13. In the future, any changes made to the source file, EX M-5, will also be made to the linked copy in the Word memo. You verify this by making a change to the source file and viewing its effect on the Word memo.

4. **Click** ⊞**, click** Save**, then close the Word memo and exit Word**

   The sales projection for other businesses has changed to $40,000.

5. **Start Excel, open the file** EX M-5.xlsx **from the drive and folder where you store your Data Files, click cell B6, type 40,000, then press** [Enter]

   You want to verify that the same change was made automatically to the linked copy of the workbook.

QUICK TIP

If the Excel workbook hasn't been saved after making changes, extra cells are displayed when the links are updated.

6. **Start Word, open** Culinary Adventures Sales Memo **from the drive and folder where you store your Data Files, then click** Yes **if asked if you want to update the document's links**

   The memo displays the new value for other businesses, and the total has been updated as shown in Figure M-14.

7. **Click the** Insert tab**, click the** Header button **in the Header & Footer group, click** Edit Header**, type your name in the Header area, then click the** Close Header and Footer button **in the Close group**

8. **Save the Word memo, preview and print it, then close the file and exit Word**

9. **Close the Excel worksheet without saving it, then exit Excel**

FIGURE M-13: Memo with linked data

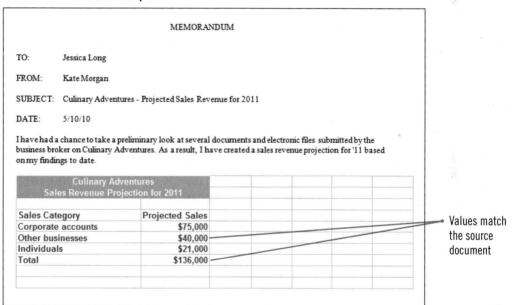

MEMORANDUM

TO: Jessica Long

FROM: Kate Morgan

SUBJECT: Culinary Adventures - Projected Sales Revenue for 2011

DATE: 5/10/10

I have had a chance to take a preliminary look at several documents and electronic files submitted by the business broker on Culinary Adventures. As a result, I have created a sales revenue projection for '11 based on my findings to date.

Linked data →

Culinary Adventures Sales Revenue Projection for 2011	
Sales Category	Projected Sales
Corporate accounts	$75,000
Other businesses	$33,000
Individuals	$21,000
Total	$129,000

FIGURE M-14: Memo with link updated

MEMORANDUM

TO: Jessica Long

FROM: Kate Morgan

SUBJECT: Culinary Adventures - Projected Sales Revenue for 2011

DATE: 5/10/10

I have had a chance to take a preliminary look at several documents and electronic files submitted by the business broker on Culinary Adventures. As a result, I have created a sales revenue projection for '11 based on my findings to date.

Culinary Adventures Sales Revenue Projection for 2011	
Sales Category	Projected Sales
Corporate accounts	$75,000
Other businesses	$40,000
Individuals	$21,000
Total	$136,000

→ Values match the source document

Managing links

When you change a source file, the link is updated automatically when you open the destination document. You can change the automatic update of links and manage the links by clicking the Office button, pointing to Prepare, and clicking Edit Links to Files. The Links dialog box opens, allowing you to change a link's update from automatic to manual and change the alert that users see when they open the file containing the link. The Links dialog box also allows you to change the link source, permanently break a link, open the source file, and manually update a link. If you send your linked files to another user, the links will be broken because the linked file path references the local machine where you inserted the links. Because the file path will not be valid on the recipient user's machine, the links will no longer be updated when the user opens the destination document.

To correct this, recipients who have both the destination and source documents can use the Links dialog box to change the link's source in the destination document to their own machines. Then the links will be automatically updated when they open the destination document in the future.

Linking an Excel Chart to a PowerPoint Slide

Microsoft PowerPoint is a **presentation graphics** program that you can use to create slide show presentations. PowerPoint slides can include a mix of text, data, and graphics. Adding an Excel chart to a slide can help to illustrate data and give your presentation more visual appeal. ▰▰▰▰ Kate asks you to add an Excel chart to one of the PowerPoint slides, illustrating the 2011 sales projection data. She wants you to link the chart in the PowerPoint file.

STEPS

1. **Click the** Start button **on the taskbar, point to** All Programs, **click** Microsoft Office, **click** Microsoft Office PowerPoint 2007, **click the** Office button 🔘, **click** Open, **navigate to the folder containing your Data Files, click** EX M-6.pptx, **then click** Open

   The presentation appears in Normal view and contains three panes, as shown in Figure M-15.

2. **Click** 🔘, **click** Save As, **navigate to the folder containing your Data Files, change the file-name to** Management Presentation, **then click** Save

   You need to open the Excel file and copy the chart that you will paste in the PowerPoint presentation.

TROUBLE

If you don't see Copy on the short-cut menu, you may have clicked the Plot area rather than the Chart area. Clicking the white area surrounding the pie will display the Copy command on the menu.

3. **Start Excel, open the file** EX M-7.xlsx **from the drive and folder where you store your Data Files, right-click the** Chart Area **on the Chart sheet, click** Copy **on the Shortcut menu, then click the** PowerPoint program button **on the taskbar**

   You need to add an Excel chart to Slide 2, "2011 Sales Projections." To add the chart, you first need to select the slide on which it will appear.

4. **Click** Slide 2 **in the Slides tab in the left pane, right-click** slide 2 **in the Slide pane, then click** Paste **on the Shortcut menu**

   After a moment, a pie chart illustrating the 2011 sales projections appears in the slide, with resizing handles. When a chart is pasted from Excel into PowerPoint, it is pasted as a link. The chart would look better if it was smaller and formatted using a style.

QUICK TIP

You can also move the selected chart using the arrow keys on the keyboard.

5. **Drag the lower-right corner sizing handle up and to the left to decrease the chart size, drag the Chart Area to move the chart to the center of the slide, resize the chart area width if necessary so the legend text doesn't wrap, click the** Chart Tools Design tab, **then click** Style 3 **in the Chart Styles gallery**

   Kate has learned that the sales projections for the Individuals category has increased based on late sales for the current year.

6. **Click the** Excel program button **on the taskbar, click the** Sales sheet tab, **change the** Individuals value in cell B7 to 45,000, **press** [Enter], **then click the** PowerPoint program button **on the taskbar**

   The chart updates to display the larger individual value in the Excel workbook. Slide Show view displays the slide on the full screen the way the audience will see it.

7. **Click the** Slide Show button 🖥 **on the status bar**

   The finished sales projection slide is complete, as shown in Figure M-16.

8. **Press** [Esc] **to return to Normal view, in the Slide pane click at the end of the Slide 2 text:** "2011 Sales Projections"; **press** [Enter], **type** by **followed by your name, deselect the chart title, then save the presentation**

9. **Click** 🔘, **click** Print, **under Print range select the** Current slide **option, click** OK, **close the presentation, close the Excel file without saving it, then exit PowerPoint and Excel**

FIGURE M-15: Presentation in Normal view

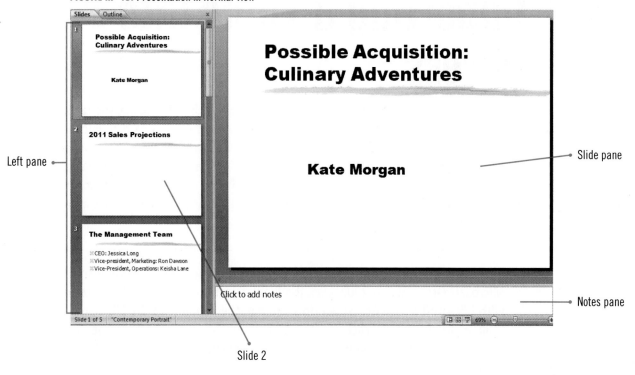

Left pane

Slide pane

Notes pane

Slide 2

FIGURE M-16: Completed Sales Projections slide in Slide Show view

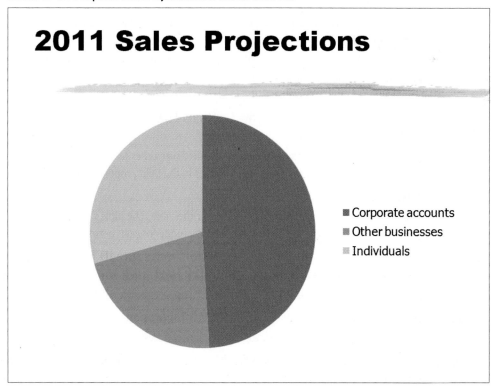

Importing a Table into Access

If you need to analyze an Excel table using the more extensive tools of a database, you can import the table into Microsoft Access, a database program. When you import Excel table data into Access, the data becomes an Access table using the same field names as the Excel table. In the process of importing an Excel table, Access specifies a primary key for the new table. A **primary key** is the field that contains unique information for each record (row) of information. Kate has just received a workbook containing salary information for the managers at Culinary Adventures organized in a table. She asks you to convert the Excel table to a Microsoft Access table.

STEPS

1. **Click the Start button on the taskbar, point to All Programs, click Microsoft Office, click Microsoft Office Access 2007, click the Blank Database button in the Getting Started with Microsoft Office Access window, change the filename in the File name text box to Culinary Management, click the Browse button 🖼 next to the filename, navigate to the folder containing your Data Files, click OK, then click Create**

   The database window for the Culinary Management database opens. You are ready to import the Excel table data.

2. **Click the External Data tab, click the Excel button in the Import group, click the Browse button, navigate to the folder containing your Data Files, click EX M-8.xlsx, then click Open**

   The Get External Data - Excel Spreadsheet dialog box opens, as shown in Figure M-17. This dialog box allows you to specify how you want the data to be stored in Access.

3. **If necessary click the Import the source data into a new table in the current database button, then click OK**

   The first Import Spreadsheet Wizard dialog box opens, with the Compensation worksheet selected, and a sample of the sheet data in the lower section. In the next dialog box, you indicate that you want to use the column headings in the Excel table as the field names in the Access database.

4. **Click Next, make sure the First Row Contains Column Headings check box is selected, then click Next**

   The Wizard allows you to review and change the field properties by clicking each column in the lower section of the window. You will not make any changes to the field properties.

5. **Click Next**

   The Wizard allows you to choose a primary key for the table. The table's primary key field contains unique information for each record; the ID Number field is unique for each person in the table.

   QUICK TIP
   Specifying a primary key allows you to retrieve data more quickly in the future.

6. **Click the Choose my own primary key option, make sure ID Number appears in the list box next to the selected option button, click Next, click Finish, then click Close**

   The name of the new Access table ("Compensation") appears in the All Tables pane.

7. **Double-click Compensation: Table in the All Tables pane**

   The data from the Excel worksheet is displayed in a new Access table, as shown in Figure M-18.

8. **Double-click the border between the Monthly Salary and Add New Field column headings, then use the last row of the table to enter your name in the First Name and Last Name columns and enter 0 for an ID Number**

9. **Click the Office button 🟠, click Save, click 🟠, click Print, click OK, close the table, then exit Access**

FIGURE M-17: Get External Data – Excel Spreadsheet dialog box

Data source

Options for storing data in Access

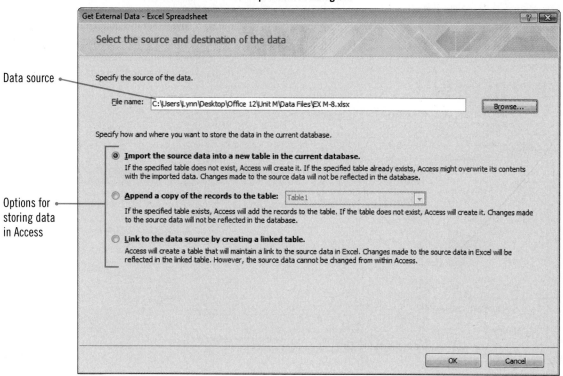

FIGURE M-18: Completed Access table

Access table

Primary key field

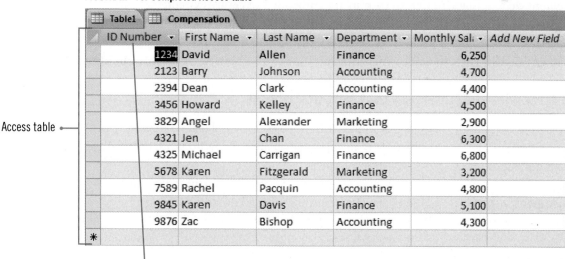

Practice

▼ CONCEPTS REVIEW

FIGURE M-19

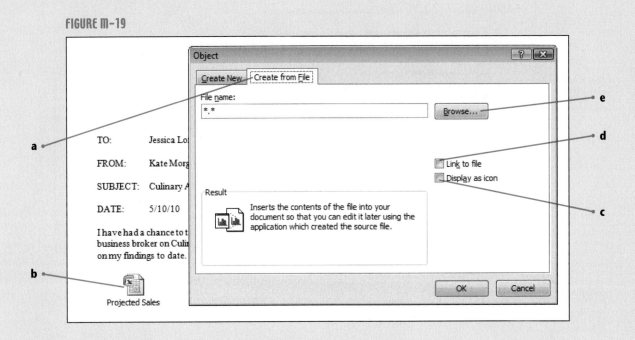

1. Which element do you click to insert an object that maintains a connection to the source document?
2. Which element do you click to find a file to be embedded or linked?
3. Which element do you double-click to display an embedded Excel workbook?
4. Which element do you click to insert an existing object into a Word document rather than creating a new file?
5. Which element do you click to embed information that can be viewed by double-clicking an icon?

Match each term with the statement that best describes it.

6. OLE
7. Linking
8. Destination document
9. Embedding
10. Source document
11. Presentation graphics program

a. File from which the object to be embedded or linked originates
b. Copies an object and retains a connection with the source program and source document
c. Document receiving the object to be embedded or linked
d. Data transfer method used in Windows programs
e. Copies an object and retains a connection with the source program only
f. Used to create slide shows

Select the best answer from the list of choices.

12. An ASCII file:

a. Contains a PowerPoint presentation.

b. Contains formatting but no text.

c. Contains text but no formatting.

d. Contains an unformatted worksheet.

13. An object consists of:

a. A worksheet only.

b. Text only.

c. Text, a worksheet, or any other type of data.

d. Database data only.

14. A column separator in a text file is called a(n):

a. Object.

b. Link.

c. Primary key.

d. Delimiter.

15. To view a workbook that has been embedded as an icon in a Word document, you need to:

a. Double-click the worksheet icon.

b. Drag the icon.

c. Click View, then click Worksheet.

d. Click File, then click Open.

16. A field that contains unique information for each record in a database table is called a(n):

a. Primary key.

b. ID Key.

c. First key.

d. Header key.

▼ SKILLS REVIEW

1. Import a text file.

a. Start Excel, open the tab-delimited text file titled EX M-9.txt from the drive and folder where you store your Data Files, then save it as a Microsoft Office Excel workbook with the name **Cosie Tea Shop**.

b. Widen the columns as necessary so that all the data is visible.

c. Format the data in columns B and C using the Accounting style with two decimal places.

d. Center the column labels and apply bold formatting, as shown in Figure M-20.

e. Add your name to the center section of the worksheet footer, save the workbook, print the worksheet in portrait orientation, then close the workbook.

FIGURE M-20

	A	B	C	D
1	**Item**	**Cost**	**Price**	
2	Pot, small	$ 10.55	$ 20.50	
3	Pot, large	$ 12.15	$ 28.00	
4	Pot, decorated	$ 17.55	$ 29.70	
5	Pot, china	$ 20.15	$ 31.90	
6	Basket, small	$ 14.95	$ 27.80	
7	Basket, large	$ 20.80	$ 33.90	
8	Kettle, small	$ 18.75	$ 28.45	
9	Kettle, large	$ 24.30	$ 33.75	
10	Mug, large	$ 1.95	$ 5.70	
11				

2. Import a database table.

a. In the Excel program, use the Get External Data button on the Data tab to import the Access Data File EX M-10.accdb from the drive and folder where you store your Data Files, then save it as a Microsoft Office Excel workbook named **Cosie Tea February Budget**.

b. Rename the sheet with the imported data **Budget**.

c. Change the column labels so they read as follows: **Budget Category**, **Budget Item**, **Month**, and **Amount Budgeted**.

d. Adjust the column widths as necessary.

e. Add a total row to the table to display the sum of the budgeted amounts in cell D26.

f. Format range D2:D26 using the Accounting style, the $ symbol, and no decimal places.

g. Save the workbook, and compare your screen to Figure M-21.

FIGURE M-21

	A	B	C	D
1	Budget Category	Budget Item	Month	Amount Budgeted
2	Compensation	Benefits	Feb	$ 62,000
3	Compensation	Bonuses	Feb	$ 49,110
4	Compensation	Commissions	Feb	$ 41,610
5	Compensation	Conferences	Feb	$ 47,654
6	Compensation	Promotions	Feb	$ 68,570
7	Compensation	Payroll Taxes	Feb	$ 44,980
8	Compensation	Salaries	Feb	$ 63,240
9	Compensation	Training	Feb	$ 59,600
10	Facility	Lease	Feb	$ 48,200
11	Facility	Maintenance	Feb	$ 61,310
12	Facility	Other	Feb	$ 58,230
13	Facility	Rent	Feb	$ 75,600
14	Facility	Telephone	Feb	$ 61,030
15	Facility	Utilities	Feb	$ 58,510
16	Supplies	Food	Feb	$ 61,430
17	Supplies	Computer	Feb	$ 45,290
18	Supplies	General Office	Feb	$ 42,520
19	Supplies	Other	Feb	$ 55,200
20	Supplies	Outside Services	Feb	$ 47,010
21	Equipment	Computer	Feb	$ 47,210
22	Equipment	Other	Feb	$ 41,450
23	Equipment	Cash Registers	Feb	$ 53,630
24	Equipment	Software	Feb	$ 63,590
25	Equipment	Telecommunications	Feb	$ 57,170
26	Total			$ 1,314,144
27				

3. Insert a graphic file in a worksheet.

  a. Add four rows above row 1 to create space for an image.

  b. In rows 1 through 4, insert the picture file EX M-11.gif from the drive and folder where you store your Data Files.

  c. Resize and reposition the picture as necessary to make it fit in rows 1 through 4.

  d. Add a style of Moderate Frame, White and change the border color to Dark Blue, Text2, Lighter 80%. Resize the picture to fit the image and the border in the first four rows.

  e. Compare your worksheet to Figure M-22, add your name to the center section of the worksheet footer, save the workbook, then print the worksheet.

4. Embed a workbook in a Word document.

  a. Start Word, create a memo header addressed to your instructor, enter your name in the From line, enter **February Salaries** as the subject, and enter the current date in the Date line.

  b. In the memo body, use the Object dialog box to embed the workbook EX M-12.xlsx from the drive and folder where your Data Files are stored, displaying it as an icon with the caption **Salary Details**.

  c. Save the document as **February Salaries** in the drive and folder where you store your Data Files, then double-click the icon to verify that the workbook opens.

  d. Close the workbook and return to Word.

  e. Compare your memo to Figure M-23 and print the memo.

5. Link a workbook to a Word document.

  a. Delete the icon in the memo body.

  b. In the memo body, link the workbook EX M-12.xlsx, displaying the data, not an icon.

  c. Save the document, then note that Mindy Guan's salary is $7,900. Close the document.

  d. Open the EX M-12 workbook in Excel and change Mindy Guan's salary to $8,900.

  e. Open the **February Salaries** document in Word, updating the links, and verify that Mindy Guan's salary has changed to $8,900 and that the new total salaries amount is $51,440, as shown in Figure M-24.

  f. Save the **February Salaries** document, print the memo, then close the document and exit Word.

  g. Close the EX M-12 workbook without saving changes, then exit Excel.

6. Link an Excel chart into a PowerPoint slide.

  a. Start PowerPoint.

  b. Open the PowerPoint file EX M-13.pptx from the drive and folder where your Data Files are stored, then save it as **Monthly Budget Meeting**.

  c. Display Slide 2, February Expenditures.

FIGURE M-22

	A	B	C	D
1				
2				
3				
4				
5	Budget Category	Budget Item	Month	Amount Budgeted
6	Compensation	Benefits	Feb	$ 62,000
7	Compensation	Bonuses	Feb	$ 49,110
8	Compensation	Commissions	Feb	$ 41,610
9	Compensation	Conferences	Feb	$ 47,654
10	Compensation	Promotions	Feb	$ 68,570
11	Compensation	Payroll Taxes	Feb	$ 44,980
12	Compensation	Salaries	Feb	$ 63,240
13	Compensation	Training	Feb	$ 59,600
14	Facility	Lease	Feb	$ 48,200
15	Facility	Maintenance	Feb	$ 61,310
16	Facility	Other	Feb	$ 58,230
17	Facility	Rent	Feb	$ 75,600
18	Facility	Telephone	Feb	$ 61,030
19	Facility	Utilities	Feb	$ 58,510
20	Supplies	Food	Feb	$ 61,430
21	Supplies	Computer	Feb	$ 45,290
22	Supplies	General Office	Feb	$ 42,520
23	Supplies	Other	Feb	$ 55,200
24	Supplies	Outside Services	Feb	$ 47,010
25	Equipment	Computer	Feb	$ 47,210
26	Equipment	Other	Feb	$ 41,450
27	Equipment	Cash Registers	Feb	$ 53,630

FIGURE M-23

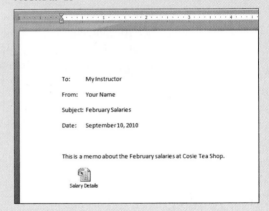

To: My Instructor
From: Your Name
Subject: February Salaries
Date: September 10, 2010

This is a memo about the February salaries at Cosie Tea Shop.

Salary Details

FIGURE M-24

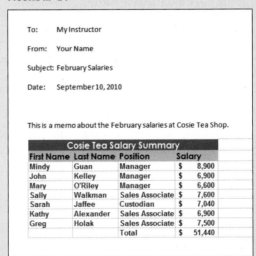

To: My Instructor
From: Your Name
Subject: February Salaries
Date: September 10, 2010

This is a memo about the February salaries at Cosie Tea Shop.

Cosie Tea Salary Summary				
First Name	Last Name	Position	Salary	
Mindy	Guan	Manager	$	8,900
John	Kelley	Manager	$	6,900
Mary	O'Riley	Manager	$	6,600
Sally	Walkman	Sales Associate	$	7,600
Sarah	Jaffee	Custodian	$	7,040
Kathy	Alexander	Sales Associate	$	6,900
Greg	Holak	Sales Associate	$	7,500
		Total	$	51,440

d. Link the chart from the Excel file EX M-14.xlsx from the drive and folder where you store your Data Files into Slide 2. Adjust the file's size and location as necessary to match Figure M-25.

e. View the slide in Slide Show view.

f. Press [Esc] to return to Normal view.

g. Replace the name Ann Lyons with your name on the first slide.

h. Save the presentation, print slides one and two as a handout (two slides to a page), then exit PowerPoint. (*Hint*: In the Print dialog box change Slides in the Print what section to Handouts, then select 2 in the Slides per page section under Handouts.)

7. Import a table into Access.

a. Start Access.

b. Create a blank database named **Budget** on the drive and folder where you store your Data Files.

c. Use the External Data tab to import the Excel table in the file EX M-15.xlsx from the drive and folder where you store your Data Files. Use the first row as column headings, store the data in a new table, let Access add the primary key, and use the default table name February Budget.

d. Open the February Budget table in Access and widen the columns as necessary to fully display the field names and field information.

e. Enter your name in the Budget category column of row 25 in the table, save the database file, compare your screen to Figure M-26, print the table, then exit Access.

FIGURE M-25

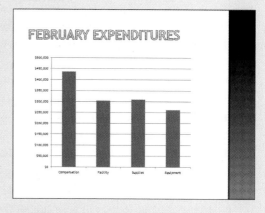

FIGURE M-26

▼ INDEPENDENT CHALLENGE 1

You are a real estate agent for the Ottawa branch of North Shore Realty. You have been asked to give a presentation to a group of agents about your sales in the past month. To illustrate your sales data, you will add an Excel chart to one of your slides, showing the different types of property sales and the sales amounts for each type.

a. Start Excel, create a new workbook, then save it as **April Sales** in the drive and folder where you store your Data Files.

b. Enter the property types and the corresponding sales amounts shown in Table M-2 into the April Sales workbook. Name the sheet with the sales data **Sales**.

c. Create a 3-D pie chart from the sales data on a new sheet named **Chart**. Apply the Office theme to the worksheet. Increase the font size to 14 in the legend. If a title appears on the chart, delete it. Your chart should look like Figure M-27.

d. Copy the chart to the clipboard.

e. Start PowerPoint, open the PowerPoint Data File EX M-16.pptx from the drive and folder where you store your Data Files, then save it as **Sales Presentation**.

f. Paste the Excel chart into Slide 2, adjusting its size and position as necessary.

g. View the slide in Slide Show view, then press [Esc] to end the show.

h. Edit Slide 1 to replace Joan Colbert with your name, then save the presentation.

i. Print Slides 1 and 2 as a handout with two slides to a page, then close the presentation and exit PowerPoint.

j. Save the workbook, then close the workbook, and exit Excel.

TABLE M-2

Property type	Sales
Condominium	$2,300,400
Single-family	$4,700,200
Commercial	$10,500,200

FIGURE M-27

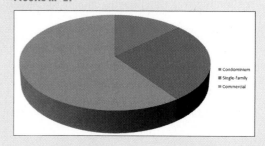

Excel 2007

▼ INDEPENDENT CHALLENGE 2

You are opening a new toy store, Ted's Toys, in San Francisco, California. The owner of SF Toys, a similar store in San Francisco, is retiring and has agreed to sell you a text file containing his list of supplier information. You need to import this text file into Excel so that you can manipulate the data. Later, you will convert the Excel file to an Access table so that you can give it to your business partner who is building a supplier database.

a. Start Excel, open the file EX M-17.txt from the drive and folder where your Data Files are stored, then save it as an Excel file named **Toy Suppliers**. (*Hint*: This is a tab-delimited text file.)

b. Adjust the column widths as necessary. Rename the worksheet **Suppliers**.

c. Create a table using data on the Suppliers sheet and apply the Table Style Dark 11 format.

d. Sort the worksheet data in ascending order, first by Item, then by Supplier. (*Hint*: Open the Sort dialog box by clicking the Sort button on the Data tab, selecting Item in the first Sort by text box, adding a level and clicking Supplier in the Then by text box.) Your worksheet should look like Figure M-28.

e. Add your name to the center section of the worksheet footer, print the worksheet in landscape orientation, save and close the workbook, then exit Excel.

FIGURE M-28

f. Start Access, create a new blank database on the drive and folder where you store your Data Files. Name the new database **Suppliers**.

g. Use the External Data tab to import the Excel file **Toy Suppliers** from the drive and folder where you store your Data Files. Use the column labels as the field names, store the data in a new table, let Access add the primary key, and accept the default table name.

h. Open the Suppliers table and AutoFit the columns.

i. Enter your name in the Supplier column in row 13, save and print the table in landscape orientation so it fits on one page (adjust column width as necessary), then close the table and exit Access. (*Hint*: You can change the orientation to landscape on the Print Preview tab.)

Advanced Challenge Exercise

- Create a copy of the Toy Suppliers.xlsx file with the name Toy Suppliers_ACE on the drive and folder where you store your Data Files.
- Using Access, create a new blank database named **Suppliers_ACE** on the drive and folder where your store your Data Files. Link the Excel data in the Toy Suppliers_ACE file to the Suppliers_ACE database file.
- Close the database file, open the Toy Suppliers_ACE.xlsx file and change the contact for the Cool Toys supplier to **J. Smith**. Save and close the Excel file.
- Open the Suppliers_ACE database and verify that the contact name was updated in the Suppliers table, then close the table and exit Access.

▼ INDEPENDENT CHALLENGE 3

You are the newly hired manager at Health Alliance, a mutual funds firm specializing in health care funds. An employee, Ed Woodman, has completed a two-year training period as an assistant and you would like to promote him to an associate position with a higher salary. You have examined the salaries of the other associates in the company and will present this information to the president, requesting permission to grant Ed a promotion and an increase in salary.

a. Start Word, open the Word file EX M-18.docx from the drive and folder where you store your Data Files, then save it as **Promotion**.

b. Add your name to the From line of the memo and change the date to the current date.

c. At the end of the memo, embed the workbook EX M-19.xlsx as an icon from the drive and folder where you store your Data Files. Change the caption for the icon to **Salaries**. Double-click the icon to verify that the workbook opens.

Exchanging Data with Other Programs

▼ INDEPENDENT CHALLENGE 3 (CONTINUED)

d. Close the workbook, return to Word, delete the Salaries icon and link the workbook EX M-19 to the memo, displaying the data, not an icon.

e. Save the Promotion memo and close the file.

f. Open the EX M-19 workbook and change Ed Woodman's salary to $54,000.

g. Open the Promotion memo, updating the links, and make sure Ed Woodman's salary is updated.

Advanced Challenge Exercise

■ Delete the worksheet at the bottom of the Promotion memo. Copy the range A1:D10 from Sheet1 of the EX M-19 workbook to the Clipboard.

■ Return to the Promotion memo and use the Paste Special dialog box to paste a link to the range A1:D10 from EX M-19 that is on the Clipboard. Use Figure M-29 as a guide. Save and close the memo.

■ Change Ed Woodman's salary to $55,000 in EX M-19. Verify the new salary information is displayed in the Promotion memo when the memo is opened.

FIGURE M-29

h. Save and print the memo.

i. Close the memo and exit Word.

j. Close EX M-19 without saving the change to Ed Woodman's salary, then exit Excel.

▼ REAL LIFE INDEPENDENT CHALLENGE

You decide to create a daily schedule of your pet's activities to give to the person who will care for your pet when you go on vacation. As part of this schedule, you record the times and corresponding activities that your pet engages in daily. You also record when medicine should be taken. You will include the schedule in a Word document that provides your contact information. You decide to link the workbook so that schedule changes will be reflected in the information you provide to the pet sitter.

a. Start Excel, open the file EX M-20.xlsx from the drive and folder where you store your Data Files, then save it as **Schedule**.

b. Use the structure of the worksheet to record your pet's schedule. Change the data in columns A and B to reflect your pet's times and activities. If you do not have any data to enter, use the data provided on the worksheet.

c. Save and close the Schedule workbook, then exit Excel.

d. Open the Data File EX M-21.docx from the drive and folder where you store your Data Files, then save it as **Contact Information**.

e. Enter your name at the bottom of the document. Change the document data to reflect your destination and contact information. If you do not have any data to enter, use the provided document data.

f. Below the line "Here is a schedule of Junior's daily activities:", create a link to Sheet1 of the Schedule workbook.

g. Save the file, then preview and print the Contact Information document.

h. Close the Word document, then exit Word.

Advanced Challenge Exercise

■ Open the Schedule.xlsx workbook from the drive and folder where you store your Data Files. Add four rows at the top of the worksheet and insert a picture of your pet. You can use the picture EX M-22.gif if you don't have a picture.

■ Resize the picture and move it to fit in the first four rows of the worksheet. Use the rotation options to flip the picture horizontally. (*Hint*: You can rotate a picture by clicking the Rotate button on the Picture Tools Format tab.)

■ Use the picture effects options to add a full reflection with an 8-point offset.

■ Save the workbook, then preview and print the worksheet.

■ Close the workbook and exit Excel.

▼ VISUAL WORKSHOP

Create the worksheet shown in Figure M-30 by importing the data from the Access database file EX M-23.accdb. If you don't have the ClipArt shown, add a ClipArt selection that is available on your computer. (*Hint*: The picture style is Beveled Matte, White and the picture border is Purple, Accent 4.) Enter your name in the center section of the worksheet footer, center the worksheet horizontally on the page, save the workbook as **Inventory**, then print the worksheet and exit Excel.

FIGURE M-30

Item Number	Category	Price	Store
1402	Desk	$40.99	Downtown
1412	Desk	$45.99	Downtown
1122	Floor	$129.99	Downtown
1128	Floor	$155.99	Downtown
1134	Floor	$141.99	Downtown
1126	Picture	$153.99	Downtown
1151	Sconce	$65.99	Downtown
1287	Sconce	$78.99	Downtown
1403	Sconce	$84.99	Downtown
1335	Table	$67.99	Downtown
1410	Table	$78.99	Downtown
1414	Table	$78.99	Downtown
1198	Ceiling	$89.99	Heights
1415	Desk	$25.99	Heights
1413	Sconce	$60.99	Heights
1221	Table	$96.99	Heights
1400	Table	$89.99	Heights
1409	Table	$76.99	Heights
1411	Table	$65.99	Heights
1124	Desk	$78.99	Uptown
1130	Desk	$37.99	Uptown
1172	Floor	$134.99	Uptown
1209	Outdoor	$40.99	Uptown
1132	Picture	$119.99	Uptown

Your Name

Sharing Excel Files and Incorporating Web Information

The Web as well as private networks are often used to share Excel files, allowing others to review, revise, and provide feedback on worksheet data. Information from the Web can easily be incorporated into workbooks, providing up-to-date information in the worksheets. Kate Morgan, the vice president of sales for Quest, wants to share information with corporate office employees and branch managers using the company's intranet and the Web.

OBJECTIVES

Share Excel files

Set up a shared workbook for
    multiple users

Track revisions in a shared workbook

Apply and modify passwords

Work with XML schemas

Import and export XML data

Run Web queries to retrieve
    external data

Import and export HTML data

Sharing Excel Files

Microsoft Excel provides many different ways to share spreadsheets with people in your office, in your organization, or anywhere on the Web. When you share workbooks, you have to consider how you will protect information that you don't want everyone to see and how you can control revisions others will make to your files. Some information you want to use might not be in Excel format. Because there is a great deal of information published on the Web in HTML format, Excel allows you to import HTML to your worksheets. XML is better suited than HTML for storing and exchanging data, so businesses store data in XML files and exchange XML data both internally and externally. Excel allows you to easily import XML data as well. You can export worksheet data to an HTML or XML file. You can also retrieve data from the Web using queries. Kate considers the best way to share her Excel workbooks with corporate employees and branch managers.

DETAILS

To share worksheet information, consider the following issues:

- **Allowing others to use a workbook**

  When you share Excel files with others, you need to set up your workbooks so that several users can **share** them, which means they can simultaneously open them from a network server, modify them electronically, and return their revisions to you for incorporation with others' changes. You can view each user's name and the date each change was made. Kate wants to obtain feedback on Quest sales data from the branch managers.

- **Controlling access to workbooks on a server**

  When you place a workbook on a network server, you will likely want to control who can open and change it. You can do this using Excel passwords. Kate assigns a password to her workbook and gives the workbook to the corporate staff and branch managers, along with the password, so only they can open the workbook and revise it.

- **HTML data**

  You can paste data from a Web page into a worksheet and then manipulate and format it using Excel. You can also save Excel workbook information in HTML format so it can be published on an intranet or on the Web. Kate decides to publish the worksheet with the North American sales information in HTML format on the company intranet, as shown in Figure N-1.

- **Working with XML data**

  You can import XML data into an Excel workbook. Once the data is in a workbook, you can manage and analyze it using Excel tools. You can also export Excel data in XML format to create an XML file. Storing data in XML format allows you to use it in different situations. For example, a company may store all of its sales data in an XML file and make different parts of the file available to various departments such as marketing and accounting. These departments can extract information that is relevant to their purposes from the file. A subset of the same XML file might be sent to vendors or other business associates who only require certain types of sales data stored in the XML file. Kate decides to import XML files that contain sales information from the Miami and New York branches to get a sales summary for Quest's eastern region.

- **Using an Excel query to retrieve data from the Web**

  You can use built-in Excel queries to import stock quotes and currency rates from the MSN Money Website. These queries import data from the Web into an Excel workbook, where you can organize and manipulate the information using Excel spreadsheet and graphics tools. Kate decides to use a query to get currency rate information for her analysis of the sales data from the Quest Canada branches, as shown in Figure N-2.

FIGURE N-1: North America sales information displayed in a Web browser

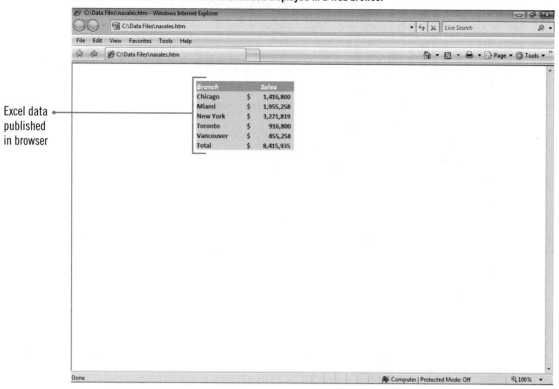

Excel data published in browser

Branch	Sales
Chicago	$ 1,416,800
Miami	$ 1,955,258
New York	$ 3,271,819
Toronto	$ 916,800
Vancouver	$ 855,258
Total	$ 8,415,935

FIGURE N-2: Data retrieved from the Web using a Web query

Excel worksheet with imported currency information

	A	B	C	D
1	**Currency Rates Provided by MSN Money**			
2	Click here to visit MSN Money			
3				
4	**Name**	**In US$**	**Per US$**	
5	United States Dollar (b) vs Argentine Peso Spot	0.32165	3.109	
6	Australian Dollar Futures Spot Price	0.74571	1.341	
7	Bahraini Dinar to US Dollar	2.6491	0.377	
8	Bolivian Boliviano to US Dollar	0.125	8	
9	Brazilian Real to US Dollar	0.45981	2.175	
10	British Pound Futures Spot Price	1.8713	0.534	
11	Canadian Dollar Futures Spot Price	0.89414	1.118	
12	United States Dollar (b) vs Chilean Peso Spot	0.00186	537	
13	Chinese Yuan to US Dollar	0.12639	7.912	
14	United States Dollar (b) vs Colombia Peso Spot	0.00042	2400	
15	United States Dollar (b) vs Cypriot Pound Spot	2.1716	0.461	
16	Czech Koruna to US Dollar	0.04473	22.357	
17	Danish Krone to US Dollar	0.16998	5.883	
18	United States Dollar (b) vs Ecuadorian Sucre Spot	0.00004	25030	
19	United States Dollar (b) vs Euro Spot	1.2674	0.789	
20	Hong Kong Dollar to US Dollar	0.12834	7.792	
21	United States Dollar (b) vs Hungary Forint Spot	0.00464	215.5	
22	Indian Rupee to US Dollar	0.02184	45.798	
23	United States Dollar (b) vs Indonesian Rupiah Spot	0.00011	9206	
24	Japanese Yen Futures Spot Price	0.00846	118.2	

Sheet1 / Sheet2 / Sheet3

Setting Up a Shared Workbook for Multiple Users

You can make an Excel file a **shared workbook** so that several users can open and modify it at the same time. This is useful for workbooks that you want others to review on a network server, where the workbook is equally accessible to all network users. When you share a workbook, you can have Excel keep a list of all changes to the workbook, which you can view and print at any time. Kate asks you to help her put a shared workbook containing customer and sales data on the company's network. She wants to get feedback from selected corporate staff and branch managers before presenting the information at the next corporate staff meeting. You begin by making her Excel file a shared workbook.

STEPS

1. **Start Excel, open the file** EX N-1.xlsx **from the drive and folder where you store your Data Files, then save it as** Sales Information

   The workbook with the sales information opens, displaying two worksheets. The first contains tour sales data for the Quest U.S. branches; the second is a breakdown of the branch sales by sales associate.

QUICK TIP

The Advanced tab of the Share Workbook dialog box allows you to specify the length of time the change history is saved and when the file will be updated with the changes.

2. **Click the** Review **tab, then click the** Share Workbook **button in the Changes group**

   The Share Workbook dialog box opens, as shown in Figure N-3.

3. **Click the** Editing **tab, if necessary**

   The dialog box lists the names of people who are currently using the workbook. You are the only user, so your name, or the name of the person entered as the computer user, appears, along with the current date and time.

QUICK TIP

You can remove users from the list by clicking their names and clicking Remove User.

4. **Click to select the check box next to** Allow changes by more than one user at the same time. This also allows workbook merging., **then click** OK

   A dialog box appears, asking if you want to save the workbook. This will resave it as a shared workbook.

5. **Click OK**

   Excel saves the file as a shared workbook. The title bar now reads Sales Information.xlsx [Shared], as shown in Figure N-4. This version replaces the unshared version.

Managing shared workbooks

A workbook remains shared as long as the Allow Changes by more than one user at the same time option is checked. Once you've obtained input from other users and no longer need to collaborate with them or keep a record of their changes, you can return a shared workbook to unshared status. To do this, click the Review tab, click the Share Workbook button in the Changes group, then deselect the Allow changes by more than one user at the same time option on the Editing tab of the Share Workbook dialog box.

FIGURE N-3: Share Workbook dialog box

Select to allow
multiple users
of the workbook
at the same time

Current users
of the workbook
are listed here

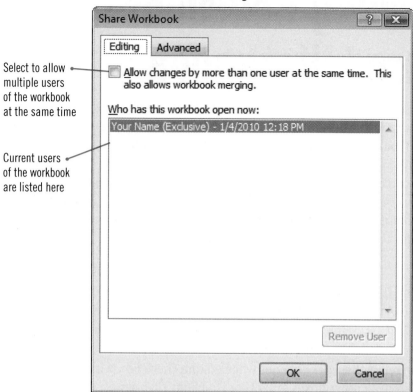

FIGURE N-4: Shared workbook

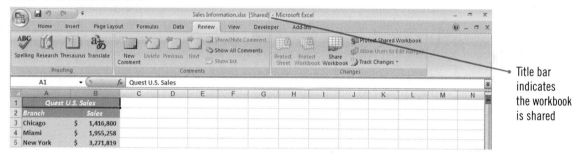

Title bar
indicates
the workbook
is shared

Merging workbooks

Instead of putting the shared workbook on a server, you might want to distribute copies to your reviewers via e-mail. Once everyone has entered their changes and returned their copies to you, you can merge the changed copies into one master workbook that will contain all the changes. Each copy you distribute must be designated as shared, and the Change History feature on the Advanced tab of the Share Workbook dialog box must be activated. Occasionally a conflict occurs when two users are trying to edit the same cells in a shared workbook. In this case, the second person to save the file will see a Resolve Conflicts dialog box and need to choose Accept Mine or Accept Other. To merge workbooks, you need to add the Compare and Merge Workbooks command to the Quick Access Toolbar by clicking the Office button, clicking Excel Options, and clicking Customize. Click All Commands in the Choose commands from list, click Compare and Merge Workbooks, click Add, then click OK. Once you get the changed copies back, open the master copy of the workbook, then click Compare and Merge Workbooks. The Select Files to Merge Into Current Workbook dialog box opens. Select the workbooks you want to merge (you can use the [Ctrl] key to select more than one workbook), then click OK.

Tracking Revisions in a Shared Workbook

When you share workbooks, it is often helpful to **track** modifications, or identify who made which changes. You can accept the changes you agree with, and if you disagree with any changes, you can reject them. When you activate the Excel change tracking feature, changes appear in a different color for each user. Each change is identified with the username and date. In addition to highlighting changes, Excel keeps track of changes in a **change history**, a list of all changes that you can place on a separate work-sheet so you can review them all at once. ▰▰▰▰ Kate asks you to set up the shared Sales Information workbook so that all future changes will be tracked. You will then open a workbook that is on the server and review the changes and the change history.

STEPS

1. **Click the Track Changes button in the Changes group, then click Highlight Changes**

   The Highlight Changes dialog box opens, as shown in Figure N-5, allowing you to turn on change tracking. You can also specify which changes to highlight and whether you want to display changes on the screen or save the change history in a separate worksheet.

2. **Click to select the Track changes while editing check box if necessary, remove check marks from all other boxes except for Highlight changes on screen, click OK, then click OK in the dialog box that informs you that you have yet to make changes**

   Leaving the When, Who, and Where check boxes blank allows you to track all changes.

   > **QUICK TIP**
   > Cells that other users change will appear in different colors.

3. **Click the Sales by Rep sheet tab, change the sales figure for Sanchez in cell C3 to 190,000, press [Enter], then move the mouse pointer over the cell you just changed**

   A border with a small triangle in the upper-left corner appears around the cell you changed, and a ScreenTip appears with your name, the date, the time, and details about the change, as shown in Figure N-6.

4. **Save and close the workbook**

5. **Open the file EX N-2.xlsx from the drive and folder where you store your Data Files, then save it as Sales Information Edits**

   Jose Silva has made changes to a version of this workbook. You want to view the details of these changes and accept the ones that appear to be correct.

   > **TROUBLE**
   > If you are working on a computer with a partitioned hard drive running Microsoft Vista and Microsoft Windows XP on different partitions, make sure you open the files and work with them on the same partition to avoid file sharing issues.

6. **Click the Review tab if necessary, click the Track Changes button in the Changes group, click Accept/Reject Changes, click the When check box in the Select Changes to Accept or Reject dialog box to deselect it, then click OK**

   You will accept the first four changes that Jose made to the workbook and reject his last change.

7. **Click Accept four times to approve the first four changes, then click Reject to undo Jose's fifth change**

8. **Click the Track Changes button in the Changes group, click Highlight Changes, click the When check box in the Highlight Changes dialog box to deselect it, click to select the List changes on a new sheet check box, then click OK**

   The History sheet appears, as shown in Figure N-7, with Jose's changes in a filtered list.

   > **QUICK TIP**
   > Because saving the file closes the History sheet, you need to print it before saving the workbook. If necessary, you can recreate the History sheet using the same steps you did earlier.

9. **Click the Insert tab, click the Header & Footer button in the Text group, click OK to unfreeze the sheet panes, enter your name in the center section of the History sheet header, print the History sheet, save the workbook, observe that the History sheet closes automatically, then close the workbook**

   The change history printout shows all of Jose's changes to the workbook.

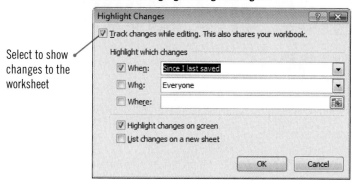

Select to show
changes to the
worksheet

FIGURE N-6: Tracked change

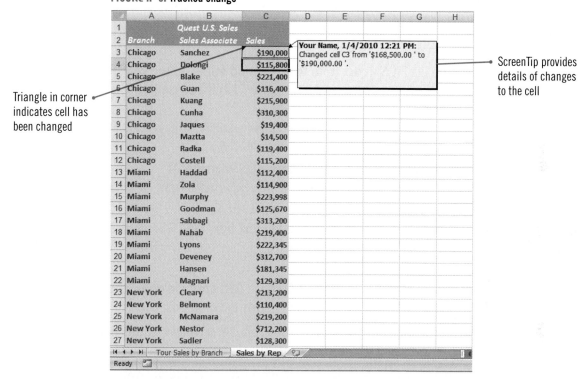

Triangle in corner
indicates cell has
been changed

ScreenTip provides
details of changes
to the cell

FIGURE N-7: History sheet tab with change history

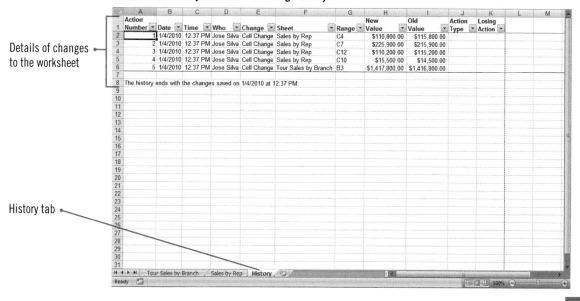

Details of changes
to the worksheet

History tab

Excel 2007

Applying and Modifying Passwords

When you place a shared workbook on a server, you may want to use a password so that only authorized people will be able to open it or make changes to it. However, it's important to remember that *if you lose your password, you will not be able to open or change the workbook.* Passwords are case sensitive, so you must type them exactly as you want users to type them, with the same spacing and using the same case. It is a good idea to include uppercase and lowercase letters and numbers in a password. ████ Kate wants you to put the workbook with sales information on one of the company's servers. You decide to save a copy of the workbook with two passwords: one that users will need to open it, and another that they will use to make changes to it.

STEPS

1. **Open the file EX N-1.xlsx from the drive and folder where you store your Data Files, click the Office button, click Save As, click the Tools list arrow in the bottom of the Save As dialog box, then click General Options**

   The General Options dialog box opens, with two password boxes: one to open the workbook, and one to allow changes to the workbook, as shown in Figure N-8.

2. **In the Password to open text box, type QSTmanager01**

   Be sure to type the letters in the correct cases. This is the password that users must type to open the workbook. When you enter passwords, the characters you type are masked with bullets (• • •) for security purposes.

QUICK TIP
You can press [Enter] rather than clicking OK after entering a password. This allows you to keep your hands on the keyboard.

3. **Press [Tab], in the Password to modify text box, type QSTsales02, then click OK**

   This is the password that users must type to make changes to the workbook. A dialog box asks you to verify the first password by reentering it.

4. **Enter QSTmanager01 in the first Confirm Password dialog box, click OK, enter QSTsales02 in the second Confirm Password dialog box, then click OK**

5. **Change the filename to Sales Information PW, navigate to the location where you store your Data Files, click Save, then close the workbook**

6. **Reopen the workbook Sales Information PW, enter the password QSTmanager01 when prompted for a password, click OK, then enter QSTsales02 to obtain write access**

   The Password dialog box is shown in Figure N-9. Obtaining write access for a workbook allows you to modify it.

7. **Click OK, change the sales figure for the Chicago branch in cell B3 to 1,500,000, then press [Enter]**

   You were able to make this change because you obtained write access privileges using the password "QSTsales02."

8. **Save and close the workbook**

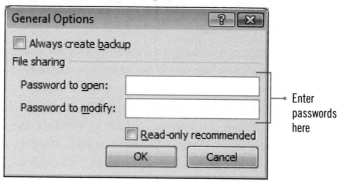

FIGURE N-8: General Options dialog box

Enter passwords here

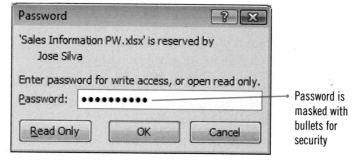

FIGURE N-9: Password entry prompt

Password is masked with bullets for security

Removing passwords

You can change or delete a workbook's password if you know what it is. Open the workbook, click the Office button, then click Save As. In the Save As dialog box, click the Tools list arrow, then click General Options. Double-click to highlight the symbols for the existing passwords in the Password to open or Password to modify text boxes, press [Delete], click OK, change the filename if desired, then click Save.

Working with XML Schemas

Using Excel you can import, export, and work with XML data. To import XML data, Excel requires a file called a schema that describes the structure of the XML file. A **schema** contains the rules for the XML file by listing all of the fields in the XML document and their characteristics, such as the type of data they contain. A schema is used to **validate** XML data, making sure the data follows the rules given in the file. Once a schema is attached to a workbook, a schema is called a map. When you **map** an element to a worksheet, you place the element name on the worksheet in a specific location. Mapping XML elements allows you to choose the XML data from a file that you want to work with in the worksheet. ████ Kate has been given XML files containing sales information from the U.S. branches. She asks you to prepare a workbook to import the sales representatives' XML data. You begin by adding a schema to a worksheet that describes the XML data.

STEPS

1. **Create a new workbook, save it as Sales Reps in the drive and folder where you store your Data Files, click the Developer tab, then click the Source button in the XML group**

   The XML Source pane opens. This is where you specify a schema, or map, to import. A schema has the extension .xsd. Kate has provided you with a schema she received from the IT department describing the XML file structure.

2. **Click the XML Maps button at the bottom of the task pane**

   The XML Maps dialog box opens, listing the XML maps or schemas in the workbook. There are no schemas in the Sales Reps workbook at this time, as shown in Figure N-10.

3. **Click Add in the XML Maps dialog box, navigate to the folder containing your Data Files in the Select XML Source dialog box, click EX N-3.xsd, click Open, then click OK**

   The schema elements appear in the XML Source task pane. Elements in a schema describe data similarly to the way field names in an Excel table describe the data in their columns. You choose the schema elements from the XML Source pane that you want to work with on your worksheet and map them to the worksheet. Once on the worksheet, the elements are called fields.

4. **Click the BRANCH element in the XML Source task pane and drag it to cell A1 on the worksheet, then use Figure N-11 as a guide to drag the FNAME, LNAME, SALES, and ENUMBER fields to the worksheet**

   The mapped elements appear in bolded format in the XML Source pane. The fields on the worksheet have filter arrows because Excel automatically creates a table on the worksheet as you map the schema elements. You decide to remove the ENUMBER field from the table.

5. **Right-click the ENUMBER element in the XML Source task pane, then click Remove element**

   ENUMBER is no longer formatted in bold because it is no longer mapped to the worksheet. This means that when XML data is imported, the ENUMBER field will not be populated with data. However, the field name remains in the table on the worksheet.

6. **Drag the table resizing arrow up and to the left to remove cell E1 from the table**

   Because you plan to import XML data from different files, you want to be sure that data from one file will not overwrite data from another file when it is imported into the worksheet. You also want to be sure that Excel validates the imported data against the rules specified in the schema.

7. **Click any cell in the table, click the Developer tab, then click the Map Properties button in the XML group**

   The XML Map Properties dialog box opens, as shown in Figure N-12.

8. **Click the Validate data against schema for import and export check box to select it, click the Append new data to existing XML tables option button to select it, then click OK**

   You are ready to import XML data into your worksheet.

FIGURE Π-10: XML Maps dialog box

XML maps in
the workbook
appear here

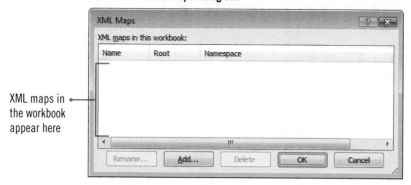

FIGURE Π-11: XML elements mapped to the worksheet

Mapped
elements

Filter arrows
appear
because a
table is
created

XML Source
task pane

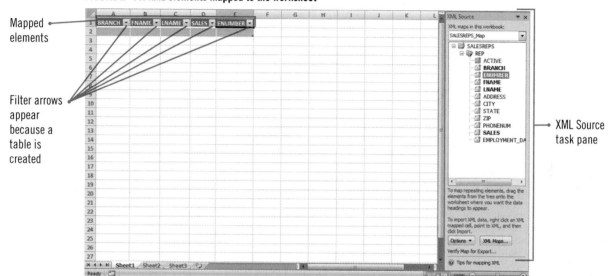

FIGURE Π-12: XML Map Properties dialog box

Click to validate
imported and
exported data

Click to add
imported data
to the bottom
of the table

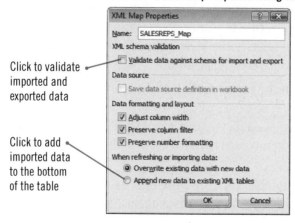

Learning more about XML

XML is a universal data format for business and industry information sharing. Using XML you can store structured information related to services, products, or business transactions and easily share and exchange the information with others. XML provides a way to express structure in data. Structured data is tagged, or marked up, to indicate its content. For example, an XML data marker (tag) that contains an item's cost might be named COST. Excel's ability to work with XML data allows you to access the large amount of information stored in the XML format. For example, organizations have developed many XML applications with a specific focus, such as MathML (Mathematical Markup Language) and RETML (Real Estate Transaction Markup Language).

Importing and Exporting XML Data

After the mapping is complete, you can import any XML file with a structure that conforms to the workbook schema. The mapped elements on the worksheet will fill with (or be **populated** with) data from the XML file. If an element is not mapped on the worksheet, then its data will not be imported. Once you import the XML data, you can analyze it using Excel tools. You can also export data from an Excel workbook to an XML file. ⬛⬛⬛ Kate asks you to combine the sales data for the Miami and New York branches that are contained in XML files. She would like you to add a total for the combined branches and export the data from Excel to an XML file.

STEPS

1. **Click cell A1, click the Developer tab if necessary, then click the Import button in the XML group**

   The Import XML dialog box opens.

2. **Navigate to the folder containing your Data Files, click EX N-4.xml, then click Import**

   The worksheet is populated with data from the XML file that contains the Miami sales rep information. The data for only the mapped elements are imported. You decide to add the sales rep data for the New York branch to the worksheet.

3. **Click the Import button in the XML group, navigate to the folder containing your Data Files in the Import XML dialog box, click EX N-5.xml, then click Import**

   The New York branch sales rep data is added to the Miami branch data. You decide to total the sales figures for all sales reps.

4. **Click the Table Tools Design tab, then click the Total Row check box to select it**

   The total sales amount of 4999777 appears in cell D25. You decide to format the table.

5. **Select the range of cells D2:D25, click the Home tab, click the Accounting Number Format button $ in the Number group, click the Decrease Decimal button ⬛ in the Number group twice, click the Table Tools Design tab, click the More button ⬛ in the Table Styles group, select Table Style Light 19, then click cell A1**

   Compare your completed table to Figure N-13.

6. **Enter your name in the center section of the worksheet footer, then preview and print the table**

   You will export the combined sales rep data as an XML file. Because not all of the elements in the schema were mapped to fields in your Excel table, you do not want the data exported from the table to be validated against the schema.

7. **Click any cell in the table, click the Developer tab, click the Map Properties button in the XML group, then click the Validate data against schema for import and export check box to deselect it**

   The Map Properties dialog box with the validation turned off is shown in Figure N-14. You are ready to export the XML data.

8. **Click OK, click the Export button in the XML group, navigate to the folder containing your Data Files in the Export XML dialog box, enter the name eastreps in the File name text box, click Export, then save and close the workbook**

   The sales data is saved in your Data File location in XML format, in the file called eastreps.xml.

FIGURE N-13: Completed table with combined sales rep data

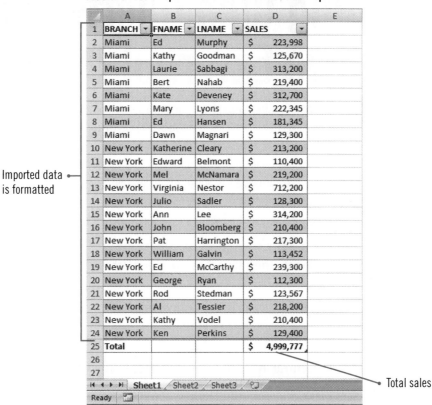

Imported data is formatted

Total sales

FIGURE N-14: XML Map Properties dialog box

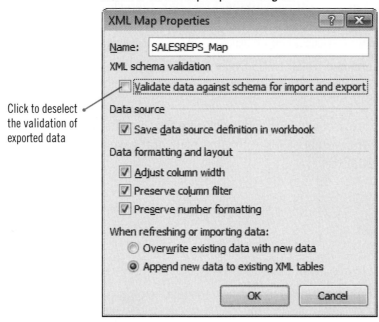

Click to deselect the validation of exported data

Importing XML data without a schema

You can import XML data without a schema and Excel will create one for you. In this situation all of the XML elements are mapped to the Excel worksheet, and the data in all of the fields is populated using the XML file. When a schema is not used, you are unable to validate the data that is imported. You also need to delete all of the fields in the table that you will not use in the worksheet, which can be time consuming.

Running Web Queries to Retrieve External Data

Often you'll want to incorporate information from the Web into an Excel worksheet for analysis. Using Excel, you can obtain data from a Web site by running a **Web query**, then save the information in an existing or new Excel workbook. You must be connected to the Internet to run a Web query. You can save Web queries to use them again later; a saved query has an .iqy file extension. Several Web query files come with Excel. As part of an effort to summarize the North American sales for Quest, Kate needs to obtain currency rate information for the Canadian dollar to adjust the data from the Toronto and Vancouver branches. She asks you to run a Web query to obtain the most current currency rate information from the Web.

STEPS

1. **Create a new workbook, then save it as Currency Rates in the drive and folder where you store your Data Files**

2. **Click the Data tab, then click Existing Connections in the Get External Data group**
   The Existing Connections dialog box opens, with all of the connections displayed, including the queries that come with Excel.

TROUBLE
Depending on the size of your monitor and the Add-Ins you have installed, you might not see a Get External Data group; you may instead see a Get External Data button. If so, click the Get External Data button, then click the Existing Connections button.

3. **Click MSN MoneyCentral Investor Currency Rates in the Connection files on this computer area if necessary, then click Open**
   The Import Data dialog box opens, as shown in Figure N-15. Here you specify the worksheet location where you want the imported data to appear.

4. **Make sure the Existing worksheet option button is selected, click cell A1 if necessary to place =$A$1 in the Existing worksheet text box, then click OK**
   Currency rate information from the Web is placed in the workbook, as shown in Figure N-16. Kate wants you to obtain the previous closing exchange rate of the Canadian dollar.

TROUBLE
If you do not see Canadian Dollar to US Dollar in column A, choose the link that will convert Canadian currency into US currency.

5. **Click the Canadian Dollar to US Dollar link**
   A Web page opens in your browser displaying currency rate details for the Canadian dollar, as shown in Figure N-17.

6. **Close your browser window, add your name to the center header section of the worksheet, save the workbook, print the first page of the worksheet, then close the workbook and exit Excel**

Creating your own Web queries

The easiest way to retrieve data from a particular Web page on a regular basis is to create a customized Web query. Click the Data tab, click the From Web button in the Get External Data group (or click the Get External Data button and click the From Web button). In the Address text box in the New Web Query dialog box, type the address of the Web page from which you want to retrieve data, then click Go. Click the yellow arrows next to the information you want to bring into a worksheet or click the upper-left arrow to import the entire page, verify that the information that you want to import has a green checkmark next to it, then click Import. The Import Data dialog box opens and allows you to specify where you want the imported data placed in the worksheet. You can save a query for future use by clicking the Save Query button in the New Web Query dialog box before you click Import. The query is saved as a file with an .iqy file extension.

FIGURE N-15: Import Data dialog box

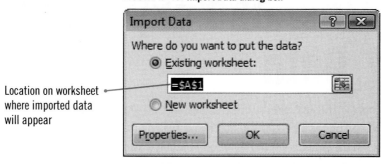

Location on worksheet
where imported data
will appear

FIGURE N-16: Currency rates quote

Currency rates
from the Web

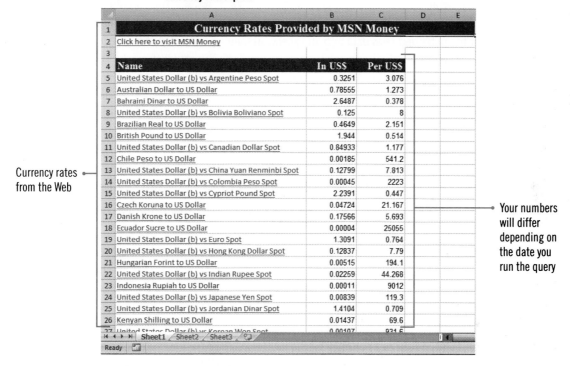

Your numbers
will differ
depending on
the date you
run the query

FIGURE N-17: Rate details for the Canadian dollar

Your values
will differ
depending
on the date
you run the
query

Sharing Excel Files and Incorporating Web Information

Importing and Exporting HTML Data

Although you can open HTML files directly in Excel, most often the information that you want to include in a worksheet is published on the Web and you don't have the HTML file. In this situation you can import the HTML data by copying the data on the Web page and pasting it into an Excel worksheet. This allows you to bring in only the information that you need from the Web page to your worksheet. Once the HTML data is in your worksheet you can analyze the imported information using Excel features. You can also export worksheet data as an HTML file that can be shared on the Web. ⬛⬛⬛ The Toronto and Vancouver branch managers have published the Canada branch sales information on the company intranet. Kate asks you to import the published sales data into an Excel worksheet so she can summarize it using Excel tools. She also wants you to export the summarized data to an HTML file so that it can be shared with all of the North American branch managers. You begin by copying the Canada sales information on the Web page.

STEPS

QUICK TIP
You can also open the htm file by navigating directly to your Data Files folder and double-clicking the filename.

1. **In Windows Explorer, navigate to the drive and folder containing your Data Files, double-click the EX N-6.htm file to open it in your browser, then copy the two table rows on the Web page containing the Toronto and Vancouver sales information**

   You are ready to paste the information from the Web page into an Excel worksheet

2. **Start Excel, open the file EX N-1.xlsx from the drive and folder where you store your Data Files, then save it as North America Sales**

3. **Click cell A6 on the Tour Sales by Branch sheet, click the Home tab, click the Paste list arrow in the Clipboard group, click Paste Special, click HTML in the As: list if necessary, then click OK**

   The Canada sales information is added to the U.S. sales data. You decide to total the sales and format the new data.

4. **Click the Paste Options list arrow ▣·, select Match Destination Formatting, click cell A8, type Total, press [Tab], click the Sum button Σ in the Editing group, then press [Enter]**

5. **Select the range A5:B5, click the Format Painter button ◈ in the Clipboard group, select the range A6:B8, then click cell A1**

   Compare your worksheet to Figure N-18. Kate is finished with the analysis and formatting of the North America branches. She wants the combined information published in a Web page.

6. **Click the Office button, then click Save As**

   The Save As dialog box opens. This dialog box allows you to specify what workbook components you want to publish.

7. **Navigate to the folder containing your Data Files, click the Save as type list arrow, click Web Page (*.htm; *.html), edit the filename to read nasales.htm, click the Selection: Sheet option button, click Publish, then click Publish again**

   The HTML file is saved in your Data Files folder.

8. **In Windows Explorer, navigate to the drive and folder containing your Data Files, then double-click the file nasales.htm**

   The HTML version of your worksheet opens in your default browser, similar to Figure N-19.

9. **Close your browser window, click the Excel window to activate it if necessary, enter your name in the center footer section of the Tour Sales by Branch worksheet, save the workbook, preview then print the worksheet, close the workbook, then exit Excel**

FIGURE N-18: Worksheet with North America sales data

Formatted table with two rows added from HTML file

FIGURE N-19: North America Sales as Web page

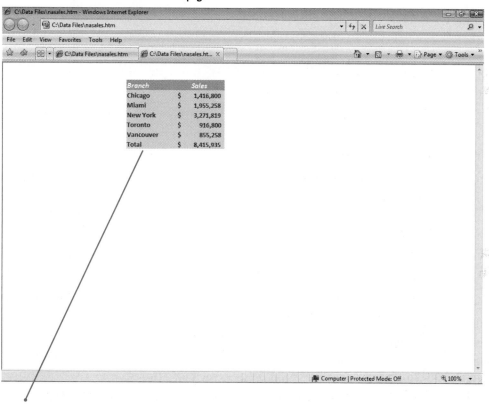

Excel worksheet data displayed in a browser

Adding Web hyperlinks to a worksheet

In Excel worksheets, you can create hyperlinks to information on the Web. Every Web page is identified by a unique Web address called a Uniform Resource Locator (URL). To create a hyperlink to a Web page, click the cell for which you want to create a hyperlink, click the Insert tab, click the Hyperlink button in the Links group, under Link to: make sure Existing File or Web Page is selected, specify the target for the hyperlink (the URL) in the Address text box, then click OK. If there is text in the cell, the text format changes to become a blue underlined hyperlink or the color the current workbook theme uses for hyperlinks. If there is no text in the cell, the Web site's URL appears in the cell.

Practice

▼ CONCEPTS REVIEW

FIGURE N-20

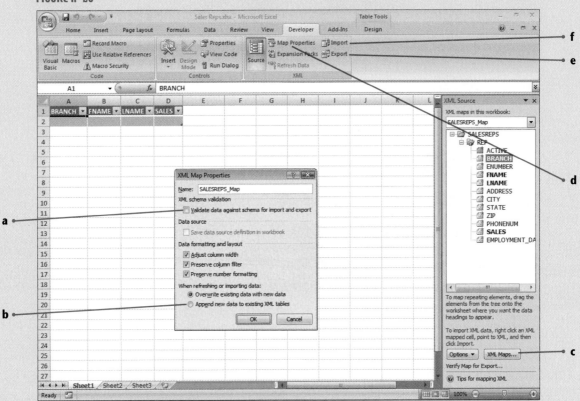

1. **Which element do you click to add a schema to an Excel workbook?**
2. **Which element do you click to bring in XML data to a workbook table?**
3. **Which element do you click to check imported XML data using the schema rules?**
4. **Which element do you click to add imported XML data below existing data in a table?**
5. **Which element do you click to save workbook data to an XML file?**
6. **Which element do you click to change the way XML data is imported and exported?**

Match each item with the statement that best describes it.

7. **iqy**	**a.** The file extension for an XML schema
8. **Shared workbook**	**b.** A record of edits others have made to a worksheet
9. **xsd**	**c.** Used to protect a workbook from unauthorized use
10. **Change history**	**d.** The file extension for a Web query
11. **Password**	**e.** A file used by many people on a network

Select the best answer from the list of choices.

12. Which of the following is the best example of a password for a workbook?

a. myfile

c. MYFILE

b. myFile

d. myFile08

13. Which of the following allows you to import data from the Web?

a. Web Wizard

c. Web query

b. Table query

d. Data query

14. The process of selecting XML elements to include on a worksheet is called:

a. Mapping.

c. Loading.

b. Selecting.

d. Sharing.

15. A file that describes the structure of XML data is called a:

a. Layout.

c. Schema.

b. Query.

d. Detail File.

▼ SKILLS REVIEW

1. Set up a shared workbook for multiple users.

a. Start Excel, open the file EX N-7.xlsx from the drive and folder where you store your Data Files, then save it as **Sales**.

b. Use the Share Workbook option on the Review tab to set up the workbook so that more than one person can use it at one time.

2. Track revisions in a shared workbook.

a. Change the Seattle sales to **$30,000** for the first quarter and **$40,000** for the second quarter.

b. Save the file.

c. Display the History sheet by opening the Highlight Changes dialog box, deselecting the When check box, then selecting the option for List changes on a new sheet.

d. Compare your History sheet to Figure N-21, enter your name in the History sheet footer, then print the History sheet.

e. Save and close the workbook.

FIGURE N-21

Action Number	Date	Time	Who	Change	Sheet	Range	New Value	Old Value	Action Type	Losing Action
1	10/1/2010	1:20 PM	Your Name	Cell Change	Sales	C2	$30,000.00	$21,000.00		
2	10/1/2010	1:20 PM	Your Name	Cell Change	Sales	D2	$40,000.00	$28,000.00		

The history ends with the changes saved on 10/1/2010 at 1:20 PM.

3. Apply and modify passwords.

a. Open the file EX N-7.xlsx from the drive and folder where you store your Data Files, open the Save As dialog box, then open the General Options dialog box.

b. Set the password to open the workbook as **Sales10** and the password to modify it as **FirstHalf02**.

c. Save the password-protected file as **Sales PW** in the location where you store your Data Files.

d. Close the workbook.

e. Use the assigned passwords to reopen the workbook and verify that you can change it by adding your name in the center section of the Sales sheet footer, save the workbook, print the Sales worksheet, then close the workbook.

4. Work with XML schemas.

a. Create a new workbook, then save it as **Contact Information** in the drive and folder where you store your Data Files.

b. Open the XML Source pane and add the XML schema EX N-8.xsd to the workbook.

c. Map the FNAME element to cell A1 on the worksheet, LNAME to cell B1, PHONENUM to cell C1, and EMPLOYMENT_DATE to cell D1.

d. Remove the EMPLOYMENT_DATE element from the map and delete the field from the table.

e. Use the XML Map Properties dialog box to make sure imported XML data is validated using the schema.

5. Import and export XML data.

   a. Import the XML file EX N-9.xml into the workbook.

   b. Sort the worksheet list in ascending order by LNAME.

   c. Add the Table Style Medium 24 to the table, and compare your screen to Figure N-22.

   d. Enter your name in the center section of the worksheet footer, save the workbook, then print the table.

   e. Use the XML Map Properties dialog box to turn off the validation for imported and exported worksheet data, export the worksheet data to an XML file named **contact**, save and close the workbook, then close the XML Source pane.

FIGURE N-22

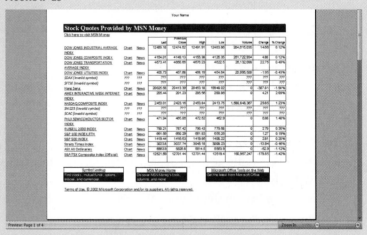

6. Run Web queries to retrieve external data.

   a. Create a new workbook, then save it as **Quotes** in the location where you store your Data Files.

   b. Use the Existing Connections dialog box to select the Web query MSN MoneyCentral Investor Major Indices.

   c. Specify that you want to place the data to cell A1 of the current worksheet.

   d. Enter your name in the center section of the worksheet header, change the page orientation to landscape, save the workbook, preview the worksheet, compare your screen to Figure N-23, then print the first page of the worksheet.

   e. Close the workbook.

FIGURE N-23

7. Import and export HTML data.

   a. Open the file EX N-7.xlsx from the drive and folder where you store your Data Files, then save it as **Sales_2**.

   b. Open the file EX N-10.htm in your browser from the drive and folder where you store your Data Files. Copy the data in the four rows of the Web page and paste it below the data in the Sales sheet of the Sales_2 workbook.

   c. On the Sales sheet, enter **Total** in cell A27 and use AutoSum in cell D27 to total the values in column D.

   d. Adjust the formatting for the new rows to match the other rows on the Sales sheet, add your name to the center section of the worksheet footer, save the workbook, then preview and print the Sales sheet.

   e. Save the data on the Sales sheet as an HTML file with the name **sales_2.htm**.

   f. Exit Excel, open the sales_2.htm file in your browser, print the Web page from your browser, compare your screen to Figure N-24, close your browser, close the workbook.

FIGURE N-24

▼ INDEPENDENT CHALLENGE 1

Shore College has three campuses, North, West, and South. The deans of the campuses work together on the scheduling of classes using shared Excel workbooks. As the registrar for the college, you are preparing the fall schedule as a shared workbook for the three campus deans. They will each make changes to the location data, and you will review all three workbooks and accept their changes.

a. Start Excel, open the file EX N-11.xlsx from the drive and folder where you store your Data Files, then save it as **Shore College**. The workbook has been shared so the other deans can modify it. Close the workbook.

b. Open the file EX N-12.xlsx from the drive and folder where you store your Data Files, then save it as **West Campus**. This workbook is a copy of the original that Joe Peabody has reviewed and changed.

c. Use the Accept or Reject dialog box to accept the change Joe made to the workbook. Save and close the workbook.

d. Open the file EX N-13.xlsx from the drive and folder where you store your Data Files, then save it **North Campus**. Nancy Brown has reviewed this workbook and made a change.

e. Use the Accept or Reject dialog box to accept the change Nancy made. Save and close the workbook.

f. Open the file EX N-14.xlsx from the drive and folder where you store your Data Files, then save it as **South Campus**.

g. Use the Accept or Reject dialog box to accept the change made to the workbook by Maureen Alberto.

h. Use the Highlight Changes dialog box to highlight Maureen's change on the screen. Review the ScreenTip details.

i. Use the Highlight Changes dialog box to create a History worksheet detailing Maureen's change to the workbook. Add your name to the left section of the History sheet footer, then print the History worksheet. Save and close the workbook.

Advanced Challenge Exercise

- Open the file EX N-11.xlsx from the drive and folder where you store your Data Files, then save it as **Merged Schedule_ACE**. Notice that the locations for the first three courses are W121, N234, and S312, respectively.
- Add the Compare and Merge Workbooks command to the Quick Access Toolbar for the Merged Schedule_ACE workbook. Do not add it to the Quick Access Toolbar for all workbooks.
- Merge the files North Campus.xlsx, South Campus.xlsx, and West Campus.xlsx into the Merged Schedule workbook. Notice the new locations for the first three courses in the worksheet. Compare your merged data with Figure N-25.
- Enter your name in the Fall 2010 worksheet footer, then save the workbook.
- Print the merged 2010 worksheet, then close the workbook.

FIGURE N-25

	A	B	C	D	E	F
1	Code	Term	Start Time	End Time	Days	Location
2	1124	Fall 2010	8:00 a.m.	8:50 a.m.	M, W, F	W100
3	1128	Fall 2010	8:00 a.m.	8:50 a.m.	M, W, F	N200
4	1135	Fall 2010	8:00 a.m.	8:50 a.m.	M, W, F	S300
5	1140	Fall 2010	9:00 a.m.	10:15 a.m.	T, TH	W214
6	1145	Fall 2010	9:00 a.m.	10:15 a.m.	T, TH	N134
7	1151	Fall 2010	9:00 a.m.	10:15 a.m.	T, TH	S230
8	1156	Fall 2010	1:00 p.m.	1:50 p.m.	M, W, F	W101
9	1162	Fall 2010	1:00 p.m.	1:50 p.m.	M, W, F	N214
10	1167	Fall 2010	1:00 p.m.	1:50 p.m.	M, W, F	S213
11	1173	Fall 2010	3:00 p.m.	4:15 p.m.	T, TH	W132
12	1178	Fall 2010	3:00 p.m.	4:15 p.m.	T, TH	N154
13	1183	Fall 2010	3:00 p.m.	4:15 p.m.	T, TH	S215
14						

j. Exit Excel.

▼ INDEPENDENT CHALLENGE 2

The Montreal Athletic Club is a fitness center with five facilities in the greater Montreal area. As the general manager you are responsible for setting and publishing the membership rate information. You decide to run a special promotion offering a 10 percent discount off of the current membership prices. You will also add two new membership categories to help attract younger members. The membership rate information is published on the company Web site. You will copy the rate information from the Web page and work with it in Excel to calculate the special discounted rates. You will save the new rate information as an HTML file so it can be published on the Web.

a. Open the file EX N-15.htm from the drive and folder where you store your Data Files to display it in your browser.

b. Start Excel, create a new workbook, then save it as **Membership Rates** in the drive and folder where you store your Data Files.

c. Copy the five rows of data from the table in the EX N-15 file and paste them in the Membership Rates workbook. Adjust the column widths and formatting as necessary. Close the EX N-15.htm file.

d. Add the new membership data from Table N-1 in rows 6 and 7 of the worksheet.

TABLE N-1

Teen	320
Youth	150

e. Enter **Special** in cell C1 and calculate each special rate in column C by discounting the prices in column B by 10%. (*Hint*: Multiply each price by .90).

f. Format the price information in columns B and C with the Accounting format using the $ English (Canada) symbol with two decimal places.

g. Add the passwords **Members11** to open the Membership Rates workbook and **Fitness01** to modify it. Save and close the workbook, then reopen it by entering the passwords.

h. Verify that you can modify the workbook by formatting the worksheet using colors of your choice. Compare your worksheet data to Figure N-26.

i. Add your name to the center footer section of the worksheet, save the workbook, then preview and print the worksheet.

j. Save the worksheet data in HTML format using the name **prices.htm**. Close the workbook and exit Excel.

k. Open the prices.htm page in your browser and print the page.

l. Close your browser.

FIGURE N-26

	A	B	C
1	Membership	Price	Special
2	Family	$ 975.00	$ 877.50
3	Adult	$ 670.00	$ 603.00
4	Senior	$ 500.00	$ 450.00
5	College	$ 450.00	$ 405.00
6	Teen	$ 320.00	$ 288.00
7	Youth	$ 150.00	$ 135.00
8			

▼ INDEPENDENT CHALLENGE 3

You are the director of development at a local educational nonprofit institution. You are preparing the phone lists for your annual fundraising phone-a-thon. The donor information for the organization is in an XML file, which you will bring into Excel to organize. You will use an XML schema to map only the donors' names and phone numbers to the worksheet. This will allow you to import the donor data and limit the information that is distributed to the phone-a-thon volunteers. You will export your worksheet data as XML for future use.

a. Start Excel, create a new workbook, then save it as **Donors** in the drive and folder where you store your Data Files.

b. Add the map EX N-16.xsd from the drive and folder where you store your Data Files to the workbook.

c. Map the FNAME element to cell A1, LNAME to cell B1, and PHONENUM to cell C1.

d. Import the XML data in file EX N-17.xml from the drive and folder where you store your Data Files. Make sure the data is validated using the schema as it is imported.

e. Add the Table Style Medium 10 to the table. Change the field name in cell A1 to **FIRST NAME**, change the field name in cell B1 to **LAST NAME**, and change the field name in cell C1 to **PHONE NUMBER**. Widen the columns as necessary to accommodate the full field names.

f. Sort the list in ascending order by LAST NAME. Compare your sorted list to Figure N-27.

g. Export the worksheet data to an XML file named **phonelist**.

FIGURE N-27

	A	B	C
1	FIRST NAME	LAST NAME	PHONE NUMBER
2	Virginia	Alexander	312-765-8756
3	Ellen	Atkins	773-167-4156
4	Shelley	Connolly	312-322-3163
5	Bill	Duran	312-322-3163
6	Katherine	Gonzales	773-379-0092
7	Keith	Jackson	773-220-9456
8	Edward	Land	312-299-4298
9	Julio	Mendez	312-765-8756
10	Laurie	Ng	312-932-9966
11	Mel	Zoll	312-765-8756
12			

▼ INDEPENDENT CHALLENGE 3 (CONTINUED)

Advanced Challenge Exercise

- Add the map EX N-18.xsd from the drive and folder where you store your Data Files to the worksheet.
- Using the INFO_Map, map the DNUMBER element to cell A14 and LEVEL to cell B14.
- Import the XML data in file EX N-19.xml from the drive and folder where you store your Data Files.

h. Enter your name in the center section of the worksheet header, save the workbook, then print the worksheet.

i. Close the workbook and exit Excel.

▼ REAL LIFE INDEPENDENT CHALLENGE

You can track the history of a stock using published Web quotes that can be entered into Excel worksheets for analysis. To eliminate the data entry step, you will use the MSN MoneyCentral Investor Stock Quotes Web query in Excel. You will run the query from an Excel workbook using the symbol of a stock that you are interested in following. The stock information will be automatically inserted into your worksheet.

a. Start Excel, create a new workbook, then save it as **Stock Analysis** in the drive and folder where you store your Data Files.

b. Run the Web Query MSN MoneyCentral Investor Stock Quotes to obtain a quote for the stock that you are interested in. Enter the symbol for your stock in the Enter Parameter Value dialog box, as shown in Figure N-28. (*Hint*: Microsoft's symbol is MSFT. Once you run the query, you can use the Symbol Lookup hyperlink to find symbols of companies that you are interested in researching.)

c. Display the chart of your stock data by clicking the Chart link on the worksheet.

FIGURE N-28

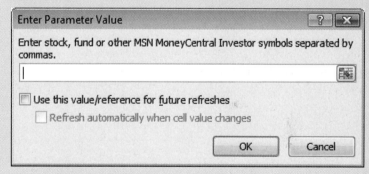

d. Print the Chart page showing the stock price history from your browser.

e. Close your browser and return to the workbook.

f. Place the name of the company that you are researching in cell A20. Use the name in cell A20 to add a hyperlink to the company's Web site. (*Hint*: Click the Insert tab, then click the Hyperlink button in the Links group.)

g. Test the link, then close the browser to return to the workbook.

h. Enter your name in the center section of the worksheet footer, save the workbook, then preview and print the worksheet in landscape orientation on one page.

i. Close the Stock Analysis workbook, saving your changes, then exit Excel.

▼ VISUAL WORKSHOP

Start Excel, create a new workbook, then save it as **Thymes.xlsx** in the drive and folder where you store your Data Files. Open the file EX N-20.htm in your browser from the drive and folder where you store your Data Files. Create the Web page shown in Figure N-29 by pasting the information from the Web page into your Thymes.xlsx file, formatting it, adding the fourth quarter information, then saving it as an HTML file named **thymes.htm.** Add your name to the footer of Sheet1 of the Thymes.xlsx workbook, and print the worksheet. Print the thymes.htm Web page from your browser. (*Hint*: The colors are in the Office theme.)

FIGURE N-29

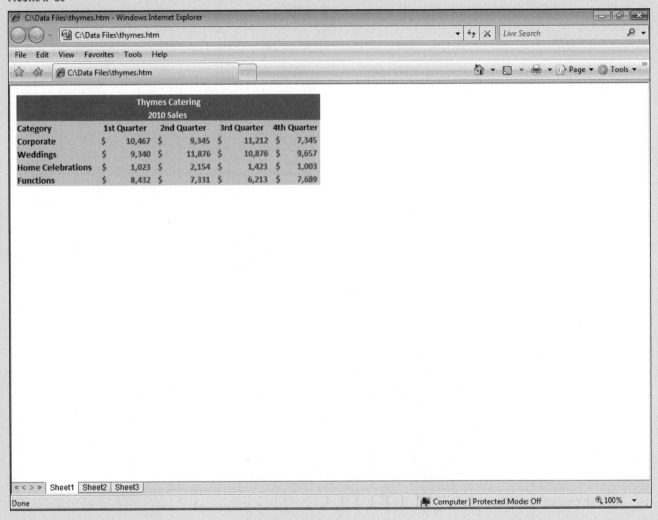

Customizing Excel and Advanced Worksheet Management

Excel includes numerous tools and options designed to help you work as efficiently as possible. In this unit, you will learn how to use some of these elements to find errors and hide the details of worksheet summaries. You'll also find out how to eliminate repetitive typing chores, save calculation time when using a large worksheet, and customize basic Excel features. Finally, you'll learn how to document your workbook and save it in a format that makes it easy to reuse. Quest's vice president of sales, Kate Morgan, asks you to help with a variety of spreadsheet-related tasks. You will use the numerous tools and options available in Excel to help Kate perform her work quickly and efficiently.

Files You Will Need:

EX O-1.xlsx
EX O-2.xlsx
EX O-3.xlsx
EX O-4.xlsx
EX O-5.xlsx
EX O-6.xlsx

OBJECTIVES

Audit a worksheet

Control worksheet calculations

Group worksheet data

Use cell comments

Create custom AutoFill lists

Customize Excel workbooks

Customize Excel options

Create a template

Auditing a Worksheet

The Excel **auditing** feature helps you track errors and check worksheet logic. The Formula Auditing group on the Formulas tab contains several error-checking tools to help you audit a worksheet. Because errors can occur at any stage of worksheet development, it is important to include auditing as part of your workbook-building process. Kate asks you to help audit the worksheet that tracks sales for the two Canadian branches to verify the accuracy of year-end totals and percentages. You use Excel Formula Auditing features to identify errors in your worksheet.

STEPS

1. **Start Excel, open the file** EX O-1.xlsx **from the drive and folder where you store your Data Files, then save it as** Canada Sales

2. **Click the** Formulas tab, **then click the** Error Checking button **in the Formula Auditing group**

   The Error Checking dialog box opens and alerts you to a Divide by Zero Error in cell O5, as shown in Figure O-1. The formula reads =N5/N8, indicating that the value in cell N5 will be divided by the value in cell N8. In Excel formulas, blank cells have a value of zero. This error means the value in cell N5 cannot be divided by the value in cell N8 (zero) because division by zero is not mathematically possible. To correct the error, you must edit the formula so that it references cell N7, the total of sales, not cell N8.

3. **Click** Edit in Formula Bar **in the Error Checking dialog box, edit the formula to read** =N5/N7, **click the Enter button** ☑ **on the formula bar, then click** Resume **in the Error Checking dialog box**

   The edited formula produces the correct result, .5576, in cell O5. The Error Checking dialog box indicates another error in cell N6, the total Vancouver sales. The formula reads =SUM(B6:L6) and should be =SUM(B6:M6). The top button in the Error Checking dialog box changes to "Copy Formula from Above". Since this formula in the cell N5 is correct, you will copy it.

4. **Click** Copy Formula from Above

   The Vancouver total changes to $322,397 in cell N6. The Error Checking dialog box finds another division-by-zero error in cell O6. You decide to use another tool in the Formula Auditing group to get more information about this error.

5. **Close the Error Checking dialog box, then click the** Trace Precedents button **in the Formula Auditing group**

   Blue arrows called **tracers** point from the cells that might have caused the error to the active cell containing the error, as shown in Figure O-2. The tracers extend from the error to cells N6 and N8. To correct the error, you must edit the formula so that it references cell N7 in the denominator, the sales total, not cell N8.

6. **Edit the formula in the formula bar to read** =N6/N7, **then click** ☑ **on the formula bar**

   The result of the formula .4424 appears in cell O6. The November sales for the Vancouver branch in cell L6 is unusually high compared with sales posted for the other months. You can investigate the other cells in the sheet that are affected by the value of cell L6 by tracing the cell's **dependents**—the cells that contain formulas referring to cell L6.

7. **Click cell** L6, **then click the** Trace Dependents button **in the Formula Auditing group**

   The tracer arrows run from cell L6 to cells L7 and N6, indicating that the formula in cell L6 affects the total November sales and the total Vancouver sales. You decide to remove the tracer arrows and format the percentages in cells O5 and O6.

8. **Click the** Remove Arrows button **in the Formula Auditing group, select the range** O5:O6, **click the** Home tab, **click the** Percent Style button ⁰∕₀ **in the Number group, click the** Increase Decimal button ⁺.₀₀ **twice, return to cell A1, then save the workbook**

   Now that all the errors have been identified and corrected, you are finished auditing the worksheet.

Cell containing error and formula

Type of error

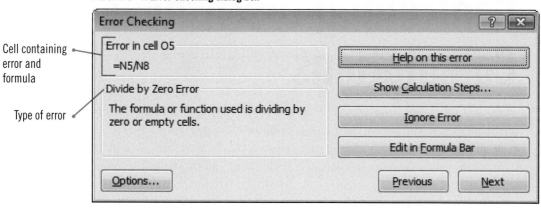

FIGURE O-2: Worksheet with traced error

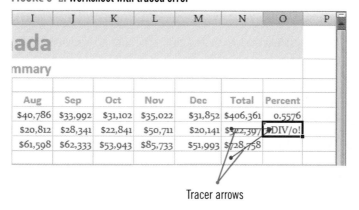

Tracer arrows

Watching and evaluating formulas

As you edit your worksheet, you can watch the effect cell changes have on selected worksheet formulas. Select the cell or cells that you want to watch, click the Formulas tab, click the Watch Window button in the Formula Auditing group, click Add Watch in the Watch Window, then click Add. The Watch Window displays the workbook name, worksheet name, the cell address you want to watch, the current cell value, and its formula. As cell values that "feed into" the formula change, the resulting formula value in the Watch Window

changes. To delete a watch you can select the cell information in the Watch Window and click Delete Watch. You can also step through the evaluation of a formula, selecting the cell that contains a formula and clicking the Evaluate Formula button in the Formula Auditing group. The formula appears in the Evaluation Window of the Evaluate Formula dialog box; as you click the Evaluate button, the cell references are replaced with their values and the formula result is calculated.

Excel 2007

Controlling Worksheet Calculations

Whenever you change a value in a cell, Excel automatically recalculates all the formulas in the worksheet based on that cell. This automatic calculation is efficient until you create a worksheet so large that the recalculation process slows down data entry and screen updating. Worksheets with many formulas, data tables, or functions may also recalculate slowly. In these cases, you might want to selectively determine if and when you want Excel to perform calculations automatically. You do this by applying the **manual calculation** option. Once you change the calculation mode to manual, Excel applies manual calculation to all open worksheets. ▚▟▞▌▌▌ Because Kate knows that using specific Excel calculation options can help make worksheet building more efficient, she asks you to change from automatic to manual calculation.

STEPS

1. **Click the Office button** 🔘**, click Excel Options, then click Formulas in the list of options**
   The options related to formula calculation and error checking are displayed, as shown in Figure O-3.

2. **Under Workbook Calculation, click to select the Manual option button**
   When you select the Manual option, the Recalculate workbook before saving check box automatically becomes active and contains a check mark. Because the workbook will not recalculate until you save or close and reopen the workbook, you must make sure to recalculate your worksheet before you print it and after you finish making changes.

3. **Click OK**
   Kate informs you that the December total for the Toronto branch is incorrect. You adjust the entry in cell M5 to reflect the actual sales figure.

4. **Click cell M5**
   Before making the change to cell M5, notice that in cell N5 the total for the Toronto branch is $406,361, and the Toronto percent in cell O5 is 55.76%.

5. **Type 39,511, then click the Enter button** ☑ **on the formula bar**
   The total and percent formulas are *not* updated. The total in cell N5 is still $406,361 and the percentage in cell O5 is still 55.76%. The word "Calculate" appears in the status bar to indicate that a specific value in the worksheet did indeed change and that the worksheet must be recalculated. You can press [F9] or click the Calculate Now button in the Calculation group to calculate the entire workbook manually. You can also use the Calculate Sheet button or [Shift][F9] to calculate just the active worksheet. Since only the active worksheet needs to be recalculated, you use the Calculate Sheet button.

6. **Click the Formulas tab, click the Calculate Sheet button** 🖩 **in the Calculation group, click cell A1, then save the workbook**
   The total in cell N5 is now $414,020 instead of $406,361 and the percentage in cell O5 is now 56.22% instead of 55.76%. The other formulas in the worksheet affected by the value in cell M5 changed as well, as shown in Figure O-4. Because this is a relatively small worksheet that recalculates quickly, you will return to automatic calculation.

7. **Click** 🔘**, click Excel Options, click Formulas in the list of options, under Workbook Calculation click to select the Automatic option button, then click OK**
   Now any additional changes you make will automatically recalculate the worksheet formulas.

8. **Place your name in the center section of the worksheet footer, fit the worksheet to one page, then save the workbook**

FIGURE O-3: Excel formula options

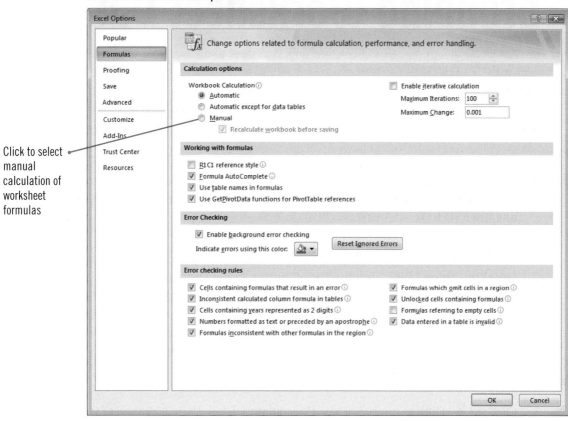

Click to select manual calculation of worksheet formulas

FIGURE O-4: Worksheet with updated values

	A	B	C	D	E	F	G	H	I	J	K	L	M	N	O	P
1							QST Canada									
2							2010 Sales Summary									
3																
4	Branch	Jan	Feb	Mar	Apr	May	Jun	Jul	Aug	Sep	Oct	Nov	Dec	Total	Percent	
5	Toronto	$37,124	$35,982	$38,942	$41,980	$15,232	$32,557	$31,790	$40,786	$33,992	$31,102	$35,022	$39,511	$414,020	56.22%	
6	Vancouver	$20,765	$22,841	$27,349	$30,943	$32,791	$22,921	$21,941	$20,812	$28,341	$22,841	$50,711	$20,141	$322,397	43.78%	
7	Total	$57,889	$58,823	$66,291	$72,923	$48,023	$55,478	$53,731	$61,598	$62,333	$53,943	$85,733	$59,652	$736,417		
8																

Updated values

Grouping Worksheet Data

You can create groups of rows and columns on a worksheet to manage your data and make it easier to work with. The Excel grouping feature provides an outline that allows you to easily expand and collapse groups as you need to show or hide related worksheet data. You can turn off the outline symbols if you are using the condensed data in a report. ▰▰▰▰ Kate needs to give Jessica Long, the Quest CEO, the quarterly sales totals for the Canadian branches. She asks you to group the worksheet data by quarters.

STEPS

1. **Click the Quarterly Summary sheet, select the range B4:D7, click the Data tab, click the Group button in the Outline group, click the Columns option button in the Group dialog box, then click OK**

   The first quarter information is grouped and **outline symbols** that are used to hide and display detail appear over the columns, as shown in Figure O-5. You continue to group the remaining quarters.

2. **Select the range F4:H7, click the Group button in the Outline group, click the Columns option button in the Group dialog box, click OK, select the range J4:L7, click the Group button in the Outline group, click the Columns option button in the Group dialog box, click OK, select the range N4:P7, click the Group button in the Outline group, click the Columns option button in the Group dialog box, click OK, then click cell A1**

   All four quarters are grouped. You decide to use the outline symbols to expand and collapse the first quarter information.

3. **Click the ⊟ Outline symbol above the column E label, then click the ⊞ Outline symbol above the column E label**

   Clicking the - symbol temporarily hides the Q1 detail columns, and the - symbol changes to a + symbol. Clicking the + symbol expands the Q1 details and redisplays the hidden columns. The Column Level symbols in the upper-left corner of the worksheet are used to display and hide levels of detail across the entire worksheet.

4. **Click the Column Level 1 button ▢1**

   All of the group details collapse and only the quarter totals are displayed.

5. **Click the Column Level 2 button ▢2**

   You see the quarter details again. Kate asks you to hide the quarter details and the outline symbols for her summary report.

6. **Click the Column Level 1 button ▢1, click the Office button ⊙, click Excel Options, click Advanced in the list of options, scroll to the Display options for this worksheet section, verify that Quarterly Summary is displayed as the worksheet name, click the Show outline symbols if an outline is applied check box to deselect it, then click OK**

   The quarter totals without outline symbols are shown in Figure O-6.

7. **Enter your name in the center footer section, save the workbook, then preview and print the worksheet**

FIGURE O-5: First quarter data grouped

Outline symbols
Column level buttons
Grouped data
Canada Sales.xlsx - Microsoft Excel
QST Canada
2010 Sales Summary

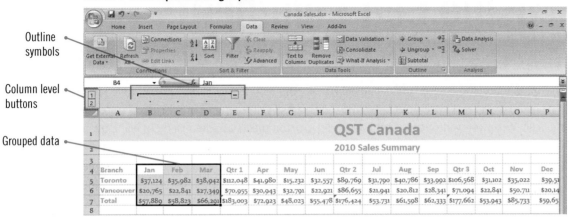

FIGURE O-6: Quarter summary

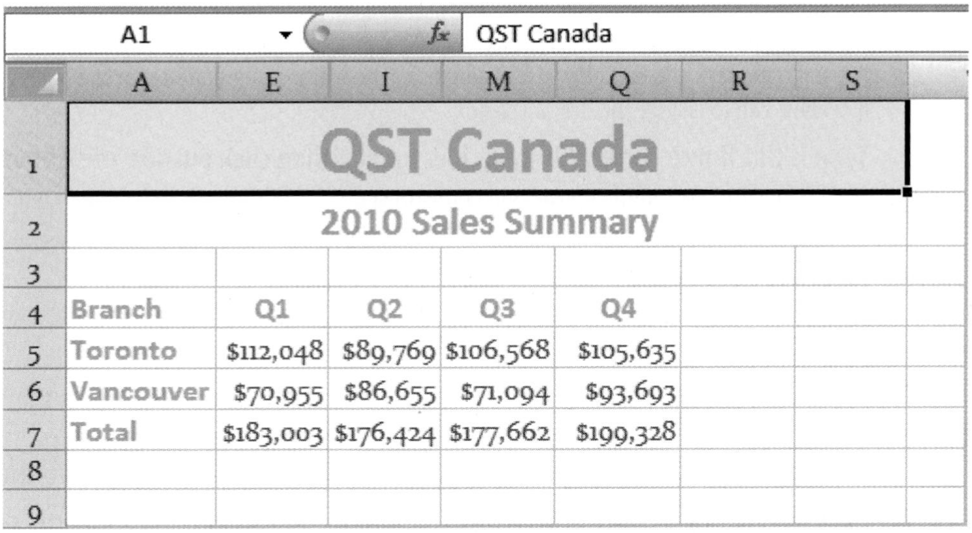

QST Canada
2010 Sales Summary
Branch
Q1
Q2
Q3
Q4
Toronto
$112,048
$89,769
$106,568
$105,635
Vancouver
$70,955
$86,655
$71,094
$93,693
Total
$183,003
$176,424
$177,662
$199,328

Excel 2007

Using Cell Comments

If you plan to share a workbook with others, it's a good idea to **document**, or make notes about, basic assumptions, complex formulas, or questionable data. By reading your documentation, a coworker can quickly become familiar with your workbook. The easiest way to document a workbook is to use **cell comments**, which are notes attached to individual cells that appear when you place the pointer over a cell. When you sort or copy and paste cells, any comments attached to them will move to the new location. In PivotTable reports, however, the comments do not move with the worksheet data. 🔲 Kate thinks one of the figures in the worksheet may be incorrect. She asks you to add a comment for Jason Ng, the Toronto branch manager, pointing out the possible error. You will start by checking the default settings for comments in a workbook.

STEPS

1. **Click the Office button 🔘, click Excel Options, click Advanced in the list of options, scroll to the Display section, click the Indicators only, and comments on hover option button to select it in the "For cells with comments, show:" section, then click OK**

   The other options in the "For cells with comments, show:" area allow you to display the comment and its indicator or no comments.

QUICK TIP

To copy only comments, copy the cell contents, right-click the destination cell, select Paste Special, click Comments, then click OK.

2. **Click the Sales sheet tab, click cell F5, click the Review tab, then click the New Comment button in the Comments group**

   The Comment box opens, as shown in Figure O-7. Excel automatically includes the computer's username at the beginning of the comment. The username is the name that appears in the User name text box in the Popular options of the Excel Options dialog box. The white sizing handles on the border of the Comment box allow you to change the size of the box.

3. **Type Is this figure correct? It looks low to me., then click outside the Comment box**

   A red triangle appears in the upper-right corner of cell F5, indicating that a comment is attached to the cell. People who use your worksheet can easily display comments.

4. **Place the pointer over cell F5**

   The comment appears next to the cell. When you move the pointer outside of cell F5, the comment disappears. Kate asks you to add a comment to cell L6.

5. **Right-click cell L6, click Insert Comment on the shortcut menu, type Is this increase due to the new advertising campaign?, then click outside the Comment box**

   Kate asks you to delete a comment and edit a comment. You start by displaying all worksheet comments.

6. **Click cell A1, then click the Show All Comments button in the Comments group**

   The two worksheet comments are displayed on the screen, as shown in Figure O-8.

7. **Click the Next button in the Comments group, with the comment in cell F5 selected click the Delete button in the Comments group, click the Next button in the Comments group, click the Edit Comment button in the Comments group, type Jason – at the beginning of the comment in the Comment box, click cell A1, then click the Show All Comments button in the Comments group**

   The Show All Comments button is a toggle button: You click it once to display comments, then click it again to hide comments. You decide to print the worksheet and the cell comment along with its associated cell reference on separate pages.

QUICK TIP

To set comment printing options, you need to open the Page Setup dialog box using the dialog box launcher in the Page Setup group. Clicking the Page Setup button in Print Preview does not allow you to control the print options for comments.

8. **Click the Page Layout tab, click the dialog box launcher 🔲 in the Page Setup group, click the Sheet tab, under Print click the Comments list arrow, click At end of sheet, click Print, then click OK**

   Your comment is printed on a separate page after the worksheet.

9. **Save the workbook**

Customizing Excel and Advanced Worksheet Management

FIGURE O-7: Comment box

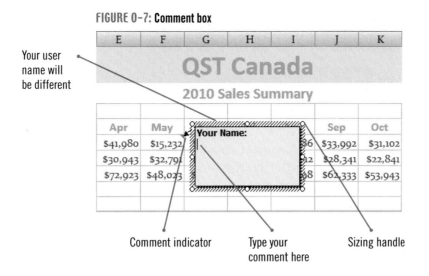

Your user name will be different

Comment indicator

Type your comment here

Sizing handle

FIGURE O-8: Worksheet with comments displayed

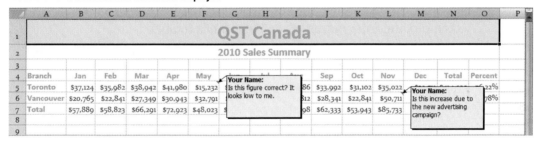

Changing the way you work with Excel

As you work with Excel you may want to change some of the settings to suit your personal preferences. For example, you may want to change the Excel color scheme from blue to black or silver. Or you may want to turn off the Mini toolbar, which provides quick access to formatting options when you select text. Other options you may want to change are the way the ScreenTips are displayed or the Live Preview feature. You can change these settings by clicking the Office button , clicking Excel Options, and selecting your settings in the Popular area of the Excel Options dialog box. Some settings have a small "i" next to them, which displays more information on the feature as you hover your mouse over it.

Creating Custom AutoFill Lists

Whenever you need to type a list of words regularly, you can save time by creating a custom AutoFill list. Then you can simply enter the first value in a blank cell and drag the AutoFill handle. Excel enters the rest of the information for you. Figure O-9 shows some examples of AutoFill lists that are built into Excel as well as Custom AutoFill lists. ▓▓▓▓▓ Kate often has to enter a list of Quest's sales representatives' names in her worksheets. She asks you to create an AutoFill list to save time in performing this task. You begin by selecting the names in the worksheet.

STEPS

1. **Click the Jan sheet tab, then select the range A5:A24**

2. **Click the Office button 🗔, click Excel Options, verify that Popular is selected, then in the Top options for working with Excel section click Edit Custom Lists**

   The Custom Lists dialog box displays the custom AutoFill lists that are already built into Excel, as shown in Figure O-10. You want to define a custom list containing the sales representatives' names you selected in column A. The Import list from cells text box contains the range you selected in Step 1.

3. **Click Import**

   The list of names is highlighted in the Custom lists box and appears in the List entries box. You decide to test the custom AutoFill list by placing it in a blank worksheet.

4. **Click OK to confirm the list, click OK again, click the Feb tab, type Sullivan in cell A1, then click the Enter button ✅ on the formula toolbar**

5. **Drag the AutoFill handle down to cell A20, then release the mouse button**

   The highlighted range now contains the custom list of sales representatives you created. Kate informs you that sales representative Bentz has been replaced by a new representative, Enrich. You update the AutoFill list to reflect this change.

6. **Click 🗔, click Excel Options, click Edit Custom Lists, click the list of sales representatives names in the Custom lists box, change Bentz to Enrich in the List entries box, click OK to confirm the change, then click OK again**

   You decide to check the new list to be sure it is accurate.

7. **Click cell C1, type Sullivan, click ✅ on the formula toolbar, drag the AutoFill handle down to cell C20, then release the mouse button**

   The highlighted range contains the updated custom list of sales representatives, as shown in Figure O-11. You've finished creating and editing your custom AutoFill list, and you need to delete it from the Custom Lists dialog box in case others will be using your computer.

8. **Click 🗔, click Excel Options, click Edit Custom Lists, click the list of sales representatives' names in the Custom lists box, click Delete, click OK to confirm the deletion, then click OK two more times**

9. **Save and close the workbook**

FIGURE O-9: Sample AutoFill lists

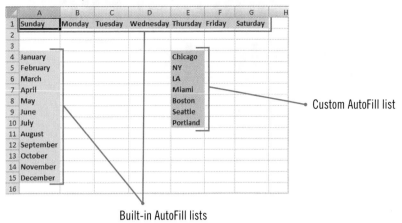

Custom AutoFill list

Built-in AutoFill lists

FIGURE O-10: Custom Lists dialog box

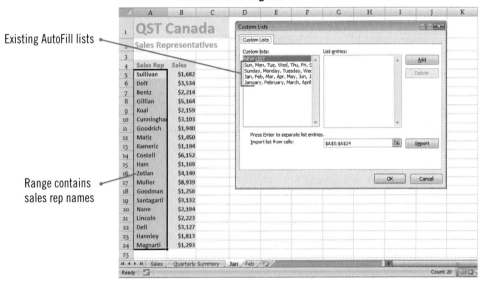

Existing AutoFill lists

Range contains
sales rep names

FIGURE O-11: Custom AutoFill lists with names of sales representatives

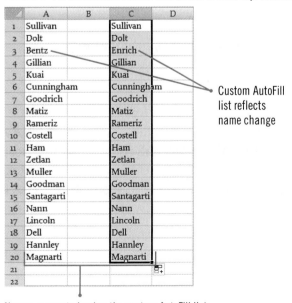

Custom AutoFill
list reflects
name change

Names generated using the custom AutoFill list

Customizing Excel Workbooks

The Excel default settings for editing and viewing a worksheet are designed to meet the needs of the majority of Excel users. You may find, however, that a particular setting doesn't always fit your particular needs, such as the default number of worksheets in a workbook, the worksheet view, or the default font. The Popular category of the Excel Options dialog box contains features that are commonly used by a large number of Excel users. You have already used the Popular category to create custom lists and the Formulas category to switch to manual calculation; you can use it to further customize Excel to suit your work habits and needs. The most commonly used categories of the Excel Options are explained in more detail in Table O-1. Kate is interested in customizing workbooks to allow her to work more efficiently. She asks you to use a blank workbook to explore features that will help her better manage her data.

STEPS

1. **Click the Office button [icon], click New, then click Create**

   In the last workbook you prepared for Kate you had to add a fourth worksheet. You would like to have four worksheets displayed rather than three when a new workbook is opened.

2. **Click [icon], click Excel Options, in the When creating new workbooks area of the Popular options select 3 in the Include this many sheets text box, then type 4**

   You can change the default font Excel displays in new workbooks, as shown in Figure O-12.

3. **Click the Use this font list arrow, then select Arial**

   You can also change the standard workbook font size.

4. **Click the Font size list arrow, then select 12**

   You can also change the default view for worksheets.

5. **Click the Default view for new sheets list arrow, select Page Layout View, click OK to close the Excel Options dialog box, then click OK to the message about quitting and restarting Excel**

   These default settings take effect after you exit and restart Excel.

6. **Close the workbook, exit Excel, then start Excel again**

   A new workbook opens with four sheet tabs in Page Layout view and a 12-point Arial font, as shown in Figure O-13. Now that you have finished exploring the Excel workbook Options, you need to reestablish the original Excel settings.

7. **Click [icon], click Excel Options, in the When creating new workbooks area of the Popular options select 4 in the Include this many sheets text box, enter 3, click the Use this font list arrow, select Body Font, select 12 in the Font size text box, type 11, click the Default view for new sheets list arrow, select Normal View, click OK twice, then close the workbook and exit Excel**

FIGURE O-12: Popular category of Excel Options

Standard font defaults

Changed default number of worksheets in a workbook

The user name for the computer

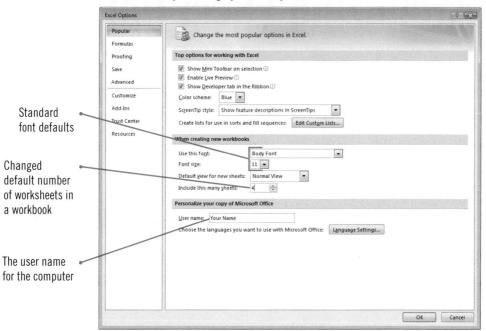

FIGURE O-13: Workbook with new default settings

New default font is 12-point Arial

Worksheet is in Page Layout view

New workbook has four worksheets

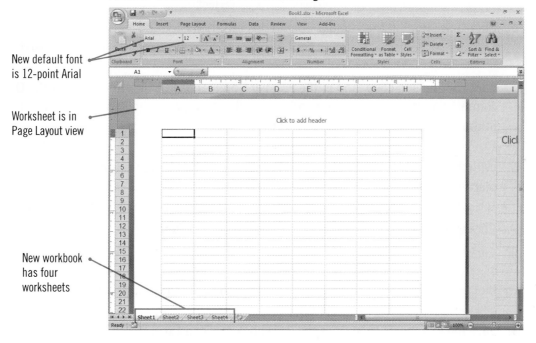

TABLE O-1: Categories of Excel Options

category	description
Popular	Allows you to create custom lists, change the user name, and change the workbook defaults
Formulas	Controls how the worksheet is calculated, error checking rules, and how formulas are referenced
Proofing	Controls AutoCorrect and spell-checking options
Save	Allows you to select a default format and location for saving files, and allows you to customize AutoRecover settings
Advanced	Allows you to customize editing and display options
Customize	Allows you to add commands to the Quick Access toolbar

Customizing Excel Options

The Customize category of the Excel Options dialog box allows you to add commands to the Quick Access toolbar. This is useful for commands that you use frequently and would like to have available with one click. Examples of commands that you might add are Quick Print, Spelling, Open, and Print Preview. You can add the commands to any open workbook or all workbooks. Kate is interested in customizing the Quick Access toolbar to include spell checking and printing. She would also like to open a document using the Quick Access toolbar. She asks you to customize the Quick Access toolbar to add commands she uses frequently.

STEPS

1. **Start Excel, then save the new file as** My Toolbar **in the drive and folder where you store your Data Files**

2. **Click the** Office button ⊙, **click** Excel Options, **then click** Customize **in the list of options**

   You can customize the Quick Access toolbar by adding any of the commands listed in the Popular Commands list, shown in Figure O-14. You want to customize the Quick Access toolbar for the My Toolbar workbook.

> **QUICK TIP**
>
> You can also add macros and commands that are not in the Ribbon to the Quick Access toolbar using the "Choose commands from" list.

3. **Make sure Popular Commands is displayed in the Choose commands from list, click the Customize Quick Access Toolbar list arrow, and select** For My Toolbar.xlsx

   You want to add the Quick Print icon to the Quick Access toolbar.

4. **Click** Quick Print **in the Popular Commands list, then click** Add >>

   The Quick Print command appears in the custom list of commands on the right side of the dialog box. You want to add the other commands that Kate uses frequently.

5. **Click the** Spelling command **in the Popular Commands list, click** Add >>, **click the** Open command **in the Popular Commands list, click** Add >>, **click the** Print Preview command **in the Popular Commands list, then click** Add >>

   You want to change the order of the icons on the toolbar.

> **TROUBLE**
>
> You may need to adjust the order of your buttons so that Print Preview is below Quick Print and above Spelling.

6. **With** Print Preview **selected in the custom list, click the** Move Up button ▲ **twice to place it under Quick Print in the commands list**

   Kate asks you to remove the Open command from the list of commands for the Quick Access toolbar.

7. **Click** Open **in the custom list of commands, then click** Remove

8. **Click** OK

   The My Toolbar workbook has six buttons on the Quick Access toolbar, the three that it opened with and the three custom commands that you added, as shown in Figure O-15. Kate is happy with the Quick Access toolbar you customized for the workbook.

9. **Save the workbook, then close the workbook and exit Excel**

Applying and creating custom number and date formats

When you use numbers and dates in worksheets or calculations, you can create your own custom cell formats. To create a custom cell format, click the Home tab, click the Format button in the Cells group, then click Format Cells. If necessary, click the Number tab in the Format Cells dialog box, click Custom in the Category list, then click a format that resembles the one you want. For example, the value –3789 appears as **(3,789)** if the cell is formatted as #,##0 _); (#,##0),To display negative numbers in green rather than red, you can replace Red with Green in the Type box, then click OK.

FIGURE O-14: Customize category of Excel options

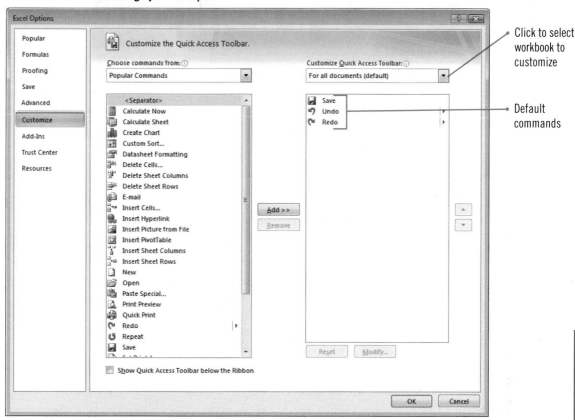

Click to select workbook to customize

Default commands

FIGURE O-15: Workbook with new Quick Access Toolbar buttons

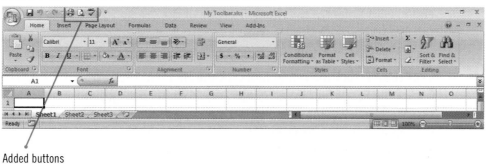

Added buttons

Customizing the Quick Access Toolbar

You can quickly add a button from the Ribbon to the Quick Access Toolbar by right-clicking it and selecting Add to Quick Access Toolbar. Right-clicking a Ribbon button also allows you to quickly open the Excel Options dialog box to access all of the customization options for the Quick Access Toolbar or move the Quick Access Toolbar from its default position above the Ribbon to display below the Ribbon.

Creating a Template

A **template** is a workbook that contains text, formulas, macros, and formatting you use repeatedly. Once you save a workbook as a template, it provides a model for creating a new workbook without your having to reenter standard data. After you save a file as a template, you can create workbooks based on the formulas and formatting you defined; the template itself remains unchanged. ▰▰▰ Kate plans to use the same formulas, titles, and row and column labels from the Sales worksheet for subsequent yearly worksheets. She asks you to create a template using Quest colors.

STEPS

1. **Start Excel, open the file Canada Sales.xlsx from the drive and folder where you store your Data Files, then delete the Quarterly Summary, Jan, and Feb sheets.**

   You decide to leave the formulas in row 7 and in columns N and O so that future users will not have to re-create them. But you want to delete the comment, the sales data, and the year 2010.

2. **Right-click cell L6, click Delete Comment, select the range B5:M6, press [Delete], double-click cell A2, delete 2010, delete the space before Sales, then click cell A1**

   The divide-by-zero error messages in column O are only temporary and will disappear as soon as Kate opens a document based on the template, saves it as a workbook, and begins to enter next year's data. You decide to create custom colors for a theme using Quest's logo colors.

3. **Click the Page Layout tab, click the Colors list arrow in the Themes group, then click Create New Theme Colors**

   The Create New Theme Colors dialog box opens, as shown in Figure O-16. The graphic designer at Quest gave you the red, green, and blue values for three of Quest's logo colors. You want to change the Text/Background Dark 1, Accent 1, and Accent 2 colors to match the logo colors.

4. **Click the Text/Background – Dark 1 list arrow, click More Colors, click the Custom tab, enter the colors for the Red, Green, and Blue boxes using the values from Table O-2, click OK, click the Accent 1 list arrow, click More Colors, enter the values from Table O-2, click OK, click the Accent 2 list arrow, click More Colors, enter the color values from Table O-2, then click OK**

TROUBLE

If the Quest colors are not available, click the Page Layout tab, click the Colors list arrow in the Themes group, click Quest Colors, then begin Step 6 again.

5. **Enter Quest Colors in the Name text box of the Create New Theme Colors dialog box, then click Save**

   You need to apply the three new theme colors and the white color.

QUICK TIP

You can save a theme for use in any Office document. Click the Page Layout tab, click the Themes list arrow in the Themes group, then click Save Current Theme. If you save it in the Document Themes folder, it will appear as a Custom Theme above the Built-In themes in the themes palette for all your Office files.

6. **Click cell A1, click the Home tab, click the Fill Color list arrow [icon], click Dark Red, Accent 2, click the Font Color list arrow [icon], click White, Background 1, select cell A2, click [icon], click Dark Red, Accent 2, apply the Orange, Accent 1 font color to the data in row 4 and column A, apply the Gray-80%, Text 1 font color to the data in the range B5:O7, then click cell A1**

   The completed template is shown in Figure O-17.

7. **Click the Office button, click Save As, click the Save as type list arrow, then click Excel Template (*.xltx)**

   Excel adds the .xltx extension to the filename and automatically switches to the Templates folder. If you are using a computer on a network, you may not have permission to save to the Templates folder, so you'll save it to your Data File location.

8. **Navigate to your Data Files folder, click Save, print the worksheet, then close the workbook and exit Excel**

   Next year, when Kate needs to compile the information for the Canada sales, she can simply open a document based on the Canada Sales template (apply the template) and begin entering data.

FIGURE O-16: Create New Theme Colors dialog box

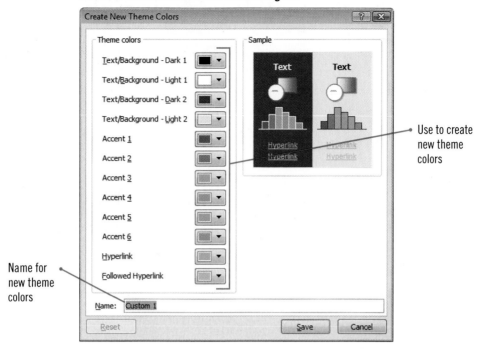

Name for new theme colors

Use to create new theme colors

FIGURE O-17: Template with Quest colors

TABLE O-2: Color settings for Quest colors

	Text/Background – Dark 1	Accent 1	Accent 2
Red	34	247	147
Green	30	147	40
Blue	31	29	34

Applying and editing templates

To create a document based on a template you have saved in the Templates folder (that is, to **apply** a template to a new document), you must use the New command on the Office menu. In the New Workbook dialog box, under Templates click My templates. Click the template you want to use, then click OK. Excel creates a new document named [Template Name]1. To edit a template, open the template (the .xltx file) from the Templates folder, change it, then save it under the same name

in the same location. The changes are applied only to new documents you create.

If you store a template in a location other than your Templates folder, such as your Data Files folder, you use a different procedure to create a document based on the template. In Excel, click the Office button, click New, click New from existing, navigate to the location where you saved the template, then double-click the template name. A new document based on the template opens.

Practice

▼ CONCEPTS REVIEW

FIGURE O-18

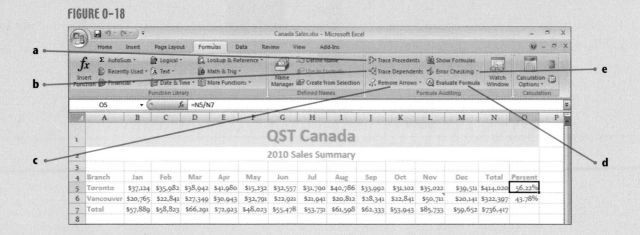

Which element do you click to:

1. Step through a formula in a selected cell?
2. Find cells that may have caused a formula error?
3. Locate formula errors in a worksheet?
4. Eliminate tracers from a worksheet?
5. Locate cells that reference the active cell?

Match each term with the statement that best describes it.

6. **Comment**
7. **AutoFill**
8. **Template**
9. **Outline symbols**
10. **[Shift][F9]**

a. Note that appears when you place the pointer over a cell
b. Used to hide and display details in grouped data
c. Calculates the worksheet manually
d. A workbook that contains text, formulas, and formatting
e. Automatically enters a list in a worksheet

Select the best answer from the list of choices.

11. Which of the following categories of Excel options allows you to change the number of default worksheets in a workbook?
    - **a.** Popular
    - **b.** Customize
    - **c.** Advanced
    - **d.** Formulas

12. Which of the following categories of Excel options allows you to customize the Quick Access Toolbar?
    - **a.** Popular
    - **b.** Customize
    - **c.** Advanced
    - **d.** Formulas

13. The _____ automatically hides everything in the worksheet except the lowest level of detail in the columns.
    - **a.** Column Level 1 button
    - **b.** Column Level 3 button
    - **c.** Column Level 2 button
    - **d.** Column Level 4 button

14. To apply a custom AutoFill list, you:
    - **a.** Press [Shift][F9].
    - **b.** Click the AutoFill tab in the Edit dialog box.
    - **c.** Type the first cell entry and drag the AutoFill handle.
    - **d.** Select the list in the worksheet.

▼ SKILLS REVIEW

1. **Audit a worksheet.**
   - **a.** Start Excel, open the file EX O-2.xlsx from the drive and folder where you store your Data Files, then save it as **Clams**.
   - **b.** Select cell B10, then use the Trace Dependents button to locate all the cells that depend on this cell.
   - **c.** Clear the arrows from the worksheet.
   - **d.** Select cell B19, use the Trace Precedents button on the Formula Auditing toolbar to find the cells on which that figure is based, then correct the formula in cell B19. (*Hint*: It should be B7-B18.)
   - **e.** Use the Error Checking button to check the worksheet for any other errors. Correct any worksheet errors using the formula bar.

2. **Control worksheet calculations.**
   - **a.** Open the Formulas category of the Excel Options dialog box.
   - **b.** Change the worksheet calculations to manual.
   - **c.** Change the figure in cell B6 to 34,000.
   - **d.** Recalculate the worksheet manually, using the appropriate key combination.
   - **e.** Turn off manual calculation and save the workbook.

3. **Group worksheet data.**
   - **a.** Group the income information in rows 5 and 6.
   - **b.** Group the expenses information in rows 10 through 17.
   - **c.** Hide the income details in rows 5 and 6.
   - **d.** Hide the expenses details in rows 10 through 17.
   - **e.** Enter your name in the center section of the worksheet footer, then print the worksheet with the income and expenses detail hidden.
   - **f.** Redisplay the income and expenses details.
   - **g.** Remove the row grouping for the income and expenses details. (*Hint*: With the grouped rows selected, click the Data tab, then click the Ungroup button in the Outline group.)
   - **h.** Save the workbook.

4. **Add a comment to a cell.**
   - **a.** Insert a comment in cell E12 that reads **Does this include newspaper advertising?**.
   - **b.** Click anywhere outside the Comment box to close it.
   - **c.** Display the comment by moving the pointer over cell E12, then check it for errors.
   - **d.** Edit the comment in cell E12 to read **Does this include newspaper and magazine advertising?**.

e. Print the worksheet and your comment, with the comment appearing at the end of the sheet.

f. Save the workbook.

5. Create custom AutoFill lists.

    a. Select the range A4:A19.

    b. Open the Custom Lists dialog box and import the selected text.

    c. Close the dialog box.

    d. On Sheet2, enter **Income** in cell A1.

    e. Use the fill handle to enter the list through cell A15.

    f. Enter your name in the center section of the Sheet2 footer, then print the worksheet.

    g. Open the Custom Lists dialog box again, delete the custom list you just created, then save and close the workbook.

6. Customize Excel workbooks.

    a. Open a new workbook, then open the Popular category of the Excel Options dialog box.

    b. Change the number of sheets in a new workbook to **5**.

    c. Change the default font of a new workbook to 14-point Times New Roman.

    d. Close the workbook and exit Excel.

    e. Start Excel and verify that the new workbook's font is 14-point Times New Roman and that it has five worksheets.

    f. Reset the default number of worksheets to **3** and the default workbook font to 11-point Body Font.

    g. Close the workbook and exit Excel.

7. Customize Excel options.

    a. Start Excel, open the Clams.xlsx workbook from the drive and folder where you store your Data Files, then activate Sheet1.

    b. Use the Customize category of the Excel Options dialog box to add the icons E-mail, New, and Quick Print to the Quick Access Toolbar for the Clams.xlsx workbook.

    c. Reorder the icons so that Quick Print appears first in the list.

    d. Remove the New icon.

    e. Verify that the Quick Print and E-mail icons have been added to the Quick Access Toolbar, then save the workbook.

8. Create a template.

    a. Delete Sheet2 and Sheet3 from the workbook.

    b. Delete the comment in cell E12.

    c. Delete the income and expense data for all four quarters. Leave the worksheet formulas intact.

    d. Create new theme colors using the Create New Theme Colors dialog box. For the Text/Background Dark 1 color, use Red 51, Green 153, and Blue 51. For the Text/Background/Light 1 color, use Red 231, Green 207, and Blue 183. Save the color palette with the name Clam Colors.

    e. Using the Clam Colors palette, apply the Green, Text 1 custom theme color to cell A1 for the fill color. Use the Tan, Background 1 fill color for the range B3:G3 and for cells A4 and A9.

    f. Save the workbook as a template named **Clams.xltx** in the folder where you store your Data Files.

    g. Close the template, then open a document based on the template. (*Hint:* If you saved the template in the Templates folder, click the Office button, click New, click My templates, then double-click the template name. If you saved the template in your Data Files folder, in the New dialog box click New from existing, navigate to the template location, then double-click the template.)

    h. Enter your own data for all four quarters and in every budget category. Adjust the column widths as necessary. Your screen should be similar to Figure O-19.

FIGURE O-19

	A	B	C	D	E	F	G
1	Ipswich Clam Shack						
2							
3		Q1	Q2	Q3	Q4	Total	% of Total
4	**Income**						
5	Beverages	$1,700	$1,600	$33,000	$1,700	$38,000	23%
6	Clams	11,000	15,200	90,000	11,000	$127,200	77%
7	**Net Sales**	$12,700	$16,800	$123,000	$12,700	$165,200	
8							
9	**Expenses**						
10	Salaries	$10,000	$12,000	$15,000	$10,000	$47,000	79%
11	Rent	1,000	1,000	1,000	1,000	$4,000	7%
12	Advertising	50	100	200	50	$400	1%
13	Cleaning	100	100	300	100	$600	1%
14	Clams	500	700	1,500	200	$2,900	5%
15	Dairy	500	300	1,000	500	$2,300	4%
16	Beverages	300	200	1,000	300	$1,800	3%
17	Flour	100	150	300	100	$650	1%
18	**Total Expenses**	$12,550	$14,550	$20,300	$12,250	$59,650	100%
19	**Net Profit**	$150	$2,250	$102,700	$450	$105,550	
20							

i. Save the workbook as **Clams1.xlsx** to the folder where you store your Data Files.

j. Print the worksheet on one page, then close the workbook and exit Excel.

▼ INDEPENDENT CHALLENGE 1

You are the human resources manager at Handy Helpers, a home repair business with franchises in the east and the west regions. You are tracking the overtime hours for workers using total and percentage formulas. Before you begin your analysis, you want to check the worksheet for formula errors. Then, you group the first quarter data, add a comment to the worksheet, and create a custom list of the east and west locations and total labels.

a. Start Excel, open the file titled EX O-3.xlsx from the drive and folder where you store your Data Files, then save it as **Overtime**.

b. Audit the worksheet, ignoring warnings that aren't errors and correcting the formula errors in the formula bar.

c. Select cell R5 and use the Trace Precedents button to show the cells used in its formula.

d. Select cell B10 and use the Trace Dependents button to show the cells affected by the value in the cell.

e. Remove all arrows from the worksheet.

f. Group the months Jan, Feb, and March, then use the Outline symbols to hide the first quarter details.

g. Add the comment **This looks low.** to cell P11. Display the comment on the worksheet so it is visible even when you are not hovering over the cell.

h. Create a custom list by importing the range A5:A15. Test the list in cells A1:A11 of Sheet2. Delete the custom list.

Advanced Challenge Exercise

- Open the Evaluate Formula dialog box with cell S5 on Sheet 1 selected.
- In the Evaluate Formula dialog box, click Evaluate three times to see the process of substituting values for cell addresses in the formula and the results of the formula calculations. Close the Evaluate Formula window.
- Open the Watch Window. Click Add Watch to add cell S6 to the Watch Window and observe its value in the window as you change cell G6 to **40**. Close the Watch Window.

i. Add your name to the center section of the worksheet footer, preview the worksheet, then save the workbook.

j. Print the worksheet and the comment on a separate page. Close the workbook, then exit Excel.

▼ INDEPENDENT CHALLENGE 2

You are the president of the Board of Trustees at Riverview Condominiums located in Montreal. One of your responsibilities is to keep track of the condominium's regular monthly expenses. You have compiled a list of fixed expenses in an Excel workbook. Because the items don't change from month to month, you want to create a custom AutoFill list including each expense item to save time in preparing similar worksheets in the future. You will also temporarily switch to manual formula calculation, check the total formula, and document the data.

a. Start Excel, open the file titled EX O-4.xlsx from the drive and folder where you store your Data Files, then save it as **Riverview**.

b. Select the range of cells **A6:A17** on the Fixed Expenses sheet, then import the list to create a Custom List.

c. Use the AutoFill handle to insert your list in cells A1:A12 in Sheet2.

d. Add your name to the Sheet2 footer, save the workbook, then preview and print Sheet2.

e. Use the Excel Options dialog box to delete your custom list, then return to the Fixed Expenses sheet.

f. Switch to manual calculation for formulas. Change the expense for Gas to $6,000.00. Calculate the worksheet formula manually. Turn on automatic calculation again.

g. Add the comment **This may increase.** to cell B6. Display the comment on the worksheet.

h. Use the Error Checking dialog box for help in correcting the error in cell B18. Verify that the formula is correctly totaling the expenses in column B.

▼ INDEPENDENT CHALLENGE 2 (CONTINUED)

i. Trace the precedents of cell B18. Compare your worksheet to Figure O-20.

j. Remove the arrow and the comment display from the worksheet, leaving only the indicator displayed. Do not delete the comment from the worksheet cell.

k. Trace the dependents of cell B6. Remove the arrow from the worksheet.

l. Edit the comment in cell B6 to **This may increase next month**. Add the comment **This seems low.** to cell B12.

m. Use the Next and Previous buttons in the Comments group of the Review tab to move between comments on the worksheet. Delete the comment in cell B12.

FIGURE O-20

	A	B	C	D	E
1	Riverview				
2	Fixed Monthly Expenses				
3					
4					
5	Item	Amount	Your Name:		
6	Gas	$ 6,000.00	This may increase.		
7	Electricity	$ 1,877.00			
8	Water & Sewer	$ 2,098.00			
9	Rubbish Removal	$ 1,009.00			
10	Parking & Garage	$ 413.00			
11	Fire Alarm Service	$ 100.00			
12	Cleaning Service	$ 298.00			
13	Building Maintenance	$ 1,160.00			
14	Payroll	$ 2,011.00			
15	Supplies	$ 509.00			
16	Landscaping	$ 1,021.00			
17	Roof Loan	$ 695.00			
18	Total	$ 17,191.00			
19					

Advanced Challenge Exercise

- Paste the comment in cell B6 to cell B11.
- The Comments group on the Review tab has a button named Show Ink. Use the Excel Help feature to find out how ink is used in Excel. (*Hint*: You may have to use Office Online help. Try using Ink in Excel for your search terms.)
- Summarize your research findings in cell A20 of the worksheet.

n. Add your name to the center section of the worksheet footer, save the workbook, then print the Fixed Expenses worksheet with any comments appearing at the end of the sheet.

o. Close the workbook and exit Excel.

▼ INDEPENDENT CHALLENGE 3

As the manager of Champion Training Center, which specializes in health and fitness, you are responsible for the yearly budget. You use Excel to track income and expenses using formulas to total each category and to calculate the net cash flow for the business. You want to customize your workbooks and settings in Excel so you can work more efficiently. You are also interested in grouping your data and creating a template that you can use to build next year's budget.

a. Start Excel, open the file titled EX O-5.xlsx from the drive and folder where you store your Data Files, then save it as **Champion**.

b. Add icons to the Quick Access Toolbar for the Champions.xlsx workbook that open a file, create a new file, and check spelling.

c. Reorder the icons so that the icon to create a new file is at the top of the list of icons.

d. Remove the icon that opens a file from the list of icons to be added to the Quick Access Toolbar.

e. Close the Excel Options dialog box and test the customized Quick Access Toolbar by checking the spelling of the worksheet.

f. Group rows 6-8 and 11-16, then use the appropriate row level button to hide the expense and income details, as shown in Figure O-21.

g. Add your name to the center section of the worksheet footer, save the workbook, then print the grouped worksheet.

FIGURE O-21

	A	B	C	D	E	F
1	Champion Training Center					
2	Yearly Budget					
3						
4	Description	1st Qtr	2nd Qtr	3rd Qtr	4th Qtr	Total
5	Income					
9	Income Total	$159,200	$159,200	$158,300	$163,300	$640,000
10	Expenses					
17	Expenses Total	$140,720	$155,100	$108,100	$143,270	$547,190
18	Net Cash Flow	$18,480	$4,100	$50,200	$20,030	$92,810
19						

h. Redisplay all rows, using the Outline symbols. Delete Sheet2 and Sheet3. Delete all data in Sheet1, leaving the formulas and labels.

▼ INDEPENDENT CHALLENGE 3 (CONTINUED)

i. Save the workbook as a template named **Budget** in the drive and folder where you store your Data Files. Close the template file and open a workbook based on the template. Save the workbook as **New Budget**.

j. Enter data for the four quarters. Save the workbook, then preview and print the worksheet.

k. Customize Excel so that your workbooks will open with four worksheets in Page Layout view and using 12-point Trebuchet MS font.

l. Close your workbook, exit Excel, and then open a new workbook to confirm the new default workbook settings. Reset the default Excel workbook to open with three sheets in Normal view and the 11-point Body Font. Close the new workbook.

Advanced Challenge Exercise

- Open the Champion.xlsx workbook and redisplay all rows in the worksheet.
- Create a custom number format that displays negative numbers using a green font. [*Hint*: Edit one of the formats that display negative numbers in a red font.]
- Apply your custom number format to cell B18. Change the first quarter membership amount in cell B6 to $1000 and verify that the value in cell B18 displays using the custom number format. Save then close the workbook.

m. Exit Excel.

▼ REAL LIFE INDEPENDENT CHALLENGE

This Independent Challenge requires an Internet connection.

Excel offers predesigned templates that you can access from the Web to create your own budgets, maintain your health records, create meeting agendas, put together expense estimates, and plan projects. You can download the templates and create Excel workbooks based on the templates. Then you can add your own data, and customize the worksheet for your purposes.

a. Start Excel, then use the Excel help feature to search for Templates.

b. Review the available templates and download a template that organizes information you commonly use at home, school, or work.

c. Save the template with the name **My Template.xltx** in the location where you store your Data Files. If your template was created using an earlier version of Excel, you will be working in compatibility mode. If this is the case, close the workbook and reopen it.

d. Create a custom color theme using as many colors as you think is appropriate for your template. Name the color theme **My Colors** and use theme colors rather than RGB values to select colors that are appropriate for your data. Select your custom color theme to replace the template color scheme with your own colors.

e. Add your name to the center section of the template's worksheet footer, save the template, preview the worksheet, and change its orientation and scale if necessary to allow a worksheet based on the template to print on one page.

f. Close the template, then open a workbook based on the template. Enter your data, save the workbook, then preview the worksheet.

g. Print the worksheet, close the workbook, close your browser, and exit Excel.

▼ VISUAL WORKSHOP

Open the Data File EX O-6.xlsx from the drive and folder where you store your Data Files, then save it as **Pet Supply**. Group the data as shown after removing any errors in the worksheet. Your grouped results should match Figure O-22. (*Hint*: The Outline symbols have been hidden for the worksheet.) The new buttons on the Quick Access Toolbar have only been added to the Pet Supply workbook. Add your name to the center section of the worksheet footer, save the workbook, then preview and print the worksheet. Close the workbook and exit Excel.

FIGURE O-22

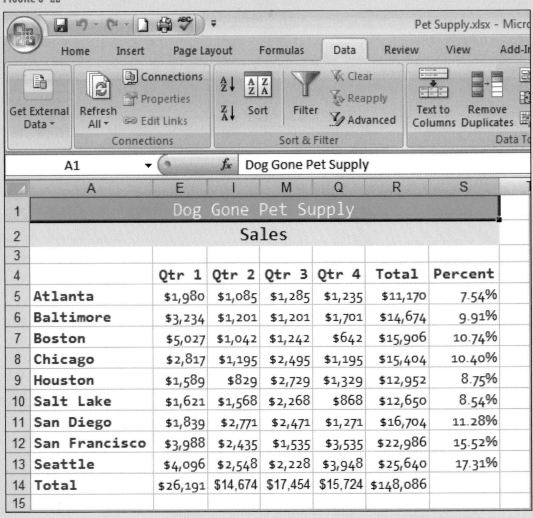

Programming with Excel

All Excel macros are written in a programming language called Visual Basic for Applications, or simply, **VBA**. When you create a macro with the Excel macro recorder, the recorder writes the VBA instructions for you. You can also create an Excel macro by entering VBA instructions manually. The sequence of VBA statements contained in a macro is called a **procedure**. In this unit, you will view and analyze existing VBA code and write VBA code on your own. You learn how to add a conditional statement to a procedure as well as how to prompt the user for information while the macro is running. You also find out how to locate any errors, or bugs, in a macro. Finally, you will combine several macros into one main procedure. Quest's vice president of sales, Kate Morgan, would like to automate some of the division's time-consuming tasks. You help Kate by creating five Excel macros for the sales division.

OBJECTIVES

View VBA code

Analyze VBA code

Write VBA code

Add a conditional statement

Prompt the user for data

Debug a macro

Create a main procedure

Run a main procedure

Viewing VBA Code

Before you can write Excel macro procedures, you must become familiar with the VBA (Visual Basic for Applications) programming language. A common method of learning any programming language is to view existing code. To view VBA code, you open the **Visual Basic Editor**, which contains a Project window, a Properties window, and a Code window. The VBA code for macro procedures appears in the Code window. The first line of a procedure, called the **procedure header**, defines the procedure's type, name, and arguments. **Arguments** are variables used by other procedures which the main procedure might run. An empty set of parentheses after the procedure name means the procedure doesn't have any arguments. Items that appear in blue are **keywords**, which are words Excel recognizes as part of the VBA programming language. **Comments** are notes explaining the code; they are displayed in green, and the remaining code is displayed in black. You use the Visual Basic Editor to view or edit an existing macro as well as to create new ones. Each month, Kate receives text files containing tour sales information from the Quest branches. Kate has already imported the text file for the Miami January sales into a worksheet, but it still needs to be formatted. She asks you to work on a macro to automate the process of formatting the imported information.

STEPS

1. **Start Excel if necessary, click the** Developer tab, **then click the** Macro Security button **in the Code group**

   The Trust Center dialog box opens, as shown in Figure P-1. You know the Quest branch files are from a trusted source, so you will allow macros to run in the workbook.

2. **Click the** Enable all macros option button **if necessary, then click** OK

   You are ready to open a file and view its VBA code. A macro-enabled workbook has the extension xlsm. Although a workbook containing a macro will open if macros are disabled, they will not function.

3. **Open the file** EX P-1.xlsm **from the drive and folder where you store your Data Files, save it as** Monthly Sales, **then click the** Macros button in the Code group

   The macro dialog box opens with the FormatFile macro procedure in the list box. If you have any macros saved in your Personal Macro workbook, they are also listed in the Macro dialog box.

4. **If it is not already selected click** FormatFile, **click** Edit, **then click** Format **in the Modules area of the Project Explorer window**

   The Project Explorer window is shown in Figure P-2. Because the FormatFile procedure is contained in the Format module, clicking Format selects the Format module and displays the FormatFile procedure in the Code window. See Table P-1 to make sure your screen matches the ones shown in this unit.

5. **Make sure both the Visual Basic window and the Code window are maximized to match Figure P-2**

6. **Examine the top three lines of code, which contain comments, and the first line of code beginning with Sub FormatFile( )**

   Notice that the different parts of the procedure appear in various colors. The first two comment lines give the procedure name and tell what the procedure does. The third comment line explains that the keyboard shortcut for this macro procedure is [Ctrl][Shift][F]. The keyword Sub in the procedure header indicates that this is a **Sub procedure**, or a series of Visual Basic statements that perform an action but do not return a value. In the next lesson, you will analyze the procedure code to see what each line does.

FIGURE P-1: Macro settings in the Trust Center dialog box

Select to allow macros to run

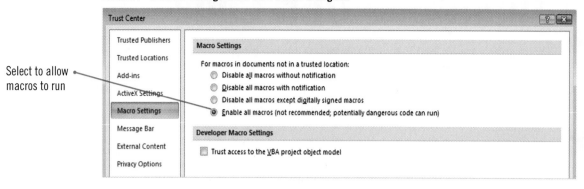

FIGURE P-2: Procedure displayed in the Visual Basic Editor

Procedure header

Project Explorer window

Properties window

Comments in green

Keywords in blue

Code window

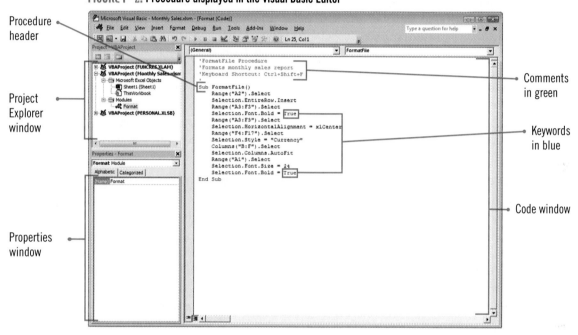

TABLE P-1: Matching your screen to the unit figures

if...	do this...
The Properties window is not displayed	Click the Properties Window button 📋 on the toolbar
The Project Explorer window is not displayed	Click the Project Explorer button 📑 on the toolbar
You see only the Code window	Click Tools on the menu bar, click Options, click the Docking tab, then make sure the Project Explorer and Properties Window options are selected
You do not see folders in the Explorer window	Click the Toggle Folders button 📁 on the Project Explorer window Project toolbar

Understanding the Visual Basic Editor

A **module** is the Visual Basic equivalent of a worksheet. In it, you store macro procedures, just as you store data in worksheets. Modules, in turn, are stored in workbooks (or projects), along with worksheets. A **project** is the collection of all procedures in a workbook. You view and edit modules in the Visual Basic Editor, which is made up of three windows: Project Explorer (also called the Project window), the Code window, and the Properties window. Project Explorer displays a list of all open projects (or workbooks) and the worksheets and modules they contain. To view the procedures stored in a module, you must first select the module in Project Explorer (just as you would select a file in Windows Explorer). The Code window then displays the selected module's procedures. The Properties window displays a list of characteristics (or properties) associated with the module. A newly inserted module has only one property, its name.

Analyzing VBA Code

You can learn a lot about the VBA language simply by analyzing the code generated by the Excel macro recorder. The more VBA code you analyze, the easier it is for you to write your own programming code. ⬛⬛⬛ Before writing any new procedures, you analyze a previously written procedure that applies formatting to a worksheet. Then you open a worksheet that you want to format and run the macro.

STEPS

1. **With the FormatFile procedure still displayed in the Code window, examine the next four lines of code, beginning with Range("A2").Select**

   Refer to Figure P-3 as you analyze the code in this lesson. Every Excel element, including a range, is considered an **object**. A **range object** represents a cell or a range of cells. The statement Range("A2").Select selects the range object cell A2. Notice that several times in the procedure, a line of code (or **statement**) selects a range, and then subsequent lines act on that selection. The next statement, Selection. EntireRow.Insert, inserts a row above the selection, which is currently cell A2. The next two lines of code select range A3:F3 and apply bold formatting to that selection. In VBA terminology, bold formatting is a value of an object's Bold property. A **property** is an attribute of an object that defines one of the object's characteristics (such as size) or an aspect of its behavior (such as whether it is enabled). To change the characteristics of an object, you change the values of its properties. For example, to apply bold formatting to a selected range, you assign the value True to the range's Bold property. To remove bold formatting, assign the value False.

2. **Examine the remaining lines of code, beginning with the second occurrence of the line Range("A3:F3").Select**

   The next two statements select the range object A3:F3 and center its contents, then the following two statements select the F4:F17 range object and format it as currency. Column objects B through F are then selected and their widths set to AutoFit. Finally, the range object cell A1 is selected, its font size is changed to 24, and its Bold property is set to True. The last line, End Sub, indicates the end of the Sub procedure and is also referred to as the **procedure footer**.

3. **Click the View Microsoft Excel button 🗗 on the Visual Basic Editor Standard toolbar to return to Excel**

   Because the macro is stored in the Monthly Sales workbook, Kate can open this workbook and repeatedly use the macro stored there each month after she receives that month's sales data. She wants you to open the workbook containing data for Miami's January sales and run the macro to format the data. You must leave the Monthly Sales workbook open to use the macro stored there.

4. **Open the file EX P-2.xlsx from the drive and folder where you store your Data Files, then save it as January Sales**

   This is the workbook containing the data you want to format.

5. **Press [Ctrl][Shift][F] to run the procedure**

   The FormatFile procedure formats the text, as shown in Figure P-4.

6. **Save the workbook**

   Now that you've successfully viewed and analyzed VBA code and run the macro, you will learn how to write your own code.

FIGURE P-3: VBA code for the FormatFile procedure

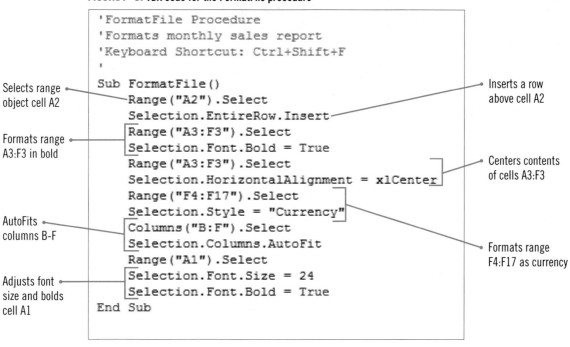

Selects range object cell A2

Formats range A3:F3 in bold

AutoFits columns B-F

Adjusts font size and bolds cell A1

Inserts a row above cell A2

Centers contents of cells A3:F3

Formats range F4:F17 as currency

```vba
'FormatFile Procedure
'Formats monthly sales report
'Keyboard Shortcut: Ctrl+Shift+F
'
Sub FormatFile()
    Range("A2").Select
    Selection.EntireRow.Insert
    Range("A3:F3").Select
    Selection.Font.Bold = True
    Range("A3:F3").Select
    Selection.HorizontalAlignment = xlCenter
    Range("F4:F17").Select
    Selection.Style = "Currency"
    Columns("B:F").Select
    Selection.Columns.AutoFit
    Range("A1").Select
    Selection.Font.Size = 24
    Selection.Font.Bold = True
End Sub
```

FIGURE P-4: Worksheet formatted using the FormatFile procedure

Formatted title

Row inserted

Formatted column headings

Range formatted as currency

Columns widened

	A	B	C	D	E	F	G
1	Quest Miami January Sales						
2							
3	Trip Code	Depart Date	Number of Days	Seats Sold	Tour	Sales	
4	452R	1/7/2010	30	30	African National Parks	$146,100.00	
5	556J	1/13/2010	14	25	Amazing Amazon	$ 71,925.00	
6	675Y	1/19/2010	14	32	Catalonia Adventure	$ 99,200.00	
7	446R	1/20/2010	7	18	Cooking in Croatia	$ 37,980.00	
8	251D	1/21/2010	7	10	Cooking in France	$ 28,220.00	
9	335P	1/22/2010	21	33	Corfu Sailing Voyage	$105,270.00	
10	431V	1/25/2010	7	21	Costa Rica Rainforests	$ 54,390.00	
11	215C	1/26/2010	14	19	Cruising the Mergui Archipelago	$ 92,663.00	
12	325B	1/27/2010	10	17	Down Under Exodus	$ 47,600.00	
13	311A	1/29/2010	18	20	Essential India	$ 78,660.00	
14	422R	1/29/2010	7	24	Exotic Morocco	$ 45,600.00	
15	331E	1/30/2010	12	21	Experience Cambodia	$ 61,068.00	
16	831P	1/30/2010	14	15	Galapagos Adventure	$ 46,500.00	
17	334Q	1/31/2010	18	10	Green Adventures in Ecuador	$ 24,500.00	
18							

Writing VBA Code

To write your own code, you first need to open the Visual Basic Editor and add a module to the workbook. You can then begin entering the procedure code. In the first few lines of a procedure, you typically include comments indicating the name of the procedure, a brief description of the procedure, and short-cut keys, if applicable. When writing Visual Basic code for Excel, you must follow the formatting rules, or **syntax**, of the VBA programming language. A misspelled keyword or variable name causes a procedure to fail. ▰▰▰▰ Kate would like to total the monthly sales. You help her by writing a procedure that auto-mates this routine task.

STEPS

1. **With the January worksheet still displayed, click the Developer tab, then click the Visual Basic button in the Code group**

   Two projects are displayed in the Project Explorer window, Monthly Sales.xlsm (which contains the FormatFile macro) and January Sales.xlsx (which contains the monthly data). The FormatFile procedure is again displayed in the Visual Basic Editor. You may have other projects in the Project Explorer window.

2. **Click the Modules folder in the Monthly Sales.xlsm project**

   You need to store all of the procedures in the Monthly Sales.xlsm project, which is in the Monthly Sales.xlsm workbook. By clicking the Modules folder, you have activated the workbook, and the title bar changes from January Sales to Monthly Sales.

3. **Click Insert on the Visual Basic Editor menu bar, then click Module**

   A new, blank module with the default name Module1 appears in the Monthly Sales.xlsm project, under the Format module. You think the property name of the module could be more descriptive.

4. **Click (Name) in the Properties window, then type Total**

   The module name is Total. The module name should not be the same as the procedure name (which will be AddTotal). In the code shown in Figure P-5, comments begin with an apostrophe, and the lines of code under Sub AddTotal( ) have been indented using the Tab key. When you enter the code in the next step, after you type the procedure header Sub AddTotal( ) and press [Enter], the Visual Basic Editor automatically enters End Sub (the procedure footer) in the Code window.

5. **Click in the Code window, then type the procedure code exactly as shown in Figure P-5 entering your name in the second line, pressing [Tab] to indent text and [Shift][Tab] to move the insertion point to the left**

   The lines that begin with ActiveCell.Formula insert the information enclosed in quotation marks into the active cell. For example, ActiveCell.Formula = "Monthly Total:" inserts the words Monthly Total: into cell E18, the active cell. As you type each line, Excel adjusts the spacing.

6. **Compare the procedure code you entered in the Code window with Figure P-5, make any corrections if necessary, then click the Save Monthly Sales.xlsm button 🖫 on the Visual Basic Editor Standard toolbar**

7. **Click the View Microsoft Excel button 🖾 on the toolbar, click January Sales.xlsx on the taskbar to activate the workbook if necessary, with the January worksheet displayed click the Developer tab, then click the Macros button in the Code group**

   Macro names have two parts. The first part ('Monthly Sales.xlsm'!) indicates the workbook where the macro is stored. The second part (AddTotal or FormatFile) is the name of the procedure, taken from the procedure header.

8. **Click 'MonthlySales.xlsm'!AddTotal to select it if necessary, then click Run**

   The AddTotal procedure inserts and formats the monthly total in cell F18, as shown in Figure P-6.

9. **Save the workbook**

Programming with Excel

FIGURE P-5: VBA code for the AddTotal procedure

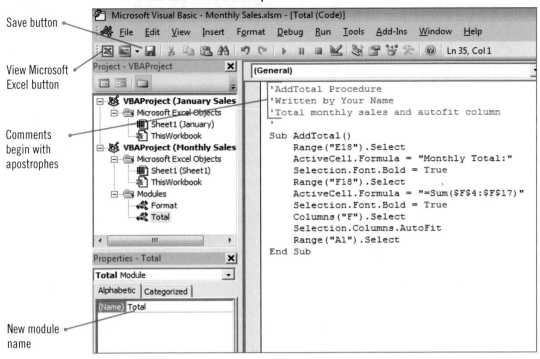

Save button

View Microsoft Excel button

Comments begin with apostrophes

New module name

```
'AddTotal Procedure
'Written by Your Name
'Total monthly sales and autofit column
'
Sub AddTotal()
    Range("E18").Select
    ActiveCell.Formula = "Monthly Total:"
    Selection.Font.Bold = True
    Range("F18").Select
    ActiveCell.Formula = "=Sum($F$4:$F$17)"
    Selection.Font.Bold = True
    Columns("F").Select
    Selection.Columns.AutoFit
    Range("A1").Select
End Sub
```

FIGURE P-6: Worksheet after running the AddTotal procedure

	A	B	C	D	E	F
1	Quest Miami January Sales					
2						
3	Trip Code	Depart Date	Number of Days	Seats Sold	Tour	Sales
4	452R	1/7/2010	30	30	African National Parks	$146,100.00
5	556J	1/13/2010	14	25	Amazing Amazon	$ 71,925.00
6	675Y	1/19/2010	14	32	Catalonia Adventure	$ 99,200.00
7	446R	1/20/2010	7	18	Cooking in Croatia	$ 37,980.00
8	251D	1/21/2010	7	10	Cooking in France	$ 28,220.00
9	335P	1/22/2010	21	33	Corfu Sailing Voyage	$105,270.00
10	431V	1/25/2010	7	21	Costa Rica Rainforests	$ 54,390.00
11	215C	1/26/2010	14	19	Cruising the Mergui Archipelago	$ 92,663.00
12	325B	1/27/2010	10	17	Down Under Exodus	$ 47,600.00
13	311A	1/29/2010	18	20	Essential India	$ 78,660.00
14	422R	1/29/2010	7	24	Exotic Morocco	$ 45,600.00
15	331E	1/30/2010	12	21	Experience Cambodia	$ 61,068.00
16	831P	1/30/2010	14	15	Galapagos Adventure	$ 46,500.00
17	334Q	1/31/2010	18	10	Green Adventures in Ecuador	$ 24,500.00
18					Monthly Total:	$939,676.00

Result of AddTotal procedure

Entering code using AutoComplete

To assist you in entering the VBA code, the Editor uses **AutoComplete**, a list of words that can be used in the macro statement and match what is typed. Typically, the list appears after you press [.] (period). To include a word from the list in the macro statement, select the word in the list, then double-click it or press [Tab].

For example, to enter the Range("E12").Select instruction, type Range(" E12"), then press [.] (period). Type s to bring up the words beginning with the letter s, select the Select command in the list, then press [Tab] to enter the word Select in the macro statement.

Adding a Conditional Statement

The formatting macros you entered in the previous lesson could have been created using the macro recorder. However, there are some situations where you cannot use the recorder and must type the VBA macro code. One of these situations is when you want a procedure to take an action based on a certain condition or set of conditions. For example, *if* a salesperson's performance rating is a 5 (top rating), *then* calculate a 10% bonus; otherwise (*else*), there is no bonus. One way of adding this type of conditional statement in Visual Basic is by using an **If...Then...Else statement**. The syntax for this statement is: "If *condition* Then *statements* Else [*else statements*]." The brackets indicate that the Else part of the statement is optional. Kate wants the worksheet to point out if the total sales figure meets or misses the $900,000 monthly quota. You use Excel to add a conditional statement that indicates this information. You start by returning to the Visual Basic Editor and inserting a new module in the Monthly Sales project.

STEPS

QUICK TIP
You can also return to the Visual Basic Editor by clicking its button on the taskbar.

1. **With the January worksheet still displayed, click the** Developer tab **if necessary, then click the** Visual Basic button **in the Code group**

2. **Verify that the Total module in the Modules folder of the Monthly Sales VBAProject is selected in the Project Explorer window, click** Insert **on the Visual Basic Editor menu bar, then click** Module

    A new, blank module named Module1 is inserted in the Monthly Sales workbook.

3. **In the Properties window click** (Name), **then type** Sales

QUICK TIP
The If...Then...Else statement is similar to the Excel IF function.

4. **Click in the** Code window, **then type the code exactly as shown in Figure P-7, entering your name in the second line**

    Notice the green comment lines in the middle of the code. These lines help explain the procedure.

5. **Compare the procedure you entered with Figure P-7, make any corrections if necessary, click the** Save Monthly Sales.xlsm button **on the Visual Basic Editor toolbar, then click the** View Microsoft Excel button **on the toolbar**

6. **If necessary, click** January Sales.xlsx **in the taskbar to display it, with the January worksheet displayed click the** Macros button **in the Code group, in the Macro dialog box click** 'Monthly Sales.xlsm'!SalesStatus, **then click** Run

    The SalesStatus procedure indicates the status "Met Quota", as shown in Figure P-8.

7. **Save the workbook**

FIGURE P-7: VBA code for the SalesStatus procedure

```
'SalesStatus Procedure
'Written by Your Name
'Tests whether total sales meets the monthly quota
'
Sub SalesStatus()
    Range("E20").Select
    ActiveCell.Formula = "Sales Status:"
    Selection.Font.Bold = True
    'If the total is less than 900000 then
    'insert "Missed Quota" in cell F20
    If Range("F18") <= 900000 Then
        Range("F20").Select
        ActiveCell.Formula = "Missed Quota"
    'otherwise, insert "Met Quota" in cell F20
    Else
        Range("F20").Select
        ActiveCell.Formula = "Met Quota"
    End If
    Range("A1").Select
End Sub
```

If . . . Then . . . Else

FIGURE P-8: Result of running the SalesStatus procedure

Quest Miami January Sales

	A	B	C	D	E	F
3	Trip Code	Depart Date	Number of Days	Seats Sold	Tour	Sales
4	452R	1/7/2010	30	30	African National Parks	$146,100.00
5	556J	1/13/2010	14	25	Amazing Amazon	$ 71,925.00
6	675Y	1/19/2010	14	32	Catalonia Adventure	$ 99,200.00
7	446R	1/20/2010	7	18	Cooking in Croatia	$ 37,980.00
8	251D	1/21/2010	7	10	Cooking in France	$ 28,220.00
9	335P	1/22/2010	21	33	Corfu Sailing Voyage	$105,270.00
10	431V	1/25/2010	7	21	Costa Rica Rainforests	$ 54,390.00
11	215C	1/26/2010	14	19	Cruising the Mergui Archipelago	$ 92,663.00
12	325B	1/27/2010	10	17	Down Under Exodus	$ 47,600.00
13	311A	1/29/2010	18	20	Essential India	$ 78,660.00
14	422R	1/29/2010	7	24	Exotic Morocco	$ 45,600.00
15	331E	1/30/2010	12	21	Experience Cambodia	$ 61,068.00
16	831P	1/30/2010	14	15	Galapagos Adventure	$ 46,500.00
17	334Q	1/31/2010	18	10	Green Adventures in Ecuador	$ 24,500.00
18					**Monthly Total:**	**$939,676.00**
19						
20					**Sales Status:**	Met Quota

Indicates status
of monthly total

Prompting the User for Data

Another situation where you must type, not record, VBA code is when you need to pause a macro to allow user input. You use the VBA InputBox function to display a dialog box that prompts the user for information. A **function** is a predefined procedure that returns (creates and displays) a value; in this case the value returned is the information the user enters. The required elements of an InputBox function are as follows: *object*.InputBox("*prompt*"), where "*prompt*" is the message that appears in the dialog box. For a detailed description of the InputBox function, use the Visual Basic Editor's Help menu. ▧▧▧▧ You decide to create a procedure that will insert the user's name in the left footer area of the worksheet. You use the InputBox function to display a dialog box in which the user can enter his or her name. You also type an intentional error into the procedure code, which you will correct in the next lesson.

STEPS

1. **With the January worksheet displayed, click the** Developer tab **if necessary, click the** Visual Basic button **in the Code group, verify that the Sales module is selected in the Monthly Sales VBAProject Modules folder, click** Insert **on the Visual Basic Editor menu bar, then click** Module

   A new, blank module named Module1 is inserted in the Monthly Sales workbook.

2. **In the Properties window click** (Name), **then type** Footer

3. **Click in the** Code window, **then type the procedure code exactly as shown in Figure P-9 entering your name in the second line**

   Like the SalesStatus procedure, this procedure also contains comments that explain the code. The first part of the code, Dim LeftFooterText As String, **declares**, or defines, LeftFooterText as a text string variable. In Visual Basic, a **variable** is a location in memory in which you can temporarily store one item of information. Dim statements are used to declare variables and must be entered in the following format: Dim *variablename* As *datatype*. The datatype here is "string." In this case, you plan to store the information received from the input box in the temporary memory location called LeftFooterText. Then you can place this text in the left footer area. The remaining statements in the procedure are explained in the comment line directly above each statement. Notice the comment pointing out the error in the procedure code. You will correct this in the next lesson.

4. **Review your code, make any necessary changes, click the** Save MonthlySales.xlsm button 🖫 **on the Visual Basic Editor toolbar, then click the** View Microsoft Excel button 🖾 **on the toolbar**

5. **With the January worksheet displayed, click the** Macros button **in the Code group, in the Macro dialog box click** 'Monthly Sales.xlsm'!FooterInput, **then click** Run

   The procedure begins, and a dialog box generated by the InputBox function opens, prompting you to enter your name, as shown in Figure P-10.

6. **With the cursor in the text box, type your name, then click** OK

7. **Click the** Office button, **point to** Print, **then click** Print Preview

   Although the customized footer with the date is inserted on the sheet, because of the error your name does *not* appear in the left section of the footer. In the next lesson, you will learn how to step through a procedure's code line by line. This will help you locate the error in the FooterInput procedure.

8. **Click the** Close Print Preview button, **then save the workbook**

   You return to the January worksheet.

FIGURE P-9: VBA code for the FooterInput procedure

```
'FooterInput Procedure
'Written by Your Name
'Customize worksheet footer
'
Sub FooterInput()
    'Declares the LeftFooterText string variable
    Dim LeftFooterText As String
    'Prompts user for left footer text and stores
    'response in LeftFooterText variable
    LeftFooterText = InputBox("Enter name:")
    'Inserts contents of LeftFooterText into left footer
    '*****THERE IS AN ERROR IN THE FOLLOWING LINE *****
    Worksheets("January").PageSetup.LeftFooter = LeftFooter
    'Inserts the date in right footer
    Worksheets("January").PageSetup.RightFooter = "&D"
End Sub
```

The phrase Enter name:
will appear in a dialog box

Comment points out an
error in the next line

FIGURE P-10: InputBox function's dialog box

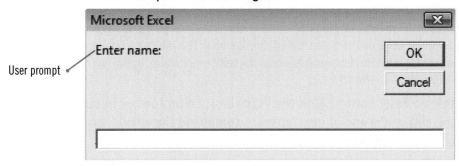

User prompt

Microsoft Excel

Enter name:

OK

Cancel

Excel 2007

Naming variables

Variable names in VBA must begin with a letter. Letters can be uppercase or lowercase. Variable names cannot include periods or spaces and can be up to 255 characters long. Each variable name in a procedure must be unique. Examples of valid and invalid variable names are shown in Table P-2

TABLE P-2: Variable names

valid	invalid
Sales_Department	Sales Department
SalesDepartment	Sales.Department
Quarter1	1stQuarter

Debugging a Macro

When a macro procedure does not run properly, it can be due to an error, referred to as a **bug**, in the code. To assist you in finding the bug(s) in a procedure, the Visual Basic Editor helps you step through the procedure's code, one line at a time. When you locate the error, you can then correct, or **debug**, it. ▟▟▟▟ You decide to debug the macro procedure to find out why it failed to insert your name in the worksheet footer.

STEPS

1. **With the January worksheet displayed click the Developer tab if necessary, click the Macros button in the Code group, in the Macro dialog box click 'Monthly Sales.xlsm'!FooterInput, then click Step Into**

   The Visual Basic Editor opens with the yellow statement selector positioned on the first statement of the procedure, as shown in Figure P-11.

2. **Press [F8] to step to the next statement**

   The statement selector skips over the comments and the line of code beginning with Dim. The Dim statement indicates that the procedure will store your name in a variable named LeftFooterText. Because Dim is a declaration of a variable and not a procedure statement, the statement selector skips it and moves to the line containing the InputBox function.

3. **Press [F8] again, with the cursor in the text box in the Microsoft Excel dialog box type your name, then click OK**

   The Visual Basic Editor opens. The statement selector is now positioned on the statement that reads Worksheets ("January").PageSetup.LeftFooter = LeftFooter. This statement should insert your name (which you just typed in the text box) in the left section of the footer. This is the instruction that does not appear to be working correctly.

4. **If necessary scroll right until the end of the LeftFooter instruction is visible, then place the mouse pointer on LeftFooter**

   The value of the LeftFooter variable is displayed as shown in Figure P-12. Rather than containing your name, the variable LeftFooter at the end of this line is empty. This is because the InputBox function assigned your name to the LeftFooterText variable, not to the LeftFooter variable. Before you can correct this bug, you need to turn off the Step Into feature.

5. **Click the Reset button ▣ on the Visual Basic Editor toolbar to turn off the Step Into feature, click at the end of the statement containing the error, then replace the variable LeftFooter with LeftFooterText**

   The revised statement now reads Worksheets("January").PageSetup.LeftFooter = LeftFooterText.

6. **Delete the comment line pointing out the error**

7. **Click the Save Monthly Sales.xlsm button ▣ on the Visual Basic Editor toolbar, then click the View Microsoft Excel button ▣ on the toolbar**

8. **With the January worksheet displayed click the Macros button in the Code group, in the Macro dialog box click 'Monthly Sales.xlsm'!FooterInput, click Run to rerun the procedure, when prompted type your name, then click OK**

9. **Click the Office button, point to Print, then click Print Preview**

   Your name now appears in the left section of the footer.

10. **Click the Close Print Preview button, save the workbook, then print the worksheet**

FIGURE P-11: Statement selector positioned on first procedure statement

```
'FooterInput Procedure
'Written by Your Name
'Customize worksheet footer
'
Sub FooterInput()
    'Declares the LeftFooterText string variable
    Dim LeftFooterText As String
    'Prompts user for left footer text and stores
    'response in LeftFooter Text variable
    LeftFooterText = InputBox("Enter name:")
    'Inserts contents of LeftFooterText into left footer
    '***** THERE IS AN ERROR IN THE FOLLOWING LINE *****
    Worksheets("January").PageSetup.LeftFooter = LeftFooter
    'Inserts the date in right footer
    Worksheets("January").PageSetup.RightFooter = "&D"
End Sub
```

Statement selector — (pointing to `Sub FooterInput()`)

FIGURE P-12: Value contained in LeftFooter variable

```
'FooterInput Procedure
'Written by Your Name
'Customize worksheet footer
'
Sub FooterInput()
    'Declares the LeftFooterText string variable
    Dim LeftFooterText As String
    'Prompts user for left footer text and stores
    'response in LeftFooter Text variable
    LeftFooterText = InputBox("Enter name:")
    'Inserts contents of LeftFooterText into left footer
    '***** THERE IS AN ERROR IN THE FOLLOWING LINE *****
    Worksheets("January").PageSetup.LeftFooter = LeftFooter
    'Inserts the date in right footer     LeftFooter = Empty
    Worksheets("January").PageSetup.RightFooter = "&D"
End Sub
```

Indicates the LeftFooter variable is empty

Adding security to your macro projects

To add security to your projects, you can add a digital signature to the project. A digital signature guarantees the project hasn't been altered since it was signed. You should sign macros only after they are tested and ready to be distributed. If the code in a digitally signed macro project is changed in any way, its digital signature is removed. To add a digital signature to a Visual Basic project, select the project that you want to sign in the Visual Basic Project Explorer window, click the Tools menu in the Visual Basic Editor, click Digital Signature, click Choose, select the certificate, then click OK twice. When you add a digital signature to a project, the macro project is automatically re-signed whenever it is saved on your computer.

Creating a Main Procedure

When you routinely need to run several macros one after another, you can save time by combining them into one procedure. The resulting procedure, which processes (or runs) multiple procedures in sequence, is referred to as the **main procedure**. To create a main procedure, you type a Call statement for each procedure you want to run. The syntax of the Call statement is Call *procedurename*, where *procedurename* is the name of the procedure you want to run. To avoid having to run her macros one after another every month, Kate asks you to create a main procedure that will run (or call) each of the procedures in the Monthly Sales workbook in sequence.

STEPS

1. **With the January worksheet displayed, click the** Developer tab **if necessary, then click the** Visual Basic button **in the Code group**

2. **Verify that Monthly Sales is the active project, click** Insert **on the menu bar, then click** Module

   A new, blank module named Module1 is inserted in the Monthly Sales workbook.

3. **In the Properties window click (Name), then type** MainProc

4. **In the Code window enter the procedure code exactly as shown in Figure P-13, entering your name in the second line**

5. **Compare your main procedure code with Figure P-13, correct any errors if necessary, then click the** Save Monthly Sales.xlsm button 🖫 **on the Visual Basic Editor Standard toolbar**

   To test the new main procedure, you need an unformatted version of the January Sales worksheet.

6. **Click the** View Microsoft Excel button 🗷 **on the toolbar, then save and close the January Sales workbook**

   The Monthly Sales workbook remains open.

7. **Open the file** EX P-2.xlsx **from the drive and folder where you store your Data Files, then save it as** January Sales 2

   In the next lesson, you'll run the main procedure.

FIGURE P-13: VBA code for the MainProcedure procedure

```
'MainProcedure Procedure
'Written by Your Name
'Calls sub procedures in sequence
'
Sub MainProcedure()
    Call FormatFile
    Call AddTotal
    Call SalesStatus
    Call FooterInput
End Sub
```

MainProcedure calls each procedure in the order shown

Excel 2007

Writing and documenting VBA code

When you write VBA code in the Visual Basic Editor, you want to make it as readable as possible. This makes it easier for you or your coworkers to edit the code when changes need to be made. The procedure statements should be indented, leaving the procedure name and its End statement easy to spot in the code. This is helpful when a module contains many procedures. It is also good practice to add comments at the beginning of each procedure that describe its purpose and any assumptions made in the procedure, such as the quota amounts. You should also explain each code statement with a comment. You have seen comments inserted into VBA code by beginning the statement with an apostrophe. You can also add comments to the end of a line of VBA code by placing an apostrophe before the comment, as shown in Figure P-14.

FIGURE P-14: VBA code with comments at the end of statements

```
'MainProcedure Procedure
'Written by Your Name
'Calls sub procedures in sequence
'
Sub MainProcedure()
    Call FormatFile 'Run FormatFile procedure
    Call AddTotal 'Run AddTotal procedure
    Call SalesStatus 'Run SalesStatus procedure
    Call FooterInput 'Run FooterInput procedure
End Sub
```

Comments at the end of the statements in green

Running a Main Procedure

Running a main procedure allows you to run several macros in sequence. You can run a main procedure just as you would any other macro procedure. ▓▓▓▓ You have finished creating Kate's main procedure, and you are ready to run it. If the main procedure works correctly, it should format the worksheet, insert the sales total, insert a sales status message, and add your name and date to the worksheet footer.

STEPS

TROUBLE

If an error message appears, click Debug, click the Reset button ▣ on the toolbar, then correct your error.

1. **With the January worksheet displayed, click the Developer tab, click the Macros button, in the Macro dialog box click 'Monthly Sales.xlsm'!MainProcedure, click Run, when prompted type your name, then click OK**

   The MainProcedure runs the FormatFile, AddTotal, SalesStatus, and FooterInput procedures in sequence. You can see the results of the FormatFile, AddTotal, and SalesStatus procedures in the worksheet window, as shown in Figure P-16. To view the results of the FooterInput procedure, you need to switch to the Preview window.

2. **Click the Office button, point to Print, click Print Preview, verify that your name appears in the left footer area and the date appears in the right footer area, then click the Close Print Preview button**

3. **Click the Visual Basic button in the Code group**

   You need to add your name to the Format module.

4. **In the Project Explorer window, double-click the Format module, add a comment line after the procedure name that reads Written by [Your Name], then click the Save Monthly Sales.xlsm button ▣**

5. **Click File on the Visual Basic Editor menu bar, then click Print**

   The Print - VBAProject dialog box opens, as shown in Figure P-17. You could print each procedure separately, but it's faster to print all the procedures in the workbook at one time.

QUICK TIP

You can assign a shortcut key combination to a macro by clicking the Options button in the Macro dialog box and entering the key combination that runs the macro.

6. **In the Print – VBAProject dialog box, click the Current Project option button, then click OK**

   Each procedure prints on a separate page.

7. **Click the View Microsoft Excel button ▣ on the toolbar**

8. **Save the January Sales 2 workbook, then print the worksheet**

   Compare your formatted worksheet to Figure P-18.

9. **Close the January Sales 2 workbook, close the Monthly Sales workbook, then exit Excel**

Running a macro using a button

You can run a macro by assigning it to a button on your worksheet. Create a button by clicking the Insert tab, clicking Shapes in the Illustrations group, choosing a shape, then drawing the shape on the worksheet. After you create the button, right-click it and select Assign Macro to choose the macro the button will run. It is a good idea to label the button with descriptive text. You can also format macro buttons using 3-D effects, clip art, photographs, fills, and shadows. To format a button, right-click it and select Format Shape from the shortcut menu. In the Format Shape dialog box you can select Fill, Line Color, Line Style, Shadow, 3-D Format, 3-D Rotation, Picture, or Text Box. To add an image to the button, click Fill in the Format Shape dialog box, then click the Picture or texture fill option button. To insert a picture from a file, click Fill in the Format Shape dialog box, click Picture or texture fill, click File, select a picture,

then click Insert. To insert a clip art picture, click Clip Art, select a picture, then click OK. You may need to resize your button to fully display a picture. You may also want to move the text on the button if it overlaps the image. Figure P-15 shows a button formatted with clip art.

FIGURE P-15: Formatted macro button

FIGURE P-16: Result of running MainProcedure procedure

Formatted title •⟶

Row inserted •⟶

Total sales calculated •⟶

Sales status message inserted •⟶

⟵• Formatted column headings

⟵• Range formatted as currency

	A	B	C	D	E	F
1	**Quest Miami January Sales**					
2						
3	Trip Code	Depart Date	Number of Days	Seats Sold	Tour	Sales
4	452R	1/7/2010	30	30	African National Parks	$146,100.00
5	556J	1/13/2010	14	25	Amazing Amazon	$ 71,925.00
6	675Y	1/19/2010	14	32	Catalonia Adventure	$ 99,200.00
7	446R	1/20/2010	7	18	Cooking in Croatia	$ 37,980.00
8	251D	1/21/2010	7	10	Cooking in France	$ 28,220.00
9	335P	1/22/2010	21	33	Corfu Sailing Voyage	$105,270.00
10	431V	1/25/2010	7	21	Costa Rica Rainforests	$ 54,390.00
11	215C	1/26/2010	14	19	Cruising the Mergui Archipelago	$ 92,663.00
12	325B	1/27/2010	10	17	Down Under Exodus	$ 47,600.00
13	311A	1/29/2010	18	20	Essential India	$ 78,660.00
14	422R	1/29/2010	7	24	Exotic Morocco	$ 45,600.00
15	331E	1/30/2010	12	21	Experience Cambodia	$ 61,068.00
16	831P	1/30/2010	14	15	Galapagos Adventure	$ 46,500.00
17	334Q	1/31/2010	18	10	Green Adventures in Ecuador	$ 24,500.00
18					Monthly Total:	$939,676.00
19						
20					Sales Status:	Met Quota
21						

FIGURE P-17: Printing the macro procedures

Current Project option button •⟶

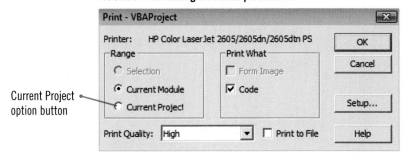

FIGURE P-18: Formatted January worksheet

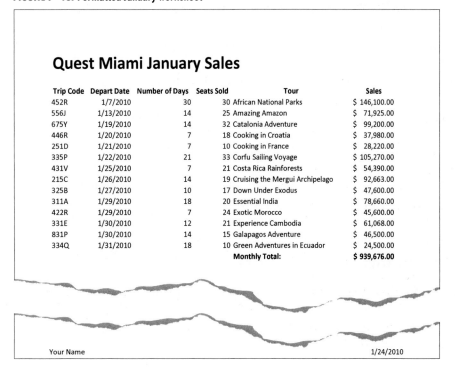

Quest Miami January Sales

Trip Code	Depart Date	Number of Days	Seats Sold	Tour	Sales
452R	1/7/2010	30	30	African National Parks	$ 146,100.00
556J	1/13/2010	14	25	Amazing Amazon	$ 71,925.00
675Y	1/19/2010	14	32	Catalonia Adventure	$ 99,200.00
446R	1/20/2010	7	18	Cooking in Croatia	$ 37,980.00
251D	1/21/2010	7	10	Cooking in France	$ 28,220.00
335P	1/22/2010	21	33	Corfu Sailing Voyage	$ 105,270.00
431V	1/25/2010	7	21	Costa Rica Rainforests	$ 54,390.00
215C	1/26/2010	14	19	Cruising the Mergui Archipelago	$ 92,663.00
325B	1/27/2010	10	17	Down Under Exodus	$ 47,600.00
311A	1/29/2010	18	20	Essential India	$ 78,660.00
422R	1/29/2010	7	24	Exotic Morocco	$ 45,600.00
331E	1/30/2010	12	21	Experience Cambodia	$ 61,068.00
831P	1/30/2010	14	15	Galapagos Adventure	$ 46,500.00
334Q	1/31/2010	18	10	Green Adventures in Ecuador	$ 24,500.00
				Monthly Total:	**$ 939,676.00**

Your Name   1/24/2010

Practice

If you have a SAM user profile, you may have access to hands-on instruction, practice, and assessment of the skills covered in this unit. Log in to your SAM account (http://sam2007.course.com/) to launch any assigned training activities or exams that relate to the skills covered in this unit.

▼ CONCEPTS REVIEW

FIGURE P-19

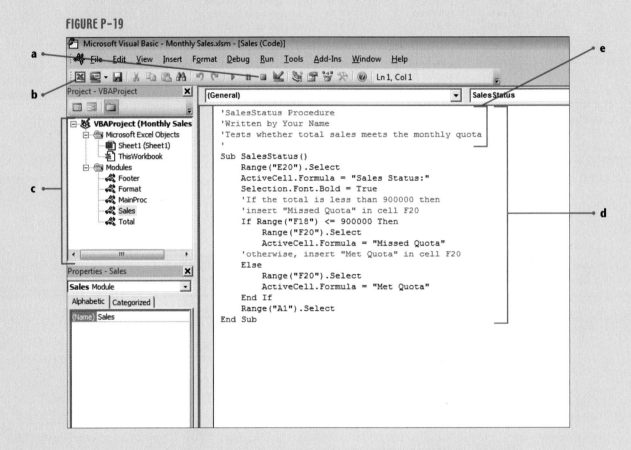

1. Which element points to comments in the VBA code?
2. Which element points to the Code window?
3. Which element points to the Project Explorer window?
4. Which element do you click to return to Excel from the Visual Basic Editor?
5. Which element do you click to turn off the Step Into feature?

Match each term with the statement that best describes it.

6. **Comments**   **a.** Another term for a macro in Visual Basic for Applications (VBA)
7. **Keywords**   **b.** A procedure that returns a value
8. **Function**   **c.** Words that are recognized as part of the programming language
9. **Sub procedure**   **d.** A series of statements that perform an action but don't return a value
10. **Procedure**   **e.** Descriptive text used to explain parts of a procedure

Select the best answer from the list of choices.

11. **A location in memory where you can temporarily store information is a:**
    a. Variable.   **c.** Sub procedure.
    b. Procedure.   **d.** Function.

12. You enter the statements of a macro in:

a. The Macro dialog box.

b. Any blank worksheet.

c. The Properties window of the Visual Basic Editor.

d. The Code window of the Visual Basic Editor.

13. If your macro doesn't run correctly, you should:

a. Create an If...Then...Else statement.

b. Click the Properties button.

c. Click the Project Explorer button.

d. Select the macro in the Macro dialog box, click Step Into, then debug the macro.

14. Comments are displayed in _____ in VBA code.

a. Black

b. Blue

c. Red

d. Green

15. Keywords are displayed in _____ in VBA code.

a. Blue

b. Black

c. Green

d. Red

▼ SKILLS REVIEW

1. View and analyze VBA code.

a. Start Excel, open the file EX P-3.xlsm from the drive and folder where you store your Data Files, enable macros, then save it as **Southeast**.

b. Review the unformatted March worksheet.

c. Open the Visual Basic Editor.

d. Select the DataFormat module and review the Format procedure.

e. Insert comments in the procedure code describing what action you think each line of code will perform. (*Hint*: One of the statements will sort the list alphabetically by state.) Add blank comment lines to the top of the procedure to describe the purpose of the macro and to enter your name.

f. Save the macro, return to the worksheet, then run the Format macro.

g. Compare the results with the code and your comments.

h. Save the workbook.

2. Write VBA code.

a. Open the Visual Basic Editor and insert a new module named **Total** in the Southeast project.

b. Enter the code for the SalesTotal procedure exactly as shown in Figure P-20. Enter your name in the second line.

c. Save the macro.

d. Return to the March worksheet and run the SalesTotal macro. Widen column E to view the total in cell E17.

e. Save the workbook.

3. Add a conditional statement

a. Open the Visual Basic Editor and insert a new module named **Goal** in the Southeast project.

b. Enter the SalesGoal procedure exactly as shown in Figure P-21. Enter your name on the second line.

FIGURE P-20

```
'SalesTotal Procedure
'Written by Your Name
'Totals March sales
Sub SalesTotal()
    Range("E17").Select
    ActiveCell.Formula = "=SUM($E$3:$E$16)"
    Selection.Font.Bold = True
    With Selection.Borders(xlTop)
        .LineStyle = xlSingle
    End With
    Range("A1").Select
End Sub
```

FIGURE P-21

```
'SalesGoal Procedure
'Written by Your Name
'Tests whether sales goal was met
Sub SalesGoal()
    'If the total is >=400000, then insert "Met Goal"
    'in cell E18
    If Range("E17") >= 400000 Then
        Range("E18").Select
        ActiveCell.Formula = "Met goal"
    'otherwise, insert "Missed goal" in cell E18
    Else
        Range("E18").Select
        ActiveCell.Formula = "Missed goal"
    End If
End Sub
```

Excel 2007

   c. Save the macro.

   d. Return to the March worksheet and run the SalesGoal macro. The procedure should enter the message **Missed goal** in cell E18. Save the workbook.

4. Prompt the user for data.

   a. Open the Visual Basic Editor and insert a new module named **Header** in the Southeast project.

   b. Enter the HeaderFooter procedure exactly as shown in Figure P-22. You are entering an error in the procedure that will be corrected in Step 5.

   c. Save the macro, then return to the March worksheet and run the HeaderFooter macro.

   d. Preview the March worksheet. Your name should be missing from the left section of the footer.

   e. Save the workbook.

FIGURE P-22

```
'HeaderFooter Procedure
'Written by Your Name
'Procedure to customize the header and footer
Sub HeaderFooter()
    'Inserts the filename in the header
    Worksheets("March").PageSetup.CenterHeader = "&F"
    'Declares the variable LeftFooterText as a string
    Dim LeftFooterText As String
    'Prompts user for left footer text
    LeftFooter = InputBox("Enter your full name:")
    'Inserts response into left footer
    Worksheets("March").PageSetup.LeftFooter = LeftFooterText
    'Inserts the date into right footer
    Worksheets("March").PageSetup.RightFooter = "&D"
End Sub
```

5. Debug a macro.

   a. Return to the Visual Basic Editor and use the Step Into feature to locate where the error occurred in the HeaderFooter procedure. Use the Reset button to turn off the debugger.

   b. Edit the procedure in the Visual Basic Editor to correct the error. [*Hint*: The error occurs on the line: LeftFooter = InputBox("Enter your full name:") The variable that will input the response text into the worksheet footer is LeftFooterText. The line should be: LeftFooterText = InputBox("Enter your full name:")]

   c. Save the macro, then return to the March worksheet and run the HeaderFooter macro again.

   d. Verify that your name now appears in the left section of the footer, then save the file.

6. Create and run a main procedure.

   a. Return to the Visual Basic Editor, insert a new module, then name it **MainProc**.

   b. Begin the main procedure by entering comments in the code window that provide the procedure's name (MainProcedure) and explain that its purpose is to run the Format, SalesTotal, SalesGoal, and HeaderFooter procedures. Enter your name in a comment.

   c. Enter the procedure header **Sub MainProcedure()**.

   d. Enter four Call statements that will run the Format, SalesTotal, SalesGoal, and HeaderFooter procedures in sequence.

   e. Save the procedure and return to Excel.

   f. Open the file EX P-3.xlsm, then save it as **Southeast 2**.

   g. Run the MainProcedure macro, entering your name when prompted. (*Hint*: In the Macro dialog box, the macro procedures you created will now have Southeast.xlsm! as part of their names. This is because the macros are stored in the Southeast workbook, not in the Southeast 2 workbook.)

   h. Verify that the macro ran successfully, widen column E to display the calculated total, select cell A1, then compare your worksheet to Figure P-23.

   i. Save the Southeast 2 workbook, print the March worksheet, then close the Southeast 2 workbook.

   j. Return to the Visual Basic Editor, then print the MainProcedure code.

   k. Return to the worksheet, save the Southeast workbook, close the workbook, then exit Excel.

FIGURE P-23

	A	B	C	D	E
1	**Book Deals Southeast Region Sales**				
2	**Store #**	**City**	**State**	**Manager**	**Sales**
3	39395	Bonita Springs	FL	Handelmann	$ 3,175.33
4	39394	Naples	FL	Hamm	$ 6,715.68
5	39398	Delray Beach	FL	Dever	$ 8,442.90
6	39397	Clearwater	FL	Erickson	$ 8,544.11
7	29396	Cape Coral	FL	Enos	$ 9,633.21
8	29393	Tampa	FL	Nelson	$ 79,654.32
9	29406	Miami	FL	Monroe	$ 82,993.22
10	29402	Forsyth	GA	Guapo	$ 1,534.34
11	11405	Leefield	GA	Clifford	$ 1,745.93
12	19404	Harding	GA	Cloutier	$ 2,656.83
13	29399	Cleveland	GA	DiBenedetto	$ 6,423.73
14	39400	Clayton	GA	Hahn	$ 8,001.34
15	39403	Franklin	GA	Lo	$ 33,643.93
16	39401	Douglas	GA	Pratt	$ 82,534.72
17					$ 335,699.59
18					Missed goal

▼ INDEPENDENT CHALLENGE 1

You work at a nonprofit public policy agency. Your coworker is on vacation for two weeks, and you have taken over her projects. The information systems manager asks you to document and test an Excel procedure that your coworker wrote for the company's accountant. You will first run the macro procedure to see what it does, then add comments to the VBA code to document it. You will also enter data to verify that the formulas in the macro work correctly.

a. Start Excel, open the file EX P-4.xlsm from the drive and folder where you store your Data Files, enable macros, then save it as **First Quarter**.

b. Run the First macro, noting anything that you think should be mentioned in your documentation.

c. Review the First procedure in the Visual Basic Editor. It is stored in the FirstQtr module.

d. Document the procedure by annotating the printed code, indicating the actions the procedure performs and the objects (ranges) that are affected.

e. Enter your name in a comment line.

f. Save the procedure, then print the documented procedure code.

g. Return to the Jan-Mar worksheet and use Figure P-24 as a guide to enter data in cells B4:D6. The totals will be displayed as you enter the income data. Format the range B4:D8 using the Accounting Number format with no decimals, as shown in Figure P-24.

h. Check the total income calculations in row 8 to verify that the macro is working correctly.

i. Enter your name in the center section of the Jan-Mar sheet footer, save the workbook, then print the worksheet.

j. Close the workbook, then exit Excel.

FIGURE P-24

	A	B	C	D
1		January	February	March
2	Income			
3				
4	Donations	$ 900	$ 800	$ 700
5	Fundraisers	$ 1,000	$ 2,000	$ 3,000
6	Grants	$ 10,000	$ 50,000	$ 90,000
7				
8	Total Income	$ 11,900	$ 52,800	$ 93,700
9				

▼ INDEPENDENT CHALLENGE 2

You work in the Toronto branch of Escapes, a timeshare brokerage specializing in Canadian resort properties. Each month you are required to produce a report stating whether sales quotas were met for the following three property categories: standard, superior, and deluxe. The sales quotas for each month are as follows: standard 10, superior 7, and deluxe 4. Your sales results this month were 8, 8, and 5, respectively. You decide to create a procedure to automate your monthly task of determining the sales quota status for the property categories. You would like your assistant to take this task over when you go on vacation next month. Because he has no previous experience with Excel, you decide to create a second procedure that prompts a user with input boxes to enter the actual sales results for the month.

a. Start Excel, open the file EX P-5.xlsm from the drive and folder where you store your Data Files, then save it as **Escapes**.

b. Use the Visual Basic Editor to insert a new module named **Quotas** in the Escapes workbook. Create a procedure in the new module named **PropertyQuota** that determines the sales quota status for each vehicle category and enters Yes or No in the Status column. The VBA code is shown in Figure P-25.

c. Add comments to the PropertyQuota procedure, including the procedure name, your name, and the purpose of the procedure, then save it.

FIGURE P-25

```
Sub PropertyQuota()

    If Range("C4") >= 10 Then
        Range("D4").Select
        ActiveCell.Formula = "Yes"
    Else
        Range("D4").Select
        ActiveCell.Formula = "No"
    End If


    If Range("C5") >= 7 Then
        Range("D5").Select
        ActiveCell.Formula = "Yes"
    Else
        Range("D5").Select
        ActiveCell.Formula = "No"
    End If


    If Range("C6") >= 4 Then
        Range("D6").Select
        ActiveCell.Formula = "Yes"
    Else
        Range("D6").Select
        ActiveCell.Formula = "No"
    End If

End Sub
```

d. Insert a new module named **MonthlySales**. Create a second procedure named **Sales** that prompts a user for sales data for each property category, enters the input data in the appropriate cells, then calls the PropertyQuota procedure. The VBA code is shown in Figure P-26.

e. Add a comment noting the procedure name on the first line. Add a comment with your name on the second line. Add a third comment line at the top of the procedure describing its purpose. Enter comments in the code to document the macro actions. Save the procedure.

f. Run the Sales macro and enter 8 for standard sales, 8 for superior sales, and 5 for deluxe sales. Correct any errors in the VBA code.

g. Print the current project's code, then return to the workbook.

FIGURE P-26

```
Sub Sales()


    Dim Standard As String
    Standard = InputBox("Enter Standard Sales")
    Range("C4").Select
    Selection = Standard

    Dim Superior As String
    Superior = InputBox("Enter Superior Sales")
    Range("C5").Select
    Selection = Superior

    Dim Deluxe As String
    Deluxe = InputBox("Enter Deluxe Sales")
    Range("C6").Select
    Selection = Deluxe


    Call PropertyQuota

End Sub
```

Advanced Challenge Exercise

- Assign a shortcut of [Ctrl][Shift][S] to the Sales macro. Insert a line on the worksheet that tells the user to press [Ctrl][Shift][S] to enter sales data.
- Edit the Visual Basic code for the PropertyQuota procedure to reflect a change in quotas to 15 for Standard, 8 for Superior, and 6 for Deluxe. Change the worksheet data in the range B4:B6 to display the new quotas.
- Delete the data in cells C4:D6.
- Run the Sales macro using the shortcut key combination entering 12 for standard sales, 10 for superior sales, and 5 for deluxe sales.

h. Add your name to the left section of the worksheet footer, save the workbook, then print the worksheet. Close the workbook, then exit Excel.

▼ INDEPENDENT CHALLENGE 3

You own a landscaping business named Green Hills. You have started to advertise your business using a local magazine, billboards, TV, radio, and local newspapers. Every month you prepare a report with the advertising expenses detailed by source. You decide to create a macro that will format the monthly reports. You add the same footers on every report, so you will create another macro that will add a footer to a document. Finally, you will create a main procedure that calls the macros to format the report and add a footer. You begin by opening a workbook with the January data. You will save the macros you create in this workbook.

a. Start Excel, open the file EX P-6.xlsm from the drive and folder where you store your Data Files, then save it as **Green Hills.**

b. Insert a module named **Format**, then create a procedure named Formatting that:
- Selects a cell in row 3 and inserts a row in the worksheet above it
- Selects the cost data in column C and formats it as currency. (*Hint*: After the row is inserted, this range is C5:C9.)
- Selects cell A1 before ending

c. Save the Formatting procedure.

d. Insert a module named **Foot**, then create a procedure named Footer that:
- Declares a string variable for text that will be placed in the left footer
- Uses an input box to prompt the user for his or her name and places the name in the left footer
- Places the date in the right footer

▼ INDEPENDENT CHALLENGE 3 (CONTINUED)

e. Save the Footer procedure.

f. Insert a module named **Main**, then create a procedure named MainProc that calls the Footer procedure and the Formatting procedure.

g. Save your work, then run the MainProc procedure. Debug each procedure as necessary. Your worksheet should look like Figure P-27.

h. Document each procedure by inserting a comment line with the procedure name, your name, and a description of the procedure.

FIGURE P-27

	A	B	C
1	Green Hills		
2	Ad Campaign		
3			
4	Advertising Type	Source	Cost
5	Magazine	Groundhog	$200.00
6	Newspaper	Reporter	$ 350.00
7	Billboard	Main Street	$ 450.00
8	TV	Local Access Station	$ 50.00
9	Radio	WAQV	$500.00
10			

Advanced Challenge Exercise

■ Insert a module named Total, then create a procedure named CostTotal that does the following:
  - Totals the advertising costs in cells C5:C9 and inserts the total in cell C10
  - Formats the total as bold and adds a green fill to the total cell. (*Hint*: The ColorIndex for green is 4.)
  - Selects cell A1
■ Document the procedure with the procedure name, your name, and a description of the procedure.
■ Run the CostTotal procedure

i. Print the code for the current project, return to the January worksheet, save the workbook, then print the worksheet.

j. Close the workbook, then exit Excel.

▼ REAL LIFE INDEPENDENT CHALLENGE

You decide to create a log of your discretionary expenses in an effort to track where you spend your paycheck each week. You will not track essential expenses such as auto expenses, rent/mortgage, groceries, necessary clothing, utilities, and tuition. Rather, your purpose is to identify optional items that may be targeted for reduction in an effort to meet a weekly budget. As part of this log, you record your expenses for each day of the week along with the daily amount spent in each category.

a. Start Excel, open the file EX P-7.xlsm from the drive and folder where you store your Data Files, then save it as **Expenses**.

b. Expand the modules folder to display the Expenses module. Edit the WeekExpenses procedure to record your expense categories. Record fewer than seven categories and remember to edit the total cells and the formatting ranges in the procedure.

c. Run the macro and debug the procedure as necessary.

d. Use the worksheet to enter your expenses for each day of the past week, as best you can remember.

e. Save your work.

f. Verify that the totals are correct for each day and each category.

g. Enter your name as a comment in the second line of the procedure, then save the procedure.

h. Print the WeekExpenses procedure.

Advanced Challenge Exercise

■ Insert a module named **PrintSheet** with a procedure named **Printdata** that prints a worksheet. Use Figure P-28 as a guide. Note that your range depends on the amount of data on your worksheet.
■ Save the macro and return to the worksheet.
■ Assign the macro Printdata to a button on the worksheet. (*Hint*: Use the Rectangle tool to create the button, label the button **Print**, then right-click one of the button's edges to assign the macro.)
■ Enter your name in the center section of the worksheet footer then test the button.

FIGURE P-28

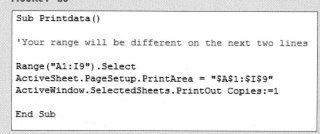

```
Sub Printdata()

'Your range will be different on the next two lines

Range("A1:I9").Select
ActiveSheet.PageSetup.PrintArea = "$A$1:$I$9"
ActiveWindow.SelectedSheets.PrintOut Copies:=1

End Sub
```

i. Save the workbook, close the workbook, then exit Excel.

▼ VISUAL WORKSHOP

Open the file EX P-8.xlsm from the drive and folder where you store your Data Files, then save it as **Tulips**. Create a macro procedure named **Formatting** in a module named **FormatFile** that will format the worksheet as shown in Figure P-29. (*Hint*: The font size is 13.) Run the macro and debug it as necessary to make the worksheet match Figure P-29. Insert your name in a comment line under the procedure name, then print the procedure code.

FIGURE P-29

	A	B	C	D	
1	Tulips				
2	Weekly Specials				
3					
4	20 Assorted	$29.00			
5	30 Assorted	$39.00			
6	20 Assorted in glass vase	$39.99			
7	30 assorted in glass vase	$49.97			
8					

Restoring Defaults in Windows Vista and Disabling and Enabling Windows Aero

Files You Will Need:

No files needed.

Windows Vista is the most recent version of the Windows operating system. An operating system controls the way you work with your computer, supervises running programs, and provides tools for completing your computing tasks. After surveying millions of computer users, Microsoft incorporated their suggestions to make Windows Vista secure, reliable, and easy to use. In fact, Windows Vista is considered the most secure version of Windows yet. Other improvements include a powerful new search feature that lets you quickly search for files and programs from the Start menu and most windows, tools that simplify accessing the Internet, especially with a wireless connection, and multimedia programs that let you enjoy, share, and organize music, photos, and recorded TV. Finally, Windows Vista offers lots of visual appeal with its transparent, three-dimensional design in the Aero experience. This appendix explains how to make sure you are using the Windows Vista default settings for appearance, personalization, security, hardware, and sound and to enable and disable Windows Aero. For more information on Windows Aero, go to *www.microsoft.com/windowsvista/experiences/aero.mspx*.

OBJECTIVES

- Restore the defaults in the Appearance and Personalization section
- Restore the defaults in the Security section
- Restore the defaults in the Hardware and Sound section
- Disable Windows Aero
- Enable Windows Aero

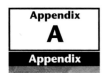

Restoring the Defaults in the Appearance and Personalization Section

The following instructions require a default Windows Vista Ultimate installation and the student logged in with an Administrator account. All of the following settings can be changed by accessing the Control Panel.

STEPS

- To restore the defaults in the Personalization section
    1. Click Start, and then click Control Panel. Click Appearance and Personalization, click Personalization, and then compare your screen to Figure A-1
    2. In the Personalization window, click Windows Color and Appearance, select the Default color, and then click OK
    3. In the Personalization window, click Mouse Pointers. In the Mouse Properties dialog box, on the Pointers tab, select Windows Aero (system scheme) in the Scheme drop-down list, and then click OK
    4. In the Personalization window, click Theme. Select Windows Vista from the Theme drop-down list, and then click OK
    5. In the Personalization window, click Display Settings. In the Display Settings dialog box, drag the Resolution bar to 1024 by 768 pixels, and then click OK

FIGURE A-1

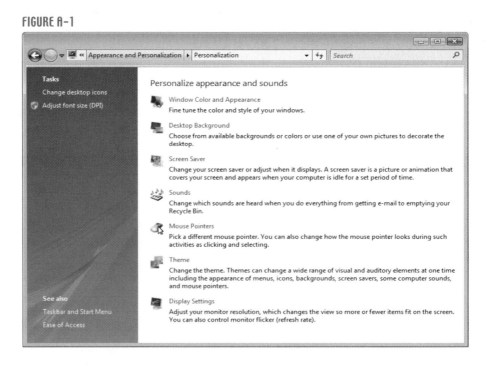

- To restore the defaults in the Taskbar and Start Menu section

  1. Click Start, and then click Control Panel. Click Appearance and Personalization, click Taskbar and Start Menu, and then compare your screen to Figure A-2

  2. In the Taskbar and Start Menu Properties dialog box, on the Taskbar tab, click to select all checkboxes except for "Auto-hide the taskbar"

  3. On the Start Menu tab, click to select the Start menu radio button and check all items in the Privacy section

  4. In the System icons section on the Notification Area tab, click to select all of the checkboxes except for "Power"

  5. On the Toolbars tab, click to select Quick Launch, none of the other items should be checked

  6. Click OK to close the Taskbar and Start Menu Properties dialog box

- To restore the defaults in the Folder Options section

  1. Click Start, and then click Control Panel. Click Appearance and Personalization, click Folder Options, and then compare your screen to Figure A-3

  2. In the Folder Options dialog box, on the General tab, click to select Show preview and filters in the Tasks section, click to select Open each folder in the same window in the Browse folders section, and click to select Double-click to open an item (single-click to select) in the Click items as follows section

  3. On the View tab, click the Reset Folders button, and then click Yes in the Folder views dialog box. Then click the Restore Defaults button

  4. On the Search tab, click the Restore Defaults button

  5. Click OK to close the Folder Options dialog box

- To restore the defaults in the Windows Sidebar Properties section

  1. Click Start, and then click Control Panel. Click Appearance and Personalization, click Windows Sidebar Properties, and then compare your screen to Figure A-4

  2. In the Windows Sidebar Properties dialog box, on the Sidebar tab, click to select Start Sidebar when Windows starts. In the Arrangement section, click to select Right, and then click to select 1 in the Display Sidebar on monitor drop-down list

  3. Click OK to close the Windows Sidebar Properties dialog box

FIGURE A-3

FIGURE A-4

FIGURE A-2

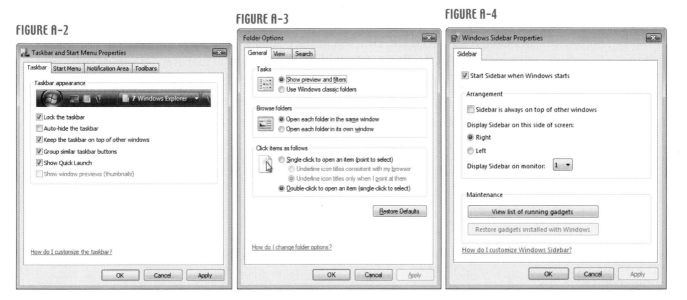

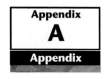

Restoring the Defaults in the Security Section

The following instructions require a default Windows Vista Ultimate installation and the student logged in with an Administrator account. All of the following settings can be changed by accessing the Control Panel.

STEPS

- To restore the defaults in the Windows Firewall section

    1. Click Start, and then click Control Panel. Click Security, click Windows Firewall, and then compare your screen to Figure A-5

    2. In the Windows Firewall dialog box, click Change settings. If the User Account Control dialog box appears, click Continue

    3. In the Windows Firewall Settings dialog box, click the Advanced tab. Click Restore Defaults, then click Yes in the Restore Defaults Confirmation dialog box

    4. Click OK to close the Windows Firewall Settings dialog box, and then close the Windows Firewall window

- To restore the defaults in the Internet Options section

    1. Click Start, and then click Control Panel. Click Security, click Internet Options, and then compare your screen to Figure A-6

    2. In the Internet Properties dialog box, on the General tab, click the Use default button. Click the Settings button in the Tabs section, and then click the Restore defaults button in the Tabbed Browsing Settings dialog box. Click OK to close the Tabbed Browsing Settings dialog box

    3. On the Security tab of the Internet Properties dialog box, click to uncheck the Enable Protected Mode checkbox, if necessary. Click the Default level button in the Security level for this zone section. If possible, click the Reset all zones to default level button

    4. On the Programs tab, click the Make default button in the Default web browser button for Internet Explorer, if possible. If Office is installed, Microsoft Office Word should be selected in the HTML editor drop-down list

    5. On the Advanced tab, click the Restore advanced settings button in the Settings section. Click the Reset button in the Reset Internet Explorer settings section, and then click Reset in the Reset Internet Explorer Settings dialog box

    6. Click Close to close the Reset Internet Explorer Settings dialog box, and then click OK to close the Internet Properties dialog box

FIGURE A-5

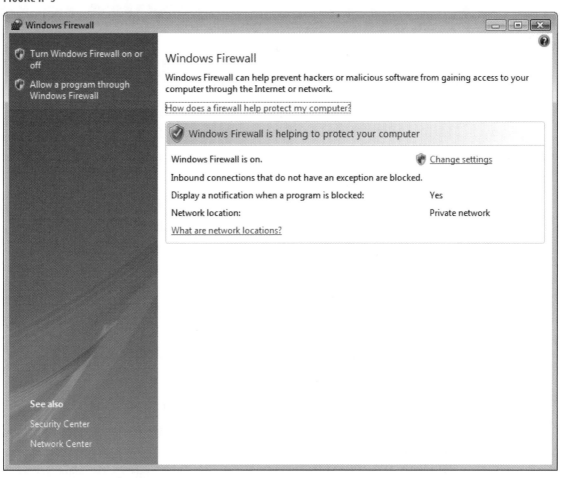

FIGURE A-6

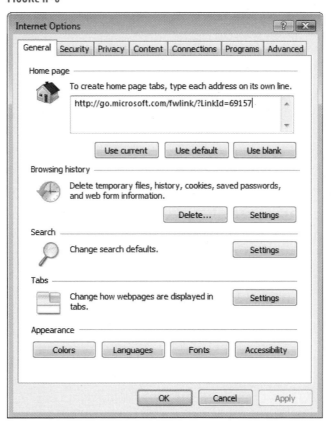

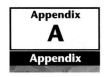

Restoring the Defaults in the Hardware and Sound Section

The following instructions require a default Windows Vista Ultimate installation and the student logged in with an Administrator account. All of the following settings can be changed by accessing the Control Panel.

STEPS

- To restore the defaults in the Autoplay section
    1. Click Start, and then click Control Panel. Click Hardware and Sound, click Autoplay, and then compare your screen to Figure A-7. Scroll down and click the Reset all defaults button in the Devices section at the bottom of the window, and then click Save

- To restore the defaults in the Sound section
    1. Click Start, and then click Control Panel. Click Hardware and Sound, click Sound, and then compare your screen to Figure A-8
    2. In the Sound dialog box, on the Sounds tab, select Windows Default from the Sound Scheme drop-down list, and then click OK

- To restore the defaults in the Mouse section
    1. Click Start, and then click Control Panel. Click Hardware and Sound, click Mouse, and then compare your screen to Figure A-9
    2. In the Mouse Properties dialog box, on the Pointers tab, select Windows Aero (system scheme) from the Scheme drop-down list
    3. Click OK to close the Mouse Properties dialog box

FIGURE A-7

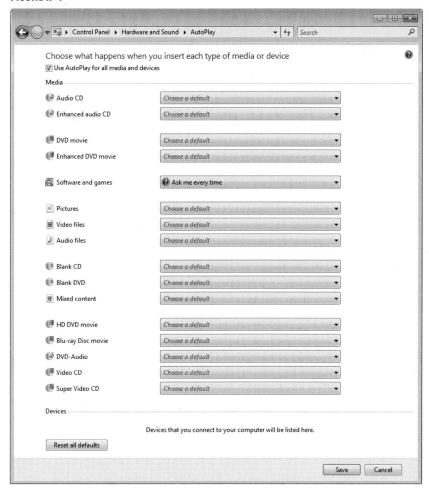

FIGURE A-8

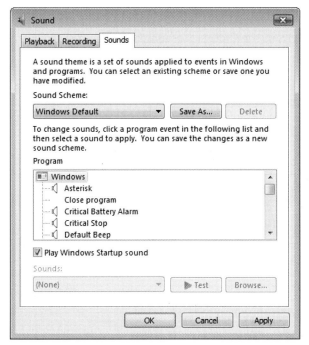

FIGURE A-9

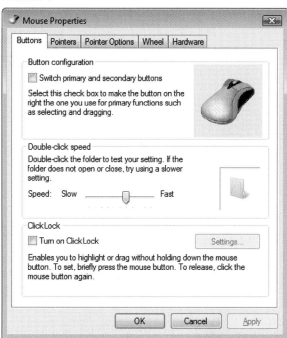

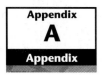
Disabling and Enabling Windows Aero

Unlike prior versions of Windows, Windows Vista provides two distinct user interface experiences: a "basic" experience for entry-level systems and more visually dynamic experience called Windows Aero. Both offer a new and intuitive navigation experience that helps you more easily find and organize your applications and files, but Aero goes further by delivering a truly next-generation desktop experience.

Windows Aero builds on the basic Windows Vista user experience and offers Microsoft's best-designed, highest-performing desktop experience. Using Aero requires a PC with compatible graphics adapter and running a Premium or Business edition of Windows Vista.

The following instructions require a computer capable of running Windows Aero, with a default Windows Vista Ultimate installation and student logged in with an Administrator account.

STEPS

- **To Disable Windows Aero**

We recommend that students using this book disable Windows Aero and restore their operating systems default settings (instructions to follow).

1. **Right-click the desktop, select** Personalize, **and then compare your screen in Figure A-10. Select** Window Color and Appearance, **and then select** Open classic appeareance properties for more color options. **In Appearance Settings dialog box, on the Appearance tab, select any non-Aero scheme (such as** Windows Vista Basic **or** Windows Vista Standard**) in the Color Scheme list, and then click OK. Figure A-11 compares Windows Aero to other color schemes. Note that this book uses Windows Vista Basic as the color scheme**

- **To Enable Windows Aero**

1. **Right-click the desktop, and then select** Personalize. **Select** Window Color and Appearance, **then select** Windows Aero **in the Color scheme list, and then click OK in the Appearance Settings dialog box**

FIGURE A-10

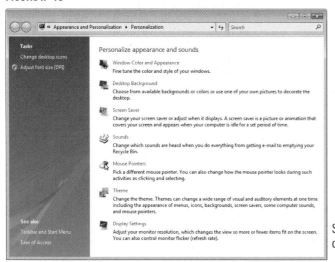

FIGURE A-11

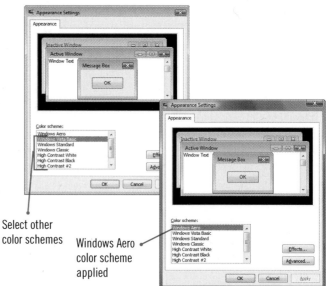

Select other color schemes

Windows Aero color scheme applied

Glossary

3-D reference A reference that uses values on other sheets or workbooks, effectively creating another dimension to a workbook.

Absolute cell reference In a formula, type of cell address that does not change when you copy the formula; indicated by a dollar sign before the column letter and/or row number. *See also* Relative cell reference.

Accessories Simple programs to perform specific tasks that come with Windows Vista, such as the Calculator for performing calculations.

Active The currently available document, program, or object; on the taskbar, the button of the active document appears in a darker shade while the buttons of other open documents are dimmed.

Active cell The cell in which you are currently working.

Active window The window you are currently using.

Add-in A supplementary program that provides additional program features; for example, the Solver add-in enables you to find a solution to a calculation that has several inputs; the Analysis ToolPak provides optional Excel features. To activate an add-in, click the Office button, click Excel options, click Add-Ins, then click Go. Select or deselect add-ins from the list.

Address Bar A horizontal box near the top of a window that shows your current location in the computer's file hierarchy as a series of links separated by arrows; used to navigate to other locations on your computer.

Alignment The placement of cell contents; for example, left, center, or right.

AND condition A filtering feature that searches for records by specifying that all entered criteria must be matched.

Apply (a template) To open a document based on an Excel template.

Argument In the Visual Basic for Applications (VBA) programming language, variable used in procedures that a main procedure might run. *See also* Main procedure.

Arithmetic operators In a formula, symbols that perform mathematical calculations, such as plus (+), minus (–), multiplication (*), division (/), or exponentiation (^).

Ascending order In sorting worksheet records, the lowest value (the beginning of the alphabet, or the earliest date) appears at the beginning of the sorted data.

ASCII file A text file that contains data but no formatting; instead of being divided into columns, ASCII file data are separated, or delimited, by tabs or commas.

Attributes Styling characteristics such as bold, italic, and underlining that you can apply to change the way text and numbers look in a worksheet or chart. In XML, the components that provides information about the document's elements.

Auditing An Excel feature that helps track errors and check worksheet logic.

AutoComplete In the Visual Basic for Applications (VBA) programming language, a list of words that appears as you enter code; helps you automatically enter elements with the correct syntax.

AutoFill Options button Feature that lets you fill cells with specific elements (such as formatting) of the copied cell.

AutoFilter A table feature that lets you click a list arrow and select criteria by which to display certain types of records; *also called* filter.

AutoFilter list arrows List arrows that appear next to field names in an Excel table; used to display portions of your data. *Also called* filter list arrows.

AutoFit A feature that automatically adjusts the width of a column or the height of a row to accommodate its widest or tallest entry.

Backsolving A problem-solving method in which you specify a solution and then find the input value that produces the answer you want; sometimes described as a what-if analysis in reverse. In Excel, the Goal Seek feature performs backsolving.

Backup A duplicate copy of a file that is stored in another location.

Backward-compatible Software feature that enables documents saved in an older version of a program to be opened in a newer version of the program.

Banding Worksheet formatting in which adjacent rows and columns are formatted differently.

Boolean filter A word or symbol for locating programs, folders, and files by specifying one or more criteria so that you have a greater chance of finding what you need.

Booting A process that Windows steps through to get the computer up and running.

Bug In programming, an error that causes a procedure to run incorrectly.

Byte One character of storage space on disk or in RAM.

Calculated columns In a table, a column that uses one formula that automatically adjusts to accommodate additional rows.

Calculation operators Symbols that indicate what type of calculation to perform on the cells, ranges or values.

Category axis Horizontal axis of a chart, usually containing the names of data groups; in a 2-dimensional chart, also known as the x-axis.

Cell The intersection of a column and a row in a worksheet, datasheet, or table.

Cell address The location of a cell, expressed by cell coordinates; for example, the cell address of the cell in column A, row 1 is A1.

Cell comments Notes you've written about a workbook that appear when you place the pointer over a cell.

Cell pointer A dark rectangle that outlines the active cell.

Cell styles Predesigned combinations of formatting attributes that can be applied to selected cells, to enhance the look of a worksheet.

Change history A worksheet containing a list of changes made to a shared workbook.

Changing cells In what-if analysis, cells that contain the values that change in order to produce multiple sets of results.

Chart sheet A separate sheet in a workbook that contains only a chart, which is linked to the workbook data.

Charts Pictorial representations of worksheet data that make it easier to see patterns, trends, and relationships; *also called* graphs.

Check box A box that turns an option on when checked or off when unchecked.

Click To quickly press and release the left button on the pointing device; also called single-click.

Clip A media file, such as art, sound, animation, or a movie.

Clip art A graphic image, such as a corporate logo, a picture, or a photo, that can be inserted into a document.

Clipboard Temporary storage area in Windows.

Code *See* Program code.

Code window In the Visual Basic Editor, the window that displays the selected module's procedures, written in the Visual Basic programming language.

Collapse button A button that shrinks a portion of a dialog box to hide some settings.

Color scale In conditional formatting, a formatting scheme that uses a set of two, three, or four fill colors to convey relative values of data.

Column heading Identifies the column letter, such as A, B, etc.; located above each column in a worksheet.

Command An instruction to perform a task.

Command button A button that completes or cancels an operation.

Comments In a Visual Basic procedure, notes that explain the purpose of the macro or procedure; they are preceded by a single apostrophe and appear in green. *See also* Cell comments.

Comparison operators In a calculation, symbols that compare values for the purpose of true/false results.

Compatible The capability of different programs to work together and exchange data.

Complex formula A formula that uses more than one arithmetic operator.

Compress To reduce the size of file so that it takes up less storage space on a disk.

Computer window The window shows the drives on your computer as well as other installed hardware components.

Conditional format A type of cell formatting that changes based on the cell's value or the outcome of a formula.

Consolidate To combine data on multiple worksheets and display the result on another worksheet.

Constraints Limitations or restrictions on input data in what-if analysis.

Contextual tab Tab on the Ribbon that appears when needed to complete a specific task; for example, if you select a chart in an Excel workbook, three contextual Chart Tool tabs (Design, Layout, and Format) appear.

Copy To make a duplicate copy of a file that is stored in another location.

Criteria range In advanced filtering, a cell range containing one row of labels (usually a copy of column labels) and at least one additional row underneath it that contains the criteria you want to match.

Custom chart type A specially formatted Excel chart.

Data entry area The unlocked portion of a worksheet where users are able to enter and change data.

Data label Descriptive text that appears above a data marker in a chart.

Data marker A graphical representation of a data point, such as a bar or column.

Data point Individual piece of data plotted in a chart.

Data series A column or row in a datasheet. Also, the selected range in a worksheet that Excel converts into a chart.

Data source Worksheet data used to create a chart or a PivotTable.

Data table A range of cells that shows the resulting values when one or more input values are varied in a formula; when one input value is changed, the table is called a one-input data table, and when two input values are changed, it is called a two-input data table. In a chart, it is a grid containing the chart data.

Data validation A feature that allows you to specify what data is allowable (valid) for a range of cells.

Database An organized collection of related information. In Excel, a database is called a table.

Debug In programming, to find and correct an error in code.

Declare In the Visual Basic programming language, to assign a type, such as numeric or text, to a variable.

Default A setting that is built into a program that is used by that program until you change the setting.

Delete To remove a folder or file.

Delimiter A separator such as a space, comma, or semicolon between elements in imported data.

Dependent cell A cell, usually containing a formula, whose value changes depending on the values in the input cells. For example, a payment formula or function that depends on an input cell containing changing interest rates is a dependent cell.

Descending order In sorting an Excel table, the order that begins with the letter Z or the highest number in a table.

Desktop The graphical user interface (GUI) displayed on your screen after you start Windows that you use to interact with Windows and other software on your computer.

Destination program In a data exchange, the program that will receive the data.

Details Pane A pane located at the bottom of a window that displays information about the selected disk, drive, folder, or file.

Device A hardware component in your computer system.

Dialog box A type of window in which you specify how you want to complete an operation.

Dialog box launcher An icon available in many groups on the Ribbon that you can click to open a dialog box or task pane, offering an alternative way to choose commands.

Document To make notes about basic worksheet assumptions, complex formulas, or questionable data. In a macro, to insert comments that explain the Visual Basic code.

Document window The portion of a program window that displays all or part of an open document.

Documents folder The folder on your hard drive used to store most of the files you create or receive from others.

Double-click To quickly click the left button on the pointing device twice.

Drag To point to an object, press and hold the left button on the pointing device, move the object to a new location, and then release the left button.

Drag and drop To use a pointing device to move or copy a file or folder to a new location.

Drive A physical location on your computer where you can store files.

Drive name A name for a drive that consists of a letter followed by a colon, such as C: for the hard disk drive.

Drop-down list button A button that opens a list with one or more options from which you can choose.

Dynamic page breaks In a larger workbook, horizontal or vertical dashed lines that represent the place where pages print separately. They also adjust automatically when you insert or delete rows or columns, or change column widths or row heights.

Edit (Excel) To make a change to the contents of an active cell. (Windows) To make changes to a file.

Electronic spreadsheet A computer program that performs calculations and presents numeric data.

Element An XML component that defines the document content.

Embed To insert a copy of data into a destination document; you can double-click the embedded object to modify it using the tools of the source program.

Embedded chart A chart displayed as an object in a worksheet.

Expand button A button that extends a dialog box to display additional settings.

Exploding pie slice A slice of a pie chart that has been pulled away from the whole pie, in order to add emphasis.

Extensible Markup Language (XML) A system for defining languages using tags to structure data.

External reference indicator The exclamation point (!) used in a formula to indicate that a referenced cell is outside the active sheet.

Extract To place a copy of a filtered table in a range you specify in the Advanced Filter dialog box.

Field In a table (an Excel database), a column that describes a characteristic about records, such as first name or city.

Field name A column label that describes a field.

File A collection of stored electronic data, such as text, pictures, video, music, and programs.

File extension Additional characters assigned by a program added to the end of a filename to identify the type of file.

File hierarchy The structure for organizing folders and files; describes the logic and layout of the folder structure on a disk.

File management A strategy for organizing folders and files.

Filename A unique, descriptive name for a file that identifies the file's content. A filename can be no more than 255 characters, including spaces, and can include letters, numbers, and certain symbols.

Filter To display data in an Excel table that meet specified criteria. *See also* AutoFilter.

Filter arrows *See* AutoFilter list arrows.

Folder A container for a group of related files. A folder may contain subfolders for organizing files into smaller groups.

Folder name A unique, descriptive name for a folder that identifies what you store in that folder.

Font The typeface or design of a set of characters (letters, numerals, symbols, and punctuation marks).

Font size The size of characters, measured in units called points (pts).

Format (n.) The appearance of text and numbers, including color, font, attributes, borders, and shading. *See also* Number format. (v.) To enhance or improve the appearance of a document.

Format bar A toolbar in the WordPad window that displays buttons for formatting, or enhancing, the appearance of a document.

Formula bar The area above the worksheet grid where you enter or edit data in the active cell.

Formula A set of instructions used to perform one or more numeric calculations, such as adding, multiplying, or averaging, on values or cells.

Formula prefix An arithmetic symbol, such as the equal sign (=), used to start a formula.

Freeze To hold in place selected columns or rows when scrolling in a worksheet that is divided in panes. *See also* Panes.

Function (Excel)A built-in formula that includes the information necessary to calculate an answer; for example, SUM (for calculating a sum) or FV (for calculating the future value of an investment) (Visual Basic) In the Visual Basic for Applications (VBA) programming language, a predefined procedure that returns a value, such as the InputBox function that prompts the user to enter information.

Gadget A mini-program on the Windows Sidebar for performing an every day task, such as the Clock gadget for viewing the current time.

Gallery A collection of choices you can browse through to make a selection. Often available with Live Preview.

Gigabyte (GB or G) One billion bytes (or one thousand megabytes).

Goal cell In backsolving, a cell containing a formula in which you can substitute values to find a specific value, or goal.

Goal Seek A problem-solving method in which you specify a solution and then find the input value that produces the answer you want; sometimes described as a what-if analysis in reverse; also called backsolving.

Gridlines Evenly spaced horizontal and/or vertical lines used in a worksheet or chart to make it easier to read.

Group On the Ribbon, a set of related commands on a tab.

Hard copy A paper copy of a file.

Hard disk A built-in, high-capacity, high-speed storage medium for all the software, folders, and files on a computer.

Header row In a table, the first row that contains the field names.

Hotspot An object that, when clicked, will run a macro or open a file.

HTML Hypertext Markup Language, the format of pages that a Web browser can read.

Hyperlink An object (a filename, a word, a phrase, or a graphic) in a worksheet that, when you click it, displays another worksheet or a Web page called the target. *See also* Target.

Icon A small image on the desktop or in a window that represents a tool, resource, folder, or file you can open and use.

Icon sets In conditional formatting, groups of images that are used to visually communicate relative cell values based on the values they contain.

If...Then...Else statement In the Visual Basic programming language, a conditional statement that directs Excel to perform specified actions under certain conditions; its syntax is "If *condition* Then *statements* Else [*elsestatements*].

Inactive window An open window you are not currently using.

Input Information that produces desired results, or output, in a worksheet.

Input cells Spreadsheet cells that contain data instead of formulas and that act as input to a what-if analysis; input values often change to produce different results. Examples include interest rates, prices, or other data.

Input values In a data table, the variable values that are substituted in the table's formula to obtain varying results, such as interest rates.

Insertion point A blinking vertical line that appears when you click in the formula bar; indicates where new text will be inserted.

Instance A worksheet in its own workbook window.

Instant Search A Windows tool you use to quickly find a folder or file on your computer.

Integrate To incorporate a document and parts of a document created in one program into another program; for example, to incorporate an Excel chart into a PowerPoint slide, or an Access table into a Word document.

Integration A process in which data is exchanged among Excel and other Windows programs; can include pasting, importing, exporting, embedding, and linking.

Interface The look and feel of a program; for example, the appearance of commands and the way they are organized in the program window.

Intranet An internal network site used by a group of people who work together.

Keyboard shortcut A key or a combination of keys that you press to perform a command.

Keyword (Excel) Terms added to a workbook's Document Properties that help locate the file in a search. (Macros) In a macro procedure, a word that is recognized as part of the Visual Basic programming language. (Windows) A descriptive word or phrase you enter to obtain a list of results that include that word or phrase.

Kilobyte (KB or K) One thousand bytes.

Labels Descriptive text or other information that identifies rows, columns, or chart data, but is not included in calculations.

Landscape orientation Print setting that positions a document so it spans the widest margins of the page, making the page wider than it is tall.

Launch To open or start a program on your computer.

Legend In a chart, information that explains how data is represented by colors or patterns.

Linear trendline In an Excel chart, a straight line representing an overall trend in a data series.

Link (Windows) A shortcut for opening a Help topic or a Web site. (Office) To insert an object into a destination program; the information you insert will be updated automatically when the data in the source document changes.

Linking The dynamic referencing of data in other workbooks, so that when data in the other workbooks is changed, the references in the current workbook are automatically updated.

List arrows *See* AutoFilter list arrows.

List box A box that displays a list of options from which you can choose (you may need to scroll and adjust your view to see additional options in the list).

Live Preview A feature that lets you point to a choice in a gallery or palette and see the results in the document without actually clicking the choice.

Live taskbar thumbnails A Windows Aero feature that displays a small image of the content within open, but not visible windows, including live content such as video.

Live view A file icon that displays the actual content in a file on the icon.

Lock (Windows) To lock your user account, then display the Welcome screen. (Excel) To secure a row, column, or sheet so that data in that location cannot be changed.

Lock button A Start menu option that locks your computer.

Lock menu button A Start menu option that displays a list of shut-down options.

Log Off To close all windows, programs, and documents, then display the Welcome screen.

Logical conditions Using the operators And and Or to narrow a custom filter criteria.

Logical formula A formula with calculations that are based on stated conditions.

Logical test The first part of an IF function; if the logical test is true, then the second part of the function is applied, and if it is false, then the third part of the function is applied.

Macro A set of instructions recorded or written in the Visual Basic programming language; used to automate worksheet tasks.

Main procedure A macro procedure containing several macros that run sequentially.

Manual calculation option An option that turns off automatic calculation of worksheet formulas, allowing you to selectively determine if and when you want Excel to perform calculations.

Map An XML schema that is attached to a workbook.

Map an XML element A process in which XML element names are placed on an Excel worksheet in specific locations.

Maximized window A window that fills the desktop.

Megabyte (MB or M) One million bytes (or one thousand kilobytes).

Menu A list of related commands.

Menu bar A horizontal bar in a window that displays menu names that represent categories of related commands.

Metadata Information that describes data and is used in Microsoft Windows document searches.

Microsoft Windows Vista An operating system.

Minimized window A window that shrinks to a button on the taskbar.

Mixed reference Cell reference that combines both absolute and relative addressing.

Mode In dialog boxes, a state that offers a limited set of possible choices.

Mode indicator An area in the lower-left corner of the status bar that informs you of a program's status. For example, when you are entering or changing the contents of a cell, the word 'Edit' appears.

Model A worksheet used to produce a what-if analysis that acts as the basis for multiple outcomes.

Modeless Describes dialog boxes that, when opened, allow you to select other elements on a chart or worksheet to change the dialog box options and format, or otherwise alter the selected elements.

Module In Visual Basic, a module is stored in a workbook and contains macro procedures.

Move To change the location of a file by physically placing it in another location.

Multilevel sort A reordering of table data using more than one column at a time.

Multitask To perform several tasks at the same time.

Name box Left-most area of the formula bar that shows the cell reference or name of the active cell.

Named range A contiguous group of cells given a meaningful name such as "July Sales"; it retains its name when moved and can be referenced in a formula.

Navigate To move around in a worksheet; for example, you can use the arrow keys on the keyboard to navigate from cell to cell, or press [Page Up] or [Page Down] to move a screen at a time.

Navigation Pane A pane on the left side of a window that contains links to your personal folders, including the Documents, Pictures, and Music folders.

Normal view Default worksheet view that shows the worksheet without features such as headers and footers; ideal for creating and editing a worksheet, but may not be detailed enough when formatting a document.

Notification area An area on the right side of the taskbar that displays the current time as well as icons for open programs, connecting to the Internet, and checking problems identified by Windows Vista.

Number format A format applied to values to express numeric concepts, such as currency, date, and percentage.

Object A chart or graphic image that can be moved and resized and contains handles when selected. In object linking and embedding (OLE), the data to be exchanged between another document or program. In Visual Basic, every Excel element, including ranges.

Object Linking and Embedding (OLE) A Microsoft Windows technology that allows you to transfer data from one document and program to another using embedding or linking.

OLE *See* Object Linking and Embedding.

One-input data table A range of cells that shows resulting values when one input value in a formula is changed.

Online collaboration The ability to incorporate feedback or share information across the Internet or a company network or intranet.

Operating system Software that manages the complete operation of your computer.

Option button A small circle you click to select only one of two or more related options.

Or condition The records in a search must match only one of the criterion.

Outline symbols In outline view, the buttons that, when clicked, change the amount of detail in the outlined worksheet.

Output The end result of a worksheet.

Output values In a data table, the calculated results that appear in the body of the table.

Page Break Preview A worksheet view that displays page break indicators which you can drag to include more or less information on each page in a worksheet.

Page Layout View Provides an accurate view of how a worksheet will look when printed, including headers and footers.

Panes Sections into which you can divide a worksheet when you want to work on separate parts of the worksheet at the same time; one pane freezes, or remains in place, while you scroll in another pane until you see the desired information.

Paste Options button Allows you to paste only specific elements of the copied selection, such as the formatting or values.

Personal macro workbook A workbook that can contain macros that are available to any open workbook. By default, the personal macro workbook is hidden.

PivotChart report An Excel feature that lets you summarize worksheet data in the form of a chart in which you can rearrange, or "pivot," parts of the chart structure to explore new data relationships.

PivotTable Interactive table format that lets you summarize worksheet data.

PivotTable Field List A window containing fields that can be used to create or modify a PivotTable.

PivotTable report An Excel feature that allows you to summarize worksheet data in the form of a table in which you can rearrange, or "pivot," parts of the table structure to explore new data relationships; also called a PivotTable.

Plot The Excel process that converts numerical information into data points on a chart.

Plot area In a chart, the area inside the horizontal and vertical axes.

Point (n.) A unit of measure used for fonts and row height. One inch equals 72 points, or a point is equal to $1/72^{nd}$ of an inch. (v.) To position the tip of the pointer over an object, option, or item.

Pointer A small arrow or other symbol on the screen that moves in the same direction as the pointing device.

Pointing device A hardware device, such as a mouse, trackball, touch pad, or pointing stick, or an onscreen object for interacting with your computer and the software you are using.

Populate a worksheet with XML data The process of importing an XML file and filling the mapped elements on the worksheet with data from the XML file.

Portrait orientation A print setting that positions the document on the page so the page is taller than it is wide.

Post To place an interactive workbook in a shared location.

Power button A Start menu option that puts your computer to sleep (your computer appears off and uses very little power).

Precedents In formula auditing, the cells that are used in the formula to calculate the value of a given cell.

Presentation graphics program A program such as Microsoft PowerPoint that you can use to create slide show presentations.

Preview Pane A pane on the right side of a window that shows the actual contents of a selected file without opening a program. Preview may not work for some types of files.

Previewing Prior to printing, to see onscreen exactly how the printed document will look.

Primary Key The field in a database that contains unique information for each record.

Print area A portion of a worksheet that you can define using the Print Area button on the Page Layout tab; after you select and define a print area, the Quick Print feature prints only that worksheet area.

Print Preview A full-page view of a document that you can use to check its layout before you print.

Print title In a table that spans more than one page, the field names that print at the top of every printed page.**Procedure** A sequence of Visual Basic statements contained in a macro that accomplishes a specific task.

Procedure footer In Visual Basic, the last line of a Sub procedure.

Procedure header The first line in a Visual Basic procedure, it defines the procedure type, name, and arguments.

Program code Macro instructions, written in the Visual Basic for Applications (VBA) programming language.

Program tab Single tab on the Ribbon specific to a particular view, such as Print Preview.

Project In the Visual Basic Editor, the equivalent of a workbook; a project contains Visual Basic modules.

Project Explorer In the Visual Basic Editor, a window that lists all open projects (or workbooks) and the worksheets and modules they contain.

Properties 1) Characteristics or settings of a component of the graphical user interface; 2) File characteristics, such as the author's name, keywords, or the title, that help others understand, identify, and locate the file.

Properties window In the Visual Basic Editor, the window that displays a list of characteristics, or properties, associated with a module.

Property In Visual Basic, an attribute of an object that describes its character or behavior.

Publish To place an Excel workbook or worksheet on a Web site or an intranet in HTML format so that others can access it using their Web browsers.

Quick Access toolbar Customizable toolbar that includes buttons for common Office commands, such as saving a file and undoing an action.

Quick Launch toolbar A toolbar on the left side of the taskbar; includes buttons for showing the desktop when it is not currently visible, switching between windows, and starting the Internet Explorer Web browser.

RAM (Random Access Memory) The physical location used to temporarily store open programs and documents.

Range A selection of two or more cells, such as B5:B14.

Range object In Visual Basic, an object that represents a cell or a range of cells.

Read-only format Data that users can view but not change.

Record In a table (an Excel database), data about an object or a person.

Recycle Bin A desktop object that stores folders and files you delete from your hard drive(s) and that enables you to restore them.

Reference operators Mathematical calculations which enable you to use ranges in calculations.

Refresh To update a PivotTable so it reflects changes to the underlying data.

Regression analysis A way of representing data with a mathematically-calculated trendline showing the overall trend represented by the data.

Relative cell reference In a formula, type of cell addressing that automatically changes when the formula is copied or moved, to reflect the new location; default type of referencing used in Excel worksheets. *See also* Absolute cell referencing.

Removable storage Storage media that you can easily transfer from one computer to another, such as DVDs, CDs, or flash drives.

Report filter A feature that allows you to specify the ranges you want summarized in a PivotTable.

Resizing button A button that you use to adjust the size of a window, such as Maximize, Restore Down, and Minimize.

Restart To shut down your computer, then start it again.

Return In a function, to display.

Ribbon Area that displays commands for the current Office program, organized into tabs and groups.

Right-click To quickly press and release the right button on the pointing device.

Ruler A horizontal bar in the WordPad window that marks a document's width in 1/8ths of an inch (also shows one-inch marks).

Run To play, as a macro.

Scenario A set of values you use to forecast results; the Excel Scenario Manager lets you store and manage different scenarios.

Scenario summary An Excel table that compiles data from various scenarios so that you can view the scenario results next to each other for easy comparison.

Schema In an XML document, a list of the fields, called elements or attributes, and their characteristics.

Scope In a named cell or range, the worksheets where the name can be used.

Screen capture A snapshot of your screen, as if you took a picture of it with a camera, which you can paste into a document.

Scroll To adjust your view in a window.

Scroll arrow button A button at each end of a scroll bar for adjusting your view in small increments in that direction.

Scroll bar A vertical or horizontal bar that appears along the right or bottom side of a window when there is more content than can be displayed within the window so that you can adjust your view.

Scroll box A box in a scroll bar that you can drag to display a different part of a window.

Search criteria (Windows) One or more pieces of information that helps Windows identify the program, folder, or file you want to locate. (Excel) In a workbook or table search, the text you are searching for.

Share *See* Shared workbook.

Shared workbook An Excel workbook that several users can open and modify at the same time.

Sheet tab Identifies sheets in a workbook and lets you switch between sheets; sheet tabs are located below the worksheet grid.

Shortcut A link that gives you quick access to a particular folder, file, or Web site.

Shortcut menu A menu of common commands for an object that opens when you right-click that object.

Shut Down To completely shut down your computer.

Sidebar A Windows Vista desktop component that displays gadgets.

Single-click *See* Click.

Single-file Web page A Web page that integrates all of the worksheets and graphical elements from a workbook into a single file in the MHTML file format, making it easier to publish to the Web.

Sizing handles Small dots at the corners and edges of a chart, indicating that the chart is selected.

Sleep To save your work, turn off the monitor, then reduce power consumption to all the hardware components in your computer so it appears off; press any key to use your computer again.

Slider A shape you drag to select a setting that falls within a range, such as between Slow and Fast.

SmartArt Predesigned diagram types for the following types of data: List, Process, Cycle, Hierarchy, Relationship, Matrix, and Pyramid.

Sort To change the order of records in a table according to one or more fields, such as Last Name.

Sort keys Criteria on which a sort, or a reordering of data, is based.

Source program In a data exchange, the program used to create the data you are embedding or linking.

Spin box A text box with up and down arrows; you can type a setting in the text box or click the arrows to increase or a decrease the setting.

Start button The button on the left side of the taskbar that opens the Start menu to start programs, find and open files, access Windows Help and Support, and more.

Stated conditions In a logical formula, criteria you create.

Statement In Visual Basic, a line of code.

Status bar (Windows) A horizontal bar at the bottom of a window that displays simple Help information and tips. (Excel) Bar at the bottom of the Excel window that provides information about various keys, commands, and processes.

Structured reference Allows table formulas to refer to table columns by names that are automatically generated when the table is created.

Sub procedure A series of Visual Basic statements that performs an action but does not return a value.

Subfolder A folder within another folder for organizing sets of related files into smaller groups.

Suite A group of programs that are bundled together and share a similar interface, making it easy to transfer skills and program content among them.

Summary function In a PivotTable, a function that determines the type of calculation applied to the PivotTable data, such as SUM or COUNT.

Switch User To lock your user account and display the Welcome screen so another user can log on.

Syntax In the Visual Basic programming language, the formatting rules that must be followed so that the macro will run correctly.

Tab 1) A set of commands on the Ribbon related to a common set of tasks or features. Tabs are further organized into groups of related commands. 2) A sheet within a dialog box that contains a group of related settings.

Table An organized collection of rows and columns of similarly structured data on a worksheet.

Table styles Preset formatting combinations for a table.

Table total row The area at the bottom of a table used for calculations with the data in the table columns.

Tag A word or phrase assigned to a file that reminds you of a file's content.

Target The location that a hyperlink displays after you click it.

Target cell In what-if analysis (specifically, in Excel Solver), the cell containing the formula.

Taskbar The horizontal bar at the bottom of the desktop; displays the Start button, the Quick Launch toolbar, and the Notification area.

Template A file whose content or formatting serves as the basis for a new workbook; Excel template files have the file extension .xltx.

Terabyte (TB or T) One trillion bytes (or one thousand gigabytes).

Text annotations Labels added to a chart to draw attention to a particular area.

Text box A box in which you type text.

Text concatenation operators Mathematical calculations that join strings of text in different cells.

Themes Predesigned combinations of colors, fonts, and formatting attributes you can apply to a document in any Office program.

Thumbnail A smaller image of the actual contents of a file.

Tick marks Notations of a scale of measure on a chart axis.

Tiled Repeated, like a graphic in a worksheet background.

Title bar Area at the top of every program window that displays the document and program name.

Title bar The top border of a window that displays the name of the window, folder, or file and the program name.

Toggle A button with two settings, on and off.

Toolbar A set of buttons you can click to open menus or select common commands that are also available from a menu bar, such as saving and printing.

ToolTip A label that appears and identifies the purpose of an object when you point to it.

Touch pointer A pointer on the screen for performing pointing operations with a finger if touch input is available on your computer.

Tracers In Excel worksheet auditing, arrows that point from cells that might have caused an error to the active cell containing an error.

Track To identify and keep a record of who makes which changes to a workbook.

Translucency The transparency feature of Windows Aero that enable you to locate content by seeing through one window to the next window.

Trendline A series of data points on a line that shows data values that represent the general direction in a series of data.

Two-input data table A range of cells that shows resulting values when two input values in a formula are changed.

USB flash drive (also called a pen drive, jump drive, keychain drive, and thumb drive) A popular, removable storage device for folders and files that provides ease of use and portability.

User interface A collective term for all the ways you interact with a software program.

Validate A process in which an xml schema makes sure the xml data follows the rules outlined in the schema.

Validation *See* Data Validation.

Value axis In a chart, vertical axis that contains numerical values; in a 2-dimensional chart, also known as the y-axis.

Values Numbers, formulas, and functions used in calculations.

Variable In the Visual Basic programming language, an area in memory in which you can temporarily store an item of information; variables are often declared in Dim statements such as *DimNameAsString*. In an Excel scenario or what-if analysis, a changing input value, such as price or interest rate, that affects a calculated result.

View A set of display or print settings that you can name and save for access at another time. You can save multiple views of a worksheet.

Views Display settings that show or hide selected elements of a document in the document window, to make it easier to focus on a certain task, such as formatting or reading text.

Virus Destructive software that can damage your computer files.

Visual Basic Editor A program that lets you display and edit macro code.

Visual Basic for Applications (VBA) A programming language used to create macros in Excel.

Wallpaper The image that fills the desktop background.

Watermark A translucent background design on a worksheet that is displayed when the worksheet is printed. Watermarks are graphic files that are inserted into the document header. Worksheet backgrounds created with the Background button on the Page Layout tab do not print.

Web query An Excel feature that lets you obtain data from a Web, Internet, or intranet site and places it in an Excel workbook for analysis.

Welcome screen An initial startup screen that displays icons for each user account on the computer.

What-if analysis A decision-making tool in which data is changed and formulas are recalculated in order to predict various possible outcomes.

Wildcard A special symbol that substitutes for unknown characters in defining search criteria in the Find and Replace dialog box. The most common types of wildcards are the question mark (?), which stands for any single character, and the asterisk (*), which represents any group of characters.

Window A rectangular-shaped work area that displays a program or file, folders and files, or Windows tools.

Windows *See* Microsoft Windows Vista.

Windows 3-D Flip A Windows Aero feature that allows you to display stacked windows at a three-dimensional angle to see even more of the content of all open windows and select the window you want to use.

Windows Aero A Windows Vista feature supported in some editions (or versions) of Windows Vista that enhances the transparency (or translucency) of the Start menu, taskbar, windows, and dialog boxes; enables live taskbar thumbnails, Windows Flip, and Windows 3-D Flip.

Windows Flip A Windows Aero feature that allows you to display a set of thumbnails, or miniature images, of all open windows so that you can select and switch to another window.

WordArt Specially formatted text, created using the WordArt button on the Drawing toolbar.

Workbook A collection of related worksheets contained within a single file.

Worksheet A single sheet within a workbook file; also, the entire area within an electronic spreadsheet that contains a grid of columns and rows.

Worksheet window An area of the program window that displays part of the current worksheet; the worksheet window displays only a small fraction of the worksheet, which can contain a total of 1,048,576 rows and 16,384 columns.

Workspace An Excel file with an .xlw extension containing information about the identity, view, and placement of a set of open workbooks. Instead of opening each workbook individually, you can open the workspace file instead.

X-axis The horizontal axis in a chart; because it often shows data categories, such as months, it is also called the category axis.

XML (Extensible Markup Language) A system for defining languages using tags to structure data.

Y-axis The vertical axis in a chart; because it often shows numerical values in a 2-dimensional chart, it is also called the value axis.

Z-axis The third axis in a true 3-D chart, lets you compare data points across both categories and values.

Zooming in A feature that makes a document appear bigger but shows less of it on screen at once; does not affect actual document size.

Zooming out A feature that shows more of a document on screen at once but at a reduced size; does not affect actual document size.

Index